Hindu Primary Sources

A Sectarian Reader

EDITED BY CARL OLSON

RUTGERS UNIVERSITY PRESS
NEW BRUNSWICK, NEW JERSEY, AND LONDON

LIBRARY OF CONGRESS CATALOGING-IN-PUBLICATION DATA

Hindu primary sources: a sectarian reader / edited by Carl Olson.

p. cm.

Includes translations from Sanskrit and from various Indic languages.

Companion text to: The many colors of Hinduism.

Includes bibliographical references and index.

ISBN 978-0-8135-4069-6 (hardcover : alk. paper) — ISBN 978-0-8135-4070-2 (pbk. : alk. paper)

1. Hinduism—Sacred books—Introductions. 2. Hindu sects. I. Olson, Carl. II. Olson, Carl. Many colors of Hinduism.

BL1111.32.E5 2007

294. 5'92—dc22

2006035926

A British Cataloging-in-Publication record for this book is available from the British Library

Manufactured in the United States of America

This book is dedicated to my grandson
Benicio and his generation in the hope that they
can also enjoy the many treasures of Indian literature.

CONTENTS

Preface and Acknowledgments ix

Introduction to Indian Religious Literature 1

PART I **5**

Classical Sanskrit Traditions

1. The Vedic Literature 7
2. Upaniṣadic Literature 28
3. Dharma Literature 49
4. Classical Philosophical-Religious Schools 73

PART II **149**

Devotional and Sectarian Traditions

5. Vaiṣṇava Tradition 151
6. Krishna Devotionalism 224
7. Rāma Devotionalism and Sant Tradition 341
8. Śaiva Devotionalism 407
9. Goddess Devotion and Tantra 503

Notes 571
Index 573

PREFACE AND ACKNOWLEDGMENTS

There have been numerous anthologies of primary sources in Hinduism. Many of these anthologies are in wide use today in college classrooms around the globe. Unfortunately, many of these anthologies focus on the classical Sanskrit literature, which gives a false and distorted view of Indian religious literature because it neglects the literature in regional languages. This anthology proposes to be more balanced, without neglecting the rich tradition of Sanskrit literature. Other anthologies also tend to neglect the sectarian nature of Hinduism, which this anthology attempts to correct in the second part of the book, after selections from the classical Sanskrit religious literature in the first part. Moreover, within the study of sectarian Hinduism, there is a tendency to overlook devotion directed toward the deity Rāma, which will be addressed in chapter 7. Prior anthologies have also been silent about the role of women in the Hindu religious tradition. I have not devoted a specific chapter to women, although I was tempted to include such a chapter of primary sources. Instead, I decided to sprinkle primary source material about women throughout the book and include a look at a goddess in the final chapter. Since this collection of primary sources is intended for use with a companion text entitled *The Many Colors of Hinduism*, and that text contains a chapter specifically devoted to Indian women, I think that the more integrated approach to women's literary material is justified.

A major omission from this anthology that might strike some readers as odd is the exclusion of any selections from the *Mahābhārata* or *Bhagavad Gītā*. The press editor and I decided that there are many inexpensive paperback editions of the Gītā that an instructor could have his or her students purchase. A major advantage to this approach is that it allows more space for other primary source material that is not readily available to students of Hinduism. Each of the chapters of this book presents representative examples of the literature to be studied. Moreover, I attempt to refrain from superficial selections of a few pages for a particular figure. By offering students more substantial selections of specific thinkers, I also try to get students more fully involved with a specific body of literature. Of course, this approach is no substitute for returning to the primary sources in their entirety.

With the exception of some figures associated with goddess devotion, this anthology does not include modern or contemporary religious thinkers or movements, even though numerous sectarian movements are still vibrant today in India, the thinkers behind them have been deceased for a long time. Again, this is intended to provide for a richer and more ample selection of material with respect to the various sectarian movements. In addition, this anthology includes hagiographical literature because of its important role in Hindu devotional movements. The arrangement of the chapters is not perfectly historical, although chapters are historically informed, and the sequence of the chapters should not be interpreted to mean that one tradition is more important than another. By including the Goddess and Tantra in the last chapter, this should not be interpreted, for instance, to mean that they are an afterthought or less important than other topics of the book. Chapters 5 through 7, on devotion directed toward Viṣṇu, Krishna, and Rāma, come one after another because they represent aspects of the Vaiṣṇava tradition to some Hindus, while these three deities also stand on their own for many ardent devotees. Because of this sequence, some parts of the Śaiva chapter, chapter 8, contain historically earlier material than chapters 5 through 7. It should also be acknowledged that Tantra overlaps with the Vaiṣṇava, Śaiva, and Goddess traditions, which was my motivation for including material from the renowned Kashmir Śaiva thinker Abhinavagupta in chapter 9 on Tantra, and selections from the *Lakṣmī Tantra* in chapter 5 on the Vaiṣṇava tradition. Needless to say, instructors can make their own decisions about how best to use the material to suit their pedagogical needs.

The division of this anthology into classical and devotional parts is an artificial construct, because many devotional themes and sectarian movements have their roots in the classical Sanskrit traditions. And designating a body of literature as classical does not imply that it is no longer relevant in some religious circles in Indian culture. There is certainly a case that could be made to refer to devotional and sectarian traditions as classical. To claim that a body of literature is classical, for instance, suggests that it represents a standard of excellence, that it stands for the highest rank or class, and that it serves as a paradigm. That which is classical stands in opposition to what is unique, novel, new, or unusual. But it is not unusual to find various sectarian movements measuring their literature against the classical Sanskrit tradition, which possesses authority and legitimacy earned over centuries, in an attempt to emulate the foundational, classical tradition, and to claim that their literature does not conflict with the earlier tradition.

I have made some translations from Sanskrit literature. I have also translated texts that originally were translated into French from Sanskrit or regional languages. The selections that are translated will, it is hoped, stimulate interested students to delve deeper into the rich treasure house of Hindu religious literature.

I want to thank a series of three Rutgers University Press editors that I have had the pleasure to work with over the past few years—David Myers, Kristi Long, and Adi Hovav—for their constructive suggestions and assistance and to thank the other staff members at the press for their professionalism. This anthology is rooted in my experience at Clare Hall, Cambridge University. The environment of colleagues and students at Allegheny College has nurtured it. Jonathan Helmreich, who originally hired me to teach at the college on the hill, never tried of inquiring about Krishna's gopī companions, and countless students in my Hinduism course over the years have always made my teaching experience enjoyable. I especially want to thank President Richard Cook, former dean and dog-walking companion LaLloyd Michaels, and current dean Linda DeMeritt for their support. A positive home environment also contributed to the completion of this book, especially after some surgery. My nurse Peggy got me functioning again, and Casey got me on my feet. In addition, Kelly, Holly, Marlon, and Benicio provided empathic support.

Finally, I want to thank the retired Malcolm McLean of the University of Otago in New Zealand for his translation of selections from the *Śrī Śrī Ramakrishna Kathamrita* from the Bengali. Malcolm's delightfully quixotic and generous nature makes academic life such an interesting place to play. Because outside reviewers play an essential part in the publishing process, I want to thank, moreover, Jack Hawley of Barnard/Columbia University, Jeff Kripal of Rice University, and an anonymous reviewer for their helpful and constructive comments for improvements in the text. Your positive karma will be great indeed. Every anthology needs a careful reader and skilled copyeditor, and Margaret Case fills this role with her usual aplomb and adroitness, for which I am deeply grateful.

Hindu Primary Sources

Introduction to Indian Religious Literature

The simplest way to began to analyze Indian religious literature is to distinguish between what has been revealed (*śruti*) and what is remembered (*smṛti*). The revealed literature includes the Vedas, and its sections that will be discussed in the next two chapters, whereas the remembered body of literature includes the following collections of literature: Dharma Sūtras (approximate dates of composition 600–200 B.C.E.), the epic *Mahābhārata* (composed between approximately 300 B.C.E. and 300 C.E.), the epic *Rāmāyaṇa* (composed between 200 B.C.E. and 200 C.E.), and the Purāṇas, which began to be composed around 400 C.E. Another large body of religious literature, frequently composed in an aphoristic style, is often attributed to individual thinkers. Because of the succinct nature of these aphorisms (*sūtras*), explanatory commentaries are absolutely necessary in order to comprehend the pithy statements. In addition, dramas, poems, and narrative works of art also cover religious themes.

The claim that the vedic hymns were revealed oral literature suggests that the poets did not create the hymns themselves. The poets saw or heard the hymns from a deep, mysterious force, and received these messages with their mind and/or heart. The mind of the poets enabled them to grasp the true nature of things. The subtle structure of knowing symbolized by the human mind represented a transformative force that could effect change, produce desired results, and establish connections between humans and divine beings. Likewise, the human heart, like the mind, enabled a person to see. What was not normally observable or knowable by ordinary social beings. These gifted, visionary poets were able to receive the revelation because they possessed an insight (*dhī*) or ability to see concealed truths. Once they possessed their visions, the poets were able to express these truths in Sanskrit, which was considered a perfect and well-formed language that allowed them to conform themselves with the divine forces giving the messages.

The inspired nature of the vedic seer is evident by considering two terms: *kavi* and *vipra*. The former term connotes an inspired sage who possesses secret wisdom and the ability to see hidden things normally inaccessible to empirical eye sight by virtue of his mental eye. The term vipra means "to tremble, shake, or vibrate." When it is applied to a vedic seer (*ṛṣi*) it suggests someone who is inspired or ecstatic. The enthusiastic seer possesses a vibrant awareness of hidden things, and he is able to perceive the truth, which is identical to the eternal knowledge embodied by the Vedas. It is possible to find references to the semidivine nature of the seers, the descent of some of them from the gods, and a description of some as friends and companions of the divine beings in the literature.

The visionary message received by the inspired vedic poets also enabled them to view the cosmos as an integrated totality. What made the triple-structured cosmos a seamless universe was the hidden structure (*ṛta*) built into and holding together the physical and moral worlds, suggesting a harmonious whole consisting of multiple parts. Thus built into the structure of the universe was an effective, universal principle that provided for harmonious concord and was closely associated with the truth (*satya*). Although not residing in a particular place or object, ṛta represented the principle upon which truth and reality were grounded. Besides its connection to truth, ṛta was also associated with *tapas* (creative heat), which ushered into being the cosmos and continuously renewed life. Therefore, the inspired vedic poets were in close touch with the very fabric and creative forces that sustained the cosmos, which gave them a prominent position within the ancient culture.

The vedic poets were also the masters and custodians of Sanskrit, which was the language of the revealed hymns and thereby sacred. Sanskrit, written in an ancient script, was associated with perfection. As an ancient Indian might say, it was "well cooked." Sanskrit embodied *brahman*, which was a mysterious and hidden power that was not only contained within the words of the sacred language but also functioned to hold the universe together. The power of brahman was revealed to the visionary poets, and was considered a sacred power that was directly associated with the sanctity of the scripture preserved in Sanskrit. Nonetheless, the sanctity of the scripture was not directly related to its intelligibility to either a hearer or a reciter of it. The holiness of the words was more likely inversely related to comprehensibility. In other words, strange, mysterious, unintelligible terms were considered more powerful. Moreover, sanctity of a term was not something extra added to a word, but the holiness of a term was rather intrinsic to the word.

The importance of poetic inspiration and knowledge is further evident in the Sanskrit term *veda*, whose root meanings are "to see," "vision," and "knowing." A master of the *veda* is a person who is able to see that which is concealed. In short, such a person can witness the eternal, powerful, divine forces of the universe. When the term *veda* is used as a noun it signifies sacred knowledge. Becoming master or recipient of the *veda* is a transforming experience because knowing the truth radically changes a person. This points to the powerful nature of knowledge, which is a conviction that runs like a thread throughout Indian cultural history.

Due to its nature and ramifications, the revealed literature takes precedence over the literature based on human memory. When there is a discrepancy between the two bodies of literature, a person must rely on the revealed literature for guidance because it possesses greater authority than the remembered literature. Holding the revealed literature in higher regard than the remembered literature does not imply that the meaning of the revealed literature is readily apparent and easy to discern. Scholarly commentaries were necessary to elicit the meaning of a hymn. Within the history of Indian culture, there is a long tradition of interpreting the meaning of and commentating on texts by learned individuals.

The revealed and remembered bodies of literature originated within the cultural context of an oral tradition, which means that the hymns of the Vedas were passed down from one generation to the next orally after they were memorized. In this sense, much of Indian classical literature is related to memory in some sense, regardless of its revealed nature. In order to preserve the sacred hymns, priestly scholars devised elaborate methods to assist memory, and particular persons specialized in specific groups of texts in order to enhance the accuracy of their oral preservation. A person might, for instance, memorize each odd-numbered word of a hymn and/or every even numbered term to ensure correct transmission of the hymn.

Due to the manner in which the sacred Vedas were orally revealed, preserved, and transmitted in the sacerdotal language of Sanskrit, these texts gave prestige to the oral transmission of literature. The oral nature of the archetypical vedic literature tended to emphasize narrative, symbol, myth, and mnemonic features of scripture. When poets recited or sang the vedic hymns, they were giving utterance to a timeless and divine power embodied in the words that originally gave birth to the universe and continue to sustain its existence along with that of human inhabitants of the cosmos.

The emphasis on the oral nature of ancient Indian sacred literature necessarily implies that scripture is not something written, which can be reified. This suggests that scripture in India is not a well-defined entity with clearly established boundaries. The significance of and emphasis upon the oral transmission of hymns can be partially understood by the traditionally negative attitude toward writing in Indian culture. According to the ancient *Aitareya Āraṇyaka* (5.5.3), the activity of writing is designated as ritually polluting, and a person thus stained should avoid reciting the Vedas along with other polluting actions such as eating meat, seeing blood or a dead body, or after sexual intercourse. Writing is an especially inappropriate vehicle for sacred mantras because the impure activity of writing risks polluting the holy utterances. This type of cultural attitude helps to explain the traditionally low social status of scribes in the culture.

In addition to the sacred Vedas, it is possible to find features connected to orality in epic, purāṇic, and sūtra style texts. Under the influence of orality and its embeddedness within Indian culture, communication and transmission are pliant in the sense of favoring a more open-ended kind of religious conceptualization, which is a tendency, along with different lineages of oral transmitters, that favors variant forms of narrative in contrast to a single, primordial version of a story. This feature helps us to comprehend the many different versions of creation narratives in the ancient literature. Even when bodies of oral literature assume a written form, the narratives do not loose their oral character. This is even true of Hindu temples and the narratives depicted on the walls and *gopurams* (pyramidal structures) that tell stories about divine beings, heroes, and ancient lore that a viewer can see at the present time.

The prestige of and reverence for the revealed Vedas influenced later thinkers, who sought to conform their teachings to the sacred literature, and later sectarian writers, who claimed to be in harmony with the spirit of the vedic literature. Moreover, some important devotional literature claimed a revealed status for itself. This suggests the continued importance of revelation within Indian culture throughout its history.

PART I

Classical Sanskrit Traditions

1

The Vedic Literature

There are four collections of vedic literature: *Rig*, *Sāma*, *Yajur*, and *Atharva*. Each of these collections of hymns is further divided into four sections: Saṃhita (mantra or sacred formula/utterance collection); Brāhmaṇa (theological and ritual commentary), Āraṇyaka (forest or wilderness texts), and Upaniṣad (speculative and secret philosophical texts). Each of these four sections is considered revealed (*śruti*). It is believed that divine beings revealed this literature orally to ancient sages (*ṛṣi*s), who heard them, preserved them within their memory, and passed the revealed hymns onto further generations in a process of oral transmission. Eventually, the revealed hymns were written down in order to preserve and protect them from faulty memory and the vicissitudes of time. Just because some vedic seers attached their names to poems does not mean that a reader should construe this signature as a claim of authorship. It is merely an acknowledgment of the identity of the person who received the revelation. The divinely revealed origin of the Vedas gives this body of literature an unquestionable authenticity and authority over other bodies of literature that would historically follow it.

The vedic literature also represents the creativity of the social elite of ancient Indian society, which was primarily priestly. Although the Vedas, give us a good window within which to see the religious life of the upper social classes, the lower strata of ancient Indian society do not appear to any great extent in this literature. The *Atharva Veda* is an exception: does give us a glimpse of some lower-class religious practices and superstitions, although this view is through the perspective of a socially elite and sacradotal class. Nonetheless, the Vedas give a reader a limited overall view of the ancient religion. What a reader will discover is a priestly worldview with respect to religion, ritual, society, and values because the literature reflects priests communicating with other priests.

The *Rig Veda* is the oldest collection of verses that form 1,028 hymns arranged in ten books called *maṇḍalas* (circles). Parts of book 1 and book 10 are the latest additions to the entire corpus, together with book 9, which includes hymns recited during the Soma sacrifice. Books 2 to 7 are designated the "family collections" because they were preserved within family clans that memorized them and transmitted them for future generations. Book 8 contains several more diminutive family collections. These family collections represent the literary products of ancient sages or their patrilinear descendants. We find references to such seers as Gṛtsamāda, Atrī, Bharadvāja, Viśvāmitra, Vasiṣṭha, and Vāmadeva. In fact, the various books are arranged according to author (that is, family or clan), deity, and meter. In addition, the hymns to specific deities are arranged according to length, with the longest at the beginning of the book. If hymns are of equal length, the hymn with a longer meter is placed first.

It is possible that the *Rig Veda* predates the introduction and common use of iron, which means that its origin can be dated to around 1200 B.C.E. According to internal textual evidence, the Vedas originated in northern India and spread to the Punjab and more eastern regions between 1500 B.C.E. and around 400 B.C.E. Members of the Angirasa and Kāṇva clans formed the bulk of its poets, who treated the hymns as the private property of the clans. In time, vedic schools called Śākhās (branches) developed to control and protect the transmission of texts, which usually resulted with a school adhering to a specific text. These various schools created an interpretive body of literature as reflected in various Brāhmaṇa and sūtra types of literature.

Although this chapter only contains translations of the *Rig Veda*, it is useful to review the other parts of the vedic literature for the sake of thoroughness. The *Sāma Veda* represents, for instance, material drawn from the *Rig Veda*, with the exception of seventy-five hymns. This collection of hymns is named for the chants (*sāmans*), which represent the earliest form of music in Indian history, that are recited during the Soma sacrifice. As the priests recite these verses during the rite, they modify the verses. Finally, the *Sāma Veda* consists of two parts: an actual text (*arcika*) and the melodies (*gāna*).

The sacred formulas (*mantras*), which literally refer to "an instrument of the mind," repeated by priests in rituals form the bulk of the *Yajur Veda*, or third vedic collection. The sacred formulas are arranged according to ritual usage and not numerically. By reciting the sacred mantras (syllables, words, or verses), the chanter expresses eternal wisdom and the preexistent sacred word itself. The oral recitation of the mantras was believed to render them more accurate and gives them a greater authority than committing them to a static written form. There were four major types of mantra chants: *ṛc*, *yajus*, *sāman*, and *atharvan*, which conformed, respectively, to each of the major vedic collections. The importance of mantras can be partially grasped by examining two types of speech. The initial type was that of the asuras, or demonic beings. This speech was without form, order, uncontrollable, and inarticulate—similar to the nature of the demonic forces of existence—whereas the vedic mantra was a type of speech that was the exact opposite of the former, and represented the measured sounds of the sacrifice such as those found in the *Yajur Veda*.

The two major branches of the *Yajur Veda* are the *Black Yajur Veda* and the *White Yajur Veda*. The former is a mixture of verses and expository prose, while the latter branch contains only mantras. In addition, the latter text is also known as the *Vājasaneyi Saṃhitā*, which consists of two recensions: *Mādhyaṃdina* and the *Kāṇva*. By contrast, there are three major versions of the *Black Yajur Veda*.

Before proceeding to the final Veda, it is important to emphasize that the meaning of the words of a sacred mantra chanted by a priest is not very relevant because what is essential is the sound, which is conceived as the very breath of the divine. It is the sound that unites and harmonizes the reciter with the deep, mysterious, cosmic forces. By uttering a mantra, the speaker is energized by a sacred force, protected from ever-lurking demonic forces, and harmoniously integrated with hidden and powerful forces beyond his comprehension. The creative nature of a mantra utterance is evident in the sounds *bhuh* (earth), *bhuvah* (atmosphere), and *svah* (sky), which are the three spheres of the vedic cosmos. When a reciter utters such mantras he is participating in an act of creation that took place at the beginning of time, when these sounds were initially uttered by sacred forces. This scenario emphatically suggests the theurgic power of the vedic hymns when they are orally recited. In fact, the power of the hymns extend to the gods and invigorates them by its inherent power (*RV* 1.15.5; 4.32.12).

The *Atharva Veda*, or fourth Veda, consists of a collection of hymns focusing on magical and healing rites. In addition, there are hymns related to harmful sorcery, speculative subjects, others concerned with rites of passage (such as initiation and marriage), and two appendixes. In sharp contrast to the *Rig Veda*, the collection begins with short works and increases to longer hymns. Even though the text provides a glimpse into the religious practices of ordinary people and is dated later than the other three Vedas, it is still considered a liturgical text along with the other three Vedas.

When the hymns were recited within a liturgical context they manifested the circular nature of the performance by the priests. Even after the Vedas assumed written form, they were not widely read, but priests were expected to perform the hymns within the ritual cult. Thus the Sanskrit Vedas represent more than a body of literary hymns, because they also embody a system of complex ritual action. Therefore, in order to grasp the meaning of the vedic texts, a person must examine the hymns within a ritualistic context.

We have also noted that the deities gave the poets a visionary insight that was conceived as a heart/mind transmission from a superior to an inferior. After receiving it from higher beings, the poet recites/chants the hymn. By orally reciting a hymn, the poet sends his inner spirit back to the realm of the divine beings who originally gave the poem its mysterious and immortal power. Moreover, the uttering of a hymn, about a particular deity sends that hymn back to its source and completes the cycle. As a person reads the vedic hymns, their cyclical nature should be remembered in order to understand the cultural context in which they were recited.

Because the ancient vedic schools represented a priestly family or clan from a specific geographical area, tribe, or kingdom, and the schools distinguished themselves by their ritual procedures and pronunciation of words, there was no single or original canon of texts that was established and authenticated by an authoritative body of religious leaders. What we have are plural textual canons of different schools. Thus the vedic canon was a collective entity of vedic texts utilized by various schools. Vedic literature became a canon by about 400 B.C.E., when it was acknowledged by the two grammarians Pāṇini and Patañjali around 150 B.C.E. It was also mentioned in the Pāli canon of Buddhism around 250 B.C.E.

Although extensive selections from the Brāhmaṇa body of literature are not included in this anthology, these texts are an important part of ancient Indian religion because they provide the rules, explanations, and guidelines for conducting the various complex rituals. The contents of this body of literature also contain speculation about the wider cosmic significance of particular rituals, along with their origin, purpose, and meaning by making essential connections (*bandhus*) between cosmic and ritual elements and actions. The Brāhmaṇas thus represent a theoretical elaboration and analytical explanation of various types of ritual. A reader discovers that these texts are concerned with the origin of sacrificial practices as well as providing practical ritual instruction. An excellent example of such sacrificial concerns and conceptualizations is the establishment of the fire according to an account from the *Śatapatha Brāhmaṇa*, included here after various hymns from the *Rig Veda*. This selection from the *Śatapatha Brāhmaṇa* is suggestive of the kinds of religious speculation and cosmic connections made by the priestly theorists about the origin, role of fire, its importance, and its association with other parts of the cosmic order.

Brāhmaṇas associated with the *Black Yajur Veda* are dated later than those connected to the *White Yajur Veda*. Two examples of Brāhmaṇas of the former Veda are the *Kaṭha* and *Taittirīya*, whereas the *Bṛhad* and the historically important *Śatapatha Brāhmaṇas* represent the White Yajur Veda. Each of the particular Brāhmaṇas represents a different priestly tradition in addition to dissimilar internal differences, and is based on various authoritative figures. The *Aitareya* and *Kausītaki Brāhmaṇas* are directly connected to the *Rig Veda*, with the former text explaining the Soma sacrifice, whereas the latter text deals with such issues as the construction of the sacred fire, daily morning and evening oblations, new and full-moon rituals, and the four monthly sacrifices. The *Pañcaviṃśa* and *Jaiminīya*

Brāhmaṇas are attached to the *Sāma Veda*, while the *Gopatha Brāhmaṇa* is connected with the *Atharva Veda*. Various Brāhmaṇa texts are associated with different Upaniṣads, but the latter texts will not be considered until the next chapter. In addition to their connection to Brāhmaṇas and Upaniṣads, each Veda is also associated with a Śrauta Sūtra, which is a ritual manual or handbook that gives instructions about the correct performance of public rites.

The Śrauta Sūtras are based on the earlier Brāhmaṇa literature with the intention of providing a manual for ritual actors. These texts are similar to an auto mechanic's manual that demonstrates, for instance, how the parts of a carburetor fit together so that a mechanic can assemble and disassemble the instrument. Thus the Śrauta Sūtras contain detailed descriptions of ritual procedures, enumerate different kinds of rites and their appropriate times, distinguish the participants in the ritual and their functions, identify the necessary instruments to be used, and finally relate the appropriate mantras. The overall purpose of these texts is to make a complex ritual system more manageable by providing a map by which a participant can navigate his way correctly and safely.

Due to the presupposed mysterious nature of the vedic hymns, students of this body of literature needed tools to assist them understand the hymns and to use them in a ritual context. Assistance was provided by the six limbs, which were auxiliary sciences called Vedāngas necessary for the study of the texts that originated around 700 B.C.E. The first limb provides instruction for the precise pronunciation of texts (*śikṣa*) and is concerned generally with phonetics. The second limb, *kalpa*, provides the details of the rituals. The limb of *vyākaraṇa* refers to grammar, *nirukta* is concerned with etymology of terms and analysis of semantic structure, *chandas* focuses on the details of verse meters, and *jyotiṣa* represents issues related to astronomy and astrology, because it is essential to determine precisely the most auspicious times for the performance of rituals in order to be in harmony with cosmic rhythms and forces.

The long-term legacy of the Vedas is evident in later devotional literature, whose authors borrow mythic themes, metaphors, and imagery to convey and illustrate religious messages. It is not impossible to find collections of devotional literature claiming status as the "fifth Veda." Later authors also link themselves genealogically with the Vedas, a divine revelation giving certainty and authority. Another strategy was for other authors to claim that their works represented a lost vedic text. It is rare to find an author asserting that his work does not conform to the Veda or embody the secret essence of the sacred literature. From a sociological perspective, the Vedas established and continued to confirm the prevailing social hierarchy with the literary, priestly class at the top of the social structure, although such a claim was not universally accepted by other members of Indian society. And the revelatory origin of the Vedas implied that this social structure was not open to change or negotiation by other social groups.

Selections from the Rig Veda

To Sky and Earth (1.160.1–5)

1. Sky and earth, these two who bring prosperity for all, maintain order, and carry the poet of space (sun). Between the divine beings, the three bowls give life beautifully; the pure sun god wanders according to fixed laws.
2. Wide and spacious, powerful, never exhausted, the father and mother guard creatures. The cosmic halves are like two beautiful women, when their father dresses them in forms and colors.
3. The daring son, who possesses the purity of the two parents, purifies the cosmos by magic strength. From the colorful cow and the bull with good seed, every day he milks the fluid that is his seed.
4. This is the most artful of the creative gods, the sky and earth, who bring prosperity to all; he generates the twofold cosmos with his power of inspiration. And he holds them together with never-decaying support.
5. Praise sky and earth, bestow on us your great power and glory, whereby we may extend control forever over all people. Let us acknowledge strength to come!

To the Uṣas and the Aśvins (1.92.1–18)

1. See the dawn establish her banner, on eastern side of the sky, she anoints herself with light as ointment. They unleash themselves like brave heroes, returning the red cows, the mothers.
2. The reddish lights flew up suddenly; they had their reddish cow-lights harnessed. Uṣas has determined the future; the red cows attained their sacred light.

3. They sing a song of praise, like women diligently at work, coming from a distance with a harnessed team, every day bringing food to a man of good actions, a generous man, and a man who prepares the Soma.
4. She puts on herself bright colors like a dancer; she exposes her breasts like a cow does her swollen udder. In that way she makes light for the whole world, Uṣas unlocks the darkness like a cow its enclosing pen.
5. Her light appears visible again; she stretches herself out, expelling the dark monster. The heavenly daughter puts on her colorful light just as the priest ties the victims on the sacrificial post.
6. We have reached the end of this darkness, which Uṣas spends lighting up her web. Already smiling like a lover, she shines forth; and with her appearance, she awakens us to happiness.
7. The daughter of the sky is praised, as bringer of donations, by the Gotamas. She shares existing rewards with children and adults; she constructs the rewards that begin with cows and end with horses, O Uṣas!
8. Uṣas! Bring such great wealth to capable sons, beginning with slaves and ending with heroes, to shine forth with fame, O Friend.
9. Overlooking all creatures, the goddess shines everywhere to every eye turned to her. Awakening into being everything that lives, she found the speech to compose poetry.
10. The ancient gods repeatedly born dressed up in the same color, making a lifetime of a mortal decrease just as the skillful gambler wins the throw.
11. She rises up exposing the ends of the sky; she drives her sister far away. Human lifetimes decrease; the young woman shines under the eyes of her wooer.
12. Her rays, extending like cattle, are lovely like a flowing stream. The spiritual order is not lessened, it allows them to see her appearing by the rays of the sun.
13. Uṣas, bring us a considerable gift, reward us with a gift that enables us to attain through our seeds descendants!
14. Uṣas, rich in cows and horses, shines, beaming plentifully riches here for us today!
15. O Uṣas, harness rewards today, such as the red steeds, and drive all good fortunes to us here!
16. O Aśvins, make your chariot turn, do not bypass us with the cows and gold. Link them here to our senses!
17. You Aśvins, awaken them at this time of the day as you rise and give humankind light, O Aśvins, give us strength!

18. To this place, the two gods, who are healing masters, drive with golden wheels to the Soma drink.

To Agni (1.1.1–9)

1. Agni appoints as his agent a priest as the god of the sacrifice; therefore, Hortṛ is the one who brings the most reward.
2. Agni was appointed by the ancient seers and those from the present too; he brings the gods here.
3. Through Agni one can gain wealth and increase day after day, and atone for the most sins.
4. Agni! Only the worship and the sacrifice that you encompass on all sides reaches to the gods.
5. Agni, the true Hotṛ (priest) with the keenest sense and most glorious being, being a god, will come with the gods.
6. If you really want to do the donor good, Agni, so that becomes true with you, O Angiras.
7. We approach you, Agni, with prayer day after day, bringing you thoughts, with devotion, offering homage.
8. The control of the order, the guardian of right custom, that shining, that grows in our own home.
9. Be you, Agni, easy to reach like a father a son! Be with us for our happiness!

To Varuṇa (5.85.1–8)

1. To the king of everyone, I build a serious song, harmonizing it like a tapestry, a hymn with which to touch Varuṇa, who struck asunder the earth and spread it beneath the sun like the slaughter with an animal skin.
2. Over time Varuṇa extended the air into the race horses; he placed victories in the milk of the cows and swift horses, intelligence into hearts, and placed fire in the waters. He placed on the mountain the Soma and the sun in heaven.
3. Varuṇa poured out the cask with an opening into both worlds and the airspace between them; so that across the whole world the king waters the ground just as rain moistures the grain.
4. He moistens the ground, earth, and heavens. When Varuṇa wants milk then, the mountains dress themselves with clouds and by virtue of conscious awareness loosen (the dress).
5. This deep magic art of Varuṇa, who stood in the middle of space and measured apart the earth with the sun as a measuring-stick.

6. Also these great clever tricks of these inspired gods—no one dares to touch that; these glittering streams, pouring down, cannot fill the one ocean with its water.
7. If we, O Varuṇa, one like Aryaman or Mitra become friends, or if we, because we have always been companions, or a brother, or an inhabitant—be it relatives or strangers—any injustice that did happen, takes that offence (from us), O Varuṇa!
8. If we have been deceived like players within the game, whether we know it for certain or not, unbind the bonds around us, O God! Thus we wish to be dear to you, O Varuṇa.

To the Maruts (1.85.1–12)

1. As women already do, the team of horses ride, good-working sons of Rudra—the Maruts raised both worlds—they become intoxicated and take delight in the sacrifices.
2. They grew up to reach a large size; the sons of Rudra have a place in heaven. Their priestly singing and creating strength like Indra have awakened the sons of the mother Pṛśṇi (dappled cow), and increased their glory.
3. When the cow-born ones adorn themselves with beautifully made ornaments, then the handsome ones radiate beaming light from their bodies. They drive each enemy away. Butter flows along their path.
4. The generous ones, who glisten with their spears, with strength itself move the immovable, when the Maruts quickly think about antelopes harnessed to their vehicles, it is like moving swift as thought.
5. If you harnessed the antelopes on the chariots, maintaining the stone forward in the race, then they unleash also rays of the reddish (steeds). Like a skin, they moisten the earth with water.
6. The high-speed teams shall become tame; with arms rapidly flying go forward! Place yourself on the sacred grass; a wide seat is prepared for you by those Maruts. You become intoxicated at the sweetened Soma tank!
7. They grew by themselves very large; they climbed the sky and made for themselves a wide seat. As Viṣṇu stood by the intoxicated bull (Indra) to help, they played immediately like birds on the beloved sacred grass.
8. Moving out like brave warriors, they contended like ambitious competitors in combat. All creatures fear the Maruts. Men of glistening sight are like the king.
9. When Tvaṣṭṛ, the artist, had constructed that well-made golden thunderbolt with its thousand spikes, Indra took it to do heroic work. He killed the dragon, releasing the flood waters.

10. They pushed up the spring with strength from above; they cleaved even the one solid rock. Blowing forth their music, the generous Maruts performed pleasant things intoxicated by Soma.
11. They forced up the spring inclined to this place and poured out a large spring for the thirsty Gotama. They came to him with assistance, the magnificent light; they satisfied the wish of the sage of the well-informed speech.
12. The shelters, which you have for a sign, continue for the threefold donor! Hold them up to us, O Maruts, bring us a treasure to master, you bulls.

To Indra (1.32.1–15)

1. I now want to proclaim Indra's heroic deeds, the first, the thunderbolt wielder did: He killed the dragon, broke open the waters; he split apart the tops of the mountains.
2. He killed the dragon, which had settled down on the mountain. Tvaṣṭṛ fashioned the roaring thunderbolt for him. Like roaring cows, the rushing waters ran down straight to the sea.
3. Greedily like a bull he took for himself the Soma; he drank from the three bowls. The generous one seized the missile to throw it; he killed the first-born of the dragons.
4. As you, Indra, killed the first-born of dragons and then deceived by your own magic the cunning of the crafty one, you brought forth the sun, sky, and red dawn. Since then you have never been mastered by anyone.
5. Indra killed Vṛtra, the greatest enemy, that shoulderless enemy with his thunderbolt, his huge weapon. As limbs of a tree cut with the ax, the dragon lies flat on the earth.
6. Because he had challenged the big hero, the strongly oppressive one caused him to drink three vats of Soma in inebriated high spirits. He could not endure the impact of his arms; his nose was smashed, as he found his master in Indra.
7. Without hands and feet he battled Indra, who hit him with his thunderbolt on his necks. As a castrated steer wanting to become like bulls, Vṛtra lay cut up there in many places.
8. Over him as he lay there like a broken reed, the rising waters of Manu ascended over him. Those waters that Vṛtra in his greatness had enclosed the dragon now lay at its feet.
9. The living strength of the mother of Vṛtra left; Indra had thrown his weapon at her. On top, the producer lay, right underneath the son. The Dānu lies as a cow with its calf.

10. Amid the never stationary and resting waters, the body lay hidden. The waters flowed over Vṛtra's secret place. Into long darkness sank the enemy of Indra.
11. As women of Dāsa watched over the dragon, the waters imprisoned them like the cows of Pani. Then the waters, which had been blocked, flowed after the killing of Vṛtra.
12. You changed into a horsehair there, Indra, as he beat you against the mouth. The single god, you conquered the cow, you won, O hero, that Soma; you freed the seven streams so that they could run.
13. Of no use was the lightning and thunder, fog and hail that he scattered, when Indra and the dragon fought. There rich offerings also continued for all the future winners.
14. Whom did you see, Indra, as avenger of the dragon, what did you fear, did it enter your heart, as you passed over the ninety-nine streams, as the frightened eagle hurries through space?
15. Indra is king over the moving, the resting, over tame and horned, who carries deer in his arms. He rules the people as their king; as the rim circles spokes, he encompasses all.

To Soma (9.74.1–9)

1. As this newborn animal roars from the woods, it runs like a reddish racing horse to win the sun. It unites with the sky's milk-rich seed. I ask it kindly for its extended umbrella.
2. It carries the fundamental already directional pillar of the sky, and as a full stalk that encompasses all, it wants these two big world-halves in order to approach them for worship. The seer holds together the united pair and all refreshments.
3. A high pleasure is that of well-made ready Soma sweetener; it is the wide way of Aditi, who follows the right way, Soma, the bull who reigns over the rain here, the bull, the father of the waters, brings help to this place.
4. The living cloud is milked for butter and milk; from the center of the sacrificial order the divine drink is born. Those that bring him gifts satisfy him; the swollen men urinate down the moving liquid.
5. The stalk roared, uniting itself with the wave; it swells for human beings the skin that arouses the gods. He puts the germ, through which we attain seeds and bodily descendants, in the lap of Aditi.
6. Out of a filter with a thousand streams, these flow downward; in the third space, it wants to have a second offspring. Four teats are appropriately below the sky. The dripping liquid carries the divine drink downward as sacrificial victims.

7. He assumes a white color, if he wants to win the goal. Soma, the rewarding Asura, knows the whole of nature. He is accompanied by poetic art and ritual action as he seeks his way. Then, full of water, he descends from heaven.
8. Now, he is the winner, because he drove the cows with milk; the racehorse reached the goal and won a hundred cows for Kakṣīvat, a man one hundred years old. In their hearts nearby, the gods demanding that they hurry up.
9. Your juice, O Soma, when you are soaked with water, you run through the sieve made of wool, O Pavamana. From the clean way created, you intoxicated are palatable for Indra to the drink, O Pavamana!

Praise to Charity (10.117.1–9)

1. Certainly, the gods do not conceal hunger after the slaughter. A death also arrives to someone well-nourished. And the wealth of generosity is not exhausted itself, but a miser does not find compassion.
2. Whoever has food and acts ungenerously toward someone desiring food, his heart hardens, and then later his unsympathetic friend also gives no food.
3. He is truly hospitable, who gives to the beggar, who has lost a lot of weight, wishing for food. He stands by him to serve if he calls him in the future, and for the future acquires a friend for himself.
4. He is no friend who doesn't give anything of his food to a friend; he looks for another donor, even if he is a stranger.
5. The wealthy should give to the needy; he considers the long way (of life), because wealth rolls like the wheels of a chariot: they turn from one to the other.
6. The fool makes the food useless. I speak the truth: it will be his death. He does not cultivate a patron for himself or a friend. Whoever eats alone also experiences the damage alone.
7. Only the plow that works the soil creates satisfaction; when we walk with our legs, we put behind us the way. The talking high priest wins more than the silent one, the giving friend is more valuable than the stingy.
8. The single foot surpasses the two-footed; the two-footed catches up with the tripod. At the shout of the two-footed, the four-footed comes, watching over his herds.
9. Two hands, although they are same, are not created equal; two cows, even if they are from the same mother, are not equal and do not give the same amount of milk. Also twins do not have the same power. Also two kinfolk do not give as much with the same charity.

The Hymn of Wisdom (10.71.1–11)

1. Bṛhaspati! That was the first beginning of speech, as he carried out the naming. The best and pure thing, which they had, this came to be revealed through intimacy to the light.
2. Where the wise ones by means of reflection formed the speech, it is like flour sifted through a strainer, then friends recognized their cooperation. Then a good sign was placed on their speech.
3. With the sacrifice, they followed the speech track; they discovered it inside the sages. They got it and distributed it among many; its seven choir singers praised it.
4. And some who see don't perceive the speech, and some that listen don't hear it. And it reveals itself to someone like a spouse in love.
5. One person says about some that he became stiff and fat in this friendship; they don't send him forward in the contests. He gives himself away to falsehood like a milkless cow, because he has a speech that carries neither fruit nor flower.
6. A man who leaves a friend has no more shares in the speech. What he also hears, he hears it in vain; he doesn't know the way of virtue.
7. Friends who have eyes and ears, their spiritual insights occur unequally. Some (like ponds) appears to reach only to the mouth, or at the shoulder; others like ponds are suitable for swimming.
8. When intuitions of the mind are created in the heart, when the Brahmans sacrifice together, some are left behind because of a lack of knowledge; the others that exit with their solemn speeches find approval.
9. This does not come near and no further; those who are not genuine Brahmans nor pressers of the Soma still participate with the Soma, they use the speech in a wrong way, and spin ignorance out of the flowing waters as a weaving.
10. All friends rejoice for a friend, who arrives as the winner in the contest, because he protects them from error and provides food. He is a man worthy to be sent forward to claim the prize.
11. The one sits there who is full of many verses that others sing, increasing them. Another sings a hymn in Śakvarī meter. The one, as Brahman, recites the existing knowledge, while another creates the measurement of the sacrifice.

To the Gods (10.72.1–9)

1. Now, we want to announce the birth of the gods hoping to visualize them in recited songs, when one is still able to chant them at a later age.

2. Brahmaṇaspati welded them together like a smith. In the earliest possible age of the gods, being was created from nothingness.
3. In first ages of the gods, being was created from the nothingness; after this, they created space: This came from the crouching one who gave birth.
4. The earth was born by the crouching one, and out of the earth began this world dream. By Aditi, Dakṣa was born and from Dakṣa the Aditi.
5. Because Aditi was born as your daughter, O Dakṣa. After she was born, the gods were born, the good friends of immortality.
6. When the gods solidly held together for you in the flood at that time, a thick cloud of mist arose from them like dust from dancers.
7. When the gods increased their enchantment with the worlds, there you pulled out the sun hidden in the sea.
8. Eight sons are there of Aditi who were born from her body. With seven, she went among the gods and threw away Mārtāṇda.
9. With seven sons, Aditi entered into the first age. But she repeated the birth of Mārtāṇda so that he could propagate soon and die.

Which God? (10.121.1–10)

1. In the beginning, he became a golden embryo. The born one became the sole lord of creation. He held together the earth and this sky. Who is this God, we should serve with sacrifice?
2. Who gives life and power, who commands all that the gods wait for, whose silhouette is immortality and death—who is the God, we should serve with sacrifice?
3. Through his power, he is the sole king over everything, over creatures that breathe and sleep, who rules over these two-footed and four-footed—who is the God, we should serve with sacrifice?
4. Through whose power each snow mountain exists, through whose (power), as they say, the ocean together with the Rāsa exists, through the (power) of both arms these heavens exist—who is the God, we should serve with sacrifice?
5. Through him the huge heaven and the earth are established, through which the sun and the sky are supported, that penetrates the air in space—who is the God, we should serve with sacrifice?
6. On these the two opposed armies, with trembling hearts, supported through his assistance, the rising sun radiates its light—who is the God, we should serve with sacrifice?

7. When the floodwaters came, conceived as an embryo, then Agni generated, he arose from it, the sole life spirit of the gods—who is the God, we should serve with sacrifice?
8. He in its greatness even looked over the flood waters that procreated Dakṣa and the sacrificial victim, who was the sole God among all the gods—who is the God, we should serve with sacrifice?
9. He must not harm us, who is the creator of the earth and the sky by valid decree, and who created the gleaming high waters—who is the God, we should serve with sacrifice?
10. O Prajāpati, no other than you encompasses all this creation. Grant our wishes for which we offer sacrifices, become our goal! Let us be rulers of riches!

The Sacrificial Horse (1.162.1–22)

1. Mitra, Varuṇa, Aryaman, Āyu, Ṛbhukṣan, the Maruts perceive nothing when we announce to the audience the heroic actions of the race horse's creation by God in wise speech.
2. When they grasp the horse, the sacrificial gift, and cover it with cloths and heirlooms, so the dappled goat goes bleating, willingly, in front to Indra's and Pūṣan's dear refuge.
3. This goat is led forward for all the gods with the steed as the share for Pūṣan. When the goat and horse are driven forward to be received by the sacrifice, so Tvaṣṭṛ encourages him on to fame.
4. When three times people circle the steed intended for the victim according to the way of the gods, so the goat victim, who is the share for Pūṣan, who reports the victim to the gods, goes on that occasion in front.
5. The Hotṛ, Advaryu, the Āvayāj, the Agnimindha, Grāvāgrābha and the deft-talking Śaṃstṛ?—fill their stomachs with this well-made, well-sacrificed victim!
6. The sacrificial stake and its carriers and those that carve the knob for the horse post, and those that collect together things to cook the steed, let their applause challenge us.
7. It entered into the realms of the gods—precisely when I prayed. The inspired seers rejoice after it. We turned it into a good companion at the banquet of the gods.
8. The horse's rope and halter, the bridle on its head, or even the grass that was put into its mouth, let all this stay with you among the gods!

9. What the fly ate of the steed's flesh, or something at the post and at the hands or nails of the slaughterer, let all this stay with you among the gods!
10. The remaining leftovers of his body evaporate as gas, whatever smell of its raw flesh remains—everything should the slaughters make right, and they should even cook the animal victim until it is well done.
11. What from the body parts flows down into the fire when it is put on the skewer, do not let it lie on the ground or the grass. This should be donated to the demanding gods!
12. This the disputed steed; if it is done, test by saying: It already smells great, remove it!—and they wait on meat alms from the horse, also let their consent be demanded by us.
13. The testing fork for the pot that cooks the flesh, the pots to pour the brew, the steaming covers of the kettles, hooks, and meat plates attend the horse.
14. On what it strides, settles, rolls itself, and the shackle of the horse, what it drank and the fodder eaten, let all of this be with you among the gods.
15. Do not let the fire smelling of smoke darken you, nor the red pot break into pieces. What is dedicated, offered, approved, is taken to the gods with Vaṣaṭ's blessed horse.
16. The garment placed underneath the horse, the head garment, the golden trappings that they put underneath the shackle and foot fetters, these dear matters should bind the horse among the gods.
17. If one has struck you too hard when riding with heel or whip, I make all this again good for you with a blessing, as they do with sacrificial food with an oblation ladle in the sacrifice.
18. The axe severs through thirty-four ribs of the racehorse, who is companion to the gods. Keep the body parts uninjured, dismantle them, announcing a limb according to each one of the pattern.
19. One is the slaughter of the steed of Tvaṣṭṛ, two others restrain him. This is the right rule. So many of your body parts I arrange according to the proper sequence, so many sacrificial lumps I place into the fire.
20. The dear soul should not hurt you when you arrive; the axe should not do your body lasting damage; a greedy, inexperienced slaughter should not cut apart limbs incorrectly with his knife sliding.
21. Really, you don't die from this, you are not harmed. You go to the gods on passable ways. The two stallions, the two mares became your chariot friends. . . .

22. Good cows and good steeds, manly children and all nourishing wealth shall be brought to us. The work of Aditi will make us innocent. Let the horse win sovereign power for us by means of sacrificial offerings!

To Puruṣa (10.90.1–16)

1. Puruṣa (cosmic man) has a thousand heads, a thousand eyes, a thousand feet. He completely covered the earth and extended himself beyond ten fingers.
2. Puruṣa alone is this whole world, the past and the future, and he is the ruler over immortality and he also grows even further through food.
3. Such is his greatness, and even more mightily therefore this is Puruṣa. All creatures are one-quarter of him, the immortal in heaven is three-quarters of him.
4. To three-quarters, Puruṣa would ascend, one-quarter of him remains here. From him, he separated out in all directions into some food that he eats and doesn't eat.
5. From him was born the Virāj, from which Virāj came the Puruṣa. He ranged beyond the earth from behind and in front when he was born.
6. As the gods with Puruṣa therefore carried out sacrifice, with him as the sacrificial victim, spring was glazed butter, summer the firewood, fall the oblation.
7. They consecrated him as the victim and the sacred grass at the beginning of the birth of Puruṣa. The gods, the Sādhyas, and the sages sacrificed.
8. From that all-encompassing sacrifice, the sacrificial fat was collected. He made this offering to the air, in the forest, and in village-living animals.
9. From this complete sacrificed victim, the verses and chants were created from him, the meters originated from him, and the sacrificial formulas.
10. From him, horses and all animals with double-row teeth were born, the cows were created from him, and the goats and sheep were created from him.
11. As they divided the Puruṣa into many parts, what would become of his many parts? For what was his mouth, his arms, his thighs, and his foot named?
12. His mouth turned into the Brahman, his two arms were made into the Kṣatriya (warrior), his two thighs to the Vaiśya, and the Śūdra was created from his feet.
13. From his spirit was built the moon, the sun came from his eyes; from his mouth Indra and Agni, the wind originated from his vital breath.
14. From his navel airspace was born, heaven followed from his head, from his two feet the earth, from the ear worldly parts of the sky. Thus, they regulated the worlds.

15. Seven enclosing sticks were created, and three times seven fuel sticks carried out the sacrifice, as the gods and Puruṣa, as sacrificial animal, prepared for it.
16. With the sacrifice, the gods sacrificed to the sacrifice. This is the first norm (of the sacrifice). This power joined itself with heaven, in which the ancient gods, the Sādhyas, can be found.

Source: *Rig-Veda-Samhitā with the Commentary of Sāyaṇāchārya*, edited by F. Max Müller. (Varanasi: Chowkhamba Sanskrit Series Office, 1969). Translated by Carl Olson.

Selections from the *Śatapatha Brāhmaṇa*

On the Establishment of the Sacred Fires (1.2.1.1–4.25)

1.1 Now when he creates the fire (Agni) from the different quarters, that is the collecting of the fire with its elements. Within whatever objects fire is inherent, he thereby collects the fire; and by thus collecting it, he gives it splendor, he connects it to cattle, and he supplies it with a mate.

1.2 Initially, the priest draws three lines, but he removes impurities from the earth when he begins. He establishes his fire on the earth in the correct way, which is the reason for drawing the lines.

1.3 The priest sprinkles them with water. . . . Thus he supplies the fire with food because water is food.

1.4–11 Because water is also female and fire is male, he creates a mate for fire. . . . He brings gold because it is found in water . . . thereby creating a fire with seed. . . . He brings salt . . . which means cattle; and therefore he supplies the fire with cattle. . . . He brings earth . . . and he supplies fire with earth. . . . He then brings small stones . . . that creates a firm resting place for the fires . . . and excludes enemies from any share in the sacrifice. . . .

3.1 The seasons of spring, summer, and the monsoon represent the gods, but the autumn, winter and wet season signify the ancestors. The waxing moon represents the gods, whereas the waning moon stands for the ancestors. The day signifies the gods while the night represents the ancestors. Furthermore, the morning represents the gods, and the afternoon signifies the ancestors.

3.2 These seasons are, then, the gods and ancestors. By knowing this, one can invoke them with one's invocation and get them to comply. . . .

3.3 When the fire of the sun moves in a northward direction, it is among the gods, and it protects them; and when it journeys southward it exists among the ancestors, and it protects them.

3.4 When the sun goes north, then a person can establish his fires. The gods free them of evil by means of the power of the sun, and the sacrificer rids himself of evil. Because the gods are immortal, the sacrificer gains a full length of life, even though there is no immortality for him, by establishing the fires at that time. If he waits to establish his fires the sun until moves toward the south, he does not get rid of evil because the ancestors have not had their evil dispelled from them. Because the ancestors are mortal, they die before their full allotment of life.

3.5 The spring is equal to the priesthood, the summer is the warriors, and the monsoon season represents ordinary people. A Brahmin sets up his fires in the spring because the spring is the priest; and the Kṣatriya sets them up in summer because the summer season is the warrior; and the Vaiśya constructs his fire during the rainy season because the monsoon season represents ordinary people. . . .

4.1 On the day prior to the establishing of the fires, a sacrificer and his wife eat food during daylight. Because the gods know the minds of humans; they are aware precisely when the establishing of fires will occur; all the gods come to the house of the sacrificer and stay there; this is a day for fasting. . . .

4.7 The sacrificer does not sleep during the night, The gods are also awake; thus the sacrificer becomes near to the gods, and he establishes his fires like a godly figure, subdued, and endowed with sacred heat (*tapas*). . . .

4.8 Some sacrifiers churn the fire before sunrise and take it eastward after sunset, which gives them both the day and night, gives them inward and outward breath, and gives them mind and speech. . . .

4.10 If they say, the fire is not established with a*rg*, *sāman*, or yajur verse, how is it created? The fire is Brahman and with Brahman it is established. The Brahman is equivalent to speech. It is the truth, which consists of mysterious utterances. Thus the sacrificer's fire is established by means of the truth.

4.11 With the mantra *bhuh* (earth), Prajāpati created the earth; with the utterance *bhuvah*, he created ether; with the mantra *svah*, he created sky. The extension of this triple world comprises this universe; the fire is established with this universe. . . .

4.15 When the gods began to establish their fires, the demonic beings prohibited them by saying, "The fire cannot be produced; you should not establish your fires!" Because they prohibited the gods, they are called Rākṣasas (demons).

4.16 Then the gods created a thunderbolt identified as a horse. It stood before the gods, and within its safe enclosure, the fire was produced. Therefore, according to this rationale the priest directs another to take the horse to the site of the fire. The horse stands in front of the priest, who raises the thunderbolt, and with this safe shelter the fire is produced. . . .

4.18 When the priests carry the fire eastward, the horse leads the way; this is done to deflect the fire from evil spirits; and the priests carry the fire safely and securely protected from the evil demons.

4.19 It is important that they carry the fire in such a way that it turns toward the sacrificer. The fire is not only the means of the sacrifice but it is also the way that the sacrifice enters the sacrificer; and it inclines toward the sacrificer. . . .

4.20 The fire is, moreover, the sacrificer's breath; they must carry the fire in a way that it turns toward him in order for the breath to enter into him. If the fire turns away from the sacrificer, breath also turns away from him. . . .

4.23 The priest makes the horse step on the fire altar. Then he leads the horse toward the east, makes it turn around, and allows it to stand facing the west. Since the horse represents strength, the priest makes it turn around again so that its vigor does not pass away from the sacrificer.

4.24 The priest rests the fire down on the horse's footprint because it represents strength. . . .

4.25 The priest silently touches the foot mark with the fire. Then, he lifts it up and repeats the gesture; repeating the gesture a third time, he lays it down by reciting earth, ether, sky. There are indeed three worlds. He thereby obtains the triple world.

Source: *The Śatapatha Brāhmaṇa*, edited by Albrecht Weber. Chowkhamba Sanskrit Series 96 (Varanasi: Chowkhamba Sanskrit Series Offcie, 1964). Translated by Carl Olson.

2

Upaniṣadic Literature

Attached to each of the four collections of the Vedas were Brāhmaṇas that explained the complex ritual system. Additional texts were added to various Brāhmaṇas to further explain the esoteric aspects of the rites. Some of these additional texts were called Āraṇyakas, whereas others were called Upaniṣads, although people did not make a sharp distinction between these new kinds of texts. In addition to explicating the ritual system, these esoteric texts also engaged in forms of cosmological and metaphysical speculation. Much like the four Vedas, these esoteric teachings were preserved orally for generations before assuming a written form. As with the Brāhmaṇa texts, particular Upaniṣad texts are associated with one of the four collections of the Vedas. The *Aitareya* and *Kausītakī Upaniṣads* are directly connected, for instance, with the *Rig Veda*, whereas the *Kaṭha* and *Maitrāyanī Upaniṣads* are associated with the *Black Yajur Veda* and the *Bṛhadāraṇyaka* and *Īśa Upaniṣads* are connection with the *White Yajur Veda*.

The Hindu religious tradition acknowledges the existence of 108 Upaniṣads, of which it is generally agreed that there are eighteen major texts. Although it appears that the Upaniṣads evolved from the Āraṇyakas (forest texts), and it is difficult to distinguish between them, the oldest Upaniṣads are the *Bṛhadāraṇyaka* and *Chāndogya*. The *Aitareya, Taittirīya*, and *Kauṣītaka* followed these texts historically. This second group was subsequently followed by the composition of the following: *Kena, Īśa, Kaṭha, Śvetāśvatara, Praśna, Muṇḍaka, Mahānārayana, Māṇḍūkya*, and

Maitrī. After the appearance of these thirteen major texts, many later Upaniṣads manifested a sectarian character by focusing on deities such as Śiva and Viṣṇu.

If one breaks the term down into its constituent components, the word *upaniṣad* suggests sitting down near a teacher to receive secret instructions characteristic of an intimate student-teacher type of relationship. In addition to being secret and personal, the teaching context was characterized as relational and dialogical. The texts mention various teachers and students. It is also not unusual to find a deity or demonic being receiving instruction, or seeing a woman playing the role of teacher. Overall, the Upaniṣads are not the result of a single mind, but rather represent the pedagogical efforts of many teachers of ancient India during a historical period of great social, economic, and religious change.

The Upaniṣads are called Vedānta (which should not be confused with the later philosophical school of thought) because they represent the deepest secrets of the Vedas. Although the Upaniṣads develop some notions of the Vedas, they also introduce new ideas, at least in a primitive form, that shape Indian religious culture, and they transform some of the old notions into something fresh and innovative. The Upaniṣads take, for instance, Vedic rites and transform them into an internal activity that is performed by the individual, who functions as priest, patron of the sacrifice, and sacrificial victim in many cases. Upaniṣads also introduce notions that formed Indian religious culture such as karma (law of cause and effect), rebirth, immortal self (ātman), ultimate reality (Brahman), and path to liberation (*mokṣa*). A reader will be able to find references to each of these notions in the following selections.

A prevalent theme in the Upaniṣads is the importance of knowing. Although there are some Upaniṣads that discuss the importance of devotion to a deity and the necessity of divine grace for salvation, such as the *Śvetāśvatara Upaniṣad*, the majority of the Upaniṣads emphasize the importance of knowledge for attaining liberation. The type of knowledge advocated by the Upaniṣads is very different from that in the West, where knowledge is something that is discovered by the individual. In Indian culture exemplified by the Upaniṣads, knowledge is to be recovered, because the truth–the object of knowledge–is always present; it has merely been lost. It simply needs to be recovered and rediscovered. This recovery occurs within an intimate teacher-student relationship. This is a not empirical or rational mode of knowledge, but it is rather an intuitive insight into the true nature of reality. This is a self-validating, transcendent, and infinite kind of knowledge.

Due to the cultural and historical importance of the renouncer (*saṃnyāsin*) in India, this chapter concludes with selections of two so-called *Saṃnyāsa Upaniṣads*–the *Paramahaṃsa Upaniṣad* and the *Āśrama Upaniṣad*. The grouping together of these texts provide a description of the renouncer, his lifestyle, and different types. To group these texts together does not reflect an indigenous form of typology. In 1905, the German scholar Paul Deussen's translation of sixty Upaniṣads represented the first reference to such texts as *Saṃnyāsa Upaniṣads*; he was probably motivated by the common subject matter of these texts. The number of these texts was expanded by F. Otto Schrader, who directed a project sponsored by the Adyar Library published in 1912. Schrader's student Joachim Friedrich Sprockhoff published a book entitled *Saṃnyāsa: Quellenstudien zur Askese im Hinduismus* on this textual material. In his work, Sprockhoff dated the *Āśrama Upaniṣad* to around 300 C.E., whereas the *Paramahaṃsa* is dated to the medieval period. Although these Upaniṣads were composed later than the selections from the earlier Upaniṣads, they give us a good glimpse into the life of a renouncer.

Selections from the Upaniṣads

Creation and the Search for Reality

From the unreal lead me to the real!
From death lead me to immortality!

The unreal is death, and the real is immortality—thus, when he says, "From the unreal lead me to the real," what he is really saying is: "From death lead me to immortality"; that is, "Make me immortal." Darkness is death, and light is immortality—thus, when he says. "From the darkness lead me to the light," what he is actually affirming is: "From death lead me to immortality"; therefore, "Make me immortal." By the statement, "From death lead me to immortality," there is nothing obscure.

He may also acquire food for himself by chanting the remaining praises. When he is singing them, therefore, he should choose as a boon anything he desires. An Udgātṛ priest who knows this is able to gain by his chanting whatever he desires, either for himself or for the patron of the sacrifice. This is genuine world conquest. When a man knows this sāman, there is no fear of his being without a world.

1.4.1. In the beginning this world was a single self (*ātman*) shaped like a person. Looking around, he saw nothing but himself. Initially, he said, "I am!" and from that utterance the name "I" came to be. Therefore, even today when you call someone, he first says, "It's I," and then speaks whatever other name he possesses. That first being received the name "person" (*puruṣa*) because he previously destroyed all evils. When someone knows this, he destroys anyone who desires to get ahead of him.

1.4.2. He became afraid; thus, one becomes afraid when one is alone. Then he thought to himself: "Of what should I be afraid, if there is only me?" Therefore, his fear left him, for what should he be afraid of? To be sure, it is from another that one becomes afraid.

1.4.3. He experienced no delight; thus one finds no pleasure when one is alone. He desired a companion. Indeed, he was as large as a man and a woman closely embraced. He split his body into two parts, creating a husband and wife. This is the reason Yājñavalkya used to say: "The two of us are like two halves of a fragment." This space, therefore, is completely filled by the wife. He copulated with her, and from their sexual union human beings were produced.

1.4.4. She then thought: "After producing me from his own body, how could he copulate with me? Let me hide myself." She became a cow. But he became a bull and copulated with her. Cattle were born from their sexual union. Then she became a mare, and he a stallion; she became a female donkey, and he, a male donkey. And again he copulated with her, and from their union single-hoofed animals were born. She became a female goat, and he, a male goat; she became a ewe, and he, a ram. And again he copulated with her, and from their union goats and sheep were born. In this way he created every male and female pair that exists, even down to ants.

1.4.5. This dawned on him: "I alone am this creation, for I created all this." From myself this "creation" came into existence. He who knows this flourishes in this creation of his.

1.4.6. Then he rubbed back and forth and, using his hands, produced fire from his mouth as from a vagina. Both these—the hands and the mouth—are without hair on the inside, just as the inside of the vagina is without hair. "People say sacrifice to this god. Sacrifice to that god." In reality each of these gods is his own creation. And he himself is all the gods. From his semen, then, he created all that is moist, which is actually Soma. Food and eater—that is, the entire world is food and its eaters.

This is Brahmā's superior creation because he created the gods, who are superior to him, and, although being a mortal himself, he created the immortals. Anyone who knows this is located within this super-creation of his.

1.4.7. At that time this world lacked any distinctions; it was distinguished by name and form, as as the expression goes—"He possesses such a name and form." Even today this world is distinguished simply by name and form, as the expression goes, "He is such a name and such a form."

He entered into this body even to the tips of the fingernails, he is similar to a razor within a case, or as a fire within its source. People do not see him, for he is incomplete when he is seen; when he is breathing he is called the vital force, when he is speaking he is called speech, when he is seeing he is called sight, when he is hearing he is called hearing, and when he is thinking he is called mind. These are only the names of his various actions. A man who considers him to be any one of activities does not understand him, for he is incomplete without any one of these. One should consider them as just his self (*ātman*), because all these become one. This same self (*ātman*) is the trace of this all, by knowing it one comes to know this all, just as by following their tracks one finds [what was lost]. He knows this finds fame and praise.

1.4.8. This self (*ātman*) is dearer than a son, it is dearer than wealth, it is dearer than everything else. If one claims that something other than his self is dear to him, and someone were to tell him that he will lose what he holds dear, that would likely happen. A person should consider only his self as dear to him. When a man considers only his self as dear to him, what he holds dear will never perish. (*Bṛhadāranyaka Upaniṣad* 1.4–1.8)

Nature of the Self (ātman)

6.9. "Just as the bees, son, prepare the honey by collecting nectar from various trees and by reducing that nectar to a unity, they are also not able to differentiate by saying: 'I am the nectar of that tree,' or 'I am the nectar of this tree.' In exactly the same way, son, when all these creatures merge into Being, they are not aware that 'We are merging into Being.' Whatever they are in this world—a tiger, a lion, a wolf, a boar, a worm, a moth, a gnat, or a mosquito—they all merge into that.

"That finest essence constitutes the self of this whole world; that is the truth; that is the self (*ātman*). And that you are, Śvetaketu."

"Sir, teach me more."

"Very well, son."

6.10. "These rivers, son, flow toward the east, and the western ones flow toward the west. From the ocean, they merge from rivers into the ocean; they become the ocean itself. In that condition they are unaware that 'I am that river,' or 'I am this river.' Precisely, son, when all these creatures reach Being, they are unaware that 'We have originated from Being.' Whatever they are in this world—whether it is a tiger, a lion, a wolf, a boar, a worm, a moth, a gnat, or a mosquito—they all merge into that."

"This finest essence constitutes the self of this whole world; that is the truth; that is the self (*ātman*). And that you are, Śvetaketu."

"Sir, teach me more."

"Very well, son."

6. 11. "Take this huge tree, son; if someone were to cut its root, sap would flow out. If someone were to cut it in the middle, its sap would flow out; and if someone were to cut it at the top, its sap would flow out. Pervaded by the self (*jīva*), this tree stands here continuously drinking moisture and flourishing. When, however, life leaves one of its branches, that branch dies. When it leaves a second branch, that likewise dies, and when it leaves a third branch, that also dies. When it leaves the entire tree, the whole tree dies."

"Indeed," he continued, "know that this body dies when life leaves it; but life does not die.

"The finest essence within this whole world constitutes the self; that is the truth; that is the self (*ātman*). And that you are, Śvetaketu."

"Sir, teach me more."

"Very well, son."

6.12. "Bring a banyan fruit."

"Here it is, sir."

"Cut it up."

"I've cut it up, sir."

"What do you see there?"

"These rather tiny seeds, sir."

"Now, take one of them and cut it up."

"I've cut one up, sir."

"What do you see there?"

"Nothing, sir."

Then he told him: "This finest essence, son, that you can't even perceive—from that finest essence this huge fig tree originates."

"Believe me, my son: the finest essence constitutes the self of this whole world; that is the truth; that is the self (*ātman*). And that you are, Śvetaketu."

"Sir, teach me more."

"Very well, son."

6.13. "Put this salt in a container of water and return tomorrow." The son did it. Then his father said to him: "The salt you put in the water last evening—bring it here." He grasped for it but could not find it, as it was completely dissolved.

"Now, take a sip from this part," said the father. "How does it taste?"

"Salty."

"Take a sip from the center. How does it taste?"

"Salty."

"Take a sip from that part. How does it taste?"

"Salty."

"Set it aside and come back later." He did as he was told and found that the container was always the same. The father told him: "You, of course, did not see Being there, son; yet it was always right there."

"The finest essence constitutes the self of this whole world; that is the truth; that is the self (*ātman*). And that you are, Śvetaketu."

"Sir, teach me more."

"Very well, son."

6.14.1–2. "Just as, son, a man might be brought here blindfolded from the land of Gandhāras and then left in a deserted region; and as he might drift about either toward the east, or the north, or the south, since he had been blindfolded and deserted, now, if someone were to free him from his blindfold and tell him, 'Go that way; the land of Gandhāras is in that direction,' being a sensible man, he would go from village to village asking for directions and finally arrive in the land of Gandhāras. In exactly the same way in this world, when a man has a teacher, he knows: 'I am delayed here only until I am freed [from ignorance]; but then I will arrive home!'"

"The finest essence constitutes the self of this whole world; that is the truth; that is the self (*ātman*). And that you are, Śvetaketu." (*Chāndogya Upaniṣad* 6.9–14)

Another Definition of the Self

8.7. "The self (*ātman*) which is free from evils, from old age and death, from sorrow, from hunger and thirst; the self whose desire is the real—that is the self that you should try to discover, that is the self that you should seek to understand. When someone discovers that self and understands it he obtains all the worlds, and all his desires are fulfilled." Thus said Prajāpati.

Both the gods and the demons heard it. Then, each side said: "Come. Let us discover that self (*ātman*), by searching for which one obtains all the worlds, and all one's desires." Then Indra set out from among the gods, and Virocana from among the demons. And without mutual communication the two arrived in the presence of Prajāpati carrying firewood in their hands.

For thirty-two years, they lived the life of celibate students. Then Prajāpati asked them: "Why have you lived here? What do you desire?"

They replied: "The self (*ātman*) that is free from evils, free from old age and death, free from sorrow, free from hunger and thirst; the self whose desires are real—that is the self that you should try to discover, that is the self that you should seek to understand. When someone discovers that self and understands it, he obtains all the worlds and all his desires."

Prajāpati then told them: "The person that one sees here in the eye—that is the self (*ātman*); that is the immortal; that is the one free from fear; that is Brahman."

"But then, sir, who is the one that is perceived in the water and in a mirror?"

"It is the same one who is seen in all these," replied Prajāpati.

8.8. "Look at yourselves in a pan of water. And let me know if there is anything you do not understand about yourselves." Then they looked into a pan of water. Prajāpati asked them:

"What do you see?"

And they replied: "Sir, we see here our entire self, corresponding precisely to the hairs of the body and fingernails."

Prajāpati told them then: "Adorn yourself, dress well, and tidy yourself, and then look into a pan of water." So they adorned themselves, dressed well, and tidied themselves, and then looked into a pan of water. Prajāpati asked them: "What do you see?"

And they replied: "Sir, as the two of us here are well adorned, well dressed, and all tidied up, in exactly the same way are these, sir, well adorned, well dressed, and all tidied."

Prajāpati told them, "That is the self (*ātman*); that is the immortal; that is the fearless one; that is Brahman," And the two of them left with tranquil hearts.

Glancing at them as the two departed, Prajāpati said: "They go, without understanding about the self (*ātman*), without discovering the self! The side that will hold to this teaching, whether it is the gods or the demons, is bound to perish."

Then, Virocana, his heart totally tranquil, went back to the demons and announced to them this teaching: "It is the embodied self that one should make happy in this world. It is the embodied self that one should care for. When someone extols the embodied self alone in this world, when he cares only for the embodied, he wins both this world and the next." Therefore, even now people here say of a person who is not generous, who is not a believer, who has no faith, and who offers no sacrifices: 'What a demonic person!' This is, indeed, the teaching that demons hold to; they perform the funerary rites for the body of a dead person with offerings of food, garments, and ornaments for which they have begged, for they believe that in this way they will win the next world. (*Chāndogya Upaniṣad* 8.7–8)

Brahman, Knowledge, and Path to Liberation

3.1.1. Two birds, companions and always united, cling to the very same tree. One of them eats a tasty fruit; the other observes, without eating.

3.1.2. On the same tree, a person, sunken, grieves, and is deluded. When he sees the other, the Lord, he is contented; when he sees the other and his greatness, his sorrow disappears.

3.1.3. When the seer sees that golden Person, the creator, the Lord, source of Brahman; then, shaking off good and evil, the wise man becomes pure, and attains the highest identity [with the Lord].

3.1.4. It is life that is visible in all beings. By understanding this, one becomes a knower and thereby a person who is a superior speaker; a person who is delighted with the self, finding pleasure in the self, and thus performing works. A person who is Brahman! Such a person is the best!

3.1.5. This self can be grasped—by truth, by austerity, by right knowledge, and by a perpetual life of chastity. It resides within the body, pure and full of light, whom ascetics perceive, when their imperfections are eliminated.

3.1.6. Truth alone he wins, never the false. By the truth runs the path to the gods, by which the sages proceed, their desires satisfied, to where that supreme treasure of the truth is found.

3.1.7. It is vast, heavenly, of inconceivable form; and yet it appears more subtle than the subtle. It is farther than the farthest, yet it is near at hand; it is right here within those who see, hidden within the secret place [of their heart].

3.1.8. Not by sight, not by speech, nor by any other sense organ; nor by austerities or rites is he grasped. Rather a person sees the one without parts, as one meditates, when one's being has become pure, through right knowledge.

3.1.9. The subtle self is known by thought within which breath has entered in five different forms; the entire thinking of people is interwoven with the senses, when it is pure, this self becomes disclosed.

3.1.10. Whatever world a person, whose being is purified, thinks with his mind, and whatever desires he covets for himself; that world, those desires, he wins. Therefore, a person who desires prosperity should praise one who knows the self.

3.2.1. He knows this highest abode of Brahman, established on which everything shines radiantly. The persons, free from desires, who worship the Person (*puruṣa*), who are wise, go beyond the seed [of rebirth] here.

3.2.2. One who entertains desires in his thoughts, due to those desires is born here and there. But when one's desires are satisfied and one's self is perfected, all one's desires disappear on this earth.

3.2.3. This self cannot be grasped by teachings or by intellect, or even by great learning. Only the person that one chooses can grasp that person, to such a person the self reveals itself.

3.2.4. This self cannot be grasped, by a weak person or through carelessness, or even by false austerity. But when a wise person strives by these means, this self enters the abode of Brahman.

3.2.5. The seers, engrossed with knowledge, become free from passion and tranquil, and their selves are made perfect when they have attained him. The wise, their selves controlled, attain him altogether, he who is omnipresent in All, they enter into the All.

3.2.6. The ascetics who have firmly ascertained full knowledge of the Vedānta have their being purified by the application of renunciation. In the worlds of Brahman, at the end time, they will all be fully liberated and immortal.

3.2.7. The fifteen parts return to their foundations; and all the senses return to their respective divinities. Works and the self consist of understanding—all are unified in the supreme immutable.

3.2.8. As the rivers flow on and disappear into the ocean, relinquishing their names and appearances; so the knower, liberated from name and form, attains the heavenly Person, beyond the highest.

3.2.9. When a person knows that highest Brahman, he himself becomes Brahman. A person with the knowledge of Brahman will not be born in one's family. Such a person passes beyond sorrow and evil. Liberated from the knots of one's heart, one becomes immortal. (*Muṇḍaka Upaniṣad* 3.1.1–3.2.9)

Kaṭha Upaniṣad *and the Narrative Approach to the Truth*

Chapter 1

1. Vājaśravas gave away all his possessions [as a sacrificial gift]. He had a son named Naciketas.
2. Although he was young, faith took hold of him, while sacrificial gifts of cows were being led away, and he reflected:
3. "They've drunk all their water, eaten all their grass, they have been milked dry, they are totally barren—'Joyless' are those worlds, to which a person goes who gives them as gifts."
4. Thus he asked his father: "Father, to whom will you give me?" He repeated it a second time, and again a third time. Then, his father asserted: "I'll give you to Death!"
5. [Naciketas reflects:] "I go as the very first of many. I go as the middlemost of many. What's it that Yama must do, that he will do with me today?"
6. [A Voice:] "Look forward! See how they have gone, those who have proceeded us! Look backward! So will they go, those who will come after us. A mortal man ripens like grain, and like grain he is born again.
7. "A Brahmin guest enters a house as a fire. They make such a person an offering. Bring water, O Vaivasvata, that is how they appease him.
8. "Hope and expectation, friendship and goodwill, children and cattle, rites and gifts—all these a Brahmin wrests from the ignorant person, in whose house he resides without any food."
9. [Death:] "Three nights, O Brahmin, you stayed in my house, a guest worthy of reverence, without any food; homage to you, O Brahmin! And may I have well-being! Therefore, choose three wishes in return."
10. [Naciketas:] "With his anxiety allayed, his anger subdued, Gautama (my father), O Death, be well-disposed to me. That he cheerfully greet me, when I'm dismissed by you—this is the first of my three wishes."

11. [Death:] "He'll be affable in the future, just as formerly; Auddālaka Āruṇi, I have dismissed you. He'll have restful nights, his anger subdued, when seeing you released from the mouth of Death."
12. [Naciketas:] "In the world of heaven there is no fear whatsoever; there one has no fear of old age or you. Transcending both—hunger and thirst, gone are all sorrows, one rejoices in heaven.
13. "You, O Death, understand the fire sacrifice that leads to heaven; describe that to me, a man who has faith; people who are in heaven enjoy immortality—this I choose with my second wish."
14. [Death:] "I shall explain to you—and learn this teaching from me, O Naciketas, you who understand—about the fire sacrifice that leads to heaven, to the attainment of an infinite world, and is its very foundation. Know that it lies hidden, in the secret place of the heart."
15. [Narrator:] He described to him that fire sacrifice—at the beginning of the world. What bricks, how many; and how they are to be laid. And he repeated it exactly as described. Then, pleased with him, Death spoke to him again;
16. Delighted, the great soul said to him: [Death:] "Here I grant you another wish today. This fire sacrifice will be named after you. Accept also this glittering chain of gold.
17. "By lighting, Naciketas, the triple fire—uniting with the three, performing the triple rite, he crosses over birth and death. By knowing Brahman that is being born, as the god who is to be praised, by recognizing this chain of gold to be that, he attains unending peace.
18. "Having this, Naciketas, a triple fire is started—knowing these three, and, with that knowledge, he builds the fire of Naciketas; he casts off the bonds of death, by passing beyond sorrow, he rejoices in heaven.
19. "This, Naciketas, is your fire that leads to heaven, what you chose with your second wish. This fire people will proclaim as your own. Choose your third wish, O Naciketas."
20. [Naciketas:] "There is this doubt about a man who is deceased. 'He exists,' say some; others say, 'He exists not.' I want to know this, so please teach me. This is the third of my wishes."
21. [Death:] "Even the ancient gods had doubts about this, for it's difficult to understand because it's a subtle doctrine. O Naciketas, make another wish. Do not press me! Release me from this."

22. [Naciketas:] "As to this, we're told, even the gods had doubts; and you say, O Death, it's hard to understand. But another teacher like you I can't find to explain it; there's no other wish that is equal to it at all."
23. [Death:] "Choose sons and grandsons who will live a hundred years! Many cattle, elephants, horses, and gold! Choose a wide expanse of earth! And you yourself live as many autumns as you wish!"
24. "And if you would think this is an equal wish, choose wealth together with a long life; achieve greatness, Naciketas, on earth; and I will make you an enjoyer of your desires."
25. "You may ask freely for all those desires, whatever desires are hard to obtain in this world. Look at these lovely girls, with chariots and lutes, such girls are unobtainable by mortals I'll give them to you; you'll be waited on by them; O Naciketas, do not ask me about death."
26. [Naciketas:] "Ephemeral are things of mortals, O Death, they sap the vigor of all the senses; and even a full life is indeed slight; thus keep your chariots, your songs and dances!"
27. "With wealth you cannot make a man satisfied; will we get to keep wealth, when we have seen you? And we get to live only as long as you will allow! This alone is the wish that I would like to choose."
28. "Having encountered it in mortals, would an insightful man, himself growing old in this wretched and lowly place, meditating on its beauties, its pleasures and joys, delight in a long life?"
29. "The point on which they have great doubts—O Death: What happens at that great passage—tell me that. This is my wish, probing the hidden mystery. Naciketas wishes for nothing other than that."

Chapter 2

1. [Death:] "The good is different, the rewarding is another thing; their aims are diverse, both bind a person. Good things await one who chooses the good; by choosing the rewarding, one misses one's goal."
2. "Both the good and the rewarding present themselves to a person; the wise assesses them, notes their difference; and chooses the good over the rewarding; the fool chooses the rewarding rather than what is good."
3. "You have examined and rejected, O Naciketas, things people desire, pleasant and pleasing to look at. This chain of gold, where many a person sinks, you have rejected as wealth."

4. "Far apart and widely different are these two: ignorance and what is known as knowledge. I think Naciketas desires knowledge; many desires do not confuse you."
5. "Abiding in ignorance, but calling themselves wise, thinking themselves learned, the fools go around, running everywhere like a group of blind people, led by a person who is himself blind."
6. "This passage lies hidden from a clueless fool, who is deluded by the delusion of wealth. Thinking 'This is the world; there is no other,' he falls under my control repeatedly."
7. "Many do not get to hear of that passage; and even when they hear, many don't comprehend it. Rare is the person who teaches it, lucky is the person who grasps it. Rare is the person who knows it, lucky is the person who has taught it."
8. "When taught by an inferior person, it is difficult to grasp, even though one may think a lot, one cannot gain access to it, unless someone else teaches it. For it is subtler than the subtle, a thing beyond the conceptual."
9. "One can't grasp this notion by reason; yet it is understandable when taught by another, dearest friend. You have grasped it! You are truly steadfast. Would that we have, O Naciketas, a questioner like you!"
10. "What you call wealth, I know to be transient; for by fleeting things one cannot gain the permanent. Therefore, I have built the fire of Naciketas. And by impermanent things I have gained the eternal."
11. "Attaining desires is the foundation of the world; uninterrupted rites bring ultimate security. Endless will and praise are the foundation—these you have seen, O wise Naciketas, and having seen, resolutely rejected."
12. "The primeval one who is hard to perceive, wrapped in mystery, hidden in the cave, residing within the impenetrable depth—by considering him as God, an insight gained by inner contemplation, the wise one abandons both sorrow and joy."
13. "When a mortal has heard it, and fully understood it; when he has drawn out the truth, and grasped this subtle point of doctrine, he rejoices, for he has found something in which he could rejoice. To the truth I declare my house to be open, Naciketas."
14. [Naciketas:] "Apart from the right doctrine and from the wrong; apart from what is done here and what is left undone; apart from what has been and what is yet to be, tell me what you see."

15. [Death:] "The word that all the Vedas reveal; and which all austerities proclaim; seeking which people live student lives. That word now I will declare to you succinctly—that is OM!"
16. "That syllable alone is truly Brahman! That syllable is alone supreme! Thus knowing that syllable indeed, a person obtains one's wishes.
17. "This is the best support! This is the supreme support! And when one knows this support, a person rejoices in Brahman's world."
18. "The wise one is not born, he does not die; this one has not come from anywhere; he has not become anyone. This one is unborn and eternal, primeval and everlasting. And is not killed, when the body is slain."
19. If the killer thinks that he slays, if the slain thinks that he is killed, both of them fail to understand. He neither slays, nor is he slain.
20. Finer than the finest, greater than the greatest, is the self (*ātman*) that lies hidden in the heart of a living being. Without desires and free from sorrow, a person perceives by the creator's grace the greatest of the self.
21. Sitting, he roams afar. Lying, he goes everywhere. Who, besides me, is able to know? That god who is ceaselessly exulting and not exulting.
22. As bodiless among bodies, as stable among unstable beings—a wise person ceases to grieve when he perceives this immense, all-pervading self.
23. This self cannot be grasped, by teachings or by intellect, nor by great learning. Only the person he chooses can grasp him, to such a person the self chooses to reveal its nature.
24. Not a man who has not ceased his evil conduct, nor a man who is not calm or composed, nor even a man who is without a peaceful mind could ever secure it by correct wisdom.
25. For whom the priest and the warrior are both like food, and death is like a sauce—who really knows where He is?

Chapter 3

1. There are two selves that partake of righteousness in the world of good works. Both have entered into the cave of the heart, the other into the highest region beyond, both drinking the truth. Brahman knowers call these two "shadow" and "light" in the world of rites rightly performed.
2. And those who maintain the five sacrificial fires, and those who perform the triple fire of Naciketas, a bridge for those who sacrifice; the imperishable, the highest Brahman, for those who wish to cross the danger of the distant shore. May we master the fire of Naciketas.

3. Know the self as a rider in a chariot, and the body as simply the chariot. Know the intellect as the charioteer, and the mind, as the reins.
4. The senses, they say, are the horses, and sense objects are the paths around them; the self is linked to the body, senses, and mind, the wise call the self the one who enjoys.
5. When a person lacks understanding, whose mind is never controlled, his senses are uncontrolled, like the bad horses of a charioteer.
6. But when a person possesses understanding, and his mind is constantly controlled, his senses are controlled, like the good horses of a charioteer.
7. When a person lacks understanding, is unmindful and always impure—such a person does not reach that final step, but proceeds to rebirth.
8. When a person has understanding, who is mindful and always pure, does reach that final goal, from which he is not reborn anymore.
9. When a person's mind is one's reins, intellect functions as his charioteer; such a person reaches the end of the journey, that highest place of Viṣṇu.
10. Higher than the senses are their objects; higher than sense objects is the mind; higher than the mind is the intellect; higher than the intellect is the great self (*ātman*);
11. Higher than the great self is the unmanifest; higher than the unmanifest is the Person; higher than the Person there is nothing at all. That is the goal, that is the highest state.
12. Though hidden in all the beings, this self is not visibly displayed. But those people with intuitive insight see him, with superior and subtle intellects.
13. A wise person should curb his speech and mind, such a person should control them within the intelligent self; he should control intelligence within the great self, and the latter, he should control within the tranquil self.
14. Arise! Awake! Obtained your wishes and understand them! A razor's sharp edge is hard to traverse. That, poets declare, is the difficulty of the path.
15. What possesses no sound or touch, no appearance, taste, or smell; without beginning or end, undecaying and eternal—when a person discerns it, stable and beyond the immense, he is freed from the jaws of death.
16. The wise person who hears or tells the tale of Naciketas, an ancient tale told by Death, will rejoice in Brahman's world.
17. If a person, pure and devout, proclaims this great secret in an assembly of priests, or during a ceremony for the dead, it will lead one to immortality!. . .

Chapter 6

1. Its roots above, its branches below, this is the eternal fig tree. That alone is the Pure! That is Brahman! That alone is called the Immortal! On it all the worlds rest; and beyond it no one can ever go. This, indeed, is that!
2. All that is this world, whatever lives, was created and moves within the breath; great is the fear, the thunderbolt is raised; those who know that become immortal.
3. Fear of it makes the fire burn; fear of it makes the sun shine; fear of it makes Indra and Wind, and Death, the fifth, run.
4. If one were able to realize it here, before the body disintegrates; according to such (knowledge), it would enable one to obtain a body within the created worlds.
5. As in a mirror, so perceived in the body, as in a dream, so in the fathers' world; as in water or in the Gandharva world, a thing becomes somewhat visible, as in shadows and light, so in the world of Brahman.
6. The separate nature of the senses, their arising and falling, as they come separately into existence—when a wise man knows this, he does not grieve.
7. Higher than the senses is the mind; higher than the mind is the essence of being; higher than the essence of being is the great self; higher than the great self is the unmanifest.
8. Higher than the unmanifest is the Self, pervading everything and without any marks. Knowing it, a person is liberated, and attains immortality.
9. His form is beyond sight; no one can see that one with one's sight; contained within the heart, with insight, with thought, those who know this become immortal.
10. When the five perceptions are calmed, together with the mind, and not even intellect stirs—that they call the highest state.
11. When senses are firmly controlled, this they call Yoga. From distractions a person is freed; Yoga is the origin, as well as the end.
12. Not by speech, not by the mind, not by sight can he be grasped. How can it be comprehended, other than by saying "It is!"
13. It can be comprehended in two ways: by saying that "It is," by affirming it is the real. To one who comprehends it as "It is," it becomes clear that it is real.
14. When they are all liberated, the desires buried in one's heart—then a mortal becomes immortal, and attains Brahman in this world.
15. When all knots are severed that bind one's heart on earth—then a mortal becomes immortal! For such is the teaching.

16. There are one hundred and one veins of the heart. One of them runs up to the crown of the head. Going up by it, he reaches the immortal. Others are ascending in all directions.
17. A person the size of a thumb is the inner soul (*ātman*), always residing within the hearts of people; a person should draw it out of the body with determination, like a reed from the grass sheath; a person should know it as immortal and pure. A person should know him as immortal and pure.
18. Then, after Naciketas received this body of knowledge, and the complete yogic rules taught by Death, he attained Brahman; and he became free from passion and death. And thus will others who know this teaching about the self.

Source: *The Principal Upaniṣads*, edited by S. Radhakrishnan (London: George Allen & Unwin, 1953; New York: Humanities Press, 1969). Translated by Carl Olson.

Selections from the Saṃnyāsa Upaniṣads

Selections from the Paramahaṃsa Upaniṣad

Para means highest or supreme, whereas *haṃsa* is a wandering wild goose or swan, which serves as a symbol of the migrating soul from one life to another, or it represents the homeless life of the renouncer.

1. At one time, Nārada approached the Lord Bhagavān and asked him: "What is the way of the Paramahaṃsas? What is their condition?"

The Lord Bhagavān replied to him: The way of Paramahaṃsas is very rare in the world and is not chosen very often. But when he walks it, he remains in a continual state of purity, he is a man of the Vedas, thus think the wise. He is a great person with his thoughts concentrating on me; thus I always live within him.

He who renounces his children, friends, wife, relatives, his topknot of hair, sacred sacrificial thread, vedic study, and all ritual works; who renounces the entire world and dons a loincloth, staff, a garment for bodily protection to help those in the world—is his position not the highest, you ask? No, it is he [the Paramahaṃsa].

2. The Paramahaṃsa carries no staff, is devoid of hair-tuft, lacks a sacrifical thread, and wanders without clothing. He is indifferent to cold and heat, pleasure and pain, respect or disrespect. He is free from the six waves of rebirth [that is,

hunger, thirst, grief, illusion, old age, and death]. He renounces censure, pride, jealousy, deceit, arrogance, desire, hatred, pain, anger, greed, illusion, joy, irration, egoism, and similar things; and while he comprehends his own body as a corpse, he rejects his body, a cause of doubt, perversity, and error, and he constantly concentrates on pure Being. He lives in that state alone. "I am that calm, blissful, timeless Being. That is my highest condition, my topknot, and sacrificial thread." By the power of knowing that the highest Self and lower self are identical, this represents true union in which time dissolves. This knowledge represents the twilight rite.

3. A person renouncing all desires and living in the Ultimate One carries the staff of knowledge alone. He is called the single-staffed ascetic. A person without knowledge carries a wooden staff, accepts food from anyone—such a person goes to a terrible hell. But a person who knows this difference is a Paramahaṃsa.

4. Clad by space [naked], he owes no obedience to anyone, and he does not sacrifice to the ancestors, utters no praise or sacred mantras, but he lives from day to day. He does not attract or repulse anything; there is nothing fit to be seen or not seen, nothing separate or inseparate, no ego, and no world. Within a homeless condition, he lives as a wanderer. He is detached from gold and other valuables, there is nothing to be seen. If one responds that it is harmless to just look at something, the renouncr knows that he can be harmed. Because he lives as an ascetic, he might become a Brahmin murderer by gazing at gold; if an ascetic touches gold, he becomes an outcaste; because he is an ascetic, he becomes a killer of the self by grasping gold. Thus, an ascetic should not gaze at, touch, or grasp gold with desire; he must renounce all desires that arise in his mind.

Not fearing pain, not longing for pleasure, forsaking desire, unattached to everything good or bad, he is devoid of hatred and without pleasure. His active senses are at rest; he is fixed in knowledge alone; and knowing the self, he represents the true yogin with perfect bliss. He knows "I am Brahman, blissful, pure consciousness." By realizing this, he becomes that Brahman, he knows it, and he achieves his goal.

Selections from the Āśrama Upaniṣad

1. There are four stages with sixteen subdivisions. There are four types of Brāhmaṇa students: Gāyatra, Brāhma, Prājāpatya, and Bṛhan.

- The Gāyatra is one who, after his initiation, abstaining from salty food, studies the *gāyatrī* verse for three nights.

- A Brāhma is he who resides as a vedic student for forty-eight years, or twelve years for each Veda, or for as long as it takes him to master the Veda.
- A Prājāpatya is he who, satisfied with his wife, approaches her at the proper time and avoids the wives of others. Or a Brāhma is one who lives in the home of his teacher for twenty-four years, whereas a Prājāpatya lives with his teacher for forty-eight years.
- A Bṛhan lives in celibacy as a perpetual student and does not leave his teacher until he dies.

2. There are also four types of householders: Vārttāvṛttis, Śālīnavṛttis, Yāyāvaras, and Ghorasaṃnyāsikas.

- Engaging in farming, cattle-breeding, and trade, the Vārttāvṛttis are without blame. They perform long-lasting sacrifices, and strive for the eternal self.
- Śālīnavṛttis [are those who] offer sacrifices, but do not officiate at a sacrifice; who study without teaching; who give without taking; who offer long-lasting sacrifices; and who seek the self.
- Yāyāvaras [are those who] offer sacrifices and officiate at them; who study and teach; who give and receive; who who offer long-lasting sacrifices; and who seek the self.
- Ghorasaṃnyāsikas [are those who] perform rites with carefully selected and purified water; who live on food obtained daily; who perform long-lasting sacrifices; and who strive for the self.

3. There are also four types of forest hermits: Vaikhānasas, Audumbaras, Vālakhilyas, and Phenapas.

- Vaikhānasas are those who tend the sacred fires with creepers and trees grown on uncultivated land external to the village; who perform the five great sacrifices, and who strive for the self.
- Audumbaras, [are those who] maintain the sacred fire with figs, jujubes, rice, and millet from the direction toward which they look; who perform the five great sacrifices; and who seek the self.
- Vālakhilyas [are those who] have matted hair; who wear rags, hides, or tree-bark; who offer flowers and fruit on the full-moon day of the month of Kārttika; obtain their living by normal means during the remaining eight months; who tend the sacred fires; who perform the five great sacrifices; and who seek the self.
- Phenapas are those who subsist on fallen leaves and fruit while they act insane; who dwell anywhere convenient; who tend the sacred fire; and who seek the self.

4. There are also four types of renouncers: Kuṭīcaras, Bahūdakas, Haṃsas, and Paramahaṃsas.

- The Kuṭīcaras are those who beg from house to house of their children, and who strive for the self.
- The Bahūdakas are those who are equipped with a triple staff, water pot, water sling, sidelocks, water strainer, drinking bowl, shoes, a seat, hair-tuft, sacred thread, loincloth, and ochre-colored garments; who beg their food from virtuous Brahmin families; and who strive for the self.
- Haṃsas are those who carry a single staff, wear a sacred thread, do not wear a topknot, carry a water sling and pot; who spend only one night in a village and five nights in a town or sacred bathing location; who perform fasts for one or two nights according to the lunar calendar; and who strive for the self.
- Paramahaṃsas are those who are without a staff; who shave their heads; who wear a loincloth and patched-together clothing; whose mark and mode of life are concealed; who act like madmen, even though they are completely sane; who discard the triple staff, water pot, water sling, water strainer, begging bowl, shoes, seat, topknot, and sacred thread; who live in deserted homes and temples; who no longer acknowledge right or wrong and no falsehood; who endure everything; who act equally toward everyone; who accept a clod, a stone, or gold as the same; who beg their food from all the four classes that they encounter; and who liberate their souls.

Source: *The Minor Upaniṣads.* Volume 1, *Saṃnyāsa Upaniṣads*, edited by F. O. Schrader. (Madras: Adyar Library, 1912). Translated by Carl Olson.

3

Dharma Literature

Falling within the limbs or supplements (vedāngas) of the Vedas, the dharma literature is the science of the *kalpa-sūtras*, which is concerned with various types of rituals, although the liturgical Brāhmaṇa literature historically preceded the dharma literature. In contrast to the verse form of the hymns of the *Rig Veda*, the dharma literature was composed in prose. Moreover, the dharma literature is grounded in the Brāhmaṇa texts, having evolved to explain the growing complexity of the ritual system, which is a development that can be dated to around the middle of the first millennium B.C.E. The verse and prose forms of the earlier literature gave way to the aphoristic style of the *sūtra* (literally, "thread"), which was probably devised from an oral tradition based on memory. The succinct sūtra style aided memory, with its brevity and lack of nonessential elements. Each individual sūtra was linked to what preceded it, forming a kind of metaphorical chain, with each sūtra sentence representing a link in the interconnected chain of words and concise sentences.

The auxiliary kalpa-sūtras include three types of texts: (1) srautasūtras that focus on major vedic rituals; (2) gṛhyasūtras that deal with domestic rituals; and (3) dharmasūtras that establish the duties and privileges related to social status. Only two Dharmasūtras have survived as original kalpa-sūtras, namely, the *Āpastamba* and *Baudhāyana*. Additional surviving Dharmasūtras include the *Gautama* and *Vasiṣṭha*. The Dharmasūtras are named after ancient seers and not historical authors, which is an excellent example of the emergence of eponymous literature, attributed to an eminent figure of the mythical past. The actual composition of these texts can be dated to between 250 and 150 B.C.E. and come from northern India. Unlike the Brāhmaṇas out of which they grow, the Dharmasūtras are not considered revelation, but are instead classified as *smṛti* (remembered) literature, although they derive from the Brahmin caste, or the same group that received the original revelation (*śruti*). These texts, based in memory, focus on dharma, which evolved from rules of correct ritual procedure to include correct moral/social behavior and eventually civil and criminal law. The texts also include legal procedure, punishment, and penances for infractions.

Covering the same types of material as the Dharmasūtras, the Dharmaśāstras are distinguished by being composed entirely in verse using the *śloka* meter (four times eight syllables to a stanza). There is no good equivalent of the term *śāstra* in English, but it refers to a tradition of expert knowledge within a specific field. Thus the English terms "expert" or "expertise" might be the best equivalents of the Sanskrit. Examples of such texts are the *Yājñavalkya*, *Nārada*, and *Parāśara*, but the earliest of these texts is the *Manu Smṛti* (*Laws of Manu*), whose original title was *Mānavadharmaśāstra*.

The *Laws of Manu* are named for the first man and also the initial king, according to some traditions. The genuine author of the text was probably a learned Brahmin of northern India, who composed the text between 200 and 300 C.E. This influential text of twelve chapters contains its own creation narrative, claiming to have originated with the Imperishable One. This creator figure taught the text to his son Manu, who in turn taught it to his students. Among these pupils there was Bhṛgu, who recited the text to the seers gathered to hear it. Again, we witness the importance of the oral nature of the literature.

It might be best to understand the Dharmaśāstra as a treatise on dharma by an expert. This is not an idle undertaking, because the balance and survival of the cosmos, human beings, and society are at stake. The ancient Indian notion of dharma included notions such as balance, harmony, rightness, way, and maintenance of the cosmic order. Ancient Indian scholars presupposed that when every element of the universe operates according to its dharma, or innate tendency, the necessary result will be harmony and maintenance of the universe. When elements go awry, the opposite of dharma occurs and the universal harmony and balance are disturbed, with disastrous consequences. Another basic presupposition of ancient scholars is that human beings cannot live in chaos; they need the safety and security of an orderly society and cosmos in order to function and thrive. This comprehension of dharma cannot be simply confined to law. Dharma rather encompasses a broad array of concerns, topics, and rules concerning social and religious life. A reader finds in these texts discussions about family life, rites of passage, ends of life, social structure, stages of life, marriage, inheritance, pollution, eating regulations, and guidelines for kings. A reader should remember that a learned elite composed these texts with their own social and political agendas at stake.

Selections from Dharma Literature

Significance of the Priest

A man is said to be purer above the navel; therefore the Self-existent one said that his mouth was the purest part of him. The priest is the Lord of this whole creation, according to the law, because he was born of the highest part of the body, because he is the eldest, and because he maintains the Veda. The Self-existent one emitted him from his own mouth, first, when he had generated inner heat, to convey the offerings to the gods and the ancestors, and to guard this whole (creation). What living being is greater than him? For it is through his mouth that those (gods) who live in the triple heaven always eat their offerings, and the ancestors (eat) their offerings. The best of living beings are those that have the breath of life; and (the best) of those that have the breath of life are those that live by their intelligence; the best of those that have intelligence are men; and priests are traditionally regarded as (the best) of men. Among priests, learned men (are the best); among learned men, those who understand their obligations; among those who understand their obligations, those who fulfil them; and among those who fulfill them, those who know the Veda.

The very birth of a priest is the eternal physical form of religion; for he is born for the sake of religion and is fit to become one with ultimate reality. For when a priest is born he is born at the top of the earth, as the lord of all living beings, to guard the treasure of religion. All of this belongs to the priest, whatever there is in the universe; the priest deserves all of this because of his excellence and his high birth. The priest eats only what is his own, he wears what is his own, and he gives what is his own; other people eat through the priest's mercy.

To distinguish the (priest's) innate activity and those of the rest (of the classes) in their order, the wise Manu, son of the Self-existent, made this teaching. A learned priest—but no one else—should study it carefully and explain it to his pupils properly. A priest who studies this teaching and has fulfilled his vow is not constantly smeared with the faults of the effects of past actions born of mind-and-heart, speech, and body. He purifies the rows for seven generations in the past and seven in the future; and he alone deserves this entire earth. This (teaching) is the best support for well-being; it increases intelligence; it is conducive to fame, long life, and the supreme good.

This (teaching) describes religion in its entirety, as well as the virtues and vices of the effects of past actions and the eternal rule of conduct for the four classes. The rule of conduct, the highest law, is described both in the revealed canon and in tradition; therefore a twice-born person who is self-possessed should always engage in it. A priest who has slipped from (proper) conduct does not reap the fruit of the Veda; but one who is engaged in (proper) conduct is traditionally said to enjoy the full fruit. When the hermits saw that the course of religion thus comes from (proper) conduct, they understood that (proper) conduct was the ultimate root of all inner heat. (*Laws of Manu* 1.92–110)

Regular Duties

The sages, ancestors, gods, disembodied spirits, and guests expect things from householders, which the understanding man should do for them. He should honor the sages with the private recitation of the Veda, the gods with offerings into the fire in accordance with the rules, the ancestors with the ceremonies for the dead, men with food, and the disembodied spirits with the ritual of the propitiatory offering. Day after day at the ceremony for the dead he should offer what gives pleasure to the ancestors: food, or water, or milk, roots, or fruits. He should feed a priest, even if it is only one, as a means of pleasing the ancestors during the ritual that is part of the five great sacrifices; but he should not feed any twice-born (priest) at this time for the purposes of fulfilling the ritual to the All-gods. Every day, a priest should take (a portion) of the sanctified (food) for the ritual to the All-gods prepared according to the rules and make an offering in the household fire to the following deities: first to Fire, then to Soma, and then to both of them together, and then to the All-gods and Dhanvantan; and then to the goddesses of the new-moon day and the full-moon day, to the Lord of Creatures, to the earth and sky together, and finally to Fire of the Perfected Offering.

And when he has offered the oblations properly in this manner, he should distribute the propitiatory offering in all the cardinal directions, in clockwise order: one each to Indra, Death, the lord of the Waters, and the Moon, together with their attendants. He should put down (a portion) at the door while saying "To the Maruts," and one in some water while saying "To the waters." Saying "To the Lord of the Trees," he should offer (one) on the mortar and pestle. He should make a propitiatory offering at the head to the goddess of Good Fortune, and at the foot to the Benevolent Dark Goddess, and in the centre of the house to ultimate reality and the Lord of the House. He should toss up into the air a propitiatory offering to the All-gods, and one to the disembodied spirits who roam in the daytime and also one to the disembodied spirits who roam at night. In the upper part of the house he should make a propitiatory offering for the Spirit of All Food, and all the remainder of the propitiatory offering should be put towards the south for the ancestors. And he should placidly scatter a propitiatory offering on the ground for the dogs, for those who have fallen, for "Dog-cookers," for those whose evil deeds have made them ill, for birds, and for worms. A priest who in this way constantly honours all the disembodied spirits takes on a physical form of brilliant energy and attains the supreme condition by the straightest route.

When he has performed this ritual of the propitiatory offering, he should first feed a guest and, in accordance with the rules, give alms to a beggar and to a chaste student of the Veda. By giving alms, the twice-born householder wins a reward for merit which is the same as the reward for merit won by giving a cow to the guru in accordance with the rule. He should present alms, or even just a vessel of water that has first been ritually prepared, to a priest who knows the true meaning of the Veda. The offerings that ignorant men make to the gods and ancestors are lost if the donors give them by mistake to priests who have become dead ashes. An offering offered in the fire which is the mouth of a priest rich in learning and inner heat rescues (the sacrificer) from an unfortunate fate and a great offence.

He should offer a guest, as soon as he arrives, a seat, some water, and food that has first been ritually prepared and perfectly cooked, to the best of his ability. If a priest stays (as a guest) and is not honoured, (when he departs) he takes away all the (credit for) good deeds even of someone who lives by gleaning (corn) and gathering (single grains), even of someone who makes regular offerings in five fires. (*Laws of Manu* 3.80–100)

Sources of the Law and Social Classes

And now we shall explain the accepted customary Laws, the authority for which rests on their acceptance by those who know the Law and on the Vedas.

There are four classes: Brahmin, Kṣatriya, Vaiśya, and Śūdra. Among these, each preceding class is superior by birth to each subsequent. Those who are not Śūdras and are not guilty of evil deeds may undergo initiation, undertake vedic study, and set up the sacred fires; and their rites bear fruit. Śūdras are to serve the other classes; the higher the class they serve, the greater their prosperity.

The Student and Initiation

Initiation is the consecration of a person seeking vedic knowledge carried out according to vedic rules, for a Brāhmaṇa declares: "The Sāvvitrī verse is recited for the sake of all the Vedas."

Teacher

"From darkness they surely enter into further darkness—an ignorant man who performs an initiation, as also the person whom he initiates," states a Brāhmaṇa. So, to perform the initiation, he should try to get a learned and steadfast man born in a family noted for vedic learning, under whom he should complete his vedic studies unless that man deviates from the Laws.

The teacher (*ācārya*) is the person from whom a man gathers the Laws. He should never offend the teacher, for he gives birth to him by means of vedic knowledge.

That is his most excellent birth; his parents give birth only to his body.

Time of Initiation

A Brahmin should be initiated in the spring, a Kṣatriya in the summer, and a Vaiśya in the autumn; a Brahmin in the eight year from conception, a Kṣatriya in the eleventh, and a Vaiśya in the twelfth.

When initiations are performed with an objective in mind, a person seeking eminence in vedic knowledge should be initiated in the seventh year, a person seeking long life in the eighth, a person seeking power in the ninth, a person seeking an abundance of food in the tenth, a person seeking strength in the eleventh, and a person seeking cattle in the twelfth.

In the case of a Brahmin there is no lapse in postponing the initiation until the sixteenth year, in the case of a Kṣatriya until the twenty-second year, and in the case of a Vaiśya until the twenty-fourth year, so as to ensure that the person has the capacity to carry out the observances that we are about to describe.

Failure to Be Initiated

If his time for initiation has lapsed, a man should live observing the rules of a student of the three Vedas for one season and then undergo initiation. For a year thereafter he should take a daily bath, after which time he may receive vedic instruction.

When both the father and grandfather of a man have not been initiated, they are all called "Brahman-killers." People should refrain from visiting them and from eating or contracting marriages with them. They may, if they so choose do a penance—such a person should perform for a year the same penance that was prescribed for a season when the initial time for initiation had lapsed and then undergo initiation. (*Dharmasūtra of Āpastamba* 1.1–36)

Importance of Sons

A man wins worlds through a son, and he gains eternity through a grandson, but he reaches the summit of the chestnut horse through the grandson of his son. Because the male child saves his father from the hell called *put*, therefore he was called a son (*putra*) by the Self-existent one himself. There is no distinction between a son's son and a daughter's son in worldly matters, for a daughter's son also saves him in the world beyond, just like a son's son.

The son of an appointed daughter should make the offering of the first ball for the dead to his mother, the second one to her father, and the third to her father's father. If a man has an adopted son endowed with all good qualities, that (son) should take his estate even if he was brought from (a family of) another lineage (of the sages). An adopted son should never take the lineage of the sages and the estate of his natural father; the balls for the dead follow the ritual lineage and the estate, and the refreshment for the dead of the man who gives (his son for adoption) dies out.

The son of a woman who has not been appointed and the son fathered by a woman's brother-in-law when she already has a son—neither of these deserves a share, since one is the son of an adulterer and the other the child of lust. The man born even in an appointed woman when the rules have not been followed does not deserve the paternal estate, for he was begotten by a fallen man. But the son born in an appointed woman should take (his share) in the estate just like a natural son, for according to law, that seed and the offspring belong to the owner of the field. A man who maintains the property and the wife of his dead brother should beget a child for his brother and give his property to him alone. If a woman who is appointed gets a son born of lust from some other man, or indeed from her brother-in-law, they say that that son is not fit to inherit the estate, and begotten in vain. (*Laws of Manu* 7. 137–147)

Duties of Husband and Wife

I will tell the eternal duties of a man and wife who stay on the path of duty both in union and in separation. Men must make their women dependent day and night, and keep under their own control those who are attached to sensory objects. Her father guards her in childhood, her husband guards her in youth, and her sons guard her in old age. A woman is not fit for independence. A father who does not give her away at the proper time should be blamed, and a husband who does not have sex with her at the proper time should be blamed; and the son who does not guard his mother when her husband is dead should be blamed.

Women should especially be guarded against addictions, even trifling ones, for unguarded (women) would bring sorrow upon both families. Regarding this as the supreme duty of all the classes, husbands, even weak ones, try to guard their wives. For by zealously guarding his wife he guards his own descendants, practices, family, and himself, as well as his own duty. The husband enters the wife, becomes an embryo, and is born here on earth. That is why a wife is called a wife (*jāyā*), because he is born (*jāyate*) again in her. The wife brings forth a son who is just like the man she makes love with; that is why he should guard his wife zealously, in order to keep his progeny clean.

No man is able to guard women entirely by force but they can be entirely guarded by using these means: he should keep her busy amassing and spending money, engaging in purification, attending to her duty, cooking food, and looking after the furniture. Women are not guarded when they are confined in a house by men who can be trusted to do their jobs well; but women who guard themselves by themselves are well guarded. Drinking, associating with bad people, being separated from their husbands, wandering about, sleeping, and living in other people's houses are the six things that corrupt women. Good looks do not matter to them, nor do they care about youth; "A man!" they say, and enjoy sex with him, whether he is good-looking or ugly. By running after men like whores, by their fickle minds, and by their natural lack of affection these women are unfaithful to their husbands even when they are zealously guarded here. Knowing that their very own nature is like this, as it was born at the creation by the Lord of Creatures, a man should make the utmost effort to guard them. The bed and the seat, jewellery, lust, anger, crookedness, a malicious nature, and bad conduct are what Manu assigned to women. There is no ritual with vedic verses for women; this is a firmly established point of law. For women, who have no virile strength and no vedic verses, are falsehood; this is well established.

There are many revealed canonical texts to this effect that are sung even in treatises on the meaning of the vedas, so that women's distinctive traits may be carefully inspected. Now listen to the redemptions for their (errors).

"If my mother has given in to her desire, going astray and violating her vow to her husband, let my father keep that semen away from me." This is a canonical example. If in her mind she thinks of anything that the man that married her would not wish, this is said as a complete reparation for that infidelity.

When a woman is joined with a husband in accordance with the rules, she takes on the very same qualities that he has, just like a river flowing down into the ocean. . . .

The ordinary life of a husband and wife, which is always auspicious, has thus been described. Now learn the duties regarding progeny, which lead to future happiness both here on earth and after death.

There is no difference at all between the goddesses of good fortune who live in houses and women who are the lamps of their houses, worthy of reverence and greatly blessed because of their progeny. The wife is the visible form of what holds together the begetting of children, the caring for them when they are born, and the ordinary business of every day. Children, the fulfillment of duties, obedience, and the ultimate sexual pleasure depend upon a wife, and so does heaven, for oneself and one's ancestors. The woman who is not unfaithful to her husband but restrains her mind-and-heart, speech, and body reaches her husband's worlds (after death), and good people call her a virtuous woman. But a woman who is unfaithful to her husband is an object of reproach in this world; (then) she is reborn in the womb of a jackal and is tormented by the diseases (born) of (her) evil.

The following discussion about a son was held by good men and great sages born long ago; listen to it, for it has merit and applies to all people.

They say that a son belongs to the husband, but the revealed canon is divided in two about who the "husband" is: some say that he is the begetter, others that he is the one who owns the field. The woman is traditionally said to be the field, and the man is traditionally said to be the seed; all creatures with bodies are born from the union of the field and the seed. Sometimes the seed prevails, and sometimes the woman's womb; but the offspring are regarded as best when both are equal. Of the seed and the womb, the seed is said to be more important, for the offspring of all living beings are marked by the mark of the seed. Whatever sort of seed is sown in a field prepared at the right season, precisely that sort of seed grows in it, manifesting its own particular qualities. For this earth is said to be the eternal womb of creatures, but the seed develops none of the qualities of the womb in the things it grows. For here on earth when farmers at the right season sow seeds of various forms in the earth, even in one single field, they grow up each according to its own nature. Rice, red rice, mung beans, sesame, pulse beans, and barley grow up according to their seed, and so do leeks and sugar-cane. It never happens that one seed is sown and another grown; for whatever seed is sown, that is precisely the one that grows.

A well-educated man who understands this and who has knowledge and understanding will never sow in another man's wife, if he wants to live a long life. People who know the past recite some songs about this sung by the wind god, which say that a man must not sow his seed on another man's property. Just as an arrow is wasted if it is shot into the wound of an animal already wounded by another shot, even so seed is immediately wasted on another man's property. Those who know the past know that this earth (*pṛthivī*) is still the wife of Pṛthu; they say that a field belongs to the man who clears it of timber, and the deer to the man who owns the arrow. "A man is only as much as his wife, himself, and his progeny," the priests say, and also this: "The wife is traditionally said to be what the husband is." A wife is not freed from her husband by sale or rejection; we recognize this as the law formulated by the Lord of Creatures long ago. The division (of inheritance) is made once, and the daughter is given (in marriage) once, and a man says "I will give" once; good people do these three things once.

Just as the stud is not the one who owns the progeny born in cows, mares, female camels, and slave girls, in buffalo-cows, she-goats, and ewes, so it is too (with progeny born) in other men's wives. People who have no field but have seed and sow it in other men's fields are never the ones who get the fruit of the crop that appears. If (one man's) bull were to beget a hundred calves in other men's cows, those calves would belong to the owners of the cows, and the bull's seed would be shed in vain. In the very same way, men who have no field but sow their seed in other men's fields are acting for the benefit of the men who own the fields, and the man whose seed it is does not get the fruit.

If no agreement about the fruit is made between the owners of the fields and the owners of the seed, it is obvious that the profit belongs to the owners of the fields; the womb is more important than the seed. But if this (field) is given over for seeding by means of an agreed contract, then in this case both the owner of the seed and the owner of the field are regarded as (equal) sharers of that (crop). Seed that is carried by a flood or a wind into someone's field and grows there belongs to the owner of the field, and the man who sowed the seed does not get the fruit. This is the law for the offspring of cows and mares, slave girls, female camels, and she-goats, and birds, and female buffalo.

The significance and insignificance of the seed and the womb have thus been proclaimed to you. After that I will explain the law for dealing with women when one is in extremity.

The wife of the elder brother is the guru's wife to the younger brother; but the wife of the younger brother is traditionally regarded as the daughter-in-law to the elder brother. If, when he is not in extremity, an elder brother has sex with the wife of a younger brother, or a younger brother with the wife of an elder brother, both of them fall even if they have been appointed (to have a child). When the line of descendants dies out, a woman who has been properly appointed should get the desired children from a brother-in-law or a co-feeding relative. The appointed man, silent and smeared with clarified butter, should beget one son upon the widow in the night, but never a second. Some people who know about this approve of a second begetting on (such) women, for they consider the purpose of the appointment of the couple incomplete in terms of duty. But when the purpose of the appointment with the widow has been completed in accordance with the rules, the two of them should behave towards one another like a guru and a daughter-in-law. If the appointed couple dispense with the rule and behave lustfully, then they both fall as violators of the bed of a daughter-in-law and a guru.

Twice-born men should not appoint a widow woman to (have a child with) another man, for when they appoint her to another man they destroy the eternal religion. The appointment of widows is never sanctioned in the Vedic verses about marriage, nor is the remarriage of widows mentioned in the marriage rules. For learned twice-born men despise this as the way of animals, which was prescribed for humans as well when Vena was ruling the kingdom. Formerly, he was a pre-eminent royal sage who enjoyed the whole earth, but his thinking was ruined by lust and he brought about a confusion of the classes. Since that time, virtuous men despise any man who is so deluded as to appoint a woman to have children when her husband has died. If the (intended) husband of a girl dies when their promises have been given verbally, her own brother-in-law should take possession of her according to this rule: when she is wearing a white dress and has made an unpolluted vow, he should have sex with her in accordance with the rule, and he should make love with her once during each of her fertile seasons, until there is a child.

An intelligent man who has given his daughter to someone should not give her again, for a man who gives and then gives again is lying to someone. Even if a man has accepted a girl in accordance with the rules, he may reject her if she is despised, ill, or corrupted, or if she was given with something concealed. If anyone gives away a daughter with a flaw and does not mention it, that (gift from the evil-hearted daughter-giver may be annulled. (*Laws of Manu* 9.1–73)

Vedic Recitation and Its Suspension

After commencing his annual course of vedic study on the full moon of July-August, he should not recite the Veda in the evening for a month and should conclude the course of study on the full moon or the lunar mansion Rohiṇī of December–January; according to some, the course of study lasts for four and a half months.

He should refrain from reciting the Veda in a market town—he may optionally recite it there after smearing an area with the dung of an ox—or in a cremation ground and the surrounding area up to a distance of a rod's throw. The recitation is not suspended, however, when a cemetery has been overtaken by a village or agricultural land, but he should not recite the Veda at a spot that he knows to have been a cemetery.

The rule pertaining to a cemetery applies also when Śūdras and outcastes are present, although, according to some, it applies only if they are in the same house. He shall suspend his vedic recitation, however, if he even exchanges glances with a Śūdra woman or any other woman who has violated class boundaries in her sexual relations. If he wants to speak with a menstruating woman when he is about to recite the Veda he should first speak with a Brahmin and then speak with her. After he has spoken with her, however, he should speak again with a Brahmin and then recite the Veda. In this way the child she bears will prosper.

Vedic recitation is suspended in a village in which there is a corpse or a Cāṇḍāla, or when corpses are being carried within its boundaries; in the wilderness when they are within slight, and for the entire day when outsiders visit the village even if they are respectable people.

When it thunders in the evening, vedic recitation is suspended during the night; and when there is lightning, until he has slept. When there is lightning about the time of dawn or at a time when one can distinguish a black cow from a red one at a distance of a rod's throw, vedic recitation is suspended for the day until the end of dusk; as also when it thunders at the end of the last watch of the night or, according to some, after midnight; and when cows have to be kept in their pens. When people condemned to death remain in prison, it is suspended until they have been executed.

Let him not recite the Veda while he is mounted on a animal.

Vedic recitation is suspended for two days and nights on new-moon days, as well as on the full-moon days that open a four-month season; or three days after the conclusion of the annual course of vedic study, the death of an elder, an ancestral offering made on the eighth day after the full moon, the commencement of the annual course of vedic study, and the death of a close relative; and for twelve days after the death of one's mother, father, or teacher.

At their death one should also bathe daily for the same period of time; in addition, the mourners should shave themselves completely. Some maintain that students who have returned home should not shave except when they are consecrated for a sacrifice. A Brāhmaṇa, moreover, declares: "Empty and uncovered, indeed, is he who is shaven-headed; the topknot is his cover." At sacrificial sessions, on the other hand, the topknot is shaved because it is explicitly enjoined.

According to some, vedic recitation is suspended for three days and nights after the death of one's teacher. It is suspended for one day upon receiving news of the death of a vedic scholar within one year of his death, but, according to some only if he was a fellow student.

If he wishes to recite or teach or if he is actually engaged in reciting or teaching the Veda during the visit of a vedic scholar, he may do so only after receiving his permission. In the presence of his teacher, moreover, he may recite or teach the Veda only after the teacher has said: "Ho, recite!" Both when he intends to recite and when he has completed his recitation he should clasp his teacher's feet. Likewise, when someone comes in during vedic recitation, he may continue the recitation only after that person utters the same words.

Vedic recitation is suspended when dogs are barking, donkeys are braying, a wolf or a solitary jackal is howling, or an owl is hooting, and whenever the sound of music, weeping, singing, or Sāman chants is heard. Likewise, when texts of another vedic branch are being recited, the recitation of Sāman chants is suspended. Vedic recitation is suspended also when there is any other noise that may blend with the recitation; after vomiting until he has slept or consumed some ghee; when there is a foul smell; and when he has indigestion. He should not recite the Veda after the evening meal or when his hands are wet. (*Dharmasūtra of Āpastamba* 1.9.1–1.10.21)

Duties of Social Classes

Do not eat carnivorous birds or any birds that live in villages, or any whole-hoofed animals that have not been specially permitted; or little finches, the sparrow, the aquatic bird, the goose, the waterbird, the village cock, the crane, the wildfowl, the moorhen, the parrot, and the starling; birds that strike with their beaks, web-footed birds, the paddy-bird, birds that scratch with their toes, and birds that dive and eat fish, or meat from a butcher or dried meat; or the heron or the crane, the raven or the wagtail; or (animals) that eat fish, or dung-heap pigs, or any fish. Someone who eats the meat of an animal is called an eater of that animal's meat; someone who eats fish is an eater of every animal's meat; therefore you should avoid eating fish. But sheat-fish and red fish may be eaten if they are used as offerings to the gods or the ancestors, and "striped," "lion-faced," and "scaly" fish can always be eaten.

You should not eat solitary or unknown wild animals or birds, nor any animals with five claws, not even those listed among the animals that may be eaten. They say that, among the animals with five claws, the porcupine, hedge-hog, iguana, rhinoceros, tortoise, and hare may be eaten, as well as animals with one row of teeth, except for the camel.

Any twice-born person who knowingly eats mushrooms, a dung-heap pig, garlic, a village cock, onions, or scallions, will fall. If he unknowingly eats (any of) these six, he should perform the "Heating" vow or the "Ascetic's Moon-course" vow; and for (eating any of) the others, he should fast for a day. A priest should perform the "Painful" vow once a year in any case, in order to clean himself from anything (forbidden) that he has unknowingly eaten; but (he should do it) specially for (anything that he has eaten) knowingly.

Wild animals and birds that are permitted (to be eaten) may be killed by priests for sacrifices and for the livelihood of dependants; for Agastya did this long ago. Indeed, in the ancient sacrifices of the sages that were offered by priests and rulers, the sacrificial cakes were made of edible wild animals and birds. Any food that is permitted (to be eaten) and is not despised may be eaten if oil is added to it, even if it has been kept overnight; and so can what is left over from an oblation. But the twice-born may eat anything that is made of barley and wheat, or dishes cooked with milk, without adding oil, even when they have been standing for a long time.

The list of what can be eaten and cannot be eaten by the twice-born has thus been declared, leaving nothing out. Now I will tell the rule for eating and not eating meat.

You may eat meat that has been consecrated by the sprinkling of water, or when priests want to have it, or when you are properly engaged in a ritual, or when your breath of life is in danger. The Lord of Creatures fashioned all this (universe) to feed the breath of life, and everything moving and stationary is the food of the breath of life. Those that do not move are food for those that move, and those that have no fangs are food for those with fangs; those that have no hands are food for those with hands; and cowards are the food of the brave. The eater who eats creatures with the breath of life who are to be eaten does nothing bad, even if he does it day after day; for the Ordainer himself created creatures with the breath of life, some to be eaten and some to be eaters. "Eating meat is (right) for the sacrifice": this is traditionally known as a rule of the gods. But doing it on occasions other than this is said to be the rule of ogres. Someone who eats meat, after honouring the gods and ancestors, when he has bought it, or killed it himself, or has been given it by someone else, does nothing bad.

A twice-born person who knows the rules should not eat meat against the rules, even in extremity; for if he eats meat against the rules, after his death he will be helplessly eaten by them (that he ate). The guilt of someone who kills wild animals to sell them for money is not so great, after his death, as that of someone who eats meat for no (religious) purpose. But when a man who is properly engaged in a ritual does not eat meat, after his death he will become a sacrificial animal during twenty-one rebirths. A priest should never eat sacrificial animals that have not been transformed by Vedic verses; but with the support of the obligatory rule, he may eat them when they have been transformed by Vedic verses. If he has an addiction (to meat), let him make a sacrificial animal out of flour; but he should never wish to kill a sacrificial animal for no (religious) purpose.

As many hairs as there are on the body of the sacrificial animal that he kills for no (religious) purpose here on earth, so many times will he, after his death, suffer a violent death in birth after birth. The Self-existent one himself created sacrificial animals for sacrifice; sacrifice is for the good of this whole (universe); and therefore killing in a sacrifice is not killing. Herbs, sacrificial animals, trees, animals (other than sacrificial animals), and birds who have been killed for sacrifice win higher births again. On the occasion of offering the honey-mixture (to a guest), at a sacrifice, and in rituals in which the ancestors are the deities, and only in these circumstances, should sacrificial animals suffer violence, but not on any other occasion; this is what Manu has said.

A twice-born person who knows the true meaning of the Vedas and injures sacrificial animals for these (correct) purposes causes both himself and the animal to go to the highest level of existence. A twice-born person who is self-possessed should never commit violence that is not sanctioned by the Veda, whether he is living in (his own) home, or with a guru, or in the wilderness, not even in extremity. The violence to those that move and those that do not move which is sanctioned by the Veda and regulated by the official restraints—that is known as non-violence, for the law comes from the Veda.

Whoever does violence to harmless creatures out of a wish for his own happiness does not increase his happiness anywhere, neither when he is alive nor when he is dead. But if someone does not desire to inflict on creatures with the breath of life the sufferings of being tied up and slaughtered, but wishes to do what is best for everyone, he experiences pleasure without end. A man who does no violence to anything obtains, effortlessly, what he thinks about, what he does, and what he takes delight in. You can never get meat without violence to creatures with the breath of life, and the killing of creatures with the breath of life does not get you to heaven; therefore you should not eat meat. Anyone who looks carefully at the source of meat, and at the tying up and slaughter of embodied creatures, should turn back from eating any meat.

A man who does not behave like the flesh-eating ghouls and does not eat meat becomes dear to people and is not tortured by diseases. The one who gives permission, the one who butchers, the one who slaughters, and the one who buys and sells, the one who prepares it, the one who serves it, and the eater—they are killers. No one is a greater wrong-doer than the person who, without reverence to the gods and the ancestors, wishes to make his flesh grow by the flesh of others. The man who offers a horse-sacrifice every year for a hundred years, and the man who does not eat meat, the two of them reap the same fruit of good deeds. A man who eats pure fruits and roots, or who eats what hermits eat, does not reap fruit (as great as that) of refraining from eating meat. "He whose meat in this world do I eat will in the other world me eat." Wise men say that this is why meat is called meat. There is nothing wrong in eating meat, nor in drinking wine, nor in sexual union, for this is how living beings engage in life, but disengagement yields great fruit. (*Laws of Manu* 5.11–44)

Food Transactions

A Brahmin may eat food given by twice-born men renowned for their devotion to their respective duties. He may also accept gifts from them.

Firewood, water, fodder, roots, fruits, honey, a promise of safety, what is given unasked, beds, seats, shelter, carriages, milk, curd, roasted grain, Śapharī fish, millet, garlands, venison, and vegetables should not be refused from anyone, as also other things needed to take care of the ancestors, gods, teacher, and dependants. If he is unable to sustain himself by other means, he may accept food from a Śūdra. A man who looks after his animals or ploughs his fields, a friend of the family, his barber, and his personal servant—these are people whose food he may eat, as also a merchant who is not an artisan.

This type of food is not fit to be eaten every day.

Unfit Food

The following are unfit to be eaten: food into which hair or an insect has fallen; what has been touched by a menstruating woman, a black bird, or someone's foot; what has been looked at by an abortionist or smelt by a cow; food that looks revolting; food that has turned sour, except curd; recooked food; food that has become stale, except vegetables, chewy or greasy foods, meat, and honey; food given by someone who has been disowned by his parents, a harlot, a heinous sinner, a hermaphrodite, a law enforcement agent, a carpenter, a miser, a jailer, a physician, a man who hunts without using the bow or eats the leftovers of others, a group of people, or an enemy, as also by those listed before a bald man as people who defile those alongside whom they eat; food prepared for no avail; a meal during which people sip water or get up against the rules, or at which different sorts of homage are paid to people of equal stature and the same homage is paid to people of different stature; and food that is given disrespectfully.

Forbidden Food

It is forbidden to drink the milk of a cow, a goat or a buffalo, during the first ten days after it gives birth; the milk of sheep, camels and one hoofed animals under any circumstances; the milk of an animal under from whose udders milk flows spontaneously or of an animal that has borne twins, gives milk while pregnant, or has lost her calf.

The following are forbidden foods: animals with five claws, with the exception of the hedgehog, hare, porcupine, Godhā monitor lizard, rhinoceros, and tortoise; animals with teeth in both jaws, with a lot of hair, or without any hair; one-hoofed animals; Kalaviṅka sparrows; Plava herons; Cakravāka geese; Haṃsa geese; crows; Kaṅka herons; vultures; falcons; water birds red-footed and red-beaked birds; village cocks and pigs; milch-cows and oxen; meat of animals whose milk-teeth have not fallen and of animals that are sick or wantonly killed; young shoots; mushrooms; garlic, resins; red juices flowing from incisions on trees; woodpeckers; Baka egrets; Balāka ibis; parrots; Madgu cormorants; Ṭiṭṭibha sandpipers; Māndhāla flying foxes; and night birds. (*Dharmasūtras of Gautama* 17. 22–34)

Internal and External Purification

Next, the method of purification. Water cleanses the body, and knowledge the understanding. Abstaining from hurting others cleanses one's inner being, and truth cleaning the mind. Internal purification is the cleansing of the mind. We will explain external purification.

The Sacrificial Cord

A sacrificial cord is made using three triple strings of Kuśa grass or cotton and reaches up to the navel. It is put on by raising the right arm and lowering the left arm and the head. The opposite procedure is used in rites for the ancestors. When it is worn around the neck, it is called "pendent"; and when it is worn below, it is called "low-hung."

Washing and Sipping

He should perform his purification seated on his haunches in a clean spot and facing the east or the north. Placing his right arm between his knees, he should wash his feet and then his hands up to the wrists. He should not use the water left over from washing his feet for sipping; or, if he uses it, he should pour some on the ground before sipping.

He should sip using the part of the hand sacred to Brahman. The base of the thumb is the part of the hand sacred to Brahman; the top of the thumb is the part sacred to ancestors; the tips of the fingers is the part sacred to gods; and the base of the fingers is the part sacred to seers.

He shall not use for sipping water that drips from the fingers; water with bubbles or froth; water that is warm, pungent, salty, muddy, or discoloured; or water that has a bad odour or taste. Three times he should sip water sufficient to reach his heart—without laughing, talking standing, or looking around; without bowing his head or stopping; never with his topknot untied, his neck wrapped, or his head covered; never hurriedly or without wearing his sacrificial cord over his left shoulder and under his right arm; never with his feet spread apart or his loins wrapped; or without holding his right arm between his knees; and without making a noise. He should wipe his lips three times; twice, according to some. Śūdras and women do both the sipping and the wiping just once. . . . Then he should apply water to the cavities of his head; to his feet, navel, and head; and finally to his left hand.

If he is sullied while he is holding a metal utensil, he should set it down, sip some water, and sprinkle water on it as he picks it up again. And if he is sullied while he is holding a dish of food, he should set it down, sip some water, and sprinkle water on it as he picks it up again. And if he is sullied while he is holding a pot of water, he should set it down, sip some water, and sprinkle water on it as he picks it up again. The same should be done, but in the opposite way, in the case of earthenware, while there is an option in the case of wooden utensils.

Purification of Things

When articles become sullied, they are purified in the following ways—if they are metal, by scrubbing them with cowdung, earth, and water, or with just one of them; if they are copper, silver, or gold, by using an acidic cleanser; if they are earthenware, by firing them; if they are wooden, by scraping them; if they are wicker, by using cowdung; if they are made of dried fruits, by using a cow's hair scourer; if they are skins of the black antelope, by using wood apple and rice; if they are goat's wool blankets, by using areca nuts; if they are woolen, by putting them in the sun; if they are linen, by using a paste of yellow mustard; and if they are cotton, by using earth. Skins are purified like cotton; stones and gems like metal; bones like wood; conch-shells, horn, mother of pearls, and ivory like linen, or by using milk.

Alternatively, when articles come into contact with urine, faeces, blood, semen, or a corpse, they are to be scrubbed twenty-one times using one of the scrubbing agents listed above, depending on how they strike one's eyes and nose. Non-metal articles that come into contact with them, however, should be discarded.

Ritual vessels used in sacrifices are cleansed in the manner prescribed in the Veda. A vedic text states: "They are not sullied by coming into contact with Soma juice." Time, fire, cleansing the mind, water and the like, applying cowdung, and ignorance—these, they say, are the six ways of purification for creatures. . . .

Purity of Persons and Things

The hand of an artisan is always clean as also goods delayed for sale. Almsfood received by a student is always pure. So states a vedic text. A calf is pure when it makes the milk to flow, a bird when it makes a fruit to fall, women when one is making love, and a dog when it catches a deer.

All factories are pure, except liquor breweries. Streams with constantly flowing water do not become polluted, as also dust blown up by the wind. Flowers and fruits of flowering and fruit bearing trees, likewise, do not become polluted even if they are growing in unclean places. If a Brahmin touches a sanctuary tree, a funeral pyre, a sacrificial post, a Cāṇḍāla, or a man who sells the Veda, he should bathe with his clothes on.

One's own bed, seat, clothes, wife, children, and water pot are pure with respect to oneself; but they are impure vis-à-vis others. When seats, beds, vehicles, boats, roads and grass come to contact with Cāṇḍālas or out-castes, they are purified by just the wind.

Grain from a threshing floor and water from a well or reservoir, as also milk from a dairy farm—these may be consumed even if they are given by someone whose food one is not allowed to eat. Gods invented three means of purification for Brahmins: being unaware that something is impure, sprinkling it with water, and getting it verbally declared as suitable.

Water collected on the ground sufficient for cows to slake their thirst may be used for purification, as long as it is not saturated with foul substances or has a bad odour, colour, or taste.

A piece of ground, on the other hand, is made pure by sweeping, sprinkling with water, smearing with cowdung, scattering clean soil, or scraping, depending on the degree of the defilement. (*Dharmasūtra of Baudhāyana* 1.8.1–9.11)

Death Impurity

A ten-day period of death impurity affects people belonging to the same ancestry as the deceased unless they are officiating as priests in or are consecrated for a sacrifice, or are vedic students. In the case of Kṣatriyas, the period of impurity lasts for eleven days; in the case of Vaiśyas for twelve days—or, according to some, for a fortnight—; and in the case of Śūdras for a month. If during that period another period of impurity arises, they become pure at the end of the time remaining from the first period of impurity; but if only one day remains, then at the end of two days; and if it happens on the morning after the conclusion of the first period, then at the end of three days.

When people are killed while defending cows or Brahmins, their relatives become pure immediately; as also when they are killed due to the king's anger or in a battle; and when they die voluntarily by walking without food or drink, by fasting, by a sword, in a fire, by poison, by drowning, by hanging, and by jumping from a precipice.

Relationship caused by ancestry ceases with the fifth or seventh generation.

These same rules of impurity come into effect also at the birth of a child; they apply to the parents or just to the mother.

When there is a miscarriage, the period of impurity lasts for as many days as the months since conception, or else for three days.

If someone hears of a relative's death after ten or more days, the period of impurity lasts two days plus the intervening night, as also at the death of a maternal relative not belonging to his ancestry or of a fellow reciter of the Veda. For a fellow student, the period of impurity lasts for a day, as also for a vedic scholar who lives close by.

Contact with a Corpse

When someone comes into contact with a corpse, the period of impurity lasts for ten days if it is done for a consideration. The period of impurity for such contact in the case of Vaiśyas and Śūdras is the same as that given above, or for as many days as there are seasons in a year. The latter rule is applicable also to the two higher classes; or else their impurity lasts for three days, as also when someone comes in contact with the corpse of his teacher, the teacher's son or wife, a man for whom he performs priestly functions, or his pupil.

If a person of a lower class comes in contact with the corpse of a higher class person, or a person of a higher class with the corpse of a lower class person, then the period of impurity is what is prescribed for the class to which the dead man belonged.

Contact with Impure Persons

When a man touches an outcaste, a Cāṇḍāla, a woman who has just given birth or is menstruating, a corpse, or someone who has touched any of these, he becomes purified by bathing with his clothes on; as also when he has gone behind a corpse or touched a dog. According to some, the spot touched by the dog should be washed. (*Dharmasūtra of Gautama*, 14.1–33).

Death of a Relative

With reference to births and deaths, they say that the period of impurity of people belonging into the same ancestry lasts for ten days, except for officiating priests, those for a sacrifice, and students. Among people belonging to the same ancestry, the relationship based on common ancestry extends to the seventh generation. Only a bath is prescribed when a child dies before it is seven months old or before teething.

When a child dies before it is three years old or before teething, no offerings of food or water are prescribed, and it should not be cremated. The same is true when unmarried girls die. Some do perform these rites for married women, but they do it just to curry favour with people; ritual formulas are thought not to apply to women.

When unmarried women die, their relatives become pure in three days, but their uterine brothers are purified by following the procedure given above.

Furthermore, one's great-grandfather, grandfather, father oneself, one's uterine brothers, son by a wife of the same class, grandson, and great-grandson—but not the great-grandson's son—they say, belong to the same ancestry; among these one's son and grandson share an undivided oblation. Those who share in separate oblations, they say, belong to the same family line. . . .

Death and Birth Impurity

If a birth and a death occur at the same time, the ten-day period of impurity is observed in common for both. If, moreover, before the completion of the ninth day of one ten-day period of impurity other periods often-day impurity arise, then the impurity ends after the first ten-day period. At a birth, meanwhile, the ten-day period of impurity affects only the mother and the father. According to some, it affects only the mother, because it is she that people avoid; while according to others, it affects only the father, because of the predominance of the semen, for the scriptures record sons who took birth outside of the womb. Without a doubt, however, both mother and father become impure, because they participate equally. . . .

Impurity from Touch

When someone accidentally touches the corpse of an outsider, he becomes pure immediately after taking a bath with his clothes on; whereas if someone does so deliberately, he remains impure for three days. The same is true in the case of a menstruating woman; the observances for her are explained in the passage: "A son born from such a woman is a heinous sinner."

If someone touches a man who sells the Veda, a sacrificial post, an outcaste, a funeral pyre, a dog, or a Cāṇḍāla, he should take a bath. If a Brahmin has an open wound filled with pus and bloody discharge and a worm appears in it, what penance should he observe? A man who has been bitten by a worm is purified after he has bathed in and drunk a mixture of cow's urine, cowdung, milk, curd, ghee, and a decoction of Kuśa grass.

If someone is touched by a dog, he should bathe with his clothes on. Alternatively, he becomes pure by washing that spot, touching it with fire, washing it again, washing his feet, and sipping some water. Now, they also quote: If a Brahmin is bitten by a dog, he is purified by going into a river that flows into the sea, controlling his breath one hundred times, and consuming some ghee. Alternatively, he becomes pure at once by bathing with water from a golden or silver pot, from a cow's horn, or from new earthen pots. (*Dharmasūtra of Baudhāyana*, 11.1–41)

Sins Causing Loss of Caste

Grievous Sins: People who murder a Brahmin; drink liquor; have sex with the wife of an elder or with a woman who is related through his mother or father, or through marriage; steal gold; become infidels; habitually commit forbidden acts; refuse to disown someone fallen from his caste; or disown someone who has not fallen from his caste—these have fallen from their caste, as also those who instigate sins causing loss of caste, and those who associate with out-castes for a year.

Consequences of Falling from Caste

Falling from one's caste entails exclusion from the occupations of twice-born people and going empty-handed into the next world. Some call this condition "hell."

Expiations

According to Manu, no expiation is possible for the first three sins. Some maintain that a man does not fall from his caste by having sex with women other than the wives of his elders.

Fall of Women

A woman falls from her caste by carrying out an abortion and by having sex with a low-caste man.

Sins Similar to Grievous Sins

Giving false evidence, slanderous statements that will reach the king's ear, and false accusations against an elder are equal to sins causing loss of caste.

Secondary Sins

People who defile those alongside whom they eat and listed before a bald man; people who kill cows, forget the Veda, or recite sacred formulas for such people; students who break their vow of chastity; and those who let the time for their initiation lapse—these are guilty of secondary sins causing loss of caste. (*Dharmasūtra of Gautama*, 21.1–11)

Sources: Some selections from *The Laws of Manu*, translated by Wendy Doniger and Brian K. Smith (London: Penguin Books, 1991). Other selections from *Dharmasūtras: The Law Codes of Āpastamba, Gautama, Baudhāyana, and Vasiṣṭha*, translated by Patrick Olivelle (Oxford: Oxford University Press, 1999).

4

Classical Philosophical-Religious Schools

The Hindu tradition recognizes six schools of thought that are called *darśanas* (viewpoints, visions). The six schools are designated as orthodox because they accept the authority of the ancient Vedas. These six orthodox schools are: Nyāya, Vaiśeṣika, Mīmāṃsā, Sāṃkhya, Yoga, and Vedānta. Members of these schools composed texts according to *sūtras* (brief prose aphorisms) and *kārikās* (verses). The brevity of this style reflects the fact that these texts were memorized and passed from teacher to student. Due to their brevity, once the texts assumed a written form, readers needed the help of a commentary (*bhāṣya*) to comprehend them. Later scholars would add their own commentaries to the original efforts. Besides these subcommentaries (*vārttika*), some thinkers added glosses (*tikā*) to further elucidate a text. The selected readings in this chapter include from all schools, sūtras, of the Sāṃkhya and commentaries from three of the other schools, in order to facilitate understanding not possible by reading just the succinct sūtras.

Selections for the Nyāya and Vaiśeṣika schools can be generally characterized as atomistic, pluralistic, realistic, and theistic. These general characteristics are derived from the atomic theory of matter, a conviction that the world is real, an interest in the analysis of nature, a belief in the plurality of selves, and an active interest in investigating the fundamental categories of reality. These schools pay considerable attention to issues of epistemology and logical analysis, although the Vaiśeṣika school possesses a strong interest in ontological issues and the Nyāya school focuses more on the nature of knowledge. The term *vaiśeṣika* is derived from *viśeṣa*, which means particularity or difference. This reflects the viewpoint of the school that diversity and not unity is at the root of the universe. The term *nyāya* is commonly understood to mean argumentation (literally, going back). It indicates the method followed in the system, which is predominantly intellectual and analytical. This point is strengthened by another designation of the school that was often applied to it, "the science of causes."

The major text of the Vaiśeṣika school is the *Vaiśeṣika Sūtra* composed by Kaṇāda in the second century B.C.E., which embodies a system of pluralistic realism in which an object possesses an independent reality separate from humans. Kaṇāda intended to establish the particulars that composed the world. He established seven philosophical categories: substance, action, universality, particularity, relation of inherence, and negation. The most important category was substance, which he argued had an atomic form with each atom being eternal and indestructible. Therefore, an object possesses an independent existence along with a transcendental reality. The philosopher Akṣapāda Gotama in his *Nyāya Sūtra* adopted this pluralistic realism in the third century C.E., but he also wanted to demonstrate the valid means of knowledge by introducing a method based on specific rules of reasoning. He thereby made important contributions to epistemological method based on inferential reasoning in order to prove a pluralistic reality. For Gotama, knowledge gained by his method had the ability to affect the salvific destiny of people.

The earliest commentary on the *Vaiśeṣika Sūtra* was by Praśastapāda (c. fifth century C.E.), and it does not follow the original text. It was more of an independent dissertation on the main contents of the text. Other commentaries followed this effort, although a couple of them have been lost. The earliest commentary on the *Nyāya Sūtra* was by Vātsyāyana (c. 400 C.E.). Around 635 C.E., Udyotakara did a commentary entitled *Pramānasamuccaya* in order to refute the criticism of the great Buddhist logician Dignāga (c. 500 C.E.). Vācaspatimiśra (c. 840 C.E.) and Udayana (c. 984 C.E.) also composed important commentaries on Nyāya philosophy, which were followed by later subcommentaries. By the tenth century, the Vaiśeṣika and Nyāya schools of philosophy were synthesized, which is reflected in the *Tarkasaṁgraha* that functions as a standard introduction to this philosophy, by

Anambhaṭṭa (seventh century), who combines Vaiśeṣika metaphysics with the Nyāya logic and epistemology.

In contrast to these schools of philosophy, Mīmāṃsā stresses the importance of language, which it believes to be the verbal expression of reality. According to Mīmāṃsā, the linguistic rules of the Sanskrit language represent the natural rhythms of the universe. The foundational text for this school is the *Mīmāṃsā Sūtra* of Jaimini (c. 200 B.C.E.–200 C.E.), with the earliest commentary by Śabara Svāmin (c. third to fourth century C.E.). Jaimini's text demonstrates a concern with ascertaining dharma (proper ethical conduct). This concern is partially reflected in some of his basic linguistic principles: direct expression (*śruti*), which enjoins a person to do something categorically, and indirect expression (*liṅga*), which is based in direct expression and refers to a term that circuitously indicates the purpose of a ritual.

The school split into two main schools, named for its founders Kumārila Bhaṭṭa and Prabhākara, around the seventh century C.E., with the former's commentary on that of Śabara marking the break. Kumārila and Prabhākara intended to grasp the nature of ritual because they presupposed that it was an essential aspect of a person's social duty. They argued that the ritual injunctions of the Vedas were self-validating. Moreover, the sacrifice was the very means of maintaining the cosmos and social order.

The philosophical position of the Mīmāṃsā school is called identity in difference because philosophical categories coexist, even though differences also exist. The color red shares coexistence, for instance, with the form of a rose. The color red and the rose flower are different, but they contribute to an identity. In other words, they cannot exist separately. Whatever is perceivable is completely different or completely identical. This suggests that items are distinct in relation to each other or identical to each other while they are items belonging to different categories. A flower such as a rose still belongs to a different category than a color, even though they share redness in common.

Due to distinctions made on different sections of the vedic literature, the Mīmāṃsā school developed two traditions of vedic interpretation: Prior Exegesis (Pūrva Mīmāṃsā) and Later Exegesis (Uttara Mīmāṃsā or Vedānta). The former tradition focused on the correct performance of ritual actions with its implications for salvation, whereas the latter concerned itself with the attainment of liberating metaphysical knowledge.

The importance of liberating knowledge is also evident in the philosophy of Sāṃkhya, whose origin is attributed to the legendary sage named Kapila, about whom we know nothing for certain. The compiler of the philosophical system is Īśvarakrishna, and he passed it on to other disciples at around the beginning of the fourth century C.E. This compiler of an older tradition claimed to summarize the contents of a work entitled the *Ṣaṣṭitantra* (Science of Sixty Topics). Īśvarakrishna composed a commentary on the *Sāṃkhyakārikā* around the sixth century C.E. called the *Light of Argumentation* (*Yuktidīpikā*), whereas *The Moonlight on the Sāṃkhya Principles of Reality* by Vācaspati Miśra appeared during the tenth century C.E. These various texts depict a fundamental dualism in the universe between matter (*prakṛti*) and self/pure consciousness (*puruṣa*), and the necessity of recognizing it for the sake of liberating the self from false notions about the nature of reality and misidentification of the self with matter.

The Yoga school of thought adopts this metaphysical dualism. The Yoga tradition credits Patañjali–to be distinguished from the second-century B.C.E. grammarian of the same name–with compiling the *Yoga-sūtras* around 300 C.E. During the sixth century C.E., the sage Vyāsa wrote an important commentary on the sūtras, whereas Vācaspati Miśra (c. 850), who was a member of the Advaita Vedānta school, also composed a gloss on Vyāsa's commentary. In addition, a subcommentary is attributed to Śaṅkara of the Vedānta school, whose authenticity is open to scholarly debate. During the eleventh century C.E., King Bhoja composed a work entitled *Royal Sun Bird* (*Rājanārtaṇḍa*). During the sixteenth century, Vijñanabhikṣu composed a commentary called the *Yoga-vārttika* and a short summary of this work entitled *Yogasāra-saṃgraha*.

Even though Śaṅkara may or may not have written a commentary on the *Yoga-sūtras*, there is little doubt that he did write a commentary on the *Vedānta Sūtras*, which were originally composed by a second-century B.C.E. figure named Bādarāyaṇa in an attempt to give consistent coherence to the philosophy of the Upaniṣads. A sage named Gauḍapāda attempted to revive the work of Bādarāyaṇa around 780 C.E. with his commentary on the *Māṇḍūkya Upaniṣad*. During probably the eighth century C.E., Śaṅkara studied with a sage named Govinda, a disciple of Gauḍapāda, and Śaṅkara's studies eventually led him to write a commentary on the Vedānta Sūtras and other important Indian texts such as the Upaniṣads and *Bhagavad Gītā*, and compose independent works such as the *Vivekacūḍāmaṇi* (The Crown Jewel of Discrimination) and *Upadeśasāhasrī* (A Thousand Teachings).

Śaṅkara accepted the Vedas as revealed literature and grounded his interpretive method on this body of texts. This is suggested by the term *vedānta*, which literally means "end of the Veda." This further implies that vedānta thought represents the essence of the secret message of the Vedas and its culmination. Based on his interpretation of the Vedas, Śaṅkara developed a philosophy called Advaita Vedānta. The term *advaita* means nondual, which implies that there is a single reality identified as Brahman.

Besides this radical nondualism, there were also other schools of Vedānta thought. During the eleventh century, the theistic thinker Rāmānuja developed a qualified nondualism (*viśiṣṭādvaita*) that argued for the reality of the world, self, and Brahman. A couple of centuries later Mādhva (c. 1238–1317) devised his unqualified dualistic (*dvaita*) version of Vedānta, which argued for a basic distinction between God, self, and world. Selections from the works of Rāmānuja and Mādhva are included in the next chapter on Vaiṣṇavism because of the strong theistic positions of these thinkers.

When reading the selections by Śaṅkara, a reader should keep in mind that he was convinced that philosophy represented a path to liberation (*mokṣa*) from ignorance and rebirth (*saṃsāra*), and that the human condition of bondage is due to one's ignorance. In order to be liberated, one's ignorance must be removed and replaced with knowledge (*vidyā*), because ignorance creates distinctions where none actually exist. Nonetheless, one's true self (*ātman*), which is pure consciousness, is not bound, does not suffer rebirth, is eternally liberated, and in unity with the ultimate and only genuine reality (Brahman). Eventually, an intuitive insight enables one to realize this monism that is untinged by difference of false distinctions.

Selections from the Nyāya and Vaiśeṣika School: *Tarkasaṁgraha* of Anambhaṭṭa

Chapter 1: Perception

1. In my heart, I devoutly cherish the Lord of the universe; my teacher, I respectfully greet; and I proceed to write this Primer of Indian Logic, called *Tarkasaṁgraha*, with a view to beginners gaining knowledge easily.
2. Substance, quality, activity, generality, particularity, inherence and non-existence are the seven categories.
3. a. Of them (the seven categories), the Substances are only nine—viz.: earth, water, light, air, ether, time, space, soul and mind.
   b. Colour, taste, smell, touch, number, size, separateness, conjunction, disjunction, remoteness, proximity, weight, fluidity, viscidity, sound, cognition, pleasure, pain, desire, dislike, volition, merit, demerit, tendency—these are the twenty-four qualities.
   c. Activity or motion is of five kinds: upward motion, downward motion, contraction, expansion and going or movement from one place to another.
   d. Generality is of two kinds—the more comprehensive and the less comprehensive.
   e. Particularities, on the other hand, abide in eternal substances and are innumerable.
   f. Whereas, inherence is merely one.
   g. Non-existence is of four kinds:—antecedent non-existence, annihilative non-existence, absolute non-existence and mutual non-existence.
4. Of them, earth is that which has smell. It is of two kinds—eternal and non-etemal. Its eternal variety consists of atoms. Its non-eternal variety consists of its products. Again, it is of three kinds—the three varieties being the body, the sense and other objectives. The earthen body is the body that belongs to the beings of our class. The earthen sense is the olfactory sense by which one perceives smell; and that sense finds its abode in the tip of the nose. The earthen objects are clay, stones and such other things.
5. Water is that which has cold touch. It is of two kinds—eternal and non-eternal. The eternal variety consists of atoms. The non-eternal variety consists of its products. Again, it is of three kinds—the three varieties being the body, the sense and other objects. The body made of water is found in the world of the Water-God. The sense made of water is the gustatory sense by which one

perceives taste; and that sense resides in the tip of the tongue. The objects made of water are rivers, ocean and such others.

6. Fire is that which has hot touch. It is of two kinds—eternal and non-eternal. Its eternal variety consists of atoms. Its non-eternal variety consists of its products. Again, it is of three kinds—the three varieties being the body, the sense, and other objects. The body made of fire is in the world of Sun. The sense made of fire is the visual sense by which one perceives colour; and that sense resides in the foremost part of the dark pupil of the eye. The objects made of fire are of four kinds, the four varieties being the light of the earth, that of the sky, that of the stomach and that of the mine. The common fire which people use and its varieties belong to the earth. Lightning and such other varieties, with water as fuel, belong to the sky. The gastric variety is what digests the food. Gold and such other lustrous metals form the variety which is dug out of a mine.
7. The air is that which has touch but no colour. It is of two kinds—eternal and non-eternal. Its eternal variety consists of atoms. Its non-eternal variety consists of its products. Again, it is of three kinds—the three varieties being the body, the sense and other objects. The body made of air is found in the world of the Wind-God. The sense made of air is the tactus by which one perceives touch; and that sense is found all over the body. The object made of air is the air that shakes trees and such other things. The air that moves about within the body is the vital air, which, though one in itself, is called differently as prana, apana, etc., according as its abodes in the body differ.
8. Ether is that which has sound as its quality. That is one, all-pervasive and eternal.
9. Time is the distinctive cause of expressions involving the term past, etc. It is one, all-pervasive and eternal.
10. Direction is the distinctive cause of expressions involving the terms east, etc. It is one, all-pervasive and eternal.
11. The substratum in which cognition inheres is the soul (*ātman*). It is of two kinds—the supreme Soul and the individual soul. Of these two, the supreme Soul is one and is the omniscient Lord. The individual soul, on the other hand, is different in association with different organisms or bodies, though it is all-pervasive and eternal.
12. Mind (*manas*) is the sense by means of which pleasure and such other (perceptible qualities of the soul) are directly apprehended. There an innumerable minds since they are specifically linked up with each soul and they are atomic and external.

13. Colour is the quality which is perceived only by the sense of vision. It is of seven kinds—the seven varieties being white, blue, yellow, red, green, brown and variegated. It is found in earth, water and light. Of these three, in earth, all the seven varieties are found. White colour, which is not brilliant, belongs to water. White colour, which is brilliant, belongs to light.
14. Taste is the quality which is perceived by the sense of taste. It is of six kinds, the six varieties being sweet, acid, salt, pungent, astringent and bitter. It is found in earth and water. Of these two, in earth, all the six varieties are found; while the sweet only belongs to water.
15. Smell is the quality which is perceived by the sense of smell. It is of two kinds—the fragrant and the non-fragrant. It is found in earth only.
16. Touch is the quality which can be perceived only by the sense of touch. It is of three kinds—the three varieties being cool, hot and lukewarm. It is found in earth, water and fire. Of these three, to water belongs the cool touch, the hot touch to fire, and the lukewarm touch to earth and air.
17. The four qualities beginning with colour are produced in earth through the application of heat and are not eternal. In the case of other substances, they are eternal in such of them as are eternal and they are not eternal in such of them as are not eternal.
18. Number is the special cause of enumerative expressions, such one, two and so on. It is present in all the nine substances and it is represented by numbers beginning from one and ending with *parārdha* (one billion). Number one may be everlasting or non-eternal—everlasting in everlasting substances and non-eternal in non-etemal substances. Number two and the higher numbers are non-eternal everywhere.
19. Size is the special cause of expressions pertaining to measurement. It is found in all four kinds—atomic, large, long and short.
20. Separateness is the special cause of expressions such as "this is separate from that." It is found in all the substances.
21. Contact is the special cause of expressions such as "these are [in] contact with each other." It is found in all the substances.
22. Disjunction is the quality which destroys contact. It is found in all the substances.
23. Remoteness and proximity are the special causes of expressions such as "this is remote," "this is near." They are found in the four substances beginning with earth and in *manas* (mind). They are of two kinds, those that are due to time and those due to space. In a remote substance, spatial remoteness is found; and

in a substance lying near, spatial proximity is found. In an older person, temporal remoteness is found; and in a younger person, temporal proximity is found.

24. Weight is the non-intimate cause of the first downward motion (of a falling substance). It is found in earth and water.
25. Fluidity is the non-intimate cause of the first flow (of a fluid substance). It is found in earth, water and light. It is of two kinds—natural fluidity and artificial fluidity. Natural fluidity is found in water. Artificial fluidity is found in earth and light. In certain varieties of earth like ghee, etc., fluidity of the artificial variety is brought about through contact with fire; and it is also found in gold and such other varieties of light.
26. Viscidity is the quality which causes the lumping up of powder etc.,—i.e. the particles of powder, etc., to adhere to each other. It belongs only to water.
27. Sound is a quality which is perceived by the ear. It belongs only to the ether. It is of two kinds: noise and alphabetic sound. Noise is found in a drum and alphabetic sounds form languages like Sanskrit.
28. a. *Buddhi* and *Jñāna* are the same thing, and stand for cognition which is the cause of all verbal expressions. It is of two kinds—recollection and experience.
    b. Recollection is the cognition which is caused only by reminiscent impression.
    c. All cognitions other than recollection come under experience. There are two kinds of experiences, real and erroneous.
    d. The experience which cognizes an attribute as belonging to a thing which really has it, is real; and this is known as prama (valid knowledge).
    e. The experience which cognizes an attribute as belonging to a thing in which it is not present, is erroneous.
    f. Valid experience is of four kinds—viz., perception, inference, assimilative experience and verbal experience.
    g. The instrument of valid experience is also of four kinds—the perceptive instrument, the instrument of inference, assimilation, and sentence or proposition.
29. a. *Karaṇa* (efficient or instrumental cause) is a special cause.
    b. The invariable antecedent of an effect is its cause.
    c. An effect is the counter-correlative of its antecedent non-existence.
    d. Cause is of three kinds, the three varieties being inherent cause, non-inherent cause, and occasioning cause.
    e. That is called inherent cause, in which the effect inheres when it is produced. For instance, threads are the inherent cause of a cloth, and a cloth of its colour and such other qualities.

f. That is called non-inherent cause, which serves as a cause, while co-inhering with its effect, or with the inherent cause of its effect. For instance, contact between threads is the non-inherent cause of cloth; and the colour of the threads is the non-inherent cause of the colour of the cloth.

g. Occasioning cause is a cause not coming under either of the above-mentioned kinds. For instance, the shuttle, the loom and such things are the occasioning causes of cloth.

h. Of these three varieties of causes, only that is called an efficient or instrumental cause (*karaṇā*), which operates as special cause.

30. a. Of those *pramāṇas*, perceptive instrument (*pratyakṣa*) is the means of perception.

b. Perception is the cognition which is produced through sense-organ coming into relation with an object. It is of two kinds:—indeterminate and determinate.

c. Indeterminate perception is a cognition which does not involve any attribute or adjunct (*prakāra*).

d. Determinate perception is cognition which involves an attribute or adjunct. It is embodied in propositions like "This is *Ḍittha*," "This is a *Brāhmaṇa*," "This is black," "This is a cook."

e. The sense-relation which causes a perceptual cognition is of six kinds—viz., contact, inherence in what has come into contact, inherence in what is inherent in a thing which has come into contact, inherence, inherence in an inherent thing and adjunct-substantive relation.

When a jar is perceived by the sense of sight, the sense-relation is "contact." When the colour of a jar is seen, the sense-relation is "inherence in a thing which has come into contact," the jar, in that case, having come into contact with the visual sense and colour being connected with the jar through the relation of inherence. When colourness in the colour of a jar is seen, the sense-relation is "inherence in what is inherent in a thing which has come into contact"; for, in that case, the jar has come into contact with the visual sense, the colour of the jar inheres in it and colourness inheres in colour.

When sound is perceived by the sense of hearing, "inherence" is the sense-relation; for the ether bound within the auricular orifice is the auditory sense, sound is a quality of ether, and the relation between a quality and its substratum is inherence. When soundness (*śabdatva*) is perceived by the auditory sense, the sense-relation is "inherence in a thing which inheres"; for, soundness inheres in sound which inheres in the auditory sense.

In the perception of non-existence, the adjunct-substantiue-relation is the sense-relation; for in the case of the visual perception which takes the form—"The seat of the non-existence of jar is floor," the "non-existence of jar" is an adjunct to the floor with which the visual sense has come into contact.

Thus the cognition which arises from one or the other of these six sense-relations is perception; and sense-organ is its efficient instrument. Therefore, the senses constitute the efficient instrument of perceptual experience (*pratyakṣa-pramāṇa*).

Chapter 2: Inference

31. a. *Anumāna* (Inference) is the efficient instrument (*karaṇa*) of inferential cognition.
    b. Inferential cognition is a cognition which arises from subsumptive reflection.
    c. Subsumptive reflection is a cognition which cognizes the presence of the invariably concomitant factor denoted by the middle term (*probans*) in the thing denoted by the minor term. For instance, the cognition, "This mountain has smoke which is invariably concomitant with fire" is a subsumptive reflection; and the cognition resulting from it and taking the form "mountain has fire" is inferential cognition.
    d. "Wherever there is smoke there is fire"—This type of invariable concomitance is *vyāpti* (co-extension).
    e. Subject-adjunctness consists in the invariable concomitant being present in things like a mountain (denoted by *pakṣa* or the minor term).
32. a. Inference is of two kinds:—inference for oneself and inference for others.
    b. Inference for oneself causes one's own inferential experience. For instance, a person may make out the relation of invariable concomitance between smoke and fire and arrive at the universal generalization—"Wherever there is smoke there is fire" from his repeated observation in the hearth and such other places and then approach a mountain. He may have doubt as to the presence of fire in that mountain. On seeing smoke there, he remembers the generalization—"Wherever there is smoke there is fire". Then, he comes to have the cognition—"This mountain has smoke which is pervaded by (or invariably concomitant with) fire." It is this cognition that is called *liṅgaparāmarśa* (the subsumptive reflection of the probans). From this

cognition arises the inferential cognition—"The mountain has fire." This is what is called inference for oneself.

c. Inference for others is the syllogistic expression which consists of five members and which a person employs after inferring for himself fire from smoke, with a view to enabling another person to have likewise the same kind of inferential cognition.

E.g.—"The mountain has fire; because it has smoke; whichever has smoke has fire, as a hearth; the mountain is such (has smoke which is invariably concomitant with fire); and therefore, it is such (has fire)." From this five-membered syllogism, the other person to whom it is addressed comes to know the probans (smoke) and infers fire from it.

33. a. The five members of a syllogism are:—(1) the thesis set down, (2) the reason, (3) the exemplification, (4) the subsumptive correlation, and (5) conclusion; e.g.—"The mountain has fire"—this is the thesis. "For it has smoke"—this is the reason. "Whichever has smoke has fire, as a hearth"—this is the exemplification. "And so is this"—this is the subsumptive correlation. "Therefore it is such"—this is the conclusion.

b. In the case of inferential cognition for oneself as well as that for others, it is the subsumptive reflection of the reason (*liṅgaparāmarśa*)that serves as the efficient and special cause. So, *liṅgaparāmarśa* in this sense is the instrument of inferential cognition (*anumāna*).

34. a. Probans (*liṅga* = literally, mark) is of three kinds—concomitant in affirmation and negative, concomitant in affirmation alone and concomitant in negation alone.

b. The [concomitant in affirmation and negation] type of probans is that which has affirmative concomitance and negative concomitance with the probandum; as smoke when fire is the probandum. "Where there is smoke, there is fire, as in a hearth"—this is affirmative concomitance. "Where there is no fire, there is no smoke, as in a tank"—this is negative concomitance.

c. The [concomitant in affirmation alone] probans has affirmative concomitance alone; as—"Jar is namable, because it is knowable, like a cloth." In this instance, negative concomitance is impossible between knowability and namability; for all things are knowable and namable.

d. The [concomitant in negation alone] probans has negative concomitance alone; as in the syllogism—"Earth is different from the rest (not-earth), for it has smell; whichever is not different from the rest (not-earth) has no smell, as water; this (earth) is not so—i.e., it does not have absence of smell or *gandhābhāva*, with which the absence of difference from not-earth is invariably concomitant; therefore, it is not so—i.e., it is not devoid of difference from non-earth." In cases like this, there is no example in which the affirmative concomitance "Whichever has smell, has difference from non-earth" may be made out; for all varieties of earth come under the *pakṣa* (subject).

35. a. *Pakṣa* (subject) is that in which the presence of the probandum is not known for certain and is yet to be proved; as a mountain, when smoke is relied upon as the probans.

    b. *Sapakṣa* is a similar instance, in which the probandum is known for certain; as a hearth, in the same case of inference.

    c. *Vipakṣa* is a counter-example in which the non-existence of the probandum is known for certain; as a tank, in the same case of inference.

36. a. Fallacious reasons are of five kinds:—viz., the reason that strays away, the adverse reason, the opposable reason, the unestablished reason, and the stultified reason.

    b. The straying reason is otherwise known as . . . not unfailing in its association with the probandum. It is of three kinds:—viz., common, uncommon, and non-conclusive.

    The common strayer is that variety of straying reason which is present in a place where the probandum is not present; as, in the argument—"The mountain has fire, because it is knowable." In this argument knowability is found in a tank where fire is not present. The uncommon strayer is that reason which is present only in the subject and not present in any similar example or counter-example; as sound-ness, in the argument—"Sound is eternal, because it is sound," sound-ness being present only in sound, and nowhere else, eternal or non-eternal.

    The non-conclusive strayer is that reason which has no affirmative or negative example; as knowableness in the argument—"All things are non-eternal, because they are knowable." Here, no example is available since all things are treated as *pakṣa*.

    c. The adverse reason is one which is invariably concomitant with the non-existence of the probandum; as producibility, in the argument—"Sound is eternal, because it is produced." Here producibility is invariably concomitant with non-eternality, which amounts to the non-existence of eternality.

    d. The opposable reason is one which admits of being counter-balanced by another reason that proves the non-existence of the probandum, as audibility in the argument—"Sound is eternal, because it is audible, like soundness." The counter-reason in this case is producibility in the counter-argument—"Sound is non-eternal, because it is producible."

e. The unestablished reason is of three kinds: viz., unestablished in respect of abode (*āśrayāsiddha*), unestablished in respect of itself (*svarūpāsiddha*) and unestablished in respect of its concomitance (*vyāpyalvāsiddha*).

   The reason is [unestablished in respect of abode] in the argument—"Sky-lotus is fragrant, because it is a lotus, like the lotus of a pond." Here, sky-lotus is the abode or subject and it never exists.

   The reason is [unestablished in respect of itself] in the argument—"Sound is a quality, because it is visible, like colour." Here, visibility cannot be predicated of sound, which is only audible.

   The reason is said to be [unestablished in respect of it concomitance] when it is associated with an adventitious condition. That is said to be an adventitious condition, which is pervasive of the probandum but not pervasive of the probans. "To be pervasive of the probandum" means "never to be the counter-correlative of non-existence which co-exists with the probandum." "Not to be pervasive of the probans" means "being the counter-correlative of non-existence which co-exists with the probans." In the argument—"The mountain has smoke, because it has fire," contact with wet fuel is the adventitious condition. "Where there is smoke, there is contact with wet fuel"—thus it is pervasive of the probandum. There is no contact with wet fuel in every place where there is fire; for instance, a red-hot iron ball has no contact with wet fuel; thus the [adventitious condition] is non-pervasive of the probans. In this manner, contact with wet fuel is the [adventitious condition] in the present instance, because it is pervasive of the probandum but not pervasive of the probans. And fire, in the argument under reference, is [unestablished in respect of its concomitance], since it is associated with an adventitious condition.

f. The stultified reason is one which is put forward to prove a probandum whose non-existence is established by another proof. "Fire is not hot, because it is a substance," the probandum is "not being hot"; its reverse—"being hot"—is perceived through tactile perception; so, the probans is stultified.

Chapter 3: Assimilation or Analogy (upamāna)

37. Assimilation is the instrument of assimilative cognition. Assimilative cognition consists in the knowledge of the relation between a name and the object

denoted by it. Knowledge of similarity is the efficient instrument of such cognition. This may be illustrated thus:—A person happens to be ignorant of the exact meaning of the word *gavaya* (a particular animal of the bovine species). From a forester, he learns that a gavaya is similar to a cow, he goes to a forest, sees the animal called gavaya, which is similar to a cow and recollects the information conveyed by the assimilative proposition. Then the assimilative cognition, "This is the animal (of the bovine species) denoted by the word gavaya arises.

Chapter 4: Valid Verbal Testimony

38. a. Valid verbal testimony is a proposition set forth by a trustworthy person. One who habitually speaks only truth is a trustworthy person. A sentence or proposition is a group of words like "Bring a cow."
    b. A word is that which has significative potency (*śakti*). "From this word, this concept should be known"—God's will to this effect is called śakti (significative potency).
39. a. Verbal expectancy, congruity and proximity—these are the causes which bring about verbal cognition or judgment from a proposition.
    b. Verbal expectancy consists in a word not being capable of conveying a complete judgment in the absence of another word.
    c. Congruity consists in the sense being not stultifiable.
    d. Proximity consists in the articulation of words without undue delay.
    e. A sentence which is devoid of expectancy and the other two requirements (congruity and proximity) does not bring about a valid cognition. For instance, a string of words like "Cow, horse, man, elephant" does not produce any judgment; for there is no verbal expectancy here. The sentence "One should sprinkle with fire" does not produce a valid judgment, as there is no congruity here. Words like "Bring a cow," uttered at long intervals, cannot produce a valid judgment, owing to want of proximity.
40. a. There are two classes of sentences: those that belong to the Veda and those that belong to secular speech. Those that belong to the Veda are all statements of God and therefore authoritative. Of those that belong to secular speech, such as [are] produced by trustworthy persons are authoritative and others are not authoritative.
    b. Verbal cognition is the knowledge of the meaning of a sentence. Its efficient instrument is sentence.
41. a. Erroneous experience is of three kinds—the three varieties being doubt, misapprehension and indirect argument (reductio ad absurdum).

b. A doubt is a cognition which relates to several incompatible attributes in the same thing—as, in the dubitative cognition—"It may be a post or a man."
c. Misapprehension is a false cognition—as in the erroneous cognition of a nacre, in the form—"This is silver."
d. Indirect argument (reductio ad absurdum) consists in the hypothetical admission of an invariably concomitant fact which leads to the admission of the pervasive concomitant; as, "If there were no fire, there would be no smoke."

42. Recollection is also of two kinds:—true and false. The former is the result of a valid experience; and the latter arises from an erroneous experience.
43. a. Pleasure is a quality which all consider agreeable.
    b. Pain is a quality which all consider disagreeable.
    c. Desire is wish.
    d. Dislike is ill-feeling.
    e. Volitional effort is the will to do.
    f. Dharma is the unseen spiritual benefit accruing from the performance of actions which are enjoined by the Vedic law.
    g. Adharma is the unseen spiritual demerit accruing from the performance of forbidden actions.
    h. Cognition and the following seven qualities (eight in all) are the specific qualities found only in the soul. Cognition, desire and volitional effort may be eternal or non-eternal; they are eternal in God and non-eternal in the ordinary souls of living beings.
    i. There are three kinds of tendencies or impressions—speed, reminiscent impression and elasticity. Speed belongs to the substances—earth, water, fire, air and mind. Reminiscent impression belongs only to the soul and it results from a previous experience and causes recollection. Elasticity is the tendency of a thing to recover its original form when it is changed.
44. Activity is of the nature of motion. Upward motion leads to contact with an upper place. Downward motion leads to contact with a lower place. Contraction leads to contact with a place near one's body. Expansion leads to contact with a place remote from one's body. All the other varieties of motion come under "going."
45. Generality is a generic attribute which is eternal and one and inheres in many things. It is found in substances, qualities and activities. Existence is the most comprehensive type of generality. Substance-ness and such others are less comprehensive.

46. Specialities are the differentiating features belonging to eternal substances.
47. Inherence is the eternal relation, which belongs to the inseparables. An inseparable pair consists of two things of which one thing, so long as it does not come to an end, exists only in the other thing:—as component part and the composite whole, quality and substance, motion and moving body, generality and the individual having it, and speciality and the eternal substance having it.
48. a. Antecedent non-existence has no beginning but has an end. It relates to the period preceding the production of an effect.
    b. Annihilative non-existence has a beginning but has no end. It relates to the period subsequent to the production of an effect.
    c. Total non-existence is the negation of a counter-correlative in respect of relation to all the three times—present, past and future—as in the statement—"There is no jar on this spot."
    d. Reciprocal non-existence is the negation of a counter-correlative in respect of its identity with another thing—as in the statement—"A jar is not a cloth."
49. All the other *padārthas* may be brought under one or the other of the seven *padārthas* enumerated at the beginning of this work. So, there are only seven categories.
50. Annambhaṭṭa has written this treatise called *Tarkasaṁgraha* with the object of introducing beginners to a study of the Nyāya and Vaiśeṣika systems of Gautama and Kaṇāda.

Source: Kuppuswami Sastri, *A Primer of Indian Logic* (Madras: Kuppuswami Research Institute, 1961).

Selections from the Mīmāṃsā Sūtra

The Law Dharma of Subject-Matter of the Vedas

Dharma

Let us now understand what is Dharma. It may be defined as the highest good; and so let us inquire into its cause.

How to Understand Dharma

The idea of dharma does not arise from sense-perception, because the latter is limited to what is present, while the idea of Dharma goes beyond the present. As it is conceived to be the highest good, its idea can best be imparted by a competent teacher, which is a valid means of acquiring knowledge, and does not require the authority of a *Bādarāyaṇa* to prove it.

Dharma and Action

Some people say that Dharma arises from action, and prove their point by referring to the actual facts of life; and so they believe that the idea of Dharma is not permanent.

Dharma and the Law of Life

Dharma is indeed linked up with action, for we often say that a person does his Dharma, and that implies action. Action is part of our nature, for we see that all of us are engaged in some kind of action at the same time; and we see it in *Prakṛti* or Nature in all its modifications. We also see that success in action is often the result of a number of persons acting together. At the same time we find that there are some who believe that we should be indifferent to all that is in the world. But even he who is said to be indifferent, acts. He might appear to be inactive, but is not really so; and we believe that he has not acted, because he has not succeeded in achieving his object. Indeed, we have to go beyond the commencement of an action to understand all this; for the sun may appear to be inactive, but it is acting all the time; and so are all creatures too.

Law of Action

There is an immutable law of action at work within all forms of life, according to which all must act. For instance, we see things growing in size, but without apparent action; yet there is sound, motion, or vibration within them unperceived.

Action Is Eternal and Universal

Action is eternal, because it is meant to be performed for the sake of something else; and also because we see it all the time everywhere. The number of creatures engaged in action is so large, that it cannot be counted; and it is not necessary to refer to the same creature again, because all are acting at the same time. We say so because we know the manner in which action takes place; and if we take necessary evidence or observe the working of *Prakṛti* or Nature, we shall find that it is so.

Natural and Deliberate Action

But it may be argued that action, performed in the ordinary course of nature, is of little importance, because it does not serve any special purpose; and those who believe that all action should be of this kind, naturally argue in this way. But we see that when people have a purpose or aim in action, it is the result of deliberate intention or precise thinking.

Vedas and Action

According to some, the Vedas deal with the problem of the soul as their principal subject-matter; but this is not correct, because we find that they deal with the world of Nature, which is not permanent. This has been stated to be their subject-matter; and that is how they are taught and explained; and all Vedic literature is of the same kind. As they deal with the problem of action, they tell us what actions to perform and how to perform them. . . .

The Vedas and The Method of Their Interpretation

Subject-matter of the Vedas

The subject-matter of the Vedas is action; and they would be meaningless if we interpret them in any other light: hence they are said to be non-eternal. They are not eternal also because they give expression to conflicting opinions; because they do not yield the desired results; because no other meaning is possible; because they are the joint composition of a number of authors; and deal with things that are not eternal. Indeed, we find that they have the meaning of laws of Nature, and are meant to be a praise of these laws. This is also the traditional view; and there is no contradiction in it; and if a person is unable to understand them in this light, he should seek the assistance of a competent teacher.

An Exposition of the Guṇas

The Vedas are really an exposition of the *Guṇas* or the attributes of Nature; and that is so because the *Guṇas* are the most important part of Nature,—for it is chiefly in this form that Nature appears to us, when we look at it from a distance (or in a broad perspective).

Guṇas and Nature

The Guṇas are said to be born of Nature or *Prakṛti* in the same sense in which a child is born; for there is a natural desire to have something that will last for some time (and that is why *Prakṛti* creates *Guṇas* and lives through them).

Knowledge and Action

It is for the same reason that we praise knowledge (for it lasts); and the more complete the knowledge, the longer it lasts; and so the most perfect knowledge belongs to the Supreme. (We find, however, that knowledge is connected with action, for) we see that certain results follow from certain causes; and so we might say, broadly speaking, that certain special results will follow from certain special causes. But the idea of knowledge and action is the same as has been explained in the previous systems. Nevertheless, there must be a law governing the two; but such a law has not yet been discovered, and a mere statement of their relation would be useless.

An Objection

We cannot deal with the question in a popular way, because that is already known (and it has no bearing on the idea of a law). It may, however, be argued that all that can be said in the matter has already been said, and nothing more is possible now. Further, it may be contended that it is impossible, in a number of places, to construe the text of the Vedas in the light of action; and so it is best to regard these books as consisting of hymns of praise addressed to the gods. Moreover, if there is consistency of this kind of meaning throughout, we must not drag in some other meaning; specially, as against it, a reference to a law would be inappropriate. Again, if it had been the intention of the authors of the Vedas to expound a law, the language of the text should have been different.

An Answer

But there is good reason for coming to the conclusion that the Vedas deal with the laws of Nature, because the same can be proved, and we can get it from the text itself. The text of the Vedas does indeed support the view that it refers to the praise of the gods; but that is its first or direct meaning, without being pressed into some other sense. But even as praise it appears to be meaningless; and we might ask if it is not improper to have praise that is meaningless. While we cannot deny that the text does refer to the praise of the gods, we hold that, in the way it is commonly understood, it is so only in a secondary sense,—the primary idea being that of a law. We are, however, prepared to agree that, if the text does really refer to the laws of Nature, this conclusion should be based on well-established facts, and not on some special statements or analogies,—for that would nullify the very idea of a law. But, as a matter of fact, we get the idea of law from the text of the sacred books themselves; for we get this meaning from the very language of the text, when we apply correct grammatical rules. But he alone will understand who is learned or wise, for the language needs to be properly understood.

How to Understand the Text

We cannot get the correct meaning of words from their common form; but we can do so by referring them to Nature, which is described as *a-chetana* or inanimate. That, however, should be done when the common meaning is contradictory; and a student of the Vedas can easily find out the real meaning of the text in this way. The reference to the laws of Nature should be made when we are unable to understand the correct meaning of the text and are confused; and (we should understand that) it would be meaningless for the Vedas to refer to something that is ephemeral.

It may, however, be argued that the meaning of words cannot be a special one; but in this connection we might repeat that the text has a secondary meaning (which refers to the praise of the gods).

Special Mention of This Method

Indeed, there is a special mention of this method of interpreting the text; and there is an explanation of its idea too; and the principal subject-matter of the Vedas is found to be consistent when interpreted in this light. Further, if we make use of this method and understand words in their correct formation, we find that the text does not contain any censure of the actions of any one; and the explanation of the meaning of words is in accordance with what is found in a dictionary. At the same time, a single thread of thought runs throughout the text, and there is no contradiction in it anywhere.

Cause of Failure to Understand

We do not know this explanation of the Vedas because of want of application and ignorance on the part of those who read them. But we find that they do refer to Nature, which is said to be non-eternal; and we get this meaning from the text itself; and so our conclusion is that the language of the Vedas refers to the laws of life.

The Law of Dharma and the Vedas

Dharma is founded on the word of the Vedas, which is the highest word. (Dharma is linked up with action, and) we find that a man is always engaged in action, and this should enable us to acquire definite knowledge in regard to the law of action. Any contradiction of the fact that there is action everywhere should be disregarded; for we know that it is impossible.

Every Action Is Not Dharma

(But every action is not Dharma; for instance,) we cannot say that an action of the body, performed by a healthy man in the ordinary course of Nature, is Dharma; for the sacred books have their own idea of Dharma, and it is based on certain principles admitted by all to be true. There is no inconsistency or contradiction in the sacred books; and if there is any inconsistency anywhere, we should take it to be in our own ideas rather than in them. We should, therefore accept what is contained in these books.

Action Due to Impulse Is Not Dharma

The action of a healthy body, performed spontaneously or in the ordinary course of nature, is obviously the result of impulse; and that is not the idea of Dharma as given in the sacred books; and it would be an incorrect application of the rules laid down by them to think that it is so. Their statement regarding Dharma is definite and complete, and leaves no gaps to be filled; and we can verify this for ourselves by making an experiment and a careful study of the sacred books.

If we do so, we shall find that there is only one inescapable conclusion,—that there is action everywhere, and all things are subject to it. It should, therefore, be deemed to have been proved, and regarded as a universal law of life,—for such is the nature of things, as we can see for ourselves. This is proved by the fact that we can find nothing in the world that is eternal.

Definition of Action

Action means that there is a material contact of an object with a place. This, however, does not limit the idea of action and make it local, for the same object can be in different places at different times,—just as when we say that a person belongs to Mathurā, we do not confine him to that place. The law of action or of the doer of the deed,—for both are the same—may be illustrated by the action of a person who is devoted to something for a while; and this is not inconsistent with the law of universal action described in the sacred books. Since, however, they speak of continuous action, we have to understand the sense in which the term is used, for otherwise we might commit a mistake.

How Described in the Vedas

(All this has been briefly expressed, and) it would be improper to demand that it should have been described in many words. We can, however, understand the real meaning if we make a special effort; and our inability to do so arises from the fact that we take only the form of words, and neglect their real meaning.

How to Understand the Text

The entire meaning of the text would be changed by changing the form of a word in a particular place; and this can be done because there are no fixed rules regarding the combination of words or their parts. But if we adopt but a single meaning, we cannot distinguish between things; and that will render the whole idea worthless. It is possible to look at the text in different ways; but the best meaning is that which refers to action. There are some, however, who believe that there is no reference to action; that there is no possibility of any other meaning than the common one; and that the words refer to one particular object only. All that we can say is that the meaning does refer to actions, and there is no break in the continuity of its idea.

The Vedas and the Method of Their Interpretation

Action in the Vedas

It has been explained that the text of the sacred books, when properly interpreted, refers to action; and it follows from this that everything should have a bearing on that meaning. It may be that this action consists in giving a new name to an object,—something that has not been done before; but so far as the main idea of action is concerned, it should refer to the *Guṇas*, which are closely connected with *Prakṛti* or *Pradhāna*. This is contained in a number of sacred books; and there is a definite statement to this effect too.

Character of a Name

There are some who believe that, in such a case, when a name is given to an object, the rule should be that there should be a clear mention of the *Guṇas*. But this is not possible, for a name may refer to two equal actions, and in such a case a single word would need to have another meaning too.

There are others who maintain that a word and its attributes should go together; that we should not divide it into parts to get the idea of action; and that there should not be different rules in connection with different words. But this is not always possible; for if a word and its attributes should always go together, so should a word and the object to which it refers. Again, suppose there is mention of the word *Barhis* (meaning sacrificial grass) and *ājya* (meaning clarified butter poured over the sacrificial fire) in the text, but no consecrating ceremony,—should we say that these words have no meaning? We should, of course, agree that they have their ordinary meanings if they were used in connection with vessels of holy water required for a sacrifice. The same would be true in connection with another word,—*Nirmanthya* (meaning, being stirred or churned). It is true that there is no variation in the meaning of the word *Vaiśva-deva* (meaning, relating to all-gods); and that is so because of the nature of what it signifies,—something that is perceptible to the senses, and requires no discussion of the thing itself; and if we were to give a different meaning to the word, it would make no sense at all. The idea of the *Guṇas*, however, is different.

No Fixed Rules

As has already been observed, we cannot lay down any hard and fast rules to get the correct meaning of words; and their only test is their suitability in connection with the context. We must, however, remember that an attribute is meant to describe the characteristics of an object; and this requires that the attributes should be in their proper place, and that nothing should be meaningless; for the whole significance of the text depends on their use. This means that nothing should be left out.

Requirements of Interpretation

Now, in order to interpret a Vedic text in the light of action or the law of creation, we have to show that the whole of it,—with all its names-remains unbroken when understood in this manner; whereas it makes little sense when understood in terms of the praise of gods. It is not necessary that there should be any authority in support of this; for the authority is the manner in which we have to fix a meaning, when we are unable to find a cause, and the text makes little sense. For instance, when there is a reference to an actor, there may be a number of causes for his action, and we have to find them out; and we fix the meaning of a word in the same manner. That is the proof of the correctness of our meaning—namely, that it fits into the text; and testifies to the glory of the Vedas, and their wealth, and shows that the matters of which they speak are eternal.

Value of This Interpretation

The value of this interpretation lies in its ability to fill all gaps of thought in case of confused, doubtful, or ambiguous expressions; but we have to understand it in the light of the meaning it yields, and conceive of it as part of a great whole.

Action, Purpose and Sacrifice

How To Understand the Text

(It is in this manner that we have to understand the meaning of the text.) For instance, the word *Svaru* is not limited to a single meaning to complete its sense, and has a number of meanings in connection with its own actions. We can find out its correct meaning from the different ways in which it is used in the text; and there it must be taken as a part of the whole context, and referred to its cause. One of the meanings of the word is "a piece of wood"; and it is also associated with a sacrificial post, as may be seen.

Action and Its Differentiation

When we say that a person does something, what is meant by doing is that he has drawn something near to himself. The most important part of action is the function of a limb of the body: he has drawn something near to himself, and, in order to be effective, it (action) must be apportioned among the different limbs of the body; and it is this that makes for diversity of action. This (idea of action) is signified by the word *Upavesha*; and we get it when we depart from its more common meaning.

Meaning of Juhoti and Harana

There are other words like *Juhoti* and *Harana*, which too have to be understood in their supplementary sense; and that is how we get the real meaning of the text.

Common Meaning Is Not the Real Meaning

We cannot say that the common meaning of a word is its real meaning, because it does not give us a proper connection between things, and so we get no meaning at all; and, as we do not get any satisfactory result, we have to think of another method of interpretation, as in the case of the word *ājya*. In some cases we have to choose the meaning that suits the context best: for instance, there are some who explain the word *Sam-yavana* in one way, and some in another; and we have to choose the best.

Mitra and Varuṇa

(The meaning of certain expressions has been defined in a special way; for instance,) when the rod of authority is handed over to what belongs to Mitra and Varuṇa (or the priests of that name), it represents the idea of one who has done his life's work, and sits in a great posture of devotion.

Purpose and Action

(There can be no action without a purpose); and when a person engages in action, his action and purpose are linked together like flowers in a garland, each following each in order. We can see this for ourselves when a person engages in action. Purpose is born with a man, according to the teachings of the Vedas; and he goes on from one action to another, because after achieving one purpose he goes on to another. This is illustrated by the *Soma* sacrifice in which we are shown how purpose is achieved.

Action and Purification

It is because a person is brought into contact with the objects of life, that a desire arises within him, and it is followed by action with a purpose. It is in this manner that action takes place, and all purposes have their place; (but they make for bondage too, and so) the Vedas speak of purification (by means of which a person can act and yet be free from taint).

Object of Action

There is no fixed rule in regard to the relation between the actor, place and time; but they are always associated together in any plan of things. But the *śruti* says that all purposes are governed by a law. That is indeed true,—but in so far as it relates to the attainment of material objects. But that, according to the *śruti*, is a secondary object of action, because it only gives rise to action and is not its end; while the highest end of action is purification. (This leads us to the idea of Sacrifice; and) Sacrifice, according to prescribed rule, means the association of a proper person with the great forces of Nature and action; and we get this in the light of the accomplishment of all things. The same idea is expressed by means of *Juhoti*, with the addition of sprinkling water. *Dāna* or an act of charity or gift is clearly connected with the idea of renunciation, because it implies an admission that some one else has a prior claim to the possession of what is given away as a gift.

Action Is without End, and It Creates

(There is no end to action, because) it is a law that when a person has done one deed, he must have another object to pursue. Again, it is action that creates; and it is for this reason that it is linked up with a purpose. This is true of all things without exception; and, so far as the commencement of an action is concerned,—the cause in every case is the same. . . .

The Method of Interpretation

When the meaning of the principal word has been explained in accordance with the authority of the *śruti*, the meaning of the rest of the text should also be explained in accordance with the same authority. It will then be found that the text, unseparated from its original meaning, comes to possess its true essence, and retains the same character throughout. We shall thus find, from the conclusions arrived at and the truth disclosed, that the direction we have followed is the correct one, as it will partake of the characteristics of the original words. Indeed, the description is so accurate, that the ideas appear in every case to be like living beings.

An Objection

It may be argued that this is not possible, because the meanings cannot be divided in such a manner as to give us this result, and so it is not possible to agree that there can be two different meanings in this way.

An Answer

But if this contention were correct, and if the meaning of the text has no bearing on the laws of life it follows that, what the text teaches should be true, and all that we are told should take place, so that if we act in conformity with it, our actions should blossom forth and produce the promised results. If the names are real names, and if this is the normal form of the text, we should be able to grasp the essential characteristics of all things. If, however, we must take the meanings as they are, and cannot divide words into parts, it is possible to say that the names are the names of objects, but the text also refers to their actions, which do not appear to be consistent with their character. Hence we cannot apply the same rule to the rest of the text (and say that the names refer to living beings).

Method Applicable to Both Śruti and Smṛti

It may be argued that this method may apply to the *smṛti*, but not to the *śruti*. But this is not possible, because the *smṛti* is nothing but conclusions drawn from what precedes it (*śruti*).

Need of Selection

The words used in the text have a number of meanings; and it is only because we restrict ourselves to a particular explanation that (a difficulty arises, and) we get a different meaning. (It is a common rule of interpretation that) if a word has similar meanings, we should accept that which has already been referred to in the text. But this does not apply to the word *śyena*, because it does not make sense. Again, if a word is quite new, and has more than one meaning, the term "similar" should apply only to such meanings as have a bearing on a law of Nature-as, for instance, that which is derived from *Jyotishṭoma*. If, however, there is a reference to "five motions" in the text, it is easy to explain its meaning; and we get it by substituting one expression for another; and this substitution can be made throughout the text, because it is one and the same idea that is expressed, which can, be understood when we see through this "disguise."

Oneness of Meaning

There are some who maintain that it is not possible to have the same meaning throughout, because the sense is fixed by the context in each case. But this cannot be accepted; for if we take the meanings as they are, we find that they are unsuitable, and we are compelled to reject them; and it is in this manner that we find that there is but one assemblage of ideas in connection with Indra and Agni.

Words with Fixed Meanings

There are certain words which have only one meaning: for instance *Viśvedevas* (all-gods) refers to Nature or *Prakṛti*; and the *āgrāyaṇa* sacrifice should be understood to include all sacrifices. There is also a reference to *avabṛtha* sacrifice, and it is only once that the word has to be divided into parts; and that too in accordance with an express direction.

Source: *Mimamsa: The Secret of the Sacred Books of the Hindus*, translated by N. V. Thadani (Delhi: Bharati Research Institute, 1952), 1–14, 83–88, 170–173.

Selections from *The Sāṃkhyakārikā* of Īśvarakṛṣṇa and Vācaspati Miśra's Commentary *The Tattva-kaumudī*

I. Because of the torment of the threefold suffering, (there arises) the desire to know the means of removing it. If (it is said that) this (desire—i.e., inquiry) is useless because perceptible (means of removal are available), (we say) no, since (perceptible means) are not final or abiding.

Commentary The three kinds of pain constitute [what is ordinarily called] the "triad of pain." These are: (1) the intrinsic, (2) the extrinsic and (3) the divine or superhuman. Of these, the intrinsic is two-fold, bodily and mental. Bodily pain is caused by the disorder of the several humours, wind, bile, and phlegm; and mental pain is due to desire, wrath, avarice, affection, fear, envy, grief, and the non-perception of particular objects. All these are called intrinsic on account of their being amenable to internal remedies. Pains amenable to external remedies are two-fold; extrinsic and superhuman. The extrinsic are caused by men, beasts, birds, reptiles, and inanimate things; and superhuman ones are due to the evil influence of plants and the various elementals.

II. The revealed (or scriptural, means of removing the torment) are like the perceptible (i.e., ultimately ineffective), for they are connected with impurity destruction and excess; a different and superior method is the (discriminative) knowledge of the manifest (*vyakta*), the unmanifest (*avyakta*) and the knowing one (or knower—i.e., *puruṣa*).

Commentary The impurity lies in the fact of the Soma and other sacrifices being accompanied by the killing of animals and the destruction of grains and seeds. . . . The literal meaning of the words of the kārikā is as follows: The means of removing pain, consisting in the direct discriminative knowledge of the spirit (*puruṣa*) as apart from matter, is contrary to the Vedic means, and hence is better. The Vedic remedy is good in as much as it is authorized by the Veda and as such capable of removing pain to a certain extent; the discriminative knowledge of the spirit as distinct from matter is also good; and, of these, the latter is better, superior.

III. Primordial nature (*mūlaprakṛti*) is uncreated. The seven—the great one (*mahat*), etc.—are both created and creative. The sixteen are created, puruṣa is neither created nor creative.

IV. The attainment of that which is to be proved (is) by means of correct knowledge. The accepted means of correct knowledge are three because (these three) comprehend all means of correct knowledge. These three means (are as follows:) (a) perception, (b) inference, (c) reliable authority.

Commentary Inference that has been just defined in its general form has three special forms, called (1) a priori, (2) a posteriori, and (3) based on general observation. . . . all other means of cognition, such as analogy and the rest, which have been posited in the other philosophical systems, are all included among those that have been described above.

V. Perception is the selective ascertainment of particular sense-objects. Inference, which is of three kinds, depends upon a characteristic mark (*liṅga*) and that which bears the mark. Reliable authority is reliable teaching.

VI. The understanding of things beyond the sense is by means of (or from) inference by analogy. That which is imperceptible and, therefore, beyond both perception and inference, is established by means of reliable authority.

VII. (Perception may be impossible due to the following:)
- (a) because something is too far away;
- (b) because something is too close;
- (c) because of an injured sense-organ;
- (d) because of inattention;
- (e) because of intervention (of an object between an organ and the object to be perceived);
- (f) because of suppression (i.e., seeing the sun but no planets);
- (g) because of intermixture with what is similar.

VIII. The non-perception (of *prakṛti*) is because of its subtlety—not because of its non-existence. Its apprehension is because of (or by means of) its effect. Its effect—the great one (*mahat*), etc.—is different from yet similar to *prakṛti*.

IX. The effect exists (before the operation of cause) (*satkārya*)
- (a) because of the non-productivity of non-being;
- (b) because of the need for an (appropriate) material cause;
- (c) because of the impossibility of all things coming from all things;
- (d) because something can only produce what it is capable of producing;
- (e) because of the nature of the cause (or, because the effect is non-different from the cause).

X. The manifest (*vyakta*) is (a) caused; (b) finite; (c) non-pervasive; (d) active; (e) plural; (f) supported; (g) emergent; (h) composite; (i) dependent; the unmanifest (*avyakta*) is the opposite.

XI. (Both) the manifest and unmanifest are (a) (characterized by the) three *guṇas* ("qualities" or "strands"); (b) undiscriminating; (c) objective; (d) general; (e) non-conscious; (f) productive; the puruṣa is the opposite of them, although similar (to the avyakta as characterized in vs. X).

Commentary That is to say, the manifest has the three attributes of pleasure, pain, and delusion. By this assertion are set aside all those theories that attribute pleasure and pain to the spirit. . . .

Some people have held that it is consciousness alone that constitutes pleasure, pain, and delusion, and that there exists nothing besides this consciousness that could possess these [pleasures, etc.] as its attributes. In opposition to this view it is asserted that the manifest is "objective"; "objective" here stands for "what can be apprehended." That is, it is exterior to the consciousness. And because it is "objective," therefore, "common," i.e., apprehended simultaneously by several persons. If it were nothing more or less than the idea, then in that case, in as much as ideas, being in the form of "functions," belong specially to particular individuals, all that is "manifest" would have to belong specially to particular individuals. That is to say, as a matter of fact, the idea of one person is not apprehended by another, the cognition of another person being always uncognizable. In the case of [manifest substance such as] the glance of a dancing girl, it is found that many persons continue to stare at it at the same time. This could not be the cause if it were otherwise (i.e., if the glance were a mere idea).

XII. The *guṇas*, whose natures are pleasure, pain and indifference, (serve to) manifest, activate and limit. They successively dominate, support, activate, and interact with one another.

Commentary That is to say, one can produce its effects only when resting on the other two. By production here is meant modification, and this is always of the same character as the parent attribute. This is the reason why this "modification" is not regarded as "caused" [produced], what brings it about not being essentially different from itself; nor is it non-eternal, transient,–there being no merging of it into anything essentially different from itself . . . they are mutual concomitants not existing apart from one another.

XIII. *Sattva* is buoyant and shining; *rajas* is stimulating and moving; *tamas* is heavy and enveloping. They function for the sake of the puruṣa like a lamp.

XIV. Lack of discrimination, etc., is established because of (the manifest) having the three guṇas and because of the absence (of the *guṇas*) in the opposite of that (i.e., in the *puruṣa*). The unmanifest is likewise established because of the *guṇa*-nature in the cause of the effect (or because the effect has the same qualities as the cause).

XV and XVI.

(a) Because of the finiteness of specific things in the world which require a cause;
(b) because of homogeneity or sameness of the finite world;
(c) because of the power or potency (of the cause) which the process of emergence or evolution implies;
(d) because of separation or distinction between cause and its effect (with respect to modification or appearance);
(e) because of the undividedness or uniformity of the entire world;

The unmanitest (*avyakta*) is the cause; it functions because of or by the interaction of the three guṇas, modified like water, due to the specific nature abiding in the respective *guṇas*.

Commentary In as much as there is no merging of Nature itself into anything else, it is unmanifest pure and simple. . . . The specific objects in question, the Great Principle and the rest, have an unmanifested entity for their cause [i.e., they have a cause in which they exist in their unmanifested state], because they are finite, like the jar and other things: the jar and other things are found to have, for their cause, clay and other things, in which inhere the unmanifested state of the effects, we have already shown that the cause is that wherein the effect already exists in the unmanifested state. Under these circumstances, the cause of the great Principle must be that highest unmanifest which must be the final cause, for there is not ground for postulating a further unmanifested reality. . . . The Great Principle and the rest–manifesting themselves as "volition" and the rest–are found to be "homogeneous" in the sense that they consist in pleasure, pain, and delusion. And whatever is invariably connected with a certain form must have, for its cause wherein it inheres, something which has that form for its constitutent element. Thus it becomes established that of the specific objects, the unmanifested [i.e., Nature] is the cause. . . . we all know how the water falling from the clouds, though naturally of itself having one taste, becomes sweet, sour, saline, bitter, pungent, and hot, according as it comes into contact with different modifications of earth and becomes transformed into the juice of fruits such as cocoanut, palm, wood-apples, and so forth; in the same manner [owing to the blending and the mutual suppression of the attributes], the attributes of Nature come to be predominant one by one and thereby bring about various modifications in the state of various products.

XVII. The *puruṣa* exists,

(a) because aggregations or combinations exist for another;
(b) because (this other) must be apart or opposite from the three guṇas;
(c) because (this other) (must be) a superintending power or control;
(d) because of the existence or need of an enjoyer;
(e) because there is functioning or activity for the sake of isolation or freedom.

The plurality of *puruṣa* is established,

(a) because of the diversity of births, deaths, and faculties;
(b) because of actions or functions (that take place) at different times;
(c) and because of differences in the proportions of the three *guṇas* (in different entities).

Commentary Nature, the great Principle, the "I-principle," and other things must exist for another's use, because they are composite like the bedstead, the chair, the unguent, and other things. Nature and the rest are all "composite," being composed as they are, of pleasure, pain, and delusion. . . .

The objects of experience are pleasure and pain, which are felt by everyone as agreeable and disagreeable respectively. That is to say, there must be something other than the feelings themselves to which they can be agreeable or otherwise. Feelings cannot be agreeable or disagreeable to the Great Principle and other products, as that would involve the anomally of things operating upon themselves, as the great principle and the rest are all themselves integrally composed of pleasure, pain, and delusion. Thus, then, something else, which does not consist of pleasure, etc., must be the one to whom things are agreeable or disagreeable, and this something else must be the spirit.

XIX. And, therefore, because (the *puruṣa*) (is) the opposite (of the unmanifest), it is established that *puruṣa* is a: (a) witness; (b) possessed of isolation or freedom; (c) indifferent; (d) a spectator; (e) and inactive. Because of the proximity (or association) of the two—i.e., *prakṛti* and *puruṣa*—the unconscious one appears as if characterized by consciousness. Similarly, the indifferent one appears as if characterized by activity, because of the activities of the three *guṇas*.

Commentary Since is it only a "sentient" being that can be a "seer," and one can be a "seer," and one can be a "witness" only when the things have [been] shown to him, as in daily life we find the two parties of a dispute showing the object of their dispute to the witness, similarly does the nature exhibit its creations before the spirit, which latter, therefore, becomes the witness. And again, no object can be shown to one who is himself an object and insentient; and since the spirit is both sentient and non-objective, it becomes the witness. For the same reasons, the spirit is also the "seer."

XXI. The proximity (or association) of the two, which is like that of a blind man and a lame man, is for the purpose of seeing the *pradhāna* and for the purpose of the isolation of the *puruṣa*. From this (association) creation proceeds.

Commentary The spirit, while in union with the "enjoyable" Nature believes the three kinds of pain–the constituents of Nature–to be his own; and from this [self-imposed bond] he seeks liberation, isolation; this isolation is dependent upon due discrimination between the spirit and the three attributes; this discrimination is not possible without the Nature . . . thus it is that for his own isolation the spirit needs Nature.

The said "union" [of spirit with Nature] cannot by itself suffice for "enjoyment" or "isolation" if the Great Principle and the rest be not there; hence the union brings about the evolution for the sake of "enjoyment" and "isolation."

XXII. From *prakṛti* (emerges) the great one (*mahat*); from that (comes) self-awareness (*ahaṃkāra*); from that (comes) the group of sixteen. Moreover, from five of the sixteen (come) the five gross elements.

Commentary The "set of sixteen" is made up of the eleven sense-organs, to be described later on, and the five primary elements. Out of these sixteen, from the five primary elements proceed respectively the five elementary substances ether, earth, water, air, and fire.

XXIII. The *buddhi* ("will" or "intellect") is (characterized by) ascertainment or determination. Virtue, knowledge, non-attachment, and possession of power are its *sāttvika* form. Its *tāmasa* form is the opposite (of these four).

XXIV. Self-awareness (*ahaṃkāra*) is self-conceit (*abhimāna*). From it a twofold creation emerges: the group of eleven and the five subtle elements.

XXV. From self-awareness (known as) *vaikṛta* ("modified") proceeds the group of eleven, characterized by *sattva* ("goodness" or "purity"); from self-awareness (known as) *bhūtādi* ("the origin of gross elements") proceed the five subtle elements (*tanmātras*), characterized by *tamas* ("darkness" or "delusion"); from self-awareness (known as) *taijasa* ("shining" or "passionate") both proceed.

Commentary The sense organs, being illuminative and buoyant, is said to abound in the sattva attribute; and it proceeds from the "I-principle." From the "I-principle" as dominated by the tamas attribute proceeds the set of rudimentary substances. How so? Because these substances abound in the sattva attribute. That is to say–though the I-principle is one and uniform, yet by reason of the domination or suppression of one or other of these attributes it evolves products of diverse kinds. . . .

From the "taijasa form," that is, from the form abounding in the rajas attribute, proceed both, the "set of eleven" as also the "set of rudimentary substances." Even though there is no separate product from the rajas attribute exclusively by itself, yet [it is necessary factor as] the sattva and tamas attributes are, by themselves, absolutely inert and as such do not perform their functions at all; it is only when they are energized and moved by the rajas attribute that they perform their functions; thus the rajas attribute is instrumental in the evolving of both the sets of products mentioned above, through the exciting of activity of the other two attributes sattva and tamas. Thus it is not true that the rajas attribute serves no useful purpose.

XXVI. The sense organs (*buddhīndriyas*) ("organs of the buddhi" or "organs of ascertainment") are called eye, ear, nose, tongue, and skin. The organs of action (*karmendriyas*) are called voice, hands, feet, and organs of excretion and generation.

XXVII. The mind (*manas*) is of the nature of both; it is characterized by reflection (or synthesis or construction) and it is a sense because it is similar (to the senses). The variety of external things and the variety (of the organs) is because of the specific modifications (or transformations) of the *guṇas*.

XXVIII. The function of the five (sense organs)—(hearing) sound, etc.—(is) mere awareness (*ālocanamātra*). The function of the five (organs of action) (is) speech, grasping, walking, excretion and orgasm.

XXIX. With respect to the specific characteristics of the three (i.e., of the *buddhi*, *ahaṁkāra* and senses) each functions differently; the five vital breaths (or winds) (make up) their common function.

XXX. With respect to that which is presently in perception, the function of the four (i.e., *buddhi*, *ahaṁkāra*, *manas* and any one of the senses) (is) simultaneous and successive. With respect to that which is not present in perception, the function of the three (i.e., *buddhi*, *ahaṁkāra*, and *manas* or the "internal organ") is based upon a prior perception.

Commentary With regard to imperceptible things . . . the three internal organs operate without the aid of the external organs. . . . The instantaneous as well as the gradual functions of the three internal organs are preceded by some perception of a visible object; since inference, testimony, and remembrance, which are means of cognizing imperceptible things, operate only when they have for their background some sort of perception [of perceptible things]. The sense is that in regards to "perceptible" as well as "imperceptible" things the functioning of the internal organs is always preceded by the perception of some external object.

XXXI. (The external and internal organs) accomplish their own particular function in coordination with one another. The only motive is for the sake of the *puruṣa*. By nothing else is the instrument (i.e., the thirteenfold instrument) motivated.

XXXII. The instrument (*karaṇa*) is thirteenfold (i.e., made up of *buddhi*, *ahaṁkāra*, *manas* and the ten senses); (it is) characterized by seizing, holding and manifesting. (The instrument's) effect is tenfold (i.e., relating to the five senses and the five actions): the seized (or to be seized), the held (or to be held), and the manifested (or to be manifested), (or to be seized), the held (or to be held), and the manifested (or to be manifested).

XXXIII. The internal organ (*antaḥkaraṇa*) is threefold (i.e., *buddhi*, *ahaṁkāra*, and *manas*); the external is tenfold and is known as the context (or range or sphere) of the threefold. The external (functions) in present time. The internal (functions) in the three times (i.e., in past, present, and future).

XXXIV. Of these, the five senses (*buddhīndriyas*) (function with) specific and non-specific (i.e., gross and subtle) objects. Speech only has sound as its object, but the remaining (organs of action) have all five as objects.

XXXV. Since the buddhi together with the other internal organs (i.e., *ahaṁkāra* and *manas*) comprehends every object; therefore, the threefold instrument is the door-keeper and the remaining (ten) are the doors.

XXXVI. These (organs—i.e., *ahaṁkāra*, *manas*, and the ten senses), which are different from one another and which are distinct specifications of the *guṇas*, present the whole (of being) to the *buddhi*, illuminating it for the sake of the *puruṣa* like a lamp.

XXXVII. (This is done) because the *buddhi* produces (or brings about) every enjoyment of the *puruṣa*; and, moreover, (because the *buddhi*) distinguishes the subtle difference between the *pradhāna* and the *puruṣa*.

XXXVIII. The subtle elements (*tanmātras*) are non-specific. From these five (emerge) the five gross elements. These (gross elements) are considered (to be) specific, and are tranquil, turbulent and delusive.

Commentary The sense is that, in as much as among the gross elements . . . some abounding in the sattva attribute are calm, pleasing, illuminating, and buoyant; others abounding in the rajas attribute are turbulent, painful, and unstable; the rest abounding in the tamas attribute are deluded, confounded, and sluggish. These gross elements, thus perceived to be distinguished from one another, are said to be specific and gross. The rudimentary elements on the contrary cannot be similarly distinguished by ordinary people; and as such they are said to be non-specific and subtle.

XXXIX. Subtle (bodies), (bodies) born of father and mother together with gross elements are the threefold kinds (of bodies). Of these the subtle (bodies) are constant; (bodies) born of father and mother are perishable.

XL. The subtle body (*liṅga*), previously arisen, unconfined, constant, inclusive of the great one (*mahat*), etc., through the subtle elements (i.e., inclusive of *buddhi*, *ahaṁkāra*, *manas*, the ten senses and the five subtle elements), not having enjoyment, transmigrates, (because of) being endowed with *bhāvas* ("conditions" or "dispositions").

XLI. As a picture (does) not (exist) without a support or as a shadow (does) not (exist) without a post, etc.; so, too, the instrument (*liṅga*, or *karaṇa*) does not exist supportless without that which is specific (i.e., a subtle body).

XLII. This subtle entity, motivated for the sake of the *puruṣa*, appears like a player (who assumes many roles) by means of its association with efficient causes and effects (i.e., by means of its association with the *bhāvas*) and because of its association with the power of *prakṛti*.

Commentary The subtle body acts like a dramatic actor, on account of its connection with the "causes," in the shape of virtue, vice, etc., and "effects" in the shape of the taking up of different kinds of physical bodies, the latter being the effects of virtue, etc. That is to say, just as a dramatic actor, playing different parts . . . so does the subtle body, occupying various physical bodies, act like a man or a brute or a tree.

XLIII. The innate *bhāvas*, both natural and acquired—i.e., virtue (*dharma*), etc.—are seen to be dependent on the instrument (*karaṇa*) (i.e., thirteenfold instrument); whereas the embryo, etc., is dependent on the effected (i.e., the gross body).

XLIV. By means of virtue (i.e., the *bhāva*, *dharma*) (there is) movement upwards (in the scale of beings); by means of vice (*adharma*) (there is) movement downward; by means of salvation-knowledge (*jñāna*) (there is) final release or salvation (*apavarga*); from the opposite (of *jñāna*) bondage results.

XLV. From non-attachment (comes) dissolution in *prakṛti*; from attachment which is passionate (*rājasa*) (comes) transmigration; from power (comes) non-obstruction; and the reverse of that from its opposite.

Commentary Those who are free from passion, but are ignorant of the true nature of the spirit, become merged into Nature. Nature here stands for the whole set consisting of Nature, will, I-principle, the elements, and the sense-organs. Those who worship these as "spirits," become absorbed into these [i.e., those mistaking the senses for the spirit become absorbed in the senses, and so on]; that is to say, they rest there till, in the course of time, they are born again.

XLVI. This is the intellectual creation, and it is distinguished as ignorance, incapacity, complacency and perfection. These are of fifty varieties because of the suppression of differing qualities.

XLVII. There are five varieties of ignorance; twenty-eight varieties of incapacity, due to defects of the instrument; nine complacencies and eight perfections.

XLVIII. There are eight varieties of obscurity and delusion; ten kinds of extreme delusion; both gloom and utter darkness are eighteenfold.

XLIX. Injuries to the eleven organs together with injuries to the buddhi are said to make up incapacity; the injuries to the buddhi are seventeen due to the failure of the (ninefold) complacency and the (eightfold) perfection.

L. The nine complacencies are thought of (in two groups); four are internal, including nature, means, time, and destiny; and five are external due to the cessation or turning away from the objects of sense.

LI. The eight perfections are proper reasoning, oral instruction, study, removal of the three kinds of suffering, friendly discussion and generosity. The previous threefold division (i.e., ignorance, incapacity, and complacency) hinders the perfections.

LII. The *liṅga* (or *karaṇa* or thirteenfold instrument together with the five subtle elements) cannot function without the *bhāvas* ("conditions," "dispositions," or "strivings"). The *bhāvas* cannot function without the *liṅga*. Therefore, a twofold creation operates (or functions) called *liṅga* and *bhāva*.

LIII. The divine of celestial (order) is eightfold; the sub-human (order) is fivefold; the human (order) is one variety; such, briefly, is the elemental or gross creation.

LIV. (In the) upper (world) (there is) a predominance of *sattva*. (In the) lower creation (there is) a predominance of *tamas*. In the middle, (there is) a predominance of *rajas*. (This is so) from Brahmā down to a blade of grass.

LV. The *puruṣa*, which is consciousness, attains there the suffering made by decay and death; until deliverance of the subtle body; therefore, suffering is of the nature of things.

LVI. This creation, brought about by *prakṛti*—from the great one (*mahat*) down to the specific gross elements—(functions) for the sake of the release of each *puruṣa*; (this is done) for the sake of another, as if it were for her own (benefit).

Commentary A cook having finished the cooking in which he was engaged retires from the work; similarly Nature, being urged to action for the emancipation of the spirit, brings about this emancipation and thereafter stops her operations with regard to that spirit whom she has already liberated [and, thus emancipation is not impossible]. This action for another's sake is just like the action for one's own benefit.

LVII. As the unknowing (or unconscious) milk functions for the sake of the nourishment of the calf; so the *prakṛti* functions for the sake of the release of the *puruṣa*.

Commentary It is a fact of observation that insentient objects also act towards definite ends, e.g., the milk, which is insentient, flows for the nourishment of the calf. Similarly, Nature though insentient could act towards the emancipation of the spirit.

LVIII. As (in) the world (a man) engages in actions for the sake of the cessation of a desire; so also does the *prakṛti* function for the sake of the release of the *puruṣa*.

LIX. As a dancer ceases from the dance after having been seen by the audience; so also *prakṛti* ceases after having manifested herself to the *puruṣa*.

LX. (She) (*prakṛti*), possessed of the *guṇas* and helpful in various ways, behaves selflessly for the sake of him (*puruṣa*), who is without the *guṇas* and who plays no helpful part.

LXI. It is my thought that there is nothing more delicate than *prakṛti*, who (says to herself) "I have been seen," and never again comes into the sight of *puruṣa*.

LXII. Nothing, therefore, is bound; nothing released, likewise not anything transmigrates. (Only) *prakṛti* in its various forms transmigrates, is bound and is released.

Commentary Verily no spirit is bound; nor does any migrate; nor is any emancipated. Nature alone, having many vehicles, is bound, migrates, and is released. Bondage, migration and release are ascribed to the spirit, in the same manner as defeat and victory are attributed to the king, though actually occurring to his soldiers, because it is the servants that take part in the undertaking, the effects of which–grief or profit–accrue to the king. In the same manner, experience and emancipation, though really belonging to nature, are attributed to the spirit, on account of the non-discrimination of spirit from Nature. . . .

LXIII. Prakṛti binds herself by herself by means of seven forms (*rūpa* or *bhāva*); she releases herself by means of one form (*rūpa* or *bhāva*) for the sake of each *puruṣa*.

LXIV. Thus, from the study (or analysis) of the principles (*tattvas*), the "knowledge" (or salvation-knowledge) arises, "I am not, nothing belongs to me, I do not exist," (and this "knowledge") is complete because free from error, pure and solitary (*kevala*).

Commentary "I am not," means that "I am the spirit, not productive" and because non-productive, "I take no action"–"Not I"; and since without action, "I can have no possession," hence "naught is mine."

LXV. Then, the *puruṣa*, comfortably situated like a spectator, sees *prakṛti* whose activity has ceased due to the completion of her purpose, and who has turned back from the seven forms (*rūpa* or *bhāva*).

LXVI. (Says the) indifferent one (or spectator), "I have seen (her)"; the other ceases (saying), "I have been seen." Though the two are still in proximity, no (further) creation (takes place).

LXVII. Having arrived at the point at which virtue, etc., has no (further) cause, because of the attainment of direct knowledge, the endowed body (i.e., the body in association with *puruṣa*) yet continues because of the force of past impressions (*saṁskāras*), like a potter's wheel.

LXVIII. With the cessation of *prakṛti* due to its purpose having been accomplished, (the *puruṣa*) on attaining separation from the body, attains isolation (*kaivalya*) which is both certain and final.

LXIX. This secret (or mysterious) "knowledge" for the sake of the *puruṣa*—wherein is analyzed the existence, origin, and termination of all beings—has been expounded or enumerated by the highest (or greatest) sage.

LXX. This excellent and pure (knowledge) the sage gave with compassion to Āsuri; Āsuri likewise to Pañcaśikha; and by him the doctrine (*tantra*) was expanded or modified.

LXXI. Handed down by disciples in succession, it has been compendiously written in *ārya* metre by the noble minded Īśvarakṛṣṇa having fully learned the demonstrated truth.

LXXII. The subjects of the complete *ṣaṣitantra* are indeed in the seventy (verses of Īśvarakṛṣṇa), although the illustrative tales together with the objections of opponents are not included.

LXXIII. Thus, this briefly expounded treatise is not defective with respect to content, and is like a reflection in a mirror of the vast material of the *tantra*.

Source: *Sāṃkhyakārikā*, translated by Gerald James Larson in *Classical Sāṃkhya: An Interpretation of Its History and Meaning* (Delhi: Motilal Banarsidass, 1969). Commentaries are from *The Tattva-kaumudī*, translated by M. G. Jha, third edition (Poona: Oriental Book Agency, 1965).

Selections from the *Yoga Sūtra* of Patañjali with the *Yoga Bhāshya* of Veda Vyāsa

Chapter 1. Concentration (Samādhi)

1. 1. Now the exposition of yoga [is to be made].

To give a provisional definition: yoga is concentration; but this is a quality of the mind-stuff (*citta*) which belongs to all the stages. The stages of the mind-stuff are these: the restless, the infatuated, the distracted, the single- intent, and the restricted. Of these [stages the first two have nothing to do with yoga and even] in the distracted state of the mind [its] concentration is [at times] overpowered by [opposite] distractions and [consequently] it cannot properly be called yoga. But that [state] which, when the mind is single-in-intent, fully illumines a distinct and real object and causes the hindrances to dwindle, slackens the bonds of karma, and sets before it as a goal the restriction [of all fluctuations], is called the yoga in which there is consciousness of an object. This [conscious yoga], however, is accompanied by deliberation [upon coarse objects], by reflection [upon subtle objects], by joy, by the feeling-of-personality. . . . But when there is restriction of all the fluctuations [of the mind-stuff], there is the concentration in which there is not consciousness [of an object].

1. 2. Yoga is the restriction of the fluctuations of mind-stuff.

By the non-use of the word "all" [before the fluctuations], [the yoga which is] conscious [of objects] is also included under the denomination of yoga. Now mind-stuff has three aspects (*guṇa*), as appears from the fact that it has a disposition to vividness (*prakhyā*), to activity (*pravṛtti*), and to inertia (*sthiti*). For the mind-stuff's [aspect] *sattva*, which is vividness, when commingled with *rajas* and *tamas*, acquires a fondness for supremacy and for objects-of-sense; while the very same [constituent-aspect, *sattva*,] when pervaded with *tamas*, tends towards demerit and non-perception and passionateness and towards a failure of [its own rightful] supremacy; [and] the very same [*sattva*],–when the covering of error has dwindled away,–illumined now in its totality (*sarvatas*), but faintly pervaded by *rajas*, tends towards merit and knowledge and passionlessness and [its own rightful] supremacy; [and] the very same [*sattva*],–the stains of the last vestige of rajas once removed,–grounded in itself and being nothing but the discernment (*khyāti*) of the difference between the *sattva* and the Self (*puruṣa*), tends towards the contemplation of the rain-cloud of [knowable] things. The designation given by contemplators (*dhyāyin*) to this [kind of mind-stuff] is the highest elevation. For the energy of intellect is immutable and does not unite [with objects]; it has objects shown to it and is undefiled [by constituent-aspects] and is unending. Whereas this discriminate discernment, whose essence is *sattva*, is [therefore] contrary to this [energy of intellect and is therefore to be rejected]. Hence the mind-stuff being disgusted with this [discriminative discernment] restricts even this insight. When it has reached this state [the mind-stuff], [after the restriction of the fluctuations] passes over to subliminal impressions (*saṁskāra).* This is the [so-called] seedless concentration. In this state nothing becomes an object of consciousness: such is concentration not conscious [of objects]. Accordingly the yoga [which we have defined as] the restriction of the fluctuations of the mind-stuff is two-fold. . . .

1. 3. Then the Seer [that is, the Self] abides in himself.

At that time the energy of intellect is grounded in its own self, as [it is] when in the state of isolation. But when the mind-stuff is in its emergent state, [the energy of intellect], although really the same, [does] not [seem] so. . . .

1. 4. At other times it [the Self] takes the same form as the fluctuations [of mind-stuff].

In the emergent state [of the subliminal-impressions], the Self has fluctuations which are not distinguished from fluctuations of the mind-stuff; and so we have a sūtra, "There is only one appearance [for both],–that appearance is knowledge." The mind-stuff is like a magnet; and, as an object suitable to be seen [by the Self as Witness], it gives its aid [to the Self] by the mere fact of being near it, and thus the relation between it and the Self is that between property and proprietor. Hence the reason why the self experiences the fluctuations of the mind-stuff is its beginning-less correlation [with the thinking-substance].

1. 5. The fluctuations are of five kinds and are hindered or unhindered.

The hindered are those which are caused by the hindrances [undifferentiated-consciousness] and are the field for growth of the accumulation of the latent-deposits of karma; the unhindered have discriminative discernment as their object and thus obstruct the task of the aspects (*guṇa*). These are still unhindered even when they occur in the stream of the hindered. For even in the midst of the hindered [fluctuations] they are unhindered; while in the midst of the unhindered [they are] hindered. Corresponding subliminal-impressions are produced by none else than [these] fluctuations, and fluctuations [are made] by subliminal-impressions. In this wise, the wheel of fluctuations and subliminal-impressions ceaselessly rolls on [until the highest concentration is attained]. Operating in this wise, this mind-stuff, having finished its task, abides in its own likeness, or [rather] becomes resolved [into primary substance].–These, either hindered or unhindered are the five-fold fluctuations.

1. 8. Misconception is an erroneous idea (*jñāna*) not based on that form [in respect of which the misconception is entertained].

Why is it not a source-of-a-valid-idea? Because it is inhibited by the source-of-a-valid-idea, for the reason that the source-of-a-valid-idea has as its object a positive fact. In such cases there is evidently an inhibition of the source-of-the-invalid-idea by the source-of-the-valid-idea, as for instance the [erroneous] visual-perception of two moons is inhibited by the actual visual-perception of one moon. . . . These same [are known] by peculiar technical designations: obscurity and infatuation and extreme infatuation and darkness and blind-darkness. These will be discussed in connection with the subject of the defilements of the mind-stuff. . . .

1. 17. [Concentration becomes] conscious [of its object] by assuming forms either of deliberation [upon coarse objects] or of reflection [upon subtle objects] or of joy or of the sense-of-personality.

1. 18. The other [concentration which is not conscious of objects] consists of subliminal-impressions only [after objects have merged], and follows upon that practice which effects the cessation [of fluctuations].

1. 19. [Concentration not conscious of objects] caused by worldly [means] is the one to which the discarnate attain and to which those [whose bodies] are resolved into primary matter attain.

1. 20. [Concentration not conscious of objects,] which follows upon belief [and] energy [and] mindfulness [and] concentration [and] insight, is that to which the others [the yogins] attain.

[That concentration not conscious of objects, which is] caused by [spiritual] means is that to which yogins attain. Belief is the mental approval [of concentration]; for, like a good mother, it protects the yogin. For him [thus] believing and setting discrimination [before him] as his goal there is the further attainment of energy. For him who has reached the further attainment of energy mindfulness is at hand. And when mindfulness is at hand the mind-stuff is self-possessed and becomes concentrated. When his mind-stuff has become concentrated he gains as his portion the discrimination of insight, by which he perceives things as they really are. Through the practice of these means and through passionlessness directed to this end there [finally] arises that concentration which is not conscious [of any object].

1. 21. For the keenly intense, [concentration] is near.

[For them] there is gaining of concentration and the result of concentration.

1. 22. Because [this keenness] is gentle or moderate or keen, there is a [concentration] superior even to this [near kind].

In that there is a gently keen and a moderately keen and a vehemently keen, there is a superior even to this [concentration]. Because there is a superior to this [near kind], the attainment of concentration and the result of concentration is near to him who follows the vehement method and is of mildly keen intensity; still more near to him who is of moderately keen intensity; and most near to him who is of vehemently, keen intensity.

1. 23. Or [concentration] is attained by devotion to the Īśvara.

1. 24. Untouched by hindrances or karmas or fruition or by latent-deposits the Īśvara is a special kind of self.

Now what is the means of attaining escape?

Chapter 2. Methods **(Sādhanā)**

2. 2. For the cultivation of concentration and for the attenuation of the hindrances.
2. 3. Undifferentiated-consciousness (*avidyā*) and the feeling-of-personality and passion and aversion and the will-to-live are the five hindrances.
2. 5. The recognition of the permanent, of the pure, of pleasure, and of a self in what is impermanent, impure, pain, and not-self is undifferentiated-consciousness.
2. 6. When the power of seeing and the power by which one sees have the appearance of being in a single-self, [that is] the feeling-of-personality.
2. 7. Passion is that which dwells upon pleasure.
2. 8. Aversion is that which dwells upon pain.
2. 9. The will-to-live swooping on [by the force of] its own nature exists in this form even in the wise.
2. 10. These [hindrances] [when they have become] subtle are to be escaped by the inverse-propagation.

These five hindrances when they have become like burned seeds, after the mind which has predominated over the deeds of the yogin is resolved [into primary matter], come with it to rest.

2. 11. The fluctuations of these should be escaped by means of contemplation.
2. 16. That which is to be escaped is pain yet to come.
2. 17. The correlation of the seer and the object-of-sight is the cause of that which is to be escaped.
2. 24. The reason for this [correlation] is undifferentiated-consciousness (*avidyā*).
2. 26. The means of attaining escape is unwavering discriminative discernment.

Discriminative discernment of the presented-idea of the difference between *sattva* and the Self. But this discernment wavers when erroneous perception is not repressed. When erroneous perception, reduced to the condition of burned seed, fails to reproduce itself, then the flow of the presented-ideas of discrimination–belonging to the *sattva*, which is cleansed from *rajas* belonging to the hindrances, and which continues in the higher clearness [and] in the higher consciousness of being master–becomes stainless. This unwavering discriminative discernment is the means (*upāya) of escape.* After this, erroneous perception tends to become reduced to the condition of burned seed. And its failure to reproduce itself is the path (*mārga*) to release, the way-of-approach (*upāya*) to escape.

2. 27. For him [there is] insight seven-fold and advancing in stages to the highest.

The words <for him> refer to him in whom discernment is re-uprisen. The word <seven-fold> means that the insight of the discriminating [yogin], after the removal of the defilements from the covering of impurity, when no other kind of presented-idea is generated in the mind-stuff, has just seven forms, as follows. 1. The thing to be escaped has been thought out; nor need [the yogin] think it out again. 2. The reasons for the thing to be escaped have dwindled away; nor need they dwindle away again. 3. The escape is directly perceived by the concentration of restriction; [nor need anything beyond this be discovered]. 4. The means of escape in the form of discriminative discernment has been cultivated; [nor need anything beyond this be cultivated]. So this is the four-fold final release (*vimukti*), belonging to insight, which may be effected. But the final release of the mind-stuff is three-fold [as follows]. 5. The authority of the thinking-substance is ended. 6. The aspects (*guṇa*), like rocks fallen from the top of the mountain peak, without support, of their own accord, incline towards dissolution and come with this [thinking-substance] to rest. And when these [aspects] are quite dissolved, they do not cause growth again, because there is no impelling-cause. 7. In this stage the Self has passed out of relation with the aspects (*guṇa*), and, enlightened by himself and nothing more, is stainless and isolated.–The Self beholding this seven-fold insight advancing in stages to the highest is denominated fortunate. Even when there is also the inverted generation of the mind-stuff the Self is said to be released [and] fortunate, because he has passed beyond the aspects (*guṇa*).

2. 28. After the aids to yoga have been followed up, when the impurity has dwindled, there is an enlightenment of perception reaching up to the discriminative discernment.

The aids to yoga are the eight which are about to be enumerated. As the result of following them up there is a dwindling or cessation of the five-sectioned misconception. Upon the dwindling of this follows the manifestation of focused thinking. And in proportion as the means [of attaining discriminative discernment are followed up], so the impurity is reduced to a state of attenuation. And .in proportion as it dwindles, the enlightenment of perception also, in accordance with the degree of dwindling, increases. . . .

2. 30. Abstinence from injury and from falsehood and from theft and from incontinence and from acceptance of gifts are the abstentions.

Of these [five] abstinence from injury means the abstinence from malice towards all living creatures in every way and at all times. And the other abstentions and observances are rooted in it. In so far as their aim is the perfection of it, they are taught in order to teach it. . . . Abstinence-from-falsehood (*satya*) means speech and mind such as correspond to the object-intended; and speech and mind correspond to the object intended; and speech and mind corresponding to what is seen or inferred or heard. If speech is spoken in order that one's own knowledge may pass to some one else, it should not be deceitful or mistaken or barren of information; [then it would be abstinence from falsehood]. It should be used for the service of all; not for the ruin of creatures. And even when used thus, should it be only for the ruin of creatures, it would not be an abstinence from falsehood; it would be nothing less than wrong.

In so far as there would be a false kind of merit [and] a resemblance of merit, it would become the worst of evils. Therefore let [the yogin] consider [first] what is good(for all creatures and [then] speak with abstinence-from-falsehood. –Theft is the unauthorized appropriation of things-of-value from another. While abstinence-from-theft, when free from coveting, is the refusal to do this. –Continence is control of the hidden organ of generation.–Abstinence-from-acceptance-of-gifts is abstinence-from-appropriating objects, because one sees the disadvantages in acquiring them or keeping them or losing them or in being attached to them or in harming them. These then are the abstentions.

Chapter 3. Supernormal Powers

3. 24. [As a result of constraint] upon powers [there arise] powers like those of an elephant.

3. 25. As a result of casting the light of a sense-activity [there arises the intuitive] knowledge of the subtle and the concealed and the obscure.

The yogin by casting the light of that sense-activity of the central organ which is called luminous upon an object whether subtle or concealed or obscure has access to that object.

3. 35. Experience is a presented-idea which fails to distinguish the *sattva* and the Self, which are absolutely uncommingled [in the presented-idea]. Since the *sattva* exists as object for another, the [intuitive] knowledge of the Self arises as the result of constraint upon that which exists for its own sake.

The *sattva* of the thinking-substance, with its disposition to brightness, by mastering the *rajas* and *tamas* which are equally dependent upon the *sattva*, enters into a mutation as a result of the presented-idea of the difference between the *sattva* and the self. Therefore the self, of which we can only say that it is intellect (*citti*), which is other [than the aspects (*guṇa*), and which is undefiled [by objects], is absolutely contrary in quality even to the *sattva* which is mutable. Experience is a presented-idea, which fails to distinguish these two which are absolutely uncommingled. Because the self has objects shown to it. This [same] presented-idea of experience is an object for sight, since the *sattva* exists for the sake of another. But as a result of constraint upon that presented-idea, which is distinguished from this [*sattva*], which is intellect and nothing more; and which is other [than the aspects (*guṇa*), and which belongs to the Self,–[as a result of this,] that insight whose object is the Self arises. The Self is not seen by that presented-idea of the Self whose essence is the *Sattva* of the thinking-substance. It is the Self which sees the presented-idea which depends upon its own self. . . .

3. 36. As a result of this [constraint upon that which exists for its own sake], there arise vividness and the organ-of-[supernal]-hearing and the organ-of-[supernal]-feeling and the organ-of-[supernal]-sight and the organ-of-[supernal]-taste and the organ-of-[supernal]-smell.

As a result of vividness, there arises an [intuitive] knowledge of the subtle or concealed or remote, whether past or future. As a result of the organ-of-[supernal]-hearing, one hears supernal sounds; as a result of the organ-of-[supernal]-feeling, one has access to supernal touch; as a result of the organ-of-[supernal]-sight, one has the consciousness of supernal colour; as a result of the organ-of-[supernal]-taste, one has a consciousness of supernal flavour; as a result of the organ-of-[supernal] smell, one has an [intuitive] knowledge of supernal fragrance. These unceasingly arise.

3. 37. In concentration these [supernal activities] are obstacles; in the emergent state they are perfections (*siddhi*).

These, the vividness and so forth, arising in the yogin whose mind-stuff is concentrated, are obstacles, in that they go counter to the sight which belongs to this [concentrated mind-stuff]. [But] arising [in the yogin] whose mind-stuff is emergent, they are perfections.

3. 38 As a result of slackening the causes of bondage and as a result of the consciousness of the procedure [of the mind-stuff], the mind-stuff penetrates into the body of another.

By virtue of the latent-deposit of karma in the body, the central-organ which is changeable and unstable becomes established. This is bondage. By virtue of concentration there is a slackening of this karma which is the cause of bondage. And the consciousness of the procedure [of the mind-stuff] comes only from concentration. As a result of the dwindling of the bondage of karma, and as a result of the consciousness of the procedure of his mind-stuff, the yogin by withdrawing mind-stuff from his own body deposits it in other bodies. The organs also fly after the mind-stuff thus deposited. Just as, for instance, when the king-bee flies up, the bees fly up after him, so the organs follow after the mind-stuff in its penetration into the body of another.

3. 39. As a result of subjugating the *udāna*, there is no adhesion to water or mud or thorns or similar objects, and [at death] the upward flight.

The fluctuation of the whole complex of organs which is distinguished by having the different vital-forces (*prāṇa*) is vitality. Its activity is five-fold. *Prāṇa* has its course through the mouth and nose and its fluctuation extends as far as the heart. And *samāna*, since it distributes equally, has its fluctuation from the navel. *Apāna*, since it leads down, has its fluctuation as far as the sole of the foot. *udāna*, since it leads up, has its fluctuation as far as the head. *Vyāna* is pervading. Among these *prāṇa* is predominant. As a result of subjugating the *udāna* there is no adhesion to water or mud or thorns or similar objects; and at the time of decease there is the upward flight. This [upward flight] he attains by mastery [of the *udāna*].

3. 40. As a result of subjugating the *samāna* [there arises] a radiance.

The yogin who has subjugated the *samāna* by causing a pulsation of the flames, becomes radiant.

3. 41. As a result of constraint upon the relation between the organ-of-hearing, and the air, [there arises] the supernal organ-of-hearing.
3. 42. Either as the result of constraint upon the relation between the body and the air, or as the result of the balanced state of lightness, such as that of the cotton-fibre, there follows the passing through air.
3. 43. An outwardly un-adjusted fluctuation is the great discarnate; as a result of this the dwindling of the covering to the brightness.

The fluctuation assumed by the central-organ outside the body is the fixed-attention called discarnate. If it is only an outer fluctuation of the central-organ which abides in the body, it is called adjusted. But if it is an outer fluctuation of the central-organ, which is itself externalized, in that it [the fluctuation] disregards the body, it is of course called unadjusted. [The yogins] by means of the adjusted one among these two accomplish the unadjusted great discarnate, by means of which yogins enter the bodies of others. And as a result of this fixed-attention, the covering of the *sattva* of the thinking-substance, whose essence is brightness, which has the three-fold fruition from the hindrances and the karma, and whose root is *rajas* and *tamas*, dwindles away.

3. 45. As a result of this, atomization and the other [perfections] come about; [there is] perfection of body; and there is no obstruction by the properties of these [elements].

As to these [eight perfections], 1. atomization occurs in case [the yogin] becomes atomic; 2. levitation occurs in case [the yogin] becomes light; 3. magnification occurs in case [the yogin] becomes magnified; 4. extension occurs in case [the yogin] touches the moon with a mere finger's tip; 5. efficacy, the non-obstruction of desire, occurs in case [the yogin] dives into the earth underground [and] emerges again, as if in water; 6. mastery occurs in case [the yogin] masters elements and products of elements and is not mastered by others; 7. sovereignty occurs in case [the yogin] is sovereign over the production, absorption, and arrangement of these [elements and products]; 8. the capacity of determining things according to desire is the capacity to will actual facts so that the elements which are the evolving-causes remain as he wills. And although having power, he does not cause reversal of things. Why not? Because at the will of another [the Īśvara], who determines things according to desire, and who from the beginning is perfected, the elements have been so willed. These are the eight powers. –Perfection of body is described later. And its external-aspects are not obstructed. Earth with its limitation-in-extent [its essential-attribute] does not restrict the action of the body and [organs] of the yogin. For he penetrates even the rock. The water, liquid as it is, wets him not. The fire, hot as it is, burns him not. The wind, motor as it is, budges him not. And even in the air, whose essence is that nothing is covered [by it], his body is covered. . . .

3. 46. Beauty and grace and power and the compactedness of the thunderbolt,—[this is] perfection of body.

The perfect body is handsome and alluring and unexcelled in power and compact as the thunderbolt.

3. 47. As a result of constraint upon the process-of-knowing and the essential-attribute and the feeling-of-personality and the inherence and the purposiveness, [there follows] the subjugation of the organs.

The object-to-be-known is the sounds and other [perceptible objects] whose essence is both the generic-form and the particular. 1. The process-of-knowing is a fluctuation of the organs with reference to these [objects]. And this [process] has not the character of being a process-of-knowing their generic-form only. . . .

3. 55. When the purity of the *sattva* and of the Self are equal [there is] isolation.

When the *sattva* of the thinking-substance is freed from the defilement of the *rajas* and *tamas*, and when it has no task other than with the presented-idea of the difference of [the *sattva*] from the self, and when the seeds of the hindrances within itself have been burned, then the *sattva* enters into a state of purity equal to that of the Self. When-this-is-so purity is the cessation of the experience which is falsely attributed to the Self. In this state [of purity] isolation follows for one-who-has-supremacy or for one-who-has-not-supremacy, for one who partakes of the [intuitive] knowledge proceeding from discrimination or for another. For if there be [intuitive] knowledge in the case of one whose hindrances have become burned seed, there is no further need of any [supernormal power]. As being the means of purifying the *sattva*, both the supremacy proceeding from concentration and the [intuitive] knowledge have been introduced-into-the-discussion. But strictly speaking the [intuitive] knowledge represses not-sight. When this is repressed there are no more hindrances. Because there are no more hindrances there is no fruition of karma. In this state the aspects, their task done, do not again submit themselves as objects-for-sight to the Self. That is the Self's isolation. Then the Self having its light within itself becomes undefiled and isolated.

Chapter 4. Isolation

4. 25. For him who sees the distinction, the pondering upon his own states-of-being ceases.

Because a blade of grass sprouts during the rains we infer the existence of seed. Just so in the case of him who betrays thrills of joy and falling tears in hearing of the way of release, we may likewise infer that there is in him [good] karma rooted in the knowledge of the difference [between the *sattva* and the Self], conducive to liberation, and brought to completion [in the past]. In him, the pondering upon his own states-of-being which is natural to him comes into activity.–When there is none of this [good karma], this has been said "For [those] who, after having renounced their own nature [of pondering upon themselves], there is by reason of lack [of good karma], a liking for the opposing view and no liking for the ascertainment of truth–, [for them there is no sight of the distinction and no cessation of the pondering]."–Now-as-to-this-point, the pondering upon his own states-of-being is in this fashion, "Who was I? How was I? What is this [birth]? How is this [birth]? What shall we become? or how shall we become?" But this pondering ceases for one who sees the distinction [between the *sattva* and the Self]. For what reason is this? Since it is this mind-stuff which undergoes this diversified mutation. But when there is no longer undifferentiated-consciousness (*avidyā*), the Self is purified and untouched by the conditions of the mind-stuff. For this reason this skilful person ceases pondering upon his own states-of-being.

4. 26. Then the mind-stuff is borne down to discrimination, onward towards isolation.

That mind-stuff of his which formerly was borne onward towards objects-of-sense, down to non-thinking, becomes changed for him. It is borne onward towards isolation, down to the thinking which comes from discrimination.

4. 27. In the intervals of this [mind-stuff] there are other presented-ideas [coming] from subliminal-impressions.

The mind-stuff which is [borne] down towards discrimination of the presented-idea and the flow of which is towards nothing but discernment of the difference between the *sattva* and the Self, has in its intervals other presented-ideas, either "It is I" or "It is mine" or "I think" or "I do not think." From what source? From the dwindling seeds, from previous subliminal-impressions.

4. 28. The escape from these [subliminal-impressions] is described as being like [the escape from] the hindrances.

The hindrances when in the condition of burned seed are unfit for generation. Just so a previous subliminal-impression, when in the condition of seed burned by the fire of [intuitive] thinking does not generate presented-ideas. But because the subliminal-impressions of [intuitive] knowledge are dormant until the task of the mind-stuff is completed, they are not considered here.

4. 29. For one who is not usurious even in respect of elevation, there follows in every case, as a result of discriminative discernment, the concentration [called] rain-cloud of [knowable] things.

This Brahman even in respect of elevation, is not usurious, [that is to say] is not looking for anything [as a reward] even from that; [and] if, even in respect of that, he be passionless, in every case nothing-less-than-the discriminative discernment becomes his. In this way, when, because the seeds of the subliminal-impressions have perished, there do not spring up for him any more presented-ideas,–then the concentration called rain-cloud of [knowable] things becomes his.

4. 30. Then follows the cessation of the hindrances and of karma.

After the attainment of this [rain-cloud of knowable things], undifferentiated-consciousness (*avidyā*) and the other hindrances are extirpated root and [branch]. And the latent-deposits of karma, good and bad, are destroyed with their roots. Upon the cessation of the hindrances and of karma, the wise man, even while yet alive, is released. Why is this? Because misconception is the cause of the world. For surely no one has ever seen the birth of any one whose misconceptions have dwindled away.

4. 31. Then, because of the endlessness of knowledge from which all obscuring defilements have passed away, what is yet to be known amounts to little.

The knowledge which is freed from all obscurations by hindrances and by karma becomes endless. The *sattva* of the obscured knowledge overwhelmed by the *tamas* which obscures it, and kept in motion here and there only by the *rajas*, is set free [from the *tamas*] and becomes fit for the process-of-knowing. In this case when it has become rid of defilement by any of the defilements of the covering, it becomes endless. In consequence of the endlessness of knowledge what is yet to be known amounts to little, to no more than a firefly in the sky. On which point this has been said "A blind man pierced a jewel; one without fingers strung it on a cord; one without a neck put it on; a dumb man paid honour to it."

4. 32. When as a result of this the aspects (*guṇa*) have fulfilled their purpose, they attain to the limit of the consequence of mutations.

As a result of the rise [into consciousness] of the rain-cloud of [knowable] things, when the aspects have fulfilled their purpose they end the sequence of their mutations. For [the aspects] having completed their experience and their liberation, and having attained the limit of their sequence, are incapable of lingering even for a moment.

4. 34. Isolation is the inverse generation of the aspects, no longer provided with a purpose by the self, or it is the energy of intellect grounded in itself.

When the aspects (*guṇa*), whose essence is causes and effects, are inversely generated,–now that experience and liberation have been accomplished [for the Self] and now that a purpose is no longer provided by the Self,–this is isolation. The Self's energy of thought becomes isolated, since it is grounded in itself and is not again related to the *sattva* of the thinking-substance. Its continuance thus for evermore is isolation.

Source: *The Yoga-System of Patañjali*, translated by James Haughton Woods. Harvard Oriental Series 17. (Cambridge: Harvard University Press, 1914; reprinted third edition, Delhi: Motilal Banarsidass, 1966).

Selections from *The Vedānta Sūtras* with the Commentary of Śaṅkara

It is a matter not requiring any proof that the object and the subject whose respective spheres are the notion of the "Thou" (the Non-Ego) and the "Ego," and which are opposed to each other as much as darkness and light are, cannot be identified. All the less can their respective attributes be identified. Hence it follows that it is wrong to superimpose upon the subject—whose Self is intelligence, and which has for its sphere the notion of the Ego—the object whose sphere is the notion of the Non-Ego, and the attributes of the object, and vice versa to superimpose the subject and the attributes of the subject on the object. In spite of this it is on the part of man a natural procedure—which has its cause in wrong knowledge—not to distinguish the two entities (object and subject) and their respective attributes, although they are absolutely distinct, but to superimpose upon each the characteristic nature and the attributes of the other, and thus, coupling the Real and the Unreal, to make use of expressions such as "That am I," "That is mine."—But what have we to understand by the term "superimposition?"—The apparent presentation, in the form of remembrance, to consciousness of something previously observed, in some other thing.

Some indeed define the term "superimposition" as the superimposition of the attributes of one thing on another thing. Others, again, define superimposition as the error founded on the non-apprehension of the difference of that which is superimposed from that on which it is super-imposed. Others, again, define it as the fictitious assumption of attributes contrary to the nature of that thing on which something else is superimposed. But all these definitions agree in so far as they represent superimposition as the apparent presentation of the attributes of one thing in another thing. And therewith agrees also the popular view which is exemplified by expressions such as the following: "Mother-of-pearl appears like silver," "The moon although one only appears as if she were double." But how is it possible that on the interior Self which itself is not an object there should be superimposed objects and their attributes? For every one superimposes an object only on such other objects as are placed before him (i.e. in contact with his sense-organs), and you have said before that the interior Self which is entirely disconnected from the idea of the Thou (the Non-Ego) is never an object. It is not, we reply, non-object in the absolute sense. For it is the object of the notion of the Ego, and the interior Self is well known to exist on account of its immediate (intuitive) presentation. Nor is it an exceptionless rule that objects can be superimposed only on such other objects as are before us, i.e. in contact with our sense-organs; for non-discerning men superimpose on the ether, which is not the object of sensuous perception, dark-blue colour.

Hence it follows that the assumption of the Non-Self being superimposed on the interior Self is not unreasonable.

This superimposition thus defined, learned men consider to be Nescience (*avidyā*), and the ascertainment of the true nature of that which is (the Self) by means of the discrimination of that (which is superimposed on the Self), they call knowledge (*vidyā*). There being such knowledge (neither the Self nor the Non-Self) are affected in the least by any blemish or (good) quality produced by their mutual superimposition. The mutual superimposition of the Self and the Non-Self, which is termed Nescience, is the presupposition on which there are based all the practical distinctions—those made in ordinary life as well as those laid down by the Veda—between means of knowledge, objects of knowledge (and knowing persons), and all scriptural texts, whether they are concerned with injunctions and prohibitions (of meritorious and non-meritorious actions), or with final release.—But how can the means of right knowledge such as perception, inference, &c., and scriptural texts have for their object that which is dependent on Nescience?—Because we reply, the means of right knowledge cannot operate unless there be a knowing personality, and because the existence of the latter depends on the erroneous notion that the body, the sense, and so on, are identical with, or belong to, the Self of the knowing person. For without the employment of the senses, perception and the other means of right knowledge cannot operate. And without a basis (i.e. the body) the senses cannot act. Nor does anybody act by means of a body on which the nature of the Self is not superimposed. Nor can, in the absence of all that, the Self which, in its own-nature is free from all contact, become a knowing agent. And if there is no knowing agent, the means of right knowledge cannot operate (as said above). Hence perception and the other means of right knowledge, and the Vedic texts have for their object that which is dependent on Nescience. . . . With reference again to that kind of activity which is founded on the Veda (sacrifices and the like), it is true indeed that the reflecting man who is qualified to enter on it, does so not without knowing that the Self has a relation to another world; yet that qualification does not depend on the knowledge, derivable from the Vedānta texts, of the true nature of the Self as free from all wants, raised above the distinctions of the Brāhmaṇa and Kṣatriya-classes and so on, transcending transmigratory existence. For such knowledge is useless and even contradictory to the claim (on the part of sacrificers, &c. to perform certain actions and enjoy their fruits). And before such knowledge of the Self has arisen, the Vedic texts continue in their operation, to have for their object that which is dependent on Nescience. For such texts as the following, "A Brāhmaṇa is to sacrifice," are operative only on the supposition that on the Self are superimposed particular conditions such as caste, state of life, age, outward circumstances, and so on. That by superimposition we have to understand the notion of something in some other thing we have already explained. (The superimposition of the Non-Self will be understood more definitely from the following examples.) Extra-personal attributes are superimposed on the Self, if a man considers himself sound and entire, or the contrary, as long as his wife, children, and so on are sound and entire or not. Attributes of the body are superimposed on the Self, if a man thinks of himself (his Self) as stout, lean, fair, as standing, walking, or jumping. Attributes of the sense-organs, if he thinks "I am mute, or deaf, or one-eyed, or blind." Attributes of the internal organ when he considers himself subject to desire, intention, doubt, determination, and so on. Thus the producer of the notion of the Ego (i.e. the internal organ) is superimposed on the interior Self which, in reality, is the witness of all the modifications of the internal organ, and vice versa the interior Self, which is the witness of everything, is superimposed on the internal organ, the senses, and so on. In this way there goes on this natural beginning and endless superimposition, which appears in the form of wrong conception, is the cause of individual souls appearing as agents and enjoyers (of the results of their actions), and is observed by every one.

Enquiry into Brahman

The word "then" is here to be taken as denoting immediate consecution; not as indicating the introduction of a new subject to be entered upon; for the enquiry into Brahman (more literally, the desire of knowing Brahman) is not of that nature. Nor has the word "then" the sense of auspiciousness (or blessing); for a word of that meaning could not be properly construed as a part of the sentence. The word "then" rather acts as an auspicious term by being pronounced and heard merely while it denotes at the same time something else, viz. immediate consecution as said above. That the latter is its meaning follows moreover from the circumstance that the relation in which the result stands to the previous topic (viewed as the cause of the result) is non-separate from the relation of immediate consecution.

. . . The special question with regard to the enquiry into Brahman is whether it presupposes as its antecedent the understanding of the acts of religious duty (which is acquired by means of the Pūrvā Mīmāṁsā.) To this question we reply in the negative, because for a man who has read the Vedānta-parts of the Veda it is possible to enter on the enquiry into Brahman even before engaging in the enquiry into religious duty. . . . The knowledge of active religious duty has for its fruit transitory felicity and that again depends on the performance of religious acts. The enquiry into Brahman, on the other hand, has for its fruit eternal bliss, and does not depend on the performance of any acts. Acts of religious duty do not yet exist at the time when they are enquired into, but are something to be accomplished (in the future); for they depend on the activity of man. In the *Brahma-mīmāṁsā*, on the other hand, the object of enquiry, i.e. Brahman, is something already accomplished (existent),—for it is eternal,—and does not depend on human energy. The two enquiries differ moreover in so far as the operation of their respective fundamental texts is concerned. For the fundamental texts on which active religious duty depend convey information to man in so far only as they enjoin on him their own particular subjects (sacrifice, &c.); while the fundamental texts about Brahman merely instruct man, without laying on him the injunction of being instructed, instruction being their immediate result. The case is analogous to that of the information regarding objects of sense which ensues as soon as the objects are approximated to the senses. It therefore is requisite that something should be stated subsequent to which the enquiry into Brahman is proposed.—Well, then, we maintain that the antecedent conditions are the discrimination of what is eternal and what is non-eternal; the renunciation of all desire to enjoy the fruit (of one's actions) both here and hereafter; the acquirement of tranquillity, self-restraint, and the other means, and the desire of final release. If these conditions exist, a man may, either before entering on an enquiry into active religious duty or after that, engage in the enquiry into Brahman and come to know it; but not otherwise. The word "then" therefore intimates that the enquiry into Brahman is subsequent to the acquisition of the above-mentioned (spiritual) means. . . .

But, it may be asked, is Brahman known or not known (previously to the enquiry into its nature)? If it is known we need not enter on an enquiry concerning it; if it is not known we can not enter on such an enquiry.

We reply that Brahman is known. Brahman, which is all-knowing and endowed with all powers, whose essential nature is eternal purity, intelligence, and freedom, exists. For if we consider the derivation of the word "Brahman," from the root *bṛh*, "to be great," we at once understand that eternal purity, and so on, belong to Brahman. Moreover the existence of Brahman is known on the ground of its being the Self of every one. For every one is conscious of the existence of (his) Self, and never thinks "I am not." If the existence of the Self were not known, every one would think "I am not." And this Self (of whose existence all are conscious) is Brahman. But if Brahman is generally known as the Self, there is no room for an enquiry into it! Not so, we reply; for there is a conflict of opinions as to its special nature. (1.1.1)

Brahman as Origin of this World

The full sense of the Sūtra . . . is: That omniscient omnipotent cause from which proceed the origin, subsistence, and dissolution of this world—which world is differentiated by names and forms, contains many agents and enjoyers, is the abode of the fruits of actions, these fruits having their definite places, time, and causes, and the nature of whose arrangement cannot even be conceived by the mind—that cause, we say, is Brahman. . . .

[T]he knowledge of the real nature of a thing does not depend on the notions of man, but only on the thing itself. For to think with regard to a post, "this is a post or a man, or something else," is not knowledge of truth; the two ideas, "it is a man" or something else, being false, and only the third idea, "it is a post," which depends on the thing itself, falling under the head of true knowledge. Thus true knowledge of all existing things depends on the things themselves, and hence the knowledge of Brahman all depends altogether on the thing, i.e. Brahman itself.—But, it might be said, as Brahman is an existing substance, it will be the object of the other means of right knowledge also, and from this it follows that a discussion of the Vedānta-texts is purposeless.—This we deny; for as Brahman is not an object of the senses, it has no connection with those other means of knowledge. For the senses have, according to their nature, only external things for their objects, not Brahman. If Brahman were an object of the senses, we might perceive that the world is connected with Brahman as its effect; but as the effect only (i.e. the world) is perceived, it is impossible to decide (through perception) whether it is connected with Brahman or something else. Therefore the Sūtra under discussion is not meant to propound inference (as the means of knowing Brahman), but rather to set forth a Vedānta-text. (1.1.2)

(The omniscience of Brahman follows) from its being the source of scripture. (1.1.3)

But that (Brahman is to be known from scripture), because it is connected (with the Vedānta-texts) as their purport. (1.1.4)

[F]rom the mere comprehension of Brahman's Self, which is not something either to be avoided or endeavoured after, there results cessation of all pain, and thereby the attainment of man's highest aim. That passages notifying certain divinities, and so on, stand in subordinate relation to acts of devout meditation mentioned in the same chapters may readily be admitted. But it is impossible that Brahman should stand in an analogous relation to injunctions of devout meditation, for if the knowledge of absolute unity has once arisen there exists no longer anything to be desired or avoided, and thereby the conception of duality, according to which we distinguish actions, agents, and the like, is destroyed. If the conception of duality is once uprooted by the conception of absolute unity, it cannot arise again, and so no longer be the cause of Brahman being looked upon as the complementary object of injunction of devotion. Other parts of the Veda may have no authority except in so far as they are connected with injunctions; still it is impossible to impugn on that ground the authoritativeness of passages conveying the knowledge of the Self; for such passages have their own result. Nor, finally, can the authoritativeness of the Veda be proved by inferential reasoning so that it would be dependent on instances observed elsewhere. From all which it follows that the Veda possesses authority as a means of right knowledge of Brahman. . . .

Among eternal things, some indeed may be "eternal, although changing" . . . But this (*mokṣa*) is eternal in the true sense, i.e. eternal without undergoing any changes, omnipresent as ether, free from all modifications, absolutely self-sufficient, not composed of parts, of self-luminous nature. That bodiless entity in fact, to which merit and demerit with their consequences and threefold time do not apply, is called release; a definition agreeing with scriptural passages, such as the following: "Different from merit and demerit, different from effect and cause, different from past and future" (Ka. Up. 1.2.14). It (i.e. *mokṣa*) is, therefore, the same as Brahman in the enquiry into which we are at present engaged. If Brahman were represented as supplementary to certain actions, and release were assumed to be the effect of those actions, it would be non-eternal, and would have to be considered merely as something holding a pre-eminent position among the described non-eternal fruits of actions with their various degrees. But that release is something eternal is acknowledged by whoever admits it at all, and the teaching concerning Brahman can therefore not be merely supplementary to actions.

. . . Nor, again, can it be said that there is a dependence on action in consequence of (Brahman or Release) being something which is to be obtained; for as Brahman constitutes a person's Self it is not something to be attained by that person. And even if Brahman were altogether different from a person's Self still it would not be something to be obtained; for as it is omnipresent it is part of its nature that it is ever present to every one, just as the (all-pervading) ether is. . . .

As long as the knowledge of the Self, which Scripture tells us to search after, has not arisen, so long the Self is knowing subject; but that same subject is that which is searched after, viz. (the highest Self free from all evil and blemish). Just as the idea of the Self being the body is assumed as valid (in ordinary life), so all the ordinary sources of knowledge (perception and the like) are valid only until the one Self is ascertained. (1.1.4)

The Individual Soul

The individual soul (*jiva*) is called awake as long as being connected with the various external objects by means of the modifications of the mind—which thus constitute limiting adjuncts of the soul—it apprehends those external objects, and identifies itself with the gross body, which is one of those external objects. When, modified by the impressions which the external objects have left, it sees dreams, it is denoted by the term "mind." When, on the cessation of the two limiting adjuncts (i.e. the subtle and the gross bodies), and the consequent absence of the modifications due to the adjuncts, it is, in the state of deep sleep, merged in the Self as it were, then it is said to be asleep (resolved into the Self). (1.1.9)

Scripture States Brahman Is the Cause of the World

Brahman is apprehended under two forms; in the first place as qualified by limiting conditions owing to the multiformity of the evolutions of name and form (i.e. the multiformity of the created world); in the second place as being the opposite of this, i.e. free from all limiting conditions whatever. (1.1.11)

Scripture Teaches Unity of Soul

But when he, by means of the cognition of absolute identity, finds absolute rest in the Self consisting of bliss, then he is freed from the fear of transmigratory existence. But this (finding absolute rest) is possible only when we understand by the Self consisting of bliss, the highest Self, and not either the *pradhāna* or the individual soul. Hence it is proved that the Self consisting of bliss is the highest Self. (1.1.19)

Omnipresence of Brahman

Against the further objection that the omnipresent Brahman cannot be viewed as bounded by heaven we remark that the assignment, to Brahman, of a special locality is not contrary to reason because it subserves the purpose of devout meditation. Nor does it avail anything to say that it is impossible to assign any place to Brahman because Brahman is out of connexion with all place. For it is possible to make such an assumption, because Brahman is connected with certain limiting adjuncts. Accordingly Scripture speaks of different kinds of devout meditation on Brahman as specially connected with certain localities, such as the sun, the eye, the heart. For the same reason it is also possible to attribute to Brahman a multiplicity of abodes, as is done in the clause (quoted above) "higher than all" (1.1.24)

Relationship between Soul and Brahman

. . . [A]s the passages, "I am Brahman," "That art thou," and others, prove, there is in reality no such thing as an individual soul absolutely different from Brahman, but Brahman, in so far as it differentiates itself through the mind (*buddhi*) and other limiting conditions, is called individual soul, agent, enjoyer.

. . . If there were no objects there would be no subjects; and if there were no subjects there would be no objects. For on either side alone nothing could be achieved. . . .(1.1.31)

[T]here is only one universal Self, there is an end to the whole practical view of the world with its distinction of bondage, final release, and the like. (1.2.6)

Two Kinds of Knowledge

[T]wo kinds of knowledge are enjoined there (in the Upaniṣad), a lower and a higher one. Of the lower one it is said that it comprises the *Ṛgveda* and so on, and then the text continues, "The higher knowledge is that by which the Indestructible is apprehended." Here the Indestructible is declared to be the subject of the higher knowledge. If we now were to assume that the Indestructible distinguished by invisibility and like qualities is something different from the highest Lord, the knowledge referring to it would not be the higher one. For the distinction of lower and higher knowledge is made on account of the diversity of their results, the former leading to mere worldly exaltation, the latter to absolute bliss; and nobody would assume absolute bliss to result from the knowledge of the *pradhāna*. (1.2.21)

Soul and Ignorance

That same highest Brahman constitutes—as we know from passages such as "that art thou"—the real nature of the individual soul, while its second nature, i.e. that aspect of it which depends on fictitious limiting conditions, is not its real nature. For as long as the individual soul does not free itself from Nescience in the form of duality—which Nescience may be compared to the mistake of him who in the twilight mistakes a post for a man—and does not rise to the knowledge of the Self, whose nature is unchangeable, eternal Cognition—which expresses itself in the form "I am Brahman"—so long it remains the individual soul. But when, discarding the aggregate of body, sense-organs and mind, it arrives, by means of Scripture, at the knowledge that it is not itself that aggregate, that it does not form part of transmigratory existence, but is the True, the Real, the Self, whose nature is pure intelligence; then knowing itself to be of the nature of unchangeable, eternal Cognition, it lifts itself above the vain conceit of being one with this body, and itself becomes the Self, whose nature is unchanging, eternal Cognition. As is declared in such scriptural passages as "He who knows the highest Brahman becomes even Brahman" (Mu. Up. 3.2.9) And this is the real nature of the individual soul by means of which it arises from the body and appears in its own form.

. . . Before the rise of discriminative knowledge the nature of the individual soul, which is (in reality) pure light, is non-discriminated as it were from its limiting adjuncts consisting of body, senses, mind, sense-objects and feelings, and appears as consisting of the energies of seeing and so on. Similarly—to quote an analogous case from ordinary experience—the true nature of a pure crystal, i.e. its transparency and whiteness, is, before the rise of discriminative knowledge (on the part of the observer,) non-discriminated as it were from any limiting adjuncts of red or blue colour; while, as soon as through some means of true cognition discriminative knowledge has arisen, it is said to have now accomplished its true nature, i.e. transparency and whiteness, although in reality it had already done so before. Thus the discriminative knowledge, effected by *śruti*, on the part of the individual soul which previously is non-discriminated as it were from its limiting adjuncts, is (according to the scriptural passage under discussion) the soul's rising from the body, and the fruit of that discriminative knowledge is its accomplishment in its true nature, i.e. the comprehension that its nature is the pure Self. Thus the embodiedness and the non-embodiedness of the Self are due merely to discrimination and non-discrimination. . . . (1.3.19)

Although the Vedānta-passages may be conflicting with regard to the order of the things created, such as ether and so on, they do not conflict with regard to the creator, "on account of his being represented as described." That means: such as the creator is described in any one Vedānta-passage, viz. as all-knowing, the Lord of all, the Self of all, without a second, so he is represented in all other Vedānta-passages also. Let us consider, for instance, the description of Brahman (given in Taitt. Up. 2.1ff). There it is said at first, "Truth, knowledge, infinite is Brahman." Here the word "knowledge," and so likewise the statement, made later on, that Brahman desired (2.6), intimate that Brahman is of the nature of intelligence. Further, the text declares that the cause of the world is the general Lord by representing it as not dependent on anything else. It further applies to the cause of the world the term "Self" (2.1), and it represents it as abiding within the series of sheaths beginning with the gross body; whereby it affirms it to be the internal Self within all beings. . . . The Vedanta-passages which are concerned with setting forth the cause of the world are thus in harmony throughout. (1.4.14)

Brahman and Causation

Brahman is to be acknowledged as the material cause as well as the operative cause; because this latter view does not conflict with the promissory statements and the illustrative instances. The promissory statement chiefly meant is the following one, "Have you ever asked for that instruction by which that which is not heard becomes heard; that which is not perceived, perceived; that which is not known, known?" (Ch. Up. 6.1.3) This passage intimates that through the cognition of one thing everything else, even if (previously) unknown, becomes known. Now the knowledge of everything is possible through the cognition of the material cause, since the effect is non-different from the material cause. On the other hand, effects are not non-different from their operative cause; for we know from ordinary experience that the carpenter, for instance, is different from the house he has built.—The illustrative example referred to is the one mentioned (Ch. Up. 6.1.4), "My dear, as by one clod of clay all that is made of clay is known, the modification (i.e. the effect) being a name merely which has its origin in speech, while the truth is that it is clay merely"; which passage again has reference to the material cause. . . . The Self is thus the operative cause, because there is no other ruling principle, and the material cause because there is no other substance from which the world could originate. (1.4.23)

The refutation contained in the preceding Sutra was set forth on the condition of the practical distinction of enjoyers and objects of enjoyment being acknowledged. In reality, however, that distinction does not exist because there is understood to be non-difference (identity) of cause and effect. The effect is this manifold world consisting of ether and so on; the cause is the highest Brahman. Of the effect it is understood that in reality it is non-different from the cause, i.e. has no existence apart from the cause.—How so?—"On account of the scriptural word "origin" and others." The word "origin" is used in connexion with a simile, in a passage undertaking to show how through the knowledge of one thing everything is known. . . . The meaning of this passage is that, if there is known a lump of clay which really and truly is nothing but clay, there are known thereby likewise all things made of clay, such as jars, dishes, pails, and so on all of which agree in having clay for their true nature. For these modifications or effects are names only, exist through or originate from speech only, while in reality there exists no such thing as a modification. In so far as they are names (individual effects distinguished by names) they are untrue; in so far as they are clay they are true.—This parallel instance is given with reference to Brahman; applying the phrase "having its origin in speech" to the case illustrated by the instance quoted we understand that the entire body of effects has no existence apart from Brahman. . . . We therefore must adopt the following view. In the same way as those parts of ethereal space which are limited by jars and waterpots are not really different from the universal ethereal space, and as the water of a mirage is not really different from the surface of the salty steppe—for the nature of that water is that it is seen in one moment and has vanished in the next, and moreover, it is not to be perceived by its own nature (i.e. apart from the surface of the desert)—; so this manifold world with its objects of enjoyment, enjoyers and so on has no existence apart from Brahman. (2.1.14)

Process of Sublation

The entire complex of phenomenal existence is considered as true as long as the knowledge of Brahman being the Self of all has not arisen; just as the phantoms of a dream are considered to be true until the sleeper wakes. For as long as a person has not reached the true knowledge of the unity of the Self, so long it does not enter his mind that the world of effects with its means and objects of right knowledge and its results of actions is untrue; he rather, in consequence of his ignorance, looks on mere effects (such as body, offspring, wealth, &c.) as forming part of and belonging to his Self, forgetful of Brahman being in reality the Self of all. Hence, as long as true knowledge does not present itself, there is no reason why the ordinary course of secular and religious activity should not hold on undisturbed. The case is analogous to that of a dreaming man who in his dream sees manifold things, and, up to the moment of waking, is convinced that his ideas are produced by real perception without suspecting the perception to be a merely apparent one.—But how (to restate an objection raised above) can the Vedānta-texts if untrue convey information about the true being of Brahman? We certainly do not observe that a man bitten by a rope-snake (i.e. a snake falsely imagined in a rope) dies, nor is the water appearing in a mirage used for drinking or bathing.—This objection, we reply, is without force (because as a matter of fact we do see real effects to result from unreal causes), for we observe that death sometimes takes place from imaginary venom, (when a man imagines himself to have been bitten by a venomous snake,) and effects (of what is perceived in a dream) such as the bite of a snake or bathing in a river take place with regard to a dreaming person.—But, it will be said, these effects themselves are unreal!—These effects themselves, we reply, are unreal indeed; but not so the consciousness which the dreaming person has of them. This consciousness is a real result; for it is not sublated by the waking consciousness. The man who has risen from sleep does indeed consider the effects perceived by him in his dream such as being bitten by a snake, bathing in a river, &c. to be unreal, but he does not on that account consider the consciousness he had of them to be unreal likewise.—(We remark in passing that) by this fact of the consciousness of the dreaming person not being sublated (by the waking consciousness) the doctrine of the body being our true Self is to be considered as refuted.—Scripture also (in the passage, "If a man who is engaged in some sacrifice undertaken for some special wish sees in his dream a woman, he is to infer there from success in his work") declares that by the unreal phantom of a dream a real result such as prosperity may be obtained. And, again, another scriptural passage, after having declared that from the observation of certain unfavourable omens a man is to conclude that he will not live long, continues "if somebody sees in his dream a black man with black teeth and that man kills him," intimating thereby that by the unreal dream-phantom a real fact, viz. death, is notified.—It is, moreover, known from the experience of persons who carefully observe positive and negative instances that such and such dreams are auspicious omens, others the reverse. And (to quote another example that something true can result from or be known through something untrue) we see that the knowledge of the real sounds A. &c. is reached by means of the unreal written letters. Moreover, the reasons which establish the unity of the Self are altogether final, so that subsequently to them nothing more is required for full satisfaction. An injunction as, for instance, "He is to sacrifice" at once renders us desirous of knowing what is to be effected, and by what means and in what manner it is to be effected; but passages such as, "Thou art that," "I am Brahman," leave nothing to be desired because the state of consciousness produced by them has for its object the unity of the universal Self. For as long as something else remains a desire is possible; but there is nothing else which could be desired in addition to the absolute unity of Brahman. . . . Nor, again, can such consciousness be objected to on the ground either of uselessness or of erroneousness, because, firstly, it is seen to have for its result the cessation of ignorance, and because, secondly, there is no other kind of knowledge by which it could be sublated. And that before the knowledge of the unity of the Self has been reached the whole real-unreal course of ordinary life, worldly as well as religious, goes on unimpeded, we have already explained. When, however, final authority having intimated the unity of the Self, the entire course of the world which was founded on the previous distinction is sublated, then there is no longer any opportunity for assuming a Brahman comprising in itself various elements. (2.1.14)

Cause and Effect

For the following reason also the effect is non-different from the cause, because only when the cause exists the effect is observed to exist, not when it does not exist. For instance, only when the clay exists the jar is observed to exist, and the cloth only when the threads exist. That it is not a general rule that when one thing exists another is also observed to exist, appears, for instance, from the fact, that a horse which is other (different) from a cow is not observed to exist only when a cow exists. Nor is the jar observed to exist only when the potter exists; for in that case non-difference does not exist, although the relation between the two is that of an operative cause and its effect.—But—it may be objected—even in the case of things other (i.e. non-identical) we find that the observation of one thing regularly depends on the existence of another; smoke, for instance, is observed only when fire exists.—We reply that this is untrue, because sometimes smoke is observed even after the fire has been extinguished; as, for instance, in the case of smoke being kept by herdsmen in jars.—Well, then—the objector will say—let us add to smoke a certain qualification enabling us to say that smoke of such and such a kind does not exist unless fire exists.—Even thus, we reply, your objection is not valid, because we declare that the reason for assuming the non-difference of cause and effect is the fact of the internal organ (*buddhi*) being affected (impressed) by cause and effect jointly. And that does not take place in the case of fire and smoke. . . . The non-difference of cause and effect results not only from Scripture but also from the existence of perception. For the non-difference of the two is perceived, for instance, in an aggregate of threads, where we do not perceive a thing called "cloth," in addition to the threads, but merely threads running lengthways and crossways. So again, in the threads we perceive finer threads (the aggregate of which is identical with the grosser threads), in them again finer threads, and so on. On the ground of this our perception we conclude that the finest parts which we can perceive are ultimately identical with their causes, viz. red, white, and black (the colours of fire, water, and earth, according to Ch. Up. 6.4); those, again, with air, the latter with ether, and ether with Brahman, which is one and without a second. (2.1.15)

For the following reason also the effect is to be considered as non-different (from the cause). That which is posterior in time, i.e. the effect, is declared by Scripture to have, previous to its actual beginning, its Being in the cause, by the Self of the cause merely. . . . A thing, on the other hand, which does not exist in another thing by the Self of the latter is not produced from that other thing; for instance, oil is not produced from sand. Hence as there is non-difference before the production (of the effect), we understand that the effect even after having been produced continues to be non-different from the cause. As the cause, i.e. Brahman, is in all time neither more nor less than that which is, so the effect also, viz. the world, is in all time only that which is. But that which is is one only; therefore the effect is non-different from the cause. (2.1.16)

Nature of the World

The beginninglessness of the world recommends itself to reason. For if it had a beginning it would follow that, the world springing into existence without a cause, the released souls also would again enter into the circle of transmigratory existence; and further, as then there would exist no determining cause of the unequal dispensation of pleasure and pain, we should have to acquiesce in the doctrine of rewards and punishments being allotted, without reference to previous good or bad actions. That the Lord is not the cause of the inequality, has already been remarked. Nor can Nescience by itself be the cause, as it is of a uniform nature. On the other hand, Nescience may be the cause of inequality, if it be considered as having regard to merit accruing from action produced by the mental impressions of wrath, hatred, and other afflicting passions. Without merit and demerit nobody can enter into existence, and again, without a body merit and demerit cannot be formed; so that—on the doctrine of the world having a beginning—we are led into a logical see-saw. The opposite doctrine, on the other hand, explains all matters in a manner analogous to the case of the seed and sprout, so that no difficulty remains. (2.1.36)

Nature of the Self and Body

[A]lthough the Self must be admitted to be one only, injunctions and prohibitions are possible owing to the difference effected by its connexion with bodies and other limiting adjuncts, the products of Nescience.—It then follows that for him who has obtained perfect knowledge, injunctions and prohibitions are purportless.—No, we reply, (they are not purportless for him, but they do not refer to him), since to him who has obtained the highest aim no obligation can apply. For obligations are imposed with reference to things to be avoided or desired; how then should he, who sees nothing, either to be wished or avoided, beyond the universal Self, stand under any obligation? The Self certainly cannot be enjoined on the Self.—Should it be said that injunctions and prohibitions apply to all those who discern that the soul is something different from the body (and therefore also to him who possesses perfect knowledge), we reply that (such an assertion is too wide, since) obligation depends on a man's imagining his Self to be (actually) connected with the body. It is true that obligation exists for him only who views the soul as something different from the body; but fundamentally all obligation is an erroneous imagination existing in the case of him only who does not see that his Self is no more connected with a body than the ether is with jars and the like. For him, on the other hand, who does not see that connexion no obligation exists, much less, therefore, for him who discerns the unity of the Self.—Nor does it result from the absence of obligation, that he who has arrived at perfect knowledge can act as he likes; for in all cases it is only the wrong imagination (as to the Self's connexion with a body) that impels to action, and that imagination is absent in the case of him who has reached perfect knowledge.—From all this it follows that injunctions and prohibitions are based on the Self's connexion with the body. (2. 3.48)

And that individual soul is to be considered a mere appearance of the highest Self, like the reflection of the sun in the water; it is neither directly that (i.e. the highest Self), nor a different thing. Hence just as, when one reflected image of the sun trembles, another reflected image does not on that account tremble also; so, when one soul is connected with actions and results of actions, another soul is not on that account connected likewise. There is therefore no confusion of actions and results. And as that "appearance" is the effect of Nescience, it follows that the *saṁsāra* which is based on it (the appearance) is also the effect of Nescience, so that from the removal of the latter there results the cognition of the soul being in reality nothing but Brahman. (2.3.50)

Illusion and Reality

It is not true that the world of dreams is real; it is mere illusion and there is not a particle of reality in it.—Why?—"On account of its nature not manifesting itself with the totality," i.e. because the nature of the dream world does not manifest itself with the totality of the attributes of real things.—What then do you mean by the "totality"?—The fulfillment of the conditions of place, time, and cause, and the circumstance of non-refutation. All these have their sphere in real things, but cannot be applied to dreams. In the first place there is, in a dream, no space for chariots and the like; for those cannot possibly find room in the limited confines of the body. . . . In the second place we see that dreams are in conflict with the conditions of time. One person lying asleep at night dreams that it is day . . . another lives, during a dream which lasts one *muhūrta* only, through many crowds of years.—In the third place there do not exist in the state of dreaming the requisite efficient causes for either thought or action; for as, in sleep, the organs are drawn inward, the dreaming person has no eyes, &c. for perceiving chariots and other things; and whence should he, in the space of the twinkling of an eye, have the power of—or procure the material for—making chariots and the like?—In the fourth place the chariots, horses, &c., which the dream creates, are refuted, i.e. shown not to exist by the waking state. And apart from this, the dream itself refutes what it creates, as its end often contradicts its beginning; what at first was considered to be a chariot turns, in a moment, into a man, and what was conceived to be a man has all at once become a tree. (3.2.3)

We only maintain that the world connected with the intermediate state (i.e. the world of dreams) is not real in the same sense as the world consisting of ether and so on is real. . . . Brahman is the Self of all; the world of dreams on the other hand is daily sublated by the waking state. That the latter is mere illusion has, therefore, to be understood with a distinction. (3.2.4)

. . . Brahman is that whose nature is permanent purity, intelligence, and freedom; it transcends speech and mind, does not fall within the category of "object," and constitutes the inward Self of all. Of this Brahman our text denies all plurality of forms; but Brahman itself it leaves untouched. . . . Now, after the two forms have been set forth, there arises the desire of knowing that to which the two forms belong, and hence the text continues, "Now then the teaching by means of 'Not so, not so.' " This passage, we conclude, conveys information regarding the nature of Brahman by denying the reality of the forms fictitiously attributed to it; for the phrase, "Not so, not so!" negatives the whole aggregate of effects superimposed on Brahman. Effects we know to have no real existence, and they can therefore be negated; not so, however. Brahman, which constitutes the necessary basis for all fictitious superimposition. (3.2.22)

There can exist nothing different from Brahman, since we are unable to observe a proof for such existence. That all existences which have a beginning spring from, subsist through, and return into Brahman we have already ascertained, and have shown that the effect is non-different from the cause.—Nor can there exist, apart from Brahman, something which has no beginning, since scripture affirms that "Being only this was in the beginning, one, without a second." The promise moreover that through the cognition of one thing everything will be known, renders it impossible that there should exist anything different from Brahman. (3.2.32)

Superimposition

Adhyāsa takes place when the idea of one of two things not being dismissed from the mind, the idea of the second thing is superimposed on that of the first thing; so that together with the superimposed idea the former idea remains attached to the thing on which the second idea is superimposed. When e.g. the idea of (the entity) Brahman superimposes itself upon the idea of the name, the latter idea continues in the mind and is not driven out by the former. A similar instance is furnished by the superimposition of the idea of the god Viṣṇu on a statue of Viṣṇu. . . . We, in the second place, have *apavāda* when an idea previously attached to some object is recognised as false and driven out by the true idea springing up after the false one. So e.g. when the false idea of the body, the senses, and so on being the Self is driven out by the true idea springing up later—and expressed by judgments such as "Thou art that"—that the idea of the Self is to be attached to the Self only. (3.3.9)

Nature of the Self

The assertion that the Self is not separate from the body cannot be maintained. The Self rather must be something separate from the body, "because the existence (of the Self) does not depend on the existence of that (i.e. the body)". For if from the circumstance that they are where the body is you conclude that the qualities of the Self are qualities of the body, you also must conclude from the fact that they are not where the body is that they are not qualities of the body, because thereby they show themselves to be different in character from the qualities of the body. Now the (real) qualities of the body, such as form and so on, may be viewed as existing as long as the body exists; life, movement, &c., on the other hand, do not exist even when the body exists, viz. in the state of death. The qualities of the body, again, such as form and so on, are perceived by others; not so the qualities of the Self, such as consciousness, remembrance, and so on. Moreover, we can indeed ascertain the presence of those latter qualities as long as the body exists in the state of life, but we cannot ascertain their non-existence when the body does not exist; for it is possible that even after this body has died the qualities of the Self should continue to exist by passing over into another body. The opposite opinion is thus precluded also for the reason of its being a mere hypothesis.—We further must question our opponent as to the nature of that consciousness which he assumes to spring from the elements; for the materialists do not admit the existence of anything but the four elements. Should he say that consciousness is the perception of the elements and what springs from the elements, we remark that in that case the elements and their products are objects of consciousness and that hence the latter cannot be a quality of them, as it is contradictory that anything should act on itself. Fire is hot indeed but does not burn itself, and the acrobat, well trained as he may be, cannot mount on his own shoulders. As little could consciousness, if it were a mere quality of the elements and their products, render them objects of itself. For form and other (undoubted) qualities do not make their own colour or the colour of something else their objects; the elements and their products, on the other hand, whether external or belonging to the Self (the organism) are rendered objects by consciousness. Hence in the same way as we admit the existence of that perceptive consciousness which has the material elements and their products for its objects, we also must admit the separateness of that consciousness from the elements. And as consciousness constitutes the character of our Self, the Self must be distinct from the body. That consciousness is permanent, follows from the uniformity of its character (and we therefore may conclude that the conscious Self is permanent also; as also follows) from the fact that the Self, although connected with a different state, recognises itself as the conscious agent—a recognition expressed in judgments such as "I saw this,"—and from the fact of remembrance and so on being possible.

The argumentation that consciousness is an attribute of the body because it is where a body is, is already refuted by the reasons stated above. Moreover, perceptive consciousness takes place where there are certain auxiliaries such as lamps and the like, and does not take place where those are absent, without its following there from that perception is an attribute of the lamp or the like. Analogously the fact that perception takes place where there is a body, and does not take place where there is none, does not imply that it is an attribute of the body; for like lamps and so on the body may be used (by the Self) as a mere auxiliary. Nor is it even true that the body is absolutely required as an auxiliary of perception; for in the state of dream we have manifold perceptions while the body lies motionless.—The view of the Self being something separate from the body is therefore free from all objections. (3.3.54)

Knowledge of Brahman

Former works, i.e. works, whether good or evil, which have been accumulated in previous forms of existence as well as in the current form of existence before the origination of knowledge, are destroyed by the attainment of knowledge only if their fruit has not yet begun to operate. Those works, on the other hand, whose effects have begun and whose results have been half enjoyed—i.e. those very works to which there is due the present state of existence in which the knowledge of Brahman arises—are not destroyed by that knowledge. . . . Were it otherwise, i.e. were all works whatever extinguished by knowledge, there would be no reason for the continuance of the current form of existence, and the rise of knowledge would therefore be immediately followed by the state of final release; in which case scripture would not teach that one has to wait for the death of the body.—But, an objection is raised, the knowledge of the Self being essentially non-active does by its intrinsic power destroy (all) works; how then should it destroy some only and leave others unaffected? We certainly have no right to assume that when fire and seeds come into contact the germinative power of some seeds only is destroyed while that of others remains unimpaired!—The origination of knowledge, we reply, cannot take place without dependence on an aggregate of works whose effects have already begun to operate, and when this dependence has once been entered into, we must—as in the case of the potter's wheel—wait until the motion of that which once has begun to move comes to an end, there being nothing to obstruct it in the interim. The knowledge of our Self being essentially non-active destroys all works by means of refuting wrong knowledge; but wrong knowledge—comparable to the appearance of a double moon—lasts for some time even after it has been refuted, owing to the impression it has made.—Moreover it is not a matter for dispute at all whether the body of him who knows Brahman continues to exist for some time or not. For how can one man contest the fact of another possessing the knowledge of Brahman—vouched for by his heart's conviction—and at the same time continuing to enjoy bodily existence? This same point is explained in scripture and smṛti, where they describe him who stands firm in the highest knowledge.—The final decision therefore is that knowledge effects the destruction of those works only—whether good or evil—whose effects have not yet begun to operate. (4.1.15)

Source: *The Vedānta Sūtras with the Commentary of Śankarācārya*, translated by George Thibaut. Sacred Books of the East. 34, 38, edited by F. Max Müller. (Oxford: Clarendon Press, 1890, 1896; reprinted Delhi: Motilal Banarsidass, 1968).

PART II

Devotional and Sectarian Traditions

5

Vaiṣṇava Tradition

This chapter marks a turn from classical Sanskrit literature and the socially elite religiosity that it embodied to more consistently devotional and sectarian varieties of Hinduism that are captured in both Sanskrit and many regional languages. The use of regional languages enhances religious communication among the different social classes, serves as a social bond, and increases the audience for its devotional message, especially by oral communication. Nonetheless, Sanskrit continued to be used by compilers of myth and creators of theological works.

Excellent examples of the use of Sanskrit are the various Purāṇas that capture the exploits of the sectarian deities. Selections for this chapter on Viṣṇu and subsequent chapters focusing on Krishna, Rāma, Śiva, and the goddess Kālī begin with narratives from the purāṇic literature. The term *purāṇa* refers to something ancient or old, and it falls with the rubric of remembered (*smṛti*) literature in sharp distinction to revealed (*śruti*) literature. The selections from purāṇic literature in this and following chapters are adopted from the major eighteen Mahāpurāṇas. Like many forms of Indian literature, the Purāṇas were orally transmitted before being written, although some scholars think that some texts appeared initially in written form. During the period between the fourth and sixth centuries C.E., the Purāṇas began to be collected by scribes and compilers. Many of the narratives became part of temple decoration that conveyed some purāṇic stories in stone to both the literate and illiterate members of society. The purāṇic literature embodies the rise of such deities as Viṣṇu, Krishna, Rāma, Śiva, and various goddesses and the eclipse of former vedic deities such as Indra and Agni along with the passing of the ancient sacrificial cult. This literature also manifests a new understanding of time in four ages and a new worldview that is dominated by devotional religion.

In addition to selections about the deity Viṣṇu and his incarnational exploits in the purānṇic literature, this chapter also includes devotional poems by two of the Ā<u>l</u>vārs: Nammā<u>l</u>vār and Āṇṭāḷ–the lone woman of the twelve Ā<u>l</u>vārs of the Vaiṣṇava tradition. In comparison to the passive character of the "heard or revealed" nature of vedic literature and the "remembered" aspect of dharmic and purāṇic literature, devotional literature adopts a more active mode, with an emphasis on utterance or saying, which reflects a shift from hearing to speaking. This shift to a more active mode takes place within the context of other changes that accompanied the advent of devotionalism: iconic representations of deities, use of local customs and language, and moves from sacrifice to worship (*pūjā*), from holding rites outdoors to holding them in temples, from abstract divine entities to more personal deities, and to greater emphasis on the nearness of God or Goddess.

Devotionalism (*bhakti*) is more than the worship of God or Goddess as expressed in poems, songs, or rites. The ardent *bhakta* (devotee) wants to possess God or Goddess and/or to be possessed by God or Goddess. It is thus not unusual to discover a devotee being labeled mad, an idiot, or a demon (someone possessed). In devotional Hinduism, God's or Goddess's oneness is stressed at the same time that his or her multiple natures are also emphasized. This suggests that the duty incarnates himself or herself often and in many different forms, in a continual process of revelation.

Many of these features of devotionalism can be discovered in the poems of Nammā<u>l</u>vār (literally, "Our saintly master," whose real name was Caṭakopan) who is considered the greatest of the twelve Ā<u>l</u>vārs; he composed four works, of which the *Tiruvāymo<u>l</u>i* (Holy Word of Mouth) is the most significant. He was born between 880–930 C.E. into a peasant caste in Tirukurukūr in the Tamil region, and he lived only thirty-five years. According to legend, he was born into a princely family, but his family abandoned him at a local Viṣṇu idol because he was assumed to be both deaf and mute. He proceeded to a tree where he assumed a yogic posture of meditation. Following a light emanating from this location, a pilgrim named Maturakavi discovered the source of the light to be the seated child. With this discovery, the light disappeared, but the pilgrim recognized that the child lived on as god. After breaking a long silence, Nammāḻvār created his initial hymns about Viṣṇu. Nammāḻvār's greatest composition–*Tiruvāymoḻi*–represents a poetic circle, which is called *antāti*, in which the last word of each verse is the first word of the next verse. In addition, the final word of the last verse is the first word of the initial verse.

Along with composing independent works of philosophical theology, Vaiṣṇava religious thinkers also wrote commentaries on such devotional poety as the *Tiruvāymoḻi*. An excellent example of such a commentary is *The Six thousand Patis* (*Āṟāyirappaṭi*) by Tirukkurukai Pirān Piḷḷān, a relative and disciple of Rāmānuja, around 1100 and 1150 C.E. According to tradition, Rāmānuja instructed Piḷḷān to write a commentary on the poem. Piḷḷān interprets Nammāḻvār's poem through the theology of Rāmānuja, and he mixes together Tamil and Sanskrit languages, demonstrating the so-called Ubhaya Vedānta (dual Vedic theology). Piḷḷān's commentary is written in the *maṇipravāḷa* style, which means that it consists of Sanskrit "gems" intermixed with Tamil "coral." A typical passage would have, for instance, a Tamil language structure and use mostly Tamil verbs, whereas a large number of nouns would be taken from Sanskrit.

From Piḷḷān's interpretive perspective, Nammāḻvār's poem suggests that God is speaking through the poet's words. This means that God enters into him and uses the poet to sing the poem, which enables God to convey his message to his devotees. Piḷḷān also interprets Nammāḻvār's poem as representing a dialogical question-and-answer format. Piḷḷān envisions the poet anticipating certain questions and providing answers within the verses. The commentary refers to various devotional themes such as longing, separation, refuge, and the gift of grace. The path to salvation is interpreted as a way of bhaktiyoga. And the notion of union is expressed as "entering" (*pukutal*) and "mingling" (*kalaivi*). Both terms also mean sexual union, which suggests the sense of intimacy embodied within the terms for the interpreter.

The only female of the twelve Āḻvārs was Āṇṭāḷ (literally, "the lady"), whose real name was Kōtai. Āṇṭāḷ's life and personality are embedded within legend. There is a narrative that she was discovered as a child under some tulsī leaves, which are especially sacred to Viṣṇu, by Periyāḻvār, a Vaiṣṇava Brahmin, living to the south of

Maturai. Viṣṇu appeared to the Brahmin in a dream to inform him that he preferred flower garlands carried by Āṇṭāḷ, which is connected to her choosing the god as her spouse. By his appearance in a dream, Viṣṇu accepts her in marriage, and Āṇṭāḷ disappears in the sanctuary of the deity.

Āṇṭāḷ expressed her love of God in personal terms and selflessly as she sought God's grace in such works as the Tiruppāvai, which appears in this chapter. In this poem the author depicts God as the master of illusion, and she proclaims God's unity beneath his various manifestations. The popularity of this Vaiṣṇava devotional text is evident by its many editions, commentaries written about it, and its numerous translations into Sanskrit. Moreover, the text anticipates later devotional Vaiṣṇava developments. The text falls within the compilation of the songs of the Āḻvārs called the *Nālāyira Divyaprabandham* (The Four Thousand Divine Compositions), which was shortened to Nālāyiran (Four Thousand) or the *Divyaprabandham* (Divine Compositions) by the tenth-century figure Nāthamuṇi, who collected the poems of the Āḻvārs and arranged them for recitation around 900 C.E. Nāthamuṇi was a priest working in the Śrīrangam temple, who was followed by his grandson Yāmuna (c. tenth to eleventh centuries). From an historical perspective, Nāthamuṇi formed a link between the poet-saints and the temples. Traditionally, Śrī Vaiṣṇavas have regarded this collection of poems as being equivalent to the four Vedas. These poems stress such themes as community, human senses (especially touch, taste, and smell), intimate contact, love with erotic connotations, and personal experience.

In contrast to this type of devotional poetry, an example of sectarian Vaiṣṇava literature is provided by the Pāñcarātras, an early Vaiṣṇava sect, in their text entitled *Lakṣmī Tantra*. This text is still relevant today because the ritual worship described is still performed in many temples in southern India and even in some northern institutions. It requires ritual worship of the deity in four places: image, water pitcher, mystic diagram, and the sacrificial fire-pit. The text is an example of issues related to Pāñcarātra philosophy, cosmogony, and the *vyūha* (emanation) theory along with *mantra-śāstra* (linguistic occultism). Its glorification of the goddess Lakṣmī, who is the feminine energy (*śakti*) of Viṣṇu, its advocacy of worshiping the feminine element, and its praise of ordinary women—these features make the text unique. And it helps to explain how it became a standard Śākta Āgama by the sixteenth century. There is a tendency within the text to overcome sectarian differences by asserting that other goddesses are merely other names for Lakṣmī. By accepting the Buddha as an incarnation and referring to devotion to the goddess Tārā, internal evidence of the text suggests a date of composition between the ninth and twelfth centuries C.E.

In addition to this text, this chapter contains theological, devotional expressions of the tradition by the thinkers including Rāmānuja, Madhva, and Vedānta Deśika. Rāmānuja's system of thought is characterized, as a qualified nondualism because Brahman, which he equates with Viṣṇu, is not devoid of qualities, and the self and world that form its divine body qualify it. Therefore, a reader should be aware that the self, world, and God form a unity for Rāmānuja. Nonetheless, human beings are slaves of a personal deity with whom they should seek refuge, which is an action that provokes the divine grace necessary for salvation.

After the death of Rāmānuja, theologians argued about the roles of human effort and divine grace in the quest for salvation. In this anthology, Piḷḷai Lokācārya (1250–1311) envisions Viṣṇu's consort playing a salvific role as an interceder with Viṣṇu. Because God originates all human acts, humans are helpless to save themselves. They must rather completely surrender to God, whose saving grace is a gift that cannot be earned by humans. This Teṉgali (cat-hold school) type of theology emphasizes human helplessness, surrender, and the importance of God's grace, which is typical of southern Vaiṣṇavism.

This type of theology is countered by thinkers such as Vedānta Deśika (1268–1369) of the northern tradition, who develops surrender into a sixfold ritual act and emphasizes the importance of righteous actions as a precursor for the saving action of God, a deity that never acts arbitrarily to save a person. Along with intellect and feelings, a person can experience an ecstatic kind of insight into the beauty of Viṣṇu that promises to transform him. The selections from the works of Vedānta Deśika are taken from an example of his lyrical theology entitled *Acyutaśatakam* (A Hundred Verses in Praise of Acyuta). The poet asks god to accept him as he would accept an aspiring bride.

Finally, the rich variety of Vaiṣṇava theological thinking is evident in the work of Madhva (c. 1238–1317) and his unqualified dualism, which means that God, self, and world are different from each another, although the self and world are dependent upon the personal and independent deity identified with Viṣṇu. As the ultimate reality or Brahman, Viṣṇu saves human beings by means of his grace. These types of notions were expressed in any number of works attributed to the prolific authorship of Madhva. The selection from his works for this chapter is the *Viṣṇu Tattva Vinirṇaya* (Complete Ascertainment of the Nature of Viṣṇu), a treatise on one specific topic. This text should be placed within the context of a response to the Advaita Vedānta school of Indian thought. Unlike the nondualism of the Advaita Vedānta, Madhva's text argues forcefully for differences, which he grounds in revealed scripture and logical reasoning. For reasons of economy, I have not included passages from this text that quote other texts to support its position.

Selections from the Purāṇas about the Exploits of Viṣṇu

Incarnation as Matsya, the Fish

Now hear, O brahmins, the ancient tale of Matsya, the Fish, which is holy, purifying and life-bestowing, as it was sung by the mace-bearer, Viṣṇu.

Long ago there was a patient king named Manu, son of the sun, practicing abundant *tapas*, who gave his kingdom to his son. In a particular place in Malaya that hero, possessed of all the fine qualities of the self, to whom grief and joy were the same, attained supreme Yoga. After a million years had passed, the boon-giving Brahmā, whose seat is a lotus, was pleased with him and said, "Choose a boon!"

Thus addressed, the king bowed to the Grandfather and replied, "I want only one thing from you, the ultimate boon: make me the protector of all standing and moving creatures when the dissolution comes."

"So be it!" said the universal soul. And then and there he disappeared, while abundant showers of flowers thrown by the gods fell from the sky.

Once while that king was making water offerings to the Fathers in his hermitage, there fell into his hands along with the water a tiny fish. When he saw the little fish, that compassionate lord of earth carefully looked after it, trying to protect it in his bowl of water. In only one day and night that fish's body grew to the length of sixteen finger-breadths, and it cried out, "Save me! Rescue me!"

So the king took the fish and put it into a large pitcher, but even there it grew to the length of three hands overnight. Once again the fish cried out in anguish to the son of the thousand-rayed sun, "Save me! Save me! I have come to you for refuge!" So that son of the sun put the fish into a well, and when that also grew too small, he put it into a pond where it grew still larger until it was a league in length. The miserable fish cried out again, "Save me, save me, excellent king!"

But even after it was tossed into the Ganges river it continued to grow, so the king threw it into the sea where it filled the entire ocean. Then Manu became alarmed, and asked, "Are you some sort of demon, or are you Vāsudeva? How could you be anyone else, such as you are? Now I recognize you, the lord, in the form of a fish! O Keśava, you have fooled me indeed; O Hṛṣīkeśa, Jagannātha, Jagaddhāma, praise be to you!"

Thus praised, the lord Janārdana in the form of a fish said, "Sādhu, sādhu! O faultless one, you have recognized me. Soon, O king, the earth shall be flooded with water, with its mountains, trees and forests. A boat has been constructed by a group of all the gods in order to rescue the great aggregate of creatures, O lord of earth, those who are sweat-born, egg-born, plant-born and live-born. Put all these helpless creatures into the boat, O faithful one, and save them! When the boat is battered by the wind at the end of the Age, O king, fasten it to my horn, O chief of kings. Thus at the end of the dissolution of the world with its standing and moving beings you shall be Prajāpati, master of creatures on earth, O king. You shall be the all-knowing wise king at the start of the Kṛta Age, and you shall rule the Manvantara, worshiped by all the gods."

Thus addressed by Madhusudana, Manu asked him, "O blessed one, how soon will this intermediary dissolution occur? And how, O guardian, shall I protect the creatures? And when shall we meet again, you and I, O Madhusudana?"

"Beginning then," said the Fish, "there will be a drought on the surface of the earth lasting a full hundred years, and a brutal famine. Seven cruel rays of the sun will deal death to the weak, and there will be seven times seventy solar rays the color of fiery coals. At the close of the Age the submarine fire will blaze forth, and burning poison will flow from the mouth of Saṃkarṣaṇa in the netherworld, and also from the third eye of Bhava. The three worlds, aflame, will crumble, great seer, and the entire earth will be burned to ashes. Space will be scorched by the heat, O enemy-burner, and the world with its gods and constellations will be utterly annihilated."

"Seven rain clouds will bring destruction: Bhīmanāda (Awful Roar), Droṇa (Bucket), Caṇḍa (Cruel), Balāhaka (Thundercloud), Vidyutpatāka (Lightning Banner) and Śoṇa (Crimson). And as they flood the earth, clouds will form because of the fire, like sweat, and the turbulent oceans will merge together into a single sea. They will turn the entire triple world into one vast sheet of water."

"Then you must take the seeds of life from everywhere and load them into the boat of the Vedas. Fasten to it the rope I shall give you, O well-vowed one, and tie the boat to my horn. When even all the gods have been burned up, O enemy-burner, you alone shall survive, by my power, along with Soma, Sūrya, Brahmā and myself, and the four directions, the holy river Narmadā, the great seer Mārkaṇḍeya, Bhava, the Vedas, the Purāṇas and all the sciences. All of these, along with yourself, shall be saved when that vast ocean is all that is left in the dissolution at the end of the Cākṣusa Manvantara. At the start of the next creation, which you shall rule, I shall again promulgate the Vedas, O lord of earth." So speaking, the lord vanished on the spot.

Manu resorted to Yoga, by the grace of Vāsudeva, until the flood began, as prophesied. When the aforementioned time came, as Vāsudeva had said, Janārdana appeared in the form of a horned fish, and a serpent in the form of a rope appproached Manu's side. The virtuous king collected all the creatures and loaded them into the boat, by Yoga. Then he fastened the boat to the fish's horn with the rope made of the snake. And prostrating himself before Janārdana, he stepped into the ship. . . .

Then in the midst of that vast flood, Manu asked Keśava, "Tell me at length the whole of Dharma, about the origin and dissolution of the world, about the lineages, genealogies and the Manvantaras, and the extent of the earth, about gifts, Dharma, rules, the eternal rituals of *śrāddha*, the divisions of caste and stage of life, the rites called *iṣṭa*, and *pūrta*, the fashioning of statues, about the gods and so on, and anything else found on earth. Tell me all this!"

So Vāsudeva replied, "At the end of the time of the great dissolution, the universe consisted of darkness, as if it were asleep, inconceivable, unknowable, without characteristics of any kind. The world with its standing and moving creatures was unknown and unknowable. Then the unmanifest, self-existent Svayambhū, the origin of good deeds, appeared in order to make manifest all this, by dispelling the darkness. He who is beyond what is manifest, both infinite and infinitesimal, eternal, known by the name of Nārāyaṇa, appeared alone, all by himself. Desiring to pour forth the manifold world from his body, he set his mind on the task. He emitted the waters and put his seed into them. Then a huge golden egg appeared that shone like ten thousand suns for a thousand years. That splendid being who was himself his own origin entered inside the egg and became Viṣṇu, pervading it by virtue of his own power. Inside the egg the lord became the sun, which is called Āditya, because it was first, long ago. And then he became Brahmā because he recited the Brahman, the Veda. He made heaven and earth from the two halves of the egg, made all the directions, and put the sky in the middle for all time. The after-birth became the mountains, with Mt. Meru as the chief mountain. The membrane became the clouds, and the umbilical cord, the lightning. Rivers, called eggs, appeared, as well as the Fathers and the Manus. The seven seas flowed from the water inside the egg: Lavaṇa (Salt), Ikṣu (Sugar cane), Surā (Wine) and the rest, filled with various jewels.

Kurma, the Tortoise

I shall relate the tortoise *avatāra* that destroys the sins of those who hear it. Long ago, in the battle between the gods and the Asuras, the gods were defeated by the Daityas. Because of Durvaśas' curse they became bereft of good fortune. Praising Viṣṇu who had gone to the ocean of milk, they said, "Protect us from the demons!"

Hari replied to Brahmā and the other gods, "Make a compact with the Asuras to churn the milky ocean for the nectar that will restore your good fortune, O gods. One should treat with one's enemies when something important is to be done. I shall see to it that you drink the nectar, not the Dānavas. Using Mt. Mandara as a churning stick and the snake Vāsuki as a rope, unflaggingly churn the milk ocean, with my help."

After making the agreement with the Daityas that Viṣṇu had advised, the gods went to the ocean of milk and taking Vāsuki's tail, began to churn. When heated by the serpent's breath, the gods were invigorated by Hari. Because the unsupported mountain sank down into the water as they stirred up the sea, Viṣṇu took the form of a tortoise and held Mt. Mandara on his back. From the milky ocean that was being churned in this way arose the poison Halāhala. Hara took it into his throat, and because of this his throat turned blue. Then the goddess Vāruṇī came forth, followed by the coral tree Pārijāta, the jewel Kaustubha, cows, celestial Apsarases and the goddess Lakṣmī, who went to Hari. Seeing and praising her, all the gods regained their good fortune.

Then Viṣṇu arose as Dhanvantari, the promulgator of the Āyurveda, holding a jar filled with nectar. The Daityas took the nectar from his grasp and gave half of it to the gods. When Jambha and the other demons had taken it, Viṣṇu assumed a female form. When they saw a beautiful woman appear, the deluded Daityas said, "Please be our wife, fair-faced one! Bring the nectar and give it to us to drink!" Agreeing to this, Hari took the nectar from the demons and gave it to the gods to drink instead.

Pretending to be the moon, one demon, Rāhu, was exposed by the sun and the moon while he drank the nectar; whereupon Hari cut off his head. This head, now separate, became immortal through the nectar's grace. So Rāhu spoke to boon-granting

Hari, "Let the sun and the moon undergo eclipses because of me!" Thus Rāhu became the cause of eclipses; gifts given at such times are inexhaustible.

"So be it," said Viṣṇu with all the immortals as he left the woman's body. Then when Hara said "Show it to me!" lord Hari exhibited his female form to Rudra. Fooled by this trick and abandoning Gaurī, Śaṃbhu went after the woman. Naked and crazy-looking, he grabbed the woman's hair. She shook herself loose and fled, with Hara in pursuit. Wherever Hara's semen spilled on the earth there appeared a sacred place of *liṅgas* which are as good as gold. After Hara had recognized her to be an illusion and had resumed his own form, Hari said to Śiva, "Rudra, you have seen through my deception. There is no other person on earth but you who can conquer it!"

Then the Daityas who had been deprived of the nectar were felled by the gods in battle and the deities went to live in heaven. Whoever recites this story will also go to heaven.

Varāha, the Boar

At the end of the last Eon when the tempest of time began, the forest trees were uprooted, the fire god burned the three worlds as if they were straw, the earth was flooded with rain and the oceans overflowed. While all the regions were sunk in vast sheets of water and the waters of destruction had begun their ferocious dances, leaping with fish and undulating with circular, arm-like waves, Brahmā as Nārāyaṇa slept peacefully in the sea. . . .

The Siddhas who lived in Janaloka, folding their hands in prayer and singing hymns, awoke the lord of the thirty gods who lay in Yogic sleep as he concentrated on Śiva, just as the Śrutis awoke the lord at the beginning of creation, long ago. Waking up and rising from his bed in the middle of the water, his eyes cloudy with Yogic sleep, the lord looked in all directions. He saw nothing whatsoever but himself! Sitting up like one bewildered, he grew deeply concerned, thinking, "Where is that lovely lady, the broad earth, with her many lofty mountains, her streams, towns and forests?" Worrying this way, Brahmā could nowhere spy the earth.

Then he called to mind his father, the lord with three eyes. Because he remembered Bhava, the god of gods with infinite splendor, the lord of the world realized that the earth was immersed in the sea. Wanting to rescue earth, Prajāpati thought of the heavenly form of the boar with a body like a mighty mountain, who delighted in water-play. This boar was terrifying, making a hissing noise like a big black cloud, booming forth with a dreadful sound. His trunk was round fat and firm, his hips high and full, his shank-ends short and rounded, his snout sharply pointed. Red as a ruby were his horrible round eyes; his body was long and tubular with shining stiff little ears, curvaceous in trunk and cheek; he was covered with a fine, waving mane of hair.

The ocean of Doomsday was roiled up by the heavy panting of this boar, who was adorned with gems, ornaments and glittering jewelry shining like lofty piles of clouds filled with lightning. Having assumed this vast, infinite, boar-like shape, the lord entered the netherworld in order to raise up the earth. There this mountainous boar blazed forth as radiantly as if he had gone to the foot of Maheśa's mountain, which is shaped like the *liṅga*.

Then the earth-upholder dug up the earth which was sunk in the sea and emerged from the netherworld holding it on his tusks. When they saw him, the inhabitants of Janaloka, the seers and Siddhas, rejoiced and danced, showering his head with flowers. The mighty boar's body covered with flowers was as beautiful as a mountain of antimony alive with fireflies on the wing.

When the boar had brought the great earth to its proper place he returned to his own form and stabilized it. Aligning the earth, the lord piled up the mountains and fashioned the four worlds and all the rest, just as it had been before. Thus having rescued the great earth from the middle of the vast ocean of dissolution, Viśvakarman once more poured forth creation with its moving and unmoving beings.

Narasiṃha, the Man-Lion

Hiraṇyakaśipu was overcome with rage and grief when his brother was failed by Hari in the form of a boar, O Vyāsa. Happily feuding with Hari, he directed the heroic Asuras, who themselves loved bloodshed, to sow destruction among creatures. When they received on their heads the command of their master, these murderous demons began to slaughter creatures and gods. When earth herself was wounded by these evil-minded Asuras, the gods left heaven and roamed the earth unseen. Mourning his dead brother, Hiraṇyakaśipu performed the water offerings for him and comforted his wife and family.

This leader of the kings of the Daityas wanted to make himself the only sovereign, unconquerable, immortal, undecaying, without an equal. In order to do so he performed the highest degree of tapas with only his big toe touching the ground, his arms raised aloft, his eyes on the sky. While he was doing this tapas, the powerful gods defeated all the other Daityas and resumed their proper places in heaven. Then a smoking fire born of Hiraṇyakaśipu's tapas arose from his head and spread in all directions, burning the worlds across, above and below. Scorched by this fire, their faces grimacing from the heat, the gods abandoned heaven and went to Brahmaloka, where they reported to the creator. Then, O

Vyāsa, instructed by these gods, the self-existent creator went to the hermitage of the Daitya lord, accompanied by Bhṛgu, Dakṣa and the other seers. Having set fire to all the worlds, the demon saw the lotus-born god approaching. To reward him for his tapas, the Grandfather said, "Choose a boon." Hearing the gracious words of the creator, the Daitya replied, his mind clear, "O god, lord, lord of creatures. Grandfather, let me never be killed by these means: the striking and throwing weapons of my enemies, thunderbolts, dried tree-trunks, high mountains, by water or fire. Let me be free from the threat of death from gods, Daityas, seers, Siddhas and whatever other beings you have created. But why go on? Let me not be slain in heaven, on earth, in the daytime, at night, from neither above nor below, O lord of creatures!"

When he heard this speech, the god whose womb is the lotus mentally praised Viṣṇu and replied with compassion, "I am indeed pleased with you, lord of the Daityas. You shall have all this. Enough of tapas! For 96,000 years your desires will be fully satisfied. Arise and resume your sovereignty of the Dānavas!" When he heard these words, Hiraṇyakaśipu's face grew content. Consecrated as king by the Grandfather, he put his mind to the destruction of the three worlds. Having destroyed all Dharmas, the wanton demon likewise conquered all the gods in battle. Then, out of fear, all the gods led by Indra who were oppressed by the Daitya chief conferred with the wise Grandfather and went to the ocean of milk where Hari lay. After propitiating Viṣṇu effusively with laudatory speech, thinking of him as a savior, they all told the gracious god of their great unhappiness. Satisfied that he had heard the full extent of their suffering, Lakṣmī's husband granted their wish. Arising from his bed, Upendra whose splendor equals Vaiśvānara's, comforted all the gods and seers and spoke at length to them with words befitting his nature, "I will kill the Daitya by force, O lords of gods. You may return home satisfied!"

When they heard what Lakṣmī's consort had said, the lords of gods, Indra and the others, were all very pleased. They went to their homes, lord of seers, thinking that Hiraṇyanetra's younger brother was already dead.

Viṣṇu then assumed a hairy form like both man and lion. It had widely gaping jaws, ferocious fangs, sharp claws, a fine snout, shining most horribly like a *koṭi* of suns, blazing forth like the fire of time at the end of the Age—but why go on? At sunset the great-souled lord went to the city of the Asuras. Doing battle with the mighty Daityas, he seized the demon hosts and killed them. This Man-Lion roamed about the city showing supernatural valor and shattering demons. When the Daityas saw his matchless might, they all panicked. Observing that lion of universal form, Prahlāda, the son of the Daitya lord, said to the king, "Why has this cosmic king of beasts come here? The everlasting lord god in the shape of a man-lion has entered your city. Turn back from battle and seek refuge in him! I see the gaping mouth of this lion whom no one can oppose in the three worlds! Act like a king and bow down to this lord of beasts!"

Hearing his son's speech, the evil-souled king replied, "Why are you so afraid, my son?" So speaking, the eminent hero among the bulls of the Daityas cried out, "Heroes, seize that lion with the contorted grimacing face!" So at his command, the best of the Daityas approached the beast in order to capture it. But they were instantly scorched, like moths nearing fire, attracted by its beauty. After the Daityas has been burned, their king himself entered the battle against the lord of beasts using all manner of striking and throwing weapons: spears, javelins, nooses, elephant hooks, fire and other means. While the two of them fought, sword in hand, with heroic outcries, most virile, their minds fixed in fury at each other, a day of Brahmā passed.

Suddenly the Daitya sprouted multiple arms, each with a sword, and attacked the Man-Lion who was fighting ferociously with him. Engaging in an unendurable battle with various striking and throwing weapons, the chief of the Daityas, carrying a spear, swiftly rushed at the Man-Lion after the weapons he threw had come to naught. Seizing the demon Hiraṇyakaśipu with his many arms hard as mountains, he threw him across his knees, and with his shoot-like claws ripped apart the tender belly of the Dānava between his arms. When the lion's claws had rent the lotus of his heart, the demon instantly dropped dead, like a log, his limbs thoroughly mangled.

After the enemy of the gods had been destroyed, the gracious Viṣṇu welcomed Prahlāda, who bowed before him. The wonderful heroic Viṣṇu consecrated him king of the Daityas and went on his incomprehensible way. All the lords of gods, the Grandfather and the others, were very happy, O brahmin. Bowing there to Viṣṇu, the blessed lord most worthy of praise who had accomplished his task, they went home.

Vāmana, the Dwarf, and Bali

When Bali saw the earth with its mountains and forests shaking, he prostrated himself before Śukra-Uśanas with folded hands and said, "O teacher, the earth covered with oceans and mountains is trembling! Why do the Fires refuse the Asuras' offerings?" The great-minded Kāvya, best among these who know the Veda, pondered Bali's question for a long time before he answered the foremost Daitya lord. "The eternal Hari, the supreme soul, womb of the world, has descended in the form of a dwarf into the house of Kaśyapa. Surely he is coming to your sacrifice, bull of the Dānavas! The earth quakes with the tread of his feet, the mountains shake and the dwelling places of the great fish are disturbed. The earth cannot support the lord, the master of creatures! Gods, demons, Gandharvas, Yakṣas, Rākṣasas and Snakes, the earth, waters, fire, wind and sky are all held up by him alone. He supports all the gods, demons and human beings. Because he is nearby, the god's enemies, the demons, are not entitled to their shares of the sacrifice. Because of him the three fires refuse the Asuras'offerings." . . .

After a while Janārdana, who consists of all the gods, assumed the body of a dwarf by illusion and arrived at Bali's sacrifice. When they saw the lord enter the sacrificial enclosure, the Asuras were shaken by his appearance, their splendor overshadowed by his. Those who had gathered at the great sacrificial site, Vasiṣṭha, Gadhi's son Viśvāmitra, Garga and the other excellent seers, began to say prayers under their breath. Bali thought that his whole life had suddenly borne fruit and none of the trembling seers dared to say a thing. One by one they worshiped the overlord of the gods with all their might. When he saw the master of the demons and the finest seers bowing before him, Viṣṇu, lord god of the gods, in the form of a dwarf, himself praised the sacrifice, the Fire, the sacrificer, the ritual acts, the officiants, the celebrants and all the offerings. The brahmin sacrificial attendants cried out, "Sādhu! Sādhu!" to Vāmana, who had appeared before them in the sacrificial enclosure, a vessel wholly worthy of their honor. Holding out the hospitality gift of water, the great Asura Bali thrilled to the worship of Govinda and said, "I shall give you this pile of gold and jewels, these herds of elephants and horses, women, clothes, ornaments, cows and many villages. All these and the entire earth as well I shall give to you. Take whatever you desire; my dearest possessions are yours!"

Thus addressed by the Daitya chief, lord Viṣṇu in the form of a dwarf spoke words filled with affection in a deep, smiling voice, "Give me three paces of land for a fire-altar, O king. Give the gold, villages, jewels and the rest to others who want them."

"What good are only three steps, best of striders? You should ask for a hundred or a hundred thousand steps!"

"I am content with only this much, lord of the Daityas. Give your wealth to other supplicants as you see fit."

When he heard this reply, Bali ordered recitations for the great-souled dwarf. As the hospitality water fell into his hand, Vāmana shed his dwarf-life shape. In the twinkling of an eye he manifested the form which consists of all the gods. His eyes were the moon and the sun; the sky was his head and the earth his feet. His toes were the Piśācas and his fingers the Guhyakas. The Viśvedevas were in his knees and the excellent deities, the Sādhyas, were in his shins. In his nails appeared the Yakṣas and in the contours of his body, the Apsarases. All the Pleiades were the lord's eyes, the rays of the sun the hairs of his head, the stars the pores of his skin and the great seers the hairs of his body. His arms were the intermediate directions, and the principal directions were in the great-souled one's two ears. In his hearing lay the Aśvins, and the wind was in the nose of that great-souled god. . . . All the luminaries and supreme tapas appeared as the splendor of this foremost god of gods. In the cavities of his body lay the Vedas, and his knees were the great sacrifices, the offerings, the cattle and the ritual acts of the brahmins. When they saw the divine form of the great-souled Viṣṇu, the Daityas crept closer like moths approaching a flame. The great demon Cikṣusa bit him on the big toe, and Hari kicked him in the neck with it. When the lord had driven off all the demons with the palms of his hands and soles of his feet, assuming a gigantic body, he quickly made off with the earth. As he stepped across the earth, the sun and moon were in the center of his chest. As he bestrode the sky, they sank to the region of his thighs. When he took his ultimate step, the sun and moon lay at the base of his knees. Thus Viṣṇu performed the task of protecting the gods.

After he had won the three worlds and had slain the bulls of demons, the masterful, blessed lord, wide-striding Viṣṇu, gave the triple world to Indra, sacker of cities, and to Bali, the netherworld named Sutala, below the surface of the earth. . . . When he had given this boon to Bali and given Śakra his heaven, Hari vanished from sight in his form as all-pervader. And so Indra ruled the three worlds as of old and Bali remained in the netherworld for all time.

Source: *Classical Hindu Mythology: A Reader in the Sanskrit Purānas*, edited and translated by Cornelia Dimmitt and J.A.B. van Buitenen (Philadephia: Temple University Press, 1978).

Selections from the Poems of Nammālvār

HE PACES THE WORLDS

First, the discus
  rose to view,

then the conch,
    the long bow,
    the mace,
    and the sword;

with blessings
  from the eight quarters,

---

he broke through
the egg-shell of heaven,
making the waters bubble;

giant head and giant feet
growing away from each other,

time itself rose to view:

how the lord
paced and measured

all three worlds! 7.4.1

CHURNING THE SEA

That moment:

with the sound
of rivers streaming backward
into their mountains

and the sound
of the serpent
wrapped around the mountain

and the sound
of the sea churning
now left now right

the lord
drew out of the gods' elixir
that rose slowly in the churning 7.4.2.

THE BOAR RESCUES THE EARTH

No, they did not come apart:

the seven islands of the earth,
they stayed in place;

and the seven mountains,
they stayed in place;

---

and the seven seas
did not go wild
but stayed in place

miraculously,
        that day

our lord pitchforked them out
with his tusks
from the deep. 7.4.3

THE MAN-LION

At the red hour of sunset,
there was blood
on the heavens and the eight directions.

Our lord
plunged the demon into despair
and slaughtered him:

a lion
tearing open
a mountain under his claws. 7.4.6

THE LORD AT PLAY

Worker of miracles,
  magical dwarf,
    and killer of the demon
      named Honey,

only you can tell us:

becoming fire, water, earth,
sky, and wind,

becoming father, mother,
  and the children too
  and all others
  and all things unnamed,

---

the way you stand there,
being yourself—

what's it all about? 7.8.1

You do stunts
with your chariots

the discus your weapon:

tell us how

managing every one of the four ages
becoming every little thing in them
harmonious now
now quite contrary

you stand there

a marvel
of contradictions! 7.8.3

THE DWARF

Dwarf,
You confuse everyone.

But make me understand:

becoming oblivion, memory,
heat, cold,
all things wonderful,
and wonder itself,

becoming every act of success,
every act of good and evil,
and every consequence,

becoming even the weariness
of lives,

you stand there—

---

and what misery you bring! 7.8.6

When I didn't know a thing
you made me love
your service

mixing inseparably
with my soul

when I
your servant
was in the illusion of unknowing:

you dwarf incognito
who once said to great Bali
"Give me space
just three steps"

and cheated him of everything
before anyone knew. 2.3.3

HE AND I

He who took the seven bulls
by the horns
he who devoured the seven worlds

made me his own cool place
in heaven

and thought of me
what I thought of him

and became my own thoughts 1.8.7

Three loves never part from him—
Lakṣmī, goddess of all good things,
the Earth,
and the simple cowherd girl.

Ruling three worlds,
devouring them altogether,
my lord rests on a banyan leaf:

darker than the sea,
Kaṇṇan,
child perching on my hip. 1.9.4

You dwell in heaven
stand on the sacred mountain
sleep on the ocean
roll around in the earth

yet hidden everywhere
you grow
invisibly:

moving within
numberless outer worlds

playing within my heart
yet showing your body

will you always play hide and seek? 6.9.5

LOVE'S MESSENGERS

Is that you, little bird?

When I asked you to go
as my messenger to the great lord
and tell him of my pain,

you dawdled, didn't go.

I've lost my looks,
my dark limbs are pale.

Go look for someone else
to put sweet things
in your beak,
go now. 1.4.8

The cold wind threads through my bones.

Remembering only my faults,
my lord doesn't show me any grace.
Go ask him,
"What wrong did she do?"

Dear parrot gnawing at a bone,
please, go ask him.

I brought you up, didn't I? 1.4.7

GOD'S IDIOTS

Mumbling and prattling
the many names
of our lord of the hill
with cool waterfalls,
long strands of water,

while onlookers say,
"They're crazy,"

entering and not entering
cities,
standing still or swaying
before a laughing world,

they dance, they leap,
undone by feeling—

and the gods bow down
before them. 3.5.8

TALKING OF MONISM

If they should merge,
That's really good:

If the two that'll never meet
should meet,

then this human thing
will become our lord,
the Dark One
with the sacred bird
on his banner—
as if that's possible.

It will always be itself.

There are yogis
who mistake fantasy
for true release

and run around
in circles
in the world
of what is and what was said
and what will be.

It takes all kinds. 8.8.9

Source: *Hymns for the Drowning: Poems for Viṣṇu by Nammāḻvār*, translated by A. K. Ramanujan (Princeton: Princeton University Press, 1981).

Selections from the *Tiruppāvai* of Āṇṭāḷ

1

On this auspicious day,
full moon in the month of Mārkaḷi,
come beloved young maidens
of blessed Āyarpāṭi,
come adorned with jewels,
come all who wish
to bathe in the limpid waters.

Dark-bodied one,
face fiery as the sun,

soft as the moon,
with eyes like pink lotus;
that young lion,
child of Yaśodā of beauteous eyes,
son of Nandagōpa
ready with the sharp spear,
that Nārāyaṇa himself
will fulfill our desires.

Come join us in this Mārkaḷi vow,
all will applaud you.

Fulfill, O song of our vow.

2

People of the world,
O listen to the rules we observe
for our *pāvai* vow.

Bathing at dawn,
we sing the praises of the supreme one
who slumbers upon the milky ocean.
We eat no ghee, drink no milk,
wear no flowers in our hair,
no kohl in our eyes,
we do no wrong, speak no evil,
we bestow in abundance,
give alms humbly to those who seek,
in this manner
we gladly live.

Fulfill, O song of our vow.

3

We bathe in the clear waters
at the break of dawn.
We sing the glories of the supreme lord
who spanned the worlds

and measured them.
Eternal prosperity surely will be ours.

Our land will be free from evil;
three times a month
there will be abundant rain;
in flooded fields of tall red paddy
carp will jump and play;
spotted beetles will idly dream
in bright blossoms of water lily;
our pots will overflow with milk
from the heavy udders
of our cows,
large, placid, yielding.
Plentiful indeed our gain.

Fulfill, O song of our vow.

4

Beloved god of rain
you dive into the ocean,
scoop and drink its waters,
you rise into the skies—
do not hold back your wealth.

Your form is dark as the hue
of the primordial lord
of the deluge.
Your lightning flashes like
the brilliant discus in the hand
of Padmanābhā
of broad-shouldered beauty.
Your thunder resembles
the resonance of his
Valampurī conch.

Like the stream of arrows
from his *sāranga* bow,
rain upon us, do not delay.

Let plenty come to all
as we joyously dip
in the Mārkaḷi waters.

Fulfill, O song of our vow.

5

O lord of illusion
who dwells on the banks
of the sacred brimming Yamunā,
lord of Maturai of the north,
radiant light of the cowherd clan,
Dāmodara whose birth
brought fame to his mother,
In purity and innocence
we come to worship at your feet
strewing fragrant flowers,
your form held in our minds,
your name upon our tongues.

Chant the names of the lord—
like cotton by fire
all past sins will be consumed,
what future sins may come
will vanish too.

Fulfill, O song of our vow.

6

Young maiden, leave your sleep.
Do you not hear the warble
of the early morning birds?
Or the deep sound
of the silvery conch
calling from the temple of Garuḍa's lord?

The primal cause
slumbers on the serpent
upon the cosmic waters.

He once sucked the poison
from the breast of the demoness.
With a single kick
he shattered the cart
of treacherous Śakaṭa.

The sages and yogis
in whose heart the lord abides
are chanting his holy name.
O maiden, sleep no more.
Arise and join us
for the melodious name of Hari
reverberating
through the air
has entered our souls,
brought us surpassing peace.

Fulfill, O song of our vow.

7

You crazy child,
do you not hear
the noisy chatter of blackbirds
that fills the morning air?
Or the jingle of necklaces
worn by the fragrant-haired
women of Āyarpāṭi?
Do you not hear
the swish of the buttermilk
as the churning rod
moves to and fro?

O noble maiden,
what prompts you to sleep
when we stand here singing
the glories of Nārāyaṇa
who came to us as Keśava?

Bright maid,
arise from your sleep,
open the door.

Fulfill, O song of our vow.

8

Pale dawn lightens the skies.
For a brief while
buffaloes move out
to graze upon the dewy grass.
Barring the way
of maidens going out to bathe,
we brought them here.
We wait, calling out to wake you.
O eager maiden
leave your sleep, join us.

If we honor and serve
the lord who destroyed the Mallas,
split open the mouth of the horse-demon,
if we beseech the supreme being,
leader of the gods,
extol him—
surely his grace
will descend upon us.

Fulfill, O song of our vow.

9

O cousin mine
asleep upon a couch
in a splendid mansion
lit by the glimmer of lamps
where incense fills the air,
leave your slumber,
open your jeweled door.

Aunt, your daughter does not speak.
Is she perhaps dumb
or is she deaf?
Or is she perchance a lazy one?
Has a spell bound her,
kept her captive?
Is she held in a stupor?

We chant the holy names of the lord,
Mādhavan̲, lord of Vaikuṇṭa,
Himself the great illusion-
Aunt, will you not awaken her?

Fulfill, O song of our vow.

10

O fortunate maiden
whose penance
has heaven as its goal,
will you not answer us?
Will you not open the door?

If we worship Nārāyaṇa
whose hair is adorned
with the fragrant holy basil,
that holy one
will grant our desires.

In ancient days
did Kumbhakarṇa lose to you?
Falling into the jaws of death
did he perhaps bequeath to you
his profound slumber?
You slothful one, bright gem,
do not sleep, open the door.

Fulfill, O song of our vow.

11

O golden creeper
of the clan of cowherds,
those innocent ones
who milk young herds of cows,
face their enemies,
strip them of strength.

O peacock of the woods,
with stomach smooth and curved
like the snake's dancing hood,
arise and join
your friends and relatives.

We have entered your porch.
we sing the glories of the
lord dark as the rain cloud.
O fortunate maiden
what avails it to slumber thus
with no movement,
no speech?

Fulfill, O song of our vow.

12

O younger sister
of a plenteous cowherd home,
your lowing buffaloes
call fondly to their calves,
the milk flows freely
from their heavy udders,
making a slush on the floor.

Dew falls upon us
as we cling to the lintel
of your doorway.
We celebrate the fame of the beloved lord
whose righteous anger

destroyed the evil king
of Southern Laṅkā.

Why this senseless slumber
when all around
have arisen?
O speak to us,
now at least awake, join us.

Fulfill, O song of our vow.

13

O maiden whose eyes
put the lotus to shame,
Venus has arisen,
Jupiter has gone to slumber;
bird sounds are ringing
through the morning air.
We extol the glorious deeds
of the lord who split open
the beak of the bird,
cut off the many heads
of wicked Rāvaṇa.

All young maidens
have gathered at the *pāvai* grounds.
Will you alone
refrain from plunging
into the cool waters?
Will you alone lie abed
on this auspicious day?
Give up your pretence,
come maiden, join us.

Fulfill, O song of our vow.

14

In the large pond
of your back garden

pink water lilies unfold,
dark blooms close.
Holy men in ochre robes
with pure white teeth
have walked their unhurried way
to blow the conch,
open the temple doors.

Maiden who promised
to come and wake us,
you are without shame.
Your tongue wags much
but you act not upon your word.
Come let us chant the fame
of the lotus-eyed lord
whose invulnerable hand
holds the discus and conch.

Fulfill, O song of our vow.

15

Young parakeet
are you still asleep?

Stop calling in shrill tones, friends,
I'll be with you soon.

Your words are real clever!
Do we not know of old
your ready tongue?

You indeed are the clever ones!
But never mind—let it be me.

Come, be quick,
what is keeping you?

Has everyone arrived?

They are all here
come count for yourself.

Come sing with us
the prowess of the lord
who killed the vicious elephant,
lord of illusion
whose enemies perish
before his might and valor.

Fulfill, O song of our vow.

16

O watchman
of the portals to the mansion
of our chieftain Nandagōpa,
you who guard
the festooned entrance,
unlock the jeweled door!

The lord of illusion
that dark-hued gem
promised yesterday
to give us the sounding drum.

In purity and innocence
we have come
to awaken him with song.
O friendly sir,
do not refuse our plea,
please open
the tight shut door.

Fulfill, O song of our vow.

17

Awake, O master Nandagōpa,
known for your largesse,
food and drink and clothes
you give to all.

Awake, O mistress Yaśodā,
light of our cowherd clan—

we young stems depend on you,
the open blossom.

O lord of the celestials
whose limitless might
spanned the worlds
and measured them,
leave your sleep, arise.

O Baladeva
adorned with heavy golden anklets,
do not sleep, arise,
your brother and you.

Fulfill, O song of our vow.

18

Daughter-in-law of Nandagōpa
who never shrinks from enemies,
whose strength rivals
an elephant in rut;
O Nappiṉṉāi,
the fragrance of your tresses
fills the air,
please open the door.

The crowing of the cocks
heralds the dawn.
The cooing of flocks of koelbirds
resounds from the bower
of *mātavī* creepers.
O you who hold the ball
between your fingers,
bracelets jingling
upon your lotus hands—
As we chant the names
of your beloved lord,
come joyously, open the door.

Fulfill, O song of our vow.

19

Lord reclining
upon your ivory-legged couch
soft with cotton and silk and down,
lit by the glimmer of tall lamps,
your head upon
the breasts of Nappiṉṉāi
whose hair is braided
with clusters of flowers,
O lord of broad-chested splendor,
speak to us.

You of large kohl-lined eyes,
you do not wish your lord to awaken
however late it be.
You cannot bear to part with him
for even a second.
Is it right to act thus?
Truly, it is not befitting.

Fulfill, O song of our vow.

20

O Redeemer
who appeared before
the thirty-three celestials
and rescued them from fear,
awake, arise.

O lord of great strength
who drives terror
into the hearts of enemies,
spotless lord,
impartial one,
arise from your slumber.

O Nappiṉṉāi of soft rounded breasts,
O lady Śrī,

slender-waisted, coral-lipped,
awaken from your sleep.

Give to us the fan and mirror,
ask your lord
to bathe us right now
in the cooling waters.

Fulfill, O song of our vow.

21

Awake
O son of Nandagōpa,
whose many herds of cows
yield streams of milk
which fill the pots
to overflowing.

O great protector,
supreme lord,
light of lights who came to earth,
awaken from your slumber.

Like those who lose their strength to you,
seek refuge at your door,
bow at your feet,
glorify you in song,
we too have come
to hymn your praises.

Fulfill, O song of our vow.

22

Subduing their pride
the monarchs of the wide earth
crowd beside your couch.
Likewise,
we too gather at your feet.

Will you not glance upon us
with your eyes
opening ever so little
like the slit in the *kiṅkiṇī* bell,
like the budding pink lotus?

If you would gaze upon us
with those two beautiful eyes
resembling the sun and moon
rising at once,
indeed,
all our sins will vanish.

Fulfill, O song of our vow.

23

The majestic lion
asleep in his mountain cave
during the season of rains
awakens, opens his fiery eyes,
shakes himself,
his fragrant mane
flying in all directions,
then roars,
stretches his length,
comes forth.

O lord dark as the *pūvai* blossom,
come forth thus
from your seclusion.
Seated upon
your resplendent lion-throne,
consider our request.
Let your grace
be with us.

Fulfill, O song of our vow.

24

Once you measured the worlds—
  glory be to your feet.
You killed the king of Southern Laṅkā—
  glory be to your valor.
You kicked and shattered the cart—
  glory be to your fame.
Like a twig,
you flung and killed the calf—
  glory be to your jeweled anklet.
You held aloft the mountain
as umbrella—
  glory be to your greatness.
You destroy all enmity—
glory be to the lance in your hand.

In these many ways
do we sing your heroic deeds.
We have come today
to ask for our heart's desire.
Let your grace touch us.

Fulfill, O song of our vow.

25

Born as one woman's son,
that same night you became
the son of another—
in secret you grew in her home.

When in fear and wrath
Kaṃsa made evil plans
seeking to kill you,
you did foil them.
O Neṭumāl,
as fire you were to him.

We come to beseech you.
If you would grant our heart's desires,

we shall ceaselessly sing
your valor, your brilliance,
your glory which befits
the luster of Śrī.
And all our sorrows
will be as yesterday—
forever
shall we rejoice.

Fulfill, O song of our vow.

26

Almighty lord
dark as the sapphire,
if you wish to know our needs
for the Mārkaḷi bath in the waters,
here is what our elders say.

Give us conches
as milky white as your Pāñcacanya
whose sound drives terror
into the hearts of enemies,
large sounding drums,
chanters of hymns of praise,
ornate lamps,
banners and canopies.

Lord who slumbers
upon the banyan leaf,
grant us your grace.

Fulfill, O song of our vow.

27

O Govinda of renown
victorious over enemies,
we sing your virtues,
you fulfill our desires.
All the world

shall marvel at
the gifts we receive—
bracelets, armlets, *tōṭus*,
ear pendants, anklets,
numerous jewels.
We shall drape ourselves
in silk.
We shall eat milk-rice
so covered with ghee
it drips down our elbows.
In joy
together we shall be.

Fulfill, O song of our vow.

28

We humble cowherds
eke out our days
roaming the forests,
grazing our herds.
Little learning ours,
but ours the fortune
that you took birth
in our clan.

O Govinda of excellence
nor you, nor we
may revoke the relationship
between us here.

O supreme lord,
we are artless children.
Forgive us
for hailing you
in familiar ways.
Let your grace be upon us,
grant us our desire.

Fulfill, O song of our vow.

29

At break of dawn
we rise to serve you,
worship at your feet.
Great indeed is our fortune.
Born in our cowherd clan
you cannot deny us,
you are bound to accept
our little services.

O Govinda we have not come
to ask for the ritual drum.
We are your slaves,
we serve only you.
Forever and a day
we shall be connected
with you.
Make all our desires
flow to you alone.

Fulfill, O song of our vow.

30

The cowherd maidens of Āyarpāṭi
adorned with bright jewels,
faces radiant like the moon,
worshipped at the feet of Keśava,
of Mādhava who churned
the ship-laden ocean.
They received from him
their heart's desire.

This tale was told
by Kōtai of the chief of *paṭṭars*
of beautiful Putuvai,
who wore a garland
of cool fresh lotuses.
This reward will be theirs

who chant together
faultlessly
this Tamil garland of thirty songs—
the grace of Tirumāl,
will be upon them—
that lord of limitless wealth,
of holy countenance and lotus eyes,
whose four great shoulders
rise high as hills.
They will live in joy
for ever more.

Fulfill, O song of our vow.

Source: Vidya Dehejia, *Āṇṭāḷ and Her Path of Love: Poems of a Woman Saint from South India* (Albany: State University of New York Press, 1990).

Selections from the Lakṣmī Tantra

Chapter 4. Vyūhas and Their Śaktis

1. Śrī:—In essence I consist of consciousness and matchless bliss like pure space. I am Nārāyaṇī, Hari's state of existence and my nature resembles His.
2. My essence being consciousness, I am neither inert nor active, nor an intermediary state between the two. I represent the nature peculiar to Hari, the all-pervasive (Viṣṇu), who is the soul of all and has the same character as myself.
3. His form is undifferentiated, homogeneous and inscrutable; and I, also undifferentiated, am of His form and possess perfect tranquility.
4. From time to time a billion-billionth particle of ourselves, composed of consciousness, stirs into activity.
5. (That particle) which is known as the urge to create is in the form "I will create according to my liking," whereupon I, with that particle of myself, instantaneously evolve into pure creation.
6. As the brilliance of a diamond shines forth in all directions, so does my pure course (of creative activity) diffuse its rays in every direction.
7. Pure creation issues from my form of concentrated (absolute) knowledge, whose (tranquility) resembles a cloudless sky or a still ocean.
8. Devoid of all activity, ever blissful, pure, all-embracing and supreme, the primeval (knowledge) becomes manifest and is called Saṃkarṣaṇa.

9. Aiśvarya (the divine attribute) is my sovereign power to create the universe without dependence on any factor outside myself. That is my (form) Pradyumna, the excellent Person.
10. My śakti that is immanent, irresistible and which pervades the whole of this variegated universe is known as my Aniruddha form.
11. These resplendent, blue lotus-eyed Puruṣas (Pradyumna, Aniruddha and Saṃkarṣaṇa) are my forms manifesting (the divine attributes) vijñāna (consciousness), aiśvarya (lordhood) and śakti [feminine energy]. Pradyumna, Aniruddha and Saṃkarṣaṇa are respectively responsible for the creation, maintenance and dissolution of creation.
12. My primordial form when the urge to create (the universe) first stirs in me is Vāsudeva, who may be compared to an absolutely waveless ocean or to a cloudless sky.
13. The manifestation of (all six of my divine attributes) jñāna, śakti, bala, aiśvarya, vīrya and tejas in equal proportion is called Vāsudeva.
14. When of these (attributes) only jñāna and bala are manifested, I am Saṃkarṣaṇa who supports the entire creation without aid. He manifests himself dimly like black marks (faintly discerned on human bodies).
15. Hence in Vedānta literature he is named Bala (Saṃkarṣaṇa). My manifestation of vīrya and aiśvarya is named Pradyumna.
16. Since vīrya signifies immutability, he (Pradyumna) is changeless. My manifestation of śakti and tejas is known as Aniruddha.
17. Tejas means absolute sovereignty and irresistibility. The sacred literature, like a clap of thunder, issues from Saṃkarṣaṇa.
18. All activities originate from god Pradyumna. All fruits of such activities are said to issue from Aniruddha.
19. Here (in the creation of this universe) Aniruddha is verily the creator; Pradyumna sustains what the former has created, and the creation thus protected by him is devoured by lord Saṃkarṣaṇa.
20. These gods function with spontaneous benevolence through the acts of creation, maintenance and dissolution in accordance with sacred texts, religious duties (*dharma*) and the fruits thereof.
21. Though each god manifests only one particular attribute (or aspect), yet all the six (divine) attributes are vested in all three of them, (so that in fact) they stand on the same footing as (lit. neither less nor more than) the eternal Vāsudeva.
22. Their major and minor limbs and intelligence etc. are not phenomenal; their bodies containing the (divine) sixfold attributes are divine and eternal.

23. O Lord of heaven, it is erroneous to think that there is any essential difference between these (manifestations). In order to stress the particular activity associated with each, (such differentiations) are envisaged (by scripture).
24. Aiśvarya is not different from knowledge; and again śakti is not different from aiśvarya. These, O Śakra, are my (forms) envisaged to focus meditation.
25. First there is only the substance (of reality); then comes the state of being; next there is the object created and, last of all, there is activity. All created beings pass through these four consecutive states.
26. I (voluntarily) divide myself into four as Vāsudeva etc., but continue to infuse all four forms with my consciousness.
27. In each form the gods Vāsudeva and the others (in turn again) divide themselves into three forms, i.e. into Keśava etc.
28. These are the Vyūhāntaras, so called by the Pāñcarātra, and these twelve gods are engaged in conducting the activities (involved in creation).
29. These projections (manifestations) as Padmanābha etc. are the Vibhava (evolution) of Hari as Aniruddha who, though omnipresent, yet assumes these manifold forms for the benefit of the worlds.
30. From time to time to benefit the world the Lord of the world appears in the form of a man or god. Such manifestations constitute a different type of Vibhava.
31. God's image conceived by Himself or by various deities, sages, manes, or demigods for favouring the worlds are His arcā forms consisting of pure knowledge.
32. Thus I have briefly explained the pure course (of creation). Now listen as I describe the other course (of creation) containing the three guṇas (components of phenomenal existence). . . .

Chapter 5. Evolution of the Material World from Prakṛti

80. Every individual subtle body differs in each living being (*jīva*). At the time of liberation this product of the evolutionary process withdraws itself from the (liberated) being.
81. These twenty-three resulting (categories), starting from mahat and ending with viśeṣa, mutually assist each other in creating the egg.
82. That golden egg became as bright as the thousand-rayed (sun). In it Prajāpati, the four-faced god, was born as Virāj.
83. Manu was born from Virāj, and the descendants of Manu are known as Mānavas. This world, consisting of both movables and immovables, has originated from them headed by Marīci.

84–85. So far I have disclosed only a fraction of my active state. Although the śakti of consciousness is pure in essence, through contact with beginningless avidyā (nescience) caused by misery, birth, decay etc., she manifests herself in an impure state. But when avidyā is destroyed through contact with pure knowledge accompanied by pure deeds, she regains her original blissfulness.

Chapter 6. The Six Kośas (Sheaths) of Śakti

1. Śrī:—I am the primordial I-hood of Hari who possesses, though in unmanifest form, the aggregate of the six divine attributes. Hari is the great ocean of consciousness and bliss and (His tranquility and pervasiveness) resemble the waveless ocean.

2–5. Although I am so pure, sometimes I project myself. Then I—Viṣṇu's absolute essence, the Goddess (Śakti) consisting of reality and consciousness, and distinguished by my urge to create—evolve into the states of the six kośas [sheaths]: śakti, māyā, prasūti, prakṛti consisting of the three guṇas, brahmāṇḍa (the cosmic egg) and the individual living being. These six are called the six kośas. Śakti, the first kośa, follows the pure course (of creation) and is the urge to create that emanated from Hari's I-hood. Kośa is a synonym for kulāya (nest), which is another name for body.

6. The supreme God Saṃkarṣaṇa, the Lord, Ego-consciousness, is manifested in this first pure kośa, which is characterized by the initial appearance of creative activity.

7. In Him all effects (created things) lie (dormant, indistinct) like faint marks on a (human) body. The goddess consisting of His I-hood is myself, called the absolute Saṃkarṣaṇī.

8. Known as Śrī, I possess (the divine attributes of) consciousness and power. My (further) emanation from her is called Pradyumna.

9. Divine Pradyumna, the supreme Puruṣa, exists as the intelligence (*buddhi*) of divine Saṃkarṣaṇa, who is manifest in śaktikośa.

10–11. There in Him, all the enjoyers and their objects of enjoyment lie dormant. That which is said to be the I-hood of the divinity who forms the (cosmic) mind, is myself, bearing the name Sarasvatī who (out of herself) evolves vīrya and aiśvarya. My emanation from her is known as Aniruddha.

12–13. I (Aniruddha) exist as the egohood of Saṃkarṣaṇa. These three ancient divinities headed by Saṃkarṣaṇa are known as jīva, buddhi and ahaṃkāra (egohood). These are indeed not phenomenal, but consist of pure consciousness. . . .

Chapter 14. The True Nature of Śakti (Lakṣmī)

1. Śrī:—God Vāsudeva is the absolute Brahman. In essence He is (higher) knowledge; undifferentiatted with regard to space, time etc.; devoid of guṇas and pure.
2. His nature is bliss. He is ever immutable, possesses six (divine) attributes, is undecaying and everlasting. I am His supreme śakti, His I-hood. I am eternal and constant (i.e. immutable).

3–5. My śakti of action is characterized by my urge to create. With a billionth fraction of myself I voluntarily embark on creation by differentiating myself in two separate (particles), of which one is conscious and the other is the object of its knowledge. Of these two, consciousness is my citśakti. In fact consciousness, consisting of myself, evolves into both sentient and insentient objects. Absolutely pure and sovereign consciousness is, indeed, my real form.

6. Like the juice of the sugar-cane, this (consciousness) becomes grosser through contact with material objects. Hence it is that in the process of cognizing material objects, the latter acquire the nature of consciousness.
7. Just as fuel, when kindled, becomes engulfed by fire, so do (perceptible material) objects pervaded by consciousness adopt its nature.
8. Polarized thinking aware of (objects such as) blue, yellow, happiness, sorrow etc., distinguishes undifferentiated pure consciousness by its variegated wealth of limiting conditions.
9. Polarized thought is also one of my forms voluntarily created by myself whereby, viewed from an internal and an external angle, perceptible (material) objects become classified as subject and object.
10. Neither the external (object) nor the internal (cognition) constitutes the essence of my absolute consciousness. My selfhood splits itself in two components: the (objects) capable of being known; and the (subjects) who do the knowing.
11. That self of mine, which is beyond all polarized knowledge, free from the taint of words and unaffected by any limiting condition, undergoes evolution in the form of perceptible (material) objects.
12. When the mind is free of polarized thought, those perceptible (material) objects that attain the middle mode become identified with consciousness.
13. Just as the form existing in the eye is seen (by that eye) as being the form belonging to a particular external object, so also the form existing in the knowledge observed (by the knower) appears to belong to the thing known.

14. Just as a burning piece of wood looks like fire, so also are perceptible (material) objects pervaded by consciousness perceived as consciousness.
15. When the object is related to cognition by the knower and he reflects upon it; it is then myself, consisting of knowledge and ever revealed (who is in fact perceived as that object).
16. I-hood is the essential characteristic of knowledge distinguishing it from the object perceived; it is unique, and that is my own self. Hence I, consisting of pure consciousness, am all-pervading.
17. When in the ocean of consciousness the only foothold left on the flooded island is the term connoting "this" and perceptible (material) objects are almost submerged I then provide them with a support to hold on to.
18. Those whose impressions have all been washed away (i.e. removed) by the nectar-like flow of meditation upon me, realize me, who am (pure) consciousness engulfing the multitudinous variety of objects, as identical with themselves.
19. People are of opinion that, since I consist of knowledge alone, my function of revealing objects of knowledge (i.e. cognition) is an effect of avidyā, about which I have spoken before. . . .

Chapter 16. Methods to Attain Ultimate Truth

1–4. Now listen attentively, O Śakra, to my description of mahat, the first disturbance (lit. activity) in the tranquil equilibrium of the guṇas. It too has three aspects (modes, manners of manifesting itself): the sattva-aspect which is buddhi (intellect); the rajas-aspect which is prāṇa (the vital air); and the tamas-aspect called kāla (time). Now hear me explain these. Buddhi is the incentive to mental effort; prāṇa is the incentive to endeavour; and kāla is the incentive to transform in the form of impulse and effective development. Ahaṃkāra [I-hood] results from a modification of mahat.

5. (Ahaṃkāra) also has three aspects resulting from the proportional difference in the guṇas. The five tanmātras (element-principles), space etc., are evolved from its tamas-aspect.

6–7. The cognitive senses owe their origin to predominance of the sattva-aspect (of ahaṃkāra); the conative senses to predominance of its rajas-aspect; while the mind originates from both (its sattva- and rajas-aspects). This is how the tattvas (cosmic principles) exist. Amongst these, only prakṛti (matter), the eternal, is the source of all (and not an effect).

8–9. The other seven (principles), starting from mahat, have both the aspects of being the source and the effect. The modifications of the five tanmātras (element-principles), viz. space etc., the cognitive and conative senses together with the mind,—these sixteen are referred to by scholars as being mere effects.

10–12. These are the twenty-four tattvas (cosmic principles). O slayer of Vṛtra, (I have already dealt with) other details and peculiarities relevant to these. O king of the gods, I have told you about this avyakta (unmanifested) prakṛti along with its own twenty-three modifications. This (prakṛti), consisting of both manifest and unmanifest objects, is characterized as continuously producing (effects).

13. Citśakti differs from this. It is imperishable; and the wise (respectable), who are versed in the scriptures dealing with the categories, call it jīva (the individual soul).

14. In essence this is pure, unmodifiable, unchangeable, concentrated consciousness, eternal, endless and unlimited (lit. unabating).

15. These, prakṛti and Puruṣa though by nature unattached, appear to be connected and are even higher than mahat (the highest).

16. Both these eternal (realities) are identifiable as indicatory mark and (at the same time) are devoid of any indicatory mark. It is therefore left for the learned to deduce their common characteristics by inference.

17–19. Now listen, Śakra, while I recount their differences. Prakṛti consists of the three guṇas, eternal and ever evolving, though it is undifferentiated, impure, and invariably identified with the jīvas. It is also the unconscious (material) object subjected to the delusion of pleasure and pain. Puruṣa is the innermost ever-existing soul which, though functioning, is uninvolved and is the the witnessing consciousness, the knowledge and at the same time the knower, who is pure, unending and incorporating the (divine) attributes.

20–21. These are the divergences between the two. Now listen to a description of their nature. She who (That which) is devoid of positive or negative material diversity, is unchangeable, ever active (in creation), ever blissful, with a form consisting of all the six attributes, is (in fact) myself, Nārāyaṇī, the Śakti of Viṣṇu, pure Śrī.

22–25. These two (viz. Puruṣa and prakṛti) originate from me and will merge in me. Containing all these, I have evolved into various objects and resting in Nārāyaṇa, once again I become active in creation (i.e. develop myself) out of Him. Nārāyaṇa is the unique Viṣṇu, the eternal Vāsudeva. Since He is not different from (His) Śakti, He is the one and undifferentiated

Brahman; the great ocean, as it were, of jñāna, śakti, bala, aiśvarya, vīrya and tejas; He is ever tranquil and embraces the entire universe containing both static and dynamic objects (i.e. living creatures and inanimate things). Thus, Śakra, the science of sāṃkhya (i.e. the knowledge of truth) has been briefly revealed to you.

26–28. The wise should first study the science of knowledge, which consists of the enumeration of the cosmic principles. Then he should master the knowledge concerning recapitulation (carcā) derived from the teaching of the principles set forth in scripture concerning their common and divergent characteristics, their nature and source etc. The true knowledge attained by the pure soul after mastering the speculative discussion on the revelation of existing reality, is that absolute knowledge bestowed through my grace.

29–30. Thus I have given you an account of the philosophy of Sāṃkhya. After applying themselves to this philosophy according to the Sāṃkhya system, these adepts of sāṃkhya attain my state of existence. The third method called yoga will (now) be described to you. There are two types of yoga, samādhi (concentration) and saṃyama (constraint).

31. Samādhi results from (practising) the components (of yoga) known as yama etc., which implies existing in a state of identity with the absolute Brahman called Śrīnivāsa, without having to return.

32. This state (condition) is proper to those who have realized Brahman; it consists of intuitive realization based on the identification of the meditator with the object meditated on, and arises through grace bestowed by me.

33. Saṃyama implies good deeds relating solely to the highest Self. That again is of two varieties, pertaining to the body and to the mind.

34–37. I shall elaborate on both saṃyama and samādhi. The first method consists of performing (religious) duties previous described by me. It generates pure consciousness by purifying the inner organ. When by confining himself to good deeds (the adept) receives my favour, I bestow (on him) buddhiyoga the realization of truth through mental communion with the Highest), which (further) purifies the inner organ. As already mentioned, this is the second method called sāṃkhya. It eludes observation and is based on study of the sacred scriptures. When this last mentioned realization of truth takes firm root (in the mind), it becomes (as vivid as) direct knowledge (of the Highest) and gains my supreme satisfaction.

38. Then I, recognized in my own form with my attributes and vibhavas (divine manifestations), disclose that direct higher knowledge which is the outcome of discrimination (between truth and falsity).

39. The third form of direct (knowledge) comprised in samādhi is inviolable and firm, resulting chiefly from sattva and is largely due to grace.
40. That (other) variety of the third (method of knowledge), which is described by the name saṃyama and includes the pure enjoyment derived from three different sources, greatly delights me.
41. There I, the soul of the universe, Śakti of Viṣṇu the all-embracing, am worshipped directly as myself, or as God Puruṣottama (and through Him as myself).
42. Thus I have carefully explained to you the three exalted methods (of attaining the highest goal). Now listen to my description of the fourth method called complete renunciation.
43. It consists of the (adept's) abandonment of every task however weighty or trifling; (whereafter) having been made thoroughly miserable (lit. burnt) by the fire of worldly existence, he (the adept) resorts to me alone.
44. When, with unwavering mind a person resorts to me, I permit him to identify himself with me after his mind has become rid of all sin.

Chapter 17. The Secret Method of Self-surrender

68–73. Repudiation of arrogance (implies) humility achieved through sacred knowledge and good conduct. (Sometimes) upāya (the prescribed method) cannot be satisfactorily followed owing to the impossibility of procuring all the requirements for performance of the supporting rites, because of inability to officiate in the prescribed manner, or perhaps again for want of an auspicious opportunity to perform such rites on account of discrepancies in place, time or qualification; whereas as against what is prescribed, what is prohibited is still more exacting. The repudiation of arrogance calls for timidity and humility. Since Śakti is innate in God who is ever merciful; and since there is a basic relationship (between God) as Master and (living beings) as His subjects, the deep-rooted conviction arises in the mind (of devotees) that, because God is benevolent, He will protect them. Such implicit trust, O śakra, destroys all demerit. Although God is the master of all embodied beings, and although He is full of compassion and capable (of showing it), yet without prayer He will not protect; (this consideration is inducement) to pray (by introducing the words) "Be my protector," which imply throwing oneself on His protection.

74. (The whole process of renunciation), which starts with waiving the right to claim the results of the deeds (performed by) those who rely solely on

God's protection and which ends with relinquishing that privilege in favour of Keśava, is called self-surrender.

75. Nyāsa, which is synonymous with nikṣepa, has five components. It is (also) referred to as saṃnyāsa, tyāga or śaraṇagati.

76–77. This is the fourth method which was spoken of earlier. It achieves quick results. Those who follow this fourth method as practised by the brahmins tend to regard the three previous methods as less attractive. Practice of the ānukūlya method and the (method) other than ānukūlya ensures the avoidance of prohibited deeds.

78–80. It has been said that the practice of kārpaṇya dispenses with the necessity of (adhering to) the upāyas: and yet confidence in God's protection makes it desirable to adhere to the upāya. . . .

81. The śāstra [sacred text] has indicated that violence, theft etc., are apāyas; and that karman (religious duties), sāṃkhya etc., are upāyas.

82–87. He who rejects both upāya and apāya and, convinced of God's protection, has recourse to the middle course by surrendering to God all that he possesses, will realize that Puruṣottama (God), the God of gods, is (his) protector.

Śakra:—O Ambikā, what is this middle course between upāya and apāya? Since all action springs from either upāya or apāya accordingly as the prohibitions and injunctions laid down in the śāstras are obeyed or disregarded, it would appear that every activity necessarily falls either under upāya or apāya.

Śrī:—O king of gods, there are three inscrutable types of karman (deeds); learn to distinguish between them by applying the prohibitions and regulations laid down in the śāstras. Some deeds produce harmful results, whilst others produce beneficial results; others again redeem sins. In the light of the śāstras recognize these three types of deeds.

88–90. The first two types known as upāya and apāya should be rejected. The third group that redeems sin (again has two subdivisions). (Of these the first consists of) deeds called prāyaścitta, which annihilate the evil consequences of misdeeds. The intelligent should avoid deeds of that nature, just as in the case of the first two groups. Only those duties, which when performed bring no reward, but when ignored result in harm, should be performed (by the adept).

91. This is the attitude taken by the Vedas, which endorse the middle way between upāya and apāya. He who follows this road seeks refuge in surrendering himself wholeheartedly to the Lord of the universe, Janārdana.

92. The method prescribed by this śāstra, if practised (even) once, will liberate the human being (adept); whereas by following both upāya and apāya he is bereft of that advantage (of prapatti [surrender].

93. If one intentionally commits some apāya deed, a redeeming rite should be performed without delay. But he who has sought refuge (*Śaraṇāgati*), discovers that act in itself to be as efficacious as prāyaścitta.

94–98. Again, even if the upāyas are accepted as such, the position remains unchanged. In order not to dislocate the laws of dharma and to maintain the family, to govern the world (*loka*) without disturbance, to establish (social) norms and to gratify me and Viṣṇu, the God of gods, the wise should not violate the Vedic laws even in thought. Just as even a king's favourite, who defiles a river—that is useful to that monarch, a source of pleasure and beneficial to the community for raising the crop—incurs the (death penalty) on the stake, even though he be indifferent to (the river in question), so also does a mortal, who disregards the norm laid down in the Vedas and thereby disobeys my command, forfeit my favour, although he be a favourite of mine.

99–103. Thus mentally giving up attachment to the upāyas, the wise adopt the fourth method; and having overcome all affliction (impediments), enter the pure state of (sattva) existence. Hence the middle course that is neither upāya nor apāya is (called) surrender; it is the foremost means (of attaining the *summum bonum*) and enables human beings to traverse the ocean of life and death. It is the only way of refuge whereby both the ignorant and the well-informed may set foot on that longed for farther shore (of ocean-like mundane existence) in order to become eternal. The redemption of sinful acts must be sought through me alone, consort of the God of gods. Abstaining from upāya, (let the human being) take refuge in me.

104–105. (Thus) gradually nearer to me (Śakti) and intent on observing upāya, after harvesting the rewards of his immaculate deeds, he finally becomes detached (from all worldly ties) and acquires the highest status. This complete self-surrender is a means (of attaining the human goal)—simple to follow, but in my opinion difficult to carry out.

106–107. (Therefore) only the cultured and the wise, who have rid their minds of all desire, choose this road. Hence in order to achieve their aim, whether rid of desire or not, men should always worship my mantra-form. In accordance with the ritual precepts, the adept should receive initiation from a preceptor, attain the fulfilment of his aspirations and worship my mantra-form with mantras consisting of me.

Source:*Laksmī Tantra: A Pāñcarātra Text*, translated by Sanjukta Gupta (Leiden: E. J. Brill, 1972).

Selections from the *Vedārthasaṃgraha* of Rāmānuja

4. In truth, all declarations of the Vedanta are meant to set forth the knowledge of the proper form and nature of the individual soul which are different from the body; the proper form and nature of the Supreme Spirit who is the inner Ruler of the soul; the worship of the Supreme Spirit; and the apprehension of Brahman as perfect boundless bliss which presupposes the revelation of the proper form of the soul that results from the worship of the Supreme Spirit. By setting forth all this the declarations of the Vedanta serve to remove the danger of rebirth which is inevitable since it results from the misconception of the individual soul that it is identical itself with that one of the four types of bodies—sc. gods, from Brahmā onwards,—men—animals—inanimate beings—, into which it has entered by the impulsion of the continuous flow of good or evil karman amassed during ageless ignorance.

Such declarations are met with in śrutis like "Thou art That, this soul is Brahman, He who, although residing in the soul, is different from that soul, whom the soul does not know, whose body is the soul, and who directs the soul from within, He is the immortal inner Ruler of thy soul, He is the inner soul of all beings, free from all evil, the divine and sole God Nārāyana,'tis He whom the Brahmans aspire to know by repeating the Vedas, by sacrifice, charity, mortification and fasting, he that knows Brahman attains the Most-High, he that knows this is immortal: there is no other way to tread," and so on and so forth.

5. The proper form of the soul is free from all various differentiations consisting in the distinctions that are brought about by the natural evolution of prakṛti [matter] into the bodies of gods, men, etc. In essence it is only characterized by knowledge and beatitude. When these differentiations of god, man, etc.,—which have been brought about by the karman of the soul—have vanished there persists a differentiation in its proper forms; it is beyond the power of expression and can only be known by the soul itself. So the soul can only be defined as essentially knowledge; and this essential nature is common to all souls.

15. With a view to explain this point that the One—as described above—when known makes everything known, the father adduces an example drawn from common experience in order to illustrate that cause and effect are not different from each other: . . . "a single substance of clay can be transformed into various structures, conditions and forms—jug, bowl etc.—so that within itself it includes diverse practical purposes. Yet, although it may assume diverse denominations, it is an established fact that it remains the same substance clay and does not become another substance for it remains differentiated by the structural peculiarities of clay. So it is possible through the knowledge of one lump of clay to know all that is differentiated by the same structural peculiarities of clay—jugs, bowls and the like."

16. The son does not know that Brahman is the sole cause of the entire Universe, so he asks: Sir, you must tell me what that is. Then the father expounds that Brahman Himself, the omniscient and omnipotent, is the universal cause. . . . He means to say that at the very time of its creation the world was still non-differentiated: so . . . he states that the world that was in the state of *sat* [being] was at that time not yet differentiated into names-and-forms. By this same exposition it is made clear that *sat* [being] is the material cause of the world; now the word [non-dual] denies that there was still another cause, or an operative cause, different from that material cause.

17 a. Then the father proceeds to develop in a lucid manner what he had tacitly borne in mind before in the passage: Have you asked about that [directing person] by whom the unheard-of is heard-of etc., namely that the Commander or Operator Himself is the material cause. So he says: "That *sat*, which Itself is at once the material and the operative cause of the world . . . that means: "That Supreme Brahman, denoted by the word *tad*, who is omniscient and omnipotent and has his every will realized and all his desires materialized, decided nonetheless, for the sake of his own sport: "I be many in the form of a world composed of an infinite variety of spiritual and non-spiritual beings; to that purpose I will multiply." He then created the primordial elements—ether etc.—out of a single portion of Himself. Then again this Supreme Deity, denoted by the name *sat* [being] declares that the living soul is itself ensouled by Brahman and points out that all non-spiritual matter becomes [a named object] when the living soul ensouled by Brahman enters into it, and that then all substance assumes name.

b. In other words: the individual soul is itself ensouled by Brahman, for the soul is a modification of Brahman because it constitutes His body, as appears from another śruti: . . . whose body is the soul etc. The non-spiritual entities in the generic structures of a god, a man etc. are modifications of this same individual soul—which is a modification of Brahman himself—because they constitute the soul's body. Consequently all these entities are ultimately ensouled by Brahman. Hence follows that all words which have a definite denotative value owing to the combination of the radical element with a suffix, e.g. god, man, yakṣa, rākṣasa, cow, game, fowl, tree, creeper, wood, rock, grass, jug, cloth etc., actually denote the entire composite entity: the body, the individual soul represented by it, and finally the inner Ruler of that soul, the Supreme Person in whom that entity terminates. All words denote this entire *compositum* by merely denoting the material mass which has a certain generic structure that is commonly known as being denoted by a certain word.

18. Then the father sets forth in some detail that *sat* [being] is the material cause, the operative cause, the substratum, the controller and the principal of the entire phenomenal world of spiritual and non-spiritual entities. . . . Thereafter the father proceeds to declare that because of the relation cause-effect, etc., the entire Universe, being ensouled by Brahman is real. . . . Finally the assertion that Brahman is the soul of all as He is the soul of the entire Universe, that this entire Universe constitutes His body and that He therefore, as He is modified by the individual soul, can be denoted by the word *tvam*, this assertion is now summed up and applied to one specific individual soul in the statement *tat tvam asi* [That you are].

19. In other words, in the above statement . . . the words *idaṃsarvam* refer to the phenomenal world of spiritual and non-spiritual entities. Thus is declared that . . . "He" is the soul of this phenomenal world, so that this *śruti* [revelation] sets forth that Brahman ensouls the evolved phenomenal world.

Now the question calls for consideration whether Brahman ensouls the world in a soul-body relation, or is essentially identical with the world. When it is supposed that Brahman is essentially identical with the world, this would mean that Brahman's perfections, such as we gathered from the beginning of the context . . . are thereby sublated. Besides, we have already learnt particularly from another śruti that He ensouls the world by constituting the soul of the world as a body. . . .

Therefore, since all spiritual and non-spiritual entities constitute Brahman's body, Brahman being thus embodied and modified by all, is denoted by all words. Hence the [logical] construction *tat tvam* [That you] denotes Brahman as "the One who is modified by the individual soul inasmuch as this soul constitutes his body."

20. When this is said the sense of the statement *tat tvam asi* beomes clear; *tvam* means "you, i.e. you that were previously held to be no more than the operator of a certain body are in reality a modification of the Supreme Spirit because you constitute his body, and therefore you terminate in this Supreme Spirit [and are incapable of separate existence and activity]." Hence *tvam* denotes only the inner Ruler of *tvam* as differentiated by the mode *tvam*. Since Brahman is the soul of the embodied individual soul, . . . He has the same name as that individual soul. It follows that both words *tat* and *tvam* coordinated in a construction, denote that one Brahman. The word *tat* refers to Brahman as the One who is the cause of the world, the abode of all perfections, the immaculate and untransmutable One; whereas *tvam* refers to that same Brahman under the aspect of inner Ruler, of the individual soul as being modified by the embodied soul. So it is said that the words *tat* and *tvam* both apply to the same Brahman but under different aspects. And in this manner all the various perfections of Brahman, e.g. that he is the perfect, untransformed abode of all beautiful qualities and the universal cause, are preserved and no one is sublated.

21. Laymen who have not received the instruction of the Vedānta do not see that all [things] and all individual souls are ensouled by Brahman, and they think that the full meaning of all words is completely exhausted by the various [things] they denote, which, however, form only part of their full significance. Now that they have heard what the Vedānta declares they know that Brahman is the soul of everything because it is His effect and He is its inner Ruler and that every word denotes Brahman as modified by everything.

But, it is objected, would that not mean that the original meaning of words like cow etc. as denoting specific [things] is sublated?

No: When we elucidated the [revelation] . . . we had occasion to say that all words denote the Supreme Spirit only in so far He is differentiated by the non-spiritual matter and the individual soul. . . .

33. . . . To resume. In the passage under discussion the words *agra*, etc., show therefore that there are a number of differentiations in Brahman Himself. There is no word to be found in it that voices a negation of differentiations such as you are

pleased to assume. On the contrary the existence of a time-differentiation shows clearly that Brahman is the cause and the world his effect:*āsīt* denotes a specific action; then there are His modes of being the material as well as the operative cause of the world; then again His quality of omnipotence as proved by the denial of difference between material and operative: thus differentiations, unsuspected before, are expounded by thousands!

34. Since this Śruti means to teach that the relation between cause and effect is one based upon substantial reality . . . i.e, an entity that has originated from *asat* (nonbeing) remains essentially *asat*, in the same way as an entity—a jug, etc.— that has originated from clay remains essentially clay. The origination of an existent entity is by definition its conjunction with a variety of modes or phases of being, and this conjunction is the ground that it may have a variety of practical purposes.

35. In other words, it is declared that one and the same entity that is a cause becomes an effect when entering upon another mode of being. The point which is sought to establish hereby is this that knowledge of all can be had through knowledge of one. But this point cannot be proved in the *asatkāryavāda* theory, for according to this theory an effect . . . because it has several causes . . . originates as a completely different entity. Hence it is impossible anyhow that the effect is known when the cause is known, inasmuch as the effect is an entity completely different from the entity that is its cause. . . .

First the fact that, as even our adversary who maintains that the effect originates as a new entity must agree—the different name, practical purpose etc., which apply to the identical entity, prove that a different phase has been entered upon by the cause; and secondly the fact that we do not see another entity appear at all. Hence it is said that the effect is nothing but the cause in another phase, and that is what our śruti declares.

36. But is the *asatkāryavāda* not rejected just to show that there can be no error without a substratum? For one and the same being which alone is real in the form of spirituality, evolves into the form of the phenomenal world when it is obscured by Nescience. If Nescience is to have a substratum, we must assume that the Real itself is its ultimate cause. Which proves that the *asatkāryavāda* theory is untenable.

This is not true. What is actually declared is this that that theory is untenable because the assertion, and the illustration that all is known when one is known can only have any bearing at all on the topic if the *satkārya* point of view is adopted. For that matter, in your own position the theory that an error without a substratum is impossible does not admit of proof itself. Your doctrine leads to this conclusion: When one holds that the defect inherent in a spiritual being is real and that this defect is a real basis for errors to arise, then, being oneself afflicted with that defect, one is proved to have a vision of a phantom, say a fairy-tale castle, which it itself is unreal. But when one holds that this defect is unreal and therefore is no real basis for errors to arise, one is proved to have that illusion all the same, because of its very basis being unreal! Actually in your position an error without a substratum is not at all impossible.

37. We have already pointed out that Brahman is declared to be differentiated by all the qualities ascribed to him: for even the so-called purifying statements . . . do not contradict the assertion that one denoted object may be qualified by a number of qualities which are established by [logical] constructions and by the original sense of the terms. . . .

65. [A]ll these srutis and smṛtis propound that Brahman Himself is modified by all spiritual and non-spiritual entities; (1) since it is learnt from them that the Supreme Brahman is the soul of all and that all entities, spiritual and non-spiritual, constitute his body; (2) since the body is a [thing] only by virtue of its function of modifying the being it embodies; and (3) since, although body and embodied being have different properties, they are not confused with each other. This doctrine of a Brahman modified by all spirit and non-spirit they propound by the use of . . . constructions etc., taken in their primary sense, which set forth Brahman's supernal manifestation by declaring that Brahman is embodied by all. For . . . the word *tat* refers to the perfect Brahman who is the universal cause and the possessor of all perfections; whereas the word *tvam*, which is used predicatively of spiritual entities, refers to Brahman as being qualified by the individual soul, or as embodied by that soul, existing as the inner Ruler of the soul that constitutes His body. . . .

66. In other words, the declaration that *Brahman is such* proves the reality—in subtle and gross phase alike—of the phenomenal world, consisting in a plurality of spiritual and non-spiritual entities, as the mode denoted by the word *such*. Thus the full meaning of the passage. . . is exhausted: the sum-total of spiritual and non-spiritual entities exists conditionally as the generic structure of this same Lord who has several generic structures, being either cause or effect.

67. —However, it is a matter of common knowledge that only class and property are modifications of a substance in the form of its generic and specific structure, so that they alone can have the attributive function denoted by the word "such," and not the substance itself. So it is improper to contend that a thing capable of independent function is merely, as an attributive "such," a modification of the Lord.

Not less common is the knowledge that a substance, too, e.g. a stick, an ear-ring etc., serves to modify another substance. . . .

68. What we mean is this: we are not concerned about whether class, or property, or substance may constitute a mode. When a certain entity serves as a distinctive feature for a certain substance, then we can properly say, by means of a [logical] construction coordinating that entity with that substance, that it has no function apart from that substance and therefore constitutes a mode of it. And if a substance that may have a separate function is in some place at some time wanted as a mode for another substance, then it has a possessive suffix; that is all the difference there is.

So, since the sum-total of all entities, animate and inanimate, constitute the Lord's body, their proper forms have real existence as the modes of the Lord. Such being the case, the Lord, who is the entity modified by all these entities, is denied by the various words that denote these entities. Therefore these entities can appropriately be terms in logical coordination with Him. . . .

69. Consequently, Brahman Himself is also all effects, since he has the generic structure of being modified by all things. . . . So by knowing solely that Brahman is the cause we know all. In this manner it is established very well that knowledge of all can be had through knowledge of one. At the same time it is stated . . . that the sum-total of spiritual and non-spiritual entities is ensouled by the Supreme Brahman inasmuch as it modifies Him. . . .

76. The relation between soul and body means the relation between substratum and dependent entity incapable of functioning separately, between transcendent controller and thing controlled, between principal and accessory. In this relation the one term is called atman or "soul" because this is the one who obtains an object since he is in all respects the substratum, the controller and the principal; the other term is called body, i.e. form, because it is a modification that is inseparably connected since it is in all respects dependent entity, thing controlled

and accessory. For such is the relation between the individual soul and its body. Consequently, inasmuch as all constitute the body of the Supreme Spirit, He can be denoted by all terms. . . .

78. This is the central meaning of all śāstras: the individual souls are as such essentially uncontracted, unlimited and perfect knowledge. But they are enveloped by ignorance in the form of karman. So they are subject to contraction of knowledge proportionate to their karman, and they enter into bodies of various kinds and classes, from Brahma to tuft of grass. Their range of knowledge is now confined to that which their various bodies encompass. So these souls are led to identify themselves with their various bodies and to perform acts that follow from this identification. Consequently they enter the continuous surge of *saṃsāra* [rebirth], in this form that they experience the pleasure and pain correlated with these acts. As it is impossible for them to release themselves from this *saṃsāra* [rebirth] without resorting to the Venerable Lord therefore, to serve this purpose, the śāstras start with setting forth the equality of all those souls: they are equal because when they are free from the differentiations god, man etc., they all have the self-same form of knowledge. Then the śāstras declare that that proper form of the soul is itself ensouled by the Venerable Lord, because it is the soul's sole proper form and essence, to be accessory to its principal. This stated, they propound subsequently the proper form of the Lord: He is categorically different from everything else as He is in absolute opposition to imperfection and solely comprises perfection; He is the abode of innumerable numbers, of beautiful qualities, boundless and absolute; He is the soul immanent in everything, because each and every spiritual and non-spiritual entity brought into existence by His will. Then the śāstras conclude by expounding that worshipping Him, as well as obtaining the necessaries for this worship, is the means of attaining Him. . . .

92. In other words, when, an aspirant to release is wholly devoted to meditation in the form of knowledge of the kind enjoined by the Vedānta and when an oceanic feeling of perfect love for that meditation itself engulfs him, then by virtue of that love is he able to grasp the Supreme Person. . . .

Bhakti is a kind of knowledge that is so excellent, precious and exclusive that it robs everything else of its interest. Now, he that has acquired this knowledge is elected by the Supreme Person, and so he can grasp Him. . . . It is through bhaktiyoga, furthered at first by karmayoga that is daily intensified in the above way and subsequently by jñānayoga, that such knowledge in the form of supreme bhakti arises. . . .

107. We have to understand that when Viṣṇu—who is the Supreme Entity as declared in the text (which deals with this topic exclusively) that only the cause is the right object of meditation—enters into an effect, then this entering into an effect is a voluntary descent of Him, so as to help the world, just for his sport: thereby He completes the number of entities of certain categories which are his own effects. So, as a matter of sport, the Supreme One becomes Upendra, completing thereby the number of divinities. Likewise the Supreme Brahman has voluntarily descended into the shape of Daśaratha's son Rāma, thereby completing the number of kings of the Solar Dynasty. Similarly the Venerable Lord has voluntarily descended in the House of Vāsudeva, to incarnate Himself in Kṛṣṇa in order to support the world, thereby completing the number of scions of the Lunar Dynasty.

108. We have explained before that it is Nārāyaṇa whom the contexts that deal with creation and resorption declare to be the supreme cause. . . . Here the ground that justifies this type of statement is mentioned: the ground is that the Infinite One is omnipresent: the Supreme Spirit is omnipresent as the immanent soul of all spiritual and non-spiritual entities which constitute his own body. So we have said that all words denote the Supreme Spirit Himself as embodied by all entities. Hence the word "I" denotes the Supreme Spirit as the substance modified by a mode of which He himself is the soul. . . . [I]t is the Supreme Spirit—either in condition of effect or of cause—who ensouls the body constituted by spiritual and non-spiritual matter in gross or subtle form respectively: this is so because everyone and everything is completed in Him. . . .

127. There are thousands of śrutis that declare that this Supreme Brahman Nārāyaṇa has a proper form of undefinable knowledge and beatitude in the purest form; He has immeasurable, innumerable, all-surpassing beautiful qualities, such as knowledge, power, strength, sovereignty, fortitude, glory etc.; the sum-total of spiritual and non-spiritual entities different from Himself are actuated by an act of His will; He possesses one invariable divine form that is in accordance with His pleasure and in harmony with Himself; He has an infinite variety of unsurpassed beautiful ornaments that suit His form, and immeasurable, endless and marvelous weapons of all kinds that are equal to His power; He has a Consort who suits his pleasure and who is in harmony with Him, possessing an immeasurable eminence of proper form, qualities, supernal power, ascendancy and character. He has an infinite entourage of attendants and necessaries, suitable to Him, the

knowledge, actions etc. of who are perfect and whose qualities are limitless; He has an infinite glorious manifestation, such as is fitting to Him, comprising all objects and all means of experience; He has a divine residence, the proper form and nature of which are beyond the ken of thought and the power of expression: all this and so forth is everlasting and irreproachable. . . .

141. We have already declared that the means of attaining Brahman is a superior bhakti in the form of re-memorization staggered to a state of extremely lucid perception, which is immeasurably and overwhelmingly dear to the devotee. It is achieved by complete devotion of bhakti which is furthered by the performance of one's proper acts preceded by knowledge of the orders of reality from the sacred texts. The word bhakti has the sense of a kind of love, and this love again that of a certain kind of knowledge. . . .

142. In other words, cognitions with a content fall either under pleasure or suffering or the state of neither pleasure nor suffering, and they become one or the other of these three according to their content or object. If knowledge particularized by a particular object excites pleasure, it is held dear accordingly. The cognition that has that pleasurable object is pleasure itself, and we do not notice any different thing: particularly because this cognition leads to the practical behaviour of being happy. The capacity of particularizing such a pleasurable cognition is but relative and impermanent in any object different from Brahman, but in Brahman Itself it is absolute and permanent: it is said that "Brahman is bliss." Since knowledge is pleasurable if its object is pleasurable, Brahman is pleasurable as such. . . . Brahman being pleasure one is happy when one has attained Brahman. The Supreme Person, being in His own right and of his own accord boundless and absolute bliss, becomes bliss to another too, because there is no differentiation in that He is beatitudinous. So the meaning of our text is: he that has Brahman as the object of his knowledge becomes happy. When it is realized that the soul stands in a relation of subservience to the Supreme Brahman because this Supreme Brahman—treasury of hosts of innumerable absolute and immeasurable beautiful qualities, irreproachable, possessing an infinite supernal manifestation—ocean of immeasurable and absolute goodness, beauty and love—is the Principal to which the soul is accessory or subservient, then the Supreme Brahman who is thus an object of absolute love leads the soul to Himself.

143. However, this would mean in order words that the soul's absolute subservience is immeasurable and absolute happiness: but this is contradicted by all

experience, for we see that literally all spiritual beings have one great wish: to be completely independent; compared with that, dependence means suffering. . . .

This attitude reveals the misconceived identification of body and soul by those who have not learnt that the soul is essentially different from the body. For the body, which, as a matter of fact, is a mass in which qualities, such as the generic structure of man, etc., subsist, is held to be independent and they who are bond to rebirth think that the body is the "I." Whatever misconception one has of one's own soul, one holds the end of life to agree with that. What is pleasure is differently determined according to the body for which the soul is mistaken . . . and these different pleasures are mutually incompatible. So everything is judged by whatever aim of life corresponds to the mistaken identity of the soul. The proper form of soul has, however, knowledge for its one and only form, and is essentially different from the body, god, etc., and the soul's essence is that it is subservient to Another. . . .

144. The smṛti that you just quoted, "all dependence means suffering," declares as a matter of fact that, since there is no mutual relationship of principal and subservient terms with entities that are different from the Supreme Person, any subservience to something different from Him is suffering. . . . [O]nly the Supreme Person is worthy of the obedience of all those who know what the true nature of the soul is. . . . This service in the form of bhakti is denoted by the word of "knowing" in the revealed texts: "He that knows Brahman attains the Most-High," "He that knows this, becomes immortal, knowing Brahman he becomes Brahman." From the specifying text: "He whom He chooses may attain Him," we understand from the clause: "whom He chooses" that one must be elected and that the most beloved one is elected. The most beloved of the Lord is he in whom boundless and absolute love for the Lord has been inspired: this is stated by the Lord in: "For I am exceedingly beloved of the knower and he is beloved by me." Therefore, it is knowledge which has risen to superior bhakti that is really the means of attaining the Lord . . . after having realized one's own soul by discrimination, one sees the Supreme Spirit by bhakti, that is, one has immediate presentation of Him, attain Him. . . . Since bhakti is taken as a form of cognition, everything is established.

Source *Rāmānuja's Vedārthasaṃgraha, translated by J.A.B. van Buitenen (Poona: Deccan College Postgraduate and Research Institute, 1956).*

Selections from the *Acutaśatakam* of Vedāntadeśika

Your chest, O Acuta lovely with its mole,
Śrīvatsa, and Lady Lakṣmī,
inseparable
from its long chapter of flowers, made most auspicious
by Kaustubhā
precious gem of the Milk Ocean

and by sprays of cool holy basil,
praises your glory.

Your yellow waist-cloth is streaked red with the blood
of Madhu and Kaitabha, demons you crushed
without mercy:

its girdle, whose bells are tinkling,
shines

like the golden fetters for the lord of elephants,
the mad God
of Love.

Your lotus foot,
blossoming at the summit of the Veda, a refuge for all creatures,
shines,

O Lord true to those who surrender:
from it streamed the heavenly Gaṅgā
born the moment you measured
the worlds,

extinguishing the sins
of the threefold
universe.

They surrender to your lotus foot, O Lord of Truth,
they'll never go to Yama's hell.

even if they stumble and fall
they'll get off light—
a punishment suited to their high place

like servants in the king's
inner rooms.

To chant your name is to taste
   sweet nectar,

O Lord true to your servants,

it's the root of the tree
of freedom's bliss, best
   of the great elixirs
to cure the aging of delusion,

the one fertile soil
   of auspiciousness.

The body has been and will always be
   like a wooden puppet
moved by treads,
at the mercy
of somebody else.

Be of good will to this body of mine
   tugged this way
and that by action, speech,
   and mind,
O Lord of gods!

Cutting the twin fetters of my karmas,
   giving the good
to my friends, and the bad
   to those who
   hate me, when

O Acuta,

will you free me from this hole of a prison-house,
  my cruel body?

When, O Lord of gods—
though I am fit never to return
  to this world—
will you enjoy me as one of your blessed friends on this earth
  in the divine play
of your incarnations
  equal to you, if
  only in
  pleasure?

Overcome by sense object, I sink
into the strong whirlpools
of the ocean of beings—

pull me out with your own hands, O Acyuta,
nurse me
back to health

like a mother
her suckling child!

My heart wallows in gifts as straw,
like honey mixed with poison:

stripped of "I" and "mine,"
fix this heart
within you, O Acyuta,
treasure of nectar.

O Lord,
having no other refuge,

I've been entrusted to you
by gentle teachers
full of mercy—
seeing them,
your dear ones, O Lord true to those who surrender,
firmly bear the burden
of my soul!

O Lord true to those who surrender,
take me back like the king
his young son,
the prince

who lived among crude hunters
snatched back from the *caṇḍāla* village
on the advice
of his ministers;

take me, like the groom takes
his young
bride-to-be.

Source: *Singing the Body of God: The Hymns of Vedāntadeśika in Their South Indian Tradition*, translated by Steven Paul Hopkins (Oxford: Oxford University Press, 2002).

Selections from the *Śrīmad Viṣṇu Tattva Vinirṇaya* of Madhva

1. I offer adoration always to Nārāyaṇa, who is cognizable in all his uniqueness only through the right scriptures, who wholly transcends the kṣara [individual selves] and the akṣara [non-individual selves] and who is flawless and abounds in all excellent attributes.
2. With a view to facilitate the comprehension on the part of good men, I will establish the truth of these adjectives (applied to Nārāyaṇa) in the order in which they have been enunciated through statements of scriptures and arguments corroborative of them. . . .

21. The validity of the Veda (as of all other sources of knowledge) is intrinsic. Otherwise the fallacy of infinite regress would result.

22. The validity cannot be said to depend upon the argument adduced (above), for arguments merely serve to remove the flaws of thought.
23. To those whose thought is flawless the validity is self-established. . . .
25. Only those with defects of thought suspect the validity of a given cognition and therefore we urge that invalidity is determinable extrinsically.
26. But validity is self-established.
27. It cannot be maintained that letters originate just when they are pronounced.
28. That would contradict the recognition of the form, "This is the same that was uttered before." . . .
45. It is not reasonable to think of the letters and words of the Vedas as non-eternal, for, as God is omniscient, they are always being intuited by him.
46. It is not tenable to say that they subsist only as impressions of former experience as in the case of transient objects like jars and so on.
47. As it is already pointed out, such a supposition would go against the fact of recognition. . . .
65. Further, if difference is established by perception and inference, scripture asserting non-difference must be construed as false just on the ground of its contradiction to what is established by these other means of knowledge. . . .
68. Even if a scripture is stronger than the other means of knowledge like perception, it cannot have validity if it conflicts with the means of knowledge on which it depends and on whose foundation it is itself built up. . . .
72. Experience itself establishes the difference between the individual self and God whose existence is supposed to be proved by inference. For it is a matter of everyone's experience that he is not the author of all. The scripture can have no validity if it contradicts experience.
73. Otherwise even the experience of the truth of the scripture becomes false. . . .
98. Therefore, as non-difference (between God and the individual self) is contradicted by all the sources of knowledge, it is not the purport of the scriptures. On the contrary, the supreme purport of all the scriptures is the pre-eminence of Viṣṇu over every other entity. . . .
102. It is reasonable that all scriptures should have as their supreme purport the absolute greatness of Viṣṇu. . . .
105. This liberation is not to be attained except by the grace of Viṣṇu. . . .
112. Love is particularly seen to arise towards an individual who acknowledges the superiority in qualities in one and it is not seen to arise in response to the affirmation of identity. . . .

117. Therefore all [remembered and revealed texts] have their supreme purport in the surpassing excellence of the attributes of Viṣṇu.
118. There is no proof for the hypothesis that their purport is the identity of the supreme being and the individual selves.
119. The argument, "Difference is apprehended as either the substantive or the adjectival factor and the apprehension of the substantive and adjectival factors (as mutually different) presupposes the grasp of difference. Similarly, the apprehension of difference presupposes the apprehension of the entity that differs and the entity from which it differs and the apprehension of these entities in such mutual exclusiveness presupposes the apprehension of their difference. Thus in both ways the fallacy of "mutual dependence is inevitable" is unsound, because difference is the very substantive essence or essential nature of entities. . . .
122. Difference is apprehended when the essential nature is apprehended. The essential nature of an entity as generally unique and different from all else is apprehended. . . .
135. Therefore the apprehension of difference is logically explicable. . . .
141. Therefore, the logic that seeks to dismiss all difference is absolutely fallacious as it is diametrically opposed to all [revelation, remembrance], perception and inference.
142. It ought not to be said that in reality there is no difference but in the practical and empirical world there is difference. . . .
149. In fact by illusion we mean precisely this misperception of the non-existent as existent and of the existent as non-existent. . . .
159. Therefore (1) as there is nothing inexplicable (as either being or non-being), (2) as the non-existent is considered to be uncognisable, and (3) as difference is a matter of experience, difference becomes real and thus the non-duality of the ultimate reality is impossible. . . .
164. Hence the supreme purport of all the scriptures is the transcendent greatness of Viṣṇu over every other entity. . . .
168. There is no scriptural passage in support of the said unity. All the scriptures indicate difference. . . .
199. The [revelation establishes] that the term jīva [self] stands for Bhagavān Aniruddha.
200. Viṣṇu is said to be jīva [self] because he sustains always the senses (in the body). He, the all-pervading one, enters the great elements, after mixing the three elements, enters the bodies, both unmoving and moving and sets in

motion from state to state the transmigrating individual self, who is defined by his everlasting difference from him. It is by the presence of Viṣṇu that the individual becomes glad even if he were to get into the condition of a tree. . . .

207. The individual self cannot be the ultimate sustainer of life. . . .

231. By the knowledge of the "one" the knowledge of "all" is attained, because the "one" is dominant, because there is some similarity between it and all and also because it is the cause of all.

232. By knowing the "one," all can be known not because everything other than the one is false.

233. By the knowledge of the real, the knowledge of the unreal is not gained.

234. One who knows the mother-of-pearl (which is) does not (by virtue of that knowledge) know silver (which is not).

235. For the two units of knowledge are contradictory of each other. . . .

257. Therefore, nowhere in the sacred texts the unreality of the world is proclaimed.

258. (On the other hand all of them are to the following effect:) "The supreme God, omniscient, ruling over all minds, superior to all else, and independent, created real entities running through all times."

259. "The supreme God, who also receives desirable offerings from the devotees and also grants to them desirable boons, created the universe and the universe created by him is real. It is not futile. O wealthy Indra and Bṛhaspati, the universe that is under your control is real. Your work in the matter of protecting the real universe and the waters, are not comprehended by any other gods (not to speak of my not comprehending). The great and real deeds of this great and real god are expounded now alone." . . .

263. The world is said to be [the illusion of unreality], because it is a product of intelligence. It is called [non-order], because it is pervaded by him, who is the activating force. It is called [illusion of reality] and [non-order] even though it is not removable by knowledge and is eternal as a process. "A" is the name of the supreme deity. By him is the world made real and its nature is maintained by him. Therefore, it is described as [non-real]. That all-pervading Lord is the Reality of realities. He is to the world what the sun is to the rainbow. . . .

270. And difference is not unreal. . . .

273. "The supreme Self is real. The individual self is real. Difference is real, difference is real, difference is real."

274. "The supreme Being is not such that he can be worshipped by sinners. The supreme Being is not such that he can be worshipped by sinners. The supreme Being is not such that he can be worshipped by sinners."

275. "The supreme Self is absolutely independent, all knowing, all powerful, supremely blissful and ultimate. But the individual self is dependent on him, knows a little, has limited power, is miserable and is finite." Such texts prove that difference is real.
276. This reality (ascribed to difference) is no lower degree of reality. . . .
299. The words of the text, "become one in the supreme ātman [imperishable self]," enunciating that Brahman is the seat of the process of becoming one, intimate difference.
300. Otherwise, the statement ought to have been that they become the supreme *ātman* itself.
301. "The unity of jīva with the Lord consists of sameness of thought or it may mean dwelling in the same place. Such sameness of habitation is relative to some particular manifestation of the Lord. It is not unity of essential being. For even the released individual is different from him. The difference between the two lies in the Lord being independent and infinite and the individual and the individual being finite and dependent." Such are the words of *Parama-śruti*. . . .
316. It is suggested that each one should consider himself the only jīva [self] in question; but such alternative points of view cannot all be true of reality; the only conclusion would be that the world is not a product of any false imagination whatever. . . .
322. There is no shred of evidence in support of the thesis that the entire world is the figment of the imagination of a single *jīva* [self]. . . .
328. The world of duality is comprehended by the supreme Lord and is protected by him and hence it is not a product of illusory imagination. . . .
340. The *Parama-śruti* says: "The universe consists of five differences. They are the differences between God and the individual self, that between God and insentient matter, that among individual selves, that between insentient matter and individual self and that among the material entities themselves. This is real and unoriginated. If it were originated, it would perish. But it does not perish. Nor is it a fabrication of illusion. If it were so, it would have disappeared. But it does not disappear. Therefore, the view that there is no duality is the view of the ignorant. The view of the enlightened is that this world is comprehended and protected by Viṣṇu. Therefore, it is proclaimed to be real. But Hari alone is supreme." . . .
349. Nowhere do we have the illusory superimposition of the non-self on the self.
350. We see no one who gets into the illusion "I am not I."

351. But the theorists under discussion hold that the world is the superimposition of the non-self on the self.
352. If it is supposed that there is an illusory superimposition of the self on the non-self independent of the superimposition of the non-self on the self, then the non-self must have reality.
353. Then if it is supposed that reality is one without a second, it follows that the non-self alone exists and the self does not. . . .
363. And there is absolutely no philosophical difficulty in the way of affirming the reality of the world of difference.
364. The school of Advaita which postulates a plurality of individual souls also asserts the unreality of differences. . . .
365. Even according to it plurality is produced by unreal adjuncts.
366. Nowhere do we see differences being generated by unreal adjuncts.
367. The very concept of an unreal adjunct is untenable, because it is of the nature of imagining the self as non-self.
368. Illusory creations occur only when there is another similar entity in reality and only on some substratum which resembles the other entity in being a substance etc. . . .
372. If it is maintained (as is done) that the single Brahman is caught up in rebirth (as one jīva) and gets liberation (as another jīva) owing to differences in adjuncts, then as the bound selves will always be there, Brahman will always be caught up in [rebirth].
373. Hence even the attainment of identity with Brahman cannot be release, for that Brahman is ever associated with adjuncts.
374. It cannot be argued that the pure Brahman is not associated as such with any adjunct; for, to postulate association with another adjunct as a pre-condition of association with the adjunct in question is to perpetrate infinite regress.
375. Nor can it be maintained that association with the same adjunct provides the requisite contamination for entering into association with it. For that lands the argument in the fallacy of "atmāśraya."
376. There is a further consideration also damaging the idea of an unreal adjunct.
377. The unreal adjunct is possible only if there is ignorance. What presents itself to consciousness in the absence of ignorance can never be proved unreal.
378. And there can be no ignorance without an unreal adjunct, for only Brahman as conditioned and differentiated by the unreal adjunct, can be ignorant.
379. If the pure Brahman (unmotivated by any adjunct) can be the seat of ignorance, then even the released soul must be liable to ignorance.

380. In that case, ignorance being natural would be real, and being real would constitute a principle besides Brahman itself; the latter cannot be regarded as the sole reality without a second.
381. As it is admitted (by the opponent) that which is natural can never cease to be, ignorance would remain an irremovable entity. "The real can never be terminated." Such is the view in the theory.
382. Thus the fallacy of reciprocal dependence results.
383. Or the fallacy of circular explanation arises, because the position is that if there is ignorance there will be the unreal adjunct, if there is the unreal adjunct there will be the individual self, and if there is the individual self, there can be ignorance in it.
384. It is not logical to hold that the pure Brahman itself is ignorant by virtue of illusion.
385. For, even in that case, the fallacy of reciprocal dependence is inevitable. If there is ignorance, illusion is possible, and if there is illusion, ignorance is possible. . . .
389. The supposition of the unreality of anything, which is a fact of observation, requires the support of stronger evidence and reasoning.
390. If such evidence and reasoning are not there, its reality gets established by the very force of that observation. . . .
392. What is ascertained through perception cannot be dismissed by mere argumentation without the aid of stronger perceptions and scripture.
393. In the matter of the apparent smallness of the length of a tree, distant from the observer, through reason we determine its greater length, because it is a settled principle that the power of the eye is enfeebled in relation to distant objects.
394. That perception is dull with regard to remote objects and that it can be mistaken in the grasp of magnitudes etc., is determined by more powerful perception itself.
395. But in the present instance of the world, the falsity of the perception of the world is not established by any mode of (direct) knowledge.
396. In particular the direct experience of knowledge and ignorance, pleasure and pain, and the uniqueness of the self, are not falsified by any direct experience.
397. Therefore, as the life of transmigratory existence is real and as what is real cannot be terminated, there can be no emancipation. . . .
407. Further, does the adjunct seize a part of the self? or does it seize the whole?
408. If it is admitted that it seizes a part only, that would imply that the self is composed of parts and according to the theory everything composed of parts is non-eternal. If the adjunct seizes the whole self, then it cannot be

the principle of differentiation. If it is supposed that the self has parts owning to an adjunct and that the adjunct is the same as the limiting adjunct whose seizing of the self is being examined, we have the fallacy of self-dependence. If on the contrary, some other adjunct is said to introduce distinctions within the self, and the adjunct under consideration seizes one of the parts differentiated by the other adjunct, we have landed ourselves in infinite regress.

409. As Īśvara is omnipresent, he cannot be said to be differentiated from Brahman as a result of the action of some adjunct.

410. There is no instance of two entities infinite in space and time being differentiated through the action of an adjunct.

411. As the self-same Īśvara dwells in all the bodily adjuncts and as differences are unreal, on the analogy of the unity of the experiencer in a body in spite of the multiplicity of its members, Īśvara himself must be the experiencer of all the pleasures and pains of all. . . .

424. It cannot also be maintained that differences are due to beginningless differences of karma (merit and demerit).

425. If difference owning to the action of adjuncts are there, there will be differences of karma. Again if differences of karma are there, there will be differences due to adjuncts. Thus reciprocal dependence arises again.

426. Thus, as the school is infected with countless fallacies, only with a view to avoid excess of volume, the discussion is being closed.

427. Thus the purport of the [revelation] is not non-difference, for that would stand contradicted by all the [means of knowledge]. . . .

435. There is no instance of knowledge without a knower and an object to be known.

436. And (as argued out before), the difference between the jīva [soul] and Īśvara is not a matter established otherwise than through scriptures. Therefore, the scripture cannot aim at the teaching of identity between jīva [soul] and Īśvara. . .

438. Thus it is established that Bhagavān Nārāyaṇa is known only through the right scriptures as different from all, and as surpassing all. . . .

Source: *Śrīmad Viṣṇu* Tattva Vinirṇaya of *Śrī Madhvācārya*, translated by S. S. Raghavachar (Mangalore: Sri Ramakrishna Ashrama, 1959).

6

Krishna Devotionalism

Krishna becomes a major figure in Indian religious culture with the appearance of the eighteen books of the *Mahābhārata,* which like the other major epic, the *Rāmāya ṇa,* focuses its attention on such topics as kingship, court intrigue, deception, exile, war, destruction, death, reunion, love, jealousy, and hate. Both epics began as bardic narratives and were orally transmitted over centuries before assuming their written forms. Brahmin scholars, who inserted pieces about dharma into them and also retold the tales from a priestly perspective, reworked both epics. A cultural tension between orthodox ritualists and more autonomous ascetics spilled over into the literature. This development overlapped with the advent of devotional religion, which lead to an additional reworking of the material. In order to understand the place of Krishna in historically later devotional Hinduism, it is worthwhile to review the narrative of the *Mahābhārata,* which is attributed by tradition to a sage named Vyāsa (meaning arranger or compiler). Vyāsa is probably a mythical or a composite figure for several compilers of the epic. He appears at points in the text itself by suddenly making an appearance. At other times, his words or actions are recalled, which again gives him a presence within the body of the text. Thus Vyāsa is not a detached compiler of the text, but is rather a direct or indirect participant in the narrative. The *Mahābhārata* is classified in Indian literature an as *itihāsa* (chronicle). The term *itihāsa* means literally the following: thus (*iti*), indeed (ha), it was (*āsa*). This prodigious epic is sometimes called the fifth Veda, which is an attempt to make two assertions: it possesses continuity with the past, and it is as authoritative as the sacred Vedas.[1]

Before the text finally gained its written form between 300 and 450 C.E. in northern India, it enjoyed a long period of oral transmission by *sūtas* or bards.[2] The title of the epic means the "Great narrative of the descendents of Bharata" (India). It origins date to around 400 B.C.E. and grew over a long period to its present substantial size of 100,000 verses divided into eighteen books, before achieving its written form around the period of the Gupta Dynasty around 400 C.E.[3] Dates of 400 B.C.E. to 200 C.E. have also been offered by scholars.[4] Another theory of the date and composition of the epic argues for a date of composition between the mid-second century B.C.E. and the beginning of the Common Era by a group of poor Brahmins who may have enjoyed the financial support of royal or merchant patrons.[5] Such a theory of composition suggests a unified process of the epic's creation and a cohesive literary character. But argument for the text being composed by a committee of Brahmins working together synchronously within a relatively short period of time does not explain the variations and discontinuities of the text.[6] A counter argument views a gradualist model as more plausible.

In addition to the eighteen books of the epic, the *Harivaṃśa* represents a supplement to the epic by forming a nineteenth book. The epic is seven times the combined size of Homer's *Iliad* and *Odyssey*. It is possible that the *Mahābhārata* evolved from a classical heroic epic, was transformed into a religious didactic epic, and also paradoxically retained some common aspects of archaic folklore.[7] The central narrative relates an apocalyptic story in the sense of uncovering a hidden divine plan for the destruction of a corrupt stratum of society. From one perspective, the narrative suggests a divine alliance of priest and divine beings by which it becomes possible to replace the unrighteous usurpers.

Vyāsa's story is about the feuding Pāṇḍava and Kaurava families from Bharata, a region of the upper Ganges basin around modern Delhi. In short, the Pāṇḍavas represent a coalition of priests and gods, whereas the Kauravas suggest demonic forces. The feuding families are related by blood of the two brothers named Pāṇḍu and Dhṛtarāṣṭra, who were educated by their uncle Bhīsma. Dhṛtarāṣṭra is forbidden to rule because of the handicap of his blindness but he marries Gāndhārī, who gives birth to a hundred sons, called the Kauravas. In contrast to the fecundity of this couple, the ruling king Pāṇḍu does not dare to have sex with his two wives named Kuntī and Mādrī because of a curse that he would die if he engaged in sexual intercourse. Using a boon, Kuntī invokes various divine beings and is able to conceive three sons by them: the gods Dharma, Vāyu, and Indra help her to conceive, respectively, Yudhiṣṭhira, Bhīma, and Arjuna. Kuntī utilizes the boon further to help Mādrī conceive the twins Nakula and Sahadeva by the twin divine Aśvins. A rationale for these incarnations is provided early in the epic (Mbh 1.58) when the Earth becomes distressed and calls for help because she is being oppressed by an overpopulation of incarnated demonic beings (*asuras*).

Each of the Pāṇḍava brothers embodies different forms of symbolic significance. Yudhiṣṭhira stands for dharma and duties of law. The impulsive Bhīma represents the energy of physical force and violence, and he stands for the protective aspect of kingship. The twins Nakula and Sahadeva symbolize abundance and multiplicity with respect to fertility and growth that characterizes the third (Vaiśya) order of society. The fifth brother, Arjuna, is an image of the king as a being of light that unites the attributes of the others within himself. After Pāṇḍu's attempt at sexual intercourse with her and his subsequent death, Mādrī becomes implicated in his death, and she voluntarily commits immolation (*sati*) on her husband's funeral pyre. This leaves Kuntī with the responsibility of raising the five sons. After the death of Pāṇḍu, the dual sets of cousins are raised together and learn the same military skills from their uncle Droṇa. The blind Dhṛtarāṣṭra functions as the regent of the kingdom until Yudhiṣṭhira reaches the proper age to assume leadership of the kingdom.

A narrative thread that runs throughout the epic is the rivalry between the cousins and jealously of the Kauravas for the Pāṇḍavas. The five Pāṇḍavas and their mother avoid an assassination attempt–a fire started by the envious party—by escaping through an underground tunnel. The rivalry is also evident when there is a contest for the hand of Draupadī, which concludes with the victory of Arjuna by means of his skill in archery. Draupadī becomes the wife of the five brothers. Draupadī represents a secret incarnation of the goddess Śrī, an embodiment of the auspiciousness and prosperity needed by any successful king. When they return home, the brothers receive half the kingdom from the blind regent, and they establish their capital of Indraprāṣṭha (Indra's Station).

After successful military campaigns, Yudhiṣṭhira becomes a universal monarch by conquering enemies in the four directions. The king's victories culminate with a celebration of a royal consecration (*rājasūya*) ritual. In reaction to the success of the Pāṇḍavas, the Kauravas become increasingly jealous, and they devise a plan to undermine their cousins by challenging them to a game of dice, which is inherently connected to fate. This connection to fate associates dicing with such negative aspects as destructiveness, disintegration, crookedness, and unbalancing forces.[8] These features suggest a future war at which time everything will be made right.

The otherwise virtuous Yudhiṣṭhira's weakness for gambling proves to be his undoing. Along with addictions to women, hunting, and drinking, the epic considers dice to be the worse vice (Mbh 3:14, 7). With the game rigged by the duplicitous Duryodhana, the king loses successively his wealth, brothers, himself, and wife jointly shared by the brothers. Draupadī is insulted and humiliated by the Kaurava Duḥśāsana even though she is menstruating. She is dragged into the assembly hall by the hair, and an attempt is made to publicly strip her, but this miraculously fails as an unending flow of fabric keeps her clothed. The outraged Draupadī challenges Yudhiṣṭhira's right to stake her in the dice game. She demands to know if he had already gambled himself away before wagering her. The blind Dhṛtarāṣṭra intervenes by calling the entire match off, restores to Yudhiṣṭhira what he lost, and grants freedom to Draupadī and her five husbands. Again, Yudhiṣṭhira is challenged to gamble everything on one final throw of the dice. The agreed wager involves a period of exile if he should lose, versus the restoration of all previous loses. After the gambling-addicted Yudhiṣṭhira loses for the last time, the brothers and their wife go into exile for twelve years in the forest and a thirteenth year in which they must live incognito before returning to reclaim their kingdom. Their exile is told in the third book of the epic called the "Book of the Forest." Within this long part of the epic, there are numerous tales, and the importance of pilgrimage is stressed.

The fourth book of the epic recounts the final year of exile at the court of king Virāta, for whom this book of the epic is named. The Pāṇḍavas disguise themselves as humble servants at the court. Draupadī becomes, for instance, a low-caste hairdresser and maid, Yudhiṣṭhira poses as a master of dicing named Kanka, which is a carrion-eating and death-dealing bird, and Arjuna, who is a paragon of manhood, becomes a eunuch and lives in a harem and teaches dancing to women of the palace.[9] Such disguises represent opposites of the genuine natures of the subjects. After nearly having their identity revealed at a couple of points, they finally reveal themselves, to the utter astonishment of Virāta; he offers his daughter to Arjuna, who accepts her as wife for his son Abhimanyu instead of himself.

When the Pāṇḍavas are unable to reclaim their kingdom and peace negotiations fail, the rival sides prepare for war by enlisting allies and appointing commanders. Krishna joins, the Pāṇḍavas, whereas his army links itself with the other party. The Kauravas are also able to recruit figures such as Bhīṣma, Droṇa, and Karṇa. The sixth book describes the furious battle and Vyāsa's granting of a boon to Dhṛtarāṣṭra to overcome his innate blindness. The boon allows his charioteer Samjaya to describe the battle in detail. When the armies are prepared for battle, Arjuna is suddenly afflicted by doubts, turns to his charioteer Krishna, and asks for advice. The eighteen chapters of the *Bhagavad Gītā* capture the ensuing dialogue between the warrior and his charioteer.

The *Bhagavad Gītā* constitutes chapters 32–40 of the sixth book, Bhīṣma Parvan, which was inserted into the larger epic sometime between 200 B.C.E. and 100 C.E. The *Gītā* was conceived and created within the context of the larger epic narrative, and was not an independent text that was simply added or wandered into the epic. The *Gītā* was developed to bring a dramatic climax and solution to the human dilemma, which was that between worldly duty (*dharma*) and worldly renunciation or liberation (mokṣa), created by a just and pernicious war. Although the text does not satisfactorily resolve the dilemma, the *Gītā* provides a unique context within which to consider the problem.

With opposing armies assembled across from each other on the field of Kurukṣetra, a flat plain near the present city of Delhi and an ancient sacred place between two sacred rivers–Yamunā and Sarasvatī–and the battle about to begin, Arjuna, greatest of the Pāṇḍava warriors, rides to the front of the battlefield with his charioteer Krishna. At this precise location between the two opposing armies, their dialogue begins, which is part of a new revelation in Hindu religion and literature that is personal, historic, and original. A reader can best grasp the teaching method of the *Gītā* as progressive and dialogical. In other words, Krishna, who functions as the primary instructor, slowly reveals the whole truth as the text unfolds his message.

The entire sixth book of the *Mahābhārata* is named for the Kauravas' commander named Bhīṣma, who becomes mortally wounded and lies on a bed of arrows. The battle continues for the next three books, bearing the names of the Kaurava commanders: Droṇa, Karṇa, and Śalya. They relate the death of Arjuna's son Abhimanyu, Arjuna's revenge, the duplicitous killing of Droṇa, Bhīma's revenge on Duḥśāsana for humiliating Draupadī, Arjuna's destruction of Karṇa, and the killing of the final commander-in-chief Śalya and his brother by Yudhiṣṭhira. The Kaurava army is finally led to defeat by Duryodhana, who at one point takes refuge in a lake before engaging in a mace dual with Bhīma. Duryodhana is eventually defeated after being struck in his thigh with the mace, which fulfils Bhīma's earlier vow to deliver such a devastating blow. Protests of foul play are leveled at the Pāṇḍavas and Krishna. Three remaining Kaurava warriors successfully execute a counterattack against the sleeping Pāṇḍava army. The army is massacred; although the five brothers and Krishna are not present, but away at the capital. The dying Duryodhana learns of the total destruction of his cousins, army. The theme of the eleventh book, entitled the "Book of the Women" is a lament over the carnage by the blind Dhṛtaraṣṭra and various women who survey the battlefield. Characters express recriminations and make confessions. Gāndāri wants to curse the Pāṇḍavas for the massive carnage, but the sage Vyāsa dissuades her; she curses Krishna instead and holds him responsible for the massive slaughter. The dead are cremated on orders of Yudhiṣṭhira, while the blind regent and others proceed to the Ganges River to make offerings to the deceased.

From one perspective, if the Pāṇḍavas represent the incarnation of divine beings and the Kauravas signify the incarnations of demonic beings, the war is an updated version of the cosmic conflict of Indra and Vṛtra of the vedic cosmogonic tale. From another perspective, the war symbolizes an all-consuming sacrificial fire. Kurukṣetra, the location of the war is referred to as a sacrificial altar (Mbh 3.81.178). The killing that occurs at this sacrificial altar of human beings becomes the offering to the gods.[10] Moreover, the scope of the destruction suggests a cosmic dissolution (*pralaya*) that occurs at regular intervals within the context of cosmic cycles of time.[11] The presence of Krishna within the epic narrative supports this view because he is the lord of cosmic dissolution, as evident in the eleventh chapter of the *Bhagavad Gītā* (11.32).

The longest book of the epic, called the "Book of the Peace," concludes the war. Yudhiṣṭhira is congratulated on his victory, but the king does not grasp the result as a reason for celebration. Vyāsa persuades the victorious king to seek the advice of the dying Bhīṣma who is still lying on his bed of arrows. Bhīṣma's advice is contained in the "Book of Instruction," which is subdivided into lessons about the duties of kings during peaceful times, the king's responsibilities during periods of conflict, the path to liberation, and the merits of giving. In order to atone for all the death and suffering, Yudhiṣṭhira decides to offer a horse sacrifice, which provides the name for the fourteenth book. The fifteenth book, called "The Stay at the Hermitage," recalls the blind Dhṛtarāṣṭra's retirement to the forest along with others, and their perishing in a forest fire.

The deaths of Krishna, his brother Balarāma, and their tribes are recalled in "The Book of the Clubs." After Krishna is killed by a hunter's arrow, the ocean submerges his capital, and his soul is merged back into Viṣṇu. After learning of the death of Krishna and his tribe, the Pāṇḍavas renounce the world, leaving Arjuna's grandson as ruler. As they make their way north to the Himālayas or polar mountain toward the heavenly realm, they die one by one during the journey, with Draupadī being the first to fall. Finally, Yudhiṣṭhira is the only person left, and he continues the journey followed by his faithful dog. With the final episode, called "The Book of the Ascent to Heaven," Yudhiṣṭhira enters heaven after enduring various tests that involve his refusal to abandon his dog, which is revealed as an incarnation of the god Dharma. A final test of his virtue occurs in heaven when Yudhiṣṭhira sees only his deceased enemies there, and he is told that his brothers are in hell. He insists on joining his brothers in hell, but their location in heaven is finally revealed to him, and he passes his final test. In general, the central narrative of the epic enables a reader to grasp that the role of the king is not necessarily glorious and that the burdens of the position test the fortitude of the best of men, especially those with innate character flaws.

Very different from the calculating, manipulative, duplicitous warrior and awe-inspiring deity of the *Gītā*, is the purāṇic Krishna, who becomes incarnated with the purpose of destroying his evil uncle Kaṃsa. He appears as a more playful, mischievous, tricky, and mirthful figure, who is also an erotic deity who as an adolescent drives women mad with passion. Selections here from the tenth book of the *Bhāgavata Purāṇa*, which probably assumed its current written form around 950 C.E., illustrate many of these features.

The epic and purāṇic images of Krishna inspired the poet Jayadeva to compose the *Gitāgovinda,* whose theme is the erotic relationship between Krishna and his consort Rādhā, in 1170; this work made a major contribution to identifying the cowherd lover of the deity. The poets Caṇḍīdāsa (c. 1350–c. 1430) and Sūrdās (born 1478) were also inspired to express their devotion in poetry. The former poet often focused on the illicit love affair of the deity and his consort, whereas the latter composed poems about Rādhā as the legitimate spouse of Krishna and the God's childhood exploits. Sūrdās is alleged to have been blind from birth, though contemporary scholarship questions the poet's blindness, which becomes a sign of divine grace, arguing that this trait of the poet developed in later hagiographical literature, two hundred years after his death.[12]

Sūrdās is famous for the work *Sūrsāgar* (Sūr's Ocean) attributed to him, although it does not represent the effort of a single poet. This sprawling text gradually evolved within a sectarian context, and it includes the poems of several artists. Within this work, Sūrdās depicts himself as an abject sinner. This self-portrait is meant to locate "all his hearers somewhere inside the pale of divine mercy at whose boundary he stands."[13]

The sixteenth-century poet Mīrābāī was a female poet with wide popularity, a Rajput princess who rejected her earthly husband for her genuine spouse, Krishna. After her marriage to a mortal prince and entry into her new home, she refused to bow humbly to her mother-in-law or embrace the goddess worshiped by the family, as required by social norms. Moreover, Mīrābāī did not execute her social duties, but rather spent her time associating with wandering holy people, who were devoted to her own secret husband Krishna. Her exasperated in-laws poisoned her with a concoction made as an offering to an icon of Krishna's feet.

Within her throat the liquid was said to have been transformed into an immortal nectar due to its contact with the feet of the god; this enabled her to survive and continue to sing poems. She left home and became a wandering ascetic; at the end of her life, she is said to have merged with the icon of Krishna in a temple. Whether this traditional legendary account possesses any historical validity is debated among scholars. Reflecting her own life, according to traditional depiction, her poems are often defiant in tone, and they exhibit the illict love between the blue god and his *gopīs*, who abandon their husbands and family due to their love of the deity.

Krishna devotionalism also inspired sectarian movements such as the Rādhāvallabha sect, Vallabhācāryas, Mahānubhāvas, and the cult of Viṭhobā in north India, and the Gauḍīya Vaiṣṇavism of the Bengal region. The Rādhāvallabha tradition was allegedly established by Śrī Hit Harivamś (1502–1552), whose theology depicted Rādhā as the ground of being in the universe, bestower of bliss, and more powerful than Krishna. Devotees can share in the blissful experience of Rādhā and Krishna in sexual union by playing the role of friends of the divine couple. The Vallabhācāryas trace their origin to the theologian named Vallabha (1479–1531), who devised a system of pure nondualism (Śuddhādvaita), which is purified by the power of devotion (*bhakti*) and rejection of the doctrine of illusion (*māyā*)–unlike the Advaita Vedānta or nondual monism of Śaṅkara. Another name used to refer to Vallabha's type of devotion was "path of grace" (*puṣṭimārga*). This chapter includes selctions from Vallabha's work entitled *Subodinī*, a commentary on book ten of the *Bhāgavata Purāṇa*. I have only include Vallabha's commentary on the text, and I have deleted his direct quotations of the text for reasons of space.

In contrast to the northern devotionalism of Harivamś and Vallabha (whose family came from south India, but who lived in the north), Caitanya (1486–1534) revived Krishna devotion in the Bengal region of India with his emotional enthusiasm and public singing for the glory of his deity. Caitanya was also instrumental in spreading Krishna devotion from Bengal to the southern and northern parts of the country. His life and exploits are entertainingly depicted in the hagiographical work entitled the *Caitanyacaritāmṛta* (Immortal Acts of Caitanya) by Kṛṣṇadāsa Kavirāja (1517–c.1615 or 1620), which captures his deep devotionalism and madness. While praying at a Krishna temple, the deeply learned Kavirāja received a sign that he should write the book, which focuses on the theme of play (*līlā*) of the saint. The emphasis on play is evident in the structure of the book, which is arranged into three parts: (1) the *ādi līlā* depicts the early life of Caitanya in seventeen chapters, including his renunciation of the world; (2) the *madhya līlā*, in twenty-five chapters, treats his life in Purī and pilgrimage to the south and to Vṛndāban, along with theological discussions, and (3) the *antya līlā* of twenty chapters deals with his later life, increasing madness, and death.

Caitanya inspired a religious devotional movement that came to be identified as Gauḍīya Vaiṣṇavism, and was centered around the theological contributions of the six Gosvāmins, who produced a prodigious number of theological works in Sanskrit. This anthology uses selections from Rūpa Gosvāmin's work entitled *Bhaktirasāmṛtasindhu* (Ocean of the Essence of Devotional Rasa), which was composed in 1541 in the area of Vṛndāban, which was sacred to Krishna devotionalism. As the title implies, the text focuses on human emotions that are analogous to waves on the ocean and develops devotion directed at Krishna in terms of aesthetic theory. The waves are the many different forms of emotion, but underlying the multitude of waves is a unity grounded in the love for Krishna. Rūpa acknowledges forty-one emotions (*rasas*) with eight being dominant. *Rasa* (literally, sap, juice, essence, taste) is produced from a combination of *vibhāva* (a stimulant that enables one to experience a primary emotion), *anubhāva* (indications that are vocal, physical, and mental that enable meaning to be expressed and conveyed), and *vyabhicāri-bhāva* (temporary emotions). If the context is right, such as watching a play about Krishna, these three aspects give rise to the eight primary rasas: love, humor, compassion, anger, heroic effort, fear, abhorrence, and wonder. This line of analysis leads to Rūpa's major focus on the two kinds of devotion: *vaidhi* (a scripturally based love by which a person seeks protection of god) and *rāgānuga* (a deep and excessive love that leads to attachment to the deity).

In some areas of northern India, Krishna is known as Viṭhoba or Viṭṭhala, who is not identified as the lover of Rādhā, but is now the lawful spouse of Rukmiṇī. This religious tradition gave birth to the Mahānubhāvas (literally, "those who have a great experience"), who were devoted to the five Krishnas—series of five incarnations of the deity. Guṇḍam Rāül, famous for his mad behavior, was also considered an incarnation. This is evident in his biography entitled *Śrī Govindaprabhu Caritra* (The Biography of Govindaprabhu), dated around 1573. The text is also called *Ṛddhipuralīlā* (Deeds of God in Ṛddhipur).

The various examples of Vaiṣṇavism and Śaivism that are reviewed in this part of the anthology are religious movements that are often connected to specific individuals. The names of these individuals are often associated with biographies called hagiographies, a type of literature that combines some truth with legend and fictive myth. A hagiography is often created to guide social and religious practice, to illustrate some desirable quality, and to create a portrait that others hearing or reading the narrative will not only commemorate but also seek to emulate in their lives. Sometimes, however, the actions of a particular subject are intended to astonish listeners or readers without any intention that others will emulate a subject's behavior.

In a hagiography, the life of the holy person is not presented as a chronological record, and hagiographies are not historical records of what actually happened, although the narratives may include actual events–that is, hagiographies are not pure fabrications. A particular religious community plays a vital and creative role in the construction of the narrative, for the hagiography is intended to enhance and promote the growth of a religious movement, while seeking to shape both the movement and the actions of its adherents. The hagiography often records the charisma of the subject, and in them, it is not unusual to find a mortal exhibiting aspects or degrees of divine nature. When a subject is claimed to be an incarnation of the sect's deity, the biography of the subject may be patterned on the mythical narrative of the deity. Caitanya's hagiography, for instance, is distinctly modeled on the play (*līlā*) of Krishna in the *Bhāgavata Purāṇa*. This anthology will include examples of hagiographies of both male and female holy figures.

Selections from the *Bhāgavata Purāṇa* Book 10

Chapter 3. Kṛṣṇa's Birth

1. In due time, an extremely auspicious moment endowed with all good qualities arrived. At the time of [Kṛṣṇa's] birth, the constellations and the stars were

all favourable. The constellation was Rohiṇī, which is presided over by Brahmā.

2. The directions were clear and the sky covered with clusters of visible stars. On the earth there was a happy abundance of mines, pastures, villages and towns.
3. The rivers contained crystal clear water and the ponds were beautiful with lotuses. Lines of trees offered eulogies with the loud sounds of bees and birds.
4. A fresh breeze blew in that region, pleasing the senses and bearing pleasant scents, and the sacred fires of the *brāhmaṇas* blazed forth, undisturbed.
5. The minds of the ascetics and the gods were peaceful, and kettledrums resounded in unison at the moment of birth of the unborn one.
6. The *kinnaras* and *gandharvas* burst into song, the *siddhas* and *cāraṇas* offered prayers, and the *vidyādharas* joyfully danced along with the *apsaras*.
7. The sages and demigods, overflowing with happiness, showered flowers, and the clouds rumbled gently, resonating with the ocean.
8. At midnight, when deep darkness had fallen, Janārdana [Kṛṣṇa], was born. Viṣṇu, who dwells in the heart of everyone, appeared in Devakī, who resembled a goddess, like the full moon appearing in the eastern direction.

9–10. Vasudeva saw that amazing, lotus-eyed child, his four arms wielding the weapons of the conch, club, lotus and disc. He bore the mark of *śrīvatsa*, and the Kaustubha jewel was radiant on his neck. Clad in a yellow garment, he appeared as beautiful as a dark rain-cloud. He was resplendent with a magnificent belt, and arm and wrist bracelets, and his profuse locks were encircled with a lustrous helmet and earrings made of valuable *vaidūrya* gems.

11. Upon seeing his son, Hari, Vasudeva was overwhelmed by the auspicious occasion of Kṛṣṇa's incarnation. His eyes were wide with amazement. Overcome with joy, he bestowed 10,000 cows on the *brāhmaṇas*.
12. Vasudeva understood that this was the supreme being illuminating the birth chamber with his radiance, O Parīṣit, descendant of Brahmā. Realizing his majesty, Vasudeva's fear was dispelled. He praised Kṛṣṇa with body bowed, hands joined in supplication, and concentrated mind. . . .

21. "O Lord of everything and omnipresent one, desiring to protect this world you have incarnated in my house. You will destroy the armies arrayed for battle with millions of demoniac leaders masquerading as kings.
22. But when the barbaric Kaṃsa heard that your birth was to be in our house, he murdered all your brothers born before you. Hearing the reports of your

incarnation from his servants, he is rushing here even now, weapons in hand."

23. Śrī Suka said: Then, Devakī, seeing this son of hers displaying the characteristics of the supreme being, went towards him in great astonishment. She was afraid of Kaṃsa.
24. Śrī Devakī said: "That form which they call *brahman*, unmanifest, original, the light, devoid of the *guṇas*, unchanging, pure being, undifferentiated and devoid of activity is you. You are Viṣṇu himself, the light of the self. . . .
28. You are he, the Lord. Protect us from Kaṃsa, the fearsome son of Ugrasena. We are terrified. But do not reveal this form as the supreme being, the object of meditation, to ordinary sight.
29. Let that sinful one not know about your birth in me, O Madhusādana [Kṛṣṇa]. My mind is disturbed and I am trembling with fear of Kaṃsa on account of you.
30. O Lord of the universe, withdraw that transcendent form. It has four arms and is adorned with the splendour of lotus, club, disc and conch.
31. That supreme person who, at the appropriate occasion at the end of Brahmā's night, bears this entire universe within his own body, is your Lordship, the same person who has entered my womb. How wonderful is this imitation of the human [ways] of the world."
32. Śrī Bhagavān said: "You, in a previous creation, during the era of Svāyambhuva Manu, were Pṛśni, O chaste lady, and this Vasudeva was a faultless *prajāpati* called Sutapā.
33. After you were both instructed by Brahmā in the creation of progeny, you restrained your senses and underwent extreme ascetic practices.
34. You endured the various features of the seasons—heat, cold, sunshine, wind and rain. The impurities of your minds were removed by breath control.
35. You endeavoured to worship me, desiring benedictions from me, your minds appeased by a diet of wind and fallen leaves.
36. In this way, absorbed in me and performing extreme and very arduous disciplines, 12,000 divine years passed by for you both.
37. Then, fully satisfied with your continual austerity, faith and devotion, I manifested in your heart in this form, O sinless one.
38. Being asked to choose a boon, you requested a son like me. So I, the Lord of boon-givers, have become manifest out of a desire to satisfy your desire.
39. You were childless as husband and wife, and had not indulged in sexual intercourse. Deluded by my divine *māyā*, you did not choose liberation.

40. After I had departed, you received the blessing of a son such as me. Having fulfilled your heart's desire, you enjoyed the pleasures of sexual intercourse.

41. Not finding anyone else in the world who was my equal in the qualities of magnanimity and virtue, I became your son, known as Pṛśnigarbha, born of Pṛśni.

42. As Upendra, I was again born from both of them—that is, you both—of Kaśyapa in the womb of Aditi. Because I was a dwarf, I became known as Vāmana [the dwarf].

43. In this third appearance, I have now again taken birth from you both through that same form [of Viṣṇu]. I have stated the facts, O chaste lady.

44. This form was shown to you to remind you of my previous birth. Otherwise, knowledge of my real nature would not arise, because of my appearance as a mortal.

45. Both of you, constantly thinking affectionately of me in my nature as *brahman*, as well as in my nature as a son, will attain my supreme destination."

46. After speaking in this way, Lord Hari [Kṛṣṇa] fell silent and immediately changed into an ordinary child through his *yogamāyā* power of illusion while his parents were watching.

47. Vasudeva, the son of Sūra, removed his son from the room of the birth as had been directed by the Lord. Then, just at the time that he wanted to leave, Yogamāyā was born to the wife of Nanda.

48–49. As Vasudeva approached carrying Kṛṣṇa, all the entrances, which had been securely shut with huge doors and iron bolts and chains, opened of their own accord through Yogamāyā's influence, just as darkness [disappears] before the sun. Meanwhile, all of the doorkeepers and citizens slept, their consciousness and all their functions overcome [by sleep]. The clouds, rumbling mildly, showered rain. Śeṣa followed, warding off the water with his hoods. . . .

51. On reaching Nanda's Vraj, Vasudeva found all the cowherd men there fast asleep. Putting his son down on Yaśodā's bed and picking up her daughter, he again returned home.

52. Vasudeva then put the infant girl down on the bed of Devakī, refastened his leg-shackles, and remained as he was before.

53. Afterwards, Yaśodā, Nanda's wife, aware of the birth but exhausted, and with her memory stolen by sleep, could not recall the gender of the child.

Chapter 4. Kaṃsa's Encounter with the Goddess and his Council with his Ministers

1. Śrī Śuka said: The doors of the house, both inside and outside, were closed as they had been previously. Then the doorkeepers, hearing the cries of a child, sprang to their feet.
2. They hurriedly approached Kaṃsa, the king of the Bhojas, and informed him of Devakī's delivery, which he had been anxiously awaiting.
3. He got up from his bed quickly, thinking "Death is here!" Stumbling along with his hair loose, he came in haste to the delivery room.
4. That pious divine and wretched lady spoke to her brother piteously: "You should not kill a female—she will be your daughter-in-law, O auspicious one.
5. Impelled by fate, you killed many infants, who were radiant as fire, O brother. You should leave me one daughter.
6. Truly, I am your younger sister, a desperate woman whose children have all been killed, O master. You should give me this last female infant, O sibling. I am a pitiful soul."
7. Śrī Śuka said: Devakī clung on to her infant like a wretched creature. Although implored by his sobbing sister, that brute reviled her and tore the infant from her clasp.
8. Having seized his sister's newborn infant by the feet, Kaṃsa dashed it against the surface of a rock, his [brotherly] affection displaced by self-interest.
9. Flying up immediately from his grasp, the younger sister of Viṣṇu rose into the sky and manifested herself as the goddess, bearing weapons in her eight mighty arms.
10. She was decorated with divine garlands, garments, ointments, jewels and decorations, and bore the bow, trident, arrows, shield, sword, conch, disc, and club.
11. As she was being praised by the *siddhas*, *cāraṇas*, *gandharvas*, *apsarās*, *kinnaras* and *uraga* serpents, and propitiated by extravagant offerings, she spoke the following words:
12. "What will be achieved by killing me, you fool? Your enemy from a former life, the bearer of your death, has already been born somewhere else. Do not kill helpless creatures capriciously."
13. The illustrious goddess Māyā spoke in this way to Kaṃsa. She became known by many names on the earth in many different places.
14. Hearing what she had spoken, Kaṃsa was astonished. Freeing Devakī and Vasudeva, he addressed them courteously:
15. "Alas, O sister! Shame on me, O brother-in-law! Like a cannibal [eating] his own offspring, I have killed many sons. I am an evil person. . . ."

29. When the night had passed, Kaṃsa summoned his ministers and told them everything that Yogamāyā had said.
30. Hearing these words of their master, the incompetent demons, who were enemies of the demigods and bore grudges against them, replied:
31. "If this is the case, O king of the Bhojas, then we will today kill all the babies who are ten days old, as well as those who are not yet ten, in all the towns, villages and pastures. . . ."
43. Śrī Suka said: After holding council with his ministers in this fashion, the wicked-minded Kaṃsa, a demon trapped in the snare of destiny, decided that persecution of the *brāhmaṇas* was the solution.
44. He commanded the demons, who could assume any form at will, and who were by nature inclined to killing, to engage in the wholesale slaughter of saintly people. Then Kaṃsa entered his residence.
45. The demons, who had *rājasic* dispositions, and whose minds were bewildered by *tamas*, undertook a campaign of enmity against saintly people. The deaths of these demons were imminent.
46. The harassment of the great destroys all good fortunes—length of life, beauty, fame, religious practice, heaven and blessings.

Chapter 5. The Meeting of Nanda and Vasudeva

1. Śrī Śuka said: After his son had been born, the noble-minded Nanda's joy blossomed. Bathed, purified and decorated, he summoned *brāhmaṇas* who knew the Veda.
2. When he had arranged for the recitation of benedictory Vedic *mantras* and the birth ceremonies for his son, he also performed the worship of the gods and the ancestors, according to the appropriate injunctions.
3. He gave 200,000 well-decorated cows, and seven mountains of sesame, decorated with gold cloth and streams of jewels, to the *brāhmaṇas.*
4. Things become purified through time, through bathing and cleansing, through rites of passage, through austerities, through oblations, through charity and through contentment. The soul becomes purified through knowledge of the self.
5. *Brāhmaṇas*, together with *sūta*, *māgadha* and *vandī* bards, and with singers, recited auspicious blessings, and drums and kettledrums resounded.
6. The gateways of Vraj [were decorated with] various leaves, pieces of cloth, garlands, banners and flags. Inside the houses, the courtyards and doors were sprinkled with water and cleansed.
7. The cows, bulls and calves were smeared with oil and turmeric, and [decorated with] garlands of gold, wreaths of peacock tail-feathers and various minerals.

8. The *gopas* were decorated with very valuable cloth, ornaments, garments and turbans, and arrived bearing various gifts, O king.
9. The *gopīs* were delighted when they heard of the birth of Yaśodā's son. They decorated themselves with garments, ornaments and mascara. . . .
19. After assigning the protection of Gokula to the *gopas*, Nanda went to Mathurā to pay the yearly tax, O Parīkṣit, descendant of the Kurus.
20. When he heard that his brother Nanda had arrived and learnt that he had paid his taxes to the king, Vasudeva went to Nanda's residential quarters.
21. Seeing him, Nanda immediately sprang up like a body that has regained its vital airs. Delighted and overwhelmed with love, he embraced his dearest Vasudeva with both arms.
22. Vasudeva was worshipped and honoured and seated comfortably, O sovereign of the people. After inquiring as to Nanda's health, Vasudeva spoke the following words, his mind fixed on his two sons:
23. "O brother, it is by good fortune that a child was born to you. Advanced in years, you had been childless up to now, and had given up hope for a child.
28. The three prescribed aims of life, *dharma*, *artha* and *kāma*, are attained for the sake of friends. But the three aims do not accomplish their purposes when these friends are experiencing distress."
29. Śrī Nanda said: "Alas, many of your sons born of Devakī were killed by Kaṃsa. Only the youngest one survived, a girl, and even she ascended into heaven.
30. People are undoubtedly subject to destiny. Such destiny is supreme. One who knows that destiny is the reality for the self is not bewildered."
31. Śrī Vasudeva said: "The yearly tax has been given to the king, and we have seen each other. Do not stay here for too many days. There are portents in Gokula."
31. Śrī Śuka said: Addressed thus by Vasudeva son of Śūra, the *gopas*, headed by Nanda, with Vasudeva's permission set out for Gokula with their carts yoked to the oxen.

Chapter 6. Pūtanā's Arrival in Vraj

1. Śrī Śuka said: On his journey, Nanda. worried about impending calamities, decided that the words of Vasudeva might not have been spoken idly and took shelter of Hari [Kṛṣṇa] [in his mind].
2. The dreadful Pūtanā, slaughterer of children, had been dispatched by Kaṃsa, and was roaming about devouring infants in towns, villages and pastures.
3. Evil beings exist wherever people do not perform their duties, nor engage in devotional activities beginning with hearing about Viṣṇu, the Lord of the Sātvatas. These activities can destroy all evil beings.

4. Pūtanā roamed about freely and was able to fly. One day, after changing herself into a woman by her own mystic power, she flew to Nanda's Gokula [Vraj], and entered it.

5–6. The *gopīs*, the cowherd women, saw a shapely, attractively dressed woman with flowers entwined in her braid. Her waist was heavy with voluptuous hips and breasts, and her face and hair were bright with shining ear-ornaments. The male residents of Vraj, their mind's bewitched by her sideways glances and beautiful smiles, thought that she was like Śrī, the goddess of fortune, coming to her husband with a lotus flower in her hand.

7. Then with her mind intent on infants, that abductor of children came by chance upon the house of Nanda, and saw the child, the scourge of the wicked, on the bed. His vast powers were concealed, just like fire is concealed in ash.

8. Knowing her to be a compulsive killer of children, Kṛṣṇa, the soul of all moving and non-moving beings, closed his eyes. She lifted the infinite Lord, who was to be her destruction, on her lap, just as a fool lifts a sleeping serpent thinking it to be a rope.

9. The two mothers, overcome by her influence, saw that this distinguished woman was inside, and stood watching her. Like a sword covered in a sheath, her heart was razor-edged—but she was careful to appear exactly the opposite.

10. The dreadful ogress placed Kṛṣṇa on her lap there, and gave the infant her breast, covered with deadly poison. Squeezing it tightly with both hands, the furious Lord sucked it, along with her life breath.

11. With all her vital parts under stress, her body drenched in sweat, writhing with convulsions, rolling her eyes and thrashing her legs and arms about incessantly, Pūtanā cried out, "Stop! Release me, release me."

12. The earth with its mountains, and space with its planets, trembled at that powerful, reverberant sound. The nether worlds and all the directions reverberated. People fell to the ground fearing that thunderbolts were falling.

13. Being tormented at her breast in this way, that roamer of the night reassumed her original form, O king. Opening her gaping mouth wide, she toppled down like Vṛtra struck by the thunderbolt. Her hair legs and arms splayed out over the pastures.

14. Even while falling, her body pulverized the trees within a twelve-mile radius, O king. It was a wondrous thing. . . .

33. The people of Vraj cut up the body with axes and deposited it at a distance. Then they covered it with wood and burnt it piece by piece.

34. The smoke rising from the burning body had the pleasant smell of aloe; its sins had been instantly destroyed when suckled by Kṛṣṇa.
35. Pūtanā, the devourer of people's children, was a demoness whose sustenance consisted of blood. But she offered her breast to Hari and so, despite intending to kill him, she attained *sadgati*, the destination of saints. . . .

Chapter 16. The Banishment of Kāliya

1. Śrī Śuka said: After seeing the Yamunā polluted by the black snake, Kṛṣṇa, the Almighty Lord, desired to purify it, and so banished that serpent.
2. The king said: "How did Bhagavān subdue the serpent in the depths of the waters? How had the snake come to reside there for so many ages? Please relate how this took place, O *brāhmaṇa*.
3. Who could be satiated from tasting the nectar of the exalted pastimes of the all-pervasive Gopāla [Kṛṣṇa], O *brāhmaṇa*? He acts according to his own pleasure."
4. Śrī Śuka said: In the Yamunā river there was a pool which was boiling from the fire of Kāliya's poison. Birds flying overhead plummeted into it.
5. All moving and non-moving living entities in the vicinity of the shore died when touched by the spray borne by the wind from the poison-laden waves of the pool.
6. Seeing the contaminated river and the potency of that highly toxic poison, Kṛṣṇa, whose incarnation was to subdue the wicked, climbed a very high *kadamba* tree. With his belt well-fastened, he slapped his arms and jumped into the poisonous water.
7. The serpent was greatly provoked by the force of the supreme being's plunge. He exhaled poison into masses of matter, which overflowed in waves on all sides of the serpent's pool. Lethal from the toxicity of the poison, these waves flooded for a distance of over one hundred bows. But what is this for Kṛṣṇa, who has unlimited power?
8. Kāliya, whose eyes were his ears, heard the commotion of the water churned by the mighty arms of Kṛṣṇa, who was sporting in the pond, as powerful as a mighty elephant, O king. Observing such a lack of respect for his abode, Kāliya came forth, unable to tolerate it.
9. Kṛṣṇa was playing without fear of anyone. Dressed in yellow, and bearing the mark of *śrīvatsa*, he was delicately youthful, gorgeous to behold and luminous as a cloud. His beautiful face was smiling, and his feet resembled the inside of a lotus. Kāliya furiously bit Kṛṣṇa's tender parts and wrapped his coils around him.

10. Seeing Kṛṣṇa apparently motionless and enveloped by the coils of the serpent, his dear friends the *gopas* collapsed in great distress, their minds overcome by fear, sorrow and pain. They had dedicated their desires, their wives, their wealth, their relatives and their own selves to Kṛṣṇa.
11. The cows, bulls and female calves were greatly distressed. With their eyes fixed on Kṛṣṇa, they were bellowing fearfully and stood as if weeping.
12. Then three kinds of extremely terrifying and ominous portents—on the earth, in the sky, and on people—arose in Vraj. They forewarned of imminent danger.
13. Learning that Kṛṣṇa had gone to graze the cows without Balarāma, the *gopas*, led by Nanda, were struck with fear on seeing these portents.
14. Because of the inauspicious signs, and unaware of who Kṛṣṇa really was, the *gopas* thought Kṛṣṇa had met his death. Their minds were absorbed in Kṛṣṇa and they had surrendered their life to him, and so they were struck by fear, distress and pain.
15. All the cowherd folk, from children to elders and women, O king, feeling miserable, left Gokula anxious for a sight of Kṛṣṇa.
16. Seeing them despairing in this way, Lord Balarāma, the descendant of Madhu, laughed, knowing the power of his younger brother. But he said nothing.
17. Searching for their beloved Kṛṣṇa along the path by means of his footprints, which were marked with the signs of God, the cowherd folk went to the banks of the Yamunā.
18. Seeing the footsteps of the Lord of their community here and there mixed in with the other footprints of the cows on the path, O king, they rushed along. These footprints bore the marks of the flag, the thunderbolt, the goad, the barley and the lotus.
19. Seeing Kṛṣṇa motionless in the body of water in the distance and enveloped in the coils of the serpent in the lake, and seeing the cows and cowherd men in distress everywhere, the cowherd folk were struck with utter despair and cried out in anguish.
20. The *gopis*' minds were attached to the unlimited Lord. Remembering his affectionate smiles, glances and words, they were overcome with utter grief as their beloved was being seized by the serpent. They perceived the three worlds as void without their dear one.
21. They prevented Kṛṣṇa's mother from following her child [into the lake], although they were as distressed as she. Pouring out their sorrow, and telling stories about the darling of Vraj, each one remained still as a corpse, their eyes fixed on the face of Kṛṣṇa.

22. Lord Balarāma was aware of the potency of Kṛṣṇa. Seeing Nanda and the others, for whom Kṛṣṇa was their very life, about to enter the lake, he restrained them.
23. Kṛṣṇa remained for some time, assuming the behavior of a human being in this manner. Then, seeing that his own Gokula community, including women and children, which had no shelter other than in him, was in great distress, he realized that it was on his account and rose up from the bonds of the serpent.
24. The serpent, his coils tormented by the extended body of Kṛṣṇa, released him. Enraged, the serpent raised his hoods and drew himself erect as he looked at the Lord. His face had unmoving eyes like burning charcoal and he was breathing through his nostrils as from pots of poison.
25. Kṛṣṇa circled around him, toying with him. Like Garuḍa [Suparṇaka], the king of birds, Kṛṣṇa manoeuvred around waiting for his opportunity. The serpent had eyes fiery with dreadful poison and repeatedly licked the two corners of his mouth with his forked tongue.
26. Bending the raised neck of the serpent, whose strength had been depleted by this circling around, Kṛṣṇa, the original being, climbed on to its massive hoods. Then, the original teacher of all art forms danced, his lotus feet made red by contact with the heaps of jewels on the serpent's head.
27. Then his followers—the celestial *gandharvas*, *siddhas*, sages, *cāraṇas*, and young wives of the gods—seeing that Kṛṣṇa had begun to dance, immediately approached in delight with eulogies, offerings, flowers, songs, musical instruments and various types of drums such as *mṛdangas*, *paṇavas* and *ānakas*.
28. Kṛṣṇa, chastiser of the wicked, crushed whichever head of that hundred-and-one-headed snake would not bend with blows of his feet, O king. The snake's span of life was running out and he was whirling around. He vomited blood profusely from his nose and mouth and was overcome by utter desperation.
29. The serpent was breathing fiercely from anger and was discharging poison from his eyes. Whichever head he raised up, Kṛṣṇa forced him to bow low, striking it with his feet as he danced. As he was being worshipped with flowers, that most ancient being forced the snake to submit in the lake.
30. The serpent, his body broken, and his 1,000 hoods battered by that extraordinary dancing, was spewing blood from his mouths, O king. He remembered that most ancient being, Nārāyaṇa, the teacher of all moving and non-moving entities, and surrendered to him in his mind.
31. The wives of the snake, whose hood umbrellas had been smashed by heel blows, saw that he had been crushed by the extreme weight of Kṛṣṇa, who

bears the universe in his abdomen. They approached the original being in distress, with the locks of their hair, ornaments and clothing loosened.

32. Deeply agitated in mind and with their children placed in front of them, they prostrated their bodies on the ground, and offered obeisance to Kṛṣṇa, the Lord of creatures. These righteous ladies folded their hands in supplication and approached the giver of shelter for shelter, desiring the liberation of their wicked husband.
33. The serpent's wives said: "Punishment is certainly fitting for this offender. Your incarnation is for the subjugation of the wicked. You view sons and even enemies with impartiality. In fact, you mete out punishment after considering its benefits.
34. In fact, what has happened to us is your Lordship's blessing. Your punishment of the unrighteous is undoubtedly that which destroys their sin. Even your anger is considered really to be a blessing for this embodied soul who has found himself in the form of this snake. . . .
52. Be merciful, O Bhagavān. This serpent is giving up his life. Our husband is our life—please return him to us. We are women, and should be pitied by those who are righteous.
53. We are your servants: tell us what we should do. One is undoubtedly freed from all kinds of fear by complying with your command with faith."
54. Śrī Śuka said: When he was extolled in this way by the wives of the serpent, Bhagavān released the broken-headed snake, who was unconscious from the blows of his feet.
55. The wretched Kāliya slowly regained his vital airs and senses. Breathing again with difficulty, he spoke to Hari with his hands joined in submission.
56. Kāliya said: "We are miscreants, full of wrath and *tāmasic* from birth. One renounces one's personal nature with difficulty, O Lord, because it clings to falsehood.
57. This universe is an emanation of the *guṇas*, and has been generated by you, O creator. It contains a variety of natures, potencies, powers, wombs, latent dispositions and forms.
58. And in this universe, O Bhagavān, we serpents are extremely wrathful as a species. How can we, who are deluded, shake off your māyā by ourselves? It is so hard to cast off.
59. Your Lordship is the means to do this. You are the all-knowing Lord of the universe. Bestow either compassion or chastisement on us as you see fit."
60. Śrī Śuka said: After listening to this, Bhagavān, who took human form for a purpose, spoke these words: "You should not remain here, serpent. Go to the

ocean with your relatives and wives. Do not delay. Let the cows and people enjoy the river. . . ."

Chapter 22. Kṛṣṇa Steals the Gopīs' *Clothes*

1. Śrī Śuka said: In the first month of the *hemanta* [winter season], the young girls of Nanda's Vraj observed the vow to worship the goddess Kātyāyanī by eating sacrificial food.

2–3. After bathing in the waters of the Kālindī river at sunrise, they made an image of the goddess from sand near the water, O king. Then they worshipped it with scents, fragrant garlands, offerings, incense, fire lamps, both simple and costly gifts, fresh shoots, fruits and rice.

4. "O goddess Kātyāyanī, great Māyā, great *yoginī*, supreme Lord; honour to you! Please make the son of Nanda, the *gopa*, my husband, O Goddess." Uttering this *mantra*, those young girls performed *pūjā* worship.

5. The young girls had their hearts fixed on Kṛṣṇa. They performed this vow in this fashion for a month and worshipped the goddess Bhadrakālī in the same way: "Please let the son of Nanda be my husband!"

6. They arose at dawn every day by [calling out] each other's family names. Then they sang loudly about Kṛṣṇa while going to the Kālindī to bathe, with their arms intertwined.

7. Once, arriving at the bank of the river, they threw down their clothes as usual and sported happily in the water, all the while singing about Kṛṣṇa.

8. Bhagavān Kṛṣṇa, the Lord of the lords of yoga, surrounded by his companions, arrived at that place. He had come to fulfil those rites.

9. Gathering up their garments, he quickly climbed a *kadamba* tree. Laughing along with the snickering boys, he said jokingly to the girls:

10. "Ladies, you are all exhausted from your vow. Come forward, ladies, and take your own clothes, if you wish. This is not a joke—I am speaking seriously.

11. These [boys] know that I have never uttered a falsehood. Collect your clothes [by coming] one by one, or even all together, O slender-waisted ones."

12. Seeing such jesting, the *gopīs*, who were deeply in love with Kṛṣṇa, were embarrassed. Exchanging glances with each other, they started to giggle, but did not go.

13. When Govinda had spoken in this way, the *gopīs* were flustered by his joking. Immersed in the cold water up to their necks, and shivering, they spoke to him:

14. "Do not behave in this way. You are the son of Nanda the *gopa*, and have a good reputation in Vraj! We regard you as our beloved, so give us back our clothes, dear one—we are shivering.

15. Syāmasundara [Kṛṣṇa]! We are your servants and do whatever you want. Give us our clothes— you know what dharma is. If you do not, hey, we will tell the king!"
16. Śrī Bhagavān said: "You girls have bright smiles! If you really are my servants, or will do whatever I have said, then come here and each take your own clothes."
17. At this, all the young girls, trembling from the cold, emerged from the pool of water. Covering their genitals with their hands, they were stricken by the cold.
18. Seeing that they were virgins, Bhagavān was pleased with their pure state of mind. He placed the clothes on his shoulder, and addressed them with a smile. He was satisfied:
19. "Intent on your vow, you all bathed in the waters without clothes, and that is an offence against the gods. Offer obeisance with your folded hands on your head in expiation for this sin, and then take your lower garments."
20. The women of Vraj conceded that, as Acyuta had pointed out, bathing without clothes was a deviation from their vow. Because they wanted that vow and all of its rites to come to fruition, they offered obeisance to Kṛṣṇa, who was before their eyes, because he is the remover of imperfection.
21. Seeing them bow down in this way, Bhagavān, the son of Devakī, was satisfied. Being compassionate, he gave them back their clothes.
22. The girls were cheated, deprived of their modesty, derided and made to perform like puppets. Moreover, their clothes were stolen. Yet, they were not really upset with Kṛṣṇa. They were delighted to be in the company of their darling.
23. When they had on their clothes, the *gopīs* could not move. Their hearts had been captured, and they were attached to the company of their dear one. So they cast bashful glances at him. . . .

Chapter 25. Kṛṣṇa Lifts Mount Govardhana

1. Śrī Śuka said: At this, O king, Indra understood that his own worship had been abandoned, and became enraged with the *gopas*, led by Nanda, who had accepted Kṛṣṇa as their Lord.
2. Considering himself Lord, Indra summoned the host of clouds called Saṃvartaka which bring about the annihilation of the universe. Furious, he spoke the following words:
3. "Just see how intoxicated the forest-dwelling *gopas* are because of the wealth [of the forest]. They have taken refuge with Kṛṣṇa, a mortal, and now they neglect the gods.

4. Abandoning meditative knowledge, they desire to cross over the ocean of material existence through ritualistic so-called sacrifices which are like unstable boats.
5. By taking refuge with Kṛṣṇa, a boastful, childish, stubborn, ignorant mortal who thinks himself to be a great scholar, the *gopas* have made an enemy of me.
6. Destroy the arrogance of these people caused by the conceit of riches. They are steeped in wealth and their egos have been inflated by Kṛṣṇa. Bring destruction to their livestock.
7. As for me, I will mount my elephant Airāvata, and follow you to Vraj accompanied by the immensely powerful host of Maruts, with the intention of destroying the cattle station of Nanda."
8. Śrī Śuka said: "Ordered on this way by Indra, the clouds, unleashed from their moorings, deluged rain on Nanda's Gokula.
9. Flashing forth with lightning and roaring with claps of thunder, they showered down hail, urged on by the fierce hosts of Maruts.
10. The clouds released incessant torrents of rain as thick as pillars, and the earth became inundated with floods. Low ground could not be distinguished from high ground.
11. The livestock, shivering because of the high wind and rain and the *gopas* and *gopīs*, afflicted by cold, approached Kṛṣṇa for protection.
12. Covering their heads and shielding their children with their bodies, shivering and tormented by the rain, they approached the soles of the feet of the Lord:
13. "Kṛṣṇa, most virtuous Kṛṣṇa, master—you are compassionate towards your devotees. Please protect Gokula, which accepts you as Lord, from the wrath of this divinity."
14. Seeing them pounded unconscious by the excessive wind and hail, Lord Hari reflected on what Indra had done in his fury:
15. "Indra unleashes rain full of hail and mighty winds out of season in order to destroy us because we neglected his offering
16. Consequently, I will employ suitable countermeasures through my mystic power. I will destroy the ignorance and pride born of opulence of those who, out of stupidity, think of themselves as lords of the world.
17. The bewilderment caused by thinking of oneself as lord is inappropriate for the demigods, who are endowed with a godly nature. If I break the pride of the impure for their peace of mind it is an appropriate thing to do.
18. Therefore, I make this pledge: I shall protect the cowherd community by my own mystic power. They accept me as their Lord, their shelter is in me and they are my family."

19. Saying this, Viṣṇu lifted up the mountain of Govardhana with one hand and held it effortlessly, as a child holds a mushroom.
20. Then the Lord spoke to the cowherds: "Mother, father and residents of Vraj, enter the cavity under the mountain with your herds of cows whenever you wish.
21. Do not be afraid that the mountain might fall from my hand during this time. Enough of your fear of the rain and wind! I have arranged shelter from them for you."
22. At this, reassured by Kṛṣṇa, they entered the cavity with their wealth, their herds and dependants as far as there was room for them.
23. Giving up concern for hunger and thirst, and any expectation of comfort, Kṛṣṇa held up the mountain for seven days. Watched by the residents of Vraj, he did not move from the spot.
24. Subdued and helpless, and with his plan thwarted, Indra reined in his clouds. He was awed by Kṛṣṇa's mystic power.
25. When he saw that the sky was cloudless, the fierce rain and wind had ceased, and that the sun had arisen, Govardhanadhara [Kṛṣṇa], he who lifted Mount Govardhana, spoke to the *gopas*:
26. "Don't be afraid, O *gopas*, and come out with your wives, possessions and children. The wind and rain have ceased, and the rivers are for the most part without [flood] water."
27. At this, the *gopas*, women, children and elders each took their own cows and their utensils, which had been loaded on to carts, and came out slowly.
28. While all watched, Bhagavān, the Lord, effortlessly put back the hill where it had been.
29. The people of Vraj were filled with the force of love, and came to embrace him, or whatever was appropriate. And with joy the *gopīs* offered auspicious blessings, and with love worshipped him with offerings of yogurt and unhusked barley, and other such items. . . .

Chapter 32. The Gopīs' *Lamentation in the Rāsa Pastime*

1. Śrī Śuka said: Thus the *gopīs* sang and spoke incoherently in various ways. Longing to see Kṛṣṇa, O king, they wept loudly.
2. Kṛṣṇa, the descendant of Śūra, bewilderer of the mind of the mind-bewilderer Kāma himself, appeared in their midst, his lotus face smiling. He was wearing yellow garments, and bore a garland.
3. Seeing that their beloved had returned, the women, their eyes wide with love, sprang up simultaneously as if the vital air of the body had returned.

4. One ecstatic woman caught hold of Kṛṣṇa's lotus hand in her folded hands. Another placed his arm, decorated with sandalwood paste, on her shoulder.
5. A slender woman accepted his chewed betel nut with folded hands. Another, burning [with desire], placed his lotus feet on her breast.
6. Yet another, trembling with the fury of love, was biting her lips with her teeth, her brows knitted in a frown. She glared at Kṛṣṇa as if she could strike him with a look of rebuke.
7. Another woman dwelt on his lotus face with unblinking eyes. Although she drank it in with her eyes, she was not fully satisfied, just as a saint is not fully satisfied [by meditating on] Kṛṣṇa's lotus feet.
8. Some other woman, drawing Kṛṣṇa into her heart through the apertures of her eyes and then sealing them shut, stood embracing him [in her heart], like a yogī immersed in bliss
9. All rejoiced at the wonder of seeing Keśava [Kṛṣṇa] and let go the distress they had felt at separation, as people are joyful after encountering a wise man.
10. Bhagavān, Acyuta, surrounded by the women who had shaken off their sorrow, shone brilliantly, like the supreme being surrounded by his *Śakti* powers.

11–12. The supreme ruler took the women along and enjoyed himself on the auspicious bank of the Kālindī [Yamunā]. There were bees with six legs and a breeze fragrant with blossoming jasmine and *mandāra* flowers. Its soft sands were lapped by waves that were like the hands of the Kṛṣṇa river [Yamunā]. The darkness of the night was dispelled by the full rays from the autumn moon.

13. The heartache of the *gopīs* had been assuaged by the bliss of seeing Kṛṣṇa, just as the Vedas attained the culmination of their hearts' desire. The *gopīs* made a seat for the friend of their heart with their outer garments, which were smeared with the *kunkum* powder from their breasts.
14. Bhagavān, the Lord, whose seat is fixed within the hearts of the masters of yoga, sat down there. He was worshipped as he sat in the company of the *gopīs*, and revealed himself in a form that was a unique embodiment of beauty in the three worlds.
15. Those women worshipped that inciter of Kāma by massaging his hands and feet, which they had placed on their laps. They praised him, their eyebrows quivering, with playful looks and laughter. Then they spoke, somewhat angrily.

16. The beautiful *gopīs* said: "Some serve those who serve them. Some do the opposite of this [i.e. serve those who do not serve them]. And some do not serve either. Can you explain this for us clearly?"
17. Śrī Bhagavān said: "Friends, there are those who serve each other reciprocally but their exchange is exclusively out of self-interest; there is no dharma or friendship there. Personal gain and nothing else is the motive. . . ."

Chapter 33. The Description of the Rāsa Pastime

1. Hearing the Lord's winning words spoken in this way, the *gopīs* relinquished their distress at separation, but their aspirations increased from touching his limbs.
2. Govinda [Kṛṣṇa] began the *rāsa* pastime there, in the company of those devoted jewels of women, who linked arms happily together.
3. The festival of the *rāsa* dance began, featuring a circle of *gopīs*. The Lord of all yogīs, Kṛṣṇa, inserted himself between each pair of *gopīs*, and put his arms about their necks. Each woman thought he was at her side only. Meanwhile, the sky was crowded with hundreds of the vehicles of the gods, who were accompanied by their wives and carried away with excitement.
4. Kettledrums resounded then, streams of flowers fell, and the chiefs of the *gandharvas* and their wives sang of Kṛṣṇa's spotless glories.
5. There was a tumultuous sound of bracelets, ankle-bracelets and the bells of the young women in the circle of the *rāsa* dance with their beloved.
6. Kṛṣṇa Bhagavān, the son of Devakī, was radiant in their company, like a great emerald in the midst of golden ornaments.
7. The consorts of Kṛṣṇa, their braids and belts securely fastened, sang about him with hand gestures and dancing feet. Their faces were sweating, their earrings rolling on their cheeks, and the garments on their breasts slipping. Their waists were bent, and they smiled, their eyebrows playful. They shone like lightning in a circle of clouds.
8. They were intent on amorous pleasure and overjoyed by Kṛṣṇa's touch. Their throats decorated with dye, they sang loudly as they danced, and the world reverberated with their songs.
9. One *gopī* led a duet in harmony with Mukunda. Kṛṣṇa was pleased and praised her: "Well done! Well done!" Then she led the refrain and he heaped praises on her.
10. Another, tired by the *rāsa* dance, her *mallikā* [jasmine] flowers and bracelets loosened, laid her arm on the shoulder of Kṛṣṇa, the wielder of the club, who was standing by her side.

11. Kṛṣṇa placed his arm on the shoulder of one of the *gopīs*. Smelling it, fragrant as a blue lotus and smeared with sandalwood, she kissed it, the hairs of her body tingling with rapture.
12. Kṛṣṇa gave his chewed betel nut to another *gopī* as she placed her cheek, adorned with the glitter of earrings in disarray from the dancing, next to his cheek.
13. Yet another *gopī* who was singing and dancing, her belt and ankle-bracelets jingling, became fatigued. She placed the soothing lotus hand of Acyuta, who was at her side, on her breast.
14. The *gopīs* won their lover Acyuta, who is the exclusive beloved of Śrī, the goddess of fortune. Their necks encircled by his arms, they delighted in him as they sang.
15. The *gopīs*, with glowing faces, cheeks adorned with locks of hair, and lotus flowers behind their ears, were beautiful. They danced with the Lord in the circle of the *rāsa* to the musical accompaniment of the bees complemented by the sound of their anklets and bangles. Wreaths of flowers fell from their hair.
16. Thus Kṛṣṇa, the Lord of Lakṣmī, sported with the beautiful girls of Vraj with freely playful smiles, amorous glances, and with caresses and embraces. He was like a child enraptured by his own reflection.
17. The senses of the women of Vraj were alive with pleasure from the contact of his limbs. Their ornaments and garlands were awry, and the women could not keep their garments or their hair or the cloth covering their breasts in order, O best of the Kuru Dynasty.
18. The women of the celestial realm travelling in the air were stricken with desire at seeing Kṛṣṇa's pastimes, and became entranced. The moon and its entourage [the stars] were full of wonder.
19. Although content within himself, the Lord became manifest in as many forms as there were *gopī* women, and enjoyed himself with them in *līlā* pastimes.
20. With great compassion, Kṛṣṇa lovingly caressed with his very soothing hands the face of those *gopīs* who were exhausted from the pleasures of love.
21. The *gopīs* paid homage to their hero with sideways looks and honeyed smiles. Their beautiful cheeks glowed with locks of hair and the glitter of golden earrings. Thrilled by the touch of Kṛṣṇa's fingernails, they sang of his auspicious deeds.
22. When he tired, Kṛṣṇa went into the water with them. He was pursued by bees, who [sang] like *gandharva*-chiefs, because of his garland. Crushed by contact

with the limbs of the *gopīs*, it was stained with the *kunkum* powder from their breasts. Kṛṣṇa was like the king of the elephants who had lost all inhibitions with his female elephants.

23. With looks of love, the young women around him laughed and splashed him vigorously, O King! Worshipped with showers beloved of Śrī, the goddess of fortune. Their necks encircled by his arms, they delighted in him as they sang. . . .
35. He lives within the *gopīs*, their husbands and all living beings. He is the supreme witness who has assumed a form in this world for the purpose of sport.
36. Manifest in a human form, he indulges in such pastime as a favour to the devotees. Hearing about these, one becomes fully devoted to him.
37. Confused by his power of illusion, the menfolk of Vraj were not resentful of Kṛṣṇa; each thought his own wife was present at his side.
38. The *gopīs* held the Lord dear. When the duration of Brahmā's night had expired, they went home unwillingly with the approval of Vasudeva.
39. The sober person who is endowed with faith should hear and describe these pastimes of Viṣṇu with the maidens of Vraj. Achieving supreme devotion to the Lord, one quickly frees oneself from lust, the disease of the heart.

Source: *Krishna: The Beautiful Legend of God: Śrīmad Bhāgavata Purāṇa, Book X*, translated by Edwin F. Bryant (London: Penguin Books, 2003).

Selections from the *Gītāgovinda* of Jayadeva

Careless Krishna

While Hari roamed in the forest
Making love to all the women,
Rādhā's hold on him loosened,
And envy drove her away.
But anywhere she tried to retreat
In her thicket of wild vines,
Sounds of bees buzzing circles overhead
Depressed her—
She told her friend the secret. (1)

THE FIFTH SONG

Sweet notes from his alluring flute echo nectar from his lips
His restless eyes glance, his head sways, earrings play at his cheeks.
My heart recalls Hari here in his love dance,
Playing seductively, laughing, mocking me. (2)

A circle of peacock plumes caressed by moonlight crowns his hair.
A rainbow colors the fine cloth on his cloud-dark body.
My heart recalls Hari here in his love dance,
Playing seductively, laughing, mocking me. (3)

Kissing mouths of round-hipped cowherd girls whets his lust.
Brilliant smiles flash from the ruby-red buds of his sweet lips.
My heart recalls Hari here in his love dance,
Playing seductively, laughing, mocking me. (4)

Vines of his great throbbing arms circle a thousand cowherdesses.
Jewel rays from his hands and feet and chest break the dark night.
My heart recalls Hari here in his love dance,
Playing seductively, laughing, mocking me. (5)

His sandalpaste browmark outshines the moon in a mass of clouds.
His cruel heart is a hard door bruising circles of swelling breasts.
My heart recalls Hari here in his love dance,
Playing seductively, laughing, mocking me. (6)

Jeweled earrings in sea-serpent form adorn his sublime cheeks.
His trailing yellow cloth is a retinue of sages, gods, and spirits.
My heart recalls Hari here in his love dance,
Playing seductively, laughing, mocking me. (7)

Meeting me under a flowering tree, he calms my fear of dark time,
Delighting me deeply by quickly glancing looks at my heart.
My heart recalls Hari here in his love dance,
Playing seductively, laughing, mocking me. (8)

Jayadeva's song evokes an image of Madhu's beautiful foe
Fit for worthy men who keep the memory of Hari's feet.
My heart recalls Hari here in his love dance,
Playing seductively, laughing, mocking me. (9)

My heart values his vulgar ways,
Refuses to admit my rage,
Feels strangely elated,
And keeps denying his guilt.
When he steals away without me
To indulge his craving
For more young women,
My perverse heart
Only wants Krishna back.
What can I do? (10)

THE SIXTH SONG

I reach the lonely forest hut where he secretly lies at night.
My trembling eyes search for him as he laughs in a mood of passion.
Friend, bring Keśi's sublime tormentor to revel with me!
I've gone mad waiting for his fickle love to change. (11)

I shy from him when we meet; he coaxes me with flattering words.
I smile at him tenderly as he loosens the silken cloth on my hips.
Friend, bring Keśi's sublime tormentor to revel with me!
I've gone mad waiting for his fickle love to change. (12)

I fall on the bed of tender ferns; he lies on my breasts forever.
I embrace him, kiss him; he clings to me drinking my lips.
Friend, bring Keśi's sublime tormentor to revel with me!
I've gone mad waiting for his fickle love to change. (13)

My eyes close languidly as I feel the flesh quiver on his cheek.
My body is moist with sweat; he is shaking from the wine of lust.
Friend, bring Keśi's sublime tormentor to revel with me!
I've gone mad waiting for his fickle love to change. (14)

I murmur like a cuckoo; he masters love's secret rite.
My hair is a tangle of wilted flowers; my breasts bear his nailmarks.
Friend, bring Keśi's sublime tormentor to revel with me!
I've gone mad waiting for his fickle love to change. (15)

Jewel anklets ring at my feet as he reaches the height of passion.
My belt falls noisily; he draws back my hair to kiss me.

Friend, bring Keśi's sublime tormentor to revel with me!
I've gone mad waiting for his fickle love to change. (16)

I savor passion's joyful time; his lotus eyes are barely open.
My body falls like a limp vine; Madhu's foe delights in my love.
Friend, bring Keśi's sublime tormentor to revel with me!
I've gone mad waiting for his fickle love to change. (17)

Jayadeva sings about Rādhā's fantasy of making love with Madhu's killer.
Let the story of a lonely cowherdess spread joy in his graceful play.
Friend, bring Keśi's sublime tormentor to revel with me!
I've gone mad waiting for his fickle love to change. (18)

The enchanting flute in his hand
Lies fallen under coy glances;
Sweat of love wets his cheeks;
His bewildered face is smiling—
When Krishna sees me watching him
Playing in the forest
In a crowd of village beauties,
I feel the joy of desire. . . . (19)

Bewildered Krishna

Krishna, demon Kaṁsa's foe,
Feeling Rādhā bind his heart with chains
Of memories buried in other wordly lives,
Abandoned the beautiful cowherd girls. (1)

As he searched for Rādhikā in vain,
Arrows of love pierced his weary mind
And Mādhava repented as he suffered
In a thicket on the Jumna riverbank. (2)

THE SEVENTH SONG

She saw me surrounded in the crowd of women,
And went away.
I was too ashamed,
Too afraid to stop her.
Damn me! My wanton ways
Made her leave in anger. (3)

What will she do, what will she say to me
For deserting her this long?
I have little use for wealth or people
Or my life or my home.
  Damn me! My wanton ways
  Made her leave in anger. (4)

I brood on her brow curving
Over her anger-shadowed face,
Like a red lotus
Shadowed by a bee hovering above.
  Damn me! My wanton ways
  Made her leave in anger. (5)

In my heart's sleepless state
I wildly enjoy her loving me.
Why do I follow her now in the woods?
Why do I cry in vain?
  Damn me! My wanton ways
  Made her leave in anger. (6)

Frail Rādhā, I know jealousy
Wastes your heart.
But I can't beg your forgiveness
When I don't know where you are.
  Damn me! My wanton ways
  Made her leave in anger. (7)

You haunt me,
Appearing, disappearing again.
Why do you deny me
Winding embraces you once gave me?
  Damn me! My wanton ways
  Made her leave in anger. (8)

Forgive me now!
I won't do this to you again!
Give me a vision, beautiful Rādhā!
I burn with passion of love.

Damn me! My wanton ways
Made her leave in anger. (9)

Hari's state is painted
With deep emotion by Jayadeva—
The poet from Kindubilva village,
The moon rising out of the sea.
Damn me! My wanton ways
Made her leave in anger. (10)

Lotus stalks garland my heart,
Not a necklace of snakes!
Blue lily petals circle my neck,
Not a streak of poison!
Sandalwood powder, not ash,
Is smeared on my lovelorn body!
Love-god, don't attack, mistaking me for Śiva!
Why do you rush at me in rage? (11)

Don't lift your mango-blossom arrow!
Don't aim your bow
Our games prove your triumph, Love.
Striking weak victims is empty valor.
Rādhā's doe eyes broke my heart
With a volley of glances
Impelled by love—
Nothing can arouse me now! (12)

Glancing arrows your brow's bow conceals
May cause pain in my soft mortal core.
Your heavy black sinuous braid
May perversely whip me to death.
Your luscious red berry lips, frail Rādhā,
May spread a strange delirium.
But how do breasts in perfect circles
Play havoc with my life? (13)

Her joyful responses to my touch,
Trembling liquid movements of her eyes,

Fragrance from her lotus mouth,
A sweet ambiguous stream of words,
Nectar from her red berry lips—
Even when the sensuous objects are gone,
My mind holds on to her in a trance.
How does the wound of her desertion deepen? (14)

Her arched brow is his bow,
Her darting glances are arrows,
Her earlobe is the bowstring—
Why are weapons guarded
In Love's living goddess of triumph?
The world is already vanquished. (15)

Tender Krishna

THE NINTH SONG

An exquisite garland lying on her breasts
Is a burden to the frail wasted girl.
  Krishna, Rādhikā suffers in your desertion. (11)

Moist sandalbalm smoothed on her body
Feels like dread poison to her.
  Krishna, Rādhikā suffers in your desertion. (12)

The strong wind of her own sighing
Feels like the burning fire of love.
  Krishna, Rādhikā suffers in your desertion. (13)

Her eyes shed tears everywhere
Like dew from lotuses with broken stems.
  Krishna, Rādhikā suffers in your desertion. (14)

Her eyes see a couch of tender shoots,
But she imagines a ritual bed of flames.
  Krishna, Rādhikā suffers in your desertion. (15)

She presses her palm against her cheek,
Wan as a crescent moon in the evening.
  Krishna, Rādhikā suffers in your desertion. (16)

"Hari! Hari!" she chants passionately,
As if destined to die through harsh neglect.
 Krishna, Rādhikā suffers in your desertion. (17)

May singing Jayadeva's song
Give pleasure to the worshipper at Krishna's feet!
 Krishna, Rādhikā suffers in your desertion. (18)

She bristles with pain, sucks in breath,
Cries, shudders, gasps,
Broods deep, reels, stammers,
Falls, raises herself, then faints.
When fevers of passion rage so high,
A frail girl may live by your charm.
If you feel sympathy, Krishna,
Play godly healer! Or Death may take her. (19)

Divine physician of her heart,
The love-sick girl can only be healed
With elixir from your body.
Free Rādhā from her torment, Krishna—
Or you are crueler
Than Indra's dread thunderbolt. (20)

While her body lies sick
From smoldering fever of love,
Her heart suffers strange slow suffocation
In mirages of sandalbalm, moonlight, lotus pools.
When exhaustion forces her to meditate on you,
On the cool body of her solitary lover,
She feels secretly revived—
For a moment the feeble girl breathes life. (21)

She found your neglect in love unbearable before,
Despairing if you closed your eyes even for a moment.
How will she live through this long desertion,
Watching flowers on tips of mango branches? (22)

Lotus-eyed Krishna Longing for Love

THE ELEVENTH SONG

He ventures in secret to savor your passion, dressed for love's delight.
Rādhā, don't let full hips idle! Follow the lord of your heart!
In woods on the wind-swept Jumna bank,
Krishna waits in wildflower garlands. (8)

He plays your name to call you on his sweet reed flute.
He cherishes breeze-blown pollen that touched your fragile body.
In woods on the wind-swept Jumna bank,
Krishna waits in wildflower garlands. (9)

When a bird feather falls or a leaf stirs, he imagines your coming.
He makes the bed of love; he eyes your pathway anxiously.
In woods on the wind-swept Jumna bank,
Krishna waits in wildflower garlands. (10)

Leave your noisy anklets! They clang like traitors in love play.
Go to the darkened thicket, friend! Hide in a cloak of night!
In woods on the wind-swept Jumna bank,
Krishna waits in wildflower garlands. (11)

Your garlands fall on Krishna's chest like white cranes on a dark cloud.
Shining lightning over him, Rādhā, you rule in the climax of love.
In woods on the wind-swept Jumna bank,
Krishna waits in wildflower garlands. (12)

Loosen your clothes, untie your belt, open your loins!
Rādhā, your gift of delight is like treasure in a bed of vines.
In woods on the wind-swept Jumna bank,
Krishna waits in wildflower garlands. (13)

Hari is proud. This night is about to end now.
Speed my promise to him! Fulfill the desire of Madhu's foe!
In woods on the wind-swept Jumna bank,
Krishna waits in wildflower garlands. (14)

While Jayadeva sings his enticing song to worship Hari,
Bow to Hari! He loves your favor-his heart is joyful and gentle.

In woods on the wind-swept Jumna bank,
Krishna waits in wildflower garlands. (15)

Sighing incessantly, he pours out his grief.
He endlessly searches the empty directions.
Each time he enters the forest thicket,
Humming to himself, he gasps for breath.
He makes your bed of love again and again,
Staring at it in empty confusion.
Lovely Rādhā, your lover suffers
Passion's mental pain. (16)

Your spitefulness ebbed
As the hot-rayed sun set.
Krishna's mad desire
Deepened with the darkness.
The pitiful cry of lonely cuckoos
Keeps echoing my plea,
"Delay is useless, you fool—
It is time for lovers to meet!". . . (17)

Four Quickening Arms

THE NINETEENTH SONG

If you speak, moonlight gleaming on your teeth
Dispels the dread darkness of fear.
Let your moon face lure my nightbird eyes
To taste nectar from your quivering lips!
Rādhā, cherished love,
Abandon your baseless pride!
Love's fire burns my heart—
Bring wine in your lotus mouth! (2)

If you feel enraged at me, Rādhā,
Inflict arrow-wounds with your sharp nails!
Bind me in your arms! Bite me with your teeth!
Or do whatever excites your pleasure!
Rādhā, cherished love,
Abandon your baseless pride!

Love's fire burns my heart—
Bring wine in your lotus mouth! (3)

You are my ornament, my life,
My jewel in the sea of existence.
Be yielding to me forever,
My heart fervently pleads!
Rādhā, cherished love,
Abandon your baseless pride!
Love's fire burns my heart—
Bring wine in your lotus mouth! (4)

Frail Rādhā, even with dark lotus pupils,
Your angry eyes are like scarlet lilies.
As your arrows of love arouse emotion,
My black form responds with red passion.
Rādhā, cherished love,
Abandon your baseless pride!
Love's fire burns my heart—
Bring wine in your lotus mouth! (5)

Let pearls quivering on full breasts
Move the depths of your heart!
Let a girdle ringing on round hips
Proclaim the command of Love!
Rādhā, cherished love,
Abandon your baseless pride!
Love's fire burns my heart—
Bring wine in your lotus mouth! (6)

Your hibiscus-blossom foot colors my heart
As your beauty fills the stage of love.
Speak, soft voiced Rādhā! Let me dye your feet
With the rich liquid of gleaming red lac!
Rādhā, cherished love,
Abandon your baseless pride!
Love's fire burns my heart—
Bring wine in your lotus mouth! (7)

Place your foot on my head—
A sublime flower destroying poison of love!

Let your foot quell the harsh sun
Burning its fiery form in me to torment Love.
Rādhā, cherished love,
Abandon your baseless pride!
Love's fire burns my heart—
Bring wine in your lotus mouth! (8)

This graceful loving coaxing
Mura's foe spoke to Rādhikā
Triumphs in the joy Jayadeva sings
To delight his muse Padmāvatī.
Rādhā, cherished love,
Abandon your baseless pride!
Love's fire burns my heart—
Bring wine in your lotus mouth! (9)

Fretful Rādhā, don't suspect me!
A rival has no place
When your voluptuous breasts and hips
Always occupy my heart.
Only the ghost of Love is potent enough
To penetrate my subtle core.
When I start to press your heavy breasts,
Fulfill our destined rite! (10)

Punish me, lovely fool!
Bite me with your cruel teeth!
Chain me with your creeper arms!
Crush me with your hard breasts!
Angry goddess, don't weaken with joy!
Let Love's despised arrows
Pierce me to sap my life's power!. . . (11)

Blissful Krishna

THE TWENTY-SECOND SONG

All his deep-locked emotions broke when he saw Rādhā's face,
Like sea waves cresting when the full moon appears.

She saw her passion reach the soul of Hari's mood—
The weight of joy strained his face; Love's ghost haunted him. (24)

He toyed with ropes of clear pearls lying on his chest,
Like the dark Jumna current churning shining swells of foam.
She saw her passion reach the soul of Hari's mood—
The weight of joy strained his face; Love's ghost haunted him. (25)

The soft black curve of his body was wrapped in fine silk cloth,
Like a dark lotus root wrapped in veils of yellow pollen.
She saw her passion reach the soul of Hari's mood—
The weight of joy strained his face; Love's ghost haunted him. (26)

Her passion rose when glances played on his seductive face,
Like an autumn pond when wagtails mate in lotus blossom hollows.
She saw her passion reach the soul of Hari's mood—
The weight of joy strained his face; Love's ghost haunted him. (27)

Earrings caressing his lotus face caught the brilliant sunlight.
Flushed lips flashing a smile aroused the lust of passion.
She saw her passion reach the soul of Hari's mood—
The weight of joy strained his face; Love's ghost haunted him. (28)

Flowers tangled his hair like moonbeams caught in cloudbreaks.
His sandal browmark was the moon's circle rising in darkness.
She saw her passion reach the soul of Hari's mood—
The weight of joy strained his face; Love's ghost haunted him. (29)

His body hair bristled to the art of her sensual play.
Gleaming jewels ornamented his graceful form.
She saw her passion reach the soul of Hari's mood—
The weight of joy strained his face; Love's ghost haunted him. (30)

Jayadeva's singing doubles the power of Krishna's adornments.
Worship Hari in your heart and consummate his favor!
She saw her passion reach the soul of Hari's mood—
The weight of joy strained his face; Love's ghost haunted him. (31)

Her eyes transgressed their bounds—
Straining to reach beyond her ears,

They fell on him with trembling pupils.
When Rādhā's eyes met her lover,
Heavy tears of joy
Fell like streaming sweat. (32)

She neared the edge of his bed,
Masking her smile by pretending to scratch
As her friends swarmed outside—
When she saw her lover's face
Graced by arrows of Love,
Even Rādhā's modesty left in shame. (33)

Ecstatic Krishna

When her friends had gone,
Smiles spread on Rādhā's lips
While love's deep fantasies
Struggled with her modesty.
Seeing the mood in Rādhā's heart,
Hari spoke to his love;
Her eyes were fixed
On his bed of buds and tender shoots. (1)

THE TWENTY-THIRD SONG

Leave lotus footprints on my bed of tender shoots, loving Rādhā!
Let my place be ravaged by your tender feet!
Nārāyaṇa is faithful now. Love me, Rādhikā (2)

I stroke your foot with my lotus hand—You have come far.
Set your golden anklet on my bed like the sun.
Nārāyaṇa is faithful now. Love me, Rādhikā! (3)

Consent to my love; let elixir pour from your face!
To end our separation I bare my chest of the silk that bars your breast.
Nārāyaṇa is faithful now. Love me, Rādhikā! (4)

Throbbing breasts aching for loving embrace are hard to touch.
Rest these vessels on my chest! Quench love's burning fire!
Nārāyaṇa is faithful now. Love me, Rādhikā! (5)

Offer your lips' nectar to revive a dying slave, Rādhā!
His obsessed mind and listless body burn in love's desolation.
Nārāyaṇa is faithful now. Love me, Rādhikā! (6)

Rādhā, make your jeweled girdle cords echo the tone of your voice!
Soothe the long torture my ears have suffered from cuckoo's shrill cries!
Nārāyaṇa is faithful now. Love me, Rādhikā! (7)

Your eyes are ashamed now to see me tortured by baseless anger;
Glance at me and end my passion's despair!
Nārāyaṇa is faithful now. Love me, Rādhikā! (8)

Each verse of Jayadeva's song echoes the delight of Madhu's foe.
Let emotion rise to a joyful mood of love in sensitive men!
Nārāyaṇa is faithful now. Love me, Rādhikā! (9)

Displaying her passion
In loveplay as the battle began,
She launched a bold offensive
Above him
And triumphed over her lover.
Her hips were still,
Her vine-like arm was slack,
Her chest was heaving,
Her eyes were closed.
Why does a mood of manly force
Succeed for women in love? (10)

Then, as he idled after passionate love,
Rādhā, wanting him to ornament her,
Freely told her lover,
Secure in her power over him. (11)

Source: *Love Song of the Dark Lord: Jayadeva's Gītagovinda*, edited and translated by Barbara Stoler Miller (New York: Columbia University Press, 1977).

Selections from the Poems of Sūrdās

THE BUTTER THIEF

1. Hari stole butter for the very first time.
   He fulfilled the furtive longings
   Of the women of the village,
   Then he ran off through the narrow lanes of Braj.
   And Hari thought to himself:
   "I'll go to every house in the land!
   I've taken birth in Gokul
   For the fun of it;
   I'm going to eat everyone's butter!
   Yośodā thinks I'm just an ordinary child;
   Oh will I have a time with the Gopīs!"

So lovingly says Sūr's Lord:
"These Braj-folk
are mine."

2. Yaśodā sits in the courtyard, churning butter;
   Hari stands laughing, his tiny teeth agleam.
   It is a sight to steal away the mind,
   a beauty beyond describing:
   Like a troupe of heavenly nymphs, adorned
   To tempt a sage from the labors of his mind.
   The mother says, "Dance!
   Mohan, dance and I'll give you butter!"
   His tiny feet pound and stamp upon the earth,
   His ankle bells ring.
   Sūr sings the praises of his name,
   earth and heaven resound with his fame;
   but the Lord of the Three Worlds dances
   for his butter.

3. "Mother, when will my topknot grow?
   How many times I've drunk my milk,
   and it's still so small!
   You keep saying it'll grow like brother's,

it'll get long and thick, you say;
And if I comb it, and braid it, and wash it,
then it'll drag along the ground
like a big black snake.
You keep feeding me plain old milk,
you never give me butter-and-bread!"
(Sūrdās says: Live long, you brothers,
Hari and Haladhara!)

4. The two boys frolic as one.
Footsteps stumbling,
swinging their dust-drawn limbs,
They toddle along the road, ankle bells tinkling,
shrieking each to each,
Like a pair of tender goslings
enraptured with their own new speech.
At a tiny waist, a gold-belled belt
gleams a slivered gleam,
As gold upon a touchstone
leaves a thin and gleaming slash.
Earrings glitter in lovely ears;
a lotus-pair, swaying, swaying,
As when Bāsava sent the sacrifice
at the Life-poet's command.
Locks of hair stray across a face,
doubling its beauty,
As when the crescent moon was embraced
by the son of Siṃhikā.
Now they dash to the door
now to father Nanda's side;
Their Gopi-mother takes the hand of Sūr's own Lord
and kisses him.

13. Yaśodā stands near and watches;
The sight of Śyām's childish play
floods her mind with love.
As Nanda performs the rituals of worship,

seated in deep mediation,
Kānha stealthily snatches the image
and pops it into his mouth.
"Now," he thinks, "let's all just see
how great this 'god' really is!"
Nanda opens his eyes; looks all around;
alarmed, amazed, he asks:
"Where did my god go? Who took him?"

Then Yaśodā points at her son's face:
"Let's take a look in your mouth, Kanhāi.
Why did you put the god in your mouth?
You've melted it now, it's ruined!"

And so he spread wide his mouth
and the Three Worlds were there revealed;
and when Nanda peered inside
O Sūr, he was stunned,
he was speechless.

14. Śyām went to the Gopī's house
He peeked through the door; nobody home.
He looked all around; he crept inside;
And the Gopī heard him coming,
and she hid.
Syām sat himself down by the butter-churns,
alone in the empty, silent house.
He found the butter-jugs and began to eat
until
in a jewel-studded pillar
he glimpsed his own reflection,
and struck up a clever conversation:
"Today's the first time I ever stole;
it's good to have a friend along!"
So he fed himself,
and tried to feed his reflection—
but the butter dropped to the floor.

He asked:
"What's wrong?
You can have the whole pot if you want,
but don't drop it like that; it's good!
It's fun, feeding you like this;
now tell me, what do you think?"

At this the Braj-girl laughed aloud;
Sūr's Lord turned around, and saw her face
and that famous Foe of Mura ran away.

15. "Take him home, Yaśodā!
You're the daughter of a fine family;
it's a fine way you've taught your son to talk!
Oh, it wouldn't be so bad
if he'd eat my butter by himself,
but he always brings along his friends.
And when I tried to catch him—well!
what can I say about that?
As soon as he saw me, he ran off and hid,
so I went in and lay down;
Then he snuck up behind me and grabbed my braid,
and he tied it to the bed!"

"Listen now, mother, let me tell you about *her*.
She called me in,
And made me pick out all the ants
that had fallen in her butter-jar;
Then she left me alone
to look after the house
while *she* went and slept with her man!"
Sūr says, Yaśodā laughed at the tale
while the Gopī hid her face in shame.

THE MEETING OF RĀDHĀ AND KRISHNA

9. Śyām the Black says:
"Who are you, white girl?

Where do you live,
who's your father,
why haven't I seen you in the streets of Braj?"

"And why should I come to Braj?
I always play at my father's house;
And I always hear of this Nanda's son
who runs around stealing butter."

"What could I steal from you?
Come on, let's go
play."

The Lord of Sūr,
Sovereign among lovers,
seduced simple Rādhā with his words.

10. "Why do you keep going to *their* house?"
When she's home her mother scolds her,
but she's not a bit afraid.
"Rādhā-Kṛṣṇa, Kṛṣṇa-Rādhā,
It's all over Braj,
it's so shameful!
You're the daughter of the great Vṛṣbhānu;
But that one has no caste, no rank.
Stay away from Gokul!
Haven't you had your fill
of shame?"

The mother lectures the daughter;
but the daughter wavers not;
she only smiles.

THE CLOTHES-STEALING

11. Kṛṣṇa, give us back our clothes!
You carried them into that *kadamba* tree
and left us here, naked, in the water!
We can't come out like this,
we'd be so ashamed;

You can keep our blouses,
and keep our garlands,
just throw us back our skirts!
Oh don't keep saying that same shocking thing—
"Women,
come out naked!"
Sūr's Śyām, show a little pity;
it's getting cold.

THE GIFT

12. Don't ask for things we'll never give you!
Every time you catch a girl in the words,
you run to block her path;
On road, and riverbank, and narrow trail,
you plague us with your silly patter!
Who ever taught you you could ask for a thing like this!
Well, we can tell
you won't be content
'til we've told you a thing or two:
You just can't have the thing you want,
but you can have all the milk you can drink!
First go get it, Mohan,
from somebody else,
and then we might give you a call!
Now stop being such a naughty little boy
with us, Sūr's Śyām!

THE EPISODE OF MOUNT GOVARDHANA

13. "Believe what I say!
If you care for the land of Braj
then worship Govardhana!
No matter how much you take from your cows,
they'll go on giving you milk;
What did *Indra* ever do for you?
He's a crutch; give him up!
If you hope to get everything

you've ever prayed for,
then listen to what I say,"
Said Sūr's Lord to the herdsmen,
"for I swear what I say is true."

14. "That Mountain looks so much like Śyām . . .
So hungrily it feasts,
stretching out its thousand arms;
And this child standing here, holding Nanda's hand—
he's the very same form as the Mountain!"

To little Rādhā her friend, Lalita, says:
"See the Form!
The same earrings,
the same garland,
the same yellow mantle;
The Mountain's splendour is as the beauty of śyām,
Śyām's beauty is matched by the Mountain!"

There was a women, Badaraulī,
a servant in Vṛṣbhānu's house,
who set out an offering of food;
The Mountain stretched its arm
down into the house,
and took it.

Little Rādhā stood stunned by the beauty of it all,
as little Śyām fixed his eyes upon her;
The Beloved succumbed to the glances of desire
cast sidelong by the Lord of Sūrdās.

THE FLUTE BEARER

1. When Hari puts the flute to his lips
The still are moved and the moving stilled;
Winds die, the river Yamunā stops,
crows fall silent and the deer fall senseless;
bird and beast are stunned by his splendor.
A cow, unmoving

dangles a grass blade from her teeth;
Even the wise can no longer
hold firm their own minds.

Sūrdās says: Lucky the man
who knows such joy.

2. Honeybee, Kṛṣṇa's flute is honey-sweet.
We hear, and our very breath is immersed in love
like a wick immersed in oil,
shining hot and bright,
And the moths see the flame,
and destroy their greedy bodies;
Like a fish who yearns for a sliver of meat,
and seizes a bamboo hook;
a crooked thorn,
It twists in the heart
and then will not come out.
As a hunter sounds a horn
and draws a herd of deer;
Aims an arrow,
looses it,
and threads their hearts upon the shaft.
As a *ṭhag* lures a pilgrim
with *laḍḍūs* sweet with wine,
Makes him drunk and trusting,
takes his money and his life;
Just so, Honeybee,
Hari takes our love by deceit.

Sūr's Lord tore up the sweet sugarcane
and planted a garden of longing.

3. The flute has become everything to him!
Now you just try to drive her away,
she who's taken Nanda's son in her power!
Sometimes on his lip,

sometimes on his hand he lays her,
sometimes he clasps her to his heart and sings;
Sometimes he plays himself into a trance
and she lies there dangling from his lips.
She for whom he's so lost his senses,
how will you get her away from him?
Sūr's Śyām's forgotten us all;
Now how could he forget her?

Source: Kenneth E. Bryant, *Poems to the Child-God: Structures and Strategies in the Poetry of Sūrdās*, (Berkeley: University of California Press, 1978).

Selections of Devotional Poems by Mīrābāī

SONGS OF LOVE

Once they are fixed upon the Lord
My thirsty eyes do not waver.
They drink in every atom of His body,
Ranging with anxious longing
From head to toe.
I was standing at the door of my house
When Mohan passed.
He was smiling gently,
His face radiant as the moon.
My relatives reproach me and crack bitter jests,
But my wayward eyes brook no obstruction.
They are sold and belong to another.
Whether they praise me or chide me,
I accept whatever is said
And raise it reverently to my forehead.
Says Mīrā: "Without my Master, Giridhara,
I cannot exist for a second."

O my companion,
Strange is the behaviour of my eyes.
That sweet form has entered my mind
And pierced its way into my heart.
How long have I been standing in my house

Gazing down the road?
My very existence depends on Shyām, the Beloved.
He is the herb that grants me life.
Mīrā has become the personal property of Giridhara:
The people say she is mad.

LOVE'S ASPIRATIONS

O my companion, I will instal
That lotus-like figure in my eyes.
Now Shyām has come
And I dare not blink.
Murāri has come to dwell in my heart,
Every instant I enjoy His sight.
I adorn myself to receive Shyām
And prepare a bed for His enjoyment.
Mīrā's Lord is the courtly Giridhara,
Again and again she offers Him her all.

Do not lose hold of such a gracious Master!
Offer thy body, mind and wealth
To Him alone.
Cherish His image in thy heart.
Come, my companion, look at His face,
Drink in the beauty with thine eyes.
Act only to please Him, in every way.
Shyām is lovely to look upon,
On a glimpse of His visage I live.
Krishna is Mīrā's Lord.
Fortunate is she to have found His favour.

I danced before my Giridhara.
Again and again I dance
To please that discerning critic,
And put His former love to the test.
I put on the anklets
Of the love of Shyām,
And behold! My Mohan stays true.
Worldly shame and family custom

I have cast to the winds.
I do not forget the beauty of the Beloved
Even for an instant.
Mīrā is dyed deeply in the dye of Hari.

OPPOSITION

Sister, I will sing the glories of Govind.
If the King shows displeasure
I can leave his kingdom,
But if Hari shows displeasure
Whither can I retreat?
The King sent me a cup of poison
And I accepted it as nectar,
As the very foot-wash of the Lord.
He sent me a black serpent,
Hidden in a basket,
And I worshipped it
As the black stone that embodies Vishnu.
Now Mīrā has gone veritably mad with love,
She has obtained Shyām for her bridegroom.

TESTING

I am dyed deep in the love of Shyām,
My King, dyed deep in the love of Shyām.
I danced before the holy men,
Beating the drum.
People think I am mad over Madan,
That love of Shyām has driven me silly.
The King sent me a cup of poison
Which I gulped down without even a look.
Mīrā's Lord is the courtly Giridhara,
His love is true, birth after birth.

I knew the Queen had sent me poison.
When gold is placed in fire
It emerges shining like the sun.
I have thrown away worldly shame

As one throws away dirty water.
You observe purdah in your place, my Queen,
But I am just a poor mad girl.
An arrow from the quiver of love
Has pierced my heart and driven me crazy.
I offer my body and mind
As a sacrifice to all holy men,
And I hug closely those lotus feet.
The Lord has taken Mīrā into his protection,
Knowing her to be His servant.

This love, Sister, is a love that endures.
I have drunk from the cup of nectar
And it has set me in a spin.
They cannot sober me, however they try.
The King sent a snake in a basket
And they gave it to the Princess of Meratā
To put on her neck.
Mīrā donned it smiling,
Thinking "This is my best necklace."
The King prepared a cup of poison
Which they gave to the princess to drink.
She drank it up
Like the foot-wash of the Lord,
Singing the glories of Govind.
I have drunk from the cup
Of the Holy Name,
And nothing else pleases me.
Mīrā's Lord is the courtly Giridhara,
His love is paint that does not peel.

SUFFERINGS IN ABSENCE

What shall I say to you,
O my Shyām Giridhara?
My love is ancient
And runs from former births,
Do not abandon me, Giridhara.

I offer myself in unconditional sacrifice, my darling,
When I behold Thy beautiful face.
Come into my courtyard, Giridhara,
The women are singing auspicious hymns.
I have set aside a square for Thy welcome,
Heaped with the pearls of my tears.
I cast myself before Thee, body and mind.
Servant Mīrā takes refuge at Thy feet:
For Thy sake she has remained a virgin
From birth to birth.

REPROACHES

Sister, behold how Hari has hardened His heart!
He said He would come,
But has not done so.
That was His promise when He went.
Food, drink and my surroundings,
Are all forgotten.
Why does my life go on?
Thy actions belie Thy words, my Master,
How couldst Thou have forgotten me?
Mīrā's Lord is the courtly Giridhara.
She says: Without Thee I am heart-broken.

HYMNS OF PRAISE

Sleep has not visited me the whole night,
Will the dawn ever come?
O my companion,
Once I awoke with a start from a dream.
Now the remembrance of that vision
Never fades.
My life is ebbing as I choke and sigh,
When will the Lord of the Afflicted come?
I have lost my senses and gone mad,
But the Lord knows my secret.
He who deals out life and death
Knows the secret of Mīrā's pain.

How can I finish a letter
When I cannot even write?
My hand trembles when I take up the pen
And my eyes flood with tears.
When I want to say anything
I cannot speak.
My heart is sore afraid.
You have beheld my plight.
Go to Hari, and beg of Mīrā's Lord,
The courtly Giridhara,
That He may keep a place for her
At His lotus feet.

THE LAND OF BRAJ

O my companion, the sight of Brindāvan
Has become very dear to me.
In every house the Lord is worshipped
By the offering of tulsi-leaves,
And they enjoy the sight of the Lord
With reverence.
The pure water of the Yamunā flows,
And their sole nourishment is milk and curds.
The Lord sits on a gem-studded throne,
Wearing a crown of tulsi-leaves.
O Shyām, I walked from bower to bower,
Listening to the sounds of Thy flute.
Mīrā's Lord is the courtly Giridhara,
She says, "Without worship of the Lord,
Man is a feeble creature."

O my mind,
Let us go to the bank of the Yamunā.
My whole body has been refreshed
By the pure waters of the Yamunā.
Krishna was playing His flute
In the company of Balvīr.
His peacock's feather crown

And yellow loincloth are charming.
The diamonds in His ear-rings sparkle.
Mīrā's Lord is the courtly Giridhara—
Behold, he is playing with Balvīr

THE CHILDISH SPORTS

Wake up, my dear flute player,
Wake up, my darling.
The night has passed,
Dawn has come,
People are opening their doors.
You can hear the gopīs churning the curds,
Harken to the clink of their bracelets.
Wake up, Lāl jī, the dawn has come,
Men and gods alike
Are waiting at Thy door to greet Thee.
The cowherd boys are in a frenzy,
Everywhere there are shouts of "Jai! Jai!"
Now the little herdsmen
Have taken their parcels of bread and butter
Ready to go out.
Mīrā's Lord is the courtly Giridhara.
He saves those
Who choose Him for their refuge.

THE PLAYING OF THE FLUTE

On the banks of the Yamunā
The flute was heard.
The Flute-Player has captured my heart,
My soul has not strength to withstand.
Dark Himself,
Krishna is seated on a dark blanket
By the dark waters of the Yamunā.
On hearing the sounds of the flute
I lose body-consciousness,
My body remaining like a stone.
Says Mīrā, O my Lord,

The courtly Giridhara,
Come quickly and end my pain.

Sister, the sound of the flute
Has driven me crazy.
Without Hari, nothing avails.
On hearing the sounds
I loose body-consciousness,
My heart well caught
In the meshes of the net.
What vows and observances have you performed,
O flute? Who is now at your side?
The magic of those seven notes
Has entrapped even Mīrā's Lord Himself.

THE SERPENT

O Thou of the lotus-leaf eyes,
Thou didst tame the black serpent.
Thou didst subdue the serpent
In a pool of the Yamunā,
Dancing on his ruffled black crests.
Thou didst leap into the water without fear,
For Thou art one,
But Thy powers are infinite.
Mīrā's Lord, the courtly Giridhara,
Is the darling of the women of Braj.

Source: *The Devotional Poems of Mīrābāī*, translated by A. J. Alston (Delhi: Motilal Banarsidass, 1980).

Selections from *The Caurāsī Pad* of ŚrīHit Harivaṃś

ONE

Whatever the Beloved does seems
Pleasant to me. Whatever seems pleasant
to me the Beloved does.

A good place for me to be is
In the eyes of the Beloved. The Beloved wants
to be in the pupils of my eyes.

To me more dear even than body,
Mind and life, the Beloved would give up
Crores of his lives for me.

Śrī Hit Harivamś says, hail to the Swan
And his Mate, the dark and the fair!
Who, pray tell, can separate waves from water?

TWO

O Sulky Lady, the Beloved has called!
How beautiful it is tonight for the meeting
Of the lightning with the fresh cloud.

O Sakhī, Mohan is the lord of lovers.
Who is the Passionate Lady
That could be angry with him in such a way?

Śrī Hit Harivamś says, hearing these words,
The Beloved, whose walk is like the elephant's,
Met the one who is Rādhā's Lover.

THREE

Early in the morning, the couple eager for love
Very joyously engaged
In the victorious battle of sexual delight.

Weary, her lotus face was bathed
With dense drops, and the ornaments
Were scattered on her limbs.

Her tilak [Forehead dot] had nearly disappeared.
Her curls were loose and appeared
Like bees, deceived by her lotus face.

Śrī Hit Harivamś says, their words and eyes
Are colored with the color of love.
The girdle of her silken skirt has come undone!

FOUR

O Young Maiden, today your face is filled with bliss,
Announcing the joy and happiness
Of your meeting with the Beloved.

Your words are very langorous.
Your cheeks are red
And red your two tired and sleepless eyes.

Your beautiful tilak has become very small.
The flowers are scattered in your hair as though
You had not adorned the hair-part on your head.

The Generous One, who is a treasure of mercy,
Keeps nothing back
But gives his essence when he begins to give his lips.

O Timid One, why do you conceal the garment
You have exchanged with the Beloved—
overpowering and instructing Śyām
In the hundredfold sports of love?

The garland has fallen down upon your breast.
The clasp of your belt of tiny bells is loosened.
Śrī Hit Harivaṃś praises that sleeping in the house of creepers!

FIVE

Today early in the morning
The splendid Couple are joyously drenched in pleasure
In the temple of creepers.

That charming pair, one dark one fair,
Filled with love's color, are swaying together.
Their feet keep them on the earth.

The saffron powder of her nipples
Stains the strands of the garland
On the chest of the Lord of erotic love, Śrī Śyām.

The Beloved is adorned with the marks of love
Which the Crown Jewel among wise men
Gave with his own hand.

The couple, filled with love and joy,
Sing so sweetly
That they capture each other's hearts.

Śrī Hit Harivaṃś says, the humming bee, intent upon their praise,
Lends a sweeter tone
To their song.

SIX

O Darling, who is
That clever, young maiden, your sweetheart,
Whom you meet by night stealthily?

Listen, my dear,
How can this fact be kept secret through pretense?
Your eyes are moist with the color of love and pleasure.

On your breast are the moon-prints of nails.
You wear someone else's clothes.
Your speech is confused.

Śrī Hit Harivaṃś says, hail to Rādhā's Lord,
Who, full of love,
Is tormented by Kāmadeva!

SEVEN

The fresh Youth and the young Maiden
Are sporting today
In the beautiful new bower.

Their mutual love
Is completely incomparable.
It is heard that this couple is unique on earth.

Where the earth is made
Of various crystals and corals
And the powder of fresh camphor is abundant,

There is a sleeping couch
Made of tender young leaves
On which Śyām has caused the Fair One to sit.

The couple is wholly occupied
With their joy-filled lovemaking.
The betel juice has stained their lotus cheeks.

There is a charming struggle
Of the fair and the dark hand
Over the unloosening of the waistband cord.

Having seen her own reflection
In the mirror on Hari's breast, the Innocent Lady,
Deluded and distressed, became very angry.

Most agreeably stroking her chin
And explaining that it was her own reflection,
The Beloved implored her to understand.

Having heard again and again
Those nectar-filled words, No! No!
Lalitā and the others gaze from where they are secretly hidden.

Śrī Hit Harivamś says that snatching
At the necklace with her hand
In the anger of love, she broke it.

TEN

Today the Clever Lady and the Youth,
That dazzling couple are pleasing to the heart.
Oh, what shall I say about such limbs of surpassing sweetness!

In their play, placing their arms
Around each other's necks—touching cheek to cheek,
They join with the elegant circle in the Rāsa Līlā.

There are the sweet sounds of flute, drum and cymbal,
Anklets and so on, the belt of tiny bells, and bangles
In Śyām and the Beautiful Lady's retreat.

Śrī Hit Harivamś, the Sakhī concealed, sees
The lovely movement of the sudhaṁg dance
And sacrifices her body's breath.

ELEVEN

In the land of lovely and peaceful groves
Rādhā and Hari wear beautiful clothes
On a night in Śarad when the moon in the heaven is full.

She has golden limbs, he is of dark blue luster:
Having met rejoicing, they are one—
As though lightning were shining in the midst of a blue jewel cloud.

He is wearing new red and yellow garments,
His love is true and without compare.
A sweet-scented, cool wind blows gently.

A sleeping couch is made of tender leaves.
The Lover speaks flattering words,
But the Passionate Lady is continually adverse and angry.

Mohan, his mind in torment with sexual desire,
Touches her nipple, waistcloth and necklace.
The Woman, throbbing, says, No! No!

The Lord in his beautiful play is a vehicle
For man to bear many kinds of burdens. In the love sport
Rāsa's form he is a River—The Purifier of the World!

THIRTY

Listen, O Sakhī,
The new bower
Looks very charming.

Having taken
Mādhavī and ketakī creepers,
He has adorned his house of love.

In the month of Śarad
On the night of the full moon,
A cool, gentle, fragrant breeze was blowing.

Greedy for pollen,
The bee has grown weary:
The parrots and cuckoos sing.

O Sakhī, there is a bed for the Beloved,
Made of petals and young leaves
In many different colors.

There are vessels of gold,
Filled with various sweet drinks.
They are arranged carefully on the earth.

On that bed
The skillful Boy and Girl
Amuse themselves a great deal.

The Lover's hand
Touches her beautiful breast.
She covers it over with a garment.

The Passionate Lady
Gazes with contracted eyebrows.
She is constantly contrary at every step of the way.

Agitated and very much subject
To his passion
Hari swiftly seizes her by the shoulder.

The Clever Boy loosens
Her waistband
And pulls away her blue scarf.

The Woman
Under the pretext of anger and obstinacy
Speaks softly the sweet words, No! No!

Embracing in the reversed position,
They present their beautiful and charming
Private sports.

It is as though a golden creeper
Shines on a tree
Made of sapphires.

On the surfaces of the foreheads
Of the Couple uniting
There are drops of perspiration.

Lalitā and the others
Fan with the borders of their cloaks.
The passion in their hearts is unassailable.

Śrī Hit Harivaṃś tells
As much as he knows
About the essence of the nectar of Kṛṣṇa's love.

He whose ears hear
Is the receiver of the love
Of Rādhā's tender lotus feet.

THIRTY-ONE

At dawn today
The Couple
Are very brilliant:

The Clever Lady and the Youth,
Immersed in the rasa
Of the color of sexual love.

Placing their arms
On each other's shoulders,
They gaze into each other's moon-like faces.

Intoxicated together,
They drink that rasa
With eyes as thirsty as the cakora bird's

Her alluring loosened locks
Are those that stole
The Darling's heart.

Embracing and kissing each other,
They sing with a slow sound—
Sweet and clear.

In the forest—unsteadily stepping,
They joyously roam
Dark lanes amid beautiful bowers.

Śrī Hit Harivamś says,
The meeting of the two Darlings
Soothes my heart.

THIRTY-TWO

Śyām Śyāmā today
Are sporting
In the forest.

The night of Śarad is beautiful.
Because of the moonlight
The bower shines in a lovely way.

Biting each other's lips,
They embrace.
He snatches away the cloth from her hips.

There are nail marks on their breasts—
They look with sidelong glances:
The Couple is equal in passion.

With his hand he touches
The firm breast and garland
Of the love with beautiful eyes, the Beloved.

Betel juice has run upon their clothing.
Their hair is disarrayed.
They have exhausted hundreds of Kāmadevas in the battle of sexual love.

At every instant
Their desire for sensual pleasure is extreme.
The beautiful, tender ones are very greedy.

Śrī Hit Harivamś says,
Today all limits are breached:
I offer myself as sacrifice in their immaculate retreat.

THIRTY-THREE

The young Couple
Shine today
In the forest.

The Son of Nanda
And the Daughter of Vṛṣbhānu
Sleepily arose at dawn.

Their footsteps fall unsteadily—
Their pace is slow.
They touch the earth with the tips of their moon-like toenails.

Their lips are bruised:
Collyrium has streaked their cheeks,
And their tilaks are small.

Even impeded by the finger-like curls,
The thieving bees—their red eyes
Cannot hide.

Śrī Hit Harivamś says,
Because of the waves on that ocean of sensual love,
There is no restraint on the body and mind.

THIRTY-FOUR

They wander in the forest's many bowers.

They pass through
Very narrow lanes,
But do not brush with their garments.

Early in the morning,
When all have awakened from the night,
The happiness in their unsteady eyes is revealing—

Drowsy, red
And very distracted:
Some movement arises in the pupils.

Their eyebrows are playful.
Their lotus faces are gentle and charming
Because of laughter and sweet words.

The Darling, very much entranced
Like a greedy bee
Was taken without cost.

Crushed, limp, black
And loosened locks of hair
Shine on their fine cheeks.

Kissing, embracing
And beautiful chin-stroking,
They unite in the reverse position.

Whenever she grows tired,
On their couch of leaves
He fans her face with his garment's fringes.

The waves of love-sport on that ocean
Drench the heart
Of the female slave, Harivaṃś.

Source: *The Caurāsi Pad of Śrī Hit Harivaṃś*, translated by Charles S. J. White (Honolulu: University Press of Hawaii, 1977).

Selections from *The Love Games of Krishna* (*Subodinī*) by Vallabha (*Bhāgavata Purāṇa* X. 35)

Four Verses: Verse I: In this thirty-second chapter we hear described how the Blessed Lord Hari filled the Gopīs, interiorly, with His own Joy. Because of this alone is He called "the One whose Joy is Full" (i.e., because He filled the Gopīs full with His own Joy).

Verse II: The Blessed Lord had entered within the Gopīs. And now, after they have drawn Him out again through their mouths. He enters within them once more, fully and perfectly, through their ears. Then is He firmly, forever established in them.

Verse III: Both word and meaning have dominant importance in this chapter; this is why the stanzas come here in mutually related pairs which together form a single sentence. And what Krishna does through all the months of the year is the matter that is expressed here.

Verse IV: And so, there is one pair of stanzas for each month here (making 24 stanzas), plus an introductory stanza, and a final one concerning the reward. And—taking the first and last stanzas as an additional pair—we come up with a total of thirteen pairs in the chapter.

Introduction to Stanza 1: Having thus described the game the Gopīs played with the Blessed Lord at night, Śuka eliminates the suspicion that they will merely set the wheel of Samsāra turning again during the day by telling us that they became totally preoccupied in these days with describing the Blessed Lord's great qualities. And, describing for us how sorrow, at the beginning, was the factor necessitating their singing of His great qualities, Śuka also explains how, at the end, joy had become the factor. Now at the beginning, and when they first set these songs in motion, the worst sort of sorrow and suffering pervaded the Gopīs' days. This is what Śuka describes for us in the first stanza:

Stanza 1: Śuka said: When Krishna had gone off to the forest, the Gopīs' minds and hearts ran off after Him. By singing very intimately, then, of Krishna's Games, they passed their days in sorrow.

Commentary: The fact that only "the Gopīs" are mentioned here means we should understand that no other women are intended here but the ones who took part in Krishna's love-games. When He who is Eternal Joy "had gone off to the forest . . . their minds ran off after Him" alone. Their minds could not bear the idea of grasping anything else. The word "ran off," or "flowed," expresses their dissolution or absorption in Him. Because of that, their minds, having attained a very subtle form of existence, flowed forth, or spread around from all sides, and thus grasped the Game of Him who is Eternal Joy. Therefore they began "singing very intimately of Krishna's Games." Just as Krishna's Form embodies Eternal Joy, so do His Games. And it is in order to indicate that these Games have Eternal Joy as their very Self that Śuka uses Krishna's name a second time in the stanza. Otherwise he would merely have used the word "His." And had he done that, Krishna's Games would achieve no more than association with Him, rather than being an embodiment of Eternal Joy. And it was necessary that this be said, because in a person's separation from Krishna Himself there is nothing apart from Him that can cause a person to go on living, because everything else is totally inferior to Him. Because to this, with great mental agony "they" somehow or other "passed their days." But when once more the Gopīs' minds are absorbed in accounts of many various deeds of the Blessed Lord, and thus achieve a real oneness, then will their desires be fulfilled. "Now every object connected with Him is shattered and scattered about," say the Gopīs, as they pass their days "in sorrow." And when Śuka uses the word "days" we should note that the Gopīs are holding their breath, somehow, for the sake of the night.

Verse 1: Hari's most excellent Game is the one which is preceded by His playing the flute. In all these following pairs of stanzas, the cause which gives rise to the meaning which is to be expressed is described in the first stanza.

Verses 2–3: The wives of the gods, and the cows as well; the rivers, the trees and the creepers; the winged creatures, and the clouds, too; Brahmā and his kind, and the Gopīs as well; the does of the forest, the gods and the Gandharvas; and the Blessed Lord Hari Himself (i.e., in the last two pairs of stanzas in the chapter), are described in the second of the pairs' stanzas as true connoisseurs of the beauty of His flute-playing.

Verse 4: But the Blessed Lord alone is the real connoisseur. Hari Himself is the only one who truly appreciates. Therefore at the end (i.e., in the last two pairs of stanzas) the Blessed Lord has been twice described as preoccupied with those who are preoccupied with nothing but Him.

Verses 5–6: The brilliant power of His flute's sound is first described as it affects three types of feminine creatures (i.e., the gods' wives in the stanza-pair 2–3; the cows in 4–5; and the rivers in 6–7); and next, as it affects types of male (the trees in 8–9; the birds in 10–11; and the clouds in 12–13). Likewise Brahmā and his peers (14–15), the Gopīs (16–17), and the does (18–19). These three groups have been described as threefold (on the basis of the three qualities). But all the gods who appear scattered throughout these stanzas (e.g., 20–21 as well as 2–3 and others), are not to be classified in these threefold three groups. For all, even those who cannot recognize the beauty of His playing, are united by the majestic power of the thing. Thus in this chapter the flute has been described as conferring its reward in twelve ways.

Introduction to Stanzas 2–3: The women predominate at first among the connoisseurs to be described in this chapter, and chief among them are the gods' wives. And so, in order to express the powerful effect of Krishna's flute-playing upon them, the Gopīs describe the way in which the song of His flute arises.

Commentary: The connection between the two stanzas is as follows: "When Mukunda . . . sets His flute upon His lower lip . . . and makes it burst into sound . . . then"—at that moment— "the women who course the sky in their heavenly chariots . . . fainted." The sound of Krishna's flute is of five kinds, depending on whether He holds His face to one or the other side, or straight, or pointed upwards or down. The first of these—when He turns His face away to the left—awakens passion (*kāma*) in women. And when He holds it to the right, this awakens passion in both men and women. When upwards—the gods; when downwards, the beasts and birds; and when straight, all the insentient beings as well. In this context His turning His face to the left awakens passion in the women who are the wives of the gods. And thus is it described in the stanzas. A doubt may well be expressed that, since existence as a god is greater than existence as a human being, these wives of the gods will not be stunned and distracted by a merely human sound. But we have the saying: "The bend of His brow is the seat of Brahmā" (Bh.P. II.1.30). And

He has here joined the graceful play of His eyebrows with the song of His flute, as the Gopīs have told us. "Resting His left cheek on His left shoulder . . . His eyebrows dancing." The eyebrow involved here is the right eyebrow, for that is precisely the way this is done in the theatre. "Dancing" means He was raising His eyebrows. The '"lower lip" has been described earlier as something which has greed as its essence (cf. Bh.P. II.1.32). If the flute is set to rest completely on that lip (i.e., on greed), it does not confer Supreme Joy; rather it awakens mere passion. Therefore, upon hearing its song these women would attain only the pain that comes from separation, and not Supreme Joy. But if the Blessed Lord's Power of Action were to become strong even when resting on greed, then the Reward could be attained even from a greedy flute. But this, too, is not the case here, say the Gopīs. For "His delicate fingers (are) lazily following or resting upon the path of its (the flute's) holes." Because it is proper that the flute should be played within the notes of the low scale at the beginning. The flute's "paths" are its holes. When the holes are stopped tightly by the fingers, a high note results; when the pressure is medium, a note in the central scale; and when "delicate" or soft, a low note results.

The form of direct address: "O Gopīs," is used to convey that this flute-playing is an experience witnessed by all of them. The Gopīs have expressed the purpose here by calling Him "Mukunda." For Mukunda says to Himself: "If the world is purified by the sound of My flute, I will grant it ultimate freedom." Since He thus played the flute for the good of the world, those persons who were not eligible for ultimate liberation experienced only passion, as the Gopīs tell us when they say: "then the women who course the sky . . ." "Heavenly chariots" are the flying vehicles in which all who are born in the race of gods ride; and the gods' wives are called "the women who course the sky in their heavenly chariots." Because they are eligible by reason of their womanhood and their fitness to be enjoyed, they are ineligible for ultimate freedom. And they are moving "along with the Siddhas." These women have the powers to grant everything except the Blessed Lord. And they themselves are great virtuosos at singing. When they first heard the sound of His flute, they were "awestruck." After that, when they perceived it was He who was playing the flute, they "became a bit ashamed" at the slight overflow of passion they felt, saying to themselves: "Our husbands will come to know." And after that, in order to protect themselves against the raging flood of passion they felt, and fearing they would die of passion, "their minds became dedicated entirely to seeking Kāma." They acted in the same way as those timid creatures who offer themselves to their slayer even before the *coup de grâce* And just after that, tormented by passion, "they fainted." The Gopīs tell us that this faint made them forget everything completely.

Thus they were "totally oblivious of their waistcloth's knot's undoing." And, the Gopīs want to point out if the sound of Mukunda's flute awakened such an overwhelming passion in these divine women, why should anyone be surprised if it makes us faint immediately?

Introduction to Stanzas 4–5: The Gopīs now describe the rising sound of Krishna's flute in another way, in order to tell us that the same thing happened to the cows, too, in reaction to the sound of His flute.

Commentary: "O helpless ones, listen to this wonder!" The connection between the stanzas is as follows "when Nanda's boy makes His flute coo like a bird," then "the bulls and the cows . . . after just biting off clumps of grass . . . stood stock still, entranced as if asleep." Passion, among animals, is directed to one's own kind, not to something higher, nor something lower. But the mule has another condition entirely! Also, the association, for the sake of lovemaking, of someone great with low persons is a pseudo-mood. Therefore, dismissing passion which is characterized by intercourse, Krishna constrains the eating which is so completely vital to the animals His previously described "resting of His left cheek on His left shoulder," and His other gestures, are continued here. But in that very context, the due specification of differences in gesture should be understood (i.e., as noted above, Krishna turns His face downwards when playing the flute to the animals). . . . He "gives happiness to the afflicted ones." And the proof of this is that this is exactly what we are seeing! For the high and mighty do not act in this way. And so this a "wonder." He "makes His flute coo like a bird" in order to communicate this idea alone.

Or, to explain it in another way: the flute is played with His face playfully pointed downwards, relative to His face's previous position. And then "His chest reflects the smile that is like a pearl-necklace." That His smile is stationary on His chest, and that even the gaps in the smile are preserved there is another wonder. Krishna's Śrīvatsa is also most excellent; and so its stability is described here in order to show His splendor. One's love grows stronger when such a one is Nanda's boy. Besides this, He helps us. "Making it coo" is a special way of playing the flute. This playing attracts to itself the inner functions and attributes of the life-breath of all. When this playing steals away the functions and attributes of the life-breath and so forth (i.e., mind, etc.) of even the beasts, what must we say about its effect on others? This is the question the Gopī raises as she describes the stealing of these things from the animals. For when such a thing happens to only one being, some other cause may be proved responsible. Therefore this Gopī has said: "by the herd," i.e., collectively. She means that wherever the sound of His flute penetrates, this happens to all who hear it. The "bulls of Braja (= Vraja)" are big-humped and full of wild frenzy. And even the bullocks who draw carts in Braja are as vigorous as the freeroaming bulls. And when she says that these bulls are in the vicinity of Braja alone, the word "Braja" signifies that she means to include all the other village animals, too. The "beasts" and "cows" mix together in herds in the forest. And so, when she uses the word "beasts," this is to signify that the forest animals are included as well as the village animals. But why multiply words? Every single animal "has its mind stolen away" by the playing of His flute! Nor are they even able to go near the place where the Blessed Lord is playing. Rather, their minds are stolen "even from far away." This shows that this attribute is entirely natural to the sound of Krishna's flute, and it is not brought about merely in the Blessed Lord's immediate vicinity.

And the "clumps of grass" have been "just bitten off"—the cows are able neither to throw them away, nor to chew them. And when this Gopī says that even the simple effort it takes to chew has been prevented, she shows that all other actions have been made all the more impossible. And the word "clumps" expresses the real necessity of what they were doing previously. And she says the animals "pick up their ears" lest they faint, as the gods' wives did. Having abandoned all other means, they "picked up their ears" as the only means to prevent their fainting. She says: "entranced as if asleep" to show that they then turned away from the outside world completely. And then, they were pervaded completely by the sound. And after that again, they became like cows and so forth "painted in a picture." They became even stiller than the most immobile objects. And the use of the word *citra* ("painting") here for the second time in this stanza-pair (*citra* meant "wonder" above) shows that its present meaning, as "painting," surpasses its previously expressed meaning.

Introduction to Stanzas 6–7: The Gopīs describe the sound of Krishna's flute once again, in order to tell us how the sound of His flute caused an intense longing to arise even in the rivers, which are completely insentient:

Commentary: The introduction of Krishna's flute-playing and its possession of the hearts of the Gopīs, as well as the external appearance of the God, have been described in the first two stanza-pairs. And now the entry of His Games is described. For the action of rivers is incessant. But the cessation of action of sentient beings can be, and indeed has been seen in their sleeping, fainting and so forth. But rivers simply never stop flowing. All the more in the case of great rivers (such as Yamunā). They cannot even be dammed up. But even they have ceased to flow at the sound of Krishna's flute. His mineral dye is, for instance, red chalk, or something of the sort. And Krishna wore "leaves." Or, He painted His body with mineral dyes in the shape of leaves. And lotus-leaves are also tied round His head to provide the proper shape. And having done all this, the result was the "outfit," decoration, and outward appearance of a wrestler. So He, by tying on Himself these clusters and so forth which make up the outfit of a wrestler was "imitating the outfit of a wrestler." Or rather He tied on an imitation. For what is unnatural is nothing but a ridiculous imitation, like someone who is merely play-acting at wrestling. By this we know that this particular sound of His flute has been suggested by this Gopī to be useful only for His dancing with them (the Gopīs). Thus has His Power of Action been described as going forth from Him and dwelling in the sound of His flute, and this is the reason why the rivers are drawn to Him. When the word "occasionally" is used, it refers to the times when Krishna has enthusiasm for using His Power of action. That is why the Gopī then says: *sabala*, which means both "powerful" and "in" the company of Balarāma."

When this Gopī addresses another Gopī as "dear girlfriend," she is saying that this following meaning is suggested as a secret, and she wants to assure her she is not deceiving her. For the Gopī who is speaking probably went to see Krishna at that time, under the pretext of bathing or something of the sort. When He has thus donned this outfit, He—who is either our Enjoyer by His very Nature, or has become our Enjoyer—is "together with the cowherd boys." By this she signifies that the Game of Vaikuṇṭha itself is being played here. Besides, Lakṣmī is present (with Him) together with us at night, and is present (with Him) together with the cowherd boys during the day. This is why this Gopī's words of direct address indicate a secret.

Then "He invites the cows" with the sound of His flute, since the sound of His flute is the subject-matter of this entire chapter (although not specifically mentioned in the stanzas). Or alternatively, He does not take up the flute, in order to call them with a sound that is equivalent to that of His flute. And the Gopī tells us the reason why He invites the cows when she says: "Mukunda." Having called them forth, He Himself bestows liberation on them because of their absence of means, saying: "For ultimate freedom should be given to these cows." Or, to establish His own Joy in them (as an alternative to liberation). In the calling of the cows the idea has been expressed that once His Power of Action has gone forth, it performs a great work. And when the Gopī says "then," she means that the rivers, too, knowing the etymological meaning of the word *gāḥ* ("cows," but deriving from the root *GAM*, "to go") and saying to themselves: "We go perpetually," stopped when they heard His invitation. At that very instant, "the flow of their waters (was) interrupted." For no one at all can transgress the Blessed Lord's command. And the word she uses for "rivers" (*saritaḥ*, from the root *SṚ* "to go, move") has captured perfectly the single reality of their nature—to flow. And their sole desire is to become Vaiṣṇava. For the ocean is their lord. But, as the Gopī says, they "long intensely for the dust of His lotus feet," so that the Blessed Lord may become their Husband. And the Gopīs, in saying "wafted on the wind," indicates the means by which they may be united with that dust. The wind has brought this dust for their sake. Thus are they related with this wind. And the wind needs water. But since only those who belong completely to the Blessed Lord attain union with the Blessed Lord, this longing for the dust of His feet has deep implications. But here the goal of these rivers is passion alone, since they are goddesses. This is the reason why, later, Yamunā will become so (i.e., a wife of Krishna; cf. Bh.P. X.58.22). But in their present state their luck does not extend so far, as the Gopī says in the words: "they . . . of little merit." Their merit is not great, so they will not simultaneously attain the form of both cows (as they try become by obeying the Lord's invitation), and protectors of cows by day (which rivers are since they furnish water, grass, etc.), and women by night (since they desire the Lord as their Husband). For desired objects are not attained without merits. And the Gopī tells us how she came to know that this is the rivers' desire when she says: "like we." "They, like we, are of little merit." Otherwise we would become cows or cowherd boys during the day. Therefore they come to know by their own example that the rivers may long as intensely as they want, but their purpose is not fulfilled. Besides, this Gopī has described how, because of the rivers' *sāttvika* expressions as well, the constant emotion that is in their heart is indicated, when she says: "the waves that are their arms trembling with love." Their waves are trembling out of love—not because of the wind. Therefore they seem to be suffering from the painful fires of separation. And besides, they show the stillness of pillars, too, as the Gopīs say in the words: "their waters numbed." Thus have the three types of *rājasa* Gopī been described (the present stanza-pair having been spoken by *tāmasa-rājasa* Gopīs).

Introduction to Stanza 8–9: In order to describe the different kinds of *sattva*, the Gopīs describe the Blessed Lord, too, in this way, in the next three stanza-pairs. The creepers, the birds and the clouds are all *sāttvika*. These become filled with devotion by the sound of His flute. First among these three we hear about the Vṛndāvana forest's creepers and trees, which are Vaiṣṇava. The sap (and mood: *rasa*) of love rise in them by reason of the sound of His flute. In order to describe this the Gopīs have spoken of His flute's sound in a different manner. And for the sake of that, the Blessed Lord, too, must be described in a different manner. And He must be described in accordance with devotion, and in accordance with the world and the Vedas. Among these the first is according to devotion.

Commentary: Like "the Primeval Person" and like the Supreme Person, whose heroic deeds of Strength, such as creating the world and so forth, are "recounted" as unparalleled in their excellence by the Vedas who are their followers, so is "His heroic Strength," by His "companions, followers," and worshippers, the cowherd boys. And this Gopī has described His greatness as superior to all others' according to worldly standards, too, when she says: "His wealth and grandeur immovable, like that of the Primeval Person." His wealth, of course, refers to Lakṣmī. And this praise has been re-echoed by all His followers—the gods and everyone else. And worldly people, because they deal with Him on an everyday level, say there is no one comparable with Him but Puruṣottama (who, of course, He is). Therefore there is no simile here (because there are no two different Beings compared). And the Gopī has given us the reason why the description is made in terms of difference (between the Primeval Person and Krishna) when she says: "He . . . moves about the forest." He who moves about the Vṛndāvana forest has adopted the *sāttvika* expressions, because He is established on the soil of *sattva*. As "the cows graze on the cliffs of the mountains," He goes there Himself, and to help the animals to level ground from the jagged edges He "calls" them. And to show that He is not an ordinary cowherd boy, He "calls them with His flute" alone. We come to know through His future conduct that He has penetrated the forest by means of His flute. Otherwise the trees would not react in such a way. When "He" is playing in different parts of the forest, whenever He "calls out" with His flute, then "the forest's trees . . . shoot forth flowing streams of honey." This is how the stanzas connect. The word "For" is used in the sense of: "And this meaning is correct." If it were otherwise, they would not recognize the sound of His flute, nor would He call them by their names. Therefore by means of His flute the Blessed Lord penetrated all the trees. Likewise later on the same principles will apply.

"The forest's creepers," realizing that the Blessed Lord was "moving about" very near them, and that He was "calling," i.e., inviting. His very own, revealed fully the Joy that was within themselves, in order to bring to fulfillment His enjoyment of them (i.e., His very own). And the "trees" did precisely the same. Just as women and men who belong to the Blessed Lord become filled with Joy when the Blessed Lord and those who belong to Him have come together, and they give what is their very own for the sake of His enjoyment, so did these creepers and trees also give. In case someone objects: "But this attribute belongs to creatures that can move—not to immobile things," the Gopī speaking here has said: "fully to reveal Viṣṇu in themselves, (they) show forth. . . ." In sentient beings alone are both the Power of Action and the Power of Knowledge of the Blessed Lord manifest. And their possession of Being, Consciousness and Joy becomes manifest gradually. All this comes about when the Blessed Lord has entered and dwelt within them. And, reasons the Gopī, if He has entered and dwelt within these trees and creepers, too, and now becomes revealed, then all this is only fitting. These trees and so forth are endowed with five attributes, and so they, "as if fully to reveal Viṣṇu in themselves, show forth . . ." The Gopī tells us that the first revelation came about in them by the power of action when she says: "(show forth) their riches of flowers and fruits." For where the Blessed Lord enters and dwells, there secondary fruit (*phalam*; also "reward") and the highest fruit come to be. Because of this action of His, the creepers and trees come to "show forth, as if fully to reveal . . ." Their flowers constitute their secondary fruits, but their fruits are their highest fruit. And they showed forth "their riches" of all these. And the Gopī points out that they show an excess of Being for the sake of the Blessed Lord when she says: "bowing low their branches with their burden." To refute the objection that it is possible that the branches are bowing because of their burden, too, she has mentioned their "bowing low" first, and their "burden" only afterwards. And she has described that excellence of Consciousness which embodies knowledge when she says: "all their limbs thrill with love." For loving devotees alone experience the thrilling of all the hairs of their body out of love. . . . And in the "flowing streams of honey" the trees and creepers make evident externally, for the Blessed Lord's sake, the Joy that is present within them. Their awareness of all this is surely their power of knowledge. . . .

Introduction to Stanzas 14–15: In order to tell us of three most excellent types of being, and that the sound of Krishna's flute had some effect on them, too, the Gopīs describe the sound of His flute, and the Blessed Lord as well, in the next three stanza-pairs. Doubt, delusion, and the renunciation of all things were brought about by the sound of His flute in the sages, the holy scriptures (i.e., the Gopīs who embody the holy scriptures), and the forest-dwellers, respectively. In the present stanza-pair the Gopī describes the sound the Blessed Lord had His flute make for the sake of creating a doubt in even those who, among the three just mentioned, are the Gurus of all, i.e., Brahmā and the others.

Commentary: . . . And the Gopīs have stated the cause for the ignorance when they say: "setting His flute beneath His lower lip red as a bimba-fruit." . . . As has already been stated, His lower lip has greed as its essence. And so it is not well known in the world; that is to say, the nectar or taste of that lip is not granted by the Blessed Lord. Moreover, having the appearance of a bimba, it is enlightening like the sun. For those who are to be enlightened do not know the real nature of the enlightener. And on that lip this flute has been placed, for the sake of proclaiming its excellence because of that fact, too. The words "all the scales and kinds of sound" refer to the different classes of sound . . . and all the other notes. "When He led forth," i.e., created anew, then, in their effort to understand this thoroughly, these gods, even though their main concern is to preside over the three qualities of worldly existence, also came together in terms of the three times. But to indicate that this time (of Krishna's Game), too, is on the divine level, the Gopīs have used the word: "libation." They "heard the sound" of His flute "from each of their libations." "Indra" is *sāttvika*, "Śiva" *tāmasa*, and "Brahmā" *rājasa*; and they "led" these gods. Indeed, all the gods are composed of the three qualities of worldly existence. And they were "poet-sages"—thus they were also skilled in sound. For Indra, the lord of the three worlds, is at all time intent on sound. But Śiva is the creator of the treatises on sound. And Brahmā is the guru of them both. Hence the Gopīs use the name Parameṣṭhī ("standing at the head, highest, chief") for Brahmā. To express the absence of distraction from their minds, the Gopī has said: "their necks and their minds bowed in appreciative homage." Their necks were bent very low in order to portray externally the bowing of their minds. The mind is what grasps. And the bowing here is complete from all sides. And they also became "no longer sure they knew all the elements of music." It mustn't be thought, either, that, out of indifference, after considering these sounds for some time they remained silent in ignorance. For we have been told that "they fell into a worried depression"—they became faint with anxiety. Or, they were deluded by His flute's sound. For this very reason, the view that this was a pseudo-sound (i.e., an uncultured expression of the notes), is also refuted. Because this sound produces transcendent joy, and the transcendent mood of love. . . .

Introduction to Stanzas 20–21: Having thus described in nine different manners the sound of His flute, the Gopīs now describe in three ways, according to the manner of (and in the words of) those who have transcended the worldly qualities, how the Blessed Lord brought the entire world under His control with His flute's sound.

Commentary: When the Blessed Lord "has played merrily in Yamunā's waters"—here too, the sound of His flute, since it is required and referred to in both the foregoing and the future stages of His game, is understood, because it is the subject-matter of this chapter; but since there is no special, particular mode of flute-playing here, it has not been mentioned separately then "the crowds of minor deities . . . have encircled Him." This is how the stanzas connect. And when the Gopīs say "in the Yamunā's waters," they use the locative case in the sense of "nearness to." Or, the locative is used in the sense of actual locus (i.e., they are literally "in" the Yamunā). It is possible that the cows and cowherd-boys are standing in the water because they are hot. And there Krishna "plays merrily" with the cowherd-boys, and thus this is a water-game. And they also wash down the cows, and so forth. The flute's sound is His helper for calming distress and anxiety everywhere.

In case someone doubts whether Krishna was decorated at this time, the Gopīs have described His decoration in the words: "Donning festive garb by wearing a garland of white jasmine or oleander." They mention the flower-garland alone because the doubter may think that Krishna would certainly be decorated with ornaments on His clothing and so forth, but He would not be decorated with flowers. Garlands are of many kinds. His "garb" is decked out in such a way with these as to make it simply stunning. But here He has decked Himself out in a fashion meant to produce the mood of humor. But since someone may raise the question as to how it happened that the Blessed Lord played such an ordinary game, the Gopīs have said: "Nanda's son . . . your darling boy." By the game by which He becomes the son of Nanda, by (and by virtue of) that very game He brings about an ordinary game, too. And the Gopīs address Yaśodā as "blameless one" to make sure she doesn't get angry and to secure her trust. And He has become "your darling boy." By this they are saying that you—Yaśodā—are the cow, and He is your calf. And by this word the Gopīs have also pointed out Yaśodā's unawareness of all Krishna's hidden moods and delights. Otherwise He would not have played the game in which He allowed Yaśodā to tie Him to the mortar. And since the Gopīs have placed the words of direct address, "O blameless one," in the middle, between "Nanda's" and "your," they have indicated the blamelessness of both Nanda and Yaśodā. And since He is the "darling boy" of such a woman, the blamelessness refers to the Blessed Lord as well. The fact that Krishna is marked by a fullness of great qualities—indeed by an excess of them—is expressed by the Gopīs' subsequent characterization of Him. That is to say: in addition, "He bestows happiness on those who love Him." This means that whatever persons possess love for Him—then just as they have loved Him in exactly the same way does He play His game with them. By these words has the cause for every one of His games been expressed! And where there is play by reason of attachment to His games, that is "playing merrily." This "playing merrily" should be understood here as including His water-game, His dancing-game, and His flute-playing game. Otherwise there would be no need of or use for the "instrumental music" of the minor deities, and so forth.

For it is beings who possess knowledge who are to be brought under control here. And in this the "breeze," or wind, is producer of knowledge. And the gods are the basis of that. Among the gods, moreover, the "crowds of minor deities" and "bards" are intent on manifesting external knowledge. And so the distinguishing characteristic which they possess, by comparison with the others, has been expressed by the Gopīs. But first of all the Gopīs describe the breeze, which is the cause. As "a lazy breeze" is "agreeable," that is how this one "blows along." And as the word "agreeably" also means "along the bank," . . . the good the breeze does is further indicated, since this describes the breeze's coolness. And the words "with the touch of sandalwood-scent" point out its fragrance. And these words also tell us that the breeze comes from the south. Or, the breeze's coolness and agreeableness are increased by its contact with the sandalwood-paste which the Blessed Lord has applied to His own body. The breeze "bears the touch of sandalwood-scent," or perhaps its touch is "as if of sandalwood-scent." Since this breeze is of such a nature, it will produce love of the Blessed Lord in all who are there, without exception. The Gopīs describe the breeze as "paying Him reverence." As the breeze may indeed pay him reverence with its own three qualities (laziness, coolness and fragrance), so, for precisely that purpose, it blows, thus showing its extreme suitability for subjection to His control. And the "crowds of minor deities" as well as the "bards"—the Gandharvas and so forth—have become proclaimers of His Fame. And they are singers as well. The Gopīs' word "who" means those who belong to the Blessed Lord. With their "instrumental music," which is a *tāmasa* means of attainment, their "songs," which are *rājas* means, and their worship, i.e., "their offerings," which are *sāttvika* means, they "have encircled Him." They have done what was desired in everything.

Introduction to Stanzas 22–23: Having thus described the variety that exists in the type of beings which transcends the worldly qualities, the Gopīs now describe, in these two final stanza-pairs, the deeds of the Blessed Lord alone.

Commentary: The herd of cows which the Blessed Lord is now leading to the cowpens. He leads by His Grace. Otherwise, even if they had been involved in only one game (cf. Stanzas 4–5), they would already be liberated. The same is true for the Gopīs. But by His Grace alone, He acts as He does in order that both these may experience the Joy of worshipping Him through love. The Gopīs tell us the cause for this when they say: "Since," i.e., because of which. He is "the Mountain-Holder." If He were not granting the Joy of worshipping Him through love, then He would not hold Mount Govardhana aloft. It is in order to tell us that this particular Greatness of the Blessed Lord is known to all people that Gopīs have said: "whose feet are hymned with worshipful homage on the path by the elders." "The elders" are well informed in every way. It is only by those who know much that the Blessed Lord can be worshipped. And so "He has gathered the" entire "great wealth of cows together," having separated them from the forest. . . . Or perhaps "gathered together" means He brought all of them together very near to Himself, or restored them to their own proper place—near Himself. "At the day's end," say the Gopīs, since it would be bad for the cows to stay in the forest after that. And the other reason is that Krishna wants to play His other game (with the Gopīs, at night). His "flute" became "songful." This was in order to remove strain and exhaustion, and also to inform the inhabitants of Vraja that He is coming. The effect of the flute's sound is to be expressed later. And Krishna makes not only the Gopīs successful and happy in attaining what they desire, but the Gopas (cowherd-boys) as well. It is to tell us this that the Gopīs have described the hymn of praise the Gopas sang: "His Fame praised in song by His followers." "His followers" means His worshipful servants. By this, we are told that the Gopas, too, sing of Him at night, just as the Gopīs do during the day. Otherwise the constraint of all would not come to pass. Precisely to tell us that Krishna alone knows the effect of such activity and constraint, and He alone produces it, the Gopīs have used the word "joy"!

Source: *Subodhinī* in *Vallabhācārya on the Love Games of Kṛṣṇa*, translated by James D. Redington, S.J. (Delhi: Motilal Banarsidass, 1983).

Selections from the *Caitanya Caritāmṛta of Kṛṣṇadāsa Kavirāja*

Ādi Līlā Chapter 13

So in the evening of the full-moon night in Phālguna, Prabhu was born. At that time, by divine power, there was an eclipse of the moon. The people were greatly delighted, and called out "Hari Hari!" Then Caitanya Prabhu was born, giving birth [also] to the Name. From his birth to his childhood, boyhood, adolescence, and youth, under many pretexts Prabhu caused people to take the name of Hari. Under the pretext of his childhood, Prabhu wept much; but hearing the names "Kṛṣṇa" and "Hari," his crying stopped. Thus the women said "Hari, Hari" to him, and friends all came to see. All the women laughing called him Gaurahari, and thus his name became Gaurahari. In his childhood he was taught to write; in his boyhood he did not marry. He married when he was in his first youth, and everywhere caused people to take the name of Kṛṣṇa. In his adolescence he studied, and taught pupils; and everywhere explained the Kṛṣṇa-name. The essential truth of the *sūtras*, *vṛttis*, *pāñjis*, and the commentaries was in the name of Kṛṣṇa, and his students were delighted at this wonderful power. To whomever he saw, he said "Speak the name of Kṛṣṇa!" and he caused the whole of the town of Navadvīpa to float in the name of Kṛṣṇa. In the days of his youth he began *saṃkīrtana*; day and night he danced in *prema*, his *bhaktas* with him. He wandered from *nagara* to *nagara*, making *kīrtana*, and caused the three worlds to float, by giving *prema-bhakti*. Twenty-four years it was thus in the town of Navadvīpa; he caused all people to take Kṛṣṇa-prema through the name. And after twenty-four years he took *saṃnyāsa*, and taking his *bhaktas* he went to live at Nīlācala. . . .

Adī Līlā Chapter 17

One day Prabhu and all his *bhaktas*, having performed *saṃkīrtana*, were wearied, and sat down. Prabhu planted a mango seed in the courtyard, and immediately a tree was born and began to grow. While they were watching the tree bore fruit; many fruits ripened, and all were astonished. Prabhu quickly gathered two hundred fruits; washing them, he offered them to Kṛṣṇa. Their color was red and yellow, and they had neither pit nor skin; and if he ate one fruit, the stomach of a man was filled. Seeing this, the son of Śacī was greatly pleased, and he fed them all before he ate. There was neither pit nor skin, and they were full of juice like nectar; if he ate one fruit, one's belly was filled with the juice. In this way there was fruit every day, throughout the full year; the Vaiṣṇavas ate the fruit, to the delight of Prabhu. The son of Śacī performed all these līlās; except for the *bhaktas*, other people knew nothing of it. In this way, for twelve months, at the end of the *kīrtana*, Prabhu made each day a great feast of mangoes. While Prabhu was having *kīrtana* the rain clouds came; but according to his own desire he prevented them [from raining].

One day Prabhu gave his instructions to Śrīvāsa, "Read the *Bṛhatsahasra-nāma*; I want to hear it." While reading he came to the praises of the name Nṛsiṃha [man-lion]; hearing it Prabhu the Gauradhāma was possessed. Under the possession of Nṛsiṃha he took a club into his hand and ran to the city to beat the disbelievers. Seeing him, possessed by Nṛsiṃha, full of great radiance, the people left the road and fled in great fear. Seeing the fear of the people, Prabhu regained consciousness, and going to the house of Śrīvāsa he threw away his club. In great dejection Prabhu said to Śrīvāsa, "People were afraid, I have offended them." Śrīvāsa said, "He who takes your name, has a crore of his offences destroyed. There was no offence, but you have saved the people; he who saw you has escaped *saṃsāra*." Saying such things, Śrīvāsa served him, and being soothed Prabhu came to his own house. . . .

Madhya Līlā Chapter 1

Previously I gave the *sūtras* of the *ādi līlā*, which Vṛndāvana Dāsa has expounded in more detail. Thus I have only given his *sūtras*, and among the *sūtras* I have spoken of a few things in more detail. Now let me state the primary *sūtras* of the *śeṣa līlā*; the *līlā* of Prabhu is unending, and cannot be described. Among them, of that part which Vṛndāvana Dasa has described in his *Caitanya Maṅgala*, I shall write *sūtras* only, and I shall elaborate on a few particular things. The Vyāsa of the Caitanya-*līlā* is Vṛndāvana Dāsa; with his permission, I shall take his leftover food. In great devotion I hold his feet upon my head, and describe the *sūtras* of the final *līlā*. For twenty-four years Prabhu remained in his home, and at that time performed the *līlā* known as the *ādi līlā*. And at the end of twenty-four years, in the month of Māgha, in the bright fortnight, he took *saṃnyāsa*. He remained a *saṃnyāsin* for twenty-four years, and this *līlā* is called the *śeṣa līlā*. The *śeṣa līlā* has two names, *madhya* and *antya*, for to the two divisions of the *līlā*, the Vaiṣṇavas give different names. Within them, six years were spent in travelling, in Nīlācala, Gauḍa, Setubandha, and Vṛndāvana. And that *līlā* is called the *madhya līlā*, and the *līlā* following that has the name *antya līlā*. So there are the *ādi*, the *madhya*, and the *antya līlās*; and now I shall describe the *madhya līlā*.

For eighteen years he remained only at Nīlācala, and according to his own practice he taught *bhakti* to the *jīvas*. And within that, for six years he was with his *bhaktas*, and he caused them to propagate *prema-bhakti* in the joy of singing and dancing. He sent Nityānanda Gosvāmī to the Gauḍa country, and he caused the Gauḍa country to float in *prema-rasa*. By nature Nityānanda was mad with Kṛṣṇa-*prema*; by the order of Prabhu he distributed *prema* to all. A crore of my obeisances to his feet, who caused the world to take the *bhakti* of Caitanya, whom Caitanya Gosvāmī called "elder brother"; but he called Caitanya Gosvāmī, "my Prabhu." Even though he himself was Prabhu Balarāma, still he was proud to be a servant of Caitanya. "Serve Caitanya, sing Caitanya, take the name of Caitanya; he who has *bhakti* toward Caitanya, he is my life." In this way he caused the people to take the *bhakti* of Caitanya; the poor and humble, the calumners, he saved them all. . . .

Madhya Līlā Chapter 2

The last twelve years that Prabhu remained were constantly agitated by separation from Kṛṣṇa. Like the condition of Rādhā at the sight of Uddhava, in just such condition was Prabhu, day and night. Eternally Prabhu was mad with *viraha*; he wandered about constantly, and his speech was raving. Blood oozed from the pores of his skin, and his teeth chattered. In a moment his body became thin, and the next moment it swelled. In the *gambhīrā* he got no sleep at all; he scraped his face and head against the wall, and was all bruised and cut. Three doors were shut, but Prabhu still got outside; once he fell in the lion-gate, and once in the water of the sea. Seeing the Caṭaka hill, he mistook it for Govarddhana, and ran weeping, with groans and cries. And seeing the groves and gardens, he thought it was Vṛndāvana; he went there and danced and sang, and in a moment fell unconscious. The manifestations of this *bhāva* were like nothing anyone had ever heard of before; just such a *bhāva* was manifested in the body of Prabhu. The joints of his hands and feet, all separated a span in measurement, and skin that remained [was all that held them together]. His hands, his feet, his head, all retracted into his body, and Prabhu seemed like a tortoise. In such ways was this wonderful bhāva manifested in his body; there was emptiness in his heart, and in his speech he groaned aloud, "Where is the lord of my heart . . . ?"

Madhya Līlā Chapter 4

Once Madhava Purī had come to Vṛndāvana, and while wandering he went to the Govarddhana mountain. Absorbed in prema, he knew neither night nor day; now he fell, now he rose up, and knew not where he was. Circumambulating the hill, he came to the Govindakuṇḍa; he bathed, and was sitting under a tree. It was evening. A cowherd boy with a pot of milk came and placed it before him, and said, smiling, "Purī, drink this milk. Why do you not beg and eat? Upon what do you meditate?" Purī was delighted with the beauty of the boy, and at the sweetness of his words, his hunger and thirst disappeared. Purī said, "Who are you? Where do you live? How did you know that I am fasting?" The boy said, "I am a cowherd, and I live in the village; and in my village, no one remains hungry. Some by begging have rice to eat, some drink milk; and to those who do not ask, I give food. The women saw you when they came to draw water, and all the women gave me milk and sent me to you. I want to milk the cows, so I will go quickly; I shall come again and take the pot." So saying, the boy went away, and was not seen again. And Mādhava Purī was astonished in his mind. He drank the milk, and washed the pot and put it aside; he watched the path, but the boy did not come again. Purī, sat, taking the name, and did not sleep. At the end of the night he felt sleepy, and the outside world was far away. He saw in a dream that the boy had come before him, and holding him by the hand had taken him into a grove. Showing him the grove, he said, "I stay in this grove, and I suffer much from cold and rain and wind and fire. Call the people of the village, and take me from this grove, and put me, well-placed, upon the hill. Build a temple there and put me in it, wash my body with much cool water. I have been watching the path for you for many days, [thinking] "When will Mādhava come and serve me?" You have served me, and I am conquered by your *prema*; I shall show myself and pervade the whole world. My name is Gopāla, the upholder of Govarddhana; I have been established by Vajra, and am the lord of this place. Taking me from the top of the hill, my servant hid me in the grove, and fled in fear of the [foreigners]. From that time I have remained in this forest-place; it is good that you have come to take me out so carefully." So saying, the boy disappeared. And awakening, Mādhava Purī reflected on it, "I have seen Kṛṣṇa, but did not recognize him." And so saying, he fell to the earth, overcome with *prema*. Having wept for a time, he calmed himself again, and decided to honor his instruction.

Having performed his morning ablutions. Purī came to the center of the town, and having gathered all the people together, he began to say to them, "The Īśvara of your village is Govardhanadhari; he is within the grove. Come, let us bring him out. The grove is very dense and thick; we cannot penetrate it. Bring axes and spades and make an opening." Hearing this, the people went with him happily; cutting into the grove, they made a path and entered. They saw the *ṭhākura* covered with grass and earth, and seeing it all the people were struck with astonishment. Having uncovered him, they informed [Purī] of it. But the image was very heavy, and no one could move it. The most powerful men gathered there, and with Purī they took the image up upon the hill. They placed the image on a throne of stone, and they put a big stone behind the image to support it. The *brāhmaṇas* of the village all brought new water-pots; having strained it, they brought water from the Govindakuṇḍa. They presented a hundred new pots of water, and many instruments and drums sounded, and the women sang. Some sang, some danced, and there was a great festival; much milk and curd and *ghi* was brought from the village. And articles for the food-offerings came, much *sandeśa* and the rest, and many presents, so many that I cannot describe them all. *Tulasī*, flowers, and cloth, many such things came; and Mādhavendra Purī himself performed the ceremony of the installation of the image. Bathing [the image], all impurities were washed away; and he put much oil on the sacred body, until it glistened. And he bathed him with the five articles from the cow, and the five sweets; and then he gave him a great bath with the hundred pots of water. And again he put on oil, and the body glistened; and he finished the bathing with scented water from a conch-shell.

Having washed the holy body he dressed it with clothing; sandal, *tulasī*, and a garland of flowers he put upon the body. Then he began the offerings of food, with incense and lamp, and he brought milk and curd and *sandeśa* sweets of various kinds. He presented sweet-scented water in new jars, and rinsing his mouth, again he presented *tāmbūla*. Having offered *ārati*, he said prayers and praises, and bowing before it, he made the dedication of himself. As much husked rice, lentil, and wheat flour as there was in the village the people brought, and the hill was covered. The earthen pots which were in the house of the potter, all were brought in the morning, and the cooking started. Ten *brāhmaṇas* cooked the food, and they made a big mound of it; and there were five who cooked various curries, and various sauces. *Śāka* and fruits and roots from the forest made many kinds of curries; and some *brāhmaṇas* prepared *baḍās* and *baḍīs* and *kaḍis*. Five or seven prepared rows and rows of *ruṭī*; and there were all kinds of other curries, drenched with *ghi*. They put new cloth on the ground and on it *palāśa* leaves, and on these cooked rice was placed. And beside it a mountainous row of *ruṭī*, containers of sauces and curries filled the four directions. Beside these were curd and milk, buttermilk, and other kinds of milk preparations, and beside these were *pāyasa*, butter, and cream. In this way mountains of food were prepared, and Purī Gosvāmī presented them to Gopāla. Having filled many pots they offered sweet-smelling water, and with a hunger of many days, Gopāla ate it all. Even though Gopāla ate all the rice and curry, at the touch of his hand it was at once restored. Mādhava Gosvāmī perceived this; from him Gopāla hid nothing.

Thus in their great zeal a great feast was prepared in a single day; it was through the power of Gopāla, though others did not know. They gave him water to rinse his mouth, and betel-rolls, and the people made *ārati*, shouting "Jaya jaya!" Then they laid him down, having brought a new bed, and on top of it they brought and spread a new cloth. They screened it off in four directions with a hedge of grass, and covered it on top with a screen. Purī Gosvāmī gave an instruction to all the *brāhmaṇas*, "Feed the women and children and old people of the village." They all sat down and ate in order, feeding the *brāhmaṇas* and their wives first. Many people came from other villages, to see; and seeing Gopāla they all [also] partook of the *prasāda*. Seeing the power of Purī the people were astonished, for it was like a manifest mountain of rice of former days. Purī made all the *brāhmaṇas* Vaiṣṇavas, and appointed them all for the service [of Gopāla]. At the end of the day, he raised up the lord again, and fed him food and water.

Madhya Līlā Chapter 6

In ecstasy Prabhu went to the temple of Jagannātha; and seeing Jagannātha, he became restless with *prema*. He went running to embrace Jagannātha, and he fell, in the temple, overcome with *prema*. By chance Sārvabhauma saw it all, and prevented a temple servant from beating him. Seeing the beauty of Prabhu and his delirium of *prema*, Sārvabhauma was greatly astonished. After much time [Caitanya] was still unconscious; and it was time for the food-offering. Sārvabhauma then thought of a way. With the help of students and temple servants he carried Prabhu, and brought him to his house and placed him lying in a clean place. There was no breathing at all, and his stomach was palpitating, and seeing this the mind of the Bhaṭṭācārya became worried. He brought some cotton and held it before the nose [of Prabhu]. It fluttered gently, and seeing this he became calmer. Sitting down, Bhaṭṭācārya decided that this was a true delirium of the *mahāprema* of Kṛṣṇa. "This is a truly burning purity, which is called *pralaya*; it is that burning *bhāva* in a *bhakta* who is eternally perfected. He who has the *adhirūḍha-bhava* has such delirium; seeing it in the body of a man is truly wonderful." So Bhaṭṭācārya was thinking as he sat there, when Nityānanda and the rest came together to the main gate.

Hearing of this the people said to one another, "A renouncer has come, and when he saw Jagannātha he fainted; there was no consciousness in his body at all. Then Sārvabhauma took him to his house." When they heard this they all knew that this was the doing of Mahāprabhu. And at the same time Gopīnāthācārya came there. He was a dweller in Nadīyā, a son-in-law of Viśārada; he was a *bhakta* of Mahāprabhu, and one who knew the true meaning of him.

He had previously met Mukunda, and seeing him he was surprised. When Mukunda saw him he made obeisance. He embraced and asked news of Prabhu. Mukunda said, "Prabhu has come here, and we all have come with him." The ācarya then made obeisance to Nityānanda Gosvāmī; and again he asked them all together for word of Prabhu. Mukunda said, "Mahāprabhu has taken a vow of renunciation, and he has come to Nīlācala, bringing us all with him. He left us all, and went ahead for *darśana* [viewing]; we all have come after in search of him. We heard from the mouths of others that Prabhu is in the house of Sārvabhauma; Prabhu was unconscious in *prema*, because of the sight of Īśvara, and Sārvabhauma has taken him and gone to his own house. Then we thought to meet you, and by chance we caught sight of you. So let us go, everyone, to the house of Sārvabhauma; after we see Prabhu, we shall have *darśana* of Īśvara." Hearing this, Gopīnātha took everyone, and went joyfully to the house of Sārvabhauma. . . .

There was a gentle *brāhmaṇa* named Vāsudeva, whose whole body was rotten with leprosy, and full of worms. From his body those worms would fall off, and he would pick the worms up and put them in their places. In the night he heard that the Gosvāmī had come, and in the morning he came to see, at the house of Kūrma. Having heard from the mouth of Kūrma of the coming of Prabhu, he fell to the earth, fainting in sorrow. In various ways he began to lament, but coming to that place, Prabhu embraced him. At the touch of Prabhu, the leprosy fled away with his sorrow, and now full of joy his body became beautiful. Witnessing the grace of

Prabhu, his heart was astonished. He recited a *śloka*, holding his feet, and praising him.

Praising him much, he said, "Hear, O you who are full of mercy! Such qualities are not in *jīvas*. But they are in you. When they see me, and get the smell of my foul disease, people flee away. But you touch me; you are the self-dependent Īśvara. But I was good while I was vile and lowly; yet now conceit will be born in me." Prabhu said, "You will never be proud. You will forever speak the name of Kṛṣṇa. Commanded by Kṛṣṇa, go and save *jīvas*, and shortly Kṛṣṇa will embrace you." So saying, Prabhu disappeared, and the two *brāhmaṇas* wept on each others' shoulders, at the qualities of Prabhu. . . .

Madhya Līlā Chapter 9

Hearing of his learning, the followers of false doctrine came; they came in pride and conceit, bringing their pupils with them. A Buddhist teacher, very learned in his own "new faith," began to speak before Prabhu with vast learning. Even though Buddhists were not to be conversed with and unworthy to be seen, still Prabhu talked with them in order to shatter their pride. In the new faith, the Buddhist *śāstras* were primarily philosophical argument; and Prabhu countered those very arguments so that they were unable to prove them. The Buddhist teacher introduced new arguments one after another, and with profound close reasoning Prabhu shattered them all. The philosophically oriented *paṇḍitas* all were defeated; the people laughed, and the Buddhists were ashamed and contrite. Realizing Prabhu was a Vaiṣṇava, the Buddhists went home; they all met together and took evil counsel. Putting impure food on a metal plate, they brought it before Prabhu, calling it "Viṣṇu-*prasāda*." Just then a bird with a great body came and took the plate of food in his beak. It dropped the impure food on the Buddhists, being impure, and with a ringing sound, the plate crashed on the head of the Buddhist teacher. The plate fell on its edge, and his head was cut; losing consciousness the ācārya fell to the ground. All his pupils wept with grief, and they all ran for refuge at the feet of Prabhu. "You are Īśvara manifest. Forgive our offences; be merciful and bring our guru back to life." Prabhu said, "Everyone say 'Kṛṣṇa, Kṛṣṇa Hari!' Loudly say the name of Kṛṣṇa into the ear of your guru. Your guru will then regain consciousness." All the Buddhists together made Kṛṣṇa-*saṃkrītana*. Into the ear of the guru they yelled, "Say Kṛṣṇa Rāma Hari." Regaining consciousness the *ācārya* got up, saying "Hari." Saying "Kṛṣṇa" the *ācārya* made obeisance to Prabhu, and when they saw it all the people were astonished. In this way the son of Śacī performed wonders; [then] he vanished, and no one could see him. . . .

***Madhya Līlā* Chapter 17**

In the deep of night he went to see Jagannātha and to take his permission, and toward the end of the night Prabhu arose and went secretly. In the morning the bhaktas did not see Prabhu; they searched everywhere, very disturbed. Svarūpa Gosvāmī explained it to them all, and dissuaded them [from following] and kept them there, knowing the mind of Prabhu. Leaving the well-known roads, Prabhu went along side paths; keeping Kaṭaka on his right he entered the forest. Prabhu went through the lonely forest, taking the name of Kṛṣṇa, and when they saw Prabhu the elephants and tigers left the path. In packs were tigers and boars and rhinoceroses and herds of elephants, and absorbed, Prabhu moved among them. When he saw them, great fear arose in the heart of Bhaṭṭācārya; but because of the power of Prabhu they remained to one side. One day a tiger was lying on the path, and Prabhu, absorbed, stepped on its body. Prabhu said "Kṛṣṇa, Kṛṣṇa" arousing the tiger; the tiger got up; and saying "Kṛṣṇa, Kṛṣṇa" the tiger began to dance. Another day Prabhu was bathing in a river, when a herd of rut elephants came to drink water there. As the elephants came before him, Prabhu splashed water on them, saying "Say the name of Kṛṣṇa." Those whose bodies were touched with the tiniest drop of water said "Kṛṣṇa, Kṛṣṇa" and danced and sang in *prema*. Some fell to the earth, and others trumpeted. And watching all this, the mind of Bhaṭṭācārya was astonished. . . .

At that time five or seven tigers came to that place, and the tigers and deer together went with Mahāprabhu. And when he saw that, Mahāprabhu remembered Vṛndāvana. . . . When Prabhu said, "Say Kṛṣṇa, Kṛṣṇa!" the tigers and deer said "Kṛṣṇa" and began to dance. The tigers danced and wept with the deer, and Balabhadra Bhaṭṭācārya was astonished when he saw it. The tigers and the deer embraced each other, and mouth to mouth they kissed each other. As he watched this play, Prabhu began to laugh, and leaving them all there he went on his way.

Peacocks and other birds, seeing Prabhu, went with him, saying "Kṛṣṇa" and dancing drunken, and Prabhu cried "Hari *bol*!" in a loud voice. The creepers on the trees blossomed, hearing that sound. As many things, moving and unmoving, as there were in Jhārikhaṇḍa, were drunk with *prema* by the name of Kṛṣṇa. Whatever village he passed through, and wherever he stayed, *prema-bhakti* was aroused in the people of all those villages. And when anyone heard the name of Kṛṣṇa from his mouth, from his mouth another heard it, and from his mouth another. And everyone, saying "Kṛṣṇa, Hari," danced and wept and sang, and throughout the country all became Vaiṣṇavas. Even though Prabhu was in fear of the crowds of people, and kept *prema* hidden and did not manifest it outwardly, still, affected by hearing him and by the sight of him, all the people of the country became Vaiṣṇavas. He had gone to Gauḍa, Vanga, Utkala, and to the south, and wherever he had wandered he saved people. Under the pretext of going to Mathurā he had come to Jhārikhaṇḍa, where people were irreligious, like Bhillas. He saved them all, by means of the name and *prema*; who has the power to understand the profundity of the *līlā* of Caitanya?

When he saw the forest he mistook it for Vṛndāvana; and when he saw the mountains he thought, "This is Govarddhana." Wherever he saw a river he thought it the Kālindī, and there, overcome with *prema*, Prabhu danced and fell weeping. While going along the path, Bhaṭṭācārya [found] vegetables and roots and fruit; whatever he could get anywhere, he took. In whatever village Prabhu rested, there five or seven *brāhmaṇas* would come and offer him invitations. And some people would bring rice and give it to Bhaṭṭācārya, and some brought milk and curd, and some brought *ghi* and *khaṇḍa*. Where there were no *brāhmaṇas*, there were worthy *śūdras*, and coming, they all offered invitations to Bhaṭṭācārya. Bhaṭṭācārya cooked curries with things of the forest, and with the forest-curry Prabhu was much delighted. [Bhaṭṭācārya] gathered food for two or four days and kept it, and when they were in the deep forest where no one lived, Bhaṭṭācārya would cook that food. He made curry with roots and fruits and many vegetables of the forest. Prabhu would eat in the forest in the highest delight, and on those days when there were no people he found great happiness. Bhaṭṭācārya served him, in affection, like a servant, and his *brāhmaṇa* carried the water-vessel and the outer clothing. He bathed three times [a day] in the water of warm springs, and in the morning and in the evening in the warmth of the fire, for wood was plentiful. . . .

Antya Līlā Chapter 3

When Haridāsa abandoned his own home, he remained many days in the forests of Beṇāpola. He was alone in the forest, and he made a hut and served the *tulasī*, and recited in *kīrtana* night and day three lakhs of names. He lived by begging at the houses of *brāhmaṇas*, and because of his glory all the people worshiped him. The ruler of that country was called Rāmacandra Khān; he had malice towards Vaiṣṇavas, and was a greatly impious man. He could not bear the worship of the people towards Haridāsa, and he devised many schemes to degrade him. In no way did Haridāsa have any fault. So as a way of degrading him, he had prostitutes brought. He said to the prostitutes, "This Haridāsa is an ascetic; all of you destroy the *dharma* of his asceticism." Among the prostitutes there was one who was young and beautiful, and she said, "In three days' time I shall have stolen his mind." And Khān said, "Let my footmen go with you, and when he unites with you they will seize him and bring him here." The prostitute said, "The first time I will go without companions; the second, I shall take your footmen to seize him."

In the nighttime that prostitute put on beautiful clothes, and went joyfully to the dwelling place of Haridāsa. Bowing to the *tulasī*, she went to the door of Haridāsa, and bowing to the Gosvāmī, she remained standing there. Uncovering her body and showing him, she sat down in the door, and began to say in a most melodious voice, "O Ṭhākura, you are most handsome and in the blush of youth; seeing you how could any woman contain herself? My mind is greedy for union with you, and if I do not have you there is no reason to live any more." Haridāsa said, "I shall make you that promise. But [my recitation of] the number of the names [of Kṛṣṇa] is still not finished. You sit there and listen to the *nāma-saṃkīrtana* until it is. When I have finished the names, I shall do what you wish." Hearing this, the prostitute remained seated, and Haridāsa made *kīrtana* until the morning. Seeing that it was morning, the prostitute arose, and going to Khān she told him everything. "Today he has given me his promise; tomorrow I will certainly have union with him."

The next day in the evening, the prostitute came, and Haridāsa encouraged her much, "Yesterday you were sorrowed; but I will not offend you, that I shall certainly promise you. Now sit here and listen to the *nāma-saṃkīrtana*, and when the names have been fulfilled, then your wish will also be fulfilled." So the prostitute made obeisance to him and to the *tulasī*, and sat in the doorway and listened to the names, and she said "Hari, Hari." The end of the night came, and the prostitute was very restless, and seeing her condition, Haridāsa said to her, "I make a sacrifice of taking a crore of names every month. This vow I have made, and I am coming to the end of it. "Today it will be completed," was my thought, and although I took names the whole night long, I was unable to complete it. Today it will be complete, and my vow will be fulfilled; then I shall have intercourse with you, as you desire." So the prostitute went and told this to the Khān, and the next day in the evening came to the place of Ṭhākura.

Bowing to Ṭhākura and to the *tulasī*, she sat in the doorway and listened to the names, saying "Hari, Hari." "The names will certainly be finished today," said Haridāsa, "and today I shall fulfill your desire." And while he was still at *kīrtana*, the end of the night came. And in the company of the Ṭhākura, the prostitute's mind was turned. Bowing deeply she fell at the feet of the Ṭhākura, and humbly told him the story of Rāmacandra Khān. "As a prostitute I have committed infinite sins; be merciful and save me, wretched as I am." Ṭhākura said: "I know all about the Khān. He is ignorant and stupid, so I do not take offence from him. That day [when you came] I was going to go from this place, but I remained for three more days, to save you." The prostitute said, "Be gracious, and instruct me; what should I do, that the agonies of *saṃsāra* pass from me?" Ṭhākura said, "Give the goods of your house to a *brāhmaṇa*, then come to this house and remain here. Take the name incessantly, and serve the *tulasī*, and quickly you will gain the feet of Kṛṣṇa." So saying, instructing her about the name, the Ṭhākura rose up and went away, saying "Hari Hari." So the prostitute took the orders of her guru, and she gave whatever there was in her house to a *brāhmaṇa*. She shaved her head and remained with one cloth in that house, and night and day she took the name three lakhs of times. She served the *tulasī* and fasted, [only] chewing; and as she controlled her senses, *prema* manifested itself. She became a famous Vaiṣṇava, a very great person, and many great Vaiṣṇavas went to have view of her. And seeing the actions of the prostitute, the people were astonished, and they spoke of the greatness of Haridāsa, and made obeisance. . . .

Antya Līlā Chapter 18

From that day the condition of Prabhu intensified, his condition of separation from Kṛṣṇa doubled. Day and night he displayed mad ravings, and incessantly his *viraha* [feeling of separation] grew, under the control of *Rādhā-bhāva*. Suddenly the journey of Kṛṣṇa to Mathurā would come to him, and the signs of madness appeared, a condition of disorientation. He raved, clinging to the neck of Rāmananda, and he asked Svarūpa questions, believing him to be a *sakhī*. . . .

Mahāprabhu's mind was whirling, under the control of *prema*, and he sat awake, making *nāma-saṃkīrtana*. Anguish of *viraha* and anxiety rose up in Prabhu, and he began to hit his face on the walls of the *gambhīrā*. His mouth and cheeks and nose were cut and bruised all over, but absorbed in *bhāva* Prabhu did not feel the streams of blood trickling down. The whole night, in his *bhāva*, he wounded his face, and then Svarūpa heard him groaning. Lighting a lamp he entered the room and saw Prabhu's face, and Svarūpa and Govinda both were dismayed. Bringing Prabhu to the cot, they calmed him down, and Svarūpa asked him, "Why have you done this?" And Prabhu replied, "I was anxious, and I could not stay in the room; so I wandered about looking for the door, so that I could go quickly outside. I could not find the door, and I hit my face on the four walls. It was bruised and the blood fell, and I could not find the way to go." In his maddened state, Prabhu's mind was not still, and what he did and what he said, in all these were the signs of madness. . . .

Antya Līlā Chapter 19

When he saw Kṛṣṇa, Mahāprabhu went running there; seeing him before him he laughed; then Kṛṣṇa disappeared. He had found Kṛṣṇa before him, and again had lost him—Prabhu fell fainting on the ground. The garden was permeated with the perfume of the holy body of Kṛṣṇa, and when he smelled that perfume, Prabhu became unconscious. The scent of Kṛṣṇa always entered his nostrils, and when he tasted the scent, Prabhu became mad.

Source: *Caitanya Caritāmṛta of Kṛṣṇadsa Kavirāja*, translated by Edward C. Dimock, Jr., and edited by Tony K. Stewart (Cambridge: Harvard University Press, 1999).

Selections from the *Bhaktisāmṛtasindhu* of Rūpa Gosvāmin

Eastern Quadrant/First Wave: The General Characteristics of Devotion

9. The first wave defines the general characteristics of devotion; the second describes the means of actualizing (*sādhana*) devotion; the third concerns the foundational emotions (*bhāva*); and the fourth explains supreme love (*prema*).
10. The distinguishing characteristics of the highest devotion, as it is fully known by the sages, are clearly described in this first wave.
11. The highest devotion is dedicated service to Kṛṣṇa that is rendered pleasantly, is devoid of desire for anything else, and is unobstructed by intellectual knowledge or purposeful action. . . .

13–15. Devotion to the Supreme Lord is without motive and is unobstructed. Even if the five kinds of *mokṣa* are offered—namely, co-residence in the same world, equality in power, proximity, similarity in form, or even union—devotees do not accept anything but my service. This very thing called bhakti-yoga has been declared to be the highest aim.

16. The indication of the superiority of the devotees expressed in these verses amounts to a definition of devotion since it shows its supreme purity.

    The Six Qualites of Devotion:

17. Devotion a) destroys difficulties, b) bestows auspiciousness, c) trivializes *mokṣa* (liberation), d) is very difficult to attain, e) consists of a special concentrated joy, and f) attracts Śrī Kṛṣṇa.

a) The Destruction of Difficulties:

18. Difficulties are of three types: sin, the seeds of sin, and ignorance.

Sin:

19. Sin is itself of two types: that which has not yet begun to take effect, and that which has already begun to take effect. . . .

Eastern Quadrant/Second Wave: Sādhana Bhakti

1. Devotion is declared to be of three types: Sādhana, Bhāva, and Prema.
   Sādhana bhakti
2. Devotion that achieves a foundational emotion (*bhāva*) through physical effort is called Sādhana. Its goal is the manifestation in the heart of an eternally perfected emotion. . . .
16. The eligible are of three types: highest, average, and lowest.
   The Highest:
17. One who has expert knowledge of scripture and its interpretation, whose conviction is completely firm, and whose faith is strong is considered the highest among those eligible for Vaidhī Bhakti.
   The Average:
18. One who has no expert knowledge of scripture and its interpretation, but possesses firm faith is average.
   The Lowest:
19. One whose faith is weak is judged to be the lowest.

20–21. Among the four types of eligible people mentioned in the *Gītā* and other scriptures, the one who receives the grace of the Lord or one of his dear devotees gets rid of an unsteady emotional nature and becomes eligible for pure devotion. . . .

273. Rāgātmikā Bhakti is of two types: Amorous (*kāmarūpā*) and Relational. . . .
274. Having absorbed their minds in the Lord through devotion motivated by such emotions as amorous love, hatred, fear, and affection and having thereby destroyed their sins, many have reached the highest end.
275. The gopīs have done this through amorous love, Kaṃsa through fear, Śiśupāl and other kings through hatred, the Vṛṣṇis through relationships, you Pāṇḍavas through affection, and we (Nārada and other sages) through devotion, O Mighty One.
276. Fear and hatred are rejected because they are contrary to the favorable nature of this devotion. Affection generally connotes friendship and thus belongs to Vaidhī Bhakti.
277. On the other hand, if affection were understood to mean supreme love (*prema*, a state beyond practice), it is not appropriate here in religious

practice. The words (of Nārada) "we through devotion" clearly refer to Vaidhī Bhakti.

278. The statement that the goal is the same for both Kṛṣṇa's enemies and his friends means that Brahman resembles Kṛṣṇa as a sunray resembles the sun.

279. The enemies of Hari are generally absorbed only in Brahman; but a few catch a glimpse of the similarity of form with the Lord and become immersed in the happiness of that state.

As the *Brahmāṇḍa Purāṇa* says:

280. Beyond the darkness is the world of perfection (*siddhaloka*) where the perfected ones and the demons killed by Hari dwell immersed in the happiness of Brahman.

281. Devotees dear to Kṛṣṇa, who worship Him by means of a passionate relationship of one type or another, attain the nectar of His lotus-feet that consists of supreme love (*prema*). . . .

283. Amorous Bhakti is that (type of Rāgātmikā Bhakti) which leads the thirst for erotic enjoyment to its perfect state, since it is undertaken exclusively for the pleasure of Kṛṣṇa.

284. It is perfectly accomplished and brilliantly displayed in the gopīs of Vraja. Their distinctive love (*prema*) attains a special sweetness; since it is the cause of various kinds of amorous activities, the wise have called it "amorous" (*kāma*).

As the Tantra says:

285. Only the supreme love of the gopīs is celebrated as amorous. . . .

290. Following the twofold division of Rāgātmikā Bhakti, Rāgānugā Bhakti is declared to be of two kinds: Imitation of Amorous Bhakti (*kāmānugā*) and Imitation of Relational Bhakti.

Those Eligible for Rāgānugā Bhakti:

291. Anyone who is desirous of attaining the emotional state (*bhāva*) of the residents of Vraja, who are situated exclusively in Rāgātmikā Bhakti, is eligible for Rāgānugā Bhakti.

292. The indication of the birth of this intense desire for those emotional states is that upon hearing of the sweetness of their various emotional states the mind proceeds without regard for either scriptural instructions or logic.

293. But the one eligible for Vaidhī Bhakti should rely on scriptural instructions and favorable reasoning until one of these emotional states appears.

294. The practitioner of Rāgānugā Bhakti should dwell continually in Vraja, absorbed in its various stories, remembering Kṛṣṇa and the intimate companions to whom he is most attracted.

295. One who is desirous of attaining one of the emotional states of the residents of Vraja should perform services in a manner that imitates them with both the practitioner's body (*sādhaka-rūpa*) and the perfected body (*siddha-rūpa*).
296. Practices such as listening (*śravaṇa*) and praising (*kīrtana*) that were described for Vaidhī Bhakti are also known by the wise to be useful here in Rāgānugā Bhakti.

Imitation of Amorous Bhakti:

297. Imitation of Amorous Bhakti (*kāmānugā*) is that special desire which imitates Amorous Bhakti.
298. It is of two types: Desire for Erotic Enjoyment and Desire to Share in Their Emotions.
299. The goal of Desire for Erotic Enjoyment is direct amorous involvement; the goal of Desire to Share in Their Emotions is appreciation of the sweetness of the various emotions (of the gopīs of Vraja).
300. Those who are desirous of the amorous emotional state, after looking at the sweetness of the beautiful image of Kṛṣṇa or after hearing of His various forms of love play, have these two ways as a means of realizing it. This is even the case for men, as is stated in the *Padma Purāṇa*.
301. Previously all the great sages living in the Daṇḍaka forest saw the enchanting Rāma and desired to enjoy his beautiful body.
302. They were all, therefore, born in Gokula as women, and attaining Hari there by means of passion, they were freed from the ocean of worldly suffering.
303. One who has intense longing for amorous enjoyment, but serves Kṛṣṇa only by means of the path of Vaidhī Bhakti, achieves the state of a queen in the city. . . .
305. Imitation of Relational Bhakti is declared by the sages to be that form of devotion that consists of meditating on a relationship with Kṛṣṇa, such as fatherhood, and ascribing that relationship to one's own self.
306. This form of devotion is to be enacted by practitioners desirous of such emotional states as parental affection and friendship by means of the emotions, actions, and postures of Nanda the king of Vraja, Subala, and other appropriate exemplary figures.
307. It is stated in the scriptures that an old carpenter who lived in Kurupuri achieved perfection by following Nārada's instructions and worshipping an image of Kṛṣṇa, the son of Nanda, as his own son. . . .
309. Rāgānugā Bhakti is called "Puṣṭi Mārga" by some, since the sole cause of its attainment is the grace of Kṛṣṇa or His devotees.

Eastern Quadrant/Third Wave: Bhāva Bhakti

1. Bhāva (as a type of devotion) is a special form of the pure and luminous quality, and is like a beam of the sun of supreme love (*prema*); its desirous rays soften the heart.

   As it says in the Tantra:
2. The first stage of supreme love (*prema*) is called Bhāva. Here the Responses, such as tears and goose bumps, are manifest in small amounts.

   There is an illustration of this in the *Padma Purāṇa*:
3. While meditating on the two lotus-feet of the Lord, King Ambarīṣa was slightly overwhelmed and his eyes filled with tears.
4. Once manifest in the mind, this love (*rati*) identifies with the mind's own nature. Even though it is self-manifesting, it appears to be manifested by the activity of the mind.
5. In reality, this love is enjoyment itself, but it also becomes the cause of the enjoyment of the actions of Kṛṣṇa and His intimate companions.
6. This loving emotion (Bhāva) is born in two ways: either from diligent dedication to spiritual practices (*sādhana*), or for the very fortunate, by the grace (*prasāda*) of Kṛṣṇa or His devotees. The first, however, is more common; the second is rare.

   Born from diligent dedication to spiritual practices:
7. Bhāva born from diligent dedication to spiritual practices is of two types, corresponding to the two paths of Vaidhī and Rāgānugā.
8. Diligent dedication to spiritual practices brings about desire for Hari, then produces attachment for Him, and then causes the birth of love (*rati*) for Him. . . .

Eastern Quadrant/Fourth Wave: Prema Bhakti

1. When the Bhāva softens the heart completely and becomes very intense, and when it is marked by a high degree of "myness," it is called Prema by the wise. . . .
5. A Bhāva that is raised to the highest state by performing outer and inner practices is called "originating from a Bhāva." . . .
6. He who acts according to these scriptural injunctions develops an intense love by singing the names of his beloved Hari, and his heart melts. Because of this, he laughs loudly, cries, shouts, sings, and dances like a mad man, thereby transgressing all worldly conventions. . . .
11. Prema Bhakti born of grace is of two kinds: that which is connected to a knowledge of the Lord's majesty, and that which is exclusive.

An illustration of the first is in the Pañcarātra:

12. Affection that is very firm and surpasses all other emotions, and is connected with a knowledge of the Lord's majesty, is called devotion. The various states of liberation are achieved by means of it; they can be achieved in no other way. . . .

14. Prema connected with knowledge of the Lord's majesty is for those following the path of Vaidhī Bhakti, whereas Exclusive Prema is generally for those engaged in Rāgānugā Bhakti.

15–16. The first stage of love for practitioners is faith (*śraddhā*), then in order comes association with the saints (*sādhu-saṅga*), acts of worship (*bhajana-kriyā*), the cessation of worthless activity, loyalty, desire, attachment, Bhāva, and then the manifestation of Prema.

17. The behavior of that fortunate one in whose heart Prema has newly manifest is difficult to fathom, even by those well versed in scripture. . . .

Southern Quadrant/First Wave: The Excitants

1. May Sanātana Gosvāmin, the destroyer of sins, who is greatly honored in Mathurā by me, his brother Rūpa who am dependent on no other, be ever victorious.

2. The general characteristics of the Rasa of devotion to the Lord are now presented in this "Southern Quadrant," the second division of the *Ocean of the Essence of Devotional Rasa.*

3. This quadrant contains five chapters, entitled respectively: Excitants (*vibhāva*), Indications (*anubhāva*), Responses (*sāttvikas*), Transitory Emotions (*vyabhicāri-bhāva*) and Foundational Emotions (*sthāyi-bhāva*).

4. I will now discuss how love (*rati*) for Keśava becomes the highest form of Rasa when developed by means of a combination of the Excitants, Indications, Responses, and Transitory Emotions.

5. Love for Kṛṣṇa is the Foundational Emotion that becomes the Rasa of devotion (*bhakti-rasa*). It is raised by means of the Excitants, Indications, Responses, and Transitory Emotions to a relishable state in the heart of devotees engaged in such actions as listening to stories about the Lord.

6. A taste for the Rasa of devotion appears only in the heart of one who has an unconscious impression of true devotion that comes from both a past life and this life.

7–8. Love dwells in the hearts of those devotees whose impurities have been removed by devotion, whose minds are bright and pure, who are fond of the *Śrī Bhāgavata Purāṇa*, enjoy the companionship of sensitive people, live for the pleasure of devotion to Govinda, and perform acts conducive to supreme love (*prema*).

9. This love, which exists in the hearts of the devotees as the manifestation of past and present unconscious impressions, is the very form of bliss that develops into the state of Rasa.
10. In the course of encountering the Excitants—Kṛṣṇa and his intimate companions—as well as the other aesthetic components, love approaches the highest limit of perfect bliss and wonder.
11. Supreme love can be experienced in small quantities, however, from merely slight exposure to the Excitants and other aesthetic components, since it is of a nature that can be readily experienced.

A general definition of the Excitants, Indications, Responses, and Transitory Emotions:

12–13. The causes of love, such as Kṛṣṇa, his devotees, and the sound of his flute; the resulting expressions, such as smiling; the eight reactions, such as stupefaction; and the assisting emotions, such as indifference, are known in the experience of Rasa to be respectively the Excitants, the Indications, the Responses, and the Transitory Emotions.

14. The Excitants are considered to be the causes of experiencing love. They are of two kinds: the first are the Substantial Excitants, and the second are the Enhancing Excitants. . . .

300. Devotees are said to be of five types: the peaceful (*śāntas*), the servants and sons (*dāsas* and *sutas*), the friends (*sakhas*), the teachers and parents (*guru-varga*), and the female lovers (*preyasīs*).

Now the Enhancing Excitants:

301. The Enhancing Excitants (*uddīpana-vibhāva*) are those things that enhance the Foundational Emotion (i.e., love for Kṛṣṇa). They are Śrī Kṛṣṇa's 1) qualities, 2) actions, 3) ornaments. . .

Southern Quadrant/Third Wave: The Responses

1. The wise call the mind pure and luminous (*sattva*) that is imbued with emotional states (*bhāvas*) associated with either direct or obscured relationships with Kṛṣṇa. . . .
2. The emotional states arising from this pure and luminous state of mind are called Responses. They are considered to be of three types: a) Affectionate, b) Accumulated, and c) Harsh. . . .

3. The Affectionate Responses are further divided into two types: primary and secondary. . . .
4. Responses produced from Primary Love (*mukya-rati*) are Primary Responses. The sages know that they result from a direct relationship with Kṛṣṇa.
   An illustration:
5. The heavenly lady (Rādhā) whose teeth resemble jasmine buds was joyfully making an exquisite garland for Mukunda out of jasmine flowers when the ambrosial sound of his flute caused her body to become motionless.
6. This is an example of the Primary Response of "stupefaction." "Perspiration" and the other Primary Responses are to be known in a like manner.
   The Secondary Affectionate Responses:
7. Responses produced from a Secondary Love are called Secondary Responses. Here the relationship with Kṛṣṇa is somehow obscured.
   An illustration:
8. After the Supreme Lord, who was the cloud that satisfied the Cātaka bird of her own eyes, was taken away to the city of Mathurā, Yaśodā, the queen of Gokula, shouted angrily with a stammering voice at the king Nanda and her face became very red.
   Here are two secondary Responses: a broken voice and a change in color.
   The Accumulated Responses:
9. When the mind is imbued with emotions that arise from neither Primary or Secondary Love, but a love for Kṛṣṇa has somehow nevertheless appeared, the Responses accompanying this love are called "Accumulated."
   An illustration:
10. Yaśodā, the queen of Vraja, saw the huge, terrifying body of the demoness Pūtanā wandering about her house in a dream; her own delicate body trembled and with a disoriented mind she got up and began searching for her son.
11. Here the Response of "trembling" that accompanies Yaśodā's love is identified as Accumulated.
    The Harsh Responses:
12. Harsh Responses are those that sometimes arise in persons who are without love for Kṛṣṇa, but are close to becoming devotees, from the joyful amazement that results from hearing the sweet and wonderful stories of Kṛṣṇa.
    An illustration:
13. His body was covered with goose bumps in response to the sweetness of the songs about the play of Mādhava and instantly he was filled with joy, even

though there was not even a trace of love within his heart and he was engaged in actions devoted only to the pursuit of worldly pleasures.

14. The wise refer to this kind of experience (goose bumps) as a Harsh Response since it is without love. It is indicative of the semblance of love found in persons desirous of mokṣa and other such persons previously described.
15. When the mind comes under the influence of a pure, luminous state (*sattvībhava*) it establishes itself in the vital breath in an extraordinary manner. The vital breath is thereby transformed and in turn excites the body in various ways. Such emotional states as stupefaction then appear in the body of the devotee.
16. The Responses are taught to be eight in number: 1) stupefaction, 2) perspiration, 3) goose bumps, 4) broken voice, 5) trembling, 6) change of color, 7) tears, 8) loss of consciousness.

Southern Quadrant/Fifth Wave: The Foundational Emotions

1. That emotion which dominates all compatible and incompatible emotions and shines forth like the best of kings is call a Foundational Emotion.
2. The Foundational Emotion here is declared to be that love (*rati*) which takes Śrī Kṛṣṇa as its object. The knowers of Rasa say it is of two types: Primary and Secondary.
   Primary Love:
3. Love, which is a special form of the pure and luminous quality, is called primary. Primary love itself is further divided into two modes: "self-supporting" and "supportive of another."
   Self-Supporting:
4. Love that clearly nourishes its own self with compatible emotions, and is not diminished by incompatible emotions is called "self-supporting" love.
   Supportive of Another:
5. Love that contracts itself and supports both compatible and incompatible emotions is called "supportive of another."
6. The Primary Foundational Emotions, which consist of love that is both self-supporting and supportive of another, are of five types: Nondistinction, Respect, Friendship. Parental Affection, and Amorousness.
7. The particular form that love takes is determined by the specific nature of the individual experiencing it, just as a reflected image of the sun is determined by the nature of the jewel through which it is being reflected.

Nondistinct Love:

8. Nondistinct Love, which is indicated by shaking limbs and blinking eyes, is of three kinds: common, clear, and peaceful. . . .

Mixed:

26. A mixed love is a combination of two or three types of love and is exemplified respectively in such characters as Uddhava, Bhīma, and Mukharā. The particular name is determined according to which love is dominant.

Respect:

27. Those who think of themselves as inferior to Hari are considered to be His favored subordinates. The love found in them, which consists of honor, is called "Respect."

28. This kind of love produces attachment to Hari and destroys affection for everything else. . . .

Friendship:

30. The wise have determined that those who consider themselves to be equal to Mukunda are his friends. Their love, which takes the form of the intimacy that comes from a sense of equality, is called "Friendship." It is free from restraint and produces such actions as joking and laughing. . . .

Amorous Love:

36. That love, which is the primary cause of the mutual sensual pleasure of Hari and the doe-eyed women, is called "Amorous Love"; it is also known as "Sweet Love" (*madhurā*). It produces such acts as sidelong-glances, raising the eyebrows, love-talk, and smiles. . . .

38. Even though Primary Love always consists of the joy of a particular taste, it is differentiated in a hierarchical manner as the five forms of love. The particular form that love takes for a given individual is determined by unconscious impressions from previous experiences (*vāsanās*). . . .

68. When it is caused by Kṛṣṇa and is associated with a contracting Primary Love, it becomes "Fearful Love" (*bhaya-rati*). The wise have said that like Angry Love, it too is of two types (i.e., that which takes Kṛṣṇa as the Excitant, and that which takes an enemy of Kṛṣṇa as the Excitant). . . .

71. Disgust is a withdrawal of the mind from an unpleasant experience. It produces such behavior as spitting, contorting the face, and words of contempt. When it is born from a supportive form of Primary Love, it is judged to be "Disgusted Love."

An illustration:

72. Ever since my mind has begun to delight in the lotus-feet of Kṛṣṇa, which are the abode of new and ever-fresh Rasas, I spit and my face becomes contorted when remembering my sexual escapades with women.

73. Until Primary Love and the seven forms of Secondary Love reach the position of a Rasa, they remain the eight Foundational Emotions.
74. The Transitory Emotions counted independently are thirty-three; when combined with the eight Foundational Emotions and the Eight Responses there are forty-nine emotions in all.
75. Since all these emotions are associated with Kṛṣṇa, they completely transcend the three ordinary qualities of existence (*guṇas*) and consist of abundant joy. Nevertheless, they appear as if they consist of the happiness and sorrow that is produced from the three ordinary qualities of existence.
76. Therefore, such emotions as shyness, awakening, and effort appear to be related to the pure quality; such emotions as arrogance, happiness, dreaming, and humor appear to be related to the energetic quality; and such emotions as grief, depression, confusion, and sorrow appear to be related to the heavy quality.
77. Happy emotions are generally cool and the sad emotions are generally hot. What is amazing here is that even though love is a concentration of the highest joy it can appear to be hot.
78. When nourished by powerful cool emotions love becomes cooling, but when nourished by hot emotions it appears very hot, as if it were heating. Therefore, in separation it is called the semblance of the burden of sorrow.
79. Both types of love (Primary and Secondary) are transformed into Rasa in the devotees when they hear, see, or remember Kṛṣṇa and related factors that function as the Excitants and the other related aesthetic components.
80. Just as a substance consisting of yogurt and other ingredients is mixed in a special way with sugar and spices becomes the drink called Rasāla,
81. so here too, in the same way, the devotees relish the inexpressible wonder of abundant joy (i.e., Rasa) from a direct experience of Kṛṣṇa and the other aesthetic components.
82. Even though the Rasa has become one with love and the other aesthetic components, such as the Excitant, the special qualities of the various components of the Rasa can be perceived distinctly.

    For as it is said:
83. The Excitants and other aesthetic components are first recognized as separate units, but upon becoming Rasa, they are mixed and achieve a seamless unity.
84. Sometimes the individual ingredients can be tasted in sherbet, even though there is a oneness of the sugar and spices. In a like manner, the individual Excitants and other aesthetic components can sometimes be experienced distinctly in Rasa, even though they have achieved a oneness.

85. Kṛṣṇa and Kṛṣṇa's dear devotees are the "cause" of love (*rati*); emotions such as stupefaction are the "results" of love, and such emotions as indifference are its "companions."
86. In the context of Rasa, the ordinary meaning of the terms "cause," "results," and "companions" is left behind and they assume the names "Excitant" (*vibhāva*), "Indications" and "Transitory Emotions."
87. The Excitants are so called by the wise because they make possible the various kinds of special experiences of love.
88. Such actions as sidelong glances, along with the Responses, are-called Indications because they allow the love to be perceived and cause a deep experience of the love to permeate the heart. . . .
115. The fivefold Primary Bhakti-Rasas are Peacefulness, Respectfulness, Companionship, Parental Affection, and Amorousness. These are to be regarded in a hierarchical manner in which the first is considered the lowest.

    Secondary Bhakti-Rasas:
116. The seven Secondary Bhakti-Rasas are: Humorousness, Wonder, Heroism, Compassion, Fury, Dreadfulness, Abhorrence.
117. Thus, from this twofold division, Bhakti-Rasa is said to be of twelve kinds. But, in fact, in the Purāṇas only five kinds are to be seen. . . .
122. Even though all the Rasas are of a nature that is entirely pleasurable, from time to time there is an inexplicable kind of special experience in the Rasas.
123. Even though such Rasas as Compassion immediately strike both the ignorant and the uncouth rustics as sorrowful, the cultured know them truly to consist of abundant joy.
124. It is well established that happiness can clearly result from such Rasas (as Compassion) when by the play of love and the instruction of the wise the extraordinary (i.e., Kṛṣṇa) becomes their Excitant. . . .
131. The Rasa associated with the Lord is incomprehensible in every respect for those without devotion; it can be relished only by those devotees who have made the lotus-feet of Kṛṣṇa their all-in-all.
132. Rasa is judged to be that which passes beyond the course of contemplation and becomes an experience of abundant amazement that is relished intensely in a heart illuminated by purity.
133. Emotion (*bhāva*), however, is said to be that state of contemplation which is experienced by means of the deep unconscious impressions in the heart of a wise person with focused intelligence. . . .

Western Quadrant/Fourth Wave: Rasa of Parentally Affectionate Devotion

1. When the Foundational Emotion of Parental Affection (*vātsalya*) is fully developed by means of the Excitants and other aesthetic components, the wise call it the Rasa of Parentally Affectionate Devotion.

   The Substantial Excitants:
2. The wise say that Kṛṣṇa and his elders are the Substantial Excitants of this Rasa.

   An illustration of Kṛṣṇa:
3. Young Kṛṣṇa's dark blue complexion resembles that of a fresh blue lotus, his limbs are very tender, and the edges of his lotus eyes are covered by waving locks of hair that attack like bumblebees. Seeing her son moving about the land of Vraja, Yaśodā, the beloved wife of the king of Vraja, became wet with milk flowing from her breasts.
4. These are the qualities of Kṛṣṇa as the Substantial Excitant of this Rasa: He is dark blue in complexion, radiantly beautiful, connected with all virtuous characteristics, gentle, sweet-voiced, sincere, shy, modest, respectful to those deserving respect, and generous.
5. Since Kṛṣṇa with these qualities is the recipient of kindness and protection, his majestic power is not manifest here in the Substantial Excitant of this Rasa. . . .

Western Quadrant/Fifth Wave: Rasa of Amorous Devotion

1. When Amorous love (*madhurā-rati*) becomes fully developed in the hearts of the devotees by means of the Excitants and other aesthetic components appropriate to it, it becomes the Rasa of Amorous Devotion.
2. Even though this Rasa is extremely vast it is written about here only in abridged form, because it has a very secret nature, because it is difficult to understand, and because a detailed description would not be useful for dispassionate people who are indifferent toward it.

   The Substantial Excitants:
3. The Substantial Excitants for this Rasa are Kṛṣṇa and his beloved beautiful-browed women.
4. The Substantial Excitant of the Amorous Rasa is considered to be Hari, the container of the perfection of the incomparable height of beauty, play, and artfulness. . . .
6. All of you should bow to those extremely wonderful young women who are charged with ever-new and excellent sweetness, whose hearts are filled with waves of love, and who worship Hari as their own lover.

7. The most excellent among Hari's beloved women is Rādhā, the daughter of Vṛṣabhānu.
8. Look! Rādhā, the vessel of sweetness, appears radiant: her eyes steal the beauty from the female cakora bird trembling with passion, her face conquers all glory of the full moon, and her beautiful complexion captures the brilliance of pure gold. . . .
11. The Enhancing Excitants are said to be such things as the sound of Kṛṣṇa's flute.

Source: *The Bhaktirasāmṛtasindhu of Rūpa Gosvāmin*, translated by David L. Haberman (New Delhi: Indira Gandhi National Centre for the Arts and Motilal Banarsidass, 2003).

Selections from *The Deeds of God in Ṛddhipur*

1. He takes on an incarnation near Ṛddhipur.

He took on a womb incarnation in the house of a Kāṇva Brāhman in Kāṇṭsareṃ (according to some, in Kāṇṭopareṃ; according to others, in Māüreṃ), a few miles from Ṛddhipur. His father was Anant Nāyak. His mother was Nemāïseṃ.

The Gosāvī's mother had had many children; none of them had survived. She was very distressed about it. Finally the Gosāvī was born as her last child. He was named Guṇḍo.

After about a year, his mother and father died, so he was raised by his mother's brother and sister.

Seven years later, his thread ceremony was performed. He was given the top-knot and the thread, and a loincloth. The *paḷasulā* ritual was performed. In this way, four days passed. On the fourth day, the priest said, "Go begging, Guṇḍo. Use the words, 'Om, give me alms, good woman.' "

He would say, "Give me alms," but he would not say "Om."

With this, his thread ceremony was completed. Then they took him to Ṛddhipur.

2. He lives in Ṛddhipur

Bopa Upādhyāya's [teacher] was Rāma Upādhyāya; his [teacher] was Tīka Upādhyāya. The Gosāvī was sent to study with Bopa Upādhyāya. He began to study the Vedas.

The Gosāvī was extraordinarily talented. What the Gosāvī learned in a day, no one else could learn in a month. What the Gosāvī learned in a month, no one else could learn in a year. He would point out the teacher's mistakes as well as the students.

The [teacher] would say, "Guṇḍo is not ordinary. He must be an incarnation of Īśvara. We don't hear him studying. We don't hear him memorizing. We hear him reciting a whole chapter at once." (According to some, [the teacher said,] "We don't hear him reciting. We don't hear him reading. We hear him memorizing it all at once. This Guṇḍo is not ordinary. He must be an incarnation of Īśvara, or he must be an incarnation of a deity.")

Bopa Upādhyāya would speak this way, and the Gosāvī would laugh and say very softly, "Drop dead! It's true, I tell you."

To the students he would say, "More than others."

3. His power becomes evident

All the students would go to get grass for the teacher's calves. Each of them would get two bundles. They would put them on their heads and carry them back.

The Gosāvī's bundle went along in the air [over his head]. The students saw this. They came to the teacher and told him about it.

The teacher said, "This Guṇḍo is not ordinary. He must be an incarnation of Īśvara, or he must be an incarnation of a deity." Then he said to his wife, "Don't give this Guṇḍo any heavy work."

(According to some, the teacher clasped the Gosāvī's holy feet [and said], "I'm a sinner, Lord. I don't know [who you are]. So please tell me, Lord." And the Gosāvī laughed, but he would not explain.)

4. His light is seen

One day the Gosāvī had fallen asleep among the students. Light was streaming from his holy body. The students saw it, and they were afraid. They came to the teacher and told him, "Teacher, light is coming from Guṇḍo's head. He is talking to himself. He is saying, 'Why have you come? Why have you gone?' "

The teacher said, "No one knows who this Guṇḍo is. He is an incarnation of Īśvara."

5. He eats with children

The Gosāvī would come along when children were eating. The Gosāvī would eat with them, and the children would cry out in protest. Their mother would say, "Why are you crying? Let him eat." Then she would portion out [the food, and say], "Rāüḷ, you eat this [serving]; the children will eat these."

They would say, "Mother! The Rāüḷ won't eat his own serving. He'll only eat ours."

She would say, "Rāūḷ, why do you pass up your own share and eat the children's share?"

Still he would eat only the children's share. So she would tell them, "Let the Rāūḷ go ahead and eat. I'll give you some more later."

They would put their plates on their heads, and then he would eat standing up. In this way, he would have a meal of their servings; his own serving he would make into *prasād* [gracious leftovers].

She would add some more to that serving, and they would eat it. . . .

8. He brings a dead child to life

The Gosāvī used to play with someone's child. It died. It was taken and buried in a pathway, at the northeast corner of the Vājeśvara temple.

The Gosāvī arrived then at its house. [Its mother] saw the Gosāvī and began to cry. Then she said, "Rāūḷ, the child you used to play with died today," and everyone began to cry. And the Rāūḷ felt compassion.

Then the Gosāvī said, "Oh, drop dead! Bring it here! Bring it here, I tell you."

"What can I bring now, Rāūḷ," she said.

"Oh, drop dead!" [he replied]. "It should be brought, I say. . . . It should not be brought, I say. . . . Yes, it must be brought, I tell you!" and he went trotting off.

He went to the place, cleared away the stones, and dug. Then he pulled out [the baby], brushed it, wiped it, and began looking at it blissfully. Then he put it on his hip and brought it back.

[Its mother] saw them, and shut the door. "Take it away! Take it away, Rāūḷ! Take the corpse back!" [she said].

Next door to them lived an old woman. He took [the child] and put it into her arms. "Rāūḷ," she said, "what am I to do? I am a hundred years old."

So the Gosāvī put her nipple into its mouth. Milk rushed into her breast. It began to suck noisily.

At this point, [the mother] opened her door. She looked, and saw what was happening.

The Gosāvī left.

She began to ask for [her child]. The old woman said, "Why wouldn't you take him when he was offered to you? And why should I give him to you now?"

With that, [the mother] set off to make a complaint to the village headmen. The headmen said, "The Rāūḷ gave him to her; the child is hers. You may love the child, but you may not have him. Now you must live near him."

So she began to live near him, and she gave him a bed and a mattress. She gave him a cow.

Eventually he lived to be a hundred years old. He became a skilled cowherd. His name was Dāmodhar. For the rest of his life, he had no fevers. He used to tell the devotees about the divine deed which he had experienced.

9. He lays a child down to sleep in a heap of cotton

A certain housewife said, "Rāüḷ, would you take my child for a moment, while I go get a potful of water?" She put her child into the Gosāvī's arms. The Gosāvī played with the child for a while.

There was a heap of cotton in a wide, shallow basket. He laid the child down to sleep in it, and the heap closed back over [the child]. Then the Gosāvī left.

The woman returned. She put down the water pot and entered the house. She began to look for her child. She looked in the cradle. She looked on the bed. She looked in the nooks and crannies. She didn't see it anywhere. Then she asked her women friends in the neighborhood, "Did the Rāüḷ hand my child to you?"

"No, he didn't," they said. "The Rāüḷ is mad. The Rāüḷ is possessed. What will you do when he throws it into a small well, or into a big well, or when he throws it into a grain cellar?"

As she was searching this way, the heap [of cotton] stirred. The child was sleeping happily in the basket. "Look at that!" she said. "The Rāüḷ is our Mother. The Rāüḷ is our Father. How well the Rāüḷ has taken care of my child!" And she became happy. . . .

12. He hides behind the Vināyaka image

The children used to play hide-and-seek. The Gosāvī would come along. He would play with the children, hiding himself.

The Gosāvī would hide behind the Vināyaka image. The children would look all around, but they would not see him. And they would cry out, "Guṇḍo!"

And right there he would say "Boo!" and stand up. And all the children would be amazed. They would play again, and again the Gosāvī would do the same thing.

The Gosāvī would play this way. Then he would leave.

13. He plays with tamarind seeds

The children used to play with tamarind seeds on the pedestal of the Vināyaka image. The Gosāvī would come along. He would agree to play.

They would roughen one side of the tamarind seeds. They would throw one down. It would fall exactly the way the Gosāvī said. In this way, he won all the tamarind seeds.

The children would say, "All the roughened seeds fall the Gosāvī's way. None fall our way. Come on," they would say, "let's get some more tamarind seeds. Then let's roughen them on one side."

And they would get some more tamarind seeds. They would roughen them on one side. They would play again, and all the roughened seeds would fall the way the Gosāvī said. In this way, he won all the tamarind seeds. Then, as he was leaving, he would say, "Whee! Whee!" and scatter [the seeds]. And the children would tussle for them.

And the Gosāvī would laugh. Then he would leave. . . .

24. He uproots and replants a grapevine

The Gosāvī went to Aḷajpur. At a certain Brahman's house, there was a grapevine. The Gosāī uprooted it. The [Brahman] said, "Hey, Rāüḷ! Why did you pull up a fruit-bearing, blooming plant?"

On the third day, the Gosāvī brought it back. Then he dug in the ground with a stick. He planted the roots. He poured on three handfuls of water from the water jar.

The [Brahman] said, "Rāüḷ, it's dry and withered. How will it take root now?"

Then the Gosāvī went off. Three days later it sprouted bunches of fruits and flowers. And the [Brahman] was amazed. He said, "The Rāüḷ is our Mother. The Rāüḷ is our Father. The Rāüḷ is Īśvara. There is nothing the Rāüḷ cannot do." He began to praise him this way.

Then the Gosāvī left. . . .

41. He predicts deaths

A member of some household would be about to die. The Gosāvī would go to the house. He would prepare a bier in the courtyard. The people would say, "Rāüḷ, we can't tell what inauspicious sign you see."

Then someone in their household would die. The Gosāvī would accompany him to the burning ground, stay until the skull cracked, and then bathe fully clothed at Sūtak well or Sīndak well.

Then, simply draping his wet clothes over his head, he would go to the house of the next person who was to die. He would go and sit in a corner. The people would say, "Rāüḷ, we can't tell what inauspicious sign you see."

In two or three days someone in their household would die, and the Gosāvī would do those same things.

42. He circumambulates a pipal tree

There was a pipal tree in the northeast corner of the Kaḷaṇkeśvara temple compound. The Gosāvī used to go there. He would circumambulate the pipal tree. Wherever there was a pit or a hole, he would touch it with his holy hand. In this way he would give his contact to the pipal tree.

Then the Gosāvī would leave.

43. A cat goes into a trance

A cat was sitting in a corner where two temples met. (According to some, it was sitting on top of the Kaḷaṅkeśvara temple.) The Gosāvī looked at it, and it went into a trance. For three days it kept sitting there in trance.

Then on the third day, the Gosāvī went there, looked at it, and said, "Go away! Go away! Go away, I tell you!" And its trance was broken and it left.

Then the Gosāvī left.

44. He bursts a prostitute's cyst

A prostitute from Aḷajpur was going on pilgrimage to Rāmṭek. She stopped in Ṛddhipur, at the Nagareśvara temple. All her companions went into the marketplace. Left all alone, she fell asleep, lying on her stomach. She had a cyst on her back.

At that time, the Gosāvī came there. He placed his holy foot on her back and, pounding, burst the cyst. The Gosāvī squeezed out the bloody pus. He took away the pain that she had had.

Then she said, "The Rāüḷ is our Mother. The Rāüḷ is our Father. The Rāüḷ has taken away my pain."

Then the Gosāvī left. Her companions returned. They asked her, "How did this happen?"

"The Rāüḷ came here," she said. "He burst my cyst. He took away the pain. The Rāüḷ is our Mother. The Rāüḷ is our Father. The Rāüḷ has taken care of me."

"You go on with the Rāmṭek pilgrimage," she added. "I'm not coming." And she returned to Aḷajpur. . . .

46. He plays in Māṅgs' houses

The Gosāvī would go to the Mahārs' quarter. He would lift storage pots down from their stack and say, "Oh, drop dead! What's in here?"

The housewife would say, "What can there be here, Rāüḷ? Why must you take them down?"

He would do the same thing in Māṅgs' houses. When he saw some kind of food, he would taste it and say, "Oh, drop dead! It's sweet, I tell you."

The Gosāvī would act this way; then he would leave.

47. The village headmen make an ordinance

The village headmen said, "The Rāüḷ goes around among the houses of Māṅgs and Mahārs, and right afterwards he goes into the houses of consecrated Brāhmans. In this way, the Rāüḷ has caused general pollution. Put [the Māṅgs' and Mahārs'] houses outside the village. Then the Rāüḷ won't go to them."

Thus they had houses built outside the city. The original Mahār quarter was razed. But the Gosāvī would go to the new one, too, [saying], "Oh, I shouldn't go, I say. . . . I should go, I say. . . . No, I must not go, I tell you." In this way, he would amuse himself, going from house to house.

48. He answers the Māṅgs' plea

One day the Māṅgs pleaded, "Rāüḷ, we are dying for lack of water. What can we do, Lord?" The Rāüḷ felt compassion.

Then the Gosāvī said, "Drop dead, I tell you!" and he went there. "You should dig here, I say. . . . You shouldn't dig, I say. . . . Yes, you must dig here, I tell you." And he pointed with his holy big toe.

They dug there, and they struck an unlimited supply of water. So they said, "The Rāüḷ is our Mother. The Rāüḷ is our Father. By the grace of the Rāüḷ we have water to drink." . . .

57. He brings a dead calf to life

Some people's calf died. They brought it and put it near the "horse" at the foot of the Low Lane. At that time the Gosāvī came along. They said to the Gosāvī, "O Lord, now what are our children going to do, without milk? We had one cow. Her calf has died."

The Gosāvī went up to it and sprinkled it with grass, and it came to life. It went lowing to the house. They were delighted because their calf had come to life.

Their house was in the High Lane, right next door to the water carrier's house.

(According to some, the Gosāvī came in the evening, when the cow came home. The people whose calf it was pleaded, "Rāüḷ, our calf has died. Now what are we going to do, without buttermilk?"

The Gosāvī answered their plea, and immediately went and grabbed it by the tail. "You get up!" he said. "Get up! Get up, I tell you!"

It got up. It went to the house. It began to suck at the cow. Then the people said, "The Rāül is our Mother. The Rāül is our Father. There is nothing the Rāül cannot do." And they were amazed and astonished.) . . .

131. He saves Māhādāï when she is bitten by a snake

One day Māhādāïseṃ got up one watch into the night. She took the copper water pots and went out. She filled the copper pots, hung them from both ends of the bamboo pole, lifted them, and set off. As she did this, a snake bit her. But she kept going, carrying the two pots slung from the pole across her shoulders.

She set down her load in the main courtyard, and fell down in a faint.

The Gosāvī was sitting on his cot at the time. Ābāïseṃ cried out to him, "Oh, Lord! Rupai, the maid-servant of Devakī, has been bitten by a snake."

The Gosāvī went straight to the main courtyard. He looked at her: the poison was extracted.

Then she got up. She prostrated herself to the Gosāvī. She touched his holy feet. . . .

319. He tells the story of the bugs

One day the Gosāvī went to the Kaḷaṅkeśvara temple. All the devotees were with him. Then the Gosāvī said, "Oh, drop dead! There were two bugs here, I tell you. At night they would come out. They would bite anyone who was staying here. They bit a good many this way, and they swallowed some of them. That's what they used to do."

Then Māhādāïseṃ asked, "But, Lord, how could there be bugs like that?"

The Gosāvī answered, "Oh, drop dead! They were an incarnation of a deity, I tell you."

So Māhādāïseṃ kept silent. . . .

322. He goes home

Then, in due course, the Gosāvī became old. In due course, his holy neck, his holy head, and his holy hands trembled shakily. Then he could no longer digest the food he ate, and he got diarrhea.

He was sick this way for thirteen days. Then all the devotees, from Abāïseṃ on down, pleaded, "Oh, Lord, please take medicine. Please stop this affliction. Please change your inclination, Gosāvī."

The Gosāvī answered, "Oh, go die! Why are you saying this? Why? Oh, I will go now, I tell you." So the Gosāvī himself accepted the diarrhea.

Then the Gosāvī would squat on a low stool. He would hold onto his cot with his holy hand, and he would defecate. Then Abāïseṃ would offer him water in a metal dish. He would make use of the water in the shelter of a curtain.

Then one day Bhat asked, "Lord, Śrī Cakradhar Rāyā entrusted us to you. Now you're leaving, Gosāvī. So to whom have you entrusted us?"

The Gosāvī answered, "Oh, drop dead! I've entrusted all these others to you, and I've entrusted you to Śrī Dattātreya Prabhu. (According to some, the Gosāvī said, "Oh, go die! Go to Mātāpur, I tell you!")

And with that, on the fourth day of the dark half of the month of Bhādrapad, in the Vyaya year, the Gosāvī left.

323. His grief-stricken daughter comes

The Gosāvī's daughter was in Sāvaḷāpur. She heard in the house that the Gosāvī had gone home. (According to some, she heard the news at the place where she had gone to get water, and she left her water pot there.)

She came to Ṛddhipur. Her eyes were blinded from her sorrow. She cried the whole way on account of her father; she was still crying when she arrived.

Meanwhile, his whole body had been anointed with sandalwood paste. Flowers were offered to him. Pan was crushed and put into his holy mouth. A new fine silk garment was draped over his holy body. Then he was laid on a bier, and Bhaṭ, Mhāïṃbhaṭ, Lakṣmīndrabhaṭ, and it's not known who the fourth was, carried away the bier. They stopped at the foot of a tamarind tree, near its eastern branches.

The Gosāvī's daughter arrived as they were digging the grave. She saw the bier and threw herself down with a loud thump. She fainted. Bhaṭ and Mhāïṃbhaṭ ran up to her and revived her. Then she began to sob and moan. She threw herself onto the holy body and began wailing, "My maternal home is gone."

Seeing her suffer this way, Bhaṭ and Mhāïmbhaṭ were broken-hearted. The devotees were all very sad. Bhaṭ and Mhāïmbhaṭ said, "She truly is the Gosāī's daughter." And Bhaṭ said, "He fondled us and kept us happy. We know that he was Īśvara. [But] our grief is not as great as [hers]."

Finally the grave was dug. Bhaṭ cut a piece of padding an arm's length wide, and placed it in the bottom. The holy body was laid on it, and draped with the fine silk garment. (According to some, he was buried with his holy body naked.)

Then all the devotees, beginning with Bhaṭ and Mhāïṃbhaṭ, set off for the monastery. Bhaṭ and Mhāïṃbhaṭ tried to lead the Gosāvī's daughter away, but she would not budge. They offered her a sari and a blouse, but she refused them. "How can I take anything now? Is this my maternal home?" And she left.

Afterwards, Bhaṭ and Mhāїṃbhaṭ deliberated, and said, "The headmen are watching." So they took him out and buried him at the wall of the compound, south of the original grave. Now, Īśvara's body is like camphor, so what could have been left behind? There must have been some reason for it.

Later the village headmen built a temple over [the original grave].

Source: *The Deeds of God in Ṛddhipur*, translated by Anne Feldhaus (New York: Oxford University Press, 1984).

7

Rāma Devotionalism and Sant Tradition

In a sense, the fundamentals of Rāma devotion that are so prevalent in northern India today are grounded in the epic *Rāmāyaṇa*, which dates from 500 B.C.E. to 300 C.E., and the devotional poetry of Tulsīdās (1532–1623). Smaller than the eighteen books that comprise the larger *Mahābhārata*, the *Rāmāyaṇa* consists of seven books of roughly 25,000 verses (which is still twice the length of Homer's two major Greek epics), and it is generally agreed among scholars that the initial and last books are later additions to the main part which comprises books two to six. Both Indian epics were orally transmitted over centuries before assuming their written forms, both epics appear in regional variations, and both of them began as bardic narratives. Moreover, Brahmin scholars, who inserted pieces about dharma into them, reworked both epics, and retold the tales from a priestly perspective. The epics both also reflect a cultural tension between orthodox ritualists and more autonomous ascetics. The period of their composition overlapped with the advent of devotional religion, which led to an additional reworking of the material.[1]

Indigenous traditions of India claim the *Rāmāyaṇa* to be a work from the Tretā Yuga, the second of the four cycles of cosmic time. This is believed to make the author named Vālmīki a contemporary of the epic hero Rāma.[2] An Indian tradition depicts Vālmīki as beginning his life as a bandit before turning to a religious way of life. His name is derived from an *anthill*, which gresw around him while he was absorbed in meditation. Unlike the alleged author Vyāsa of the *Mahābhārata*, some scholars agree that the traditional ascription of the *Rāmāyaṇa* to a single author possesses some validity because of the uniformity of language with its compact vocabulary and style. But there is no way to be certain that the legendary Vālmīki is that author.[3] If one examines references to Vālmīki external to the epic, it is possible to find two allusions, one referring to an expert in vedic pronunciation and another to a mythological snake-eating bird.[4] Within the context of the epic, all information about Vālmīki appears in the first and last books. He is described in these books as a great *muni* (ascetic), eloquent speaker, a saintly man, great-souled, and learned. This ascetic and wise author reinforces traditional patriarchal attitudes in the text.

The first book, called the Bālakāṇḍa, frames the entire work by relating the birth of the hero Rāma, his early exploits, and marriage to the comely Sītā. The birth part of the narrative opens with a childless king named Daśaratha anxious about having an heir to inherit his kingdom. He performs a horse sacrifice and another one for sons; these sacrificial actions, along with pleas from other gods to destroy a demonic being persecuting them, prompt a response by Viṣṇu, who decides to become incarnate as the king's four sons in order to destroy Rāvaṇa, a demonic creature immune to death from any nonhuman source. Daśaratha's queens give birth to four sons: Rāma, Bharata, and twin half-brothers Lakṣmaṇa and Śatrughna. Lakṣmaṇa becomes an unshakable shadow of Rāma and symbolizes brotherly love and submissive obedience. At the age of fifteen, Rāma takes his younger brother Lakṣmaṇa on an initiatory journey, after an irascible sage Viśvāmitra demands the old king lend him his son to defend the sage's hermitage from demons who are interfering with his sacrificial rites. Besides defeating the demons Mārīca and Subāhu, Rāma learns mythological lore, and is initiated into the secrets of divine weapons. Even before the defeat of these two demons, Rāma is reluctant to kill the female demon Tāṭakā because of her gender, but the hero does so to fulfil a promise that he made to the sage Viśvāmitra. The sage takes Rāma and Lakṣmaṇa to King Janaka's sacrifice, where they learn of the miraculous birth of Sītā. The heroes also learn about the existence of Śiva's bow, which no mortal can bend to string it. Rāma not only bends the bow, he also breaks it. By proving his prowess, he is able to marry Sītā, and Lakṣmaṇa marries her sister, while the other brothers marry her cousins before returning to the capital of Ayodhyā.

Before these events, King Janaka related the origin of Sītā (literally furrow) by explaining how he had been ploughing when he discovered her in a furrow, and how he reared her as his daughter. This origin story thus recounts the nonhuman birth of Sītā.

In the second book of the epic, the aging king decides to appoint Rāma his heir apparent. But the old hunchback servant Mantharā convinces the king's wife Kaikeyī to supplant Rāma with her son Bharata by twisting the truth. The king is at a decisive disadvantage because he had given her a promise of two boons as a reward for her curing him of battle wounds. Kaikeyī revives the promises and pressures the king for their fulfillment. Kaikeyī's plot includes the banishment of Rāma for fourteen years to the forest. The dutiful Rāma submissively follows his father's command, and he even suggests recalling the absent Bharata, who is totally unaware of his mother's political machinations. Without protesting the unjust nature of his exile, Rāma goes to the forest accompanied by his wife and faithful brother Lakṣmaṇa. Rāma's brother and wife are paradigms of loyalty and obedience throughout the epic. As the narrative unfolds, Sītā is revealed as the ideal virtuous wife (*pativratā*). On mount Citrakūta, the trio construct a hermitage and live happily for a period of time.

The king grieves for his departed son and dies soon after Rāma leaves Ayodhyā. Before the king dies, he tells his wife Kausalyā, the mother of Rāma, that he is fulfilling a curse leveled against him by the blind parents of an ascetic that he accidentally killed. The king relates that he had been cursed to die when he became separated from his son.

Meanwhile, Bharata is recalled to Ayodhyā to assume the leadership of a kingless state, but he angrily rejects the offer to assume the kingship and overturns his mother's devious plot. Accompanied by a huge retinue that includes three queens, Bharata proceeds to retrieve Rāma with the objective of placing him on the vacant throne. When the estranged brothers encounter each other, the calm demeanor of Rāma is sharply contrasted with that of the emotionally volatile Lakṣmaṇa. Rāma declines his brother's impassioned offer to return to the capital and assume the throne, and he insists on executing his father's command to live in exile for fourteen years. After returning to the capital, and unable to convince Rāma to assume the role of king, Bharata places the sandals of the hero on the throne as a symbol of his authority. Bharata retires from the palace, but he functions as the administrative regent for his exiled brother. Rāma and his companions move to an even more remote part of the Daṇḍaka forest.

This remote part of the forest is the home of hospitable sages and malevolent demons. Although he is resolved to live an ascetic lifestyle, Rāma's warrior traits become more evident when he is forced to rescue his wife from a demonic *rākṣasa*, and he pledges to protect the sages from other demons. Rāma, his wife, and brother spend ten years among the sages, and the hero receives weapons from Agastya and the promise of protection from the vulture Jaṭāyus. After building a hermitage at Pañcavatī at the suggestion of Agastya, the brothers encounter a demoness named Śūrpanakhā, who makes amorous overtures to them only to be ridiculed by them. The infuriated demoness attacks Sītā, but she is mutilated by Lakṣmaṇa. After Rāma defeats the demoness's avenging brother and his horde, she concocts revenge with her brother Rāvaṇa, king of the island of Laṅkā, to abduct Sītā. The *rākṣasa* Mārīca attempts to dissuade Rāvaṇa from his sinister plan. In fact, Mārīca accuses Rāvaṇa of departing from the path of righteousness (*dharma*), which rather than his demonic nature–becomes the demon's root problem. Defeated, the unwilling Mārīca is disguised as a golden deer and, in the Daṇḍaka forest, falsely calls for assistance. In response, Sītā sends the two brothers to help. While the brothers are going to assist the distressed deer, Rāvaṇa appears at the hermitage as a holy mendicant and abducts Sītā. Jaṭāyus is mortally wounded as he attempts to stop the abduction. Rāvaṇa takes Sītā across the ocean to the island of Laṅkā, where she rejects his lustful advances and offer of marriage within a year or face death. Meanwhile, the brothers learn of the abduction from a dying Jaṭāyus, and Rāma despairs over his loss. The monster Kabandha gives them an element of hope by advising to forge an alliance with Sugrīva, a king of the Vānaras who are identified as monkeys, in order to rescue Sītā.

The fourth book of the epic finds the brothers in the capital of Sugrīva, and the monkey Hanumān takes them to meet the king. Rāma and Sugrīva form an alliance, and the former is shown evidence of clothes and ornaments discarded by his wife as she was being abducted. Rāma urges Sugrīva to challenge his usurping brother Vālin to single combat. With the covert help of Rāma, who hides behind a tree, Sugrīva is victorious, cremates his defeated brother, and assumes the kingship. Before his demise Vālin reproaches Rāma for his deception and lack of dharmic behavior, even though his death by an instrument of the hero results in his salvation. Rāma counters Vālin by arguing that ordinary rules of chivalric combat are not applicable in his case because the hero is an authoritative figure rightfully punishing an adulterer, the death of Vālin fulfills a promise that he made with Sugrīva, and he is a king rightfully hunting a simple beast. With Vālin destroyed and Sugrīva secured on the throne, preparations are made to amass an army to rescue Sītā, and search parties are sent to find her location. Having the most confidence of success in the search party led by Hanumān, Rāma gives the monkey a ring by which to identify himself as an emissary of the hero. Although three of the search parties return unsuccessfully, Hanumān's group encounter Sampāti, brother of the slain Jaṭāyus, who informs them of Sītā's location across the ocean.

After an account of the beauty of the island of Laṅkā, Hanumān's prodigious leap to the island is described by the text. After vainly searching for her in the palace of the demon, Hanumān finds her among a grove of trees, and he hears her reject Rāvaṇa's personal pressure and threats. Hanumān reveals himself to the incredulous Sītā. The monkey proves his identity by showing to Sītā her husband's ring, but she refuses to be rescued by Hanumān and insists that Rāma complete her rescue. Sītā gives Hanumān a jewel as a token for her heroic husband. Hanumān allows himself to be captured by Indrajit, a son of the demonic king. Vibhīṣaṇa, who is the virtuous brother of Rāvaṇa, dissuades the king from killing Hanumān because of diplomatic protocol with respect to foreign envoys. Instead the angry Rāvaṇa sets fire to the monkey's tail, which Hanumān uses to set fire to Laṅkā. Once reassured of Sītā's safety, Hanumān returns to the mainland to report his discovery to those waiting.

The sixth book of the epic recounts the battle between Rāma and Rāvaṇa. After Rāvaṇa rejects his conciliatory advice, Vibhīṣaṇa defects, is welcomed by Rāma's group, and is consecrated king of Laṅkā. A causeway is constructed to traverse the sea in order to invade the island. Meanwhile, Rāvaṇa attempts to emotionally break Sītā and get her to submit by showing her an illusion of Rāma's severed head, but she remains steadfast in her devotion to her husband. Initially, the battle goes favorably for Rāvaṇa and his army as Indrajit disables Rāma and

Lakṣmaṇa, who are assisted by the half man-celestial bird Garuḍa, many combatants perish as the conflict begins to swing against the demonic forces. Indrajit's use of magic and resort to sacrifice to ensure victory prove fruitless, and Lakṣmaṇa finally kills him. The battle culminates with a duel between Rāvaṇa and Rāma, who receives divine assistance from Indra's chariot and charioteer in order to dispatch the demon. Rāma and his wife are reunited, but the hero treats her coldly by claiming that he engaged in battle for the sake of family honor and not for her benefit. As Sītā prepares to prove her virtue by self-immolation on a funeral pyre, divine beings reveal to Rāma his genuine status as an incarnation of Viṣṇu. The deity Agni restores Sītā unharmed to a delighted Rāma. The hero's deceased father appears to instruct his son to return to Ayodhyā and resume his rule. And the victors fly back to the capital using the aerial chariot of Rāvaṇa. Rāma's brother Bharata, who had been acting as regent of the kingdom, is happy to restore the kingdom to the rightful sovereign and to participate in the installation ceremony.

The epic concludes with the seventh book, called "Further Exploits." There is general agreement among textual scholars that his book is a later addition to the epic, much like the initial book.[5] This last book recalls the sage Agastya narrating the crimes of Rāvaṇa before his encounter with Rāma, and the heroic exploits of Hanumān. The narrative then turns to the happy life and prosperous reign of Rāma and Sītā. Malicious gossip calling into question Sītā's virtue while a prisoner of Rāvaṇa disrupts their harmonious rule. Rāma is forced by public pressure to unjustly exile Sītā to Vālmīki's hermitage. While staying at the sage's hermitage, Śatrughna learns of the birth of Rāma's twin sons, Kuśa and Lava. Eventually, Sītā is recalled to court from her exile. Rāma's decision to banish his wife appears to be ruthless and cruel, but his decision is based on his vision of the perfect monarch who is willing to sacrifice everything for righteousness (*dharma*). Sītā publicly reaffirms her purity and innocence. In order to prove her truthfulness, she calls upon Mother Earth to accept her, if what she swears is correct. The Earth opens to accept Sītā, and she descends into it. Rāma mourns the disappearance of his beloved, and he commemorates her loss with a golden statue. After an ideal reign of peace and prosperity, Rāma is visited by Time, which prefigures the end of his rule. His brother Lakṣmaṇa is the first to immolate himself, and he is followed by

Rāma and the final two brothers. As Rāma's twin sons rule in his place, all the brothers are welcomed into heaven by the gods.

It is possible to identify numerous themes with sociopolitical and religious significance in the epic. There are the struggles of dharma against its opposite, along with the responsibility to fulfill one's duty. These themes are evident when the demonic Vibhīṣana joins Rāma and the side of righteousness, and it is clear in the struggle to rescue Sītā. Moreover, the licentious and violent Rāvaṇa represents the precise opposite of restraint, decorum, and righteousness of figures from the victorious group. When Bharata places Rāma's sandals on the throne, this represents the beginning of righteous rule of the Rāmarājya. The strict adherence to dharma is emphasized throughout the epic. Queen Kaikeyī and her misshapen servant are examples of the manipulation and distortion of the truth, whereas the brother Lakṣmaṇa is a paradigm of loyalty and obedience.

The heroic conflict between Rāma and the demons is a cosmic and religious battle of good and evil. This gargantuan struggle suggests continuity with the earlier Vedic cosmogonic conflict between Indra and Vṛtra now being represented, respectively, by Rāma and the demon Rāvaṇa. Of the two warrior gods, the former becomes king of the gods, whereas Rāma becomes king of men. In the second book, called the Ayodhyākāṇḍa, Rāma delivers Ahalya, wife of the cuckold ascetic Gautama who had cursed her to become invisible after her sexual affair with Indra. When she encounters Rāma she becomes visible again, which symbolizes his power to save. Another religious theme is Rāma's forgiveness of karmic transgressions, which is prefigured by the joyful reunion of the four brothers. The salvific and forgiving power of Rāma is connected to his compassion to all beings. This is poignantly suggested by the help extended by Guha, to the three exiles when they attempt to cross the Ganges River; Guha is a person of low caste embraced by Rāma. Another religious theme with environmental and human relational implications is the intimate relationship established between Rāma, humans, and nature. When the hero leaves the capital nature mourns his departure, and the text refers to trees loving him (Rām 2.42.12). Throughout the epic, animals such as the vulture Jaṭāyus and the monkey Hanumān assist Rāma. Finally, Rāma is haled as a protector by, for instance, the sages of the Daṇḍaka forest (Rām 3.1.19). Finally, there is the theme of suffering at the death of his father and separation from his wife.

The devotional themes manifested in the *Rāmāyaṇa* were more fully developed by later theological thinkers and poets in northern India, in what is generally labeled the Sant tradition. During the thirteenth century, Jñāneśvara (1275–1296) wrote an extensive commentary on the Bhagavad Gītā in Marathi, which was one of the earliest works in this language. Jñāneśvara's commentary, entitled the *Jñāneśvarī*, is considered the textual foundation of the devotional tradition in the Maharashtra region, and it functioned as the source of the Sant movement. Moreover, Jñāneśvara also tends to obscure sectarian distinctions between Vaiṣṇavism and Śaivism; his text is a hybrid, teaching the Bhagavata ideal through the mouth of Krishna, though in other works he composes treatises from a Śaiva perspective. Jñāneśvara is therefore no narrow sectarian thinker, although he does consistently exalt the guru as the primary object of devotion and the power of the divine name, as does the Sant tradition. From the perspective of Jñāneśvara, the sacred name of the deity is what mediates different religious traditions.

From the thirteenth to the seventeenth centuries, the Sant tradition developed through the leadership of many prominent figures. Three major such figures were Kabīr (1398–1448), Ravidās (Raidās c. 1450–1520), and Dādū Dayāl (c. 1543–1603). Kabīr's poems are famous for their devotion, opposition to asceticism and the caste system, iconoclastic, and paradoxical language. This anthology includes selections from the poems of Kabīr, a Hindi hagiography of Ravidās by Anantadās around 1600 C.E., and selections from a Hindi biography of Dādū entitled the *Dādū Janma Līlā*. These three Sants share humble social origins. Ravidās was a leatherworker (*camār*), who appealed to others of his social standing who call themselves Raidāsis (Ravidāsis) in north India, rather than using their common caste designation.

In contrast to Ravidās, Kabīr was a member of a weaver community, although he historically is an elastic figure with an ability to assume different guises depending on the social context. There is a tradition that depicts him as an apostle of Hindu-Muslim unity, whereas a western Indian tradition pictures him as an intimately devotional figure. An eastern Indian version of Kabīr portrays him as a more confrontational person who challenges social norms. It is this version of the poet that is adopted by the Kabīr Panth (path), which embraces ascetics and lay people within its community. Kabīr's poems are collected into his *Bījak* ("Inventory" of poems or "Guide" to the location of treasure). His poems are also called *sākhīs,* which means witness. This Muslim weaver was indebted to the Nāths, who were yogis practicing the bodily discipline advocated by haṭha yoga. It is possible to discover haṭha yoga themes in his poems. When reading these poems it is important to know that they were rhymed lyric creations of about six to eight lines in length that were intended to be sung. Therefore, the poems represented a performative event.

The historical period of the Sant poets was followed by a reworking of the *Rāmāyaṇa* by the poet Tulsīdās (1532–1623) in his major work the *Rāmacaritmānas* (The Sacred Lake of Rāma's Deeds) in the Hindi language, which enabled this work to communicate its message to a wider audience. Tulsīdās advocates a deity with attributes rather than one without attributes, as did some members of the Sant tradition that influenced him. Nonetheless, Tulsīdās shows his independent thinking by combining his devotionalism with the thought of both the qualified nondualism of Rāmānuja and the absolute nondualism of Śaṅkara.

Selections from the *Rāmāyaṇa* (Volume 1)

Sarga 1

1. Vālmīki, the ascetic, questioned the eloquent Nārada, bull among sages, always devoted to asceticism and study of the sacred texts.
2. "Is there a man in the world today who is truly virtuous? Who is there who is mighty and yet knows both what is right and how to act upon it? Who always speaks the truth and holds firmly to his vows?
3. "Who exemplifies proper conduct and is benevolent to all creatures? Who is learned, capable, and a pleasure to behold?
4. "Who is self-controlled, having subdued his anger? Who is both judicious and free from envy? Who, when his fury is aroused in battle, is feared even by the gods?
5. "This is what I want to hear, for my desire to know is very strong. Great seer, you must know of such a man."

6. When Nārada, who was familiar with all the three worlds, heard Vālmīki's words, he was delighted. "Listen," he replied and spoke these words:
7. "The many virtues you have named are hard to find. Let me think a moment, sage, before I speak. Hear now of a man who has them all.
8. "His name is Rāma and he was born in the House of Ikṣvāku. All men know of him, for he is self-controlled, mighty, radiant, steadfast, and masterful.
9. "He is wise and grounded in proper conduct. Eloquent and majestic, he annihilates his enemies. His shoulders are broad and his arms mighty. His neck is like a conch shell and his jaws are powerful.
10. "His chest is vast, and a subduer of his enemies, he wields a huge bow. His collarbone is set deep in muscle, his arms reach down to his knees, and his head is finely made. His brow is noble and his gait full of grace.
11. "His proportions are perfect and his limbs well-formed and symmetrical. Dark is his complexion and he is valorous. His chest is fully fleshed; he has large eyes. He is splendid and marked with all auspicious signs.
12. "He knows the ways of righteousness and is always true to his word. The welfare of his subjects is his constant concern. He is renowned, learned, pure, disciplined, and contemplative.
13. "He is the protector of all living things and the guardian of righteousness. Versed in the essence of the vedas and their subsidiary sciences, he is equally expert in the science of arms.
14. "He is versed in the essence of every science, learned in traditional lore, and highly intelligent. All the people love him, for he is good, cheerful, and clever.
15. "He is the constant resort of good men, as is the ocean of rivers. For he is noble and equable in all circumstances and always a pleasure to behold.
16. "The delight of his mother Kausalyā, he is gifted with every virtue. For he is as deep as the ocean and as unyielding as the Himalayas.
17. "He is as mighty as Viṣṇu, but as pleasant to behold as the moon. In his wrath he resembles the fire at the end of time, yet he rivals the earth in forbearance.

18–19. "In charity he is the equal of Kubera, giver of wealth, and in truthfulness like a second Dharma, the god of righteousness. Moved by affection for him, Daśaratha, lord of the earth, wished to appoint this Rāma, his beloved eldest son, as prince regent. For he was truly valorous, possessed all these virtues, and was gifted with other excellent virtues.

20. "Seeing the preparations for the consecration, the king's wife, Queen Kaikeyī, who had long before been granted a boon, now asked for it. She demanded that Rāma be exiled and that Bharata be consecrated in his place.
21. "Because he was a man true to his word, King Daśaratha was caught in the trap of his own righteousness and had to exile his dear son Rāma.
22. "Keeping the promise, the hero entered the forest, because of the command implicit in a father's word and in order to please Kaikeyī.
23. "Out of love for him, his beloved and obedient brother Lakṣmaṇa, the delight of Sumitrā, followed him as he set forth.
24. "And his wife Sītā, the best of women, possessed of every grace, followed Rāma as Rohiṇī does the hare-marked moon.
25. "He was followed far on his way by his father, Daśaratha, and the people of the city. But at the town of Śṛngavera on the banks of the Ganges he dismissed his charioteer.
26. "Wandering from wood to wood, they crossed great rivers until, on the instructions of Bharadvāja, they came to Mount Citrakūṭa.
27. "There the three of them built a pleasant dwelling. Delighting in the forest and resembling celestial gandharvas, they lived there happily.
28. "When Rāma had gone to Mount Citrakuṭā, King Daśaratha was stricken with grief for his son and loudly lamenting him, went to heaven.
29. "When he was dead, the brahmans, led by Vasiṣṭha, urged Bharata to become king, but that mighty man did not desire kingship. Instead the hero went to the forest to beg for grace at Rāma's feet.
30. "But Bharata's elder brother only gave his sandals as a token of his sovereignty and repeatedly urged Bharata to return.
31. "Unable to accomplish his desire, Bharata touched Rāma's feet and ruled the kingdom from the village of Nandigrāma in expectation of Rāma's return.
32. "But Rāma, seeing that the people of the city had come there, entered the Daṇḍaka forest with single-minded resolution.
33. "He killed the rākṣasa Virādha and met Śarabhanga, Sutīksṇa, Agastya, and Agastya's brother.
34. "On the advice of Agastya, and with the greatest pleasure, he accepted Indra's bow as well as a sword and two quivers, whose arrows were inexhaustible.
35. "While Rāma was living in the forest with the woodland creatures, all the seers came to see him about killing the asuras and rākṣasas.
36. "While dwelling there, he disfigured the rākṣasa woman Śūrpaṇakhā, who lived in Janasthāna and could take any form at will.

37–38. "Then Rama slew in battle all the rākṣasas who had been sent against him on the strength of śūrpaṇakhā's report—Khara, Triśiras, and the rākṣasa Dūṣaṇa, as well as all of their followers. Fourteen thousand rākṣasas were slain.

39. "But Rāvaṇa, hearing of the slaughter of his kinsmen, went mad with rage and chose a rākṣasa named Mārīca to assist him.

40. "Mārīca tried to dissuade Rāvaṇa many times, saying, 'Rāvaṇa, you would do well not to meddle with this mighty man.'

41. "But Rāvaṇa, who was driven by his fate, paid no heed to Mārīca's words and went with him to Rāma's ashram.

42. "With the help of that master of illusion, he lured both sons of the king far away. Then, having slain the vulture Jaṭāyus, he carried off Rāma's wife.

43. "Finding the vulture dying and hearing that Maithilī had been abducted, Rāghava was consumed with grief. Beside himself with grief, he lamented loudly.

44–45. "In sorrow, he cremated the vulture Jaṭāyus. Then, searching the forest for Sītā, he met a rākṣasa named Kabandha, deformed and dreadful to behold. The great-armed man killed and cremated him so that he went to heaven.

46. "But Kabandha had first told him, 'Rāghava, you must go to the hermit woman Śabarī, for she is cunning in all ways of righteousness and lives accordingly.' And so the powerful destroyer of his foes came to Śabarī.

47. "Rāma, the son of Daśaratha, was duly honored by Śabarī. Then, on the shores of Lake Pampā, he met the monkey Hanumān.

48. "Acting on Hanumān's advice, mighty Rāma met Sugrīva and told him all that had happened.

49. "Sensing that he had found a friend, the sorrowful king of the monkeys told Rāma the whole story of his feud. And the monkey told him also of Vālin's might.

50. "Rāma vowed to kill Vālin, but Sugrīva remained doubtful of Rāghava's strength.

51. "So to reassure him, Rāghava kicked the great corpse of Dundubhi ten whole leagues with his big toe.

52. "Furthermore, with a single mighty arrow he pierced seven sāla trees, a hill, and even the underworld Rasātala, thus inspiring confidence.

53. "The great monkey was confident, and, his mind at ease, he went with Rāma to the cave Kiṣkindhā.

54. "Then the foremost of monkeys, Sugrīva, yellow as gold, gave a great roar. At that roar, the lord of the monkeys, Vālin, came forth.
55. "Rāghava then killed Vālin in battle at the request of Sugrīva and made Sugrīva king in his place.
56. "Eager to find Janaka's daughter, that bull among monkeys assembled all the monkeys and sent them out in all directions.
57. "On the advice of the vulture Sampāti, mighty Hanumān leaped over the salt sea, a hundred leagues in breadth.
58. "Reaching the city of Laṅkā, which was ruled by Rāvaṇa, he saw Sītā brooding in a grove of aśoka trees.
59. "He gave her a token of recognition and told her all that had happened. Then, when he had comforted Vaidehī, he smashed the gate.
60. "He killed five generals of the army and seven ministers' sons as well. Then, after crushing the hero Akṣa, he was captured.
61. "Knowing that he could free himself from their magic weapon by means of a boon he had received from Grandfather Brahmā, the hero suffered the rākṣasas to bind him as they would.
62. "The great monkey then burned the city of Laṅkā, sparing Sītā Maithilī, and returned to tell the good news to Rāma.
63. "Approaching great Rāma, the immeasurable monkey walked reverently around him and told him just what had happened, saying, 'I have seen Sītā.'
64. "Rāma went with Sugrīva to the seashore, where he made the ocean tremble with arrows blazing like the sun.
65. "The ocean, lord of rivers, revealed himself, and, following the ocean's advice, Rāma had Nala build a bridge.
66. "By this means he went to the city of Laṅkā, and having killed Rāvaṇa in battle, he consecrated Vibhīṣaṇa as lord of the rākṣasas in Laṅkā.
67. "The three worlds, including all that moves and is fixed, and the hosts of gods and seers were delighted by that mighty feat of great Rāma.
68. "All the gods were thoroughly delighted and worshiped Rāma. Having accomplished what he had to do, he was freed from anxiety and rejoiced.
69. "He received boons from the gods and revived the fallen monkeys. Then, mounting the flying chariot Puṣpaka, he went to Nandigrāma.
70. "In Nandigrāma the blameless man and his brothers put off the knotted hair of ascetics. Thus did Rāma regain Sītā and recover his kingdom.
71. "His people are pleased and joyful, contented, well-fed, and righteous. They are also free from physical and mental afflictions and the danger of famine.

72. "Nowhere in his realm do men experience the death of a son. Women are never widowed and remain always faithful to their husbands.
73. "Just as in the Golden Age, there is no danger whatever of fire or wind, and no creatures are lost in floods.
74. "He performs hundreds of Horse Sacrifices involving vast quantities of gold. And, in accordance with custom, he donates tens and hundreds of millions of cows to the learned.
75. "Rāghava is establishing hundreds of royal lines and has set the four social orders each to its own work in the world.
76. "When he has ruled the kingdom for 11,000 years, Rāma will go to the world of Brahmā.
77. "Whoever reads this history of Rāma, which is purifying, destructive of sin, holy, and the equal of the vedas, is freed from all sins.
78. "A man who reads this *Rāmāyaṇa* story, which leads to long life, will after death rejoice in heaven together with his sons, grandsons, and attendants.
79. "A brahman who reads it becomes eloquent, a kshatriya becomes a lord of the earth, a vaiśya acquires profit from his goods, and even a lowly śūdra achieves greatness." The end of the first sarga of the Bālakāṇḍa of the *Śrī Rāmāyaṇa*.

Sarga 17

1. When the great man's Horse Sacrifice was completed, the gods accepted their portions and departed as they had come.
2. The king, his state of ritual consecration now at an end, entered the city accompanied by his host of wives, his servants, troops, and mounts.
3. The lords of the earth, honored by the king according to their rank, went gladdened to their own countries after paying homage to the bull among sages.
4. And when they had departed, the majestic King Daśaratha once more entered the city, preceded by the most eminent of the brahmans.
5. With all due honor, Ṛśyaśṛnga set out with Śāntā, escorted by the wise king and his attendants.
6. Kausalyā gave birth to an illustrious son named Rāma, the delight of the Ikṣvākus. He bore the signs of divinity, for he was one-half of Viṣṇu.
7. An immeasurably resplendent son, he glorified Kausalyā as does Indra, the foremost of the gods and wielder of the thunderbolt, his mother Aditi.
8. Kaikeyī bore a truly valorous son named Bharata, one-quarter of the incarnate Viṣṇu, endowed with every virtue.

9. Sumitrā gave birth to two sons, Lakṣmaṇa and Śatrughna, heroes skilled in all weapons and infused with portions of Viṣṇu.

10. Four great, worthy, and virtuous sons were born to the king, one after the other, equal in beauty to the constellation Proṣṭhapāda.

11–12. On the twelfth day after the births, Daśaratha held the naming ceremony. With great delight, Vasiṣṭha pronounced the names. The eldest and greatest was named Rāma, and Kaikeyī's son was called Bharata. One of Sumitrā's sons was called Lakṣmaṇa and the other Śatrughna. He saw to it that all the ceremonies, beginning with the birth ritual, were performed for them.

13. Of all the king's sons it was the eldest, Rāma, who, like a royal pennant, gave his father the greatest joy. For he was the one among the brothers held in most esteem, just as the self-existent Brahmā is most esteemed among all beings.

14–17. All of them were heroes, learned in the vedas and devoted to the welfare of the people. All were imbued with knowledge and endowed with virtues, but even among such men as these, it was the mighty Rāma who was accounted truly valorous. From earliest childhood Lakṣmaṇa, bringer of glory, was always especially fond of his eldest brother, Rāma, delight of the world. Performing every service for him, glorious Lakṣmaṇa was like another life breath outside his body, for without him, the best of men could get no sleep. Without him, he would not eat the savory food that was brought to him.

18. Whenever Rāghava went out hunting on horseback, he followed behind, guarding him with his bow.

19. Just so did Bharata love Śatrughna, Lakṣmaṇa's younger brother, more than the breath of life itself, while Śatrughna loved him just as much.

20. Daśaratha took as much joy in his four illustrious and beloved sons as does Brahmā, the Grandfather, in his sons, the gods.

21–22. When the brothers had completed their education, had cultivated all the virtues, were modest, renowned, wise in the ways of the world, and gifted with foresight, then righteous Daśaratha, with his preceptors and kinsmen, began to give thought to their marriage.

23. While the great man was pondering this in the midst of his counsellors, the great and powerful sage Viśvāmitra arrived.

24. Eager to see the king, he said to the gatekeepers, "Announce at once that I, Kauśika, the son of Gādhi, have come."

25. Hearing these words and driven by his command, they all ran to the royal dwelling, their minds in a flurry of agitation.
26. Reaching the palace, they announced to the Ikṣvāku king that the seer Viśvāmitra had come.
27. Upon hearing their words, he was delighted and, dropping all other concerns, he went out with his family priest to receive him, as Vāsava might for Brahmā.
28. When the king saw that ascetic, rigorous in his vows and blazing with an inner radiance, his face grew joyful, and he made the welcome offering.
29. Receiving the king's welcome offering as prescribed in the traditional texts, the sage asked the lord of men about his well-being and prosperity.
30. The bull among sages then embraced Vasiṣṭha and the illustrious seers, and spoke to them as is customary concerning their health.
31. All of them were glad at heart and entered the king's residence where, duly honored, they seated themselves according to their rank.
32. Glad at heart, the noble king spoke to the great sage Viśvāmitra, honoring him:
33. "The acquisition of nectar, rain in the desert, a son born to a childless man by a proper wife, the recovery of something lost, delight in great advancement—your arrival is as welcome to me as all these things. Welcome, great sage.
34. "What great desire of yours may I find joy in granting? Righteous brahman, you are a worthy recipient. What luck for me that you have come! Today my birth has borne fruit, and it is clear that I have lived a good life.
35. "Possessed of blazing splendor, once you were called a royal-seer. But through austerity, you gained a radiant splendor and reached the status of a brahman-seer. Therefore, you are doubly worthy of my homage.
36. "This is wonderful, brahman, and highly sanctifying for me. The sight of you, lord, is like a journey to a holy place of pilgrimage.
37. "Tell me what cherished purpose has brought you here. If you favor me, I would wish only to aid in the attainment of your goals.
38. "You should not hesitate about what you wish done, Kauśika. I will carry it out fully, for you are as a god to me."
39. When the great and virtuous seer, the fame of whose virtues had spread far and wide, heard these words so pleasant both to heart and ear, so modestly spoken by that wise man, he felt the greatest delight.

The end of the seventeenth sarga of the Bālakāṇḍa of the *Śrī Rāmāyaṇa*.

Source: *The Rāmāyaṇa of Vālmīki: An Epic of Ancient India*, translated by Robert P. Goldman. (Princeton: Princeton University Press, 1984).

Selections from the *Jñāneshvarī*

Chapter X

39. I have expounded the first nine chapters in accordance with my views. Now begins the second part of this book, to which please listen.
40. In this chapter Shri Krishna will explain to Arjuna in a skillful and interesting way his special and his general powers.
41. With the eloquence of our Marāthi language, the sentiment of tranquillity will be found to surpass that of love, and even the Ovi metre will be an ornament to poetic composition.
42. If my Marāthi version of the original Sanskrit [Gītā] is read carefully, with a clear understanding of its meaning, no one could say which is the original.
43. Owing to the beauty of the body, it becomes an ornament to the very ornaments that it wears, and one cannot say which of the two beautifies the other.
44. So do the Sanskrit and Marāthi languages display their beauty in the place of honour in the meaning of the Gītā; listen carefully.
45. If one has to express the feelings aroused [by the Gītā] one needs showers of the nine sentiments, whereby one's literary powers are enriched.
46. So, taking the beauty of the Marāthi tongue and adding to it the youth of the sentiments, the precious truths of the Gītā are set forth.
47. Hear now what is said by the Lord of the Yādavas, who is the greatest teacher in the whole world and who causes the minds of men of intelligence to marvel.
48. Jñānadeva, disciple of Nivritti, says: Hear what the Lord Krishna said, O Arjuna, thy mind is well able to understand all these things. . . .
49. [I wished to see whether] thou hast paid attention to the exposition of the truth previously given, and [I find that] thou hast done very well.
50. As by pouring a little water into a pot one can see whether it leaks and then more can be added, so I have tested thee to see whether I can teach thee more.
51. If one wishes to leave a stranger in charge of one's possessions one makes him treasurer only if he is honest; so now I can place confidence in thee, O Kiriti.
52. Thus the Lord of all addressed Arjuna with respect, as clouds, on perceiving a mountain, gather around it.
53. That Prince of all compassionate ones said, O Mighty-armed, listen. I will explain again the truths which I have imparted to thee.
54. When a field is sown every year and yields a drop, it will yield more and more if the farmer does not weary of cultivating it.
55. Gold which is heated again and again in a crucible should not be said to deteriorate [for its quality increases].

56. So here, O Pārtha, I am not speaking for your sake but for My own purposes.
57. When a child is covered with ornaments it does not really appreciate them; it is the mother who is delighted at the sight of them.
58. So one should say that as it benefits thee more and more, so My love for thee is doubled.
59. O Arjuna, enough of this elaboration, clearly I love thee and there is no end to my satisfaction in talking with thee.
60. For this reason I repeat these things; listen to Me with full attention.
61. Arjuna, hear this secret, My sublime teaching; it is the highest Brahma, taking on the form of words, which comes to embrace thee.

II. Neither the hosts of gods nor the great sages know any origin of Me for I am the source of the gods and the great sages in every way.

62. But, O Kiriti, dost thou not truly know Me? It is I who am here; the universe is but a dream.
63. Here the Vedas are silent, the mind and the vital air become powerless, and the sun and the moon set in darkness, though it is not night.
64. As the child in the womb does not know its mother's age so am I unknown to all the gods.
65. As fish cannot measure the ocean, as a gnat cannot traverse the whole sky, so the great sages even with their wisdom cannot know Me.
66. Aeons have passed in trying to know clearly who I am, how great, whence I come and when.
67. O Pandava, though I am the primal source from which all the gods, the great rishis and the whole of creation have sprung, it is very difficult for them to know Me.
68. If water having flowed downwards could flow up again to a mountain or a grown tree return to its own roots, then could I be known by the world which has emanated from Me;
69. or if it were possible for a banyan tree to be contained in one of its shoots, if the sea could be contained in a single wave, or the whole earth be stored in a single atom,
70. then there would be a possibility of My being known by the souls of men, the great rishis and the gods who have been created by Me.

III. He who knows Me, the unborn, without beginning, also the mighty lord of the worlds, he, among mortals is undeluded and freed from all sins.

71. Though I am thus, one who by chance withdraws from further worldly life, and turns away from all activities of the senses,
72. even though he is drawn back into these he can quickly recover and, abandoning the life of the body, can rise above the power of the elements.
73. His mind being firmly established thus, by the light of his own Self-illumination, he realizes clearly that by nature I am unborn.
74. He is as the touchstone compared with other stones, as nectar in comparison with all fluids, or as a part of Me in human form.
75. He is the living image of wisdom and the limbs of his body are as the offshoots of bliss. His human form is an illusion for ordinary men.
76. If by chance a diamond were found in a lump of camphor and water fall upon it, would it not emerge with its form preserved?
77. So though this man may seem in the human world to be an ordinary man, the weaknesses of nature are unknown in him.
78. Sins avoid him, for fear of their lives, and as a serpent will leave a burning sandalwood tree, so desires will pass by the man who knows Me.
79. Now if thou desirest to learn how I may be known, hear what I am and what are My states of being.
80. These are spread throughout the whole world, expressing themselves in many and various creatures according to their individual nature.

IV. Understanding, knowledge, freedom from bewilderment, patience, truth, self-control and calmness; pleasure and pain, existence and non-existence, fear and fearlessness.

V. Non-violence, equal-mindedness, contentment, austerity, charity, fame and ill-fame [are] the different states of beings proceed from Me alone.

81. Of these the first is intellect, then follows limitless wisdom, freedom from confusion, forbearance, forgiveness and truth,
82. then tranquility and restraint, joy and grief found among men, birth and destruction, these all exist in my nature.
83. Fear and fearlessness, harmlessness and equanimity, contentment, austerity and charity, O Son of Pāndu,
84. fame and disgrace, success and failure, all these moods which are found in every place, emanate from Me, in all creatures.
85. Just as all men are different, so regard also these moods. Some proceed from My wisdom, some know nothing of me.

86. As light and darkness are caused by the sun; when it rises light appears and darkness comes with its setting.
87. Similarly knowledge and ignorance of Me are due to the destiny of creatures; for this reason they are of different kinds.
88. Thou shouldst know, O Son of Pāndu, that the whole world of sentient beings is involved in My nature.

VI. The seven great sages of old, and the four Manus also are of My nature and born of My mind and from them are all these creatures in the world.

89. Now will I speak of eleven other manifestations of Myself, those which protect the created world and under whose power the worlds live.
90. [There are] those illustrious seven seers, Kashyapa and others, most advanced [in all virtues], and wisest among the sages;
91. fourteen Manus will be mentioned, of whom there are four principal ones and of these Svayambhu is the chief.
92. These eleven were conceived in My mind, O Wielder of the bow, for the conduct of the affairs of the created world.
93. Before the order of men had been evolved or individuality developed, the group of the primary elements was still undivided.
94. These being created they then established [the guardians of] the world; these created the peoples.
95. So these eleven are as kings and the evolved worlds are their subjects, therefore know that all this world-manifestation is Mine.
96. [As an example] first there is only a seed, from that there grows a stem, and out of that branches shoot out;
97. from the main branches others shoot out and from all these appears the foliage,
98. then the flowers and fruit; so the whole tree grows; and, if we consider rightly, the seed is all this.
99. So, in the beginning I alone was; then awareness of mind was born. Out of that arose the seven great rishis and the four Manus.
100. They created the guardians [of different worlds], and these brought into being the various worlds. From the worlds were created the whole of mankind.
101. In this way, the whole universe has developed from Me. Only through faith is this realized.

VII. He who knows in truth this glory and power of Mine is united [with Me] by unfaltering yoga; of this there is no doubt.

VIII. I am the origin of all; from Me all [the whole creation] proceeds. Knowing this the wise worship Me, endowed with meditation.

102. Therefore, O Consort of Subhadrā, these are the aspects of My powers and the whole universe is pervaded by them.
103. In this manner, [from Brahma the Creator down] to the ant, there is nothing else but me.
104. One who knows this to be true has indeed attained the awakened state of wisdom and is not aware of the illusion of distinctions between superior and inferior.
105. Thou shouldst know, through experience of oneness, that I Myself, those manifestations of Me, and all separate things comprised in them, all these are one.
106. So, therefore, he who by means of the yoga of certainty is united with Me through his mind, has attained his goal; concerning this there is no doubt.

IX. Their thoughts [are fixed] on Me, their lives [are wholly] given up to Me, enlightening each other and ever conversing of Me, they are contented and rejoicing in Me.

107. As though the sun were to encircle the sun with light, or the moon embrace the moon, or two brooks of like size meet,
108. so the streams of union with the Supreme meet, the quality of purity floating as plant leaves on the surface of the waters, and [these devotees] become as the image of Ganesha, seated in a group of four for discussion together.
109. In their great delight they leave the village of their bodies and begin to proclaim aloud their joy in Me.
110. The great truth of Brahma which the teacher conveys to his disciples, withdrawing to a quiet place, these men proclaim like the clouds in heaven till it resounds throughout the three worlds.
111. Just as the lotus bud, on opening, knows not how to keep its fragrance to itself, but offers it as a feast of fragrance alike to king and beggar,
112. so do these enlightened ones tell of Me throughout the universe. In the joy of the telling they forget their tale; in this forgetfulness they lose all awareness of body and soul.
113. In the fullness of their love they know neither day nor night; they have made themselves one with the perfect bliss of union with Me.

X. To these who are in constant union with Me and worship Me with love, I grant the power of understanding by which they come to Me.

114. Then they win for themselves the priceless gift, O Arjuna, which I Myself should grant them
115. and, O good warrior, compared with the path by which they set out, both heaven and final emancipation are as a by-path.
116. So, that love which they have for Me is the gift I have to bestow, but they have made it their own before even I could grant it.
117. All therefore that remains to be done is [to ensure that] such love increases and that the evi1 eye of death does not fall on them. This is what I have always to do.
118. O Kiriti, as a mother follows after her beloved child and watches over it lovingly while it plays,
119. and she turns into gold whatever game it wants to play so do I foster m them every kind of worship.
120. I take special delight in encouraging them along the path which brings them joyfully to Me.
121. I love all creatures who are devoted to Me, and they are devoted to Me as their only resort; for there are few such lovers in My abode.
122. The two paths leading to heaven and to liberation have been made for them to travel, I Myself and My consort Lakshmi spend ourselves [in their service].
123. But the supreme and selfless joy is reserved for those devotees who are united with Me through their loving devotion.
124. O Kiriti, to such a degree [am I attached to them] that I take these loving ones to Myself. These things are such that they are not to be spoken of.

XI. Out of compassion for those same ones, remaining within My own true state, I destroy the darkness born of ignorance by the shining lamp of wisdom.

125. They who have made of Me, who am the true Self the only centre of their lives, thinking of nought else but Me,
126. for those pure enlightened ones, O great warrior, I Myself am the torch bearer, going before them with the camphor torch.
127. I dispel the thick cloud of the night of ignorance, and I create for them the dawn.
128. When He who is best of all, beloved of the hearts of His steadfast devotees, had spoken thus, Arjuna said. My mind is at rest.

Arjuna said:

XII. Thou art the Supreme Brahman, the Supreme Abode and the Supreme Purifier, the Eternal Divine Person, the First of the gods, the Unborn, the All-pervading.

129. Hear, O Lord, well hast Thou swept away the dust of worldly life and I am set free from the pains of human birth and rebirth.
130. Today have I seen my [spiritual] birth and found my own true life. I am content.
131. Wisdom has been born, the day of my good fortune has dawned, in that I have received the grace of Thy words from Thy divine lips.
132. With the light of Thy teaching the inner and outer darkness has been dispelled and I see Thy nature in its full reality.
133. Thou art the Supreme Brahma, the resting place of the great elements, the most holy abode, O Lord of all the worlds.
134. The highest among the three gods art Thou, the spirit of the twenty-fifth principle, the divine one beyond all forms of matter.
135. Thou art without origin, O Lord, free from the grasp of the birth and action. Thee I have realized this day.
136. Thou dost control this wheel of time. Thou dost govern all life. Thou dost rule over the cauldron of the universe. Now I understand this clearly.

XIII. All the sages say this of Thee, as well as the divine seer Nārada, so also Asita, Devala, Vyāsa and Thou Thyself declare it to me.

137. In another way I see the greatness of this experience; the great sages of old have spoken of Thee thus,
138. but through Thy grace my heart understands the truth of all they taught.
139. Though Nārada always came to us and sang of Thee, yet, in spite of not understanding the meaning of his words, I merely enjoyed his singing.
140. If the sun shines on a habitation of blind men, they would feel its warmth, but how could they know its light?
141. In the same way when the great sage sang of the Supreme, I enjoyed the sweetness of the melody, but did not understand anything else with my mind.
142. I heard also from Asita and Devala that "Thou art thus"; but then my mind was overpowered by the poison of sense desires.
143. Why mention the names of others? Even when the great Vyāsa came to us he always spoke of Thy nature.
144. His teachings were like the desire-stone found in the dark, which remains unnoticed; but when daylight comes it appears and we say it is here.
145. Thus the teachings of Vyāsa and other sages were a mine of precious truth for me; but they were as though wasted without Thee, O Krishna,

XIV. I hold as true all this that Thou sayest to Me, O Keśava [Kṛṣṇa]; neither the gods nor the demons, O Lord, know Thy manifestation.

146. Now the rays of the sun [of Thy teaching] have shone forth and my ignorance of all the paths spoken of by the sages has been dispelled.
147. Their teaching, the seeds of life, have fallen deep into the soil [of my heart] and, watered by Thy grace, they have borne fruit in this conversation.
148. The discourse of Krishna has brought juice into the flowers and these have given me delight.
149. The sayings of Nārada and the other saints are as rivers in the form of devotion and I, O Ananta, am the ocean of the joy of this dialogue [into which they flow].
150. O Lord, what all the merit which I have accumulated in past lives could not achieve, Thou, O Teacher, [hast given to me].
151. Often I have heard the elders speak of Thee, but until Thy grace was bestowed on me, I could understand nothing.
152. When a man's fortune is favorable, whatever he undertakes prospers. Similarly, all that is heard or studied bears fruit through the favour of the teacher.
153. My Lord, a gardener spends his life toiling and tending his trees, but the fruit will be seen only when the spring comes.
154. When fever abates, what is sweet [again] tastes sweet and even medicine is thought sweet when health returns.
155. Moreover, as the senses, speech and breath serve their purpose only when consciousness is active in the body,
156. so all enquiry into the scriptures, all exercises practiced in yoga, can only become our own under the direction of the teacher.
157. With the realization of this experience, Arjuna, dancing with the joy of conviction, said, O Lord, I know Thy words are true.
158. O Lord of blessedness, I have indeed had the clearest realization that Thy nature is beyond even the understanding of the gods and demons.
159. Now I realize that unless Thy teaching is revealed to us, we can never understand it with only our own intelligence.

XV. Verily Thou Thyself knowest Thyself by Thyself, O Supreme Person; the Source of beings, the Lord of Creatures; the God of gods, the Lord of the world.

160. As the sky is aware of its own vastness, and the earth knows its own weight,
161. so also Thou knowest Thyself through Thy omnipotence, O Lord of Lakshmi! The Vedas even boast in vain of their knowledge of Thee.
162. How may [the speed of] the mind be outrun, or the wind be measured in a fathom? How can the original void be crossed [by swimming] with human arms?

163. So it is with the knowledge of Thee; there are none who can grasp it. Thou alone art able to impart knowledge of Thyself.
164. Thou alone knowest Thyself and art able to reveal Thyself [to others]; so wipe from thy brow once and for all, the sweat of my desire to know.
165. Hast Thou heard me, O Creator of all beings, who art as a lion to [the elephant of] worldly existence, and revered by all gods and deities, O Lord of the universe?
166. If we see Thy greatness [we know that] we are not worthy to stand before Thee; on account of this unworthiness we fear to approach Thee, yet we have no other way.
167. Everywhere seas and rivers are full, but to the chātaka bird they seem dry, for only when rain falls from the clouds does it drink.
168. Similarly are there many teachers, O Krishna, but Thou alone art our refuge. Describe to me, then. Thy divine manifestations.

XVI. Thou shoutdst tell me of Thy divine manifestations, without exception, whereby, pervading these worlds. Thou dost abide [in them and beyond].

169. Show to me those of Thy manifestations which are most permeated with Thy divinity.
170. O Ananta, reveal to me those principal and best known manifestations which pervade all worlds.

XVII. How may I know Thee, O Yogin, by constant meditation? In what various aspects art Thou, O Blessed Lord, to he thought of by me?

171. How may I know Thee? What must I know in order to meditate constantly on Thee? Were I to say that Thou art all, meditation on Thee would be impossible.
172. So do Thou once more describe to me in detail those manifestations to which Thou has earlier referred.
173. Speak to me clearly of them all, that I may find no difficulty in meditating on Thee in them. . . .

XXI. Of the Ādityas I am Viṣṇu; of the lights I am the radiant Sun; I am Marīci of the Maruts; of the stars I am the moon.

202. With these words the Compassionate One continued, among the heavenly deities I am Vishnu; among the radiant worlds of light I am the Sun,
203. Among the companies of winds I am Marici, said Shārngi and of all the stars of heaven I am the moon. . . .

228. Of all those who persecute I, Gopāla, say that I am Death and among all beasts the lion is the manifestation of Me.
229. Of birds know Me to be Garuda; that is why he is able to carry Me safely on his back.

XXXI. Of purifiers I am the wind; of warriors I am Rāma; of fishes I am the alligator and of rivers I am the Ganges.

230. Of those that can traverse the world in a moment of time, O Wielder of the bow, I am that which can circle the earth in one leap.
231. Of all such swiftly moving things I am the wind, O Son of Pāndu. Among all who wield weapons, I am Rāma,
232. who, when righteousness was in peril, transformed himself into a bow in its defence, and in the Tretā age made the glory of success his goal.
233. Then, standing on the summit of Mount Suvela, he boldly presented Rāvana's ten heads as an offering to those in heaven who were praying for his victory.
234. That Rāma restored to the gods their rightful dignity, re-established righteousness, rising as the sun of the great Solar Race.
235. I am that Rāma, the consort of Jānaki, among all the great wielders of weapons. Among all creatures dwelling in the waters, I am the tailed crocodile.
236. Of all streams I am the Ganges brought down from heaven by Bhāgirathi, who was swallowed [by Janhu] and was given forth again from his thigh, ripped open.
237. Among all rivers know Me to be the Ganges, the only river of the three worlds, O Son of Pāndu.

XXXII. Of creations I am the beginning, the end, and also the middle, O Arjuna; of the sciences [I am] the science of the self; of those who debate I am the dialectic.

238. Were I to attempt to name all the various manifestations of Myself in the universe, a thousand births would not be enough to mention even half.

XXXIII. Of letters I am [the letter] A and of compounds [I am] the dual; I also am imperishable time and I the creator whose face is turned on all sides.

239. If one desired to gather together all the stars, he would need to enclose the whole heavens in a cloth.

240. If one wished to count all the atoms of which the earth is composed, one would have to hold it under the arm. So anyone who wishes to see the whole extent [of My manifestations] must first know Me.
241. If a man wanted to grasp all the branches, flowers and fruit of a tree at the same moment, it would be necessary for him to pull up the root;
242. so if My different manifestations are to be known entirely, My faultless nature must first be known.
243. Otherwise, of all these varied forms how many canst thou listen to? Therefore know once and for all, O wise one that everything is indeed Me.
244. I am the beginning, the middle and the end of all creation, O Kiriti, as the thread is woven throughout the warp and woof of cloth.
245. When a man understands Me as pervading all, what need is there to know My separate manifestations? Thou art not yet worthy [to realize this].
246. So, O Lord of Subhadrā, as thou hast asked me, listen while I tell thee more of those manifestations. Now of all branches of knowledge, I am the knowledge of the Self.
247. Among speakers I am the discourse of which there is no end, in spite of the principles laid down in the traditional teachings.
248. It grows as the discussion develops, it adds strength to the power of imagination in all who listen, and adds value to the words of the speaker.
249. So I, Mukunda, say. I am the argument in all controversy. Of all letters I am the pure A.
250. Of compounds know Me to be the dvandva and I the one who, as death, seizes all, from the smallest gnat to the Creator Himself.
251. O Kiriti, I am he who, grasping the light of the universal dissolution, swallows up the winds and into whose belly the whole of space is absorbed.
252. I who sport with Lakshmi am death, the infinite; and again I recreate everything.

XXXIV. I am death, the all-devouring and [am] the origin of things that are yet to be; and of feminine beings, [I am] fame, prosperity, speech, memory, intelligence, firmness and patience.

253. I sustain all created things; I am their very life, and at the end, when I destroy them all, I am death; hear this. . . .
280. For this reason I will now reveal to thee My great secret: I am the seed from which all created beings arise and grow.

281. Therefore thou shouldst regard Me as everything that is without considering such concepts as great or small high and low.
282. Listen now to one more simple sign by which thou mayest recognize a manifestation of Me. . . .
305. But let us leave [what Sanjaya said]. Arjuna's respect for non-duality had so increased that his eagerness to hear more was intensified.

Source: *Jnāneshvari*, translated by V. G. Pradhan (Albany: State University of New York Press, 1987).

Selections from the Sākhīs of Kabīr

THE GURU'S GREATNESS

1. What can I give in return,
   so great is the Name of Rām?
   What gift of mine could please the Guru?
   the wish remains [unfulfilled] in my heart.

2. There is no relative closer than the Satguru,
   no bounty equal to spiritual awakening,
   There is no greater Benefactor than Hari,
   no community equal to that of Hari's devotees.

3. Even when sixty-four lamps burn
   and fourteen moons shine within,
   There can be no moonlight at all
   in the house where the Satguru is not. . . .

6. If the Guru be blind
   the disciple is born blind:
   When the blind lead the blind
   both fall into the well!

7. Doubt has devoured the whole world
   But none has ever eaten Doubt:
   Only those pierced by the Guru's Word
   Have picked and eaten Doubt. . . .

10. I was drowning but I was saved
    when the Guru's wave rose up:
    I saw the vessel fall to pieces
    and I myself jumped clear!

11. I found stability and salvation
    when the Satguru gave me firmness:
    Kabīr, the Diamond is for sale
    on the bank of Mānsarovar.

12. I became mute and witless
    and my ears no longer heard,
    My legs became paralysed
    when the Satguru's arrow struck me.

13. The grandeur of the Satguru is infinite,
    infinite is His bounty,
    He opened my eyes to the Infinite
    and showed me Infinity.

14. I was just tagging along
    in the wake of the world and the Veda,
    Then the Satguru met me on the path
    and He put a Lamp in my hand.

15. A Lamp full of oil He gave me,
    whose wick will never run dry:
    All bartering is over,
    I will go to that market no more.

16. When the Guru, the Giver of wisdom, is found,
    never, never stray from Him:
    Only through the grace of Govind,
    is the Guru ever found.

17. The one found no Guru, the other no disciple,
    out of greed they cheated:
    They both drowned in the current,
    sailing in a boat of stone!

18. The Satguru is found—but what then
    if the mind be steeped in error?
    If the cloth is already soiled,
    what is the poor red dye to do?

19. I offer myself in sacrifice to the Guru
    a hundred times a day,
    He who from man made me a God
    and that in no time at all!

20. I have dedicated myself to the Satguru
    with sincerity of heart:
    In vain did Kaliyug attack me
    for staunch was my resolve!

21. The Satguru took his bow in hand
    and he began to loose his arrows:
    One which he shot with Love
    pierced me through and through!

22. It can no longer laugh or talk,
    the fickle Mind—it is undone!
    Says Kabīr, it pierced me through and through,
    that Weapon of the Guru!

23. The Satguru fitted his arrow and let fly,
    keeping his aim steady:
    It hit my naked body
    and the Forest burst in flames.

24. Kabīr, when I have found a perfect Guru,
    the salt has vanished in the flour:
    Caste, family, and lineage are no more,
    what name then will you give me ?

25. To find the Guru is a great boon:
    without Him, you are lost,
    As the moth attracted by the lamp's flame
    falls into it in full knowledge!

26. Māyā is the Lamp, man is the moth,
    circling around [the flame], he falls:
  Says Kabīr, thanks to the Guru's wisdom,
    a few are saved.

27. Seated on the throne of Consciousness,
    the Satguru granted me firmness:
  Free from fear and doubt,
    Kabīr adores the One.

28. Guru and Govind are but One,
    all there is are but His forms:
  By crushing the self and adoring Hari,
    man obtains the Vision.

29. Kabīr, they have not found the Satguru,
    they have remained only half-taught:
  Clad in ascetic's garb,
    they go begging from door to door!

THE GREATNESS OF PRAYER

1. Kabīr, what are you doing, sleeping?
    get up and lament your fate!
  He whose dwelling is in the tomb,
    how can he sleep happily?

2. Kabīr, what are you doing, sleeping?
    Wake up and adore Murāri!
  One day you'll be made to sleep
    and then with outstretched legs!

3. If you can plunder, plunder,
    let the Name of Rām be your booty!
  [Otherwise] later you'll repent,
    when you breathe your last!. . .

6. Repeating "Thou, Thou," I became Thou,
    in me, no "I" remained:
  Offering myself unto Thy Name,
    wherever I look. Thou art!

7. [True] Bhakti is adoration of Hari's Name,
   all else is boundless torment!
   [To worship] in soul, words, and deeds,
   such is the essence of Prayer, [says] Kabīr.

8. If the devotee has a thought,
   let it be [but] of Hari's Name:
   Any thought which is not for Rām
   is but the noose of Kāl!

9. They who know not love and tenderness,
   whose tongue repeats not [the Name of] Rām,
   Those men were born in the world in vain
   and so went to perdition!

10. Through his previous wrongdoings,
    man has collected a bundle of poison,
    But millions of actions are erased in one moment
    if he but takes refuge in Hari.

11. Millions of actions are instantly erased
    by invoking the Name, just a little,
    But merits heaped up for endless ages,
    without the Name, will lead you nowhere!

12. Long is the road, far off is the house,
    rugged is the path, beset with dangers:
    O Saints, tell me, how can man obtain
    the inaccessible Vision of Hari?

THE RECOGNITION OF THE SPOUSE

1. Though the musk is held within its pod,
   the musk-deer searches in the forest:
   Likewise Rām dwells in the bodies of all,
   yet the world perceives Him not!

2. As the pupil within the eye,
   so is the Lord within the body,
   Foolish men recognize Him not
   and they go searching without.

3. What is contained in a casket
   cannot be the Lord,
   But that which pervades the whole creation,
   that you should call the Lord!

4. Kabīr, I have taken that One as my Companion,
   who knows neither pleasure nor pain:
   In close union shall I sport with Him
   and never be separated!

5. Led astray, the wife has forgotten her Spouse,
   she betrayed Him so many times,
   But the Satguru enlightened her
   and showed her again her first Husband.

6. The Lord Himself dwells within the body
   yet people grasp not this mystery,
   As the musk-deer roams around,
   sniffing the grass [for musk]!

7. He has neither face nor forehead,
   nor form of any kind,
   He is more subtle than the fragrance of flowers,
   such is His transcendent Reality.

8. Talk not about that mysterious One,
   rather hide his mystery:
   Veda and Koran cannot encompass Him,
   if you talked, who would believe you ?

9. If I say He is heavy, I am afraid,
   if I say He is light, I lie:
   What can I know of Rām,
   when my eyes have never seen Him ?

10. Had I seen Him, what would I say?
    and if I spoke, none would believe me!
    Hari is only like Hari:
    joyful, sing His praise!

11. He who remains apart from creation,
    yet holds creation in Himself,
    This One does Kabīr worship
    and he will not worship another.

12. Hidden within the blade of grass,
    is the Mountain of Rām, such is my sentiment:
    Finding the Satguru, man tastes the Experience
    and he discovers [God] within his own body.

THE EXPERIENCE

1. When I was, Hari was not,
   now Hari is and I am no more:
   All darkness vanished,
   when I saw the Lamp within my heart.

2. The effulgence of the supreme Being
   is beyond the imagination:
   Ineffable is His beauty,
   to see it is the only "proof".

3. It was a good thing the hail fell on the ground,
   for it lost its own selfhood:
   Melting, it turned into water
   and rolled down to the pond.

4. Him whom I went out to seek,
   I found just where I was:
   He now has become myself
   whom before I called "Another"!

5. In the Unattainable, the Inaccessible,
   there shines the Light,
   There Kabīr has brought his homage
   where "merits" and "sins" cannot reach.

6. The bird has flown to the sky
   while its body remained in a strange land:
   There, the bird drinks without a beak
   and has forgotten this country.

7. Love lit up the cage,
   an eternal flame sprang up,
   Doubt vanished, joy awoke,
   when I met my beloved Spouse.

8. My mind entered the *unmani* stage,
   heaven was scaled:
   Where moonlight shines without a moon,
   there dwells Niranjan, the invisible King!

9. Water turned into ice,
   then the ice itself melted:
   All that was has become Himself,
   what is there left now to say?

10. *surati* was reabsorbed into *nirati*,
    japa into *ajapa*,
    The visible into the Invisible
    and the self into the Self.

11. When I found the True One, joy was born,
    the river of my heart overflowed,
    All sins were "easily" washed away,
    when I obtained my Lord's Presence.

12. Kabīr has seen the One, the Inaccessible,
    whose glory is ineffable:
    That luminous Being, that Spouse who is Pāras,
    He was enclosed in my eyes!

13. Without foundation the temple,
    without body, the deity:
    There Kabīr has remained attached
    to the service of the Invisible. . . .

16. Kabīr, the Mind has become a Bee,
    which has found its eternal dwelling:
    That lotus which blooms without water
    [God's] servants alone can see.

17. A lotus has blossomed within,
    where Brahman makes his dwelling:
    The bee-like mind was there enclosed,
    but few will understand!

18. Though there is neither ocean nor shell,
    nor a drop of Svāti rain,
    Says Kabīr, yet the Pearl is born
    in the Fortress whose summit is the Void.

19. Within the body, the Inaccessible was found,
    to the Inaccessible a path:
    Says Kabīr, I obtained the Experience,
    when the Guru showed me the way.

20. The Sun merged into the Moon,
    both dwelt in one house together:
    Then was the longing of my mind fulfilled—
    so fortunate was my fate!

21. Crossing the boundary, I entered the Boundless,
    I took my dwelling in the Void:
    In that Palace which the Munis cannot reach,
    there I have my repose!

22. See what has happened to Kabīr,
    so fortunate was his fate:
    He whose mansion the Munis cannot reach,
    The Invisible One has become my Friend!

23. When Love lit up the cage,
    my soul was flooded with light,
    My mouth became fragrant with musk,
    perfuming all my words.

24. *surati* was reabsorbed into *nirati*
    and *nirati* remained unsupported:
    From *surati* and *nirati*, the Experience was born,
    then the Gate opened by itself.

25. I had come into this world
    and many forms there were to see:
    Says Kabīr, O Saints,
    I caught sight of the Incomparable [form]!

26. Embracing Him with open arms [is of no avail],
    if the mind is not bound firmly:
    Says Kabīr, there is no true union,
    as long as the two bodies remain distinct!

Source: *Kabīr*, translated by Ch. Vaudeville, volume 1 (Oxford: Clarendon Press, 1974).

Selections from *The Hagiographies of Anantadās* on the life of Raidās

Birth of Raidās

One

1. In Benares, that best of cities
   no evil ever visits men.
   No one who dies ever goes to hell:
   Shankar himself comes with the Name of Rām.
2. Where Śruti and Smriti have authority
   there Raidās was reborn,
   in the home of a low-caste Shākta—
   his father and mother were both Chamārs.
3. In his previous birth he was a Brahmin;
   he listened all the time to religious recitation, but did not give up meat.
   For this sin he was born into a low-caste family,
   but he remembered his previous birth.
4. He did not drink milk but only cried
   causing anxiety in his family.
   "In great pain our son has been born.
   Has in pain the unique child of a great house been born here?"
5. The women did not sing auspicious songs, and
   in their anxiety they did not play any instruments.
   They summoned many a sorcerer and healer
   to work magic and minister potions.

6. "Whoever saves this dying child, (they said),
   will be hailed as Dhanvantari [divine physician].
   We will do whatever he says
   and heap things in front of him."
7. Four days passed,
   while the mother despaired
   and the father grieved with the rest of the family.
   Only Raidas found pleasure in dying.
8. Dying is better than living,
   for life without Hari is tasteless.
   The man who lives but has forgotten Hari,
   is like one who drinks poison and is punished by the god of death.
9. Whether poor or wealthy,
   powerless or powerful,
   a fool or a wise man—
   a king or a beggar, nobody can cross the ocean of being without the grace of Hari.
10. As Raidās lay thinking of death,
    Hari, the compassionate one had mercy on his follower.
    In the night a heavenly voice was heard,
    which in his heart Rāmānanda understood:
11. "The son born in a Chamār's house is my devotee born again," and
    Hari related the whole story
    of what had happened in the past.
12. "With great compassion, give him initiation—
    you must by all means save this dying child."
    Then Rāmānanda decided
    to enlighten the whole family:
13. "If you become devotees, brothers,
    Hari will revive your child."
    The Chamār touched Rāmānanda's feet, and said:
    "Do what you like, O Gosvami."
14. Without further ado, Rāmānanda
    put his hand on the Chamār's forehead.
    He gave them understanding and had the child shaven,
    removing and rubbing away his past.

15. And everyone's hearts were gladdened when
    Raidās started to suckle at his mother's breast.
    People congratulated them, while drums were beaten
    and in every home the sacred pitchers were decorated.
16. In telling the birth story of Raidās
    even the Lord finds pleasure.
    The bonds of *karma* are severed:
    so sings the devotee, Ananta.

Two

1. In this manner, Hari is the benevolent master.
   In every age he has removed the misfortunes of his people.
   Day by day Raidās grew bigger and
   with every new day his love for Hari grew stronger.
2. By the time he was seven
   he could practice the nine forms of *bhakti*.
   He served the Lord with all his heart
   and never strayed from the path shown by the Satguru.
3. Seven more years passed
   and his love for the Lord grew.
   The narration of his childhood may be pleasing,
   but the family soon grew weary of his devotion.
4. As he grew up he was forsaken by the others.
   They shared the family's wealth among themselves,
   and relegated poor Raidās to the rear of the house;
   but he never uttered a word of protest.
5. He would buy leather from the market
   and make fine shoes from it.
   He mended broken and torn old shoes as well,
   never asking anyone for anything while he toiled.
6. Easily he made money,
   not considering any work inferior.
   He offered food to the deity in a separate temple,
   where only devotees came.
7. He performed the rituals with extreme care
   and he knew all manner of worship.

Another seven years thus passed,
while Raidās endured many bodily privations.

8. Until finally Hari came in the guise of a devotee,
much to the delight of Raidās.
With all due respect, he seated him
and spoke humble words and washed his feet.

9. For a while he narrated stories of Hari,
while food was prepared for him.
After the Lord had eaten and sat back,
the conversation turned towards the joys and sorrows of life. . . .

Seven

1. An interval of five years passed
and now I come to the stories of Chittor.
Queen Jhālī was a very intelligent woman,
a perfect example of almsgiving, religious duty and good association.

2. All enjoyments were available to her
but she had no *mālā*, mantra or guru.
Suddenly a desire arose in her mind,
and she happily wanted initiation.

3. She called a devotee and inquired of him,
from whom she should receive initiation.
The devotee told her:
"In my mind I have searched in all directions.

4. There are so many devotees, what can I say?
Let me tell you about one, your majesty.
Go quickly to the city of Kashi,
if you have any trust in my words.

5. There is a *julāhā* named Kabīr,
whom you can consider as Shukdev embodied.
He truly recognizes *nirguṇ* Brahman,
you should ask him for initiation. Majesty.

6. There is also Raidās the Chamār,
who is like an incarnation of Nārad.
I feel shy but I should call him a Shūdra,
but even kings are eager to come and see him.

7. Brahmins do not understand this mystery
   but both Kabīr and Raidās are *avatār*-s of Vishnu."
   Hearing this, the queen was very pleased,
   and arrangements were made for her journey to Banaras.
8. Brahmins wanted to go with her in the conviction
   that the queen would receive initiation from them.
   Jhālī tried to stop them, but they insisted on going,
   for the initiation and for a bath in the Ganges.
9. They came to Kashi after twenty days
   and the queen secretly sent two messengers:
   "Go and tell the respected Kabīr,
   that Jhālī wants to receive initiation from him."
10. But Kabīr was very hesitant:
    "I don't have any business with kings or queens."
    He was dressed in a torn blanket
    when the queen arrived to see him.
11. She saw all the dispassionate *nirguṇ* devotees,
    who were seated devoid of all attachment.
    She saw the hut made from grass
    and covered with torn patched robes.
12. There was no worship, no offering, no gods or goddesses,
    contemplation of God was their service.
    This service the Lord knows
    and some rare ascetics understand.
    There was no plate, pitcher, money or cloth,
    and not even water for a second day.
    This *nirguṇ* devotion concentrating only on the Name
    could not at all appeal to the queen.
13. When the queen saw the austere lifestyle,
    she felt misgivings in her heart.
    She went to the home of Raidās the Chamār,
    to see how he did things there.
14. She went quickly there,
    and she saw an enclosure with a high gate.
    When she saw the temple she was very happy,
    for Gobinda was always seated there.

15. Over sixty canopies were spread out, and
    the queen had never before seen such happiness.
    There were golden pots and silken cloths
    and plenty of small pots filled with perfume.
16. Cymbals were ringing and drums beating,
    and there were all sorts of flower garlands.
    There she saw the master, Raidās,
    sitting surrounded by many heads of monasteries.
17. He was wearing fine clothes and had a splendid body,
    while from his mouth came sweet speech.
    At that moment all pride left the queen,
    and she prostrated herself in front of the devotees.
18. She grasped the feet of Raidās,
    and then he placed his hands on her forehead.
    The queen was very happy,
    taking part in the fellowship of the devotees.

Eight

1. None of the Brahmins knew this secret,
   the queen did not reveal that she had received this initiation.
   Jhālī donated plenty of money to cover the expenses and returned home.
   "Take this money
   and spend it in beautiful celebrations."
   Then Raidās sponsored some festivals
   and fed all the devotees.
2. When they had gone five *kos* out of the city,
   her Brahmins made a great complaint.
   The priests heard that she had accepted a *mālā*,
   and they turned black in anger.
   "You have accepted initiation from a low caste man,
   you did not bother about caste and tradition,
   accepting the mantra and the garland."
   The Brahmins became like the god of death.
3. Their anger flamed up like fire,
   they picked up stones and gashed their heads.
   But the queen grasped the reins and turned back
   and arrived back in Benares.

4. The angry Brahmins cursed her, saying:
   "Your *jap* will be fruitless."
   Some of them threw down their almanacs in anger,
   others threw off their sacred threads.
5. Some burnt themselves with a piece of iron,
   while Keśava Pande cut his wrist.
   Some sat in the burning sun,
   while others threw themselves on the ground.
6. Some of them bit their tongues,
   some of them rent their clothing.
   Some of them swallowed lumps of poison,
   some of them ran off to court.
7. Some of them sliced open their bellies with daggers,
   some of them threatened they would kill themselves in the king's house.
   Some gave their blood as offering
   and some refused to drink water.
8. They arrived at the Chamār's house to kill themselves.
   At this tumult the Baghelā king came out running, and
   hiding in a shawl the queen arrived,
   regretting what she had done.
9. "Only the Lord can protect me in this crisis,"
   Jhāī said this again and again.
   If one does good which turns out badly,
   the doer has no power over this.
10. The whole city of Kashi turned up,
    and people were relating what had first happened.
    How the *śāligrām* came into the lap of Raidās,
    and how both the king and the people saw this happening.
    "Saying 'killing and beating' won't complete your work,"
    the king tried to stop the quarrel.
    "The great Raidās is a saint;
    it is a great sin to hurt him.
    If you want to enjoy greater respect,
    then you must immerse your body in love."
11. A close devotee of Hari, the barber Sen
    came from the Bādhau fort.

The Brahmins did not accept his intervention,
but he was insistent and was ready to die.
With great efforts he made them understand,
but they refused to listen to him.
"All the saints and ascetics confirm this
and even the great Kabīr has spoken like this."
But the furious Brahmins went on hurting themselves,
and no religious argument could convince them.
Then Raidās had an idea
and he told the saints what to do:
"If people do not listen to true words,
they can never find success in life."

12. He dispatched one of his devotees,
to go and ask Kabīr for advice.
"The Brahmins have come to kill themselves—
give me advice on what I should do!"

13. Kabīr said: "They will not listen to what you say,
as they have been eating from the hands of kings.
Even if Brahmā were to teach them they would not listen.
You and me are beneath their notice."
Very humbly the devotees replied:
"You are like Brahmā for us.
All good advice always comes from you
for those who carefully listen to you."
Then Kabīr spoke in this way,
removing all their doubts:
"Do not be afraid, Hari will take care of everything,
and all the Brahmins will get tired and give up."

14. Leave it to the *śāligrām* to decide,
if you want to be freed from this problem.
From age to age the devotees bear witness,
"Do not be afraid! Take Hari as your protector."

15. Kabīr gave them these instructions
and Raidās liked this idea.
The Brahmins remained intent upon killing themselves
and did not listen to anything about knowledge and meditation.

16. Then Raidās instructed them:
    "Whatever the Lord says you must do,"
    and the *sāligrām* was brought.
    Everyone was pleased with this.
17. All the quarrels disappeared,
    and the Sants started to meditate.
    They accepted as true,
    what God himself has said. . . .

Eleven

1. In the morning they started to walk,
   with their associates absorbed in Hari.
   Well behaved and absorbed in meditation
   all the followers joined the company.
2. With *nirguṇ* knowledge and concentration firm in their hearts,
   they meditated on the unproduced sound.
   One should always lake pleasure in the company of such people—
   not only men, but also gods are attracted.
3. Wherever Hari's devotees travel,
   seeing them everyone finds happiness.
   When Hari's devotees lovingly sing songs of devotion,
   everyone's mind is taken up in love.
4. If devotees cross someone's threshold,
   then his evil deeds are destroyed and he finds liberation.
   Showing great enthusiasm they make their love greater—
   whom would they not please?
5. Wandering on like this many days passed,
   while Jhālī was impatient to see him.
   When they had come near Chittor,
   then Raidās sent two devotees.
6. The devotees came and conveyed [his] words,
   and the queen was very enthusiastic:
   "Blessed is this day and blessed is this hour,
   when you came and gave me this message."
7. Then Raidās approached,
   and at first he made a camp in a garden.

The queen summoned all of her ministers,
and dispatched the entire capital to his presence.

8. Both ordinary and important people went to see him,
but the Brahmins were very resentful.
While everyone was happy,
the Brahmins died of jealousy.

Source: *The Hagiographies of Anantadās: The Bhakti Poets of North India*, translated by Winand M. Callewaert (Richmond: Curzon, 2000).

Selections from the *Janmalīlā* of Dādū Dayāl

Chapter 2

1. He left for Sāmbhar, full of love, but suffering *virah*. He was suffering for the Supreme Brahman and the hidden light within him shone brighter.
2. He meditated deeply on the Name, with detached soul and composed body. Beholding the light, glimmering or bright, he realized his life was very successful.
3. Boundless knowledge of Divine Reality dawned after he met the blessed Kabīr in *samādhi*, and they discussed his doubts about the divine experience.
4. He continually sang Kabīr's poems and verses and became his equal in word and deed. After his meeting with Kabīr, he became an authority on Divine Reality.
5. He ignored all Muslim customs and abandoned Hindu practices. He did not mix with other ascetics, but stayed immersed in Rām day and night.
6. He abstained from hypocrisy, vanity, partiality and sectarianism, knowing only the Supreme Brahma as the total truth. He rejected all temple-worship of gods, pilgrimages and fasts and did not visit holy persons or shrines.
7. Both Hindus and Muslims began to clash with him, but he had a ready answer for all. Finally, Qāzīs and Brahmans all gave up: Hari was his protector, so what could they do?
    1. "If I do not adhere to Muslim customs, what does it matter to you? Who has said that such worship is essential?"
    2. "When a boat is wrecked on the ocean and all are sinking, everybody flees to save his life, Dādū."

8. The Brahmans and Baniyas deliberated and reported to the Council. They wrote a letter and announced publicly that people should take note of their decision:
9. "Anybody going to see Dādū will be fined 500 Rupees." The clerk wrote out the order correctly, but the words were changed when the order was read:
10. "Anybody not going to see Dādū will be fined 500 Rupees." From that moment faith started to grow in Sāmbhar and famous holy men came to see him.
11. A Qāzī came from Ajmer with the Qurān in his hands: "Why have you upturned the true path? A Muslim lives by the Divine Word, if a person calls on Rām he is an infidel."
    1. "An infidel is he who speaks untruth, who does not keep his heart pure, who does not recognize the Lord and who is full of deceit, Dādū."
12. Svāmiji said: "Listen, Qāzī, why have you been deluded by this deception? For the Muslim the basis is Religion (*dīn*), while the Hindu is equally zealous about his own conviction.
13. Which belief is agreeable to the Almighty, if you know tell me quickly. What Religion (*pantha*) can it be, where creatures are killed?"
14. The Qāzī became furious and hit Dādū—blessed Svāmījī did not even try to protect himself. When he received a blow on his other cheek, Dādū said: "Now will happen as I tell you, brother.
15. The first blow was perceived in this world, at the second blow the Creator came to know. My body is very hard, Qāzī, and your hand will go on aching."
16. The Qāzī, feeling ashamed, went home, and the Almighty made his arm very painful. The Qāzī thought: "I have sinned hitting the Master in the face."
17. Three months later the Qāzī died in great suffering, but full of repentance. He who harms a saint, meets utter destruction.
18. A person will find liberation, if he sings or hears this joy-giving story of the life of Dādū Dīndayāl, says Jan Gopāl.

Chapter 3

1. In Sāmbhar a proud Qāzī intent on harming Svāmījī thought: "I shall go to my village and punish him.
2. I will dig a pit, bury him up to his neck and pierce his head with arrows. A musket, an arrow or a spear would be suitable, a stony club or a hatchet should be fetched.
3. It is written in the Book: "How can Muslims spread heresy? The truth of Religion (din) will remain firm, if frauds and rogues disappear."

4. That came to the attention of the Indweller, for enmity with a saint is sure to end in adversity. The Qāzī had 700 bundles of cotton in his house: it all started to burn, although there was no fire around.
5. The whole house burnt down and the Qāzī was very frightened. He no longer thought of harming Svāmījī, but left him in peace.
6. Then Svāmījī came out of town, totally concentrated on the Indweller. A mad elephant came running towards him and everyone with him fled.
7. Svāmījī had no fear at all, since the Indweller was aware of his situation: "This elephant comes, mad and intoxicated with illusion. I continue to taste the nectar of Rām."
8. The elephant stood still and seeing this the people experienced great joy. The elephant bent down and touched the feet of Svāmījī, who placed his hand on its forehead.
9. Another time, a thief broke into Svāmījī's house, but there was nothing of value. He found only threads and starting to take them away, made a noise which woke the family.
10. Dādū's wife and mother-in-law said: "What's happening? There is a man in the house, he must be a thief because he doesn't reply."
11. Svāmījī said: "Go away quickly, my friend, while no one is fully awake. If a watchman wakes up, your death would grieve me."
    1. The thief repented and said: "This great soul has saved my life." He took *prasād*, vowed to leave all stealing and became his disciple.
12. When they saw Svāmījī singing hymns inside a temple, the Qāzī and the Muslims were offended. A crowd gathering all around came and carried him away to kill him.
13. He kept the divine awareness constantly alive in his body, but his outer skin became dead. Usually moving to give the rhythm, his hands now were motionless by his sides.
14. Even in the presence of the evil, angry and sensual people, Svāmījī kept beholding the Indweller. Whether people honor him or beat him, a holy man sees Rām in all.
15. He was taken to the commander-in-chief, who would later suffer and repent his sin. The commander was again stubborn and threw Svāmījī into a dungeon.
16. They mocked: "What miraculous power do you have now? Savior of the world, you are lost." But the Almighty took pity on him, like a mother on her suffering child.

17. Svāmījī appeared to all inside and outside the prison and the darkness in which the commander was caught disappeared: "Forgive me my sin, how could I know your true nature?"
18. Svāmījī said: "You are not to blame, whatever the Creator orders pleases me." When the people in town heard this, they arranged seven celebrations.
19. Svāmījī stayed at home, resting, as if he did not know about the devotional celebrations. The Creator performed a miracle, but nobody understood the significance.
20. Whenever devotees came to take him somewhere, Svāmījī's form appeared there. Everyone derived much joy from the celebrations, their affection increased and they enjoyed this display of love.
21. Everyone tells this story of Dādū's appearance in seven different places. Svāmījī asked that the matter be given little attention: only the Unknown knows His own ways.
22. Dādū's honor and renown increased everywhere and people crowded to see him.
    1. Two Siddhas came to him, proud of their power to see (faraway) horses. Svāmiji said: "What are you giving your attention to?", and showed them (a horse with) blue ears.
    2. "You haven't achieved anything supernatural" yet. What is there in mastering a mere siddhi?" The two Siddhas reported that the perfect guru had put the mystic truth within their reach.
    3 "There is no marvel in what you see, but in what you cannot see. Do not weep for what is visible but for what is invisible, Dādū." All the devotees came to see him; he mysteriously appeared to all of them in turn.
23. Then the question of dress arose and Svāmījī was not pleased.
    1. "Like a garland strung on a thread, the Sadguru has given me a mind controlled by breathing. Not moving my hands I can pray day and night, this is the highest recitation."

    "How can I please the Muslims and what should I wear for the Hindus?"

24. Then Svāmījī decided to go to Āmer, which is a good place for meditation. Jan Gopāl sings the well-known story of Dādū Dīndayāl: whoever hears it knows the right way. . . .

Chapter 7

1. The discussions lasted for 40 days, there seemed to be no end to it. Dādū spoke with the firmness of Prahlād and with the wisdom of Kabīr.

2. He radiated the contemplative mind of Sukhdev and had the ascetic appearance of Gorakhnāth. Illusions and attachments did not distress or bother him, when you looked at him, he was all bliss.
3. The Emperor wondered what should be done and asked the King for his opinion. The King said: "If you can go and see him now, greet him with folded hands and head bent.
4. Please him with your humble speech, ask for his blessing and take his hand on your head. The blessing of a saint gives a vision of Khudā, without a blessing disaster will befall you."
5. Akbar ordered: "Bring Dādū quickly, if he does not mind meeting me." The King went to his palace. No one knew how Svāmījī would react.
6. A nobleman was sent to invite Dādū, who appeared to live close to the King's palace: "If you wish, the King will come and see you, or if you come to his palace, he can see you there."
7. Svāmījī decided to go along immediately, and took his disciple Jan Gopāl with him. Jagjīvan was asked to stay back, while Svāmījī went to see the King.
8. The King came to meet him and said: "May the Almighty always keep me in your shelter. I wish to inform you of the Emperor's desire to see you again, O joygiver."
9. The King accompanied Dādū to the imperial court, where they were at once received by the Emperor. When the King had announced that Dādū was present, the discussions with the Emperor started.
10. Svāmījī did not express any greeting; he remained indifferent, avoiding all involvement. "Tell me about the Gosvāmī," said Akbar, "tell me how to discern milk from water."
11. Svāmījī replied: "If the body is not pure, how can one appreciate about Gosvāmī?" "If I wasn't sure you had experienced Gosvāmī, I wouldn't have invited you here," said Akbar.
12. "Working hard day and night, there are plenty of cotton-carders in Sīkrī." Svāmījī replied: "It is all a matter of luck, if you see the way people get around.
13. All sorts of people have come in the world, how many of them have found Gosvāmī?" Emperor Akbar asked Svāmījī to explain that mystery:
14. "My mind is so involved in worldly affairs, how can I experience the Creator? With my whole being I want to commit myself to the path you prescribe.
15. I shall infuse my heart with truth, if in that way I may find Gosvāmī. "Wonderful," said Svāmījī, may Gosvāmī always keep you to this resolve.
16. If you listen to what I say, Gosvāmī will always give you this attitude. Emperor Akbar bowed his head: "You have given and I have received."

1. Dādū, the beloved of our heart, gave a blessing to the ruler of Delhi: "May the Master always keep you in prosperity and kindness."

17. Akbar then begged him to take whatever he liked as a gift. But Svāmījīī replied he could use nothing, except for the love of the Almighty.
18. Akbar said: "Please take whatever you like, so you can worship, eat and give to eat. Svāmījī: "True worship consists of serving day and night."
19. Akbar: "How can you support yourself? You should accept gifts if you do not work." "We all have a job and share our food with the devotees."
20. "I am the servant of the Able One, I am never without work, Kabīr. The husband gets the blame, if his wife is clothed in rags."
21. Akbar: "Take gold, silver or clothes, whatever I give you is too little. Villages or districts, horses and elephants, I give them as a mark of my praise."
22. "Clothed in rags and hungry, the ascetic only gathers the richness of Hari. The Emperor should leave his empire and leaving his throne the King should sit on the ground.
23. Staying away from gold and women, one enters the presence of the Master. As long as an ascetic keeps touching wealth, he commits a grave sin."
    1. "For your sake, Master, I have given up the city of Bulkh, with 16 thousand women and 18 million horses."
24. Akbar: "I am aware of all this, but accept and distribute these and I'll he happy." Svāmījī: "I would like this as your present that you treat all beings impartially.
25. "Let no being suffer and the Creator will be pleased. Stay always in the presence of the Master, give alms and encourage others to do the same."
    1. From that moment Akbar stopped hurting living beings, since he had found Dādū, the excellent *pīr*. He made his decision into a religious law, that no one should hurt living beings.

2. Akbar's attitude of mercy did not suit the Qāzīs and the Mullās. They all agreed they should try to reduce Dādū's power.
    3. They prayed to the Prophet: "Beloved, please take note of that power. You have helped us with clear instructions; please perform a miracle for us."
    4. Akbar had a throne prepared on which no other person was allowed to sit. He was eager to see with whom real power was. "Who knows the ways of the Unknowable?"
    5. The throne was nicely arranged and King Birbal was sent to Svāmījī. The King invited Dādū, who already "knew" what was happening.
    6. "Why have you come," Svāmījī asked. "I was sent to invite you," the King replied. Svāmījī saw his inner thoughts and disclosed what was being planned.

7. Abdul Fazl and King Birbal stared at Svāmījī, in wonder. He said: "You may go and say that I am coming; do not worry."
8. Svāmījī then became the embodiment of love and took his disciple Jaggā with him. Via a secret road he went to the Emperor, who was greatly astonished at what he saw.
9. A strange throne appeared in the sky, radiating bright light and splendid beauty Svāmījī sat on it, like the Highest-above-all, the Indweller.
10. Akbar was terrified: Who can know the ways of Dādū? The Emperor came down from his throne, bowing low: "You are the Master, I am your slave."
11. With this miraculous display, the ignorance of the Emperor disappeared: "I am satisfied, God has appeared, my doubts have gone."
26. Be contented, your head bowed in humility, fully concentrated on the Compassionate, as the goldsmith only thinks of precious stones and the jeweller knows even the smallest stone.
27. Emperor Akbar is very intelligent, discerning good from evil." Svāmījī took his leave and went away, but the King kept asking him (to stay).
28. Hear how Dādū Dindayāl gave up *māyā*. Give up everything yourself, if you want to, says Jan Gopāl. . . .

Chapter 16

25. Even if the entire earth were made into paper, (it would not suffice to write) the merits of Rām and His devotees. What I have said is limited by my understanding. Let no one be pleased or hurt.
26. Dādū spent twelve years as a child and then he met his guru who appeared before him. In 1573 he came to Sambhar and in 1575 Garib Dās was born.
27. In 1585 he met Emperor Akbar and in 1593 he went to Kalyānpur. In 1602 he came to the town of Narainā and in 1603 he became one with Rām.
28. I am the devotee Gopāl, an ascetic and a Baniyā. My true guru is Dādū, the merciful one. It was my great good fortune that I found shelter with him. I sang the praises of that greatest of Sants.
29. I have sung of the great festival organized for Dādū. 1 have firm faith in Garib Dās to whom I surrender myself.

Thus ends the *Janmalīlā* of Dādū.

Source: *The Hindī Biography of Dādū Dayāl*, translated by Winand M. Callewaert (Delhi: Motilal Banarsidass, 1988).

Selections from *Sriramacharitamanasa* by Tulasīdasā

Name of Rama

I reverence the Lord Hari, whose name is Rama, who is supreme over all causes, whose maya (illusive power) holds sway over the entire universe with Brahma and all the gods and demons; by whose light all this unreal world seems true, as when a rope is thought to be a snake; and whose feet are the only boat for those who are eager to cross the sea of birth and death. In accord with the Puranas, the Vedas and the Agamas, and with what has been told in the Ramayana (of Valmiki) and elsewhere, I, Tulasi, for his own soul's delight, have composed these exceedingly elegant plays of Raghunatha in modern speech.

May Ganesha, lord of Shiva's retinue, by thinking on whom success is won, whose face is the face of a noble elephant, storehouse of wisdom, abode of all good qualities be gracious to me! May that merciful Lord, whose grace enables the dumb to loose his tongue and the cripple to climb the steepest hill, and who burns to ashes the impurities of the Kaliyuga, be compassionate to me! May the Lord who ever rests upon me the Sea of Milk, with body dark as the dark-blue lotus, and eyes bright as a budding water-lily, make his dwelling in my heart! May the destroyer of Kamdeva, Shiva, whose form resembles in color the jasmine flower or the moon, who is the beloved spouse of Parvati and an abode of compassion and who loves the humble, show me his grace! I reverence the lotus feet of my guru, ocean of grace, Hari in human form, whose words are like a flood of sunlight on the deep darkness of powerful ignorance! I reverence the pollen-like dust of the lotus feet of my guru, bright, fragrant, sweet to the taste and full of the flavor of love; pure powder of the root of ambrosia that heals all the attendant ills of life. . . .

Devotion to Rahupati is for Tulasidasa the season of rain; his faithful servants are the growing rice, and the glorious consonants in Rama's name are the months of Shravana and Bhadon. The two letter-sounds of the name are sweet and attractive; they are the eyes; as it were, of the alphabet and the life of the faithful, easy to remember, bringing happiness to all, a gain in this world and salvation in the next. They are most delightful to hear and to contemplate; as dear to Tulasi as the inseparable Rama and Lakshmana. When they are uttered, devotion separates them, but they are as naturally bound together as Brahma and the individual soul. These two letters are twin brothers, like Nara and Narayana; preservers of the world and, especially, redeemers of the elect; lovely jewels in the ears of the beauteous faith; the sun and the moon shining clear for the good of the world. Sweet taste and contentment they bring, like the nectar of salvation; like the tortoise and the serpent, upholding the world; like a bee to the lovely lotus of the devotee's mind; as sweet to the tongue as Krishna and Haladhara to Yashoda. Of the two letter of the name of Raghunatha one gleams like a royal umbrella and the other like a crest-jewel over all the letters of the alphabet, O Tulasidasa. The name and the object named are regarded as one and the same, but the close connection between them is that of master and servant. Both name and form are two attributes of God; they are ineffable and without origin and can be rightly understood only by pious understanding. It is presumptuous to ask which of the two is the greater and which is the less; when they hear the difference between the, the wise will understand. Forms are found to be subordinate to names; the form cannot be known apart from the name. . . .

Rama assumed the form of man to help the faithful and endured misery to make the pious happy; but votaries who lovingly repeat the name easily becomes abodes of joy and blessings. Rama himself redeemed one ascetic's wife (Ahalya), but the name has converted the sinful hearts of millions of sinners. For the seer's (Vishvamitra's) sake Rama put an end to Suketu's daughter (Tadaka), her army and her son (Subahu); but the name destroys its servant's sins and woes and despairs as the sun puts an end to night. With his own right hand Rama broke the bow of Shiva; but the glory of the name dispels the fear of death and rebirth. The lord made beautiful only the Dandaka forest; but the name has sanctified the souls of countless votaries. Raghunatha massacred the demon host; but the name has destroyed all the sins of the Kaliyuga. Raghunatha granted the bliss of final release to Shabari, the vulture Jatayu and other righteous servants; but the name has delivered innumerable evil-doers, and the story of its virtues is celebrated in the Vedas. Rama, as everyone knows, took both Sugriva and Vibhishana under his protection; but the name has protected many a poor supplicant, shining forth gloriously both in the world and in the Vedas. Rama assembled a host of bears and monkeys and labored hard to build a bridge; but at the mention of the name the ocean of birth and death is dried up; meditate thereon, O you saints! Rama slew Ravana with all his family in battle and returned to his own city with Sita; he was then crowned king in the capital of Ayodhya, and gods and sages hymned his virtues in melodious strains; but by devoutly thinking on the name his servants overcome the mighty forces of ignorance without effort and, absorbed in devotion, wander in the paths of their own joy; by the grace of the name they live at ease without even a dream of sorrow. Therefore the name is greater than either the impersonal Absolute or the personal Rama and blesses even those that bless. This Shiva knew well when he chose it from among the thousand million verses in the Ramayana. By the grace of the name, Shambhu attained immortality, an auspicious figure in an inauspicious attire. Shukadeva and Sanaka and all the saints, sages, and ascetics by the grace of the name enjoy heavenly bliss. Narada too acknowledged the power of the name, for all the world loves Hari, and Hari and Hara love Narada. When Prahlada repeated the name, the Lord showed him his grace and he became the crown of the faithful. Dhruva in his distress repeated the name of Hari and won a place fixed, incomparable. The son of the wind (Hanuman) thought on that holy name and made Rama subject to himself. Ajamila the sinner, the elephant and the harlot of the legend were liberated by the power of hair's name; but why should I any more extol Hari's name; but why should I any more extol the name? Rama himself cannot adequately glorify the name. In this Kaliyuga the name of Rama is a wish-yielding tree (the tree of paradise); the very home of blessing, thinking whereon Tulasidasa, who was nothing by intoxicating hemp, has become the sacred tulasi plant (the holy basil). In all the four ages, at all times past, present, and future, and in all the three spheres creatures have been freed from care by the repetition of the name. The Vedas, the Puranas and the saints agree that the reward of all virtuous deeds is the love of Rama. In the first age the Lord is pleased by contemplation, in the second by the rite of sacrifice, and in the Dvapara by ritual worship; but the Kaliyuga is nothing but the root of all impurities when the hearts of men wallow like fish in the ocean of sin. . . .

The Story of Rama

The story of Rama is mysterious and he who hears it and he who tells it must be repositories of wisdom; how could I, a stupid creature, grasp its meaning—an ignorant dolt, in the toils of the sin of the Kaliyuga? Nevertheless, when my guru (the preceptor) had repeated the story over and over again, I began partially to understand it as well as I could. That same story I shall versify in the popular tongue, to enlighten myself.

Equipped with what little understanding and judgment I possess I shall write with a heart inspired by Hari. The story I am going to tell is such as will dispel my own doubts, ignorance and error and will serve as a boat for crossing the stream of mundane existence. The story of Rama brings peace to the learned and is a source of delight to all men, and wipes out the impurities of the Kaliyuga. Rama's story is a powerful spell to subdue the serpent of the Kaliyuga and a wooden stick for kindling the sacred fire of wisdom. The story of Rama is the cow of plenty in this age of Kali; it is a beautiful life-giving herb to the virtuous; a veritable river of nectar on earth; it shatters the fear of birth and death and is a virtual snake to swallow the frogs of delusion. . . .

Nature of Rama

In Rama, who is the sun, truth, consciousness and bliss combined, the night of delusion can have no part whatever. He is the blessed Lord, whose very being is light, and in him there can be no dawn of wisdom. Joy and sorrow, knowledge and ignorance, egoism and pride—these are the characteristics of a jiva (finite being); but Rama, as all the world knows, is the all-pervading Brahma, supreme bliss personified, the highest lord and the most ancient being. He who is universally known as the spirit, the fount of all light, manifests in all forms and is the Lord of life as well as of matter (i.e., of the whole sum of things), that jewel of Raghu's race is my master. So saying, Shiva bowed his head.

Fools do not understand their own error; on the other hand; those stupid creatures attribute their delusion to the Lord, just as senseless men, seeing a clouded sky, say that the sun has been hidden by the curtain of clouds. He who looks at the moon with his eye pressed with a finger, fancies that there are two moons in sight. To fancy the existence of such delusion in Rama (or that Rama is subject to such delusion) is like seeing darkness, smoke and dust in the sky. (Delusion, says Shiva, affects Rama in the same way as smoke, or a cloud, or dust affects the brightness of the heavens). The objects of sense, the organs of sense, their presiding deities and the individual souls—all these derive their conscious existence one from the other. (That is to say, the objects are illumined by the senses, the senses by their presiding deities and the deities presiding over the senses by the conscious self.) The supreme illuminator of them all is the eternal Rama, lord of Ayodhya. The world of matter is the object of illumination, and Rama is the illuminator; he is the lord of illusion and the home of wisdom and virtue. It is due to his reality that even unconscious matter appears to be real, ignorance contributing to the deception.

Though (a polished) oyster-shell is mistaken for silver and in a mirage for water, and these appearances are false at all times (in the past, present, and future), yet no one can rid himself of the delusion. In the same way is this world of matter dependent on Hari. Though unreal, it gives us pain nonetheless, as when a man's head is cut off in a dream, he is not rid of pain till he awakes. . . . If men even involuntarily repeat his name, the sins committed by them in many previous existences are burnt away, and those who devoutly meditate upon him are able to cross the ocean of mundane existence as if it were a paddle (a mere hollow made by the hoof of a cow). . . .

Reason for Incarnation

Perceiving that the gods and earth were terror-stricken and hearing their loving entreaties, a solemn voice came from heaven which dispelled their doubt and anxiety.

"Fear not, O sages, adepts and high gods! For your sake I will assume the form of a man with every element of my divinity incarnate in the glorious solar race. (The sage) Kashyapa and (his wife) Aditi practiced severe penance; to them I have already granted a boon. They have taken birth in the city of Ayodhya as Dasharath and Kausalya, a royal pair. In their house I shall become incarnate as four brothers, the pride of the house of Raghu. I shall fulfill all that Narada predicted and descend to earth with my supreme energy (my eternal consort). I shall relieve the earth of all its burden; be fearless, O company of gods." As the divine voice from heaven reached the gods' ears, they straightway returned with their hearts comforted. Then Brahma consoled Earth, who was rid of all fear and felt reassured in her heart. Then Brahma returned to his own realm after thus instructing the gods: "Assume, each of you, the form of a monkey and go to the earth and wait on the feet of Hari." All the gods went to their several homes along with Earth; they all felt relieved in their hearts. The gods were delighted to receive the orders that Brahma gave and lost no time in carrying them out. They assumed the form of monkeys on the earth, of incomparable strength and power. They were all mighty warriors and had mountains, trees and claws for their weapons. Resolute of mind, they awaited the advent of Hari. . . .

Devotees and God

Never harbor in your mind, O lord of the immortals, even the thought of injuring a devotee of Rama, for it would bring you infamy in this world, sorrow in the next and an ever-increasing burden of remorse in your day-to-day life. Listen O king of the gods, to my advice; a devotee is supremely dear to Rama; he is gratified when one serves his devotees, and bears great enmity to those who are hostile to them. Even though the lord is alike to all without either love or anger and contracts neither sin nor virtue, neither merit nor demerit, and even though he has appointed fate the sovereign of the universe, so that one reaps what one sows, yet according as one possesses the heart of a devotee or an unbeliever he appears to be impartial or hostile in his dealings. Though devoid of attributes, unattached, free from pride and ever immutable, yet for love of his votaries has he assumed a form with attributes. Rama has ever respected the wishes of his servants, as the Vedas and Puranas and holy men and gods bear witness. Knowing this, abandon perversity and show fitting devotion to the feet of Bharats. Rama's devotees, O Indra, are devoted to the good of others, share the sorrows of others, and are compassionate by nature; and Bharata is the very crest-jewel of devotees; then be not afraid of him, O king of heaven. . . .

Monkeys Sent to Locate Sita

Then with a smile, Raghunatha spoke to Sugriva, "You are, brother, as dear to me as Bharata! Now then, with all your heart endeavor to get tidings of Sita." While they were thus conversing, multitudes of monkey's arrived; throngs of monkeys of every hue could be seen here, there and everywhere. I myself, Uma, saw the army of monkeys; only a fool would try to count them. They came and bowed their heads at Rama's feet and found their Lord in him when they saw his face. In the whole host there was not one single monkey after whose well-being Rama did not ask. This was no great marvel for my master, Raghunatha, of cosmic form and omnipresent. They stood in martial array at the word of command and Sugriva exhorted them all: "I commission you to do Rama's work; therefore, you monkey squadrons, go forth in every direction; go, search for Janaka's daughter and return, my brothers, within a month. He who comes back after that period without nay news shall die at my hands." Hearing these words and driven by Sugriva's command, the monkeys set out at once in every direction. Sugriva then summoned Angad, Nala, and Hanuman and said, "Listen, O Nila, Angad, Jambavan and Hanuman, resolute and sagacious champions all, go you together to the south and inquire of everyone you meet the whereabouts of Sita. Let every thought and word and deed be applied to devising some ways of accomplishing Rama's purpose. One must wait on the sun with one's back turned towards it and on fire with the breast facing it; but a master must be served with one's whole being, without any subterfuges. One must turn from things illusory (mine-ness and attachment) and be devoted to things spiritual, so shall all the cares connected with birth and death be destroyed. The consummation of human birth, brothers, lies in forsaking all worldly desires and worshipping Rama only. He only is truly discriminative and greatly blessed who is devoted to Raghunatha's feet." Taking leave of Sugriva and bowing their heads at his feet, the monkeys set out rejoicing with their thoughts fixed on Raghunatha. The last to make obeisance was Hanuman (the son of the wind). The Lord, knowing that his work was going to be accomplished by him, called him to himself. He touched his head with his lotus hands and recognizing him to be his devotee, gave him the ring from his finger and said, "Do what you can to comfort Sita; tell her of my might, and the agony I endure in her absence and return with all speed." Upon hearing this, Hanuman considered his life blest, and set out with the image of the all-merciful enshrined in his heart. Although the Lord knew everything, yet as protector of the gods he respected the recognized principles of statecraft. All monkeys went forth, ransacking woods and streams and lakes and hills and ravines with their minds also wholly absorbed in Rama's concerns that they forgot all about their own bodily needs. . . .

Hanuman

On the seashore stood a majestic hill and on to it he sprang as if in sport. Then, again and again invoking Raguhubira, the son of the wind leapt with a mighty bound. The hill on Hanuman had planted his foot sank down at once into the nethermost world. On sped Hanuman like Raghunatha's own unerring shaft. Knowing him to be Raghunatha's envoy, Ocean bade Mainaka relieve him of his fatigue. (Don't hide yourself, he said; rise higher and offer him rest.) Hanuman only touched the mountain with his hand and then made obeisance to him, saying, "How can I rest before I have done Rama's business?" When the gods saw the son of the wind sweeping along, they wished to try his mighty strength and wisdom. So they sent Surasa, the Mother of Serpents, who came and said, "Today the gods have given me a meal!" Upon hearing these words, the son of the wind replied, "When I have performed Rama's commission and return and give my lord the news about Sita, then will I enter your mouth: I tell you the truth, mother, only let me go just now." But when she would not let him go any account, Hanuman said, "Then why not swallow me?" She opened her jaws full three leagues wide, but Hanuman made his body twice as broad. She stretched her mouth to a breath of fifty leagues, but Hanuman at once became a hundred leagues in breath. However much Surasa expanded her jaws, Hanuman displayed a form twice as large again. But when at last she made her mouth three hundred leagues wide, Hanuman assumed a very minute form and crept into her mouth and then came out again and bowing his head to her, begged leave to proceed. "I have gauged the extent of your wit and strength," said Surasa, "and it was to this end that the gods had sent me. You will carry out all that Rama has commanded, for in you dwell such might and wisdom." Having blessed him thus, she departed, and Hanuman joyfully resumed his journey. There dwelt a female demon in the ocean who by magic caught the birds of the air. Seeing in the water the reflections of the creatures that flew though the sky, she would catch their shadowy forms, so that they could not fly away; and in this manner she always had birds to eat. She practiced the same craft on Hanuman, but the monkey at once saw through her trickery. The son of the wind, steadfast and valiant, slew her and swept across the ocean. Reaching the further shore of the sea, he gazed on the loveliness of the woods, with the bees buzzing in their greed for honey. . . .

Hanuman's Capture and Torture by Ravana

"Listen, Ten-headed; I tell you on oath that there is none to protect him who is opposed to Rama, Shankara, Vishnu and Brahma in their thousands are unable to save you if you are Rama's army. Abandon pride, a sin born of tamas (darkness) and infatuation, a source of many woes, and adore Rama, chief of the house of Raghu, ocean of grace, the blessed Lord!" Though Hanuman gave him exceeding salutary advice, full of devotion and discretion, dispassion and wisdom, that most arrogant demon, Ravana, laughed and said, "What a sage guru we have found in this monkey! Wretch, since death hangs over your head, you have dared, O vile creature, to offer me advice!" "Nay," retorted Hanuman, "it will be contrariwise; I clearly perceive that you are laboring under some mental delusion." On hearing the monkey's retort, Ravana was beside himself with rage. "Quick, some of you," he cried, "and put an end to this fool's life." As soon as the demons heard it, they ran to slay him, but that very moment came Vibhishana (Ravana's youngest brother) with his ministers. Bowing his head before Ravana, he made humble entreaty: "Slay not an envoy, sire; it is against all diplomatic usage; punish him in some other way." All said, "This is sound counsel, brother." When he heard it, the Ten-headed said with a laugh, " All right, let the monkey go, but then mutilate him first. A monkey is deeply attached to his tail: I tell you this secret. Swathe his tail with rags soaked in oil and then set fire to it. When the tailless monkey goes back home, the wretch will bring back his master with him, and then I shall see what power he has, whom he has so extravagantly exalted." Upon hearing these threats, the monkey smiled to himself and thought, "Sarasvati, I believe, has helped me (by putting this idea into the demon's mind)." At Ravana's command the stupid demons set about doing as they were bid. Not a rag nor a drop of ghi or oil was left in the city, to such a length had the monkey grown his tail in sport. The citizens thronged to see the fun; they kicked Hanuman and jeered at him with loud guffaws. With beating of drums and clapping of hands they took him round the city and then set fire to his tail. When Hanuman saw the fire blazing, he immediately assumed an utterly diminutive form, and then slipping out of his bonds, leapt on to the attics of gold, to the dismay of the demons' wives. At that moment all the forty-nine winds, impelled by Hari, began to blow. Hanuman roared with a loud laugh and swelled to such a size that he touched the sky. Though enormous in size, Hanuman appeared most nimble-bodied; he rushed and sprang from palace to palace. The city was all ablaze and the people were distraught as many millions of fierce flames leapt up and piteous cries were heard everywhere: "Alas! Father! Mother! Who will save us at this hour? Did we not say that this was no monkey, but some god in monkey form? Such is the result of scorning a nobler soul; the city is burning as though it had no protector." In the twinkling of an eye Hanuman burnt down the city, save only Vibhishana's house. The reason why Hanuman went unscathed, Girija, was that he was the envoy of him who created the fire. Thus he consumed whole of Lanka from one end to the other and then leapt into the ocean.

After extinguishing his tail and relieving his fatigue, he resumed his diminutive form and went and stood before Janaka's daughter with folded hands. "Be pleased, mother," he said, "to give me some token, such as Raghunatha gave me." She unfastened the jewel in her hair and gave it to the son of the wind, who gladly accepted it. . . . Reassuring Janaka's daughter, he consoled her in many ways and, bowing his head at her lotus feet, set forth to rejoin Rama.

Reunion of Sita and Rama

Forthwith they went to the spot where Sita was and found all the demon ladies waiting on her in all humility. Promptly Vibhishana gave them their instructions, and they attended her to the bath with all formality; they also adorned her with jewels of every description and then brought a charming palanquin duly equipped. Sita joyously mounted it with her thoughts fixed on her loving lord Rama, abode of bliss. On all four sides (of the palanquin) went guards with staves in their hands, all supremely delighted at heart. The bears and the monkeys all came to catch a glimpse of her, but the guards darted in a fury to keep them back. But said Raghubira, "Attend to what I say, my friend, and bring Sita on foot, that the monkeys my look on her as they would on their own mothers." Thus said the holy lord Rama and smiled. The bears and monkeys rejoiced to hear the lord's words, while from the heavens the gods rained down a great shower of blossoms.

The real Sita had earlier been lodged in the fire, and now the blessed lord who witnesses the secrets of all hearts sought to bring her back to light. For this reason, the all-merciful addressed some reproachful words, on hearing which the female demons all began to grieve. Sita, who was ever pure in thought and word and deed, bowed to her lord's command and said, "Lakshmana, be sharer in this pious rite and prepare the fire forthwith." When Laksmana had heard Sita's words, so full of desolation, discretion, piety and prudence, tears rushed to his eyes and he folded his palms in prayer but could not speak a word to his lord. Reading Rama's tacit approval in his looks, Lakshmana ran and after kindling a fire, brought a heap of fire-wood. Sita rejoiced at heart to see the fiercely blazing flames, and felt no fear. "If in thought and word and deed," she said, "I have never set my heart on anyone other than Raghubira, may this fire, who knows the thoughts of all, become as cooling as sandal-paste!" With her thoughts fixed on the lord, Janaki entered the flames as though they were cool like sandal-paste, saying, "Glory to the lord of Kosala, whose feet Mahadeva adores and for which I cherish the purest devotion!" Both her shadow-form as well as the stigma of public shame were consumed in the blazing fire; but no one understood the secret of the lord's doings. Even the gods, adepts and sages stood gazing in the heavens. Then fire assumed a bodily form and, taking by the hand the real Sita famed alike in the Vedas and the world, escorted her and committed her to Rama, even as the ocean of milk committed Lakshmi to lord Vishnu. Standing on the left side of Rama, she shone like a golden lotus beside a blue lotus newly opened. The gods in their delight showered down flowers and kettledrums sounded in the sky; Kinnaras sang their melodies and the celestial nymphs danced, all mounted on their celestial cars.

Rama Ascends the Throne and Its Results

When Rama ascended the throne, all the three spheres rejoiced and all sorrow was at an end. No one felt any enmity towards another, for Rama's glorious grace had extinguished every variance. Devoted to duty, the people trod the path of the Vedas, each according to his caste and stage of life, and enjoyed happiness, unvexed by fear, or sorrow, or sickness. Nowhere in Rama's realm could one find a person who suffered from bodily pain, ill fortune or evil circumstance. All the men and women loved one another, conducted themselves in accordance with righteousness and were devoted to the injunctions of the Vedas. Righteousness with its four pillars (truth, purity, compassion, and charity) reigned throughout the world and no one ever dreamt of sin. Men and women alike, all earnestly devoted to Rama, were heirs of final beatitude. There was no premature death nor suffering of any kind; everyone was comely and healthy. No one was destitute or sorrowful or miserable; no one was ignorant or devoid of auspicious marks. All men and women were unaffectedly good, pious and upright, clever and accomplished; all recognized the merits of others, all were learned and wise; all were grateful for kindnesses and guilelessly prudent. Listen, O king of birds, during Rama's reign there was not a creature in the world, moving or unmoving, that suffered from any of the ills caused by time, past action, personal temperament or character. Undisputed sovereign of the entire globe girdled by the seven seas was Raghunatha, the lord of Kosala. This lordship (of the entire globe) was nothing great for him, each of whose several hairs contained many a sphere of creation. To him who rightly understands that infinite greatness of the lord, this description of his universal sovereignty will sound highly disparaging. But even they, O king of birds, who have realized that greatness of the lord take supreme delight in these actions of his. Delight in these divine exploits is the reward of knowing his infinite greatness—so declare the greatest of sages and ascetics. The bliss and prosperity of Rama's reign were more than the Serpent King and Sarasvati could describe. All the men and women were generous and charitable and devoted to the feet of the Brahmans. Every husband was pledged to a vow of monogamy and each wife was devoted to her husband in thought and word and deed. Throughout all Ramachandra's realm a rod was never seen save in the hands of ascetics; the word "difference" had ceased to exist except in relation to tune and measure in the dancer's troupes; and the word "conquer" was heard only with reference to the mind (for the only victory was self-conquest). The trees in the forest blossomed and bore fruit throughout the year; the elephant and the lion lived together as friends; birds and beasts of every description forgot their instinctive animosities and lived in the greatest harmony with one another. Birds sang and beasts wandered fearlessly through the forest in distinct herds, making merry all the time. Cool, mild and fragrant blew the breezes, and bees made a pleasant humming even as they moved about laden with honey. Creepers and trees dropped honey to those who asked for it; cows yielded milk to one's heart's content. The earth was ever rich in crops; even in the Tretayuga every feature of the Satyayuga was repeated. Conscious of the fact that the universal spirit was no other than king of the world, the hills disclosed their mines of jewels of every description. Every river flowed with fair water, cool, transparent, refreshing and delicious to the taste. The oceans kept within their bounds and cast forth jewels on the shore for men to gather. All the ponds were thick with lotuses, and all the cardinal and intermediate directions enjoyed perfect happiness. The moon flooded the earth with her radiance; the sun gave as much heat as was necessary; the clouds poured forth showers for the mere asking in the days when Rama was king.

Theological Implications of Rama Devotion

Desire is a worm and the body is wood; is there anyone so resolute of mind whose body is not consumed by desire as wood by the wood-louse? Whose mind has not been sullied by the three passions—the desire of progeny, of wealth and of renown? All these constitute the retinue of illusion formidable and infinite in number, more than any can tell. Even Shiva and Brahma stand in awe of her; of what account, then, are other creatures? Illusion's formidable army is spread over the whole world; lust and its fellows (e.g., anger and greed) are her generals;

hypocrisy, deceit and heresy her champions. That illusion is Raghubira's own handmaid; though unreal when understood, there is no release from her grip except by Rama's grace; this I assert, my lord, and vouch for the truth of it. The same illusion that has made a puppet of the whole world and whose ways are unknown to anyone, is herself set a-dancing with all her troupe, like an actress on the stage, O king of birds, by the play of the lord's eyebrows.

For Rama is the sum of truth and intelligence and bliss (the One self-existing Brahma), the uncreated, wisdom personified, the home of all perfections, pervading all and all that is pervaded, indivisible, infinite, the blessed lord of unfailing power, unqualified, supreme, transcending speech and the other senses, all-seeing, irreproachable and invincible, unattached, formless, without illusion, eternal and untainted by maya, very bliss, beyond nature, the omnipotent word who dwells in every heart, desireless, free from passion and imperishable absolute. In him delusion finds no ground to stand upon; can the shades of darkness ever face the sun?

For the sake of his devotees, the blessed lord Rama assumed the form of an earthly sovereign and played his most holy part in the manner of an ordinary man, just as an actor, while playing upon the stage, assumes a variety of disguises and exhibits different characters in keeping with his dress, but himself remains the same. Such, O Garuda, is the pastime of Raghunatha, a bewilderment to the demons but a delight to the faithful. Those who are dull-witted, victims of the pleasures of sense and slaves of passion, impute such infatuation to the lord, my master. . . .

Now, O king of birds, I tell you the story of Rama's kindness and my own stupidity; listen attentively. Whenever Rama appears in human form and plays his many parts for his votaries' sake, I always betake myself to the city of Ayodhya and delight to watch his childish pranks. I go there and witness his birthday rejoicings and, fascinated (by the charm of his childish sports), stay there for full five years. The child Rama is my patron deity, who sums up in his person the beauty of myriad loves. Even gazing on the face of my lord, I satisfy the desire of my eyes, O Garuda! Assuming the form of a little crow, I keep close to Hari and witness his manifold childish sports. Wherever he roams in his boyish play, I flutter about close to him and pick up and eat whatever crumbs he lets fall in the courtyard. One day Ragubira played all the merry pranks of his early childhood. As soon as Kakabhushundi recalled the lord's playfulness, the hair of his body bristled with rapture. . . .

The soul is dependent (subject to illusion), God is self-dependent. Jivas (souls) are many, but Lakshmi's lord is one (without a second). Even though this distinction, created by illusion is false, yet it cannot disappear except by Hari's grace, whatever you may do. The man who hopes for liberation (from the bondage of karma and the wheel of birth and death) without worshipping Ramachandra is but a beast without tail and horns, however wise he may be. Though the moon were to rise with all its sixteen kalas (fullness) and the whole starry host, and though the forest on every mountain were set on fire, night would not yield except to the sun. Even so, O Garuda, men's souls cannot be rid of their suffering without worshipping Hari. Ignorance affects not a servant of Hari, for it is knowledge, directed by the lord, that pervades his whole being. Therefore, best of birds, the servant is not destroyed; on the other hand his devotion to his master grows ever stronger. When Rama saw me bewildered by confusion, he laughed. Now hear that wondrous act as well.

The secret of this diversion nobody could comprehend, neither his younger brothers not yet his father or mother. With his swarthy form and rosy hands and feet Rama crawled on his hands and knees to catch me. Then, O enemy of serpents, I took to flight and Rama stretched out his arms to seize me. High as I flew into the sky, I still saw Rama's arms close beside me. I flew off to Brahman's realm, but when I looked back in my flight, O my friend, two finger's breath was all the distance between me and Rama's arms! Piercing the seven veils of the universe (consisting of earth, water, fire, ether, the cosmic ego and the cosmic intellect), I mounted to the utmost height I could reach; but when I saw the lord's arms even there, I was again dumbfounded. In my terror I closed my eyes, and when I opened them again, I found myself in the city of Ayodhya. Rama looked at me with a smile, and as he laughed, I was straightway driven into his mouth. Listen, king of birds; in his belly I beheld a cluster of multitudinous universes, with many strange spheres, each more wonderful than the other, with millions of Brahmas and Shivas, countless stars and suns and moons, innumerable guardians of the spheres and gods of death and times, numberless mountains and vast terrestrial plains, oceans, rivers, lakes and forests without end and manifold over varieties of creation, with gods and sages, adepts, serpents, human beings and Kinnaras, and all the four kinds of creatures, moving and unmoved. I saw there all such marvels as I had ever seen or heard of, such as had never entered my mind; how, then, can I describe them? . . .

Now listen to my words, most simple and true and easily intelligible, which have also been echoed by the Vedas and other scriptures. I declare to you my own doctrine; listen to it and imprint it on your mind and abjuring everything else, worship only me. The world with all its varieties of life, both moving and unmoved, is a creation of my illusion. All are dear to me, for all are my creation;

but man is the creature I delight in most. Of men, the brahmans, and of the brahmans, those well-versed in the Vedas; of these, those who follow the course of conduct prescribed in the Vedas; of these again, celibates are my favorites, and yet more the wise; of the wise too I love best the spiritually wise, but dearer to me than these is my own servant (devotee), who looks to me for refuge and has not other hope. Again and again I declare to you the doctrine that none is so dear to me as my servant. One without devotion, be he the creator himself, is no dearer to me than any other creature, but the humblest creature that breathes, if he be possessed of devotion, is dear to me as my own life; such is my doctrine. . . .

Source: *Shriramacharitamanasa of Tulasīdasā*, edited and translated by R. C. Prasad (Delhi: Motilal Banarsidass, 1988).

8

Śaiva Devotionalism

In Hindu mythology, Śiva is a deity who plays paradoxical roles: married householder and ascetic; inert and dancer; creator and destroyer of the cosmos; terrible and compassionate; anti-erotic and erotic; chaste and sexually active. Śiva's position as a householder is emphasized when he is iconographically seated with his consort Pārvatī with his arm wrapped around her. His ascetic nature is iconographically symbolized by his *liṅga* (sign, phallus) rising from the *yoni* (womb).

Being the archetypical ascetic, Śiva inspired ascetic movements, which is exemplified by the selections from the *Pāsupata Sūtra* and the *Gorakṣa Śataka* of the Kānphata Yogis. The Pāśupatas sought to imitate Śiva as the Lord of Beasts, which sometimes meant acting mad and incurring the censure of others in order to reduce the mad ascetic's karmic residues. Kānphata Yogis were noted for inserting large earrings into their ears in an attempt to acquire yogic powers. The alleged leader of this ascetic group was Gorakhnāth; they were also known as the Nātha-Yogins, who conceived of themselves as being in the tradition of eighty-four siddhas, immortal demi-gods.

In addition to inspiring ascetic movements, Śiva also stimulated devotional hymns by Tamil devotees who transmitted these poems orally as they spread their emotional enthusiasm for Śiva and converted countless people to the spirit of devotionalism. Many of the Śaiva poems from the *Tēvāram* are recited even today in temples throughout southern India; the *Tēvāram* contains the poems of the

Nāyaṉārs with selections from such poets as Campantar, Cuntarar, Appar, and Māṇikkavācakar. Although his dates are uncertain, Māṇikkavācakar is the most revered of the poets saints of south India; his poem the *Tiruvācakam* (Sacred Verses) and his twenty-verse hymn entitled *Tiruvempāvai* are still recited today in temples of the south. After a career as a court official, Māṇikkavācakar retired and became closely associated with the temple at Cidamabaram, where Śiva is enshrined as the Naṭarāja, or Lord of Dance.

Śiva also inspired theological developments in north and south India. In the latter region, a school called Śaiva Siddhānta (culmination of the knowledge of Śiva) emerged around the thirteenth century. This conservative and dualistic school relied on the Śaiva Āgamas that formed the basis of the theology. This chapter includes selections from the Śaiva Āgama entitled the *Tantra of Svayambhu Vidyapada* with a commentary by a sage named Sadyojyoti, whose dates are uncertain. This text represents number thirteen of the twenty-eight Āgamas that constitutes the literary corpus of the Śaiva Siddhānta school, whereas the Kashmir school is based on a collection of sixty-four Āgamas, which might be an ideal number without a basis in history. According to the literary theory of the Śaiva Siddhānta school, all twenty-eight basic texts and the 207 ancillary texts (*upāgama*) were created by Śiva and given to humans through a succession of supernatural souls.

Although the *Svāyaṃbhusūtrasaṃgraha* (another name for the text) represents a major work of the school, it is impossible to determine its date and location of origin. An outline of the initial four chapters includes the following four subjects: bound soul (*paśu*), the bondage (*pāśa*), power of divine grace, and path of liberation. A reader should be aware that the text introduces itself as an emanation from the consciousness of God, which is identified with his śakti (power, grace), in the form of language. The commentary to the text is provided by Sadyojyoti, who is the most ancient of the known teachers of this school. In addition to this text, he also commented on two other works and composed some independent treatises.

This chapter also contains an example of a theological composition from the Śaiva theologian Umāpati Civācāyār's work entitled *Tiruvaruṭpayan* (Fruit of Divine Grace), which was composed around 1307, and explains how the grace of God operates for the soul to gain the highest stage of love of God by using analogies from ordinary life.

In the north, what came to be called Kashmir Śaivism culminated with the many scholarly contributions of Abhinavagupta (c. 975–1025), who combined three traditions of thought: Karma, Kaula, and Pratyabhijñā. Abhinavagupta combined these three streams of thought and practice into a sophisticated philosophic system, a path of knowledge with an important place for ritual as in the Krama system, and a way to liberation by means of enjoyment by way of Kaulism and its advocacy of tantric methods. This chapter contains selections by Abhinavagupta from his *Paramārthasāra* (Essence of Ultimate Reality) in which he makes a distinction between different levels of manifestation of the absolute and presents the essential principles of the Trika (a term used for the entire system) philosophy, and the next chapter contains selections from his tantric work entitled *Tantrāloka* (Light of the Tantras), a work of his early middle age.

Another important Śaiva sectarian movement was represented by the Vīraśaiva sect (literally, heroic Śaivas), which was also called the Liṅgāyats (literally, wearers of the liṅga) during the twelfth century. The inspired poems of the sect's religious poets were transmitted orally for a long period before being preserved in writing in a collection called the *Śūnyasampādane* in the fifteenth century. This work embodied what sect members called *vacanas* (what is said), which stresses its original oral nature. Sect leaders thought that its oral nature manifested its dynamic nature versus vedic revelation (*śruti*, what is heard), which they envisioned as static. They also rejected the remembered tradition (*smṛti*) because it was likewise too static. The Vīraśaivas wanted to stress the active and dynamic nature of their compositions. In contrast to passive action and witnessing, the movement stressed experience and active participation in their religion. The selections from the *Śūnyasampādane* includes poems from a male figure and a female saint named Mahādēviyakka, who married against her will, eventually left her husband, and became a wandering naked ascetic. Besides autobiographical aspects of her poems, she also refers to feeling connected to love in separation and unitive love.

Within the religious context of Vīraśaiva devotionalism, there is an excellent example of Śaiva hagiography in the story of Siriyāla, his wife, and son in the *Basava Purāṇa* of Pālkuriki Somanātha (1160–1230) composed in the Telugu language, which he adopted from the story entitled *Ciṟuttṇṭar* (Little Devotee) in Tamil by the composer Cekkilār in the mid-twelfth century in his *Tiruttoṇṭar Purāṇa* or *Periya Purāṇa*. Similar to other stories from the Basava Purāṇa, violence plays a major role, and is connected to love of God, surrender, and radical devotion. The proclivity toward violence signifies a devotee's allegiance to his God, sect, and opposition to outsiders in an attempt to create a closely knit movement.

Selections from the Purāṇas about the exploits of Śiva

The Burning of Tripura

Hear how lord Bhava destroyed Tripura. Once there was a demon called Maya, of great magical power, who produced Māyā, Illusion. Defeated in battle, he began to practice severe *tapas*. When they saw what he was doing, O brahmins, two other Daityas, the mighty Vidyunmālin and the heroic Tāraka began to do supreme tapas too, in sympathy. Approaching Maya in brilliance as they performed tapas at his side, they resembled the three fires incarnate in little flames.

These Dānavas continued their tapas, and it consumed the triple world. Sitting in cold water in winter, amid the five fires in summer, and staying outside during the rains, they mortified their precious bodies by eating only fruits, roots, flowers and water. Not observing regular meal-times, their bark garments caked with mud, immersed in duckweed and slime, both pure and impure, they became emaciated, fleshless, held together only by sinews. Because of the power of their tapas, the whole world was deprived of energy, glowing feebly without its luster.

While the three fires, those Dānavas, were burning up the three worlds, there appeared before them the Grandfather, friend of the world. And those Daityas, creators of havoc, greeted the Grandfather as he arrived. Then Brahmā, face and eyes filled with joy, spoke to those Dānavas who shone like the sun due to their tapas, "*Bhoḥ*! I am the giver of boons! I have come, my children, because I am pleased with your tapas. Choose what you desire! Tell me what you want!"

Maya, the master builder, eyes wide with happiness, answered the Grandfather who had made this promise, "O god, long ago in the battle over Tāraka the Daityas were defeated, beaten and killed by the gods with their weapons. Because of the continued hostility of the gods, the demons fled in fear and trembling. We found no haven or refuge to shelter us. Now, by my devotion to you, and through the power of tapas, I want to build a fortress that will be impregnable to the gods. This fort called Tripura which I shall build, O supreme successful one, by your grace, let it be invulnerable to creatures of both land and sea, to curses, to the power of the seers, to the weapons of the gods and to the gods themselves!"

Thus addressed by the all-maker Maya, the all-creator replied to that lord of the hosts of Daityas with a smile, "O Dānava, such total immortality does not exist for one who does not have good conduct. So you should build your fort of straw."

At the Grandfather's words, the demon Maya joined his palms and spoke once again to the lotus-born Brahmā, "Then let this fortress be destroyed by only one means: a single arrow shot once by Śaṃbhu. Otherwise it should be immune to attack."

"So be it," said the lord Grandfather to Maya. And he vanished like wealth won in a dream.

After the Grandfather had gone, those powerful demon Daityas radiated brilliantly with their tapas and with the gift of that boon. And the excellent, wise bull of the Dānavas, Maya, resolved to build his fortress, thinking, "How should I construct this fort? I shall build a triple city!". . .

Thus did Maya, who knew about city construction, build the fortress of Tripura according to the design in his mind. So we have heard.

Maya built one city of black iron. Tāraka was its king and he lived in the royal palace. He built a second city of silver, which shone like the full moon. Vidyunmālin was its lord, resembling a cloud garlanded with lightning. Maya built a third city of gold, in which he himself was lord and master. Tāraka's city was a hundred leagues wide, and so was the city of Vidyunmālin. Maya's vast city was as brilliant as Mt. Meru. The three cities came together during the time of the conjunction of the constellation Puṣya, a long time ago. . . .

When the demon artist Maya built that fortress, he made it impregnable to his enemies, both gods and demons alike. The delighted demons, looking like death, entered the houses Maya had assigned them with their wives, sons and weapons. Like a pride of lions entering a forest, or sea monsters in the sea, or virulent diseases concentrated in a human body, those mighty enemies of the gods overran that city. Tripura teemed with a billion Daityas! . . .

But then Misfortune, Envy, Thirst, Hunger, Discord and Quarrel entered Tripura. At twilight those fearful evils stole into the city and settled in Tripura like diseases infiltrating a body. And Maya witnessed in a dream all those evils that had penetrated Tripura to possess the Dānavas. . . .

So the demons who lived in Tripura were ruined by fate. They deserted truth and virtue and did instead what was forbidden. They despised the holy brahmins, failed to revere the gods, ignored their teachers and even began to hate each other. They quarreled, mocked their own duty, ridiculed each other, and cried, "Me first!" They shouted at their teachers, refused to greet those who were worthy of respect, and they grew anxious for no reason, their eyes filling with tears. Lying around, they ate curds and barley with sour milk and kapittha fruit at night, and thus became impure. They urinated and touched water without washing their feet, and then went to bed without purifying themselves. They shrank from danger like rats from cats. And shameless in the practice of intercourse, they did not wash themselves after going to their women. . . .

When the Dānavas had become wicked and corrupt, and the groves of the tapas-rich sages had been devastated, all the creatures were terrorized by the lion roars of the demons as they stormed heaven. The triple world was stupefied with fear and grew dark with despair. The frightened Ādityas, Vasus, Sādhyas, Fathers and hosts of Maruts went for refuge to Brahmā, the great-grandfather. They gathered together before Brahmā who was seated on a golden lotus, and praised that god with five mouths and four faces, saying, "The Dānavas who live in Tripura are oppressing us, O faultless one. They are protected by your boon, so reprimand them as you would your servants! From fear of the Dānavas, O Grandfather, we scurry around like geese at the start of the rains, or deer in fear of a lion. So deranged are we because of the Dānavas, O sinless one, that we have even forgotten the names of our wives and sons! The god's houses are smashed, and the hermitages of the seers laid waste by the deluded and greedy demons, and now they are roaming around the world at will. If you do not rescue the earth at once, it will become devoid of men, sages and gods as they grind it to dust."

After this speech by the thirty gods, the lotus-born Grandfather spoke to them, and to Indra, his face lustrous as the moon, "The boon that I gave to Maya has now come to an end, O gods, just as I foretold. And Tripura, their city, shall be destroyed, O bulls of the thirty, not by a rain of arrows, but by a single shot. I do not see any one among you, bulls of the gods, who with a single arrow could put an end to the Dānavas' city, for Tripura cannot be annihilated by one of little valor, but only by the one great god, the Prajāpati Mahādeva. If all you gods together request this of Hara, the destroyer of sacrifices, he will destroy Tripura. Each city is 10,000 leagues wide, so they can only be destroyed by a single mighty arrow if it is shot at that one moment when they are all three in conjunction with the constellation Puṣya."

At this, the Grandfather said, "Let us go!" to all the unhappy gods, and went to Bhava's seat. There they saw the mountain lord, trident in hand, the lord of past and future, in the company of Umā and the great-souled Nandin.

After all the gods entitled to their shares of the sacrifice and Brahmā were warmly welcomed by the god Śiva Rudra, they said to him, "The demons of fierce valor have performed awesome tapas, and oppress us. We have come to you for refuge! Maya, son of Diti, who built the fortress of Tripura with its shining gates, loves war, O three-eyed one. Fearless because of the boon which Brahmā gave them, the Dānavas have retreated into their fortified city, O chief of the gods, and they torment us, Mahādeva, as if we were servants with no master! . . .

Thus addressed by the gods led by Śakra, the three-eyed, boon-granting lord of the gods whose mount is the bull, said to the gods, "Fear the Dānavas no more, O gods. I shall burn up Tripura! Now do as I say. If you want me to set that Dānava city afire, then build me a proper chariot, and wait."

At the words of the naked Mahādeva, the gods said "So be it!" along with the Grandfather, and began to construct a marvelous chariot. The earth was its support, Rudra's two attendants its yoke-pole, Mt. Meru's peak the seat, and Mt. Mandara the axle. The lords of the gods made the sun and the moon the gold and silver wheels, the dark and light fortnights their two rims, and the gods Brahmā and all the other celestials the other moving parts. The encircling ropes were the two snakes Kambala and Aśvatara, while the planets Budha (Mercury), Āngāraka (Mars), Śanaiścara (Saturn), all the supreme deities and the sky itself formed the beautifully built bumper ring of that chariot. The golden triveṇu on the front was fashioned from the eyes of fork-tongued snakes, studded with gems, pearls, and sapphires by the joyous gods. . . .

As the battle between the gods and Dānavas began, women and children were killed in that embattled city, while the furious great demon lords with their attendants rolled forward like the sea. The dreadful battle raged on with battle axes, boulders, tridents, thunder-bolts and *kampanas*, fed by relentless hatred, until the battlefield was littered with bodies. As they attacked and bruised and killed each other, the bellowing of the immortals and the Dānavas was like the roaring of the ocean at the end of the Age. The streets of the city that had been bright with chips of gold and crystal ran red with blood. In an instant those streets were reduced to rubble and littered with severed heads, feet and hands. . . .

Then the mountainous Tāraka, acting like a crazed elephant, tried to seize Rudra's chariot, but was checked like an ocean creeping beyond its shores when Śiva, the three-eyed mountain lord with his mighty bow, and the four-faced Brahmā together challenged the Daitya, who was shaken like the ocean tossed about by the power of the wind. . . . The horrible Tāraka, eyes red with rage, was halted near Rudra by Nandin, who brings joy to his family. Nandin chopped down that lord of the

Dānavas with his sharp axe like a perfume-selling wood-cutter fells a sandal tree. Struck down by that axe like a deer, the brave Tāraka drew his sword and attacked the lord of the *gaṇas*. But Nandin stripped him of his sacred thread and cut him down, bellowing raucously.

At Tāraka's death, a ghastly lion's roar rose up from the gaṇa lords along with the awful screech of conches. When Maya, standing nearby, heard the delighted shouts of the Pramāthas and the sound of their instruments, he said to Vidyunmālin who stood at his side, "What is this great noise I hear coming from many mouths, sounding like the ocean's roar? Tell me Vidyunmālin, what is the reason for these drums? The gaṇa lords attack, and the bulls of elephants flee!" Snared by the hook of Maya's words, that foe-conqueror Vidyunmālin, blazing like the sun, went to the front of the battle with the gods and reported excitedly, "A hero as great as Yama, Varuṇa, Mahendra and Rudra, the brave Tāraka who was the storehouse of your glory, the chief mainstay of every battle, has fallen to the gaṇas in the fight!" When the Pramāthas saw Tāraka crushed, his terrified eyes wide open and blazing with fire like the sun, their hair bristled with delight, and they began to roar like the clouds. . . .

When the Dānavas saw that huge and terrifying army marching on them, they began to shiver like the trembling seas. Gripping their swords, three-pointed spears, pikes, tridents, sticks and battle-axes, their thunderbolts and heavy clubs, their eyes red with rage and looking like winged mountains, they rushed to attack, like clouds assaulting the mountains in the rainy season. Happy at heart, those sons of Diti, the foes of the gods, along with Vidyunmālin and Maya, confronted the god of gods.

The army of the gods, whose minds were ready for death, grew doubtful of victory at the sight, their limbs suddenly weak. Roaring like thunderclouds, their fury like the thunder itself, the demons, ready to fight, attacked, and the two armies did awful things to each other. Pouring forth smoke from flaming weapons like the sun, those warriors, loving the fight, pulverized each other in rage. . . .

Then, when the city of the Daityas came into conjunction with the constellation Puṣya, the three cities were joined together in a row. And Hara, the three-eyed master of the three strides, immediately shot his three-pronged arrow made of the three deities at Tripura. As he released his arrow, the sky which had been the color of the blue bāṇa tree, glowed golden, reddened as if by the sun. After he had shot that arrow made of the three gods at Tripura, Hara cried out, "Shame, shame!" When he saw Maheśvara so miserable, the elephant-gaited Nandin asked the trident-bearer, "What is the matter?" And the skull-bearer, marked with the moon, spoke piteously to Nandin, "Now Maya, my devotee, will die!"

At this, the powerful Nandīśvara sped quickly to Tripura, swift as the wind, or thought, and entered the city while the arrow was still traveling through the sky. That fierce gaṇa lord who glowed like gold spotted Maya and said, "O Maya, Tripura is about to be destroyed! I am telling you to escape, with your household!"

At Nandin's words, that demon who was steadfastly loyal to Maheśvara, stole out of Tripura with the principal members of his household. And Fire, in three forms, namely Hutāśa, Soma and Nārāyaṇa, burned up that city like a pile of straw. The three cities were destroyed by that flaming arrow just as prominent families are ruined by the wickedness of an evil son. . . .

Looking like Mt. Mandara, the lord of the mountains with a thousand peaks, that excellent city of Tripura with its towers and thousands of turreted mansions, decorated with necklaces of fire, fell into the sea with a monstrous roar, leaving only its name behind. . . .

Whoever recites this victory-winning story of Rudra's exploits will receive victory in his own undertakings from the bull-bannered lord. Whoever has this story recited at the *śrāddha* of his Fathers shall win that eternal merit which bestows the fruits of all sacrifices. This story is a blessed benediction; it is the means of getting a son. Whoever hears or recites this story goes to Rudra's heaven.

The Destruction of Dakṣa's Sacrifice

King Dakṣa, Pracetas' son, who had been cursed long ago by Śaṃbhu for having insulted Bhava due to an old feud, was offering a sacrifice at the gate of the Ganges, Gangādvāra. All the gods were invited for their shares, along with Viṣṇu, and the chief sages came along with all the other seers. When the learned sage Dadhīci saw the entire family of the gods gathered there without Śankara, he spoke to the son of Pracetas, "Lord Rudra is followed by all beings from Brahmā down to the Piśācas. Why is he not being properly worshiped here as is his due?" To this Dakṣa replied, "In all the sacrifices there is no share assigned to him, nor are there any mantras to be offered to Śankara and his wife!"

The angry seer, a paragon of wisdom, spoke with a scowl to Dakṣa while the gods listened in, "Śankara is the source of all beings, the supreme lord of the universe! Surely when you realize this, you will worship him in every sacrifice."

"Hara is not beneficent; he is the terrifying Rudra, a devastator full of tamas!" replied Dakṣa. "He is naked and deformed, and he carries a skull. He cannot be the soul of the universe! Lord Nārāyaṇa is the king, the creator of the world. I worship this blessed god who consists of *sattva*, in all my actions."

Then Dadhīca said, "Don't you see the blessed lord of a thousand rays, the destroyer of all worlds, Parameśvara who consists of time? The keen-rayed Sun whom the learned reciters of the Veda extol, is himself an embodiment of Śankara. This fiery Rudra, the great god who carries a skull, whose neck is blue, the ruddy Hara, is the blessed Āditya the Sun, that god of a thousand rays who is to be praised by the sāman, adhvaryu and hotar priests! Witness this god who has fashioned the universe, whose form is Rudra, purpose of the three Vedas!"

Dakṣa answered, "These twelve Ādityas who have come for their shares of the sacrifice are the only known suns. There is no other sun." At his words, the assistant seers who had assembled to observe the sacrifice agreed, "Surely, this is so." Their minds pervaded by darkness, they failed to see the bull-bannered god whom they reviled hundreds of thousands of times more. The sages insulted both Hara, master of all creatures, and the Vedic mantras which, deluded by Viṣṇu's *māyā*, continued to honor Dakṣa's word. And all the gods who had come for their shares, led by Vāsava, failed to see lord Śiva, all except lord Hari Nārāyaṇa. The Golden Embryo, lord Brahmā, choicest among the knowers of Brahman, vanished in a flash before the eyes of all. When the lord had disappeared, Dakṣa himself went for refuge to Hari Nārāyaṇa, the god who protects the world. And Dakṣa fearlessly commenced the sacrifice while lord Viṣṇu, guardian of those who seek refuge in him, watched over it.

But the noble seer Dadhīca spoke up once again, seeing the hosts of seers and all the gods inimical to the Brahman of the Vedas. "There is not the slightest doubt that a man who neglects those worthy of honor and honors the unworthy acquires great evil. Wherever evil is embraced while good is ignored the gods send down harsh punishment at once!"

So speaking, the learned seer cursed the enemies of the lord who had gathered there, the brahmins, Dakṣa and his retinue. "Because you have ignored the Vedas and because you have reviled the supreme lord Mahādeva Śankara, whom the world adores, all of you whose minds follow despicable scriptures that insult the way of the lord, you who are hostile to the lord, will be deprived of the three Vedas. You whose learning and conduct have come to naught, who chatter with false knowledge, you shall all be crushed when the Kali Age comes, along with those born properly in that Age. The power born of tapas will utterly desert you and you will go to Hell. Hṛṣīkeśa will turn his face away from you even if you beseech him!" After saying this, the wise sage, treasure-house of tapas, stopped talking and turned his mind to Rudra, the annihilator of all sins.

Meanwhile, the all-seeing goddess, knowing of this, spoke to her husband Mahādeva, the great lord, the god who is master of creatures: "Dakṣa, who was my father in a previous birth, is holding a sacrifice without inviting you, Śankara. He is insulting both you and myself. The gods and the sages are accomplices in this deed. I want one boon from you. Destroy this sacrifice immediately!"

At her request, the lord god, supreme among the gods, suddenly emitted Rudra out of the desire to destroy Dakṣa's sacrifice. He had a thousand heads, a thousand feet, a thousand eyes, long arms with a thousand hands. He was invincible like the Fire at the end of the Age with fangs terrible to behold, bearing conch, discuss and mace, cudgel in hand, roaring horribly, armed with the Śārnga bow and smeared with ashes He was called Vīrabhadra, brimming over with the god of gods himself; just born, he attended the lord of gods with folded hands.

"Blessings upon you!" Śiva said to him. "Dakṣa is holding a sacrifice at Gangādvāra where he has insulted me. O lord of the *gaṇas*, destroy his celebration!" So Vīrabhadra, sent by his friend took the form of a lion and devastated Dakṣa's sacrifice for fun. And the great goddess Bhadrakālī, emitted by the furious Umā, went forth together with the gaṇa who rode a bull. Thousands more Rudras poured out of the blessed lord. Known as the Romajas (Hair-Born) because they were born from his hairs, they were his helpers. With spears swords and maces in their hands, carrying spades and rocks, blazing like Rudra, the Fire of Time, they made the ten directions reverberate with their roars. They all proceeded towards Dakṣa's feast, surrounding the gaṇa leader, mounted on bulls and accompanied by their wives; they were a terrifying sight to see.

When they arrived at the place called Gangādvāra, they saw there the sacrifice of Dakṣa of infinite splendor. It abounded with thousands of celestial women and resounded with the songs of Apsarases, with the music of lutes and flutes and with the chanting of Vedas. When he saw Prajāpati seated near the gods and sages, Vīrabhadra accompanied by Bhadrakālī and the Rudras, said with the ghost of a smile: "We are all the servants of Śarva of infinite splendor. We have come out of desire for our shares of the sacrifice. Give us the portions we want! Or else tell us who gave the order that you are to receive the shares and not we, so that we may know who he is!"

Thus addressed by the gaṇa chief, the gods led by Prajāpati said to the lord, "There are no mantras prescribing your share of the sacrifice!"

When they heard this, those gods whose minds were obscured by illusion still ignored the lord, so the mantras deserted the gods and went to their own home. Then lord Rudra touched the divine sage Dadhīca with his hand, and in the company of his wife and the gaṇa lords, addressed the deities: "You are arrogant with power, refusing as you do the authority of the mantras. Because of this I shall humble you and destroy your conceit!"

After announcing this, the leader of the gaṇas set fire to the sacrificial enclosure while the furious gaṇa lords tore up the sacrificial posts and threw them away. Seizing the *prastotṛ* priest, the *hotṛ* priest and the sacrificial horse, the terrifying gaṇa chiefs hurled them into the Ganges river.

Vīrabhadra too, his soul afire, gleefully paralyzed the outstretched hand of Śakra and those of the other deities as well; playfully plucking out Bhaga's eyes with his fingernail, he struck Pūṣan with his fist and knocked his teeth out. Then the mighty gaṇa with a smile boldly attacked the god Candramās with his big toe, in play. He ripped off both hands of Fire and pulled out his tongue for fun. Then, O lords of seers, he pounded the seers with blows in the head with his feet.

Next this huge and powerful being immobilized Sudarśana, Viṣṇu's discus which had arrived with Garuḍa, and pierced the god with sharpened arrows. When he saw this happen, the large-winged Garuḍa went for the gaṇa and beat at him rapidly with his wings, roaring like the ocean. But Bhadra himself poured out Garuḍas by the thousands. Greater than Vinatā's son, they began to pursue Garuḍa. When he saw them, the clever bird who was most fleet, quickly threw off Mādhava, marvelous though he was, and fled.

At the disappearance of Vainateya, Brahmā, the lotus-born god, arrived to stop Vīrabhadra and Keśava. He sang the praises of Parameṣṭhin and reverently appeased him. The blessed lord Viṣṇu himself appeared along with Ambā. When he saw the lord who had arrived with Ambā, that overlord of the gods surrounded by all his hosts, lord Brahmā, Dakṣa and all the celestials praised him. Dakṣa bowed with folded hands and celebrated the goddess Pārvatī, whose body was half the lord's, with various sorts of hymns.

Then the blessed goddess, ocean of compassion, smiled at Maheśvara, her mind content, and said to Rudra, "You are the creator, ruler and protector of the world. Show favor to Dakṣa and the gods!" At this the blue and red lord Hara with matted hair spoke to the prostrate gods and to the son of Pracetas with a slight smile, "I am pleased with all you gods. I am not only not to be reviled but I am to be shown particular honor in every sacrifice. You too, Dakṣa, heed my word that protects all things. Abandon your worldly cravings and become my zealous devotee. By my grace you will become the lord of the gaṇas at the end of the Eon. Until then you will continue to rule your domain under the constraint of my commands." So speaking, the blessed one, along with his wife, and attendants, vanished from the boundlessly august Dakṣa's sight.

After that great god Śankara had disappeared the lotus-born Brahmā himself addressed to Dakṣa these words for the benefit of the whole world. "Now that you have gratified the bull-bannered god is your illusion dispelled? You should observe assiduously what the god has told you. The lord dwells in the innermost heart of all creatures. It is he that is seen by the wise reciters of the Veda who are absorbed in Brahman. He is the Self of all creatures, the seed, the supreme goal. Maheśvara, the god of gods, is he who is praised with Vedic mantras. He who worships only the eternal Rudra within himself, his mind yoked with love, gains the supreme goal. Therefore know the supreme lord to be without beginning, middle or end. Propitiate him zealously in act, mind and speech. With all your might and main avoid giving offense to lord Hara, for insulting acts destroy the self and lead inevitably to sin. The great Yogin who is your lord is the immortal Viṣṇu, the protector. Assuredly he is Mahādeva the blessed god of gods. Those who believe that Viṣṇu, womb of the universe is separate from lord Śiva will go to Hell because they are deluded, not grounded in the Veda. Those who follow the Veda see Rudra and Nārāyaṇa as a single god; they will enjoy release. He who knows Viṣṇu to be Rudra himself and Rudra to be Janārdana truly worships god and gains the supreme goal. Viṣṇu has poured forth this entire creation and Īśvara looks over it; thus this whole world has sprung from Rudra and Nārāyaṇa. Therefore cease your insult of Hara, but in your devotion to Viṣṇu also seek refuge in Mahādeva, who shelters the reciters of the Veda."

When he heard this speech of Viriñca, the Prajāpati Dakṣa sought shelter with the god who is master of the cows, garbed in a lion-skin. The rest of the great sages who had been scorched by the fire of Dadhīca's curse remained deluded and hostile to the god and were born henceforth in the Kali Ages. They were born into the families of brahmins on the strength of their earlier perfections, according to Brahmā's word, but they lost completely the power they had won through tapas. All of those who have fallen into Raurava and the other hells will be released from the curse at the end of the Eon, attaining in due time the sun-hued Brahmā, lord of the worlds. After being sent away by Svayambhū, they will propitiate Indra, the lord who rules the thirty gods, by the practice of tapas, and they will become as they were before through the favor of Śankara. Thus you have heard the whole story of the destruction of Dakṣa's sacrifice.

Gaṇeśa

Once upon a time while Pārvatī was taking a bath, the always auspicious Śiva threatened Nandin, who was guarding her door, and went into the house. When that lovely woman, the mother of the world, saw Śankara arrive so unexpectedly, she stood up, embarrassed. After this happened, the auspicious Pārvatī, supreme Māyā, the supernal goddess, became eager to follow the good advice given earlier by a friend, thinking to herself, "I should have a servant of my very own! He should be favorable to me, a man of accomplishment who will obey my command and no other, one who will not stray even a hair's breadth from my side!"

Thinking these thoughts, the goddess fashioned from the dirt of her body a young man who possessed all these good characteristics. He was handsome, flawless of limb, sturdy, well-adorned, and most valorous and strong. She gave to him various garments, abundant ornaments and an incomparable blessing. "You are my very own son!" she said, "I have no one else here who is mine alone."

At her words, the youth bowed and said to Śivā [Pārvatī], "What task have you found for me? I shall do as you tell me." Thus addressed, Śiva answered her son, "Dear son, hear my words. From now on you shall be my doorkeeper. You are my very own child; I have no one whatsoever here but you who belongs to me. Let no one into my house without my permission, my son, no matter who, no matter where. Use force if necessary, dear son. I mean this truly!" And so speaking, she gave him a hard stick, O seer. Gazing at his handsome body, she was thrilled with delight.

Then she kissed his face lovingly, embraced him with affection and stationed him, staff in hand, at her door as chief of her gaṇas. And the beloved son of the goddess, the great heroic gaṇa, stood at the door of her house, holding the staff in his hand, out of desire to please Pārvatī. After she had put her son Gaṇeśa, lord of the gaṇas, in front of her door, Śivā herself stayed inside to bathe with her companions.

At that moment Śiva, skilled in various sports, arrived eagerly at the door, O lion among seers. Not knowing he was lord Śiva, Gaṇeśa said, "You may not enter here, O god, without permission of my mother who is inside bathing. Where do you think you're going? Get out at once!" Saying this, Gaṇeśa brandished his staff to stop Śiva. Looking at him, Śiva said, "You silly fool, who are you to keep me out? Don't you recognize me, stupid? I am none other than Śiva himself!" But Gaṇeśa struck the great lord of many sports with his stick. This infuriated Śiva who said once again to his son, "You are an imbecile not to know me! I am Śiva, the husband of Pārvatī, daughter of the mountain! I shall go into my own house, idiot. Why are you standing in my way?"

After the god had spoken Gaṇeśa grew angry with Maheśa, who was going into the house, O brahmin, so he hit him again with his staff. At this Śiva became enraged. Mustering his own gaṇas, he asked them, "Who is this person? What is he up to? What is going on here, gaṇas, while you just stand there and watch?" . . .

The gaṇas, filled with fury, went to the guardian of the door at Śiva's behest and questioned the son of the mountain daughter. "Who are you? Where have you come from? What are you going to do? Get out now if you want to live! Now listen to us. We are Śiva's best gaṇas and doorkeepers. We have come to stop you, by order of lord Śankara. We can see that you are a gaṇa too, so we will spare your life, but otherwise you would be killed! For your own sake, stay far away from us. Why risk death by staying here?"

Even after this speech, Pārvatī's son Gaṇeśa showed no fear. Rebuking Śankara's gaṇas, he refused to budge from the doorway. When they had heard all he had to say, the gaṇas of Śivā who had gone there returned to the lord and told him what had happened. . . .

After hearing their words, Śiva said, "Listen, all you gaṇas. It is not right to go to battle over this, for you are my very own gaṇas and that other gaṇa belongs to my wife Gaurī. On the other hand, if I back down, O gaṇas, people might say, 'Śambhu is always cowed by his wife!' It is a weighty matter to know the right thing to do. That gaṇa by himself is only a mere child. What power can he have? Moreover, gaṇas, in the world you are experts in battle, and you belong to me. Why should you avoid a fight and thereby become useless to me? How can a woman be so obstinate, especially to her husband? It is she who is responsible for this! Now the mountain daughter will reap the fruit of her act! Listen carefully to what I say, all my heroes: wage all-out war! Let it come out as it will!" After making this speech, O brahmin, Śankara who is skilled in various sports stopped talking, excellent seer, according to the way of the world.

Thus addressed by their lord, the gaṇas made a supreme resolve to do his bidding. United, they went to Śivā's house. When Gaṇeśa saw the eminent gaṇas approach, armed for battle, he said to them, "Come if you will, all you lords of the gaṇas following Śiva's command! I am only one boy who obeys the order of Śivā. Nevertheless, the goddess Pārvatī shall witness the strength of her son, while Śiva shall see the power of his own gaṇas! The fight that is about to take place between a child and mighty men is a contest between Bhavānī and Śiva. You are skilled in warfare, since you have fought before; I am a boy who has never been to battle. Nevertheless, I shall put you to shame in this conflict between the mountain-born woman and Śiva! For my part, I have nothing against you, but I shall humble you before Pārvatī and Śiva! Now that you know this, O gaṇa lords, let the battle be joined! Look to your master and I shall look to my mother. Let the outcome be as it will be, for no one in the three worlds can stop it now!"

Thus challenged, the gaṇas grabbed up all kinds of weapons and assaulted him, their arms bristling with sticks. They ground their teeth, cried "*Hūṃ*!" over and over again and attacked him shouting, "Look at him! There he is!" Nandin approached first, seized Gaṇeśa's foot and tugged at it while Bhṛgin grabbed the other foot. As they pulled at his feet, the gaṇa beat back their hands which clung to his sandals.

Then Gaṇapati, the heroic son of the goddess, seized a huge iron-stubbed club and stood at the door, bashing them all with it. Some had their hands severed, the backs of others were shattered, while still others had their heads and skulls cut off. The knees of some were smashed, the shoulders of others. All those who faced Gaṇeśa were hit in the chest. Some fell to the ground, while others fled in all directions. Some had their feet cut off while others retreated towards Śarva. There was not a one among them who faced up to Gaṇeśa in battle. Like deer who sees a lion, they fled in all the ten directions. When all the gaṇas by the thousands had run away, Gaṇeśa returned to stand at the beautiful door. That destroyer of them all was a terrifying sight, looking like Time at the end of the Eon. . . .

After waging war with his army for a long time, O seer, even Śiva grew dismayed at the sight of his formidable foe. He stood in the middle of his troops thinking, "Gaṇeśa can only be killed by a trick! For surely there is no other way." Then all the gods and Maheśa's gaṇas were delighted to see both Śiva, embodied with qualities, and Viṣṇu come to the battle. Greeting each other with affection, they all celebrated. And Gaṇeśa, the heroic son of *śakti*, with his staff, following the way of heroes, was the first to worship Viṣṇu who brings happiness to all.

Then Viṣṇu said to Śiva, "You shall kill your enemy, O lord, but not without trickery, for he is hard to reach and full of tamas. I shall create a delusion." He conferred with Śambhu, and after receiving Śiva's command, Viṣṇu began to prepare his trick. . . .

The heroic son of Śivā, endowed with great strength, saw the great lord Śambhu arrive, trident in hand, eager for the kill. Recalling his mother's lotus feet, and emboldened by the *śakti* of Śiva, the mighty hero Gaṇeśa struck him in the hand with his spear. When Śiva whose protection is good saw the trident fall from his hand, he took up the Pināka bow, but the lord of the gaṇas made that too fall to the ground with a blow of his iron-studded staff. Since five of his hands had been clubbed, Śiva took up the trident with five others. "Aho!" he cried in the way of the world, "a great calamity has befallen me! Surely nothing worse than this can happen to the gaṇas!"

Meanwhile, the heroic Gaṇeśa, full of the power bestowed by śakti, attacked all the gods and gaṇas with his cudgel. Set upon by his club, they dispersed into the ten directions. None remained in combat with that wondrous fighter. When Viṣṇu saw that gaṇa, he exclaimed, "This is a lucky one! He is most powerful, most manly, a great hero fond of battle! I have seen many deities, Daityas, Dānavas, Yakṣas, Gandharvas and Rākṣasas, but there is none to equal this guardian in brilliance, beauty, valor and other fine qualities in any of the three worlds!"

As he was speaking in this manner, the gaṇa lord, son of śakti, brandished his club and hurled it at Viṣṇu. Recollecting the lotus-like feet of Śiva, Hari took up his discus and swiftly shattered that iron-studded club. The gaṇa then hurled a chip of the club at Hari, but the bird Garuḍa caught it and rendered it powerless. Thus did the time pass as the two mighty heroes, Viṣṇu and Gaṇeśa, fought with each other.

Once again, the choicest hero, the mighty son of śakti, recalling Śivā, took up his matchless staff and struck Viṣṇu with it. Unable to withstand the blow, Viṣṇu fell to the ground. But he sprang up at once and battled again with that son of Śivā. Seizing his opportunity at last, the trident-wielding Śiva took his stand in the north and cut off the head of Gaṇeśa with his trident. When Gaṇeśa lost his head, both the army of the gaṇas and the army of the gods stood stock still, rooted to the earth.

After Gaṇeśa was killed, the gaṇas held a great festival to the sound of hand drums and kettle drums. Śiva was sorry that he had cut off Gaṇeśa's head, O lord of seers, but the mountain-born goddess Pārvatī was furious: "What will I do? Where will I go? Alas, alas, misery engulfs me. How will I ever lose this grief and sorrow that now are mine? All the gods and gaṇas have killed my son. I shall wreak utter havoc! I shall bring about the dissolution of the world!"

Grieving in this manner, the great goddess of the universe, enraged, fashioned in an instant hundreds of thousands of śaktis, or powers. Once created, they bowed to the mother of the world, blazed forth and said, "O Mother, tell us what to do!" At their words, O lord of seers, Mahāmāyā, Śaṃbhu's śakti, she who is Prakṛti, full of fury, answered them all. "O śaktis, O goddesses, you are to annihilate the world without a moment's pause. O my companions, devour with a vengeance the gods, sages, Yakṣas, Rākṣasas, my very own followers and all the rest as well!"

At her command, all the śaktis, consumed with rage, prepared to destroy all the gods and other creatures. They went forth to spread devastation, as fire licks up grass. The leaders of the gaṇas—Viṣṇu, Brahmā, Śankara and Indra, Kubera, king of the Yakṣas, Skanda and Sūrya—all these they sought to obliterate without ceasing. No matter where one looked, there were the śaktis! There were multitudes of them—Karālī (Gape-Mouth), Kubjakā (Hunch-Back), Khaṃjā (Cripple), Lambaśīrsā (Droop-Head)—and they all snatched up the gods in their hands and hurled them into their open mouths.

Witnessing this devastation, Hara, Brahmā, Hari, Indra and all the rest of the gods, gaṇas and seers said to themselves, "What is this goddess doing, this untimely annihilation of the world?" Thus they were uncertain and lost hope for their own lives. Gathering together, they conferred with each other, saying, "We must consider what to do!" Thus deliberating, they talked rapidly among themselves.

"Only when the mountain goddess is satisfied will peace return to the world, and not otherwise, not even with a myriad efforts! Even Śiva, skilled in all sports, the deluder of the world, is filled with sorrow like the rest of us!"

A million gods were annihilated while Śivā was enraged; none could prevail. There was no one whatsoever to withstand the mountain-born goddess, O seer, whether her own devotee or that of another, whether god or Dānava, gaṇa or guardian of the quarters, whether Yakṣa, Kinnara or seer, not even Viṣṇu, Brahmā or lord Śankara himself! When they beheld her dazzling splendor flashing in all directions, all the gods were terrified and retreated to some distance away.

Meanwhile Nārada of divine sight arrived—you, O seer—to benefit the gods and gaṇas. After bowing to Brahma, Viṣṇu, Śankara and myself, he met with them and spoke, reflecting on what was to be done. All the gods conferred with the great-souled Nārada, saying in unison, "How can our suffering be ended?" To this he replied, "As long as the mountain-born goddess is without compassion, you will be miserable. Make no mistake about this!"

And then the seers headed by Nārada went to Śiva and all propitiated her in order to appease her fury. Over and over again they bowed, singing hymns by the numbers. . . .

Thus hymned by the seers led by Nārada, the supreme goddess continued to look furious and spoke not a word to them. So all the seers bowed again to her lotus feet and spoke diplomatically once more to Śivā with devotion, their hands folded in reverence: "Forgive us, O goddess! Devastation is upon us! Your master stands before you, Ambikā, look at him! We are the gods Viṣṇu, Brahmā and the others, O goddess. We are your very own creatures who stand before you with our hands folded in worship. Forgive our fault, supreme goddess! All of us are utterly miserable. O Śivā, grant us peace!"

So speaking, all the seers, wretched and confused, stood together in front of Caṇḍikā with their hands folded in obeisance. When she heard what they said, Caṇḍikā grew pleased. And she answered those seers with a mind filled with compassion: "If you can revive my son, I shall stop my devastation. If you honor him and make him overseer of everything, then there will be peace in the world. In no other way will you be happy again."

Thus addressed, all the seers led by Nārada went to tell the gods what had happened. After they heard the story, all the miserable gods led by Śakra bowed, folded their hands, and related it all to Śankara. At their words, Śiva said, "Do whatever is necessary to benefit the worlds. Go the north and cut off the head of whomever you first encounter. After doing this, join that head to Gaṇeśa's body."

All this was done by the gods according to Śiva's order. They brought the body, washed it by the rules and worshiped it. Then turning their faces to the north, they went out. The first thing they met was an elephant with a single tusk. Taking its head, all the deities fastened it firmly to the body of Gaṇeśa. Worshiping Śiva, Viṣṇu and Brahmā, they bowed and said, "We have done as you told us. Now you must finish the task." And the gods and attendants beamed with happiness at these words, having obeyed the command of Śiva.

Again Brahmā, Viṣṇu and the gods bowed to their master, the lord who is without characteristics, god Śiva himself, and said, "Since all of us were born from your tejas, or energy, now let your tejas enter this body by means of the recitation of Vedic mantras!" And calling Śiva to mind, they all sprinkled blessed holy water on the corpse while reciting mantras. At the mere touch of the drops of water, Gaṇeśa regained both consciousness and life. The boy arose, by Śiva's wish, as though from sleep. He was handsome, noble and resplendent, with a pleasing shape, a jolly manner and a ruddy elephant head.

Everyone rejoiced, their sorrows banished, O lord of seers, at the sight of Śivā's son restored to life. Filled with happiness, they showed him to the goddess. When she saw her son alive, she too was overcome with joy.

The Tāṇḍava Dance of Śiva

Dāruka, born of the demons, had achieved his prowess through tapas and was butchering both gods and eminent brahmins like the Fire of Time. Severely oppressed and beaten by Dāruka, the gods approached Brahmā, Īśāna, Kumāra, Viṣṇu, Yama and Indra. Knowing that the demon could only be killed by a woman, Brahmā and the other gods disguised themselves as women and went to do battle with him. But he overcame them, too, O brahmins, so they all went to Brahma and told him what had happened. In his company they went to Śiva, Umā's lord, and led by the Grandfather they bowed before the lord of the gods in manifold ways. Then Brahmā spoke up, "O lord, Dāru is a cruel demon! Protect us by killing this Daitya Dāruka, who is to be slain by a woman!"

When he had heard Brahmā's report, the lord of the gods, smiter of Bhaga's eyes, said to the mountain-born goddess with a hint of laughter, "I ask your help, my beauty, for the sake of the world. Go and destroy Dāruka who can only be slain by a woman, O fair-faced, one!" At his words the lord's mistress, who is the fire-drilling block of the world, entered the body of the god, intending to be born for Dāruka's destruction. Meanwhile, Brahmā and the gods, who were led by Indra, were unaware that she had entered that supreme deity, the lord of the gods, with a portion of herself.

When the omniscient four-faced god Brahmā saw the lustrous daughter of the mountain standing at Śaṃbhu's side as before, even he was fooled by her tricks. For as Pārvatī entered the body of the god of gods, she made for herself another body from the poison that stood in his throat. Knowing with his third eye that she had done this, Śiva, Kāma's foe, emitted the black-throated goddess from his own throat. When this goddess, Kālī, with the pitch-black throat, was born, there arose at the same time ample, abundant, auspicious Victory. And Parameṣṭhin was pleased with Bhavānī because she would accomplish the defeat of the demons.

When the hosts of the gods and the Siddhas, led by Śakra, Upendra and the lotus-born Brahmā, witnessed the birth of this luminous goddess with the inky-black poison-filled throat, they fled in terror. Also terrifying were the eye that appeared in her forehead, the crescent moon on the crown of her head, the sharp fangs in her mouth, the spiky trident in her hand and the ornaments adorning her body. Along with the goddess were born the chief Siddhas and the ghoulish Piśācas, all of them adorned with ornaments and robed in celestial garb.

At Pārvatī's command, the supreme goddess with the black throat slew the Dānava Dāruka, who had been tormenting the overlords of the gods. Her violence, however, knew no bounds, O brahmins, so the whole world became sick with the fever of her rage. Then Bhava, the lord, took the form of a boy by illusion, and began to howl aloud at a ghost-filled cremation ground in order to quell the fire of her rage.

When she saw the lord in the form of a child, she was fooled by his Māyā and offered him milk from her breasts, O brahmins. This clever boy drank up her wrath along with the breast milk; with this anger he became the guardian of the fields, adopting eight different forms for the protection of the fields. Thus was the goddess weaned of her anger by this boy.

Then at twilight the joyous trident-wielding god of gods performed a frenzied dance to gain her favor, accompanied by all his ghosts and goblins. Drinking the nectar of Śaṃbhu's dance only as far as her throat, the supreme goddess herself danced with glee in that place of ghosts and witches. All the gods, together with Brahmā, Indra and Upendra, bowed before Kālī and the goddess Pārvatī and sang their praises.

Thus you have heard in brief the story of the Tāṇḍava dance of the trident-bearing god. There are others, however, who hold that the dance of the lord is really the bliss of Yoga.

Source: *Classical Hindu Mythology: A Reader in the Sanskrit Purāṇas*, edited and translated by Cornelia Dimmitt and J.A.B. van Buitenen (Philadelphia: Temple University Press, 1978).

***Selections from the* Pāśupata Sūtram with the Pañchārtha-bhāṣya of Kauṇḍinya**

1. Now then we shall expound the Pāśupata Union and rites of Paśupati.

After offering obeisance with the head (bent) to that Paśupati, the Lord of the house (world) who created the entire world beginning with Brahma for the good (of all), Kauṇḍinya, following the tradition of his predecessors makes the commentary known as Pañchārtha (five categories), the best of its kind, enriched with significance and knowledge of the highest order. Now Bhagavān will expound five categories. . . .

Now how can that end of pains be attained? Or by which means? The answer is by Paśupati. The concluding part of the proposition—by the grace (of Paśupati). Here Paśupati means the Lord of Paśus (the effect or created world). Here the paśus are all sentient beings except the emancipated souls. . . . And the paśu-s are both those who are manifested in the shape of [body and senses] and those who are not so manifested. Now what is the state of a paśu? The answer is—want of excellence is bondage. Bondage is want of excellence and want of independence; and its characteristic is the obstruction of the power of the cause. It is beginningless. By bondage is meant the imposition of its quality. If you ask what is its characteristic, the answer is that the paśu-s are due to their capacity to be seen and to be enchained. There the paśu-s are the 23 elements of the Sāṃkhya system. . . . Being enchained, bound and obstructed by those [elements] they (paśu-s) remain dependent on the objects like sound, etc. and so it is understood that bondage is want of independence and of excellence. . . . The Paśus are so called because they are seen. Because though they are all-pervasive and possessed of pure consciousness, they see and realize only the body and not the outside world. And those who are averse to the object-world do neither accept nor reject it. And the object-world depends on merit and demerit, manifestation, space, time and guidance and others. So it is well said that the Paśu-s are due to seeing and binding. . . .

He who creates and protects those Paśus is, therefore, the ruler (Pati). How does He get and protect them? So by the all-pervading power. Because they can not surpass His infinite power. Because he is a learned Being, he possesses unending and immeasureable power of knowledge. By that immeasurable power the Lord gets the innumerable Paśus directly. The power of the master protects them. How? His will determines their likes and dislikes, their existence and their attainment of desirable and undesirable states of existence or places, bodies, senses and others. That means they are supervised and prompted by Him. . . . The end of pains is attainable by that grace and not simply by knowledge, aversion, piety and renunciation of all excellences (or miraculous powers). . . .

What is that? The answer is—Yoga. Here Yoga means the conjunction of the (individual) soul with God through the intellect. And that is born of one-sided activity on the part of a person because of the instrumentality of study, etc., as in the case of contact between a pillar and a hawk. Because there are rules for both guidance and studying, this (Yoga) is born of reciprocity of actions as in the case of contact between two sheep. Because the Lord is all-pervading, there is no scope for separation. And the unification is advised only in the case of separated ones. In the Yoga of actions it is like one who was once attached to the object-world but now averse to it. But in this scripture Yoga is restricted to activity which is characterized by concentration (samādhi).

The question is—"Is Yoga attainable simply by knowledge?" The answer is, because it is said—for the attainment of that we shall expound the practices (*vidhi*). Here the term "Yoga-vidhi" means the practices of Yoga, a certain course of action. . . . Here the technical term "Vidhi" is used as in the "Yajnavidhi" in the sense of all (particular) actions, subtle and gross. . . . The temporary activities can not be taken as a whole. If so, why "Vidhi"? It is called "Vidhi" because it enjoins and because it creates the idea of the means and the end. "Vidhim" is used in the sense of action.

Thus with the end of pains the Effect (Kārya or Egos or Jīvas or Paśu-s), the cause (Karana, the Lord or Paśupati), the union (Yoga) and the practices (*vidhi*)—these five categories are briefly referred to. These are to be explained. Their explanation lies in extension, classification, characterization, concision and conclusion. Here something is to be explained and something else is the explanation. That is why it is said—we shall explain. Hence the element "Vi" means extension, classification and specialisation. There the term "Vistara" means the perception, inference and testimony, sources of knowledge. Now perception is of two classes, the direct knowledge, gained by senses and by Self. Perception by senses means the objects of senses like sound, touch, color, taste, smell and pots, etc., as established by the exposition, heat, urine, stool, flesh, salt and breath-control. . . . Perception by Self is the totality of the relations produced by mind and the internal organ. Inference also is preceded by perception; the totality of the relations between mind, Self and inner organs and it is the cause of memories and diverse things like dharma, adharma, manifestation, space, time and guidance, etc., and time of creation, preservation and disappearance, etc. And by these is inferred that the cause is the doer of the future creation. Hence it is not beyond the range of the causal relation. And that is of two types:—perceived and perceived through universals. . . . Comparison, postulation, possibility, non-cognition (*abhava*), tradition (*aitihya*) and pratibha, etc., are regarded as falling with in these only (perception, inference and testimony). So these three are valid sources of knowledge. The Supreme Lord (Bhagavān) is the guide and cause of all valid knowledge. The individual being (*puruṣa*) is the knower. The five padarthas (categories) beginning with Kārya and Kāraṇa are the knowables. Knowledge is consciousness. Consciousness is right thinking, right understanding and the expression of Vidyā (knowledge). . . . Here ends this exposition of the categories.

2. One must take bath by ashes in three periods of the day.

Here ashes mean the object which is given to Paśupati) and which is produced by fuel set on fire. That is made by others, it is an earthly food and shining. Ashes should be acquired like alms from the villages etc. Because ashes are helpful to the observance of bath, lying down and rebath, they must be taken and because they have nothing to do with injury, they are the purest and best things and they should be taken profusely as the means (of spiritual rise). If not available, at least a slight quantity must be taken. . . . So it is said—he should bathe. Here bath means removal of dirt like oily substance, refuses of skin, excretion, bad scent, etc., coming to bodies by ashes as a matter of purification. But bath means the conjunction of body with ashes. Really speaking, bath, etc., are nothing but acts of self-purification. . . . That means one must bathe with ashes and not with water which leads to opposite results.

Is it that only bath is prescribed to be done by ashes? The answer is—because it is said—

3. One should lie down in ashes.

. . . Staying during day at a place on earth which has been washed, spreading ashes one aspirant, intent on study, teaching and meditation and tired of thoughts on texts and of concentration on them should sleep at night on ashes, purified by . . . mantras using his own arm as a pillow. . . .

Now by ashes are only the double interests, bath and lying down served or something else? What will be a remedy for him who, even after bath three times, becomes impure? So it is said—

4. Re-bath.

. . . But bath is only the application of ashes. If one becomes impure by the residue of the meal taken, by hunger, by spitting, or by reason of urine or excretion in between the baths in three periods of prayer, then he should have bath for the second time. Why so? For purification and for the manifestation of the mark (of the Pāśupata sect). One should bathe.

Now are the ashes the only way of manifestation of the mark? What is the means of something, not prohibited for the increase of devotion? Here it is said:—

5. Garland.

Here garland is an important thing of this world like ashes. . . .

Now the question is—where is it established that his mark is manifested by ashes and garland? So it is said. In this scripture. Because it is said:—

6. The bearer of the mark.

. . . the mark of a Pāśupata-Yoga means the distinctive mark of the stage as for example, ashes-bath, lying down in ashes, re-bath, garland, single cloth, etc. and this mark becomes a part of his own body creating the idea of Pāśupatas among the people. The Liṅgam is due to the act of merging and that of marking. Bearing that he becomes the holder of the mark. Like the wielder of staff.

Next—where these duties of bath, lying down, re-bath, etc., are to be performed? And whence the garland has to be procured? And where should it be taken? Where to live after taking the marks? So it is said—in the temple, because the sūtra is—

7. A resident in a temple. . . .

8. One should worship with laughter, songs, dance, sounds of ḍuṅ-ḍuṅ, salutations, muttering and presents. . . .

9.2. And celebacy has been established in the Tantra. How ? Because of prohibition of women and also of instruction to control senses. By celibacy is meant the conquest of thirteen senses, specially of tongue and the sex-organ. . . .

The inclination of the mind towards women is the rope for tying. The meritorious go severing it but the bad men do not forsake it. One goes out of a village for woman, commercial dealings are also due to woman, woman is the source of all evils and the wise should never embrace her. She, whom people regard as woman, is poison, fire, sword, arrow and more clearly a terror and māyā (illusion) incarnate. The fools and not the learned revel in a body, full of impurities and worms, foul-smelling by nature, unclean and the store-house of urine and excretion and ephemeral. One gets maddened at the sight of a woman and not by drinking wine; so one must shun a woman whose sight creates madness from a distance. The world is bitten by the snake in the shape of the sex-organ of woman, which has its mouth cast downward, which moves in between the thighs and which can not be controlled by all scriptures. The entire world is blinded by a woman like the foot-step of the female deer, having hairs, ugly appearance, foul smell and bad skin. Woman is like burning flames and man is like a pitcher of clarified butter. Those who are attached (to women), are lost and those who stand (controlled), go to heaven. As the fire, fed with fuel manifests great light, so the light of one's self is manifested by the control over senses. Patience lies in celibacy, penance lies in celibacy and those brāhmaṇas who live with celibacy go to heaven. Those brāhmaṇas who practice celibacy, drink milk, honey and soma-juice with ambrosia and become immortal after death. Thus celibacy is established in the Tantra.

9.3. And truthfulness is established in the Tantra. And it is of two classes, the statement of fact as seen in the object-world and truthfulness in speech. There truth as the statement of fact is established in the scripture. . . .

9.4. And non-transaction is also established in the Tantra. . . . Transaction is of two classes, that of purchase and sale, and that of the royal family. So for one who is engaged in either of the two, causing pain to oneself and to others becomes unavoidable. There if one torments the self, in this world itself one becomes afflicted with pain. If one causes pain to others, then also one's demerit increases to produce sorrows and others. Thereby in this world one experiences the bitter pain. So commercial dealing in both ways should be forsaken. . . .

9.5. So non-stealing is established in the Tantra. How? Because of instruction for nakedness and for prohibition of meals, not offered. Here there is instruction for wearing no garment, even if there is still one garment lying with him, filled with dirt ; and so giving up of accepting gifts has been advised, moreover, because food and drink, etc., which are rejected are found to be utilized. So here non-stealing is established in the Tantra. . . .

9.6. Non-irritability is established in the Tantra. How? By prohibition of Śūdras and by instruction for the highest type of austerity. Here toleration of all pains, personal, physical and hyperphysical, which frequent body and mind and non-revenge are prescribed and so here non-irritability is established in the scripture. Anger is again of four classes, i.e., characterised with emotions, efforts, disfiguration and torture. There anger of emotion-type is that which arouses emotions like envy, jealousy, pride, conceit and desire for the evil of others, etc. Anger of effort-type means that which creates ideas of quarrel, enmity, fighting, etc. Anger of disfiguration is that which brings about disfigurement of one's hands, feet, nose, eyes and figures, etc. Anger causing torture is that which causes taking away of life of one's ownself or of others. These are four types of anger. . . .

9.7. And service to teachers is established in the Tantra. . . . He receives Vidyā (knowledge) from the teacher and imparts it to many persons and by this distribution of Vidyā the teachers are served. . . . Śiva imparts knowledge assuming the shape of the teachers and so the teacher should never be disregarded by one, desirous of bliss. The wise man should ever satisfy with his everything (the teacher) who, knows the meaning of the textbook and who teaches the path of Yoga. . . .

9.8. And purification is established in the scripture. Because of instruction for bath by ashes. And that purification is of three types, viz., purification of body, of thought and of Self. There purification of the body by ashes is reputed for the instruction for bath by ashes. . . .

Ashes burn all those defects which are born of company, which owe their origin to parents, which are due to food and drink, which are caused by cross-breeding and which resort to the body, bones and marrows. . . .

9.10. So carefulness is established in the Tantra. Because of instruction for carefulness and for muttering. Here one should always be careful in Yama-s and should not be forgetful of them. . . .

Thus carefulness is established in the Tantra. So non-injury and other Yama-s are famous.

10. Having only one garment.

. . . His garment is of five classes, made of something born of eggs, made of skin of bulls, made of hairs, of barks and of hides. One cloth is to be worn for removal of shame, that is only the covering in the shape of loin-cloth, that is of one knot or of more than one knot, that is produced by good means from the villages, etc. and is not accepted as a possession. . . .

11. Without any garment.

Here "a" denotes prohibition of cloth. He should live without cloth, naked as he was born and without any possession. Now what is your need in being naked? So it should be mentioned—like the state of having one garment. . . .

12. He should not look at urine and excretion.

. . . Urine and excretion of men and others should not be seen by one's own sense of intellect and by one's eyes. But not that of cows etc. . . .

15. By touching.

. . . That means by approaching one gets one's mind polluted. . . .

16. By the exercise of the breath-control.

. . . The characteristic of the controlled is—when there are currents of air in and out in the inner part of the body like that of a tortoise, when his senses get cleared from impurities, then the breaths are thought to be controlled. Then the breathing air is to be released by nose very slowly so that even a petal of a lotus, put in the nostril does not waver. . . .

17. He should mutter the Gāyatrī hymn addressed to Rudra, and Bahurūpa.

. . . Why Gāyatrī? This hymn, sung of, saves the singer. . . .

Now what is the result of touching, breath-control and muttering? The answer is sinlessness. . . .

18. Of one whose mind is free from sins. . . .

19. Of one who wanders.

. . . As begging is practised, penance should be practised, one should wander and acquire penance; that means, he should not stay (in a place). . . .

20. Thereby he gains yoga.

. . . Yoga is that which is started by one who has withdrawn one's mind (from the objects of senses). By which process it acts? By degrees. By which means it acts—by penance. . . .

Here the question is—is this Tantra intended for some material need? The answer is—no. It is intended for yoga. Because it is said that though the stage after yoga is itself a peculiar end, like a (coloured) screen in the theatre it (the mention of miraculous powers), begins for inducing the disciples— . . .

21. He gains the (miraculous) powers of seeing, hearing, thinking and knowing from a distance.

. . . There the knower is the Siddha, knowledge is his (extra-ordinary) success in the act of knowing (all śāstras). The inclinations or mental operations are the knowables. These begin spontaneously when he attains spiritual success. . . .

22. Omniscience.

. . . There the knower is the Siddha, knowledge is success in the shape of knowledge. And the knowables are effect, cause and the Siddhas. So one's power of knowing is taken in the sense of innumerable knowables in various ways. And his knowledge is expressed in all directions like the sun on the crystal stone. Now the question is—"Is this Siddha (the enlightened Sādhaka) satisfied with only knowledge and does he remain like a lame person or has he also active power or not?" The answer is—yes, he has. Because it is said—

23. The possession of swiftness of thought.

Here as it comes from outside, the power of knowing all is said. . . . The answer is—as the mind has swiftness and the function of doing quickly, so this

Siddha has the power of doing quickly. Because of (the efficacy of) penance the inclination of the Siddha is not like that of Prajāpati whose inclination is followed by execution. But (as a result of penance) the Siddha has his character grown out of his inclination, because execution (of any action) is stronger than inclination in him. As soon as he resolves "I shall do," the thing is done. Whenever he resolves, "I shall destroy," it is destroyed. How? Because of the unobstructed nature of his vision and active power. . . .

Now what is to be done by the Siddha? Or how does he do it? Hence it is said—

24. The quality of assuming forms at will.

. . . He assumes forms, according to his desires, both in quality and quantity. His assuming forms beginning with earth etc., is again regulated by his Self. And because of the supremacy of the organs, wherever he assumes forms, his organs beginning with "buddhi" gain scope of work. . . . By his power of supremacy he is identical with Maheśvara. . . .

25. He wins the faculty of expatiation, i.e., the possession of transcendent supremacy even when organs are not employed. . . .

26. The state of possessing special power.

Here this (Sādhaka) becomes the possessor of an active power by virtue of a special quality. When he acquires the excellence of Maheśvara beginning with seeing and ending with the faculty of expatiation as a result of the grace of God, he becomes the possessor of an active power by virtue of the special quality within himself. . . . Here "cha" is used in the sense of imposing visual and active power (upon the aspirant). Thus here as this Siddha is said to be possessor of power of assuming forms at sweet will and of transcendent supremacy even when all organs are not employed, he is explained as possessing mastery, pervasiveness and a special quality in the forms, made by himself. Thus after reaching the state of Yoga, by the grace of God the qualities come to him.

Here ends the principal section on excellences.

Now does this siddha (enlightened soul) possess the power of mastery and pervasiveness over the forms, made even by others, in the shape of devas (gods), men and birds? Yes—he has (the power). Because it is said—

27. And all become controlled by this (*siddha*). . . .

28. And he becomes uncontrollable to them.

. . . (The Siddha) becomes superior (to all), gains the best status and becomes distinct (from all). He is uncontrollable. . . . The disciple becomes powerful by (the power of) the Guru and is not taken over.

29. He enters into all.

. . . Though he is the pervader of his knowledge and action, he (Siddha) is able to make him unconscious by the exercise of his power.

Now is this Siddha liable to be overpowered by them or not? The answer is—no.

30. He is not to be overpowered by any of them.

. . . The Siddha becomes superior, (to all paśu-s), the best and distinguished person. . . . He attains the quality of being above the stage of being overpowered. He exists not like the residue of a disease. . . .

Now the question is—is he able only to overpower like a Yakṣa, rākṣasa or a demon? Or is he able to kill or affect anybody with pain? The answer is—he is able. Because it is said—

31. And all become liable to be killed by him.

. . . When the Siddha gains qualities and excellences, all are liable to be killed by him.

Now is this Siddha liable to be killed by them? No. Because it is said—

32. He is not to be killed by them.

. . . Being thus equipped with qualities and excellences the Siddha is not to be killed by them. Thus is explained the power of mastery and pervasiveness over the forms in the shape of bodies of gods etc., also made by others. . . .

33. Fearless.

. . . Hence he has not fear for the past, present and future and so he is fearless.

But the question is—with the destruction of Brahmā and others also who are fearless, destruction (of the world) is heard of. So it (the excellence of the Siddha) can not be eternal because of fearlessness. Or what is the characteristic of the fearless? So it is said—

34. Indestructible.

. . . But this man is said to be eternal because of his union with the eternal excellence of Maheśvara. Like the royal treasury and like the commodities of a householder (who lives with his family).

Now whether this (Siddha) wears out with old age or not, because even Yayāti and other gods are found to be worn out with age. Or what is the characteristic of an indestructible one? So it is said—

35. He is without old age.

. . . Now even gods and others who are above the state of old age are found to meet death before the destruction (of the world). Now is this Siddha free from death or not? Or what is the special feature of being free from (wrinkles of) old age? That is why it is said—

36. Death-less.

... He is free from death because of his power of assuming forms at will and of expatiation. So he is called death-less. . . .

37. And he moves unobstructed everywhere. He knows no obstruction even from Maheśvara, in all objects of his desire where he is inclined.

38. Being equipped with all these qualities he becomes the Great chief of the Gaṇas of Mahādeva.

He becomes the Great chief of the Gaṇas of Bhagavān Mahādeva when he becomes equipped with all these eight qualities, marks of spiritual success, as mentioned before—viz., the state of being uncontrollable, the state of being not to be overpowered, the state of being not to be killed, fearlessness, indestructibility, freedom from old age and death and unobstructed movement. His greatness consists in his superiority to all paśus because of supremacy of his excellence. . . .

Source: *Pāśupata Sūtram with Pañchārtha-bhāṣya of Kauṇḍinya*, translated by Haripada Chakraborti (Calcutta: Academic Publishers, 1970).

Selections from the *Gorakṣa Śataka*

Om, the beginning of the One Hundred (verses) of the Haṭha Yoga of Gorakṣa!

1. I bow down to the venerable guru (who is) supreme bliss, embodiment of his own bliss; simply by means of proximity to whom the body becomes nothing but knowledge and bliss.
2. Who (= That Yogī) by reason of (his practice of) *ādhārbandha* and the other (postures), in the rays of the inner steady light of his soul is highly praised as a Yogī and as the essence of the reckoning of time (manifested) in the *yugas* and *kalpas* (or, as reality on account of his making time consisting of yugas and kalpas), in whom (= who) the primeval Lord himself, the ocean of the bliss of knowledge took form, who (= who above) is superior to qualities both manifest and unmanifest (i.e., matter), him (= who, that guru) Śrī Mīnanath, I revere continually.
3. Having saluted his guru with devotion, Gorakṣa describes the supreme knowledge, desired by Yogīs, bringing about supreme bliss.

4. With desire for the benefit of Yogīs, Gorakṣa proclaims (the) One Hundred (verses) by the knowledge of which is surely brought about the highest state.
5. This (by which) the mind is turned away from (sensual) enjoyments, and (is) attached to the supreme spirit, (is) a ladder to final release; this (is) a cheating of death.
6. O excellent men! Practice Yoga, the fruit of the-tree-of-wishes, the sacred word whose branches (punning "schools") are frequented by birds (punningly called Brāmans, *dvīja*), (which) brings to an end the misery of world.
7. Postures, control of the breath, withdrawal of the senses from their external objects, fixing of the mind upon a single object, abstract meditation and identification of self with the object of meditation, these they say, are the six stages of the Yoga.
8. (There are) as many postures as (there are) species of living beings. The distinctions between them all Śiva (alone) fully understands.
9. Every single one of the 8,400,000 (of postures) has been described (by Śiva). From them eighty-four postures have been selected by Śiva.
10. From amongst all these (eighty-four) postures these two have been selected: the first, "the perfect posture" (*siddhāsana*); the second "the lotus posture" (*kamalāsana*).
11. The Yogī should press firmly the heel of the (left) foot against the perineum and the right foot just above the male organ, keeping the body fixedly erect, immovable; the senses under control; and with motion a gaze should look at the spot between the eyebrows. This (posture), which is the opener of the door of release, is called the perfect posture (*siddhāsana*).
12. And having placed the right foot upon the left thigh, and likewise the left (foot) upon the right thigh, and having grasped firmly the great toes with the hands crossed from behind (and) fixing the chin on the chest, (the Yogī) should gaze at the tip of the nose. This (posture), the destroyer of diseases and mental and physical disturbances is called the lotus posture (*padmāsana*).

The *Haṭhayogapradīpika* gives a second padmāsana, which the commentary attributes to Matsyendranāth. "Place the feet on the thighs, with the soles upwards, and place the two hands on the thighs, palms upwards. Gaze on the tip of the nose, keeping the tongue pressed against the root of the teeth of the upper jaw, and the chin against the chest, and raise the air up slowly (pull the *apana vāyu* gently upward.) This is called *padmāsana*, the destroyer of all diseases. It is difficult of attainment by everybody, but can be learned by intelligent people in this world."

13. How can Yogīs, who do not know the six centers (*cakra*), the sixteen props (*ādhāra*), the 300,000 ("channels," *nāḍī*) (and) the five sheathes (*vyoma*) in their (own) body, attain perfection (in Yoga)?
14. How can those Yogīs who do not know their own body (as) a house of one column (with) nine doors, and (as presided over by) five tutelary divinities, attain perfection (in Yoga)?
15. The four-leaved (lotus) should be the *ādhāra*, and the six-leaved the *svādhiṣṭhāna*. In the navel (is) the ten-leaved (lotus) and in the heart the twelve-leaved (lotus).
16. The sixteen-leaved (lotus) should be in the throat; similarly the two-leaved (lotus) between the eyebrows; in the hole-in-the-skull, in the great path, the one-thousand-leaved lotus).
17. *Ādhāra* is the first cakra; *svādhiṣṭhāna* the second; *yonisthāna*, between these two, is named *kāmarūpa*.
18. And the *gudasthāna* (is) the four-leaved lotus called *ādhāra*. In the midst of it is said to be the *yoni*, the "eye of love," praised by adepts.
19. In the midst of the *yoni*, with its face towards the back, there stands the great liṅga: Who knows the disk of light, like a luminous jewel, in its head, (is) an adept.
20. Flashing even like forks of lightning, looking like molten gold, the triangular place (*yonisthāna*) of fire (is) situated below the *membrum virile*.
21. Having seen that, the supreme light unending, shining in all directions, in samādhi, the adept does not experience (any more) transient existence.
22. By means of the word *sva*, prāṇa arises; the resting place of that prāṇa (is) svādhiṣṭhana. For it is from this very place, the svādhiṣṭhāna (that) the meḍhra is named.
23. Where the kanda (uterus?) is strung on the suṣumṇā, like a jewel on a thread, that region of the navel is called *maṇipūrakam*.
24. The soul wanders only so long as it does not find the Real in the great twelve-spoked cakra (where there is) freedom from (the fruits of) merit and demerit.
25. Below the navel and above the male organ (is) the *kandayoni* shaped like the egg of a bird. There (are) the origins of the seventy-two thousand nāḍis.
26. Among these thousands of nāḍis seventy-two have been specially noted. Again, among these ten carriers of the praṇa are designated as the most important.
27. *Iḍā* and *piṅgalā* and also the third *suṣumṇā*, *gāndhārī*, *hastijihvā*, *pūṣā*, and also *yaśasvinī*.

28. *Almabuṣā*, *kuhūś*, and also *śaṃkhinī* the tenth are taught (authoritatively as the ten chief nāḍis). The centers containing these nāḍis should be known always by Yogīs.
29. Iḍā (is) situated on the left side, piṅgalā on the right, and suṣumṇā in the mid region (e.g., between them); and gāndhārī in the left eye;
30. And the hastijihvā in the right (eye) and pūṣā in the right ear, yaśasvinī in the left ear, and likewise the alamhuṣā in the mouth:
31. And Kuhuś in the region of the linga and in the mūlādhāra the śaṁkhinī. Thus are the ten nāḍis (each) attached to a door (of the body).
32. Iḍā, piṅgalā and suṣumṇā in the path of the prāṇa are connected. (They are) always the conductors of the prāṇa. (Their) presiding deities are the moon, the sun and fire.
33. (The breaths are) prāṇa (air of breathing), apāṇa (air of the rectum), samāna (digestive air), udāna (air in the throat), vyānā (air circulating through the body), nāga (air of eructation), kūrma (air of blinking), similarly kṛkara (air of sneezing), devadatta (air of yawning) (and) dhanañjaya.
34. Prāṇa always lies in the chest (heart), apāna in the region of the rectum, samāna is in the region of the navel; udāna moves in the midst of the throat.
35. But the vyānā pervades the (whole) body. The five airs beginning with prāṇa are said to be chief; the other five airs are nāga, etc.
36. Nāga is said to be the air (that functions in) eructation; kūrma in winking; kṛkara (is) known as causing sneezing, (and) devadatta in yawning.
37. Dhanañjaya, pervading the whole (body) does not quit even the dead (body). These (prāṇas), vital functions, wander through all the nāḍis.
38. As a (wooden) ball struck by the hand-club flies up, so the jīva struck (in turn) by prāṇa and apāna, does not rest (is kept moving).
39. Because the soul is under the control of prāṇa and apāna, it moves up and down through the left and right paths (iḍā and piṅgalā). Because of restlessness it is not perceived (clearly).
40. As a hawk tied with a string, even though it flies (away) is drawn back; so the jīva, bound by the guṇas, is controlled by prāṇa and upāna.
41. Apāna pulls prāṇa and prāṇa pulls apāna (alternately); an adept in Yoga causes the union of these two, lower and upper (airs).
42. With the sound of "ha" jīva (in the form of prāṇa) goes out; with the sound of "sa" (in the form of apāna) it enters (the body) again. The jīva repeats continually that mantra "*haṁsa, haṁsa.*"

43. The jīva recites continually this mantra, twenty-one thousand six-hundred times in a day and a night.
44. The gāyatrī called ajapā (is) the giver of liberation to Yogis; simply with the desire to recite this (*gāyatrī*) is he freed from all demerit.
45. Knowledge like this, repetition like this, insight like this neither was nor shall be.
46. The gāyatrī is sprung from Kuṇḍalinī and supports the prāṇa. Knowledge of the prāṇa is the great knowledge. Who knows this is an adept.
47. Above the kanda Kuṇḍali-śakti forms an eight-fold coil. She remains there constantly with her mouth (face) covering the "door of Brahmā."
48. Having covered with her face that door by which (the soul), free from disease, should go to the seat of Brahmā, the goddess (Kuṇḍalinī) lies asleep.
49. By the mind aroused through the union of fire (*buddhi*) and prāṇa (Kuṇḍalinī) is drawn upward through the suṣumṇā as a needle draws a thread.
50. Through the suṣumṇā (she), aroused through union with fire, goes upwards, like a serpent, auspicious, gleaming like a filament of a lotus.
51. As one might open a door by force with a key, so the Yogī may break open the door of release by means of Kuṇḍalinī.
52. Having closed the two hands firmly, having taken the lotus posture, having pressed down the chin on the chest, (and) it (Kuṇḍalinī) having been looked at; he should expel again and again the apāna breath after he (has filled) it in; he attains at the time of expelling the prāṇa unequalled knowledge through the awakening of Śakti.
53. One should rub his limbs with the perspiration that results from (the above) effort. Let him drink milk and abstain from bitter, acid and salty (food).
54. (He should be) chaste, one who eats little, an abstainer from worldly pleasures, a practiser of Yoga. After a year he will have perfected this skill. One must have no doubt concerning this.
55. One (by whom) very soft, sweet, good-tasting (food), leaving one fourth of it, is taken with enjoyment, is called *mitāhāra*.
56. Kuṇḍalinī-śakti, coiled eight times above the kanda (is) said to be the giver of release to Yogīs and of bondage to the uninitiated.
57. That Yogī is ready for release who knows *mahāmudrā, nabhomudrā, uḍḍīyāna, jalandhara* and *mūlabhanda.*
58. The purification of the collection of the nāḍis, the moving of both the moon and the sun, and also the drying up of the liquids of the body, is called mahāmudrā.
59. Having rested the chin on the chest, and pressing for a long time the yoni with the left great toe, with the two hands grasping the extended right foot,

having filled with breath both sides of the abdomen and having held it, one should expel it slowly. This is said to be the very great mudrā, the destroyer of the diseases of men.

60. Having practiced it first with the iḍā and then with the piṅgalā an equal number of times, he should discontinue the mudrā.
61. (There is) neither wholesome nor unwholesome (food). All tastes (are) indeed tasteless. Even deadly poison (food) (when) eaten is digested as if it were nectar.
62. His diseases, consumption, leprosy, constipation, enlargement of the spleen, decrepitude go to destruction who practices mahāmudrā.
63. This mahāmudrā has been described, which secures all kinds of success for men. It should be kept secret by all means. It (is) not to be revealed to all sorts of people (literally, "any one"),
64. By turning the tongue over backwards into the hollow above the throat and by fixing, the sight between the eye-brows the khecarīmudrā is performed.
65. Neither disease nor death nor sleep nor hunger nor fainting is there for him who knows the khecarīmudrā,
66. He is not troubled by affliction; he is not besmeared (bound) by the fruits of deeds, he is not troubled by death who knows the khecarīmudrā.
67. The *citta* wanders in space (*khe*) because the tongue having entered khe (the hollow above the throat) moves about. For that very reason the khecarīmudrā is highly valued by all adepts.
68. But the bindu is the cause of the body. In it arise all the channels which together constitute the body, from head to foot.
69. By whom the hollow in the top of the throat is sealed by khecarī, his bindu, even (though he be) embraced by a woman, does not fall.
70. While the bindu remains in the body, there is no fear of death. As long as the khecarīmudrā is continued, so long the bindu does not go down.
71. Even if the bindu has reached the fire (*yonisthānam*), it straightway returns (goes up) arrested by Śakti, by the yonimudrā.
72. Further, the bindu (is) of two kinds, pale-white and blood-red. The pale-white they call semen virile, the blood-red menstrual fluid.
73. Rajas (menstrual fluid) secreted in the place of the sun, resembling vermilion, and the bindu secreted in the place of the moon—the mingling of these two is very difficult to accomplish.
74. Bindu is Śiva, rajas (is) Śakti; bindu (is) the moon, rajas the sun; from the mingling of these two, verily, one obtains the highest state.

75. Then by moving Śakti, by vayu the rajas (is) impelled and united with bindu. Then (the body) becomes divine, wonderful in appearance.
76. *Śukra* (bindu) is joined with the moon, rajas is joined with the sun. One who knows (the means of) uniting the two is an adept.
77. Even as a great bird is able to fly without taking rest; so indeed *uḍḍīyāna* may become the lion (which is) the death of the elephant.
78. This *bandha* at the back of the abdomen and below the navel is called bandha of the uḍḍīyāna; there bandā (mudrā) is to be practised.
79. Because the jālandharabandha closes the network of channels (all the nāḍis) and stops the water from flowing down from the head; therefore, it destroys the host of disorders of the throat.
80. The jālandharabandha, characterized by the closing of the throat, having been performed, the nectar does not fall into the fire, nor is the air disturbed.
81. Having pressed the yoni with the back of the left heel, one should contract the rectum; (and then), draw the apāna upward—(thus) is the mūlabandha performed.
82. From the union of prāṇa and apāna, from the decrease of urine and faeces, even an old man becomes young by much (practice) of the mūlabandha.
83. Having taken the lotus posture, holding the body and neck steady, fixing the sight on the tip of the nose, in a secluded place, one should repeat the unperishable oṁ.
84. That supreme light, oṁ, is (that) in whose elements the worlds *bhūḥ, bhavaḥ* and *svaḥ* and the divinities moon, sun and fire exist.
85. In which the three times, the three Vedas, the three worlds, the three accents, and the three gods are situated, that, oṁ, is the supreme light.
86. In which action and desire and knowledge, Brahmī, Rāudrī and Vāiṣṇavī, the threefold śakti, is contained, that, oṁ, is the supreme light.
87. That oṁ, in which these three letters A, and likewise U and M, which has the bindu as its mark, exist, is the supreme light.
88. With the voice one should repeat that bījam; one should practice it with the body; with the mind one should remember it. That, oṁ, is the supreme light.
89. Whether (he be) either pure or impure, one who recites oṁ continually is not besmeared by sin, even as the leaf of the lotus (is not wet) by water.
90. So long as the air moves, bindu moves; (and) it becomes stationary (when the air) ceases to move. The Yogī should, therefore, control the air (and) obtain immovability.

91. As long as prāṇa remains in the body, life (jīva) does not depart. Its departure (is) death. Therefore, one should become proficient in restraining the prāṇa.
92. As long as prāṇa is held in the body, so long consciousness (*cittam*) (is) free from disease. What cause is there for fear of death so long as the sight (remains fixed) between the eyebrows?
93. Therefore, from the fear of death, Brahmā (is) intent on prāṇāyāma, as are also Yogīs and sages, Therefore, one should restrain the prāṇa.
94. The prāṇa goes out to a distance of thirty-six fingers through the left and right nostrils. Therefore it is called prāṇa.
95. When the whole group of nāḍis, full of secretions, is purified, then indeed the Yogī becomes capable of restraining the prāṇa.
96. Assuming the lotus posture, the Yogi should fill in the prāṇa through the left nostril; then, having held it as long as possible, he should expel it through the right nostril.
97. Having meditated on the circular image of the moon, nectar as white as curds (and) cow's milk, (or) of the colour of purest silver, one practising prāṇāyāma should find peace.
98. Having filled in the breath through the right nostril, one should fill the abdomen slowly; having held it according to the rules he should expel (it slowly) through the left nostril.
99. Having meditated on the circle of the sun, full of a mass of flame of fire burning very brightly in the navel, the Yogī who practices prāṇāyāma should find peace.
100. Meditating in turn on the two images, moon and sun, a (Yogī) should draw in the breath through the left nostril; he should expel it again through the other, according to the limit (of the times already explained): then having drawn in the breath through the right nostril, and having held it, he should expel it through the left nostril. After three months the group of nāḍis of the practicer becomes pure.
101. By cleansing the nāḍis the prāṇa (is) restrained as desired, the digestive fire (is) kindled, internal sound is heard (becomes manifest), (and) one becomes diseaseless.

Thus the completion of the one-hundred of Śrī Gorakṣa.

Source: George Weston Briggs, *Gorakhnāth and the Kānphata Yogīs* (Calcutta: Associated Press; reprint Delhi: Motilal Banarsidass, 1973).

Selections from the *Tēvāram*

THE LORD IS ALL THINGS

Appar VI.301.1 Civapuram

See the god!
See him who is higher than the gods!
See him who is Sanskrit of the North
and southern Tamil and the four Vedas!
See him who bathes in milk and ghee,
see the Lord, see him who dances, holding fire,
in the wilderness of the burning-ground,
see him who blessed the hunter-saint!
See him who wells up as honey
in the heart-lotus of his lovers!
See him who has the unattainable treasure!
See Śiva! See him who is our treasure
here in Civapuram!

Appar IV.54.8 Pukalūr

As water, as fire, as earth, as sky,
as the glorious rays of the sun and moon,
as the lord whom the Himalayan gods supplicate,
as the deity hard to comprehend,
the Lord of holy Pukalūr,
who dances in many places,
is the highest god among the gods.

Campantar I.134.4 Pariyalūr Vīraṭṭam

He who has no beginning in birth
is the brilliant god who makes
the beginning and end,
and the birth and flourishing
of those who are born.
He is the god who lives
Surrounded by fierce spirits
in the Vīraṭṭam Shrine
of the splendid holy town of Pariyalūr

NAṬARĀJA: LORD OF THE DANCE

Appar IV.81.4 Kōyil (Tillai)

If you could see
the arch of his brow,
the budding smile
on lips red as the *kovvai* fruit,
cool matted hair,
the milk-white ash on coral skin,
and the sweet golden foot
raised up in dance,
then even human birth on this wide earth
would become a thing worth having.

Campantar I.39.1 Vēṭkaḷam (Tiruvēṭkaḷam)

When our Lord who is both end and beginning
dances to the deep sound of the *mulavam* drum,
holding blazing fire in the hollow of his hand,
as the mountain's daughter watches,
the Gaṅgā's murmuring stream with foaming waves
flows over the cool crescent moon.
He who smears his body
with ash from the burning-ground
is our Lord who dwells
in Vēṭkaḷam's fine town.

Appar IV.2.6 Atikai Vīraṭṭāṉam

We belong to him whose light
is the flickering firebrand in the burning-ground;
the throbbing beat of the *tuṭi* drum
and his host of eighteen kinds of spirits
surround him;
the Vedic song that few may learn,
and, on the stage, the dance
that even the learned may not know—
all these, and the broad Keṭilam river, are his.
We fear nothing; there is nothing for us to fear.

Campantar I.134.5 Pariyalūr Vīraṭṭam

The skullbearer who dances
in the burning-ground for the dead,
the god who dances the *paṭutam* dance
in the cremation-ground,
is the Lord of the Vīraṭṭam shrine
in Pariyalūr of blossoming groves
and wise scholars of the sacred Veda.

Appar IV.121.1 Ārūr

The Lord of Ārūr,
who wears the *akṣa* beads
along with the snake,
is the dancer who delights
in performing to the band
of attendant goblins with gaping mouths,
who play the *kokkarai* and flute,
the lute and the *koṭukoṭṭi* drum.

THE BEGGAR

Campantar II.138 Valañcli

O god bright with a budding white smile,
you who live in Valañculi
where the large white egret
and the heron with open bill
look for prey among surging white waves,
tell me why you roamed the world,
carrying a dank white skull.

O you who smear the chalk-white ash
all over your body,
and live in Valañculi
where the wild goose walks
on fine sand, colored gold from the pollen
of full-bloomed lotuses,
tell me why, though the gods themselves praised you,
you begged for alms in a white skull.

O treasure and light
who holds the little fawn,
living in Valañcuḻi
where you end the troubles
of those who bathe in Ponni's swelling current,
fragrant with many flowers,
on the festival day of Pūcam,
tell me, why this pretense of poverty,
this begging with a disgusting white skull?

Appar VI.223 Āmāttūr

He came to us singing songs in varied rhythms,
and took us by force.
He shot the arrows of his eyes at us;
with speeches that stir up passion
he skillfully seduced us, made us sick with love.
The skullbearer god has mounted his swift bull;
wearing a skin, his body covered with white ash,
a sacred thread adorning his form,
come, see the Master as he goes riding where all can see him.
The Lord of Āmāttūr is a handsome man, indeed!

When he lingered at my door, wearing the white ash,
his spreading matted hair crowned with a white wreath,
singing the Kāntāram mode to the *vīṇā's* tune,
I asked: "What is your town,
O man with the throat dark as a sapphire?"
Pretending to be in pain, he entered my house.
Then, saying, "O girl with the slim waist,
if you wish to know my town, I'll tell you—
it is Āmāttūr, where bees buzz on the cool lotus flower,"
the Lord disappeared.

Bearing the axe, the skullbearer came
riding on a swift bull;
making sweet speeches, he entered our homes;
he won't take alms from us, nor will he leave.

Instead, he speaks only deceptions and wiles,
as if to seduce all who look at him.
The Lord of Āmāttūr, who will neither accept
the petty alms we offer him,
nor reveal his designs,
is a handsome man, indeed!

The white bull he rides is in no way inferior
to rolling chariots, horses, and elephants.
The dark-throated one with the fiery red form,
the god whom the Himalayan gods praise,
owns no wealth, yet is a rich man.
The Lord of Āmāttūr, who wears a tigerskin,
and a garland of cool blossoms,
and rides surrounded by his demons,
is a handsome man indeed!

We agree that you ride a truly excellent white bull.
Tell me, do you come from a town called Orriyūr?
Why do you stay? Or, if you wish to go,
why have you seduced us with a glance
of your forehead-eye?
O you who always torment us thus,
we think we know your town—
Ēkampam is its name.
Surely you leave us in anger, my Lord!
Our Lord of Āmāttūr is a handsome man, indeed!

In plain sight of all,
the man from Kāḷatti who carries a sharp axe
mounted his swift bull, appeared at my door,
entered my house, and begged for alms.
Yet when I rose to meet him, he disappeared
without a proper farewell.
"What town do you really come from?
Is it Turutti, or Palanam, or Neyttānam?"
The Lord of Āmāttūr, who has left me to suffer,
is a handsome man, indeed!

PAIN AND GRACE

Appar IV.79 Kur̄ainta Tirunēricai

Why was I born,
I who cared only for my pride,
I who was caught in women's snares,
I who failed to think of my dear kinsman,
my ambrosia, the world's beginning and end,
my Lord whose form bright as the sunset sky
lay buried within my heart?

Once, a slave of past karma,
I failed to remember my Lord.
Now, having gone mad,
I babble like a fool.
I cannot hold in my heart
the god who is all the goodness
that dwells in me.
Why was I born?

Cuntarar VII.51 Tiruvārūr

I know the nature of the disease
that afflicts me, makes me a sinner,
makes me stop loving and serving the Lord;
I hasten to worship him.
How long must I, a fool,
be parted from my Lord,
the one whom karma cannot bind,
great gem, my diamond,
my God in Ārūr?

How can I,
fool born into this miserable body
destined for death, bear to die,
parted from my Father who devoured the poison
to calm the distress of the suppliant gods
who were buried by the venom that arose
from the vast ocean rich in shells—
my God in Ārūr?

Appar V.133.9 Kaṭampūr

The Lord of the holy *karakkōyil* temple
in South Kaṭampūr,
the spouse of the Goddess,
mother of our Kaṭampaṉ—
his task is to save
even this lowly servant.
My task is only to serve.

Appar IV. 103.5 Ārūr (Tiruvārūr)

You destroyed the god who held the sugar cane bow
and gave happiness to the boy who wielded the axe
as his weapon.
Seeing these,
O Lord who lives in pretty Ārūr
surrounded by cool, blossoming groves,
how should I know your heart's pleasure,
and what should I ask of you?

Campantar II.176.6 Piramapuram (Cīrkāli)

Wherever his devotees are born,
into whatever form or birth,
to bless them with his grace
in that very form
is the nature of Śaṅkara,
my bull-riding Lord
with body bright as the white conch,
who lives in Piramapuram, cool with
groves of fragrant flowers.

Appar V.161.11 Kacci Ēkampam

Our Lord is the one
who bore down with his toe
when Rāvaṇa, Lanka's king,
lifted his hill.
And he is the one
who gave the demon the good course

when he cried in distress:
"Save me, O Ēkampan of Kacci!"

Cuntarar VII.21 Kacci Mērraḷi

O everlasting light burning bright,
I thought only of you.
You came to me,
and have never left me since.
Focus of all my thoughts,
Lord who dwells in the holy Western shrine,
Father, I will sing
no one but you.

I thought only of your feet.
At once you entered this carnal frame.
O my bright flame,
honey, sweet ambrosia,
King who dwells in the holy Western shrine,
I will joyfully sing
no one but you.

Cuntarar VII.23.2 Kalippālai

You who abide in Kalippālai,
wherever I, your servant,
think of you, you join me there
and grant me grace.
You are Gaṅgā's Lord
who severs my karmic bonds,
and takes me right here!

ACTS OF DEVOTION

Appar IV.81.5 Kōyil (Tillai)

Treasure our human birth as a blessing,
O dear devotees of him who blessed Arjuna
with the Pāśupata shaft!
Have we not been born to serve him,
to be possessed
by the dancer of Tillai's Ampalam hall,

who once set the three citadels
aflame with his arrow?

Campantar II.176 Piramapuram (Cīrkāli)

I beg you, good heart,
if you seek release,
think only of my Lord's holy feet.
Mouth, always sing the good fame
of the sweet ambrosia
of Piramapuram where wild geese live.
Eyes, always look upon
the Lord alone,
that he might show you his grace.

O mind, offer fresh flowers
only to the majestic holy feet
of the King who helps us overcome
the fear of death.
Tongue, keeping daily the good ritual path,
speak the praise
of the fire-hued god who lives
in Piramapuram of groves full of honey.

Campantar II.177.3 Cāykkāṭu

Good heart,
think of the Lord every day.
Who knows the course
of life and death?
If for my Lord of Cāykkāṭu alone
will my head daily bear flowers,
my ear hear his great name,
and tongue praise him in song,
good karma will surely be mine.

Appar IV.9 Tiruvaṅkamālai

Hands, join in worship,
strew fragrant flowers
on the Lord who binds

the hooded snake around his waist!
Hands, join in worship!

Of what use is the body
that never walked around
the temple of Śiva,
offering him flowers in the worship rite?
Of what use is this body?

Appar IV.20 Ārūr (Tiruvārūr)

O Father, you dwell in Tiruvārūr,
abounding in sacred waters
in which the whole world joyfully gathers
to bathe,
knowing: "To worship the Lord's feet with love
is to get rid of karma,"
and where women eager for water-play
swim and dive, and splash about,
and wash their hair.

Ayan of the lotus flower seat
and the slayer of Iraṇiyan
sought in vain to see the King of Tiruvārūr
in his flaming form.
I sought and found him
when I entered the hearts of his devotees
who worship and praise him,
and sing his ritual hymns.

Campantar I.86.7 Nallūr

The men who never leave Nallūr,
who lift up their hands in worship,
crying, "Possess me!"
those whose hearts rest in the shade
of the feet of our Lord
whom the Himalayan gods praise as their king,
will no longer be perplexed.

Campantar I.89.3 Erukkattampuliyūr

Karma cannot touch
those who can cry, "Lord of the gods!
God, bull rider, madman who is
man, woman, and in-between,
moon-crowned god,
our King who lives in Erukkatampuliyūr's
shrine, which we revere!"

Campantar I.35.3 Vīlimiḻalai

The devotees who know
how to weep,
to dance and sing and rise, and again
fall at the father's feet,
to worship Vīlimiḻalai—
they are worthy servants of the Lord.

Cuntarar VII.22.3 Palamaṇṇippaṭikkarai

Dance, lovers of Śiva,
become devotees of the Lord, crown yourselves
with dust from his feet!
Give up worldly life, end your suffering,
O devotees, gather together,
go straight to Palamaṇṇippaṭikkarai,
and sing of the place!

Appar V.135.81 Iṉṉampar

Our Lord of Iṉṉampar keeps account
of those who worship him
with flowers and praise,
and weep for love of him,
and cry out in their love,
as well as
those who waste their days
unaware of him.

Appar V.177.8 Kuraṅkāṭuturai

O devotees who have joined our group
out of love,

dance, weep, worship him,
sing his feet,
gather at Kuraṅkāṭuturai,
place of our Lord!

Appar V.162 Kacci Ēkampam

Let us hasten to make a proper pilgrimage,
to offer worship at Ēkampam
in Kacci of flowering groves,
abode of the Lord with the dark throat,
the eight-armed, three-eyed god,
chanter of the Veda,
first among the gods.

Source: Indira Viswanathan Peterson, *Poems to Śiva: The Hymns of the Tamil Saints* (Princeton: Princeton University Press, 1989).

Selections from the *Tiruvācakam* of Māṇikkavācakar

HUMAN SITUATION

O boundless One
Who transcends my thoughts,
I with my evil karma
don't know any way to praise Your great glory.
As grass, shrub, worm, tree,
As many sorts of animals, birds, snakes,
As stone, man, demon, *gaṇas*,
As mighty *asuras*, ascetics, gods—
among these immobile forms,
in every kind of birth,
I was born and grew weary
O great Lord!
O Truth!
Today I saw Your golden feet and was released. (1: 24–32)

Alone,
dashed by afflicting huge waves
in the great sea of births,

Without anything to hold on to,
agitated by the winds
of lips red like sweet ripe fruit,
caught in the jaws
of the big shark called lust,
Pondering, pondering,
"How shall I escape now?"
I grasped the five-lettered raft,
And you O God,
showed foolish me,
who was just (passively) lying there,
the abundant shore,
which has neither beginning nor end,
And You enslaved me. (5: 27)

In this mad world
of hoarded wealth,
of wives,
of children,
of family,
of learning,
where birth and death fluster the mind,
Go to God
Whose enlightening wisdom dispels this perplexity
And hum to Him, O Kingly bee! (10: 6)

THE GREAT DEITY ŚIVA

O Lord Śiva,
who severed my births,
You dwell right here in southern Peruntuṟai
where the celestial ones can't know You.
Our Lord,
on that day when You looked at me
You enslaved me,
in grace entered me,
and out of love melted my mind. (38: 7)

Look here, don't leave me!
O real One,
who wears skulls as ornaments,
who is adorned with a cluster of flowers,
who wreathes himself with a long garland of entrails,
who smears himself with ashes,
who wears red sandal paste. (6: 30)

O King of loving devotees!
O Father who owns me as Your slave!
You entered me body and soul,
abiding in me
so that all my bones become soft and melt.
O Light of truth who dispels the darkness of falsehood!
O abiding, clear, calm Sea of ambrosia!
O Śiva who dwells in holy Perunturai!
O unique Consciousness
which is realized as standing firm,
transcending words and (ordinary) consciousness
O, let me know a way to tell of You! (22: 3)

We entered the crowded, wide tank.
We scooped up water and splashed while bathing.
And we sang about your foot.
See, O Lord, how we generations of devotees have flourished.

O One who is red like a blazing fire!
O One besmeared with white ashes!
O blessed One!
O Bridegroom of the slender-waisted Lady
whose wide eyes are black with collyrium!
O Lord,
because of Your sport of enslaving and granting grace
we've lived in all the ways
in which those who've been released live.
Watch over us so that we don't grow weary. (7: 11)

Let us praise
the Dancer,

who in good Tillai's hall
dances with fire,

who sports,
creating,
protecting,
destroying
this heaven and earth
and all else. (7: 12)

LOVE AND SERVICE

O Master!
I've seen how
those who possess great love
which melts their minds
think about You
and become united with Your feet.
Yet here I am
Lower than a village dog.
My heart dosen't grow tender.
I have a mind like stone.
I won't melt.
I'm here safe-guarding
this worm-infested sheath (of a body)
which stinks of flesh.
Oh, when will You put an end to this? (5: 56)

Ah, when shall I get to gaze upon
the unique One to whom no other compares,
Him who is fire, water, wind, earth, and ether,
Him whom others cannot understand?
With voice stammering,
a cataract of tears gushing forth,
hands joined in worship,
when am I going to adorn Him with fragrant flowers?
When shall I be united with my uncut Gem?
With mind melting, melting,
growing more and more tender—

standing, sitting, lying, rising,
laughing, weeping, serving, praising—
when shall I dancing do all these things?
With hair bristling, bristling,
When am I going to gaze upon His holy form,
which gleams like the sunset,
and enter (union) with Him?
When shall I be united with my uncut Gem? (27: 7–8)

MADNESS

While unperishing love melted my bones,
I cried.
I shouted again and again,
louder than the waves of the billowing sea,
I became confused,
I fell,
I rolled,
I wailed.
Bewildered like a madman,
intoxicated like a crazy drunk,
so that people were puzzled
and those who heard wondered,
wild as a rutting elephant which cannot be mounted,
I could not contain myself. (3: 150–156)

I don't know that I am me.
I don't know day from night.
He who lies beyond thought and speech
Made me into a frenzied madman.
The Master of the great angry bull,
the Brahmin
who dwells in enduring holy Perunturai—
I don't know the mischief he played on me!
O supreme Light! (34: 3)

Thinking only abut the feet
of the supreme One,
the Father,
the Master,

my mind melting with madness,
and wandering from place to place
saying whatever is consistent with that state of mind,
so that people say,
"This fellow is confused,"
everyone speaking his own mind—
when shall I thus die? (5: 3)

The King of all came and enslaved me.
We're not subject to anyone.
We don't fear anything.
We've joined His devotees.
We'll dive (into the sea of bliss) again and again
and cavort there with His devotees (5: 30)

Source: Glenn E. Yocum, *Hymns to the Dancing Śiva: A Study of Manikkavācakar's Tiruvācakam* (Columbia, Mo.: South Asia Books, 1982).

Selections from the *Svāyaṃbhūvasūtrasaṃgraha with the Commentary of Sadyojyoti*

I. Disquisition of the Soul

I bow to the Supreme Śiva, and to the Lord who ends [the cycle of rebirths]; and then I will speak about knowledge and dīkṣā; listen to these two subjects with utmost attention. (1)

And here, by the first quarter [of the stanza], Svayaṃbhū salutes Śiva who is endowed with śiva-ness characterised as the nature of agent and knower of all objects, who, for the sake of the souls, is the cause of destruction of obstacles, eliminates evil and gives liberation. Because the distinctive characteristic of Śiva belongs also to the liberated souls, [Svayaṃbhū says] "paramam (supreme)," [qualification which excludes the liberated souls,] since the realisation of śiva-ness has a beginning for them. [Thus the meaning of the first pāda is:] having saluted the supreme Śiva whose śiva-ness has no beginning. In the second [quarter of the stanza, Svayaṃbhū] salutes Nidhaneśa, his guru, in whom the bonds have been severed by Śiva's grace, in whom universal knowledge and action have been manifested, and who gives his grace to all. Then in the third [quarter] he announces his subject, knowledge, dīkṣā, etc., which is a subject-matter found in all tantras. And here in "jñānadīkṣe" a *dvandva* compound is used to signify the equal importance of both subjects. For one person knowledge is more important, for another dīkṣā is more important: knowledge is the main subject for one who undertakes the dīkṣā [of others] and the explanation [of the doctrine]; dīkṣā is the main subject for one who aspires to liberation.

And the mention of the purpose is placed below (stanza 2). By the announcement of the subject here undertaken, [done] by him seeing the purpose [contained in] the saying of his guru (stanza 2), [Svayaṃbhū] gives to understand that he also is an author regarding mentioning facts in some cases, regarding the division of the sayings and the summarising. And here summarising is not expressing the meaning of a long original text through a new short text, it is the formulation of a new text leaving aside the formulae which in the original text repeat auxiliary facts already told of a basic rite and which are obtainable from the meaning in the case of a derived rite, and leaving aside also the formulae mentioning the purpose. One may object that in the guru's formula (stanza 2) the knowledge is mentioned, whereas here there is a mention of dīkṣā and knowledge. We answer that not only in the guru's formula knowledge is mentioned, but also the dīkṣā will be dealt with below. Thus [the author] here reveals that in the initial formula [of the guru] (stanza 2) the word "knowledge" includes dīkṣā also.

By the fourth [part of the stanza Svayaṃbhū] places in a state of psychic fixation (*samādhi*), and maintains in that state, his disciples, the Vālakhilyas, etc., who have been prepared for that by the fall on them of Śiva's power (*śakti*) and by dīkṣā, who strive after knowledge and are fit for the charge [of receiving it]. Those whose mind is fixed are able to determine with reasoning the objective reality of Śiva.

[Having thus performed] the salutation to a deity and to his guru, [having made] the announcement of the subject, having placed in the state of psychic fixation and maintained in that state the mind of his disciples, the Vālakhilyas, in order to impart knowledge to them, [Svayaṃbhū] recites his guru's saying which summarises the meaning of all then tantras: "atha . . ."

Then in order to free the souls from the bonds, i. e. from mala, māyā and karman, in order to manifest their śiva-ness, from Śiva knowledge proceeds forth. (2)

"Atha (then)": immediately after the souls engaged in existence have been turned towards the end of their change of agent, an obstruction to their full-consciousness, immediately after that time, in order to grace them, knowledge proceeds forth [for them from Śiva]. The soul is pervading, eternal, similar to Śiva. The mala is the obstructer of her śiva-ness. Therefore its śiva-ness being obstructed by the mala, the soul cannot know an object to be known or accomplish a [right] action, without some means. For the soul which depends upon a means to achieve any experience, there is the bond called māyā, i.e. kalā, etc. Māyā is the matrix of the universe. The bond which is produced by māyā is named after her. The karman is that which is experienced by the soul, equipped with the instrument of experience and having the intention to have an experience; it is called dharma or adharma. Mala, māyā and karman are a treble bond of the soul, because, when the soul is united with them, her śiva-ness is not manifested with regard to everything simultaneously. In order to free the soul from this treble bond, and in order to manifest the śiva-ness, from Śiva, because of his desire to bestow his grace, knowledge proceeds forth. On the contrary the knowledge which proceeds forth from bound souls and from bonds produces a reinforcement of the bonds, because it is manifested by bonds and is a bond itself. But Śiva is different from the bound souls and from the bonds, he is the antagonist of the bonds and he is endowed with all powers. What proceeds forth from him has the ability and the strength to eliminate these bonds. For an entity of a certain class, the power of which is obstructed, there is an entity of the same class, the power of which is not obstructed and which manifests the power [of the first]. Śiva is of the same class as the soul. It is appropriate that Śiva whose śiva-ness is not obstructed, emits forth his own knowledge in order to manifest the obstructed śiva-ness of the soul. This knowledge [of Śiva] is twofold, consisting of speech and of thought. That one which is thought, riding the other which is speech, applies itself to objects.

One may object that this [manifestation of śiva-ness] is the fruit of dīkṣā. That is true, but that knowledge [proceeding from Śiva] informs the preceptor of the aim and the means to achieve [dīkṣā]. And [the preceptor], knowing thus the aim and the means, in order to realise dīkṣā for the souls deserving grace, is able to use the means.

And the upholders of liberation propose knowledge alone for achieving liberation, in all the cases. Now liberation cannot exist without performing [any rite]. Even in the case [it is told that] "liberation comes from knowledge alone" the observance of instructions regarding what is to be avoided, etc. is necessary.

Or in the sentence "from Śiva knowledge proceeds forth" jñāna means śakti; "power." And the śakti is two-fold, consisting of thought and dīkṣā. And as a ray of the sun, which sheds light on things, heats them also but by doing so does not lose its nature of light-giver, and thus is called "light-giver" in both its functions, in the same way Śiva's śakti is called "knowledge" as she sheds light on things, and is called "dīkṣā" when she removes the bonds and manifests the śiva-ness of the soul; even in that case she does not lose her nature of knowledge and she is called "knowledge" in both her forms.

The property to be united with the bonds, i.e. mala, māyā and karman, is the characteristic property of the soul deserving grace. And this property is mentioned with the intention that it may be partially or entirely possessed. There is grace for souls who are united with mala only, for some who are united with mala and karman, for some who are united with mala and māyā, for some who are united with mala, māyā and karman. Why? Because this property is mentioned with the intention that it may be partially or entirely possessed. In fact even the souls who are not connected with kalā will be said deserving purification and awakening. And these souls are two-fold, Vijñānākalā, "freed from kalā through knowledge," and Pralayākalā, "freed from kalā during pralaya." For these two there is no māyā or its products. The souls freed from kalā through knowledge have consumed their karman; for them there is only mala. For the souls freed from kalā during pralaya there is mala and karman. Among these akala souls of both categories, those who receive grace non-accompanied with a function, are equal to Śiva; those who receive grace accompanied with a function, are Mantras and Vidyeśvaras above the domain of māyā. Grace will be possible also for souls united with mala and the products of māyā. When karman has been consumed by some means, the bond of the products of māyā goes to resorption in its own material cause. Since the śakti of the supreme Lord does not have any fixed time for bestowing grace, since [the mala] does not have any fixed time for coming to the consummation of its charge of obstructing the śakti of consciousness in the soul, there is possibility of grace for that soul [united with mala and māyā] sometimes only in the period of the advent of the resorption [of māyā products]. And for souls like us and others who stand in the realm of māyā, etc., i.e. for Mantras and Vidyeśvaras as well as souls united with mala, māyā and karman, there is grace, since there is grace even for Mantras and Vidyeśvaras who stand in the realm of māyā, etc., who are united with kalā, etc. and who enjoy experiences. . . .

That [knowledge] born from the lotus-like mouth of Śiva, though unique, becomes manifold through being divided in superior and inferior varieties on account of its objective support. (3)

But this knowledge is unique, because of the revelation of the uniqueness of Śiva's śakti. Being unique, nevertheless it becomes manifold. "Born from the lotus-like face of Śiva": Śiva's *vaktra* means Śiva's śakti consisting in manifestation and protection; or that which is the vaktra, "mouth" of a guru is the mouth of Śiva, because Śiva has taken residence in the guru. Śiva enunciates knowledge through the guru. Knowledge is [thus] of two kinds. Therefore [it is compared] with a lotus, because both are full-blown and pure. [The knowledge] is "-udbhavam" i.e. has proceeded forth from that vaktra.

Therefore by what differentiation does knowledge become manifold? . . . That [śakti of Śiva] which consists of knowledge is superior, firstly, when it sheds light on the pure path, and inferior, when it sheds light on the impure path. The knowledge which sheds light on the pure path is again superior and inferior, as it shows Śiva on one side and Sadāśiva, etc. on another side, etc. The knowledge which sheds light on the impure path is also superior and inferior as it shows the bound soul on one side and māyā on another side, etc. That [śakti of Śiva] which consists of dīkṣā is also superior as "comprising total accomplishment" and inferior as "comprising [intermediary] enjoyments." The naiṣṭhika one is again superior and inferior as "having no seed" and "having seed." The bhautika one also is superior as dealing with Śiva and inferior as dealing with enjoyments in different worlds. That which consists of speech also is a variety of [Śiva's śakti] which consists of knowledge. It is also one, because of the uniqueness of the letter-matrix. Though it is one, through differentiation in superior and inferior it becomes manifold. This knowledge of Śiva [consisting of speech] is superior, as it is issued by Śiva without dependence from [the form of] a preceptor. Rudra's knowledge is inferior, as it is issued by Śiva, taking residence in Rudra, under this form. Śiva's knowledge is again superior and inferior according to the course of its proceeding forth, the course of worship and the course of disciples. Rudra's knowledge also is superior and inferior for the same reason. There are also superior and inferior varieties for subsidiary texts. In these conditions knowledge is again superior and inferior, as it becomes manifold [after being one].

In the case of that [knowledge] which, though one, becomes manifold, manifoldness is not told as a main property, but as a superimposed property. What is the origin of the superimposition? "on account of the objective support": [knowledge, Śiva's śakti, is manifold] under the influence of the property of its artha. Now the artha is manifold. Because of this manifoldness, knowledge also becomes manifold. Firstly, for that [śakti of Śiva] which consists of thought the artha is the object which is manifold. Then for [that śakti of Śiva] which consists of dīkṣā the artha is the fruit aimed at and the means of accomplishing it, i.e. mantras, etc.; and that is manifold. For that [śakti of Śiva] which consists of speech the artha is the object [signified by words] and the subject matter of the composition; and that is manifold. Thus because of the manifoldness of its object knowledge becomes manifold. . . .

The Lord of gods [Nidhaneśa] having thus summarised the supreme real intent of the teaching in two utterances, enunciated it again in an extended form. (4) . . .

Then the soul is non-devoid of mala, bound or liberated through dīkṣā. It should be known as going through three states, isolated, united with kalā, freed from mala. (5)

"Atha": the commentary in extended form comes immediately after the summary of the real intent of the teachings. The soul mentioned in the beginning of this [summary] of the real intent of the teachings is [now] analysed. It goes through three states: non-devoid of mala, bound, liberated. "Avimalah" means "non-devoid of mala," i.e. extremely attached to mala. This same soul again, being united with mala and coloured by karman, is "bound" by the bond of kalā, etc. This same soul again is "liberated" from mala, etc. through that which is called dīkṣā and which is a means of realisation [of liberation].

[One could object:] there is no difference between the soul non-devoid of mala and the bound soul, because they have a bond, as there is the quality of being non-devoid of mala in both of them; there is no difference between the liberated soul which has a knowledge of a bound one and the liberated soul which is Śiva. [To answer to that, Nidhaneśa] says the difference: "*kevalaḥ sakalo' malaḥ* (isolated, united with kalā, freed from mala)." The soul non-devoid of mala is a soul who, being devoid of the group of kalā, etc., is isolated [i.e. liberated], even though it has a bond.

The bound soul is a soul who, being united with the group of kalā, etc. is "united with kalā," even though it is non-devoid of mala. The liberated soul whose knowledge is that of bound souls is united with mala, but the liberated soul who has the nature of Śiva is freed from mala.

The soul has been thus described but not in details. Now an exposition of the same with the maximum of details is done up to the end of the chapter.

The bound soul which is non-tied to kalā is deprived of consciousness, ubiquitous, eternal, devoid of auxiliaries, devoid of action, non-sovereign, subject to occultation, devoid of power, fit for purification, fit for awakening. (6)

This is the description of the meaning of [the word] *kevala*, "isolated." Consciousness which consists of knowledge and the quality of agent, is the power of the soul. It is eternal. In the immediate context only its form of knowledge is intended. It is not fully manifested, because this soul is obstructed by mala. It does not apply to the objects. Thus this soul is acetana, "deprived of [fully manifested] consciousness." It is vibhu, "ubiquitous" according to the revelation about the manifestation of consciousness, because wherever there is a factor of manifestation, there will be a secondary manifestation of consciousness, as [a manifestation of consciousness] qualified by a particular state is revealed. And it is this state which will have an end [not the consciousness]. Therefore this soul is nitya, "eternal." And the eternal is not fit to have an end by the end of a state. The soul does not have that non-eternity which is the resorption of other non-eternal entities born from a material cause, into their material cause. *Guṇahīna*: devoid of the guṇas which are kalā, etc., auxiliaries of the soul in the realisation of experience. This soul does not have the type of action done without instrument, because her power of action is obstructed. Thus it is "devoid of action." The sovereign-ship which is power, i.e. the faculty of ruling all the factors of action, is obstructed [in this soul] which is thus aprabhu "non-sovereign." Vyāghāta means an occultation coming from Śiva; this soul is subject to this occultation; thus it is "subject to occultation." This soul is not by itself able to apply its own power towards the objects, after having destroyed the mala; thus it is aśakta, "devoid of power." In that state this soul is śodhya, "fit to be purified" from mala itself by Śiva. And it is bodhya, "fit for awakening": having its set of powers closed, it must be made to have its set of powers open. . . .

Now I tell the soul, which is the agent fit for experience, which is bound by the bond consisting of kalā, etc. which bond, being such by its nature of inciter to experience, puts in motion towards many types of experiences. (8)

. . . A new object is presented here. *Bhoktṛ* means "able to perform the action of experience": the soul united with mala, connected to karman and turned by Śiva towards experience, is fit to perform the action of experience. Being such the soul is "bound by the bond of kalā, etc.)." [Bond] in what respect? "Bhojakabhāvena": as impeller to experience. That property itself to impel the agent to experience, makes kalā, etc. a bond. How is this bond qualified? "Nānābhogavisarpiṇā": which has the habit "visarpayitum" i.e. to put in motion the agent of experience towards many types of experiences to be accomplished. The soul bound by this bond of kalā, etc. is now told [by me through a composition of stanzas] told by the guru. This is a new object: a type of soul bound by a bond of such kind, binding in virtue of such property. . . .

The essence kalā, following Śiva's will, comes and sticks to this afore-mentioned, unchangeable [soul], intensely affected by mala. (9)

"Asya" means: for this akala soul, made inactive by dense mala. For the bound soul also there is intensity of its connection with mala. [But] because for that [bound soul] one sees the application of consciousness to some objects here and there, whereas such application does not occur for this [akala one], [this one is more] intensely united to mala. . . .

[One could object:] everyone sees that milk, etc. which takes different states is subject to alteration, i.e. transformation; it follows that the soul also may be subject to transformation, since it takes different states. Therefore [Nidhaneśa] says "avikāriṇaḥ": even though the soul takes different states, it is not subject to transformation. A transformation is the establishment of an individual which had a first state, as a new individual, its previous individuality being lost. But the soul whose power is made inactive by mala, takes a different state which is the manifestation of its power through a factor eliminating mala; therefore there is no transformation of it. For a pot the form of which is covered by a cloth, the manifestation of its form by some factor which removes the cloth, is not a transformation.

Thus, in order to remove the mala of this akala soul intensely bound by mala, firstly the essence kalā comes and sticks to it. And this kalā is not independent, because it is deprived of consciousness, but it follows Śiva's will. Afterwards the [essences (tattva] vidyā, etc. following Śiva's will come and stick to the soul. . . .

Having its consciousness fortified by kala, having a field of objects shown to itself by vidyā, being impelled to desire by rāga, by means of buddhi, etc. . . . (10)

The soul whose consciousness is udbalita, i. e. made able, manifested, by kalā which is the agent [of the manifestation]. Kalā manifests only the power of agent [in the soul], whereas vidyā, etc. manifest the power of knowledge. Vidyā itself is a factor of manifestation of that [power of agent], because that manifestation occurs after the activity of vidyā regarding the object of the action. There exists another group of essences, which is told to be a factor of manifestation of the same power of agent, because it helps the agent and the action. And this group has two forms, means of knowledge and fruit. When through it [the soul] sees a field of objects, it is a means of knowledge. When through the activity of the factors of action something final is accomplished, it is a fruit. Its form of means of knowledge will be told immediately. . . .

[One could object:] even though its power of agent is manifested by its association with kalā, the soul does not enter in activity with regard to an object it has not seen; and there is no seeing of the object without an instrument. . . . Vidyā shows the field of objects; thus it has the position of an instrument for the soul. And for the soul the field of objects is, on one side, directly, a transformation of the psychism in the form of pleasure, pain, delusion, coloured by sound, etc., on another side, indirectly, sounds, etc.

[One could object:] even though the soul has perceived its field of objects, it does not enter into activity, because it has no attachment. . . . When rāga has produced attachment in the soul, not otherwise, the soul takes as pleasure even an object of experience which overflows with pain and delusion, and strives to take possession of it.

The soul which has been thus set into activity by these three essences, produces the position of object of experience [for its field of objects] through instruments which are buddhi, etc. . . . Moreover time and fate are not mentioned here, because they act as impellers [of the soul] which is already set into activity. Time impels the soul already set into activity through instants, etc. Fate also controls the soul already set into activity [to go] where is the fruit of its actions. . . .

By Śiva's desire, before [dīkṣā], the infinite prime Śakti which resides in Śiva and gives śiva-ness, comes to the soul in its last birth. (16)

Impelled by Śiva's desire his śakti comes. Now śakti is Śiva's desire itself. Therefore how is that told? Even if there is non-difference of these two, there is no defect, because the author says "by Śiva's desire śakti comes" having in mind that firstly there is the action of Śiva's śakti called desire: "I give grace to this soul"; subsequently śakti comes [to that soul]. "Purā" i.e. before dīkṣā. "Anantā (infinite)": because she is not limited, as she has none of the two extremities which are characterised as birth and death, and because her activity is infinite. Because she is impelled by Śiva's desire, so that she will not be taken as a different entity residing in the soul and having the nature of a bond, she is told to be "śaivī" i.e. residing in the proper self of Śiva. . . . Mala's power has its function obscured by Śiva's śakti and goes to its end. That is the last birth. There is no other birth than this one.

By the advent of this śakti the mala of that [soul], cause of transmigration, flows away. When it has disappeared, there may be a desire to go towards the supreme, highest good. (17)

"Nipātāt" (by the advent) of this śakti [means:] by the relation of object of grace to bestower of grace. . . . firstly mala does not flow away by itself, nor does the bond give away its binding agency by itself. Then the soul is not the cause of mala's flowing away, because it is weaker compared to mala. And the soul is weak, since its śakti is obstructed by this very mala. Śiva's śakti is stronger than those two. Therefore by the advent of Śiva's śakti the mala "asya" i.e. of the soul "kṣarati" i.e. goes down. And this flowing away is understood from its effect which is the action of the soul to turn itself towards [the supreme good], because that was not seen before, since the soul had its power obstructed by mala. The flowing away bears only upon mala's action to lead [the soul] downwards, because it is qualified by "saṃsārakāraṇam": mala flows away as cause of transmigration. This is what has been told: "the property of mala to be a cause of transmigration, its action to lead [the soul] downwards comes to an end". Thus the dīkṣā is purposeful. . . .

The soul which by this process has gone to the superior liberation, because it is devoid of the beginningless mala, does not obtain any new existence. (19)

Karmayoga means a union with a succession [of events]: firstly there is union with Śiva's śakti, then union with the flowing away of the mala, then with the desire to go, then with the preceptor, then with dīkṣā, then with the state in which the bonds are severed. Thus by undergoing this succession [of events, a soul] has gone "to the superior liberation": kevalatā means the nature of the isolated one, i.e. isolation. This isolation is not superior, because even in this state there is a second. . . . But the isolation which is characterised by equality with Śiva is superior, because in this state nothing is second. . . . An effect is not produced without a cause. Even if there is karman the seed of a new existence is the impurity or mala. Since [the liberated soul] is devoid of this [seed], how will it go to another existence? There is an impurity which has a beginning; it is the illusion of five sorts, etc.; now it is seen that there is obtention of a new existence for a soul which is devoid of this [illusion]. Therefore the mention of the word "anādi- (without beginning)" is done to eliminate it. . . .

III. The Power of Grace

This unique [Śakti] is well-established in manifold divisions, following Śiva's desire; she rules the Lords of vidyās and avidyās; she shines in a domain which is ahead of bhava. (2)

One and same ray of the sun, which has the property to shed light and to open [flowers], being in contact with a lotus-bud, sheds light upon it and is, therefore, called "illuminator"; but when the bud has reached maturity and when, being in contact with it, it opens it, then it is called "opener." In the same way the one and same śakti of Śiva, who has the property of knowledge and action, is called "knowledge," when, being in contact with objects, she gives knowledge of them; and she is called "action," when through the same contact she is action with regard to them, being different from the activity signified by verbal root and having such characteristics as pushing upwards, etc. Though it is unique, it is well-established in manifold divisions, i.e. it is established in as many divisions as there are classes of conscious and unconscious things; and it is established in as many divisions as there are actions, differentiated by the order of their sequence, called creation, maintenance, resorption, obscuration and grace; it is established in as many divisions as there are means of realisation of the soul's aims, for instance, a body, etc.

for Śiva. "Śivecchayā": in the beginning there is activity of the Lord's śakti called "desire"; then the manifold śakti establishes itself in divisions; therefore, because actions have a sequence in time, when it is impelled by Śiva's desire, the śakti is told to be established in manifold divisions.

. . . since one sees that action is always preceded by knowledge, one should see as many differentiations of the śakti of knowledge, as there are for the śakti of action. And because Śiva is never non-connected with the śakti, we should understand that he has as many differentiations as his śakti. Because Śiva is seen to reside in beings having a body, sense-organs, etc., by the difference of these bodies, sense-organs, etc. of Śiva his śakti is again differentiated. Thus Śiva is possessed of parts because he is united with the parts of his śakti. But the ultimate truth is that Śiva is without parts, because he is devoid of any association with the parts of the bonds. . . .

This property of the śakti to be ruling resident everywhere has been thus told. Now the following matter has to be told. Is Śiva's śakti connected directly with all the beings, or directly with some, through intermediaries with others ? And what help does she give to those with whom she is connected? . . .

Some souls had their power strengthened by [Śiva's] desire to make them act and became able to dominate everything; they are the Vidyeśas, Ananta, etc., then others than them, whose power is immeasurable, then others than these, who are under the order [of the previous ones], souls without mala who give pure and impure fruits, then others than these affected with mala, accomplishing the desire of the Lord and from whom is born the whole world of moving and unmoving beings. (3–5). . . .

From Lord's śakti Mantras whose power is not vain, are issued; by Śiva's desire they act in the vast path ending in Śiva. (6)

. . . At first, for some souls, the nature of Mantra, called Śiva, characterised as omniscience and omni-action is covered by mala. This nature of Mantra is made manifest for those souls by Lord's śakti who destroy their mala. Therefore it is told that Mantras are born from Lord's śakti. . . .

A path is a road to a destination. But there is no such [road] to the Lord and there is no motion of the soul aiming at this destination, because both are ubiquitous. (7)

A path, in fact, is a road to a destination, for instance a village. Here the Lord is the destination. But there is no such [road] to him. Now an ultimate goal is revealed for the soul which goes [to the said destination].To realise this there will be a road. But there is no motion of the soul. Why is there no road to the Lord as destination and no motion of the soul? Because both are ubiquitous, since one has never seen a road to reach something which is ubiquitous, nor a motion of an ubiquitous entity. That is told in: "Since they are ubiquitous, the Lord and the soul have already attained each other. Why should we imagine a path leading one to the other?". . .

Since, if there is ubiquitousness, the possession of motion is not at all proper, nor the ubiquitousness if there is possession of motion, how can there really be a path regarding these two? (8) . . .

IV. The Path

Now, in order to eliminate the nature of bound soul, cause of the soul's bonds, and in order to manifest the nature of Śiva, the six-fold path is described. (1) . . .

What are these six kinds of path? And do they all go to the same place? Or do they diverge? To these questions the author answers:

The path of essences, the path of words, the path of phonemes, the path of worlds, the path of mantras and the path of kalās go all to a unique entity, Śiva. (2). . .

He is immeasurable, unexprimable, incomparable, without stain, subtle, ubiquitous, eternal, fixed, non-declining, he is the Lord. (3)

He is immeasurable, because he is infinite; he is unexprimable, because he is unknowable; he is incomparable, because nothing is similar to him; he is without stain, because he has no mala; he is subtle, because he is non-perceptible; he is ubiquitous, because he pervades [everything]; he is eternal, because he does not have any cause; he is fixed, because he has no motion; he is non-declining, because he possesses his full integrity; he is the Lord, because of his state of master; this essence Śiva has been thus told; it is situated above all paths. (4–6)

Source: *The Tantra of Svayambhū vidyāpāda with the Commentary of Sadyojyoti*, translated by Pierre-Sylvain Filliozat (New Delhi: Indira Gandhi National Centre for the Arts and Motilal Banarsidass, 1994).

Selections from the *Tiruvaruṭpayan̲* of Umāpati

1. The Nature before Pati

1.1 The Lord is like the vowel *a*, permanently pervading everywhere as knowledge; yet he is incomparable.

1.2 Our Lord is not separate from śakti, which gives its essence to eternal souls as their nature.

1.3 The Lord is unequaled in his unique benefit, his wide grace, his subtlety, and his greatness.

1.4 After making all things become and maintaining them, the Lord destroys them along with the fault and becomes the refuge from which they will not depart.

1.5 The Lord has no form and form; to the learned his form is knowledge.

1.6 Our Lord has no one above him that compares to his nature, by which the numerous souls possess knowledge.

1.7 The celestials do not understand his greatness, but for his servants he remains as inseparable knowledge.

1.8 He remains as one with everything everywhere like heat in hot water; yet he is himself alone.

1.9 To those who do not approach him he is not good; to those who do approach him he is good. Caṅkaraṉ is the name of the impartial one.

1.10 Set your mind upon him without doubt, for he is the medicine that will cure your everlasting births.

2. *The Nature of Categories of the Soul*

2.1 The number of those who have been and will be released is the same as the number of days that have passed and those yet to arise.

2.2 The souls are divided into those that have three malas [bonds], those that have gone beyond one of them, and those that possess only one.

2.3 All three categories possess the root mala [*āṇava mala*]; those who are most bound do not know of [the Lord's] succor.

2.4 The agency of āṇava mala is of such great power it makes things seen everyday confused in dreams.

2.5 *Aṟivu* is [hardly] the best name for understanding perceived only through the sense organs.

2.6 What can light, darkness, and the world affect if there is no clarity in the open eye?

2.7 *Sat* [reality] does not join *asat*; *asat* does not know the place of *sat*; therefore, the soul experiences these two as *satasat*.

2.8 Are there not things in the world that become completely dark in darkness and illuminated in light?

2.9 Like the eye of the owl for which even light is great darkness we cannot see certain things but for the eye of God.

2.10 Alas! The souls will continue to bear up until that day when, knowing the Lord's grace, their afflictions will be no more.

3. *The Nature of the Bond That Is Dark*

3.1 It is not possible by any means to say that the sorrows of many births, bliss, and their auxiliaries do not exist.

3.2 The reality that persists as one with everything is nothing but that which is dark.

3.3 Darkness does not reveal anything but it does show its form; this [*āṇavamala*] does not reveal either.

3.4 Since the beginning, darkness has been contained in the midst of the soul with its inner light, and remains there up until today.

3.5 The base lady of darkness embraces many persons, though her "chastity" is unknown to her husband.

3.6 Why use many words? Darkness makes truth unknown to the intelligent soul.

3.7 If darkness does not exist then why is there suffering? If it is of the soul's essence then when it is made to go they will depart as one.

3.8 If the fault has a beginning, what is the reason that it binds? If we cannot say, then the bonds will attach even in the state of mukti.

3.9 If the soul does not grasp the increasing light of grace, then darkness will never leave it.

3.10 Like a lamp that lasts up until dawn, māyā comes to karma through the body and other instruments.

4. *The Nature of Grace*

4.1 There is nothing in this world that is greater than grace, just as there is nothing above the things that the soul needs.

4.2 Grace pervades everywhere like the great light of the sun and touches the karma that is ripe.

4.3 The body does not know anything; nor does the soul know these things. How can one who does not know become one who knows?

4.4 Though the souls have grace as their nature, they flounder about in a sea of confusion like fish in an ocean of milk.

4.5 The soul will not realize knowledge with the five senses, like a wanderer who does not realize that help approaches.

4.6 Even those who move about the earth do not know the earth; how much less do those of the world understand higher things.

4.7 Those who would bring the mountain to ruin, those who would bring the earth to ruin, those who would bring the heavens to ruin, and those who would bring the highest knowledge to ruin have only brought themselves to ruin.

4.8 The person who is most deceived feels thirst even though up to his neck in a flood, and takes complete darkness for dawn.

4.9 Listen to this teaching after subduing your desires; else you will be like a cat on top of a full jug of milk who yet desires to eat a cockroach.

4.10 "Release" is too much to expect for the empty souls who are not at all familiar with Grace though they have been joined to it up to today.

5. *The Nature of the Form of Grace*

5.1 The Lord's grace, which will never depart, protected you during the state of ignorance and will appear again as a sign.

5.2 Aside from the one who has a disease inside himself, will the people of the world know anything about it?

5.3 Who of the earth would recognize the sign that came to bestow grace in ways not previously granted?

5.4 The one who lacks intellect because perception and mind are darkened by falsehood can barely see the two truths.

5.5 The world does not know that the Lord comes in the cloak of human form to catch and hold people, like a decoy for animals.

5.6 Think not, "What is to me and which things are to others;" for authority [in spiritual matters] you require him [the guru].

5.7 The vision of the guru will make darkness go, just as a vision [of a mongoose] in true meditation cures snake poison better than a mongoose itself.

5.8 The Lord Himself graciously comes to the Sakalas, removes the karma of the Pralayakalas, and bestows the grace that gives release to the Vijñānakalas.

5.9 Who will know anything if the Great Knower who gracefully manifests the path of release for all does not come?

5.10 Wisdom will arise without the guru if crystal can glow without light.

6. *The Method of Knowing*

6.1 When the endless twofold karma becomes balanced it is possible to receive the Lord's śakti.

6.2 One, many, darkness, karma, and the twofold māyā; these six are beginningless.

6.3 Know that the one who is saved exists as the one who performs actions, the actions that are performed, the fruit of these actions, and as the one who attains the fruit of these actions.

6.4 The body lives because of the soul, and the soul is one with the body; similarly, the soul is one with the Supreme Intellect.

6.5 Like the golden sun that gives the crystal its own color and many other colors, grace gives the world its own and many colors.

6.6 As with the way of conventional seeing, if the light of grace is not in its midst the eye of the soul cannot see.

6.7 Consider that the Lord's actions are related to yours in the manner that actions of the senses are related to mundane activities.

6.8 Do not undertake research or scrutinize anything; do not project from yourself; see the Lord who has seen you.

6.9 After you recognize that worldly pleasures are only excesses of the senses, take refuge as a ray in the light of knowledge.

6.10 Take things in this way of taking them: see things in the way they have been shown to you, and do not see things that have not been shown to you.

7. *The Enlightenment of the Soul*

7.1 Just as no one need be told to seek refuge under cool shade, the soul will join with grace in the same way.

7.2 At the time of bilious affliction, even milk that is sweet will be bitter; after the tongue recovers, the bitterness will subside.

7.3 He will see only when the light shows itself in darkness; on what day will the vain sin of seeing by his own agency depart?

7.4 Light and darkness are of one nature, but the action of the former is enlightenment and the latter, unenlightenment.

7.5 Except for those of worthy and good friendship, who will bear your burdens now?

7.6 When the thief stole the valuables that were kept, was the owner asleep or had he gone out? Say.

7.7 As a crystal prism catches light without shadow to itself, grace renders darkness powerless to take hold.

7.8 One who has attained the state of grace should stand behind truth just as one who holds a torch stands behind the emitted light.

7.9 If what you see is dependent upon the five senses, then besides grace what is the competence of the senses and the soul to know?

7.10 Is it possible to consider that his giving to you is due to your own will? What is the competence of the soul to know?

8. *The Nature of Experiencing Bliss*

8.1 Those who experience bliss go behind the light that arises in darkness; those who experience sorrow go before it; therefore, go behind.

8.2 There will not be any fruit of bliss between two women; it is experienced between a man and a woman.

8.3 The Lord of bliss bestows it upon those who reach him; therefore, the weight of bliss does not remain with his own form.

8.4 As the words join to make *tāṭalai* [*tāḷ* + *talai*], losing their otherness, take your joining with bliss as one.

8.5 If there is only one then it cannot unite; if there are two then sound will not arise [from the two hands that are held apart]; if this be the case, there is neither one nor two.

8.6 The ones who are freed from the cycle of birth and death are those who join with bliss, those who receive bliss, and those who adhere silently without cease.

8.7 Remain without performing any actions up until the nature of a pēy arises.

8.8 Only the fruit of grace and nothing else is experienced by those who join the highest truth; they view all else as things that drop from the hand of those who sleep.

8.9 Bliss does not appear separately from the three natures that are completely joined together; what else is there to say?

8.10 This is the state of love: If he finds sweetness in bliss today, he will attain it today.

9. *The Nature of the Grace of the Five Syllables*

9.1 The books of grace, the Vedas, and others besides elucidate the threads of truth in the five syllables.

9.2 Lord, śakti, pāśa, the power of māyā, and the soul all remain within the syllable Ōṃ.

9.3 Seek the soul between the actions of the flesh on one side and the dance of knowledge on the other.

9.4 The expanding "na" and "ma" will not release the soul that combines with them until the soul is able to end the great karma [of birth and death].

9.5 If concealment [na] and fault [ma], fraught with illusion, come first, will things ever change? The things that are highest are what set the soul free.

9.6 Who is your basic foundation? The Mūlātāram? Alas, do not continue to think this way! Recite the highest things first.

9.7 If you adopt the method of recitation with Śiva first, your births will end; recite it in this way.

9.8 "Vā" gracefully endows the soul and causes it to prosper in "Śi," Śiva-bliss. That same grace becomes the unblemished form of the soul.

9.9 Because of the grace this flawless form will not stand between "na" and "vā"; it will stand between "Śi" and "vā."

9.10 All of these methods are mentioned knowing that the soul cannot remain separated from the Lord.

10. The State of Those Who Have Attained

10.1 Those in the state of samādhi are submerged in the highest knowledge and overcome by bliss in their minds; what else is there to say?

10.2 They do not desire to perform the five cosmic actions, or to be the agents of actions, or to seek the enjoyment of passionate actions.

10.3 Even though they are in a position to know everything, they do not want to know anything except the One.

10.4 After subduing the senses they enter into their own essences without reemerging, like a tortoise that withdraws its limbs into its shell.

10.5 Where is a place that is separate from the Lord? Even if a place does not exist, he is everywhere. His existence is not separate from the liberated soul.

10.6 For those who view things internal and external as of one nature, there is nothing whose nature is reproachful.

10.7 The world is the fruit of gainful work, while truth is the fruit of selfless action.

10.8 The accumulated karma will end with the death of the body; if more karma appears in the midst of this birth, then grace alone will burn it.

10.9 For those of mature understanding, actions that give the threefold result will not be kindled; even the actions of future births will come to fruition in this birth.

10.10 When those committed to the truth reflect upon the sorrows of those committed to deceit, they are filled with compassion.

Source: *Tiruvaruṭpayaṉ* of Umāpati Civācāryār, translated by Karen Pechilis Prentiss in *The Embodiment of Bhakti*, (New York: Oxford University Press, 1999).

Selections from the *Paramārthasāra* of Abhinavagupta

1. O Lord, Śambhu, you are a great God who transcends the abyss; you are without beginning, unique, and penetrating multiple ways to the bottom of everyone's heart. You are present in all static and dynamic phenomena. I take only you as my refuge.
2. A disciple, being reborn in the cycle of suffering that begins with confinement in a mother's womb and ends with death, a disciple could approach the venerable Ādhāra and ask him about the real truth. . . .
3. The Lord discussed the topic with him through the work named Ādhārakārikā, the essence of which is being expressed by Abhinavagupta through the perspective of Śaivism.
4. It is by the expansion of His internal energy that these four spheres with their distinctions are known: Śakti (energy), Māyā (illusion), Prakṛti (nature), and Pṛthivī (earth) by means of the powers of the Lord.
5. Within the interior of the four spheres lies the whole universe along with its diverse types of worlds, organs, and bodies. This is where Śiva himself assumes the forms of a body and reveals the condition of the individual soul.
6. Just as a pure and colorless crystal assumes the appearance of different types of colors, so does the Lord also assume the forms of gods, human beings, animals, and plants.
7. Just as the reflection of moon appears to be moving when reflected in flowing waters and rests tranquil in still waters, so does this great master appear in multifarious ways in the different categories of bodies, organs and worlds.
8. Just as Rāhu shines and appears in the disk of moon, though it is otherwise invisible, so does this Ātman shine only in the mirror of the mind while witnessing some objects, though it is present everywhere.
9. Just as one's face appears lucidly in a clean mirror, so does this Ātman shine as pure consciousness in a mind purified by the bestowal of the divine Śakti of Śiva.

10–11. Resplendently, a perfect blissful event that rests on its Ātman, abandoning will, shines as the light of pure consciousness; free from all mental duality, pure, peaceful, free from appearance and from disappearance, this is in him, the superman category that consists in this world of 26 categories. . . .

12–13. Just as the reflection of some objects, such as a village, a forest, and so forth, are reflected in a mirror are devoid of distinctions, but even appear as mutually distinct and separate from an elegant mirror; proceeding from the absolute is the pure intelligence of the supreme Bhairava; this entire universe is also free of all distinctions that appear as mutually distinct parts, but are not equally distinct from this intelligence.

14. The manifest categories are called: Śiva, Śakti, Sad Śiva (eternal Śiva), and Īśvara (Lord) and the pure knowledge, projecting out worldly the five categories.
15. The goddess "Māyā-śakti," energy of illusion, is the supreme autonomy of the great Lord. She realizes different external things. She is the veil that covers the seed of Śiva. His five powers are consciousness, bliss, will, knowledge, and ability to differentiate entities from Himself.
16. From our embrace of the illusion of consciousness, it becomes soiled; it reveals an individual self being enslaved. It is tied by time, determined, and restricted to the way of desire and of limited knowledge.
17. "I know only now and just a little of it." Associated with illusion, this constitutes the six sheaths and is named part of the interior atomic soul.
18. The covering on balls of rice grains are inseparable from their goodness from (which in reality) she is distinct. But each is perfectly purified then in its ardent journey of yoga practice toward Śiva.
19. Thus the consistent, unique nature of pleasure, suffering, and delusion constitutes the internal organ made from three that is intelligence, mind, and egoism.
20. The ears, skin, eyes, tongue, and nose are the facultities of the intellect relative to itself and other objects of the senses. From other parts, the speech, hands, feet, organs of excretion, and of generation are the faculties of action.
21. The subtle and indivisible domain of the senses, which can apprehend, consists of five subtle elements: sound, touch, light, taste and smell.
22. Thus, from the combination of these (subtle elements) proceed the objects of sense that are five physical elements: ether, air, fire, water, and earth.
23. As a husk covers a grain of rice, this creation, which begins from nature and is achieved on the earth, conceals consciousness with bodily existence.
24. The major covering is here hereditary impurity. The subtle coverings are the cause of illusion, etc. (When) a greater covering appears, it is external and assumes the aspect of the physical body. It is thus the soul that is enveloped by the three sheaths.
25. A reason for the troubles associated with ignorance is concerned with a perception of the multiplicity of various subjects and objects, while consciousness is identical to the soul in reality.

26. Just as thin juice, thick juice, still thicker molasses, coarse sugar, and refined sugar are all really the same juice of sugarcane, thus all phenomena are different states of Śiva, the supreme Ātman.
27. The flow of direct, internal consciousness, cosmic bodies, ordinary bodies, and individual species are not pure experiences, which flowing from the transcendent viewpoint do not really exist.
28. No serpent exists in a rope and yet it provokes a terror even unto death. In truth, the great Śakti of delusion cannot be perceived at any time.
29. Thus goodness and evil, heaven and hell, birth and death, pleasure and pain, castes and stages of life, and so on, never exist in reality; they appear in truth on account of delusion.
30. Blindness is for the imaginer not what it is for the Ātman . . . since constant light is revealed to it.
31. This is the problem with the vision that springs from the problems associated with egoism; it is a pimple born on a tumor; it is a great calamity when one imagines an Ātman by means that cannot be it, such as the body, breath, etc.
32. It is an extraordinary vision that resembles a spider that creates its web; it envelops itself in its web like consciousness determined by the body, breath to the science of the intellect, or to the expansion of ether.
33. By means of its concentration on the revelation of the majestic self-consciousness of the Ātman, the inner self is revealed. Thus the supreme Śiva unfolds his wonderful game of bondage and deliverance.
34. Creation, preservation, and destruction (of the world), as well as wakefulness, illusion, and deep sleep appear inside the light of the fourth state. However, this fourth state is more revealed because it is not covered by these (diverse conditions).
35. The waking state is *viśva*, all illuminated by reason of its diversity. The dream state is called *tejas*, the splendor, by virtue of its majestic light. The deep sleep is called *prājña*, wisdom, because it is massive consciousness. The transcendent is the fourth.
36. Just as the surface of the firmament is not polluted by smoke and dust, thus the supreme spirit is not affected by the modifications of illusion.
37. When the space contained within a vase is covered with dust, the content of other vases are not polluted. It is the same for these individual souls that are subject to differences of pleasure and pain.
38. The Lord is also peaceful when the collective categories are tranquil, excited when they are excited. He is dazed when they are bewildered. But from the transcendent viewpoint, it is not thus.

39. Having at first rejected the false impressions of the Ātman by confusing it with what it is not, the supreme Ātman destroyed afterward the delusion which apprehends the Ātman with that which is not the self.
40. Thus when this double illusion connected to being is torn away from its roots, the supreme yogin, attending to his aim, is not more assuredly obligated to accomplish another duty.
41. Because this trinity of earth, nature, and illusion becomes objective, it is reduced to pure existence, although grace affects mystic realization of non-duality.
42. If abstraction is made of their differences (in various forms), belts, earrings, and bracelets are perceived as gold. From the same universe, all entities appear as pure being when one abstracts the different phenomena.
43. That Brahman, which is supreme, pure, tranquil, immaterial, eternally identical to itself, integral, immortal, and real, reabsorbs within itself the energy whose essence is luminous.
44. From other aspects, this does not affect its luminous essence, which one calls the object of desire, object of consciousness, or object of activity; it is not a flower within space.
45. The God of gods enables one to understand the realization of the trident of Śakti (energy), who projects the cosmic totality herself within the supreme Lord called Śiva, the absolute Truth.
46. And likewise inversely, because one acquires the consciousness of the Ātman in the external (world), this marvelous triad of spheres (Māyā, Prakṛti, Pṛthivī) is deployed with exterior grace to manifest the gradual emanation of the five energies.
47. And also God, who through his play encounters the movement of this cosmic machine, the wheel of Śakti, is the I, the immaculate essence, situated at the place of the conductor of the grand wheel of Śakti.
48. This is me who the universe reveals as the vessels and other objects in a mirror without a stain. For me, the whole emanates as multiple forms revealed in sleep.
49. It is me who forms the universe as a body to the hands, feet, etc. It is me who illumines all things as a light within its modes.
50. Without body and organs, and inaction, I see, hear, and sense. It is me who composes the diverse doctrines, religious traditions, and texts of logic.
51. When the concept of duality disappears and overcomes the illusion that misleads, one is plunged into Brahman as milk is immersed into milk and the water into water.

52. Having attained mystic realization, he arrives at a state of identity with Śiva within the totality of categories. Could suffering, delusion, and deviation from social norms be known by seeing everything as Brahman?
53. The result of one's deeds agreeing or disagreeing with an act is based on attachment to erroneous consciousness, because the vice of attachment is troublesome much like the union of a will of a human who does not have a will.
54. Stupid beings, who produce homage to ignorance formed of practical, ordinary experience, undergo birth and death, enchained by the fetters of merit and demerit.
55. But the acts of merit and demerit, however well accumulated during perceived ignorance, disappear like the flame of discrimination as from cotton gathered a long time ago.
56. From that one acquires consciousness, (the work) itself not accomplished through the door of the fruit. Is he born again then? Being no longer associated with the servitude to rebirth, the rays of the self are revealed similar to the sun who is Śiva.
57. Like the grain striped from the outer husk, the inner covering cannot become a seedling; thus the Ātman is delivered (from impurities) of finitude, illusion, and action that does not produce the rejection of existence.
58. The one who knows the Ātman does not dread anything from any quarter because everything is his own self. He does not experience suffering because, in reality, there is no destruction.
59. From the fact that one gained the joy of ultimate reality that gathers within the treasure room at the bottom of the heart, one says "I am (the universe) itself." In (this) state of the supreme Lord to whom one arrives, could misfortune happen, and to whom?
60. The state of liberation is not (determined) by access to another more exalted place. Liberation is the revelation of the energies of the Ātman when the bond of ignorance is broken.
61. The one who breaks the bond of ignorance, from whom uncertainties disappear, who overcomes error, from whom good and evil actions are annihilated, that one is delivered in comparison to some who remains united to the body.
62. Just as a grain consumed by the fire is incapable of growing, thus the acts also consumed by the fire of consciousness cannot produce birth.
63. In effect, ego-consciousness is the ability to imagine a future body, conforming to actions (which it performs) and by placing burdens on a limited intellect; consciousness proportionally commits itself to a dissolution of the actual body. . . .

68. Thus awakened by the stimulant of mystic realization, a person sacrifices all mental bipartitions in the luminous flame of the Ātman becoming identified with its light.
69. Nourishing oneself on this which one finds, clothed modestly, peaceful, dwelling not knowing where, one is delivered, becoming the soul of all beings.
70. Even if one performed a hundred million horse sacrifices or, committed as many murders of brahmins, those who know ultimate reality are not affected by the pious or impious; they are without pollution.
71. Rejecting distant infatuation, excitement, rage, passion, depression, fear, greed, and deviations from the correct course, he wanders without praise or ritual benefits like an insane person without speech or thought.
72. This group of infatuation, excitation, etc., arises from this trap that is difference. Is a person with a nondual understanding of the self affected like those who possess a dual grasp of the Ātman?
73. It is not more insignificant who agrees with the distinction. . . . A person rejoices in the praise, etc., bestowed by others; those who are delivered and discover what is beyond respect and ritual exclamation.
74. His temple is his proper body that contains the 26 categories. . . .
75. It is he who lives, making pure offerings of full consciousness of the self to divine power (Śiva), the grand Bhairava, the supreme self who accompanies his proper offerings.
76. In the hot flame of his consciousness, he throws offerings that accumulate from the grand gems (that consist) in a distinguishing of internal and external conceptual constructions. His oblation to fire is made without effort.
77. (His) meditation is not relaxed, because the Lord believes these marvelous forms vary. The fundamental reality that shapes concepts is precisely (his) meditation.
78. When, in an interior vision, he creates the unfolding of the entire world, (to know) the gradual construction of categories and also the multiplicity of elements, it is this that is called his repetitive recitation (*japa*).

79–80. His religious duty, which is very difficult (to accomplish) but also very easy, consists to all appearances as a unity and represents consciousness as the cremation ground of the universe; carrying symbols of the human skeleton, he carries a skull of a dead person, fragment of a knowable object, which he holds in his hand, full of liquor representing the essence of the universe.

81. Having thus realized this which one calls the transcendent Lord, supreme truth, liberated from origin and destruction, all duty being accomplished, he lives here with perfect satisfaction, because he receives a revelation of being by means of breaking through the subject.

82. Those who know the universal Ātman, omnipresent, from where all multipilicity is excluded (the Ātman) thus reveals what is the supreme and incomparable happiness, to those that become identified with it.

83. Who abandons his body (at death) in a holy place or in the house of a low caste family, as if it were memory; he is delivered at the precise moment when he acquires knowledge (and) arrives at the absolute, surmounting all suffering.

84. Visiting holy places is meritorious; dying in the home of a low-caste person leads to hell. (But) who are not affected by suffering from acts of virtue and vice?

86. Purified consciousness is here separated from the sheaths that cover it, then it remains (in a state of purity) being the liberated Ātman escaped from its contact with the world. . . .

92. The self imprisoned in the interior of its body is to such a person its proper heaven or hell. At the dissolution (of the body), it is united to another body according to its actual deeds.

93. Thus, at the instant of consciousness, its actual Ātman is revealed to him one time forever and he becomes like it. With the death of the body, there is no more change.

94–95. Paralysis of senses and organs, loss of memory, uncontrollable breathing, looseness in vital joints and particular types of pain are all trials. Are the outcome of one's deeds based on bodily predispositions that are not produced through the union with a body? When one comes into contact with the misguided, those who are united with consciousness do not depart at the moment of death from the transcendent reality of the Ātman.

96. According to one who follows this view of the transcendent reality by following the teaching of a Master, suddenly, one finds a forceful grace, extremely intense, and one indisputably becomes united to Śiva himself.

97. Gradually, step by step one climbs toward the transcendental position, attains unity with Śiva, whose true essence transcends all things; one realizes the ascent as an ultimate principle, and is at last identified with Śiva.

98–99. Those who, though desirous to attain the highest position, stop at some intermediary step or die before reaching the highest state, fail to attain union. If one falls from the path, he can become the master of some (divine) realm, marvelously joyful, and attain a place of relaxation for himself. He becomes identified with Śiva in his next life.

100. One who, in truth, in spite of repeated efforts fails to achieve this view of transcendent reality does not attain union; he participates, however, in the happiness of the divine world where he rejoices forever in spiritual joy.
101. Just as people venerate the sovereign of the entire earth, those who reach union with him are adored in the (celestial) worlds by all the gods.
102. After a long time, he is born again as a new human being, practices the path, and attains immortality, he never returns to this mortal existence. . . .
104. Because he meditates on the supreme Brahman like Abhinavagupta, it is revealed quickly to his heart, because having a little of the nature of Śiva penetrate to his heart.
105. It is me, Abhinavagupta, who inspired by the constant remembrance of the feet of Śiva, have summarized in about one hundred pure verses this very profound work.

Source: *Le Paramārthasāra*, translated into French by Liliane Silburn (Paris: E. De Boccard Éditeur, 1957); translated from the French by Carl Olson.

Selections from the *Śūnyasampādane*

As a spark in stone,
As an image in water,
As a tree in the seed,
As silence in speech,
So Thou in Thy devotee,
O Guhēśvara.

Can the spark in the stone
Kindle?
Can the tree in the seed
Rustle?

Guhēśvara's majesty,
Being unapparent,
Does not shine out

For the common eye:
He only knows it
Who has tasted the joy
Of The Experience!

When neither Source nor Substance was,
When neither I nor mine,
When neither Form nor formless was,
When neither Void was nor non-Void,
Nor that which moves or moves not,
Then was Guhēśvara's votary born.

When Brahma and Viṣṇu were trampled by Māyā,
When gods and demons were eaten up by Māyā,
When the Rudragaṇa and the Pramathagaṇa were teased and
fooled by Māyā,
When the third-eyed, the five-faced and the
ten-armed were wedded to Māyā,
When the eight-and-eighty thousand sages
succumbed to Māyā through pride of penance,
Lo, didn't I make her yell in pain,
O Guhēśvara!

In the Kṛtayuga, I appeared as Sthūlakāyagaṇēśvara
For Bhakti's sake.
In the Trētāyuga, I appeared as Śūnyakayagaṇēśvara
For Bhakti's sake.
In the Dvāparayuga, I appeared as Animiṣagaṇēśvara
For Bhakti's sake.
In the Kaliyuga, I now appear as Allamaprabhugaṇēśvara
For Bhakti's sake,
O Guhēśvara.

The whole world knows not
What seed was there before
The body was . . .
The senses are not the seed,
Nay, not the elements one by one.
Delusions of Dream

Have swooped upon us.
Verily, because
No one understands,
There's no real peace,
  O Guhēśvara.

The froth and foam of a flowing stream
Must touch the floating driftwood.
The pain and pleasure of the world's ocean
Must touch the creatures that sink or swim.
How can he that has taken a form
Not perish, O Guhēśvara?

Sunrise and sunset are coming and going:
We perish, alas! Being made all of water!
Darkness has shrouded the three worlds.
Tell us, O Guhēśvara, what means this riddle!

Look how they wrangle, the dogs
Come to feast on
This carcass of a world!
And as the dogs wrangle, look
How the carcass laughs!
For you see, Sir, the Guhēśvara Himself
Is not there.

Creatures
That are clad as a doll, made of water—
Creatures
That are wrapped in a shawl of fire—
Creatures
That are blown about with the wind's speed—
How shall they apprehend God,
  O Guhēśvara?

Who is the Engineer who has moulded
  This doll of clay,
Draped it in a fabric of water,
  Bound to it, in diverse states of life,

A jingle of tinkling bells;
Dowered it with air and fire,
Crowned it with adornments,
And now sets it playing?
When this Formless one has been bound to form,
When you have attained the Self
And made it the temple of the Divine,
There is no more one and two,
O Guhēśvara.

A pint-size cow with a gallon-size udder,
And twin horns, palmyra-high!
Search it for six days, it has vanished in three . . .
Let's then, O Guhēśvara,
Seek Him, Him only
To Whom all things impossible are possible.

The thieves in the wood
Are looking for the ascetic
With the deer-skin.
But their torches are out, and they cannot see.
And still they seek—
The gluttons, the sots and amorists!
And the knowing pedant, relieved of his head,
Has been swilling, O Guhēśvara,
The blood of the soul's red sin.

A merchant of Jambu Isle,
Gathering his bales and bundles,
Set up his stall
In the womb of Mother Earth.
Stricken with a crazy thirst,
He drank up the seven oceans
Until, to his own dismay
At the unquenchable thirst,
He sucked the ooze itself.
An infant carries his mother's corpse
Upon his back and goes

Mumbling her name. . . .
Behold, an earth-round shape
  Has swallowed the glory of Guhēśvara.

On heaven's expanse
A strange parrot was born,
And she built her a house
In vainglorious pomp.
But of that one parrot
There were born five and twenty.
Brahma was the parrot's cage,
Viṣṇu her victuals,
And Rudra her perch.
When she swallowed a young one
In front of those Three,
  Behold O Guhēśvara,
  The visible ceases to be!

What is this show within a show?
The court of Brahmā is blown up quite
And shattered to a mess.
Move aside, says Viṣṇu, and straight he goes,
And, swallowing the Unborn, he hides himself
In Rudra's loins. . . .
What shall I say, O Guhēśvara,
What shall I say
Of the rootless tree's image
Seen in waterless shadow?

On the tip of a buffalo's horn
There be seven hundred and seventy
Wells. . . .
In each well there's a spring,
In each spring, look, a harlot!
And there, around the harlot's neck,
Seven hundred and seventy elephants I see
  Climb and crawl,
  O Guhēśvara!

This monkey of a mind sits atop
  This tree of a body,
And swings and bounds from bough to bough:
But here's a wonder, O Guhēśvara!
Hold but your hand out, he swallows you whole;
Call out to him gently, he comes and stands still;
But challenge him, he's just not there!

In the wide waters of the deep
Look! A dark fisherman has cast his net.
And see, what fish he has caught:
Five, with heads that know;
Five, with heads that know not;
And five, with heads for doing.
When the dark fisherman goes home,
  Shouldering his net,
Watch for the flush of joy in his eye,
  O Guhēśvara!

My body I have made a garden,
My mind a spade.
I have dug up illusion's weeds,
Broken up the clouds of worldliness,
Harrowed the earth, and sown
  The Spirit's seed.
The thousand-fold lotus is my well,
My water-wheel my breath;
From my subtle nerve I have
  Channeled the water.
And to keep out the five
  Bulls of sense
That might trample my crops,
I have set up all round
Patience and poise as fence.
  Behold, O Guhēśvara!
Night and day I have lain awake,
To protect my tender plants.

When Grace strikes, earth is turned to gold;
The common stone is charged with alchemy,
When Grace strikes.

Like a poor man stumbling upon a trove,
With a seeker's tireless steps I have come
And seen, O Lord, the Inconceivable,
Beheld the sweep of my consciousness!
My whole being, within and without,
Bathes in supernal splendor,
I have gazed at the Source of all light!
I have seen my Supreme Master
With his gaze of unfathomable wonder,
Concentrate, beyond all emblems,
Upon the emblem on his palm.
And having seen, I have been saved,
  O Guhēśvara.

If, seeing the Guru who is silent and still,
I beseech Him for a word of grace,
He neither speaks nor listens.
How can the first act and the last
  Be done?
The fragrance in my heart
Is as the meeting of mute and mute,
Whose silence is but the outer form
Of inward sympathy.
How could I describe
This unaccustomed loveliness!
Only by becoming one's Self,
Never as twain, O Guhēśvara!

Among our offerings,
Who can tell
Which is the true, which false?
Interested offering is no offering;
Disinterested offering is.
  If thou accept'st, O Guhēśvara,

That which I offer as if not offered,
  Then, indeed,
I'm a partaker of Thy grace.

Water has frozen to a form
And stands upon the base.
The primal seat is installed
In the body. City of Śiva.
The breath has turned priest,
And, culling a fragrant nosegay,
Has offered the holy rites
At the gate, in the sanctuary
  Of the nine-door shrine.
And lo! Guhēśvara is there!

Unimaginable the light in the eye!
Indescribable the ring in the ear!
Incomparable the taste on the tongue!
  Immeasurable the peace
Of the inconceivable central nerve!
Everywhere you will find Him:
In minutest particles of dust,
  In the hard wood,
  Or tender blade of grass.
Everywhere He is!
The subtle, the imperishable, the unchanging Guhēśvara!

All memory is dead;
All error burnt;
Awareness is forgot;
All symbols have crumbled.
Where is now Motion or Mind?
No Motion, for the body is naught;
No Mind, for it's lost in the Liṅga;
  And gone, gone too,
  O Guhēśvara,
All that came between
The eyes and Light!

Poems of the Māhadēviyakka, a Vīraśaiva female saint

Through joy of Liṅga I achieved
The body's defeat;
By way of knowledge I achieved
Defeat of mind;
Through God-experience I achieved
Defeat of soul;
Donning the Light as garment, I subdued
The darkness of the senses.
Look at the ashes I have worn
When Kāma burnt who shows himself to you
Within the outer gloss of youth!
If Cennamallikārjuna
After slaying Kāma let him live
As the heart-born. I erased
The writing on the heart-born's head!

Guru was kinsman to officiate;
Liṅga the bridegroom, I the bride;
This all the worlds do know:
My father and my mother were
The innumerable saints;
Behold, they gave me, to a groom
Becoming Prabhu's house.
Therefore, Cennamallikārjuna is my lord:
No other husbands in the world
Are aught to me, Prabhu!
Is it true that you laid the blame
And left him? By shedding your dress,
And laying the body bare,
The error of your mind cannot be stilled;
The garment of your hair yet screens your form.
How is it that your shame is shed?
This sort of dress does not befit
Guhēśvaraliṅga!

O Sir, I love the beautiful One,
The formless One, who is beyond

Or death or dissolution;
The beautiful One,
The fearless, dauntless One,
Who is past birth . . .
Cennamallikārjuna is my groom:
All other husbands in the world
Are naught to me!

The form dissolves,
The formless thing does not:
How can there be
Marriage between the form and formlessness?
That means a bond
With what cannot be bound . . .
So long as thee must be
The natural taint of body and of sense,
So long you cannot reach
Guhēśvaraliṅga: hear that, Mother!

When you have understood the body, the mind
Ought to be purified;
When you have understood the mind, the sense
Ought to be purified;
Hear me, O Mother:
Until the body, mind and senses are
Made pure and tranquil, and
Turned Liṅga-ward,
You cannot make a prayer
To Guhēśvara!

By taking gifts from Śiva's devotees,
My body is purified;
By calling to my mind the countless ones,
My mind is purified;
By seeing all the ancient ones,
My eyes are purified;
By listening to their praise,
My ears are purified . . .

Hear me, O Father Liṅga:
This feeling has become my life . . .
Mark you, Cennamallikārjuna:
Worshipping Thee with all my heart,
My wheel of births has ceased!

If you just say your body is made pure,
If does not mean that Liṅga is firm in you—
If you just say your life is purified
It does not mean that Liṅga is firm in you;
If you just say your will is purified,
It does not mean that Liṅga is firm in you.

Within my body there is now
A disembodied state;
Within my life there is a state
Transcending life;
Within my will there is
A will-lessness.
The Absolute has become the thought
Of my whole mind.
Because you, seeing my woman's head and breasts,
Befriended me, I now belong
To Cennamallikārjuna's grace.

Is there a difference, Sir,
Between condensed and liquid ghee?
A difference between
A lamp and light?
Between the body and soul?
Because the holy Guru has proved
My body to be a charm,
There is no difference
Between the partite and the Impartite.
Why do you, Prabhu, make me speak
Who lost my consciousness
The moment I merged
In Lord Cennamallikārjuna?

In dedicating the body unto Liṅga,
The body is made bodiless;
In dedicating the mind to Consciousness,
The mind is turned to naught;
In dedicating the will to Bliss,
The will is turned to void;
Because my body, mind and will
Have perished, my body has attained
A disembodied state.
Because it is the Liṅga that enjoys
The body's joys, I have become
A dedicated spouse
To my Lord Liṅga.
Therefore, I've entered my lord
Cennamallikārjuna
And merged in Him.

Wherefore for me? I am
A puppet of this world, a vessel filled
With Māyā's filth;
A worldly mansion by the passions torn.
Why for this earthly house
Which leaks as through a water-pitcher's crack?
Is it possible to chew
The nut of a palmyra tree
If you squeeze it with your finger?
Whatever has been sown is soul:
Be mine the nature of the rind.
Do you condone my faults.
You, brothers, you are yourselves
Cennamallikārjuna, God of gods!

If you have achieved
Union with Liṅga while in body, and
Union with body when in Liṅga,
Tell us the manner you removed
The cleft and breach dividing them.
If you would achieve

Union with Liṅga while in body, then
Śiva shall tease you
By blocking up your further way.
Śiva shall make you toil and toss
In the desire of lust.
If you would lodge
Your body firm in Liṅga,
Śiva shall, in disgust,
Flee from the body far away.
Hear me, O mother: Śiva loves
A union where the woman becomes man.
If you would unite yourself
With Kūḍala Sangama, you must
Without a sense of difference be
A valiant man: that is so!

If you would consider thoughtfully,
It's body; but after I have
Transcended body's nature I have become
Your body; and after I have shed
All taste of difference and learned
The taste of Liṅga, it means I've killed
Cennamallikārjuna and died myself.

Through your grace, Sir, Basavaṇṇa,
I have conquered lust;
Through your grace, Sir, Basavaṇṇa,
I will make captive of
The Holder of the Moon;
Through your grace, lo, Basavaṇṇa,
A woman though in name,
I am, if you consider well,
The masculine principle.
And if I have
Ensnared Cennainallikārjuna's
Intemperate love
And, being one with him,
Transcending the Twain,

Have quite forgot myself,
It's through your grace,
Basavaṇṇa, Sir!

Transcending the company of both,
I have attained to peace.
After forgetting this cluster of words,
What if one lives
An integral life?
Once I am joined
To Lord Cennamallikārjuna,
I do not recognise myself
As anything.

The body is a woman's form;
The mind, one with
The spirit of the Thing.
And yet you came down here
Because you had a reason to come,
And this you have done!
You have, dear sister, transcended the sense
Of twain, in Guhēśvaraliṅga, sister mine.

You cut and saw and rub the sandal-wood:
Does it, being burnt, refuse its scent?
You cut and rub a piece of gold:
Does it, being heated, take in dross?
You cut a sugarcane joint by joint,
Put it and squeeze it in a press;
When heated, it gives sugar and jaggery:
Does it, being hurt, refuse its sweet?
When you rake up my bygone sins
And cast them in my face,
The loss is yours. . . .
O Father Cennamallikārjuna Lord,
Though you may slay me,
I'll never cease
To love the hand that slays!

Becoming Body in body, I
Have joined Body to Liṅga;
Becoming Mind in mind, I have
Joined Mind to Liṅga;
Becoming Will in will, I have
Joined Will to Liṅga;
Becoming Knowledge in knowledge, I
Have joined Knowledge to Liṅga.
Suspending action and going beyond
Inaction, I have attained
Union with the ultimate Liṅga;
Suspending the I, erasing the Thou,
I have united both with Liṅga;
Having dissolved myself
In Cennamallikārjuna, I have
Dissolved the Absolute called Liṅga
Within myself: mark that,
Sangana Basavaṇṇa!

Source: *Śūnyasampādane*, 5 volumes, translated by S. C. Nandimath, M. A. Menezes, R. C. Hiremath, et al. (Dharwar: Karnatak University, 1970).

Selection from the *Basava Purāṇa* of Pālkuriki Somanātha

The Story of Siriyāla

In Kañci a pious man named Siriyāla faithfully kept his vows; daily he served food and drink to five jaṅgamas, according to their wishes. The lord of all decided to test the depth of Siriyāla's devotion and came in the guise of a good jaṅgama, a veteran of severe austerities. The merchant folded his hands above his head, praised the sage, bowed to his lotus feet, and said "O Lord! Come quickly, great soul! Help your grandson keep his daily vow."

Hearing this, the veteran of severe austerities said: "Good man, if you give us what we wish, what more could we want for our enjoyment?" Then pleasantly, like a kind man, showering compassion on Siriyāla, he made a strange request for human flesh.

"Since you know everything, you must know that I have a son whom you gave to me. He has a perfect body and all the good qualities. Is there any need for me to go to a neighboring house to purchase human flesh? I gladly pledge to accomplish your rarest of vows this very day," said Siriyāla and fell on the sage's feet like a penitent. He then went home and told his wife what had transpired and what was to be.

"Have no fear," said Saṅgaḷavva, and at once she called her son home from school, "Today is a festival day in our house," she said and adorned him for the sacrifice.

Devoutly, acting as if it were no more than a game, the mother and father killed the boy devotee, Sirāla, dressed him out, and prepared all kinds of curries without letting the people know what they were doing.

Quickly they called Poison Throat, and washing his two lotus feet, they drank the water. When they had seated him comfortably on a suitable seat, the lady and the merchant praised, worshiped, served, and prostrated themselves before him.

Joyfully the sage surveyed the curries. But they had kept the head aside, and not seeing it anywhere, he said: "You have hidden the head with the idea that by seeing it, you can cherish your affection for your son. That is not right! There is not even a little head-meat here. This does not fulfill my vow. The word of the Vedas that 'the head is the most important of all the limbs of the body' will have to be followed. Unless you bring the boy's head and give it to me, you will be unfulfilled."

When he said this, the husband and wife were afraid, "Good sir! Great soul! What you say is true. We were afraid you might reject a curry polluted by hair, and so we put it aside. Now Candanaṅga will cook it without further delay," they said.

Again they brought the food and offered the head curry. Black Throat looked at it from the corner of his eye.

"In the whole world there are not other donors of food like yourselves. Now the ritual has been well performed. You have made an offering that can never be equaled. In keeping with the occasion, I must sit on your left and you on my right. Now after the preliminaries, if we do not sit together and eat the liṅga sacrifice, it will be unacceptable to me. If you rescind your pledge, I will be on my way," he said.

Then the merchant was dizzy and afraid and, looking at his wife, he said, "Why do you hestitate? Come!"

When the liṅga ceremony was finished, and she had begun to serve, the veteran of austerities said, "When entertaining a guest, the host should eat with his son sitting joyfully by his side. So how can you eat? I do not see your son. Where is your son? I told you that before, Siriyāla. Tell me, how is it right for me to eat in a house where there is no son? It is said that a person without a son has no path. Can sages eat in the homes of men who have no path? If you have a son, call him. If you do not, is this fit for one such as I?"

Then the man shook with fright, bowed down, and said, "I heard what you told me before. I do have a son; he must be studying or playing. He will come soon to receive your blessings. Eat the rice and curries and protect us, immortal soul. The food is getting cold."

Then the jaṅgama said to the woman, "Won't you do as I say and call him? Can there be a son who will not come when his mother calls? Look in the four directions in succession, raise your voice, and call so that we, too, can hear you. Can he fail to come if you do that?"

"How can I refuse to do what he says?" she said and went out and began by facing the east. As the sage had commanded her, she raised her voice and began to call.

"Come, my son! You destroy the tenacious karma acquired in past lives. Come, my little one! You are more than a match for the god of the south. Come, my boy! You are capable of eliminating the death and sorrow of future births. Come, my son! You are most dear to the praise of yogis who rules the north. Come, my lord, You will gain a state more blissful than heaven. Come, my child. You are capable of destroying the weapon of the lord of death. Come, my little man! You will be able to break the fetters of attachments. Come, my father! You have not become entangled in the net of desire for money, women, and sons. Come, my little bachelor! The ascetic king of the gods who is ready to give boons praises you. Come, my master! The king of ascetics who cancels death will be pleased. Come, my baby boy! You force us to swim across the terrible and senseless ocean of the cycle of birth and death. Come, O eldest son of the one who lives a meritorious life in Kañci. Come, bridgegroom of devotion! The divine maiden of liberation comes with her retinue to marry you. Come, my son! Your father's right shoulder is throbbing. Come, my Sirāla, resident of the house of riches, for the sun is setting in the west. Come, my dear, and eat this blessed food with the companion of the lord of wealth. Your presence will make it tasty for him," she said, calling for her son. And as she did so, mentioned the names of the four corners of the earth.

Earrings shone; locks tossed; jewelry glittered; bells gently tinkled; forehead ornaments shook; fate was amazed; the joy of it was universal. While his ankle bells jingled; while the lady of liberation approached; while everyone's doubts were cleared up and everyone was surprised; while the bystanders sang songs of praise; while the gods doubted themselves; while the ascetic looked on; while the father swelled with pleasure; while the mother stretched out her arms to embrace him; while the atmosphere was electric; while the people of the three worlds watched; the boy came home!

Suddenly Īśvara manifested and stood before Siriyāla, who, along with his wife and son, fell prostrate on the earth. As if they had just awakened from a dream, they looked about with wonder, and they sang praises.

Lord of wealth, lord of speech, lord of the gods, best of sages, lords of the directions, all of them, praised. The rudra gaṇas, the ancient assembly of devotees, Vīrabhadra, and others gathered around to worship. The good devotees sang praises with hearts full of amazement. And the God of gods took Candanaṅga and all her dear ones, Tiruveṅgāṇi and her friends, Siriyāla, Sirāla, and the seven neighborhoods of Kañci to Kailāsa in his divine, golden flying chariot.

Source: Velcheru Narayana Rao, *Śiva's Warriors: The Basava Purāṇa of Pālkuriki Somanātha* (Princeton: Princeton University Press, 1990).

9

Goddess Devotion and Tantra

Traditionally in Indian religious history, there has been an overlap between the cult of goddess devotion called Śāktism with Śaivism and Tantra. Rather than attempt to cover the many goddesses, their forms of devotion, and their literature, this chapter concentrates on the single goddess Kālī. I have chosen the so-called *Devī-māhātmya* section of the larger *Mārkaṇḍaya Purāṇa* because this part of the purāṇic text is historically important for the development of the goddess Kālī, and the text is still recited at the conclusion of the annual Durgā festival. Prior to the arrival of Kālī, the goddess Cāndikā is engaged in a cosmic struggle with demonic forces, who defeated the gods and drove them from heaven, where the demon Mahiṣa now reigns supreme. In response to this dire development, the gods have combine their energies to form the goddess Cāndikā, and they have given her their weapons in order for her to battle and defeat the demons, which she does successfully in single combat. In another episode, the demons Śumbha and Niśumbha conquer the gods and drive them from heaven. Whereupon, the gods turn to the goddess, who issues forth from the body of Pārvatī, consort of Śiva. Cāndikā appears beautiful to the servants of the demons, who report their findings to the demon leader Śumbha, who proposes to marry her, but she explains that because of a previous vow she can only marry a being who could defeat her in battle. After she defeats one army, the demons Caṇḍa and Muṇḍa are dispatched with another army to defeat the goddess. This second army and its leaders are destroyed by the goddess Kālī who emerges from the forehead of Cāndikā, and she also assists in the slaying of the demon Raktabīja.

In addition to myths associated with the goddess, this chapter includes selections from the poetry by Rāmprasād Sen (c. 1718–1755), an ardent devotee of the goddess, who directly reflects her devotional cult in the region of Bengal. It is virtually impossible to discern the identity of the historical figure of the poet, but a Śākta tradition evolved that created a figure to serve its own purposes as an acceptable model of a holy person and poet. There are two fundamental traditions according to which he was a member of the physician caste (*boidyā*) located in West Bengal or, alternatively, a Brahmin living in East Bengal. During his adult life, he worked as a clerk in the office of a wealthy person near Calcutta. Instead of working diligently on his job, he devoted his time to composing poetry about the goddess. He was caught wasting time on an idle pursuit, and he was declared "mad or drunk." His employer was, however, emotionally influenced by his songs, and gave the poet a stipend of thirty rupees per month to devote full time to his avocation. But this stipend became a source of friction with his family, because it was inadequate to sustain them. Nonetheless, Rāmprasād was able to relate to poor people within a cultural context in which social poverty functions as a metaphor for spiritual poverty.[1] Before the annual event of the ritual immersion of the image of the goddess into the Ganges River, Rāmprasād publicly declared that he would join the goddess while others sang his poems. He descended the steps of the bathing ghat carrying the image, and he died singing to his beloved goddess. Thus the saintly poet and goddess become immersed in the holy river with the two figures merging with each other, much like the merging of Mīrābāī with the image of Krishna at the end of her life, according to hagiographical accounts. From an historical perspective, Rāmprasād became a leader and central figure for a Śākta revival, which makes him similar to Caitanya of Gauḍīya Vaiṣṇavism.[2]

Rāmprasād pioneered the genre of Śākta Padāvalī, which can be divided into two types: those poems about Kālī categorized as *Śyāmā-sangīta* (Songs to the Black One), which recall the dark features of the goddess Kālī; and those about the goddess Umā called *Umā-sangīta*, which refer to the goddess at the yearly Durgā Pūjā festival, when she comes to Bengal as the region's beloved daughter. A further division reflects songs in anticipation of Umā's coming (*āgamanī*) and other songs recounting grief over her departure.[3] These devotional songs contributed to altering the image of the goddess to a more maternal and loving figure rather than the terrible, frightening shrew found in earlier mythology. Rāmprasād also composed his own version of a popular love story with double song cycles called *Kālikīrtan* and *Krishnarītan*. In addition to being a skilled extemporaneous versifier, Rāmprasād was deeply influenced by an esoteric tantric tradition, while being affiliated with sectarian Śāktism.

Rāmprasād uses interchangeable names for the goddess–Kālī, Durgā, and Tārā–and various epithets. Some of the themes that can be discovered in his poems include the role of warrior, good and bad mother, and, daughter of the poet; eroticism, madness, playfulness, and power. The primary successor of Rāmprasād was Kamalākānta Bhattācārya (c. 1769-1821), but it is not possible to include selections of his poems due to limitations of length.

Devotion to the goddess by Rāmprāsad was shared by the Bengali saint Rāmakrishna (1836-1886). During the life of the saint, a disciple named Mahendranath Gupta, who was more commonly and simply known as M, keep a diary of his encounters with Rāmakrishna over a four-year period (from 1882 when Gupta initially met the saint until a few months prior to Rāmakrishna's death in 1886). This four-year diary was entitled *Śrīśrīrāmakrishnāmṛta*, which was sequentially published in 1902, 1904, 1908, 1910, and 1932 (the last being the shortest volume). The five volumes are arranged cyclically, which means that each volume begins in 1882 when Gupta first encountered the saint and ends in 1886. Although the five volumes are repetitive, each text contains new material neglected in previous volumes. This personal record kept by a highly educated follower of the saint combined literary elements of personal observation, dialogue with the saint, and hagiography. The selections demonstrate the almost child-like personality of the saint, his madness, devotion to Kālī, and his playful nature. M's text is called *Kathāmṛta* in Bengali, and the author supplies dramatic scenes and dates, instead of sayings of the saint, devoid of any context, recorded by others. An English translation entitled *The Gospel of Sri Ramakrishna* was made by Swami Nikhilananda and initially published in 1942. Nikhilananda changed the original diary of M by rearranging it into a chronological sequence, and he bowdlerized the text for Western readers in order to protect the official image of Rāmakrishna perpetuated by the organizers of the movement. In this anthology, I have used selections graciously translated from the original and shared by Malcolm Mclean of the University of Otago in New Zealand.

The diaries of Gupta relating his encounters with Rāmakrishna have to be placed within the context of a community of followers of the Bengali saint. The community surrounding the saint was composed of an inner circle and an outer circle. The former consisted of both lay peope (householders) and renouncers, whereas the latter circle was constituted by vistors, guests, and women.

Like to Śāktism, Tantra was not a coherent or unified religious tradition. It was changing and fluid, but it was centered on particular texts and practices. It became established between the sixth and seventh centuries, when it originated in classes (*kula*) with ascetic origins. Tantric texts are secret and esoteric, and they use polysemic terminology in which words and sentences can convey multiple meanings. The secretive nature of the texts means that they are intended and written only for insiders. The texts have a dialogical structure, with divine beings communicating with each other, and they assume that the human body is a microcosm of the universe. Tantric texts are usually anonymous works, whereas the digests (*nibandhas*) have known authors, who often identify themselves in the text. The anonymous works are frequently said to originate with Śiva, and its original recipients is usually his spouse, or one of her maniferstations, whereas the digests do not claim to be revealed texts. Tantric practitioners use rituals, mantras (repetitive sacred utterances), and mudras (hand gestures), and they emphasize the need for a guru for initiation into its secrets.

This anthology includes selections from the *Kulārṇava Tantra* (Ocean of the Kula), which has been traditionally regarded as the fifth section of the *Ūrdhvāmnāya Tantra*, a work that has been lost. The *Kulār ṇava Tantra* consists of 2,060 verses divided among seventeen chapters called waves. The text, which can be dated between 1000 and 1400 C.E., views itself as the quintessential kula (or kaula) text. The term *kula* refers to the highest or the most secret teachings of the "heart," and represents a secretive body of teachings and practices intended for an elite initiate. A practitioner is one who engages in the secret of the heart and also penetrates into the heart of the divine. Witin the Kaula system, it is common to find worship of the human female because she represents the universal Śakti.

Dating to the late fourteenth century C.E., the *Toḍala Tantra* consists of ten chapters with 398 verses, which focus on ritual worship to Kālī and the other ten Mahāvidyās (literally, great knowledge). The ten Mahāvidyās are a strange collection of goddesses. In addition to Kālī, there are Tārā, Tripurasundarī (beautiful one of the three worlds, who is also known as Ṣoḍaśī or Sundarī), Bhuvaneśvarī (Sovereign of the Three Worlds), Tripurabhairavī (Fierce Lady, also shortened to Bhairavī), Chinnamastā (who is depicted holding her severed head, with two streams of blood streaming from her headless torso), Dhūmāvatī (Gray Lady, who is depicted as a widow with a crow as her symbol), Bagalā (goddess of battle), Mātaṇgī (goddess of the hunter tribes), and Kamalā.

The *Toḍala Tantra* is structured as a dialogue between Śiva and his consort. The former plays the role of instructor, whereas his consort is the inquiring student. Śiva teaches about proper mantras (sacred formulas) for the Mahāvidyās, tantric yoga, ritual, and microcosmic and macrocosmic symbolism. The text represents the mantra path (*mārga*) of tantric scriptures. Hand gestures (*mudrās*), sacred diagrams (*yantras*), and placing sacred mantras onto the limbs of the practitioner, which transforms one's mundane body into something sacred, are all important actions discussed by the text.

Other tantric selections are from the *Tantrāloka* (Light of the Tantras) of the Kashmiri thinker named Abhinavagupta, who asserts in the text that he is a transmitter of a tradition and not an innovator. This tantric tradition grew from the eastern transmission of the Kaula tradition, which is known as the Trika branch, or also called Kashmir Śaivism, of this text because it provides an excellent example of the secret sexual rites of the movement.

The final tantric selections are taken from the *Yoginīhṛdaya* (The Heart of the Yoginī), which dates not earlier than the eleventh century and could be later. The "heart" is understood as a great mystery and supreme plane where the goddess, consciousness of oneself, manifests her glory and power by means of the Śrīcakra (auspicious center) and Śrīvidyā (auspicious knowledge), which represent visual and phonic forms of the goddess. To clarify the title of the text further, Yoginīs are secondary deities grouped into lines (*gotra*) or families (*kula*). It is the kula that constitutes the inner, esoteric core of the various Kaula systems, and represents both the human and the cosmic body, which is the totality of the cosmos with which the individual is correlated because both have the same constitutent elements.

The Heart of the Yoginī is presented as a dialogue between Bhairava, a fearsome form of Śiva, and Tripurasundarī or Mahātripurasundarī (The Beautiful Goddess of the Three Cities), who is the main deity of the tantric Śaiva tradition called Śrīvidyā, although it might be preferable to call the system Tripurā. The system is sometimes called Saubhāgyasaṃpradāya, which means good fortune, success, happiness, and beauty. The text consists of three chapters: *cakrasaṃketa* (from which selections for this anthology are drawn), *mantrasaṃketa*, and *pūjāsaṃketa*. The text begins with the teacher vowing to realize the threefold *saṃketa* of the goddess Tripurā. The term *saṃketa* means agreement, appointment, or meeting with the promise of salvation because of the presence of Śiva and Śakti in the center (*cakra*), the knowledge (*vidyā*), and worship (*pūjā*), whose power and efficacy are traced to the presence of these male and female deities. Within the context of such a structure, the text informs its reader that the universe is created by play and represents the manifest form of the goddess, that the universe is pervaded by a divine power (*śakti*) that is feminine, that the goddess is identified with luminous consciousness, and that she vibrates throughout the universe, is immersed in bliss, and is transcendent and immanent. The text culminates with the nondual realization of the absolute.

Selections from the *The Devī-Māhātmya* (87–89) section of the *Mārkaṇḍeya Purāṇa*

Can to 87

The rishi spoke:

Then at his command the Daityas, led by Caṇḍa and Muṇḍa, and arrayed in the four-fold order of an army, marched with weapons uplifted. Soon they saw the goddess, slightly smiling, seated upon the lion, on a huge golden peak of the majestic mountain. On seeing her some of them made a strenuous effort to capture her, and others approached her holding their bows bent and their swords drawn.

Thereat Ambikā uttered her wrath aloud against those foes, and her countenance then grew dark as ink in her wrath. Out from the surface of her forehead, which was rugged with frowns, issued suddenly Kālī of the terrible countenance, armed with a sword and noose, bearing a many-coloured skull-topped staff, decorated with a garland of skulls, clad in a tiger's skin, very appalling because of her emaciated flesh, exceedingly wide of mouth, lolling out her tongue terribly, having deep-sunk reddish eyes, and filling the regions of the sky with her roars. She fell upon the great Asuras impetuously, dealing slaughter among the host, and devoured that army of the gods' foes there. Taking up the elephants with one hand she flung them into her mouth, together with their rear-men and drivers and their warrior-riders and bells. Flinging likewise warrior with his horses, and chariot with its driver into her mouth, she ground them most frightfully with her teeth. She seized one by the hair, and another by the neck; and she kicked another with her foot, and crushed another against her breast. And she seized with her mouth the weapons and the great arms which those Asuras abandoned, and crunched them up with her teeth in her fury. She crushed all that host of mighty and high-spirited Asuras; and devoured some and battered others; some were slain with her sword, some were struck with her skull-topped staff, and other Asuras met their death being wounded with the edge of her teeth.

Seeing all that host of Asuras laid low in a moment, Caṇḍa rushed against her, Kālī, who was exceedingly appalling. Muṇḍa the great Asura covered her, the terrible-eyed goddess, with very terrible showers of arrows and with discuses hurled in thousands. Those discuses seemed to be penetrating her countenance in multitudes, like as very many solar orbs might penetrate the body of a thundercloud. Thereat Kālī, who was roaring frightfully, laughed terribly with excessive fury, showing the gleam of her unsightly teeth within her dreadful mouth. And the goddess, mounting upon her great lion, rushed at Caṇḍa, and seizing him by his hair struck off his head with her sword. And Muṇḍa also rushed at her when he saw Caṇḍa laid low; him also she felled to the ground, stricken with her scimitar in her fury. Then the army, so much as escaped unslain, seeing Caṇḍa laid low and most valiant Muṇḍa also, seized with panic fled in all directions.

And Kālī, holding Caṇḍa's head and Muṇḍa also, approached Cāndikā and said, her voice mingled with passionate loud laughter—"Here I have brought thee Caṇḍa and Muṇḍa, two great beasts; thou thyself shalt slay Śumbha and Niśumbha in the battle-sacrifice."

The rishi spoke:

Thereon, seeing those two great Asuras Caṇḍa and Muṇḍa brought to her, auspicious Cāndikā spoke to Kālī this witty speech, "Because thou hast seized both

Caṇḍa and Muṇḍa and brought them, thou, O goddess, shall therefore be famed in the world by the name Cāmuṇḍa!"

Can to 88. The Slaying of Rakta-bīja

The rishi spoke:

After both the Daitya Caṇḍa was slain and Muṇḍa was laid low, and many soldiers were destroyed, the lord of the Asuras, majestic Śumbha, with mind overcome by wrath, gave command then to array all the Daitya hosts,—"Now let the eighty-six Daityas, upraising their weapons, march forth with all their forces; let the eighty-four Kambūs march forth surrounded by their own forces; let the fifty Asura families who excel in valour go forth; let the hundred families of Dhaumras go forth at my command. Let the Kālakas, the Daurhṛitas, the Mauryas, and the Kālakeyas,—let these Asuras, hastening at my command, march forth ready for battle."

After issuing these commands Śumbha, the lord of the Asuras, who ruled with fear, went forth, attended by many thousands of great soldiers. Cāndikā, seeing that most terrible army at hand, filled the space between the earth and the firmament with the twanging of her bow-string. Thereon her lion roared exceedingly loud, O king, and Ambikā augmented those roars with the clanging of her bell. Kālī, filling the regions of the sky with the noise from her bowstring, from her lion, and from her bell, and expanding her mouth wide with her terrific roars, had the predominance. On hearing that roar which filled the four regions of the sky, the Daitya armies enraged surrounded the goddess' lion, and Kālī.

At this moment, O king, in order to destroy the gods' foes, and for the well-being of the lion-like immortals, there issued forth endowed with excessive vigour and strength the energies from the bodies of Brahmā, Śiva, Guha and Vishnu and of Indra also, and went in the forms of those gods to Cāndikā. Whatever was the form of each god, and whatever his ornaments and vehicle, in that very appearance his Energy advanced to fight with the Asuras. In the front of a heavenly car drawn by swans advanced Brahma's Energy, bearing a rosary of seeds and an earthen water-pot; she is called Brahmāṇī. Maheśvara's Energy, seated on a bull grasping a fine trident, and wearing a girdle of large snakes, arrived, adorned with a digit of the moon. And Kumāra's Energy, Ambikā, with spear in hand and riding on a choice peacock, advanced in Guha's shape to attack the Daityas. Likewise Vishnu's Energy, seated upon Garuḍa, advanced with conch, discus, club, bow and scimitar in hand. The Energy of Hari, who assumes the peerless form of a sacrificial boar, she also advanced assuming a hog-like form. Nṛisiṁha's Energy assuming a body like Nṛisiṁha's arrived there, adorned with a cluster of constellations hurled down by the tossing of his mane. Likewise Indra's Energy, with thunder-bolt in hand, seated upon the lord of elephants and having a thousand eyes, arrived; as is Śakra, such indeed was she. Then those Energies of the gods surrounded Śiva. He said to Cāndikā, "Let the Asuras be slain forthwith through my good-will."

Thereupon from the goddess' body there came forth Cāndikā's Energy, most terrific, exceedingly fierce, howling like a hundred jackals. And she the unconquered said to Śiva, who was smoke-coloured and had matted locks, "Be thou, my lord, a messenger to the presence of Śumbha and Niśumbha. Say unto the two overweening Dānavas, Śumbha and Niśumbha, and to whatever other Dānavas are assembled there to do battle—'Let Indra obtain the three worlds, let the gods be the enjoyers of the oblations; go ye to Pātāla if ye wish to live. Yet if through pride in your strength you are longing for battle, come ye on then! let my jackals be glutted with your flesh.' " Because the goddess appointed Śiva himself to be ambassador, she has hence attained fame as Śiva-dūtī in this world. . . .

Raktabīja, a great Asura, seeing the Daityas, who were hard-pressed by the band of Mothers, intent on fleeing, strode forward to fight in wrath. When from his body there falls to the ground a drop of blood, at that moment starts up from the earth an Asura of his stature. He, a great Asura, with club in hand fought with Indra's Energy, and Indra's Energy then struck Raktabīja with her thunder-bolt; blood flowed quickly from him when wounded by the thunder-bolt. Thereupon stood up together fresh combatants, like him in body, like him in valour; for as many blood-drops fell from his body, so many men came into being, like him in courage, strength and valour. And those men also who sprang from his blood fought there with the Mothers in a combat, dreadful because of the sweep of their very sharp weapons. And again when his head was wounded by the fall of her thunder-bolt his blood poured forth; therefrom were born men by thousands. And Vishnu's Energy struck at this foe with her discus in the battle. Indra's Energy beat that lord of the Asuras with her club. The world was filled by the thousands of great Asuras, who were his equals, and who sprang from the blood that flowed from him when cloven by the discus of Vishnu's Energy. Kumāra's energy struck the great Asura Raktabīja with her spear, and Varaha's Energy also struck him with her sword, and Maheśvara's Energy with her trident. And the Daitya Raktabīja, that great Asura, filled full of wrath, struck every one of the Mothers in turn with his club. By the stream of blood, which fell on the earth from him when he received many wounds from the spears, darts and other weapons, Asuras came verily into being in hundreds. And those Asuras who sprang from that Asara's blood pervaded the whole world; thereat the gods fell into the utmost terror.

Seeing the gods dejected, Cāndikā spoke with haste; she said to Kālī, "O Cāmuṇḍa! stretch out thy mouth wide; with this mouth do thou quickly take in the great Asuras, which are the drops of blood, that have come into being out of Raktabīja at the descent of my weapon on him. Roam about in the battle, devouring the great Asuras who sprang from him; so shall this Daitya with his blood ebbing away meet destruction. These fierce demons are being devoured by thee and at the same time no others will be produced."

Having enjoined her thus, the goddess next smote him with her dart. Kālī swallowed Raktabīja's blood with her mouth. Then he struck Cāndikā with his club there; and the blow of his club caused her no pain, even the slightest, but from his stricken body blood flowed copiously, and from whatever direction it came, Cāmundā takes it then with her mouth. The great Asuras, who sprang up from the flow of blood in her mouth, Cāmundā both devoured them and quaffed his blood. The goddess smote Raktabīja with her dart, her thunder-bolt arrows, swords and speaks, when Cāmundā drank up his blood. Stricken with that multitude of weapons, he fell on the earth's surface, and the great Asura Raktabīja became bloodless, O king. Thereat the thirty gods gained joy unparalleled, O king. The band of Mothers, which sprang from them broke into a dance, being intoxicated with blood.

Canto 89. The Slaying of Niśumbha

The king spoke:

Wonderful is this that then, Sir, hast related to me the majesty of the goddess' exploits in connexion with the slaying of Raktabīja; and I wish to hear further what deed did Śumbha do after Raktabīja was killed, and what the very irascible Niśumbha did.

The rishi spoke:

After Raktabīja was slain other demons were killed in the fight, the Asura Śumbha gave way to abounded wrath, and Niśumbha also. Pouring out his indignation at beholding his great army being slaughtered, Niśumbha then rushed forward with the flower of the Asura army. In front of him and behind and on both sides great Asuras, biting their lips and enraged, advanced to slay the goddess. Śumbha also went forward mighty in valor, surrounded with his own troops, to slay Cāndikā in his rage, after engaging in battle with the Mothers. Then occurred a desperate combat between the goddess and Śumbha and Niśumbha, who both, like two thunder-clouds, rained a most tempestuous shower of arrows on her.

Cāndikā with multitudes of arrows quickly split the arrows shot by them, and smote the two Asura lords on their limbs with her numerous weapons.

Niśumbha grasping a sharp scimitar and glittering shield struck the lion, the noble beast that bore the goddess, on the head. When her animal was struck, the goddess quickly clove Niśumbha's superb sword with a horse-shoe-shaped arrow, and also his shield on which eight moons were portrayed. When his shield was cloven and his sword too, the Asura hurled his spear; and that his missile also, as it came towards her, she split in two with her discus. Then Niśumbha, the Dānava, puffed up with wrath, seized a dart; and that also, when it came, the goddess shattered with a blow of her fist. And then aiming his club he flung it against Cāndikā, yet that was shivered by the goddess' trident and became ashes. As that lordly Daitya then advanced with battle-axe in hand, the goddess struck him with a multitude of arrows and laid him low on the ground.

When his brother Niśumbha, who was terrible in prowess, fell to the ground, Śumbha, in utmost fury strode forward to slay Ambikā. And he, standing in his chariot, appeared to fill the entire sky with his eight arms, which were lifted far on high grasping his superb weapons.

Beholding him approaching, the goddess sounded her conch, and made her bow also give forth from its string a note, which was exceedingly hard to endure. And she filled all regions with the clanging of her bell, which caused the vigour of all the Daitya hosts to die away. Then her lion filled the heaven, the earth and the ten regions of the sky with loud roars, which checked the copious flow of the exudation from the demons' rutting elephants. Kālī springing upward then struck the heaven and the earth with both her hands; the boom thereof drowned those previous sounds. Śiva-dūtī uttered a loud inauspicious laugh. At those sounds the Asuras trembled; Śumbha gave way to utmost rage. When Ambikā cried out "Stand, O evil-souled! stand!" the gods who had taken their stations in the air then called to her, "Be thou victorious!"

The spear flaming most terribly, which Śumbha approaching hurled, that, gleaming like a mass of fire as it came along, was driven aside by a great fire-brand. The vault between the three worlds reverberated with Śumbha's lion-like roaring, but the dreadful sound of the slaughter among his soldiers surpassed that, O king. The goddess split the arrows shot by Śumbha, and Śumbha the arrows that she discharged, each with her and his sharp arrows in hundreds and thousands. Cāndikā enraged thereat smote him with a dart. Wounded therewith he fell in a faint to the ground.

Thereupon Niśumbha, regaining consciousness, seized his bow again and struck the goddess, and Kālī and the lion with arrows. And the Dānava lord, that son of Diti, putting forth a myriad arms, again covered Cāndikā with a myriad discuses. The goddess then enraged, she, Durgā who destroys the afflictions of adversity, split those discuses and those arrows with her own arrows. Then Niśumbha seizing his club rushed impetuously at Cāndikā to slay her outright, with the Daitya impetuously at Cāndikā to slay her outright, with the Daitya host surrounding him. As he was just falling upon her, Cāndikā swiftly clove his club with her sharp-edged scimitar. And he took hold of a dart. Cāndikā with a dart hurled swiftly pierced Niśumbha, the afflicter of the immortals, in the heart, as he approached with dart in hand. When he was pierced by the dart, out of his heart issued another man of great strength and great valour, exclaiming "Stand!" When he stepped forth, the goddess laughing aloud then struck off his head with her scimitar; thereupon he fell to the ground.

The lion then devoured those Asuras whose necks he had crushed with his savage teeth, and Kālī and Śiva-dūtī devoured the others. Some great Asuras perished, being pierced through by the spear held by Kumāra's Energy; others were driven back by the water purified by the spell uttered by Brahma's Energy; and others fell, pierced by the trident wielded by Śiva's Energy; some were pounded to dust on the ground by blows from the snout of Varāha's Energy; some Dānavas were out to pieces by the discus hurled by Vishnu's Energy; and others again by the thunder-bolt discharged from the fingers of Indra's Energy. Some Asuras perished outright, some perished by reason of the great battle, and others were devoured by Kālī, Śiva-dūtī and the lion.

Source: *The Mārkaṇḍeya Purāṇa*, translated by F. Eden Pargiter. (Calcutta: the Asiatic Society, 1904; reprint Delhi: Indological Book House, 1969).

Selections from the poetry of Rāmprasād Sen

What a joke!
She's a young woman
From a good family
        yes, but
    She's naked—and flirts, hips cocked
    when she stands.

With messy hair
roars awful and grim
this gentlewoman tramples demons

in a corpse-strewn battle.
But the God of Love
looks and swoons.

While ghosts, ghouls, and goblins
from Śiva's retinue, and her own companions
nude just like Her
dance and frolic on the field,
She swallows elephants
chariots, and charioteers
striking terror into the hearts
of gods, demons, and men.

She walks fast,
Enjoying herself tremendously.
Human arms hang from Her waist.

Rāmprasād says: Mother Kālikā,
preserver of the world,
have mercy!
Take the burden:
ferry me across this ocean of becoming.
Hara's woman,
destroy my sorrows.

Who can understand Kālī?
You can't get Her vision
through the six philosophies.

She plays with Śiva
two swans
amorous amidst lush lotuses.
Ascetics ponder Her
from *mūlādhāra* to *sahasrāra*.

Like "Oṃ," the root of all,
Kālī is the self
of one who delights in the self.
Just for fun

She dwells in body after body,
encasing our universe
in Her belly. Can you imagine
measuring *that*?
The Destructive Lord has grasped Her core,
But who else can?

Prasād says, People laugh at me
trying to swim across the sea.
My heart knows but my mind does not—and so
 through a dwarf
I try to catch the moon!

Can someone
called Daughter of a Stone
have compassion in Her heart?
If She weren't pitiless, could
She kick Her husband in the chest?

The world knows You
as the Compassionate, but
there isn't a trace of compassion
in You. You wear a necklace
of heads, cut
from other mother's sons!

The more I cry "Mā Mā!"
the more
 though I know You hear me
You don't listen.
Prasād gets kicked
for no reason. Still
he calls out
 "Durgā!"

At least I have a way to understand
Kālī's blackness:
the black resin
that stains me in Her world.

Her movements are frenzied;
how can I tame Her?
I'll dance Her on my lotus heart
  to mental music.
Mind, I can teach you
to get Kālī's feet.

As for those six saucy rogues
I'll chop them up. I'll spend my time
thinking Kālī,
being Kālī,
speaking Kālī.
At any time
  good or bad
I'm set to smear soot
on Death's face.

Prasād says, Mā,
how much more can I say?
I'll take Your blows
and I won't fight back.
  But nor will I stop
  calling "Kālī!"

So, Mind—
you've decided to go on pilgrimage?
If you abandon the nectar of Kālī's lotus feet
you'll fall in a well
and ruin yourself.

Life is old age, sin, and disease;
These are the sufferings they offer at Puri.
Kashi—or do I mean a cough?—can kill you when you have a fever,
and bathing at Tribeni will only make your sickness worse.

Kālī's name is a powerful medicine, the best prescription:
drink it with devotion. Oh sing! Drink!
You'll become the Self, delighting in your Self!
Śiva is the Lord of Death; if you serve Him well

liberation will quickly follow.
In Him all things are possible: even you
will merge with the Supreme.

Prasād says, Brother Mind,
you've traded the shade of the wish-filling tree
for the roots of a thorn bush. Is this the way
to lose the fear of death?

Mind, how do you think you'll find Her?
You're crazy; your house is dark!
If you have no realization,
can you catch the object of realization?
Mind, to the best of your ability
first bring yourself under control.
Otherwise, like the moon hiding at daybreak
She'll hide Herself in your small, dark room
in a secret cupboard.

I couldn't see Her
looking through the six philosophies
or the Āgamas, Nigamas, or *Tantrasāra*;
but he who appreciates the flavor of devotion
lives in that home in bliss.
Thristing for realization, that supreme yogi
inside you
meditates from age to age.
Once realization dawns, he'll catch hold of you
Like a magnet grabbing iron.

Prasād says, I worship that yogi as the Mother.
Shall I break this pot in public?
Mind, understand through hints and gestures.

Source: Rachel Fell McDermott, *Singing to the Goddess: Poems to Kālī and Umā from Bengal* (New York: Oxford University Press, 2001).

Selections from the *Srī Śrī Ramakrishna Kathamrita*

Ramakrishna was sitting with his devotees and describing his own religious practice (*sadhana*) and various of his different spiritual states. "When I was doing that sadhana I could actually see someone sitting by me with a trident in his hand. It was as if he was trying to frighten me—either I fixed my mind on God or he would kill me with his trident. Unless I fixed my mind on God he would pierce me to the heart. Sometimes the Mother put me in such a state that my mind descended from the absolute to the relative, then it would rise again to the absolute.

"When my mind descended like that sometimes I would think day and night about Sita and Rama. I would see them everywhere—I would carry the metal image of Ramlala around with me all the time, sometimes bathing him, sometimes feeding him. Sometimes my mind dwelt on Radha and Krishna and I would see them all the time. Sometimes I would think constantly of Caitanya, the union of the two modes, prakriti and purusa, I would see him all the time. . . .

"I did all kinds of sadhana. There are basically three kinds, sattvic, rajasic and tamasic. In sattvic sadhana you call out for God with earnest longing and repeat her name, you've no desire for rewards. In rajasic sadhana there are many kinds of rituals—you must offer worship so many times, visit so many holy places, practice austerities, worship with all the ritual details, and so on. Tamasic sadhana is sadhana with the help of passion—'Oh Kali, please show yourself to me! I'll cut my throat with this knife if you don't!' In this kind of sadhana one sets aside morality—as in Tantric sadhana." (3:137–138)

Ramakrishna: "One day Nangta and Haldhari were reading the *Adhyatma Ramayana* in the Kali temple. Suddenly I saw a river, with forests of green trees bordering it, and Rama and Lakshman walking beside it. One day in front of the hut I saw Arjuna's chariot with the Lord Krishna in it, dressed as a charioteer. I can still remember it. One day at Kamarpukur while we were singing *kirtans* I saw the form of Caitanya in front of me. A naked man used to stay with me all the time. I used to joke with him and laugh out loud. This naked form used to come out of me. It was like a boy, and looked like a *paramahamsa*.

"It's impossible to say how many visions of God I had then. At the time I had a stomach upset and the visions I saw used to make it worse. So when I had a vision I would spit, but they would follow me around and catch hold of me like ghosts! I used to be quite overwhelmed by my trances and couldn't tell day from night! Next day the mood would pass with my bowel motions! . . ."

Girish: "Why did you perform sadhana?"

Ramakrishna: "Bhagavati performed a lot of difficult sadhana for Siva, immersing her body in water during winter, staring at the sun! Krishna himself had to do much sadhana with Radha. She was the *Brahmayoni* and he had to worship it and meditate on it. From this *Brahmayoni* many universes were born.

It's very mysterious! I used to see visions under the bel tree—flashing like fire! I did a lot of Tantric sadhana with skull under the bel tree. The Brahmini used to gather all the things I needed. (Moving towards Haripada) I couldn't remain in that state unless I worshipped the boys' cocks with flowers and sandal paste. I also used to experience another state, one day I felt proud and the next I would be sick." Mani was amazed to hear such words from his holy mouth, and sat motionless, listening. (4:231–232)

Ramakrishna: "How does one subdue the passions? He should take the attitude of a woman. I did just that for a long time, I wore women's clothes and a scarf, I even used to worship with the scarf on! Otherwise how could I have kept my wife with me for eight months. We were both companions of the Mother. I can't call myself a man. Once when I was in a trance my wife asked, 'What am I to you?' I replied, 'You are Durga.'. . ."

"Krishna had a peacock feather on his head, and the peacock feather is a sign of the female yoni (vagina). That means Krishna carries the symbol of the female principle on his head. Krishna once went to the Rasa festival, but he went there as a woman. That's why he's always shown at the Rasa festival in women's clothes. Unless a man takes the nature of a woman he is not fit for their company. If he assumes the nature of a woman then he can join them in the dalliance of the gopis' dance and share their enjoyment. But if one is a sadhaka he must be very careful! He must stay well clear of women. He mustn't go near female devotees." (2:154–155)

Ramakrishna was sitting on his bed delighting in the company of the pure-souled devotees who were laughing at his imitations of a *kirtani.* A kirtani puts on lots of ornaments and fancy clothes when she sings. She stands with a coloured handkerchief in her hand, and every now and then coughs and lifts her nose-ring to blow her nose. If some important person arrives during her performance she welcomes them, and from time to time lifts the border of her sari to show off her amulets and her jewelery.

The devotees were laughing uproariously at his performance. Paltu was rolling about on the floor with laughter. Looking at him Ramakrishna said to Mani, "He's only a boy, that's why he rolls about like that. (To Paltu) Don't tell your father about all this or he'll lose the little respect he still has for me.". . .

Ramakrishna gazed at Young Naren, and went into samadhi as he did so. Could he perhaps see God in such a pure devotee? All the devotees watched Ramakrishna. A short while ago they were all laughing and joking, now they were all still, as if the room was empty. Ramakrishna was absolutely motionless. After a while he emerged from his samadhi. His breathing had stopped and now he let go a deep sigh. Slowly his mind returned to this world, and he looked at the devotees, still partially in a trance. He spoke to all the devotees about their spiritual progress. (3:118–119)

Ramakrishna was sitting on his couch. He said to Nilakantha, "Sing me something about the Mother." Nilakantha and his followers sang "Come to Shyama's feet" and "O Durga, destroyer of the buffalo demon." As he listened to the songs Ramakrishna stood up and went into samadhi. Nilakantha sang "Siva has the queen of the world in his heart." Intoxicated with love Ramakrishna danced, and Nilakantha and the devotees circled round him singing and dancing as they went. . . . Nilakantha sang the song "O Gauranga, in your beautiful sun-gold body" and when he came to the refrain "Swept away on the flood of love" Ramakrishna again danced with Nilakantha and the devotees. Those who were watching will never forget the scene, the room was filled with people all intoxicated with love. It was just like Srivasa's courtyard when Caitanya danced there. . . .

Hearing the sound of the singing people gathered from all around. People were standing on all the verandahs, even people passing in boats on the river were drawn by the beautiful singing. When it ended Ramakrishna bowed to the Mother, saying "Bhagavata, Bhakta, Bhagavan—I salute the jnanis, I salute the yogis, I salute the bhaktas." (4:209–210)

Ramakrishna was sitting on the small bed in his room. Narendra, Bhavanath and Mani were sitting on the floor. Narendra was talking about the Ghoshpara, Panchnami and other such sects. Ramakrishna described these groups and began to criticise them. He said, "They don't do proper sadhana, they gratify the senses in the name of religion. (To Narendra) There's no need for you to listen to all this.

"The bhairavas and bhairavis are also like that. When I went to Benares I went one day to a bhairavi cakra where each bhairava was accompanied by a bhairavi. They asked me to drink some of their wine, but I said, 'Mother, I can't touch wine.' Then they began to drink. I thought, now they'll meditate and chant the name of God, but no, they began to dance! I was afraid they would fall into the Ganges, because the cakra was held beside the river.

"If bhairava and bhairavi are husband and wife, then that's very honourable. Do you know what? I prefer to think of a woman as mother and myself as her son. That's a pure way, and not so dangerous. Regarding them as sisters isn't bad either. But as wives—the way of the hero (*virabhava*), that's very difficult. Tarak's father used to practice that sadhana. It's very hard, you can't always keep the right attitude of mind.

"There are many sects, many paths, and not all of them are good ones. We don't follow them all here; you can make up your own minds, but I would say to you that I've finally come to the point where I say, 'The Goddess is the whole and I am part of her, she's the Lord and I am her servant; and sometimes I think that she is me and I am her.'" (From 2:142–143)

Ramakrishna: "You know, some people say that after samadhi the atman flies through the sky like a bird. Once a holy man from Hrishikesh who came here said that there are five kinds of samadhi, and he saw them all in me. They are the antlike, the fish-like, monkey-like, bird-like and snake-like. Sometimes the current rises like an ant, with a tingling feeling. Sometimes in samadhi the self plays joyfully like a fish in the sea of ecstacy. Sometimes the current's like a monkey, it plays with me and makes me turn over. Then I keep silent. Then suddenly it leaps like a monkey into the sahasrara. It makes me jump up. And sometimes the current rises like a bird flitting from branch to branch in a tree. When it settles on a branch it seems to burn. Then it flies from the muladhara to the svadhisthana, from the svadhisthana to the heart, and slowly rises to the head. Sometimes it moves like a snake, wriggling this way and that. It wriggles up to the head and I go into samadhi.

"Unless the Kundalini is awakened there'll be no consciousness. The Kundalini is in the muladhara. When consciousness is awakened it moves up the susumna canal piercing the cakras until finally it reaches the head. Finally it leads to samadhi. You don't awaken the consciousness by reading books, you have to call out to Her, when you long for Her the Kundalini awakens. All you get from books is knowledge—where will that get you?

"Just before I attained that state I was shown how the Kundalini sakti awakens. Slowly all the lotuses open and samadhi comes. It's a very mysterious thing. I saw a twenty-two-year-old youth, just like me, enter into the susumna canal and have intercourse with his tongue in the vagina-like lotuses! He started at the anus, then moved to the penis, then the navel, and so on up through the lotuses which were hanging down, and made them all lift their heads. When he came to the heart—I remember this very well—after having intercourse with his tongue the lotus which had been hanging down lifted its face and opened completely. Then he moved to the lotus at the throat and the one at the forehead. Finally the thousand-petalled lotus opened up! Since then I've been like this." (From 4:237–238)

Amrita: "What do you feel when you are in samadhi?"
Ramakrishna: "You've heard about how the cockroach turns into a fruit beetle by thinking about one; do you know what it's like? It's like a fish released from a pot into the Ganges."
Amrita: "Doesn't even a trace of ego remain?"
Ramakrishna: "Yes, generally a little does remain. However much you rub gold on a grindstone a little gold remains. Or you could say that it's like a spark from a large fire. Consciousness of the outer world goes, but She keeps a little of the ego there, so that I can enjoy it! This enjoyment is only possible when 'I' and 'you' remain. Sometimes She takes away even that trace of 'I.' This is called inactive samadhi—*nirvikalpa samadhi*. No one can say what that's like. A salt doll went to measure the depth of the sea, but after it had gone a little way into the water it disappeared, it assumed the same form as the water. Then who was there to return to the surface and say how deep the ocean was?" (1.5.2.4.)

Ramakrishna and His Disciples

It was evening. The lamps were lit and incense was burning in Ramakrishna's room. Lamps were also burning in the temples and the music was playing. Soon evening worship would begin in all the temples. Ramakrishna was sitting on his bed repeating the names of the deities and meditating on the Mother. The evening worship had begun. After a while he began to stroll up and down the room, occasionally talking with the devotees and consulting with Mani about going to Calcutta.

Just then Narendra arrived, with Sarat and two other young men. They prostrated themselves before him. When he saw Narendra Ramakrishna became very affectionate. He began to fondle Narendra as one fondles a young child, and said, in an affectionate voice, "You've come!" He was standing facing west. Narendra and the other youths stood in front of him. Ramakrishna glanced at Mani and said, "Narendra's arrived, how can I go out now? What do you think?" Mani replied, "Then stay here today." (3:194–195)

Ramakrishna: "Sometimes Hazra comes and says to me, 'Why do you think so much of those young fellows?' One day while going to Balaram's house by carriage I thought a lot about it. I said, 'Mother, Hazra asks me why I think so much about

Narendra and the other young men; he asks why I think so much about them instead of thinking about God.' Even while I was saying this I suddenly saw that she herself has become human. But she's only manifested through clear vessels. When I saw this I went into samadhi for a while, then I began to get angry at Hazra. I said, 'That bastard had me worried.' Then I thought, 'Why should I blame the poor fellow, how would he know about that?'

"I know that these young men are incarnations of Narayan. When first I saw Narendra I noticed that he had no bodily awareness. I merely touched his chest with my hand and he lost consciousness. When he regained his senses he said, 'What have you done to me? I have a mother and father!' Exactly the same thing happened at Jadu Mallick's house. I became more and more anxious to see him, my spirit panted for him. Then I said to Bholonath, 'Why do I feel this way?' Bholonath said, 'The answer to that's in the *Mahabharata*. When a man comes down from samadhi he delights in the company of people with a sattvic nature. When he finds a sattvic person, his mind becomes restful.' When I heard this I was at peace. From time to time I would sit and cry to see Narendra."

"Oh, what a state I was in! At first when I found myself in this state I couldn't distinguish night from day. Everyone said I was mad. So they had me married. It was a state of intoxication. At first I was concerned about my wife, then thought that she could live like me too. . . ."

"What a state I was in! Even the slightest thing would set me off. I performed Sundari puja with a fourteen-year-old girl, seeing in her an incarnation of the Mother. Then I offered a rupee at her feet. Once I used to bring young girls here and worship them. I used to see them as incarnations of the Mother. One day I noticed a girl dressed in blue standing under the trees, a prostitute. But she immediately kindled in me a vision of Sita. I forgot the woman, but I saw the incarnate Sita liberated and returning to Rama from Lanka. For a long time I was unconscious in a state of samadhi. . . ." (2:48–49)

Ramakrishna: "I'm telling you something very personal. Why do I love Purna and Narendra so much? I once felt such love for Jagannath that I went to embrace the image and broke my arm. Then it was revealed to me, You have assumed a human body, now with this human form you should adopt all spiritual attitudes, such as lover and mother."

"When I saw Purna and the others I felt for them what I used to feel for the image of Ramlala. I used to bathe him, feed him, put him to bed, and carry him about with me. I would sit crying for him, now I feel exactly the same way about these boys. Look at Niranjan. He's not the slightest bit attached to the world. He takes poor people to the hospital and pays for them with his own money. When his family talk about marriage he says, 'Oh, what a fate!' I see him in my visions sitting on a light. . . ."

"Narendra is on a very high plane—he accepts God as formless—the essence of the Supreme Being. Of all the devotees who come here there is none like him."(4:227–228)

All Religions Are Paths to God

Ramakrishna: "If one is sincere, God may be realised through all religions. Vaisnavas, Saktas, Vedantists, Brahmos, all will receive God; as will Muslim and Christian. All who are sincere will receive her. Some people quarrel saying, 'If you don't worship our Mother Kali you will gain nothing,' 'If you don't follow our Christian religion you will attain nothing.' That kind or reasoning is fanatical, saying 'My religion is right and all others are wrong.' That kind of judgement is bad. It's possible to reach God by many paths."

"Again some people say that God has form, that she isn't formless. This also leads to quarreling, Vaisnava quarrels with Vedantist. If someone has directly seen God, then he can speak about her. One who has seen knows that God really has form and is formless. More than that he can't say."

"Once a group of blind men came upon an animal which someone told them was called an elephant. They began to ask, 'What is an elephant like?' and to feel its body. One said, 'The elephant is like a pillar' because he had touched only the elephant's leg. Another said, 'The elephant is like a winnowing fan' because he had examined only its ear with his hand. Those who had felt its trunk and belly gave different descriptions. In just such a way one who had only a partial vision of God thinks that that is what God is like, that there's nothing else." (2:19)

Ramakrishna: "Hindu, Muslim, Christian, Sakta, Saivite, Vaisnava, the ancient rishis and you modern Brahmos—all look for the same thing. A mother prepares food to suit the tastes of her family. When she cooks fish for her five children she doesn't give pullao or curry to them all, their tastes are not all the same. For some she prepares fish soup. But she loves them all equally. Do you know what my position is? I love to eat all kinds of fish. I have a feminine nature. (Everyone laughed.) I like fried fish, fish prepared with turmeric, pickled fish and fish curry. And I like fish heads, curry and pullao too."

"You know what? God has made different religions to suit different countries, times and peoples. They're all paths to her, but she is not herself to be identified with any one path. If you follow any of these paths with sincere devotion you will reach God. If there are any faults in the path you have chosen, she will correct them if you are sincere. If someone goes to see Jagannath with great sincerity, and by some mistake travels north instead of south, then certainly someone on the way will say to him, don't go this way—you must go south. Sooner or later he'll see Jagannath. There is no need for us to point out the faults in other religions. She who made the world knows them all. What we should do is find some way to see Jagannath. I think your way is a good way. You say God is formless, and that's good. You can eat cake straight or sideways, it still tastes sweet.

"But dogmatism is bad. You know the story of the chameleon. While he was sitting under a tree a man saw a chameleon, and he said to his friend, I've seen a red lizard. He believed it to be completely red. Another man came back from the tree and said that he'd seen a green lizard. He believed it to be completely green. But the man who lived under the tree said, 'You are both right in what you say, that animal is sometimes red and sometimes green. Sometimes it is yellow, and sometimes it has no colour at all.' It says in the Vedas that God is saguna and nirguna. You say God is formless. That's very boring, but never mind. If you know one thing properly, you can learn another. She'll teach you." (2:125–126)

Ramakrishna: "The Brahmos say that God is formless, and maybe they're right; it's possible to call on Her within the heart. If you're sincere, She who knows all that goes on in our minds will certainly tell you what Her true nature is. But it's not good to say that everything we understand is right and what others say is mistaken. 'We say that She is formless, therefore she is formless, she has no form.' 'We say that She has form, therefore She has form, she isn't formless.' This is why there's ill-feeling between the Vaisnavas and the Saktas. The Vaisnavas say 'Our Krishna is the only saviour' and the Saktas say 'Our Goddess is the only saviour.' "

"Once I went to see Vaisnavacharan with Mathur babu. Vaisnavacharan is very detached and scholarly, but he's a very orthodox Vaisnava. And Mathur babu is a devotee of the Goddess. They talked a lot, and Vaisnavacharan said that Krishna is the only one who can grant release (*mukti*). When he said that Mathur babu became very red in the face. He said, 'You bastard!' (Everyone laughed.) He was a Sakta, wouldn't he say that? I gave Vaisnavacharan a nudge.

"I see many men who appear to be very religious, who are all the time quarrelling with this one and that, Hindus, Muslims, Brahmo Samajis, Saktas, Vaisnavas, Saivites, they all fight with each other. They don't understand that the one they call Krishna or Siva is also called Adyasakti; the one they call Jesus is also called

Allah. The one Rama has a thousand names. Reality is one, but goes by many different names. A pond has many different steps; the Hindus go to one lot of steps and take what they call 'jal' in a pitcher. The Muslims at another lot of steps take in their skin buckets what they call 'pani.' And the Christians take from other steps what they call 'water.' (Everyone laughed.)

"If someone says, 'No, what you have there isn't 'jal' it's 'pani,' or 'That isn't pani' it's 'water,' or 'That isn't 'water' it's 'jal,' that would be very amusing, wouldn't it. But so is party strife, disagreement and quarrelling; it's wrong to resort to fighting with sticks and mutual slaughter in the name of religion. Each man should go his own way, and if he is sincere and earnest, he will realise God." (2:103–104)

On Women and Gold

Ramakrishna: "Remember, however often you wash the garlic bowl, some of the smell will remain. Young men are pure vessels! They haven't even a speck of women and gold on them; but if they spend a long time in contact with them, then like the garlic the smell will stick."

"It's like a mango pecked by crows. You can't offer it to any deity, and you'd be suspicious about eating it yourself. Compare a new pot with one that has had curd in it. You'd be afraid to keep milk in the latter, because it might turn sour."

"People like Girish are quite different, they practice both yoga and bhoga (enjoyment). Their attitude's like that of Ravana, who wanted to take brides from both serpents and deities, and at the same time realize Rama. Asuras want to continue their life of enjoyment and to realise Narayan too." (2:199)

Ramakrishna: "If a woman touches my body I become ill; the place where she has touched me aches, as if a scorpion-fish had stung me."

Doctor: "That's possible, but where would we be without them?"

Ramakrishna: "If I touch money my hand twists! My breathing stops. But if one uses money for education, or serving God, or sadhus and devotees, then that's all right.

"If a man has a wife he gets tangled in the world's maya! Then he forgets God. The Mother of the world, she has the form of maya, and she also takes the form of woman. Once you realize this you have no desire to get entangled with the world's maya. If you think of woman as being really the Mother then you can live in the world. Unless you've seen God you can't understand what woman is."

Ramakrishna was talking with Mani, telling him about his attitude to women. "They say we can't live without women and gold. They don't know much about my condition then. If I touch a woman my hand goes numb, and aches. If I approach a woman to speak to her in a friendly way, it's as if there were a screen between us, through which I can't go. If a woman comes when I'm sitting alone in my room then I immediately become like a child, and I see the woman as my mother."

Mani was quite amazed as he sat by the bed and heard all this. A little distance away from them Bhavanath was talking with Narendra. Bhavanath had just got married and was trying to find a job, so he wasn't able to come to the Cossipore house to see Ramakrishna very often. Ramakrishna used to think about Bhavanath a lot because of his lapse into the world. He was about twenty-three years old.

Ramakrishna said to Narendra, "Encourage him as much as you can." Narendra and Bhavanath looked at the Thakur and began to smile. He spoke to Bhavanath again by means of signs, "Be a great hero. Don't forget yourself when she cries behind her veil. Women even cry when they blow their noses! Keep your mind fixed on God. A hero is one who lives with a woman without having sex with her. You must only speak to her about spiritual things." (2: 231–232)

After his trance Ramakrishna went and sat on his bed with Mani on the floor at his feet. He was talking to him, expressing his anger and hatred for those who enjoy sexual intercourse while seeking God. "You've no shame, you have children, but you still enjoy sex! You love a body which is veins, blood, urine, and so on! One who meditates on God should think of even the most beautiful woman as no more than ash from the cremation ground. You enjoy as impermanent body which has worms, filth, mucus and so many other impure things in it! You've no shame at all."

Mani, rebuked like this, sat in silence with his head bowed. Ramakrishna spoke again, "Anyone who has even a tiny drop of God's love should think of women and gold as empty things. Once you've tasted sugar-candy sherbet, that made from treacle doesn't tempt you. If you pray earnestly to God, and sing her praises, then your love for her will gradually increase." (4:28–29)

The Nature of God

Ramakrishna: "The Mother showed me in the temple that she herself has become everything. She showed me that everything is full of consciousness! The vessels of worship are full of consciousness, the image is full of consciousness, the dais is full of consciousness, the door sill is full of consciousness, the marble floor, all are full of consciousness. It seemed to me that everything in the temple was saturated with bliss, the bliss of saccidananda (being, consciousness, and bliss). Outside the temple I saw a wicked man, but even in him I saw God's power shining!

"That's why I gave some of the offerings to the cat. I saw that the Mother has become everything, even the cat. . . . Once you've realised God then you'll really see that she has become all living things, the world and the twenty-four cosmic principles. Then when she wipes out the ego completely no-one can describe what happens." (4:35)

Ramakrishna: "You must have devotion, that is, you must love God. That which is Brahman may also be called 'Mother.' Ramprasad says, 'She I know as the Mother, must I openly reveal? You must understand her, O mind, from the hints I have given.' Ramprasad says to his mind, know her by hints. He is talking about knowing that which is called Brahman in the Vedas—that is what I call Mother. That which is nirguna is also saguna. That which is Brahman is also Sakti. In its inactive state it is known as Brahman. In its nature as creator, sustainer and destroyer it is known as Adyasakti, or Kali.

"Brahman and Sakti are the same, like fire and its burning power. When we speak of fire, we mean also its power to burn. If we talk about burning power we understand by that 'fire.' The meaning of the one is contained in the other. So Brahman may also also be called 'Mother.' Mothers are the objects of intense love. If you love God you will realise Brahman." (3:14)

Ramakrishna: "Do you believe God has form or not?"
Mani (to himself, astonished): "If one believes God has form, how can she be formless? And if God is formless, how can one believe she has form? Is it possible for a white substance like milk to become black?"
Mani: "I prefer to think of God as formless."
Ramakrishna: "That's good. It is possible to believe either one. It's good to think of God as formless. But it is not right to say, 'Only this is true and all other views are false.' Remember, it is right to say 'God is formless' is true and also that 'God has form' is true. Whatever you believe, hold firmly to that." . . .
Mani: "Suppose one believes God has form. But she is not the clay image. . . ."
Ramakrishna: "Why clay? It is a spiritual image."
Mani did not understand this "spiritual image." He said, "All right, those who worship clay images ought to know that the clay image is not God, and worship God rather than the image. They ought not to worship clay."
Ramakrishna (annoyed): "You Calcutta people are all the same! You just give lectures and teach others, you don't think about who will teach you. Who are you to teach? She to whom the world belongs will teach us. She has made the world, the

sun, moon, the seasons, men and animals. She has made provision for the animals' food, for parents to nurture them, and has taught parents to be affectionate. She has made so much provision for her creatures, will she not allow this also? If learning is necessary, will she not teach us? She lives within us. Even if it is wrong to worship a clay image, won't she know that it is she herself who is being invoked? She will be pleased even with that worship. Why should you worry about that? You should try to acquire knowledge and devotion for yourself." (1:20–21)

Ramakrishna: "What's wrong with worshipping images? It says in the Vedanta, wherever there is 'existence, light and love' there Brahman is manifested. So there's nothing at all which exists without it. How long do little girls play with dolls? Until they are married, and go to live with their husbands. When they get married they put their dolls away in a box. After you've realised God, will image worship be necessary?" (2:89–90)

Ramakrishna: "In one form reality is relative and in another it is absolute. What do you find in the Vedanta? Brahman is real and the world is unreal. But as long as you retain the 'I of devotion' the relative is also real. When God wipes out the 'I' then what remains is what is. But no-one can say what that is. As long as the 'I' remains you should accept everything. If you strip away the sheaths from the banana palm you get to the pith, but even when the sheaths are intact the pith is there. As long as the pith is there the sheaths are there and as long as the sheaths are there the pith is there. Similarly when you talk about the absolute it presupposes the existence of the relative, and when you speak about the relative it presupposes the existence of the absolute."

"God has become the whole creation, the twenty-four cosmic principles. When it is inactive I call it Brahman, when it is creating, sustaining and destroying, then I call it Kali. But Brahman and Sakti are the same, just as water is water whether it is still or disturbed."

"You can't eliminate the consciousness of the 'I.' And as long as you retain that consciousness you can't say that the created world is unreal! You can't determine the weight of a bel fruit if you've already thrown away the skin and the seeds. From the same bricks and mortar you can make the roof or the stairs of a house. The created world partakes of the same existence as that which is Brahman. Devotees (*vijnanis*) accept both God with form and as formless. In the cooling wind of devotion the water turns to ice, but when the sun of knowledge rises that ice becomes water once more." (4:219)

The Religious Life

Ramakrishna: "Do all your work, but keep your mind on God. Live with your wife and children, mother and father, and serve them as if they belong to you. But know in your heart that no-one belongs to you. The maidservant of a rich man works in her house, but her thoughts are all the time on her own home. She brings up her master's children as if they were her own, she calls them 'my Rama' and 'my Hari' but she knows they are not hers. The tortoise moves about in the water, but do you know where her thoughts are? They are on the land where her eggs are. Do all your worldly tasks but keep your mind on God."

"If you live in the world without devotion to God you will become more attached to it. Danger, sorrow and distress will make you uneasy and you will become attached to whatever your thoughts dwell on. You rub oil on your hands before you break open a jack-fruit because if you don't your hands will be covered with gum. Protect your hands with the oil of devotion to God, then you can immerse them in the affairs of this world."

"But a desire for solitude is necessary if one is to have this devotion. If you want to make butter you must put the curd aside to settle. If it is constantly moved about it can't settle. Then putting all other work aside you must sit down and churn the curd, and you will get butter. If you meditate on God in solitude you will gain wisdom, indifference to the world, and devotion. But the mind that dwells on the world will sink. In the world people think only of women and gold."

"The world is like water and the mind is like milk. If you pour the water into the milk they become one, and you can't find the unadulterated milk. If you make curd from the milk and turn that into butter, then put that into the water, it will float. By doing solitary sadhana you will gain the butter of wisdom and devotion. That butter will not mix with the water of the world; it will float on it." (1:21–22)

Ramakrishna: "Some people think of themselves as Her servants and devotees even after attaining samadhi. The devotee is proud to say, 'I am a servant, you are the Lord; I am a devotee, you are my Goddess.' Even after realising Her, not everyone can get rid of their ego. So a man uses this practice as a means of realising Her. This is what is meant by bhakti-yoga.

"You can gain knowledge of Brahman by means of the bhakti path. She is all powerful, she can give knowledge of Brahman if she wants to. But most devotees don't want knowledge of Brahman, they want to keep thinking of Her as Lord and themselves as servants, of God as mother and themselves as her children."

Vijay: "Those who discriminate according to the Vedanta philosophy, don't they also realise God?"

Ramakrishna: "Yes, those who follow the path of discrimination also realize her. That is the same as jnana-yoga. But the path of discrimination is a very difficult one. I explained to you about the seven planes. Samadhi comes when you reach the seventh plane. Samadhi comes when you fully understand that Brahman is real and the world is unreal, but how can a man have such understanding in this Kali Age? He can't unless he loses consciousness of the body, 'I am neither body, nor mind, nor the twenty-four principles, I am beyond pleasure and pain, what are grief, old age and death to me?'—in the Kali Age it is difficult to feel these things. However much you discriminate consciousness of the embodied self will appear from somewhere. Cut down the peepul tree and you think that only the roots remain, but next morning you will see that it has sent out more shoots. You can't get rid of consciousness of the body. That's why for the Kali Age bhakti is best, easiest."

"'I want to eat sugar, not become sugar.' I personally never want to say 'I am Brahman.' I prefer to say 'You are God, and I am your servant.' Its better to stay between the fifth and sixth planes like a boat moving between two points. I don't want to go beyond the sixth plane and remain for a long time at the seventh. I sing the praises of God's name, that's what I want. The attitude of server-and-served is a good one. It isn't good to say, 'I am That.' If a man thinks this way while still thinking of the body as the self then he can cause great harm; he can't go forward, and slowly he regresses. He deceives others and he deceives himself. He doesn't understand his own condition."

"You don't realise God through just any kind of bhakti. It's impossible without prema-bhakti (love-devotion). Prema-bhakti is also known as raga-bhakti. You can't realise God without love and devotion. You must have a great love for God or you will never realize her." (1:78–79)

Ramakrishna: "Imagine the sun shining on ten pots full of water, with the sun reflected in each one. First you see one sun and ten reflections of the sun. If nine of the pots are broken you are left with one sun and one reflection of the sun. Each pot is like a person. If you follow the reflection you'll reach the real sun, from the individual self you arrive at the Supreme Self. If the individual practices meditation and worship he'll see the Supreme Self. But no one can say what remains when the final pot is broken."

"At first the individual is in ignorance, with awareness of many different things but no awareness of God. When he has knowledge he realises that God is in all things. When you get a thorn in your foot you take another thorn to get the first one out, so you use the thorn of knowledge to remove the thorn of ignorance. But when you have vijnana, special knowledge, you throw them both away, the thorn of ignorance and the thorn of knowledge. Then you speak with God day and night, you don't just see her. . . ."

"There's a difference between the jnani and the vijnani. The jnani sits there stroking his moustache and when someone comes he says, 'Well, do you want to ask me something?' But the vijnani, the man who sees God all the time and talks with her, is quite different; sometimes he is absolutely motionless, sometimes like one spirit-possessed, sometimes like a child, sometimes like a madman. Sometimes when he's unconscious, in samadhi, he's absolutely motionless. When he's full of Brahman he seems to be possessed by a spirit, he's not aware of any distinction between good and evil, he's as naive as a child about his toilet habits, he has no sense of uncleanness after a nocturnal emossion. He doesn't have any understanding of filth as such, because everything is full of Brahman. Even food goes rotten if kept for too long."

"Sometimes he's like a madman, when people see him they think him insane. And sometimes he's quite childlike, no ties, no shame, no hatred, no shyness or anything like that. That's what it's like when you've seen God." (5:112–113)

The End

Ramakrishna was living with the devotees in a house in Cossipore. He was now very ill, but he was always concerned about the devotees' welfare. It was Saturday, 17th April 1886, and the full moon. For the previous few days Narendra had been going almost daily to Dakshineswar to meditate in the *panchavati*. On this day he had returned in the evening with Tarak and Kali.

It was now eight o'clock. Moonlight bathed the garden and a southerly breeze was blowing. Many of the devotees were meditating in a downstairs room. Narendra said to Mani, "They are letting go (renouncing the world)."

The next morning Ramakrishna called for Mani. After he had bathed in the river he went to see him and they went up onto the roof. At that time Mani's wife was almost mad with grief at the loss of her son. Ramakrishna told Mani to bring her to the house and let her take some *prasad*. He motioned to him with signs, "Ask her to come and stay for a few days. She can bring the baby, and she can eat here."

Mani: "All right. If she develops devotion for God that will be good."

Again Ramakrishna spoke, using signs, "Grief drives out devotion. What a big boy he was. Krishnakishore had two sons and they both died. He was such a great jnani, but for a long time he couldn't get over it. I'm lucky God has given me none. . . .

Flowers and sandalwood were placed in front of Ramakrishna in a vase. He was sitting on his bed, and worshipped himself with the flowers and sandalwood. He placed them in turn on his forehead, his throat, his heart and his navel. A devotee named Manmohan arrived, bowed to him and sat down. Ramakrishna was still worshipping himself. He placed a flower garland around his neck. After a while, as if pleased with Manmohan, he gave him the remains of the flowers he had used in his worship, and gave a champak flower to Mani. (4:288–289)

It was some months now since Ramakrishna had gone to the boundless sea of rest of all devotees. The cord of affection which had bound together the married and unmarried devotees in nursing him had been broken with his death. But though leaderless and afraid they were all of one mind and could hardly live without each other. They had no desire even to talk with anyone else, they wanted to talk about nothing but Ramakrishna. They all thought, Will we never see him again? He had said that if they called out with great longing and in sincerity the Goddess would reveal herself to them, that if they were sincere she would certainly hear them. Now they were alone their minds were full of him. They wandered about weeping, purposeless and alone. Knowing what they would be like, Ramakrishna had said to Mani, “When I'm gone you will wander the streets crying, that makes it more difficult for me to depart!” Some thought, why is it that he has gone and we are still alive? We still want to stay in this transient world.

The younger devotees had spent day and night at the Cossipore house nursing Ramakrishna. After his death they went like reluctant puppets back to their homes. He had asked them not to take the outward signs of the sannyasi (red robes, etc), or to renounce the role of householder. So for a while they did so, but he had made them renounce it all in their hearts. (2:244–245)

Soon after this some of the devotees stayed together in the house, never again to return to their homes. Thus was founded the first monastery of the Ramakrishna Movement.

Source: *Śrī Śrī Ramakrishna Kathamrita*, translated by Malcom McLean (PhD dissertation, University of Otago, 1983).

Selections from *The Kulārṇava Tantra*

The Nature of the Absolute and Embodiments Confusion

1.7. Śiva, O Goddess, is by his own nature the supreme absolute, without aspects; He is omniscient, the agent of all, lord of all, without any taint and without a second.

1.8. He is his very own light, beginningless and endless, without change, the supreme of the supreme, without qualities, being, consciousness, and bliss. Sentient beings are but a portion of that Śiva: they have come about from their own beginningless ignorance, just as sparks indicate the fire from which they arise.

1.19. One should protect oneself who is the Self of all; the Self is the vessel of the all. For the sake of protection one should make every effort [toward Self-realization], for there is otherwise no true vision of reality.

1.24. For one who does not make every effort for suggestive cures of hell-like bodily diseases here in this body, and so has gone to a place without medicines, what could a person do when such diseases are in place?

1.35. He does not see what he sees, nor even hear what he hears, nor does he know what he recites, and so he is deluded by your māyā.

The True Spiritual Discipline: The Sources of Truth and Error

1.42. One should do today what is for tomorrow and what is meant for the latter part of the day in the earlier part of the day. Death does not wait around to see what has been done or has not been done.

1.96. Not knowing that the truth is situated within one's Self, the deluded is confused by looking for it in treatises. One whose judgment is so poor is like the shepherd who sees his goat in a well when it is actually already within the flock.

1.107. The one true knowledge that gives liberation comes from what the guru teaches; all else is imitative, bearing confusion and error. The supreme is the one reality that embodies.

1.109. However, the nondual truth has been spoken by Śiva, freed from rituals and tormenting efforts. Obtained directly from the guru's mouth, it is not otherwise obtained, even by studying tens of thousands of scriptures.

1.115. So long as there is false attachment to the body and so long as there is sense of "mine-ness"; so long as there is no compassion from the guru, how then can there be truth?

The Kula Teaching: The Heart's Secret Teaching

2.6. You must keep this teaching secret; it is not to be given to just anyone but given only to a disciple and to one truly devoted. Otherwise one will surely fall into disaster.

2.7. The Veda is superior. Higher than the Veda is the path that worships Viṣṇu; the worship of Śiva is superior to worship of Viṣṇu; and the Right path is superior to Śiva worship. The Left path is superior to the Right; the Doctrinal path of Śaivism superior to the Left. The Heart path is superior to the Doctrinal, and there is nothing higher than the Heart.

2.9. The most secret of the secret, O Goddess; the most essential of the essential; the best of the best. The Heart path, which comes directly from Śiva, O Goddess, is transmitted from ear to ear.

2.23. In other paths, if one is a yogin, then one cannot be an enjoyer of life. Nor can an enjoyer of life be a yogin. The Heart path has the nature of being for both enjoyment of life and yoga and so, beloved, it is greater than all others.

2.33. The knowledge of the Heart shines in one whose consciousness is pure, peaceful, whose actions serve the guru, who is extremely devoted, and who can keep a secret.

2.50. Even if one performs no other rituals or actions, leaving aside what is commanded according to one's social estate and stage of life, the one who dwells within the Heart is a vessel of enjoyment and liberation, O Goddess of the Heart.

2.68. One yoked to the compassion of the guru, for whom a fallen state has been shaken off by initiation, who finds delight in the worship following the Heart—such a person, O Goddess, comes from the Heart [he is a Kaula], and not another.

2.80. The followers of the Heart, knowers of the essence, do not consider other religion, just as bees who serve themselves the blossom of the coral tree don't seek to obtain other flowers.

The Path of the Mantra, the Highest Path is the Heart Path

3.49. The supreme mantra that bestows the grace of the Auspicious One (Śrī) is the foundation of the highest path. He who knows this as our supreme form is himself Śiva.

3.50. This mantra is performed, O beloved, with each exhalation [which makes the sound *ham*] and inhalation [which makes the sound *sa*] of breath, repeated by all breathing beings, from Śiva all the way down to the worms.

3.56. Just as the fig tree exists in its subtle form in its incipient seed, so too the three worlds that make up the universe exist within this supreme mantra that bestows supreme grace.

3.63. He who attains loving devotion to the auspicious guru who is my own form is said to achieve the supreme, knowing the supreme mantra that bestows the grace of the auspicious one.

3.82. He who knows the mantra that bestows the grace of the auspicious one knows all mantras, including those belonging to Śiva, Viṣṇu, the Goddess, the sun, Gaṇapati, and the moon.

[commentary by D.R. Brooks:]

The esoteric etymology of the mantra, that is, why it is called *prasāda-para* ("grace-giving supreme") is given next, focusing on the two elements of the mantra's name, the prefix *pra-* and the word *para*. Next follow the instructions for "laying down" or nyāsa of the divinities in the form of mantra-names, invoking and placing them within the subtle body. The mudrās or gestures that should accompany the nyāsa process are next mentioned. In this way, the mantra in all its subtle divine forms is identified and invoked onto the subtle body of the Kula practitioner. The details of nyāsa involve the recitation of mantras, gestures of placement on the physical body, and mental identifications. The process of inter-identification brings the ritual of the Kula Dharma into its distinct focus: specific mantras, specific actions and intentions, and specific goals are enunciated. These ritual details need not detain us; more importantly, the text implies their distinctiveness and superiority.

4.12. Performing this inter-identification, O Goddess, wherever a human being goes he shall experience preeminence, benefits, esteem, and human dignity, beloved one.

4.127. Why say too much, O Goddess? This inter-identification is beloved to me. It should not be spoken about to one who is not like a son, nor should it be explained to one who is not a true disciple.

[commentary by D.R. Brooks]

Next follow the ritual prescriptions for the vessels and offerings, including the five M-word substances–māṃsa (flesh), matsya (fish), madya (wine), mudrā (fermented grain), and maithuna (sexual intercourse). These and other offerings are called the kula-dravyas, or heart oblations. They are strictly regulated and their qualifications and benefits detailed. Considered privileged and dangerous, these ritual actions are a distinctive (but not unique) aspect of the Kula path.

The Five M-Word Oblations on the Ritual Path of the Heart

5.71. Those who offer with loving devotion to us both flesh and drink, they create a blissful experience and, being beloved by us, are the followers of the Heart.

5.72. Our supreme mark—characterized as being, consciousness, and bliss manifests effulgently when there occurs the true enjoyment of the Kula oblations [the five M-word offerings], and not otherwise.

5.75. For example, just as a dwelling enveloped in darkness becomes lit by a lamp, so the Self covered in Illusion is seen by drinking the oblation [of wine].

5.77. Wine truly is the Terrifying Divinity (Bhairava) and wine is even called Power (Śakti). Ah yes! The enjoyer of wine can delude even the immortals!

5.78. A man who, having drunk a potent wine, is not adversely affected and has become supremely one-pointed in meditation on us, he is liberated and he is the true Follower of the Heart.

5.79. Drink is Power, Śakti; and flesh is Auspicious, Śiva: the Enjoyer becomes the Terrifying One, Bhairava himself. The bliss that arises from this union of the two is called liberation.

5.88. One who serves oneself for the sake of pleasure with wine and the rest is fallen. Having dispensed with one's own lassitudes one should indulge only for the sake of pleasing the gods.

5.89. It is said that indulging in intoxicants such as fish, flesh, and drink, and so on, other than at the time of ritual sacrifice, is prohibited and errant my beloved.

5.90. Just as the brahman is enjoined to drink intoxicating soma on the occasion of Vedic sacrifice, so drinking wine and the like at prescribed times gives enjoyment and liberation [on the path of the Heart].

5.91. Only when one knows the meaning of the Heart treatises directly from the auspicious guru should one take upon oneself the practice of the five imprinting ritual acts [that is, the five M words], for otherwise one becomes fallen.

5.105. He who practices the five imprinting ritual acts without the proper imprimatur, O Goddess of the Heart, becomes contemptible even though he may experience the Absolute.

5.111. The divine Śakti of animalistic persons is unawakened and that of the follower of the Heart is awakened. One who offers service to that awakened power truly serves Śakti herself.

5.112. One who experiences the bliss of union in sexual relationship as being between the Supreme Power (Parāśakti) and the Self—such a person knows the meaning of sexual relations; others are inferior, indulging only to pursue women.

5.113. Knowing, O entrance of the Heart (*kula-nāyikā*), the true condition of the five imprinting ritual acts in all these ways directly from the mouth of the guru, O Goddess, one truly serves and is liberated.

6.6. Pure in Self and deeply joyous within, bereft of anger and greed, having turned away from the avowed ways of animalistic persons, one should offer sacrificial ritual with a sweet disposition, my beloved.

6.7–8. When by my grace a person has, after a long time, become firm in his feelings of devotion, he should perform the rituals, offering the libations together with the offerings as it has been taught by the Auspicious Terrifying Lord (Śrī Bhairava) and according to the instructions of the guru—for otherwise he will fall.

6.9. One should perform the worship of the auspicious wheel (Śrī Cakra) with the discipline of mantras, O Goddess of Light. Being then in your company I accept that [worship] myself.

6.10. With the experience, "I am the Terrifying Lord," and so possessed of qualities such as omniscience, the lordly yogin should become a performer of the Heart worship.

Worship and Deity Presence within a Yantra

6.85. A yantra or diagrammatical form is said to consist [actually] of mantras; the deity has the form of mantras as well. The Goddess worshiped in the yantra, O Goddess, is pleased spontaneously.

6.87. As the body is for an embodied soul like oil for a lamp, my beloved, so likewise the yantra is the place of all divinities.

6.88. Therefore, drawing the yantra and meditating on Śiva in the proper manner, and gaining knowledge directly from the guru, one should worship all according to the prescribed rules, my beloved.

As are the Gods, So Are the Worshipers of the Heart

8.106. Just as We the Divine Couple are inseparable; just as the goddess Lakṣmī [is inseparable] from Lord Nārāyaṇa, or the goddess Sarasvatī from Lord Brahmā, so is the Courageous Practitioner with his Śakti consort.

9.3. Meditation is said to be of two sorts, divided accordingly as gross and subtle. The gross sort is said to include a particular form, while the subtle centers on the formless.

9.9. When there is no longer any reflective consciousness and one is as calm as the still sea—the innate form itself being empty—such meditation is called samādhi or Equanimity Consciousness.

9.10. The purely self-illuminating truth is nothing like a cognitive process; one can become that self-illuminating truth instantaneously.

9.22. For one immersed in the state of the singular Self, whatever is done is worship, whatever is recited is a mantra, whatever one sees is a meditation.

9.23. When one has experienced the Supreme Self (Paramātman), the sensation of identifying with bodily consciousness ceases; wherever such a heart goes, there consciousness is in equanimity.

9.24. When the knot of the heart is severed, so all doubts are cut away; and karmas, actions, and intentions—past, present, and future—are destroyed when one sees the Supreme Self from within.

9.41. The body is the abode of God, O Goddess; the embodied self is God Ever-abiding Śiva (Sadāśiva). Abandon ignorance as if it was old flowers offered in worship and perform worship with the contemplation "I am He," *so 'ham.*

9.42. The embodied self is Śiva; Śiva is the embodied self; that embodied self is only Śiva. The experience of bondage to one's animal nature is how one thinks of the embodied self; liberated from this animal nature identity one has the experience of the Ever-abiding Śiva.

9.52. Drinking wine, eating flesh, carrying out the practices of one's own initiatory teaching, contemplating the unitive experience of both "I" and "That," so the Heart yogin dwells in true happiness.

9.55. Valuing what is devalued in the world and devaluing what the world values, this the Terrifying Lord who is the supreme Self has pointed out is the path of the Heart.

9.59. There are no commands; there are no prohibitions. There is neither merit nor fall; no heaven and truly no hell for the followers of the Heart, O Goddess of the Heart.

9.62. What is poorly characterized becomes well characterized; otherness becomes one's own heart and what is contrary to righteousness becomes righteous for the followers of the Heart, O Goddess of the Heart.

9.65. Living anywhere, taking on any disguise, and [living] unrecognized by everyone, in whatever social position he may be, he remains a Heart yogin, O Goddess of the Heart.

9.66. Yogins in various guises act for the sake of humanity; they wander the earth, their true nature unrecognized by others.

9.67. They do not reveal their true experience immediately, O Goddess of the Heart, living in the midst of the world as if they were intoxicated, mute, or just idiots.

9.73. The yogin goes about his own life while the world looks upon him laughing, reproaching, and with contempt, keeping its distance from him.

9.74. The yogin wanders about the ordinary world in different guises, acting on some occasions like a dignified person, sometimes like a vagrant, sometimes like demon or a ghoul!

9.75. The yogin enjoys the pleasures of life only for the sake of serving the world, [and] not out of his own desire. Offering grace to all people, he traverses the earth out of compassion.

9.77. Just as the wind touches everything and space extends everywhere, just as all who bathe in rivers become pure, so the yogin is always pure.

9.81. Wherever the elephant walks becomes a path, and similarly wherever the Heart yogin goes becomes a path, O Goddess of the Heart.

9.88. Whosoever knows the truth of the Heart and is well-versed in the treatises on the Heart should perform the worship of the Heart; he is truly the Heart follower [and] not another, my beloved.

9.90. By initiation (*dīkṣā*) one is a Heart follower who knows the triadic truth [as supreme, ordinary, and both], who surrenders to the auspicious feet of the divine, who possesses the meaning of the root mantras, and who offers loving devotion to God and guru.

9.94. I do not dwell on Mount Kailāsa nor on Meru or Mandara: wherever reside the Heart knowers, I reside there, O my divine contemplation!

9.131. Just as a tree gives up its flowers regardless of [whether it has] once obtained its fruit, so the yogin obtaining the truth gives up attachment to actions and rituals.

Ultimate Identity and Identification

13.64. Just as words such as "pot," "vessel," and "jar" all mean the same object [*artha*: goal, meaning, thing], so too are god and mantra and guru said to be the same object.

13.65. Just as divinity is, so is the mantra; just as there is mantra, so there is the guru.

13.66. The fruits of worship are the same for god, mantra, and guru. For the sake of establishing myself in the form of Śiva, I seize upon worship, O Goddess of the Mountain (Pārvatī); for the sake of taking on the form of the guru I break the stranglehold of fear.

Secrecy, Intimacy, and Privacy on the Heart Path

10.44. One should not enunciate the guru's name except at the time of ritual recitation, my beloved, calling him instead over the course of spiritual life by such titles as Auspicious Lord, Deity, and Svāmī, and the like.

10.45 One should not tell anyone other than one's own disciple the mantras praising the guru's sandals, the imprinting gestures, the root mantra, and one's own grace-giving sandal mantra.

10.46. Lineage, scripture, levels of teaching, the practice of mantras, and such must all be obtained directly from the guru in order to bear fruit—and not otherwise.

14.3. Without initiation, there can be no liberation: This has been said in the sacred Śiva teachings. And there can be no initiation without the preceptor of a lineage.

14.7. Therefore one should make every effort to seek always the guru of unbroken lineage who is in origin the immediate Supreme Śiva.

14.14. The experiential knowledge of the mantra cannot establish itself in the unworthy. So there should be an examination of the disciple; otherwise [initiation, worship, and knowledge] bear no fruits.

14.30. Those persons who at the outset have no true loving devotion, who then in the midst of their spiritual practice gain loving devotion, and at the end experience the expansion of loving devotion, they assimilate the inner practice of yoga.

14.34. Initiation, you will recall O Goddess, is threefold: It is given by touch, by deliberate sight, and by mere mental intention without acts, ritual, efforts, or any other such things, great Goddess!

14.38. The disciple becomes worthy of grace by stepping into the current of the divine Śakti's initiatory power; where Śakti does not descend, no accomplishment can be claimed.

14.78. Initiation is said to be twofold, divided accordingly as outward and inner. Initiation into actions such as ritual is the outer; the inner one creates the experience of pervasive penetration into one's being.

14.86. That initiation by which those who indulge themselves in their animalistic nature become Śivas, opening the eyes to the Self, O Goddess: that is liberation from the noose of being a mere animal.

14.97. O Goddess, for one who is without initiation there is no fulfillment nor true path. So by every effort one should seek initiation from a guru.

Liberation Is the Experience of the Heart

15.19 There are innumerable hundreds of thousands of mantras and they unsettle the heart of one's own divine consciousness. The one mantra obtained by the grace of the guru will provide every goal and accomplishment.

15.34. Placing oneself in postures such as the lotus, the cross-legged, or warrior pose, one should perform repetition of the mantra and offer worship. Otherwise [initiation, grace, and effort] will bear no fruit.

15.113. One should perform the recitation of the mantra by fixing oneself on it, with life breath coursing through it, setting it within one's consciousness, and making the deep connections that form the meaning of its syllables.

The Nature of the Divine as Mantra Imparts the Supreme Grace

16.40ab. Male divinities' mantras are called mantras while those of female divinities are called vidyās, my beloved.

16.116. One who knows the mantra of supreme grace is liberated whether he dwells in a place of true pilgrimage, or a place without means to ford across the world, or even in the midst of the ocean of worldliness—there is no doubt about it.

17.102. This treatise called the Ocean of the Heart exists within the heart of divine yoginis. I have illumined it today; and with true effort it should be kept secret.

Source: *The Kulārṇava Tantra*, Edited by Arthur Avalon (Sir John Woodroffe) (Delhi: Motilal Banarsidass, 1965); translated by Douglas Renfrew Brooks in *Tantra in Practice*, edited by David Gordon White (Princeton: Princeton University Press, 2000).

Selections from the *Toḍala Tantra*

Chapter One

The Names of Different Forms of the Great God Śiva as Spouse of the Deities of Great Sacred Formulas

The goddess spoke:

1–2. O Lord of the universe, my master, who are the embodiment of all the sacred formulas (*vidyās*), [please] tell me when all the great formulas (*mahavidyās*) are venerated in the three worlds, [and] what are the specific forms of the trumpet-holding Mahādeva who is seated on the right side of each of these [*mahavidyās*], O Lord! please enumerate [these forms] to me.

Śrī Śiva spoke:

3–4. Listen O beautiful and blessed one! Bhairava Mahākāla [a form of Mahādeva] should be worshiped by the right side of the benevolent (*dakṣiṇā*) Kālī, [because] Dakṣiṇā is always engaged in love-play with Mahākāla. One should worship Akṣobhya by the right side of Tārā.

5–7ab. O goddess, at the time of the churning of the [cosmic] ocean there arose [the poison called] Kālakūṭa. Then all the gods, together with their wives, became greatly disturbed. Since [Śiva, even when he] drank that deadly poison, remained unaffected by any kind of agitation, therefore, O great sovereign lady, he is famous as Akṣobhya ("Unagitated"). With him [the goddess] Tāriṇī, the great goddess of delusion, is ever engaged in love-play.

7cd–9ab. O sovereign of the gods, one should worship the five-faced Śiva who has three eyes on each of his faces, on the right side of the great Tripurasundarī. Since the great Goddess is erotically excited [and is] ever [engaged in love-play] with him [who has five faces], therefore, O great Goddess, she is known as the fifth.

9cd–llab. One should worship Tryambaka [Śiva] by the right side of the blessed Bhuvanasundarī [Bhuvaneśvarī]. [Śiva] is called Tryambaka [associated with three mothers] because he makes love to the primaeval sovereign Goddess of the creation, in heaven, earth, and the nether region (*pātāla*). Accordingly he [Śiva] is renowned for being always united with Śakti and is venerated in all the Tantras.

11cd–12ab. One should with great care worship [Śiva] called Dakṣiṇāmūrti by the right side of Bhairavī. He is indeed the same as the five-faced [Sadāśiva].

12cd–13cd. One should worship Śiva as a headless trunk (*kabandha*) by the right side of Chinnamastā [the Beheaded Goddess]. He who does tantric ritual worship of Kabandha [Śiva] certainly becomes the lord of all tantric perfection (*siddhi*). Dhūmāvatī, the great Vidyā, is manifest in the form of a widow [hence there is no form of Śiva by her side].

14. The one-faced great Rudra (the Fierce One) is worshiped by the right hand side of Bagalā. He is famed as the annihilator [performing the contraction] of the creation.

15. By Mātaṅgī's right side one should worship Mātaṅga Śiva. He indeed is the Dakṣiṇāmūrtī who is in the form of universal bliss.

16. [A worshiper (*sādhaka*)] should worship Sadāśiva in the form of Viṣṇu by Kamalā's right side. O great sovereign Goddess, there is no doubt that he would achieve perfection (*siddhi*).

17. By the right side of Annapūrṇā [a sādhaka] should worship the great sovereign god [Śiva], the bestower of great liberation (*mokṣa*), who is the manifest brahman and who possesses ten faces.

18–19ab. [He] should carefully worship [Śiva as] Nārada by the right side of Durgā. The syllable *nā* stands for the creator, and the syllable *da* always represents the protector. Because the syllable *ra* symbolizes the destroyer Nārada, it is held [to represent the great god Śiva who creates, sustains, and destroys the universe].

19cd–19ef. For all other Vidyās, the seer (*ṛṣi*) [of the vidyā] mentioned in the formula is indeed her [the vidyā-śakti's] husband and should be worshiped by her right side.

Explanation of Śiva's Transformation into a Corpse Who Nonetheless Has Sexual Union with the Goddess

The blessed Goddess asked:

20. The [great Śakti] who is the first great Vidyā and also the second supreme Bhairavī who is the mother of the three worlds and is eternal—how can she be mounted on a corpse?

The blessed Śiva answered:

21–23. O great Goddess! she who is the primordial [divine being], herself Death/Time, exists [identified] as the heart [essence] of the glorious Śiva in the form of the destroyer. Therefore the supreme Death/Time (Mahākāla) is the destroyer of the universe. But when Kālī as the embodiment of destruction manifests herself in her true form, immediately at that very moment, O Goddess, Sadāśiva appears in the form of a corpse and at that instant, O Lady with dancing eyes, she [Kālī] appears mounted on a corpse.

The blessed Goddess said:

24. The great god Sadāśiva as a corpse is a lifeless body. How could it then perform the sex act?

The blessed Śiva answered:

25. At the time that great Kālī [actively] manifests herself, Sadāśiva is devoid of active power. When, O Goddess, he is united with śakti, then he appears in the form of Śiva; [but though] when devoid of śakti he is virtually a corpse, he still does not lose his manliness [his phallus].

End of the first chapter, called a dialogue between Hara and Gaurī, of the most excellent of all Tantras, the *Toḍala-tantra*

Chapter Two

Brief Enumeration of Kuṇḍalinī Yoga

The blessed Śiva said:

1–4. Listen O Goddess! I shall briefly recount the essence of yoga [meditation and Tantric mental adoration].

The [human] body is like a tree [in reverse form] whose roots are on top and branches hanging beneath. All the sacred places of the universe exist within this body. The very form of the macrocosm exists in the microcosm [of the human body]. There are thirty and a half million sacred places in the macrocosm, O You who are praised by the heroes [Tantric practitioners]! Out of all of these, only a hundred and forty thousand sacred places are visible. Out of these, only fourteen [are noteworthy], and out of these [fourteen], only three are auspicious. Amongst these [three again], O supreme sovereign Goddess, [the one called] Mahādhīrā bestows liberation (*mukti*).

5. Vasukī [the divine serpent] is indeed Mahāmayā [the cosmic goddess of delusion], who is manifest in the form of a serpent, coiled three and a half times, and resides in the region under the nether region (*pātāla*).

6–8. O supreme sovereign Goddess, listen carefully while I recount the seven heavens [upper regions] in their proper order. [These are] the region of the earth, of the atmosphere, of the celestials, then the region of maha [of the great saints], the region of jana [generation], the region of tapa [austerity] and, O Lady with an elegant face, the region of satya [truth]. Here ends the list of seven regions. O eminent lady! now listen carefully to the enumeration of the nether regions. [These are the regions of] atala, vitala, sutala, talātala, mahātala, pātāla, and after that rasātala.

9–17ab. The liberating [yogic duct, called nāḍī] Mahādhīrā ranges from rasātala to the end of satya, which exists inside the central [channel, that is, the spinal column, meru]. Mahāviṣṇu Śiva resides in the satya region and Vāsukī is full of intense longing to meet him. When Vāsukī, having pierced the six regions (*cakras*), rises up [to that region of satya], all the other flowing rivers [that is, the ducts] become upward flowing. In the body [the microcosm], O sovereign Goddess, the ducts remain in the following order. If [the sādhaka] presses down air through both the iḍā and piṅgalā ducts, which have the suṣumṇā between them, O sovereign Goddess, while repeating the prāṇa mantra [*so'haṃ*], then the coiled one [Vāsukī] starts [moving upward through the suṣumṇā] following the order of the [six cakras], until she approaches the eternal and immutable lotus [the sahasrāra cakra]. With anxiety the coiled one enters that eternal abode. Simultaneously all other down-flowing [ducts] start flowing upstream. At that moment, O Goddess! [the sādhaka] should concentrate on the garland of letters. Then while repeating mentally 108 times his chief (*mūla*) mantra [received from his preceptor at the time of initiation] the intelligent [sādhaka] should bring the coiled one back to his mūlādhāra cakra [her original resting-place] in the same way, while refreshing the gods of the six cakras with the nectar [from the thousand-petaled lotus].

Yogic Mudrās, or Special Physical Positions/or Kuṇḍalinī Yoga

17cd–22ab. Now, my dear, I shall describe another yoga posture called the yonimudrā [the previous one was called śakti-cālanī].

The mantra practitioner first sits down on his seat facing the east or the north. With his arms he firmly holds his two knees and then, O Queen of the gods, he brings his nose near the knees while sitting upright [that is, keeping his back straight]. O Queen of the gods, [as before] he presses air down by inhaling (but, O great Goddess! does not let the air escape by exhaling), and simultaneously continues repeating the prāṇa mantra. At the same time, as described before, he should repeat [his chief mantra] 108 times in his upright pose, [only this time] he repeats [the mantra] in reverse order. While thus [repeating his mantra], O You of glorious face, he brings [the kuṇḍalinī] back to the basic root cakra [*mūlādhāra*] through the same path while refreshing the gods of the six cakras with nectar.

22cd–25. My dear, this yonimudrā removes all illness. O Goddess, without elaborating I can just say that it destroys great diseases and, O Goddess, without exaggerating I can say that this mudrā causes the realization of the mantra, brings about the direct perception of one's [true] self, and bestows on the practitioner the great liberation, mahāmokṣa. Had I possessed a hundreḍ faces I would not have been able to exhaust all its details; but with only five faces how much can I enumerate? A Tantric practitioner practicing this mudrā becomes as beautiful as Cupid even if he began as a leper.

Here ends the second chapter of the Śiva-Pārvatī dialogue in the *Toḍala Tantra* which is the best of all Tantras

Chapter Three

The blessed goddess asked:

1. O God of gods, great God, the saver from the ocean of transient and recurring life [*saṃsāra*], O Ocean of compassion, please tell me the great mudrā called baddhayoni.

Śiva answered:

2–4ab. Listen, O Goddess, I shall briefly tell you the method of baddhayoni. O great Goddess, the mantra practitioner covers his anus with the tip of his penis. Then, O great Goddess, the intelligent practitioner gradually applies his fingers [to cover other apertures of his body] starting with the thumbs, to [cover] his ears, [and then in turn [covering his] eyes, nose, and mouth [with rest of the pairs of fingers of his hands].

4cd–7. [Thus covering all his bodily apertures] he should then inhale through his nose and fill his mouth with air and as before press it downward [through the iḍā and piṅgalā ducts]. When [the coiled goddess unites with Śiva] the practitioner should envisage the primaeval Sound (*śabda-brahman*) and then envisage the garland of syllables (*varṇāmālā*) while repeating his main mantra. Then, repeating the mantra *so'ham*, he brings, O Goddess, [the kuṇḍalinī back to the mūlādhāra cakra] through the same central channel. On the way he refreshes all the cakra gods [with the nectar produced by the union of the goddess and Sadāśiva]. O great sovereign Goddess! O spotless One! I shall tell you [later] the achievements of one who peforms this [kuṇḍalinī yoga seated in baddhayoni posture].

Kālī's Mantra or Vidyā

The blessed Pārvatī asked:

8. O omniscient Īśāna! O most excellent of the erudite, who possesses all wisdom! O master of gods! please tell me the rare description of Kālikā's mantra system.

The Bīja [Seed] Mantra

The blessed Śiva answered:

9–13. O ever-blissful Goddess, listen to my account of the excellent Kālikā mantra; even the mere discussion of its nature makes a man liberated in this life.

For the first [seed mantra], cull the syllable *ka*, add to it *ī*, *r*, and the *bindunāda* [double nasalization, symbolized by a sickle shape topped by a point representing the normal nasalization]. O auspicious One! this is the very rare perfect vidyā, the queen of all vidyās.

The Vidyā

Now listen to me explaining the next one. First utter this seed [mantra *krīṃ*] three times. Then cull the syllable *ha* connected with the nasal *bindu* and the vowel *u* [*hūṃ*], [and utter] it twice [after the first three], and now I tell you the next one [that is the third seed mantra]. Then, O sovereign Goddess [utter the syllable *ha* joined with *r*, *ī*, and the nasal, and repeat it again [*hrīṃ hrīṃ*]; then add [Kālikā's] vocative, then again three of the first seed mantra then twice the kūrca mantra [*hūṃ*] and twice the māyā mantra [*hrīṃ*] and finally *svāhā*. This mantra of twenty-five syllables is the queen of all vidyās and is very rare.

14. When this great vidyā is preceded by the vāgbhava mantra [*aiṃ* the seed mantra of the supreme speech, Vāc], its inherent deity is Śrīkālī; when preceded by the praṇava mantra [*Oṃ*], its deity is known as Siddhikālikā.

15–16. When the mantra consists of two of the goddess's own mantras [*krīṃ*] followed by one kūrca mantra [*hūṃ*], O great Goddess, this trisyllabic supreme vidyā is known as Cāmuṇḍākālikā. There is no vidyā like this one for bringing about success. The six-syllabled vidyā [*krīṃ krīṃ krīṃ phaṭ svāhā*] and the three-syllabled vidyā [*krīṃ krīṃ hūṃ*] are of equal power.

17–18ab. O auspicious one! three of [Kālikā's] own seed mantra [*krīṃ krīṃ krīṃ*] followed by the [vocative] *śmaśānakālike*, then again the three seed mantras and finally *svāhā*, [together] constitute the fourteen-syllabled mantra that is worshiped in all the three worlds.

Eight Forms of the Kālī Vidyā

18cd–21ab. Dakṣiṇākālikā, Siddhikālikā, Guhyakālikā, Śrīkālikā, Bhadrakālī, Cāmuṇḍākālikā, and the supreme Śmaśānakālikā and Mahākālī O Goddess! These are the eight (forms of goddess Kālī]. O sovereign Goddess! First utter Kālī's own seed mantra, then her name in the vocative followed by another Kālikā seed mantra, and finally add *svāhā* [*krīṃ kālike krīṃ svāhā*]. These eight forms of Kālikā's mantra are secretly expressed in all Tantras.

The blessed Goddess said:

21cd–23ab. I have [now] heard the very secret mantras of the great Kālikā. Now I wish to hear Tārā's royal mantra. O Īsāna! if you love me do tell me her mantra, whose mere mention prevents one from drowning in the ocean of [transitory] existence.

Tārā Bijas
Śrī Śiva answered:

Having uttered the moon seed [*saṃ*] add the syllable of fire [*r*] and *t* to it, together with the left eye [*ī*]. My beloved, this royal mantra, this single-syllabled vidyā [*strīṃ*] is venerated in three worlds. Īśāna [*h*] united with the nasal and the left ear [*ū*] [forms] the monosyllabic vidyā [*hūṃ*], which is [Tārā's] second royal mantra.

The Tārā Vidyā
23cd–32ab. Śiva [*h*] with the fire [*r*] and the left eye [*ī*] and the nasal added to it [*hrīṃ*] [should first be uttered]. Then the first seed [*strīṃ*] and then the second [*hūṃ*], then utter the weapon, astra mantra [*hrīṃ strīṃ hūṃ phaṭ*].

Different Forms and Efficacies of the Tārā Vidyā
When this vidyā is preceded by praṇava [*Oṃ*], then [the Goddess] is called Ugratātā. When without the praṇava this vidyā is called Ekajaṭā, the bestower of supreme liberation (*mokṣa*). With neither praṇava nor astra mantra [that is, *hrīṃ strīṃ hūṃ*], this trisyllabic vidyā is called Mahānīlasarasvatī. When the [trisyllabic] vidyā is preceded by the vāgbhava [seed mantra], it bestows [on the practitioner] the status of the god of speech. This supreme vidyā when preceded by the seed mantra *śrīṃ* bestows wealth and prosperity. When this great vidyā is preceded by the seed mantra māyā [*hrīṃ*], it bestows sure success and perfection (*siddhi*). When it is preceded by the kūrca [*hūṃ*], it reveals the entire system of speech. When this supreme vidyā is preceded by the seed of the sky [*haṃ*], it bestows the liberation of total resorption. When this great vidyā starts with the prāsāda [seed mantra, *hauṃ*] it brings about the union of the practitioner with Śiva. When this mantra starts with the seed [mantra] of prāṇa [*prūṃ*] it bestows on the practitioner the fulfillment of whatever he wishes. When this supreme vidyā opens with the seed of Kālī [*krīṃ*] it bestows both liberation and prosperity.

Ritual Worship of the Deity

32cd–50abc. Now I shall describe the method of worshiping Kālī and Tārā. Arising in the morning, the practitioner who knows his mantra [and its method of meditation] first mentally worships his guru in the topmost cakra consisting of a thousand petals. Then, having pierced the six cakras, he should repeat his main mantra 108 times. Thereafter, having bowed down [to his preferred deity] he should perform his ritual bathing. He should start this bathing ritual with the following declaration of his intention (*saṃkalpa*): "Today [here he mentions the day and date and then] the solar month, [I bathe myself] for the pleasure of the deity." Then he bathes in the pure water. Then he should utter *Oṃ* and then gaṅge ca, followed by *yamune*, then having uttered *godāvari, sarasvati, narmade* and *sindhu kāveri* he utters the words *asmin jale sannidhiṃ kuru* [*Oṃ* the rivers Ganges, Yamuna, Godavarī, Sarasvati, Narmada, Sindhu, and Kaveri please abide in this water]. [While uttering this mantra the practitioner] with the hand gesture called the goad (aṅkuśa) should [in imagination] pull these sacred rivers from the orb of the sun and settle them [in the water in which he is bathing] by carefully showing four relevant hand gestures. Then having protected the water with the hand gesture called the fish [and scooping a palm full of water and covering it with the other palm], the worshiper repeats his [deity's seed] mantra [*krīṃ*] eleven times. Then, throwing this water toward the sun, he should repeat his main mantra twelve times while [in imagination] washing [Kālikā's] feet three times. Then [in imagination] he should three times bathe himself with that rinse water flowing from [Kālī's] feet while repeating the mantra. This is done by showing the gesture of the water pot (*kumbha*) while repeating his main mantra three times.

Then, O Queen of gods! he should decorate his forehead according to the custom of his sect. Then he performs ācamana [ritual cleansing of his mouth and hands] with water while uttering the mantras of the three tattvas—ātmatattva, vidyātattva, and śivatattva. The mantras consist of each tattva preceded by praṇava and ending with *svāhā* [this is the name of the wife of the god Agni, Fire].

[At this point he has left his bathing place, cleanly and decorously attired, and reached the actual place of worship, carrying a pitcher full of water brought from the water source. In this water pitcher] he invokes the sacred rivers with the same *gaṅge ca*, etc., mantra [following the aforesaid procedure]. Then he dips a bunch of kuśa grass into the sanctified water and with it sprinkles water on the ground [where he will hold his ritual worship]. Then in the same way he should sprinkle himself seven times. Then he performs his aṅganyāsa. Then, O Goddess of the celestials, he with his left hand [scoops up water] and repeats three times the [pañcabhūta] bīja mantras: *haṃ, vaṃ, yaṃ, laṃ* and *raṃ*. Having thus encapsulated that water with that pañcabhūta mantra, the practitioner should sprinkle himself seven times with his finger in the gesture of tattva [reality] while uttering his main mantra. This act at once removes all his sins.

Then, O great sovereign Queen, the adept transfers the rest of the water from his left hand to his right and in imagination inhales it through his iḍā duct [inside his left nostril], which water then cleanses his inner body. Thereafter, he should exhale that water through his piṅgalā duct [inside his right nostril]. Here he imagines that water to be black and the embodiment of sins; he immediately throws the water onto a slab of rock with the mantra *phaṭ*. Then he should wash his hands, perform ācamana and, having performed breath control, offer libation to his lineage god and then offer arghya [an offering of a few rice grains, tips of durvā grass and sanctified water] to the Sun god and arghya to his chosen deity.

50d–53. Thereafter he should repeat the great words of the [Kālikā] gāyatrī [the famous Vedic mantra with which brahmans worship the Sun every day, as follows]: first one should take the praṇava [*Oṃ*], then utter *kālikāyai*, then *vidmahe*; then *śmaśānavāsinyai dhīmahi*, then *tan no ghore pracodayāt*. While uttering this mantra, the worshiper should three times scatter the consecrated water upward.
54ab. Then, O great Goddess, having performed aṅganyāsa the worshiper again performs ācamana.

Tārā's Gāyatrī Is Described with a Brief Mention of the Deity's Dhyāna as the Sun Deity

54cd–56ab. O great Goddess! Having envisaged in meditation one's chosen deity [here Tārā] in the orb of the sun, one should utter *Oṃ tārāyai vidmahe mahogrāyai dhīmahi tan no devī pracodayāt*. Then, having performed breath control, he should repeat this mantra 108 times.

Now, O Queen of gods, I offer in the form of aphorisms (*sūtrākāra*) an account of the system of worship.

Preliminaries

56cd–58. First proclaim universal well-being (*svasti-vacana*), then the announcement of one's intention to worship (*saṃkalpa*). Next, one should carefully place the pitcher [full of consecrated water], followed by the act of ācamana with mantras; next comes the setting the pitcher of water for arghya for general purposes; then sprinkling the entrance [with consecrated water for purification], finishing that ritual by worshiping the entrance. Then, having removed the three categories of hindrances [concretized as evil spirits, belonging to the ground, atmosphere, and close to the body of the worshiper and the material objects around him gathered for the ritual] he removes [other evil] spirits [with mantras, sprinkling of water and threatening gestures].

Starting the Actual Worship

59–60ab. Having adored the seat, the intelligent worshiper first of all bows down to his guru. Then he purifies his hands, claps them three times, and then performs the rite of consolidating and safeguarding the area surrounding his person (*digbandhana*). Then he encompasses himself with fire. Then he performs bhūtaśuddhi.

Nyāsa

60cd–64ab. He should then first perform the nyāsa of the six limbs of the mātṛkā [the full Sanskrit alphabet], then the nyāsa of the mātṛkā on his inner body. Then he utters the dhyāna mantra [the mantra that gives the deity's iconography] of the mātṛkā. He should perform the same nyāsa on his external body. Then he performs the nyāsa of the seat of the deity (*pīṭha*) before completing his breath control. Then he performs the nyāsa of the sage, and so on [the sage poet, the meter, and the deity of his mantra]. Then he performs nyāsa of his hands and his limbs [identifying them with] the letters of the Sanskrit alphabet. Then he performs the six types of nyāsa [of his main mantra]. Then he performs vyāpaka [extended] nyāsa. With concentration he performs the nyāsa of the tattvas; then, O Goddess!, he performs the nyāsa of the seed mantra. He performs the vyāpaka nyāsa in seven different ways using his main mantra. Then in deep concentration he visualizes his deity, whereafter he worships that deity mentally [with imagined ingredients].

Adoration of the Deity

64cd–68ab. [The adept] prepares the consecrated special liquid for special argyha. Then he worships [the deity's] seat. Next he again performs the visualization of the deity in deep meditation (*dhyāna*) and this time he sees her with her eyes open. [All the time he utters specific mantras and appropriate gestures to accompany his ritual acts.] Then he in similar manner welcomes the deity. Then while purifying all objects of offering he shows the gestures of the cow's udder, and so on. [These are called the dhenu mudrā, the symbol for the celestial cow whose milk is nectar; the avaguṇṭhana mudrā, which symbolizes safety and cover; the gālinī mudrā which symbolizes the fusing of the sacred and the mundane water; and the nārāca mudrā, which symbolizes iron arrowheads toward off any polluting evil spirits]. Then he performs the nyāsa of the deity's six limbs. Then he performs the rite of establishing life [in the image or other representation of the deity]. Then he worships [with offerings] his principal mantra and its deity, the Goddess. Then he requests the Goddess to authorize him [to exercise the power of the mantra]. Then he worships the deity's attendant deities like Kālī, and so on. . . . Then he worships her attendant mother-goddesses Brāhmī, and so on, and their Bhairavas, Asitāṅga, and so on. . . . Then he worships [the deity's consort] Mahākāla. Then he worships the Goddess's [weapons, that is,] her sword, and so on. Next he worships the lineage of his guru. Then the ritualist repeats the worship of Kālī. This is followed by the offering of bali [a sacrificial animal, or in some cases nonvegetarian food for the spirits]. This is followed by the fire sacrifice. Then, having performed prāṇāyāma [as a preparation for japa], he performs mantra repetition (*japa*) of his main mantra [which is a form of one-pointed meditation]. Finally, the intelligent worshiper dedicates the merit of his japa to the deity and then performs prāṇāyāma for a second time.

Esoteric Worship of the Goddess with Alcohol and Other Ingredients

68cd. At this moment the worshiper may, O Goddess, collect [esoteric ingredients such as] alcohol [meat, fish, fried food/a partner for intercourse, and the sexual fluids].

Concluding Section of the Worship

69–71. Afterward, the worshiper offers the deity arghya and also dedicates himself to the Goddess. Then he recites the Goddess's eulogy and then recites her protective kavaca ["armor," a special hymn used as a mantra, which guards every part of the worshiper's body]. Finally he prostrates himself. Afterward he mentally utters the formula, "I am Śiva," while making the gesture of bidding her farewell. He then draws a diagram on the southwestern corner and offers arghya and other offerings to the goddess Ucchiṣṭacaṇḍālī. He then himself puts a mark on his forehead with the sandal paste offered to the Goddess and partakes of some of the offered food. Thereafter he can do whatever he wishes.

Alternative Brief Ritual

Alternatively, the initiated Tantric ritualist who has composed and fixed his mind in devotion and meditation may perform a shortened version of the worship.

First he performs the nyāsa of the poet-sage, and so on, of his main mantra; then he purifies his hands [with nyāsa] followed by nyāsa of his fingers and the extensive nyāsa of his body. Then he performs the nyāsa of his six limbs. Then he claps his hands three times [to remove obstructing spirits], then encircles his surroundings with [a fiery barrier]. Then he performs breath control followed by dhyāna on his mantra deity and then mentally performs her worship. Then he prepares and places the pitcher of arghya water, and worships the seat [of the Goddess]. On that he invokes the Goddess after having meditated on her image. Then he performs her ritual welcome, and so forth, followed by establishing life in her symbol, jīvanyāsa or prāṇapratiṣṭhā, and finally worships the supreme Goddess. Then he worships the attendant deities Kālī, and so on, as well as the eight śaktis, Brāhmī, and so on, along with their bhairavas. Then having worshiped Mahākāla he worships his guru's lineage as well as the Goddess's attributes and weapons such as the sword. This is followed by a repeat of the worship of the Goddess. Then the foremost of all worshipers practices breath control before performing his japa. He dedicates the [merit of his] japa to the Goddess's hand. He performs the concluding breath control, prostrates himself, recites the Goddess's panegyric and kavaca and causes the special arghya to be offered. He then dedicates himself [to the Goddess] and bids her farewell with the gesture of resorption. He draws a diagram on his southwestern side and worships Ucchiṣṭacaṇḍālī. In conclusion, he partakes of some of the offered food and then he may do as he pleases.

Source: *Toḍala Tantra*, translated by Sanjikta Gupta in *Tantra in Practice*, edited by David Gordon White (Princeton: Princeton University Press, 2000).

Selections from the *Tantraloka* of Abhinavagupta

1. Now is described the secret rite which is designed for master and disciple who are well qualified.

2–3. In the *Kramapūjātantra* the Lord has revealed the essence of the ritual. That which is achieved in a month with a single [mantra] by the method of the siddha—perfected being—cannot be achieved in a thousand years through the ordinary ceremonies or of a flood of mantras. . . .

4. Kula is the energy (*śakti*) of the Lord, his ability, eminence, freedom, vitality, virile potency, consciousness, and body.

5. This sacrifice is intended only for someone who thus sees everything in the same light, freed from all doubts.

6. Whatever the hero accomplishes in thought, word, or action, through any activity that reveals a state of mind is called kula sacrifice.
7. Regardless of conditions, the sacrifice may be performed in six different ways: in worldly activities, in relation to a woman, in the couple's union, as well as in body breath, and thought.
8. It needs no meditational circle, fire-pit, ritual purifications, baths, etc. . . . in short, none of the objects and instruments usually associated with rites.
9. According to the *Triśirobhairava*: ". . . the kaula is nothing but knowledge and knowable."
10. Still, the wise should use practices which are forbidden in other religious scriptures: It is associated with the method of the left [the use of meat, of alcoholic liquors, and sexual union].
11. The *Brahayāmala* states: "Alcohol is the external essence of Śiva." There is no enjoyment or liberation without it. . . .
22. By means of an identity with the mantra, he brings himself to the state of Bhairava. . . .
40. Being familiar with such marks, he acquires whatever is possible from the mouth of the yoginī. . . .
64. He says: "I am not, no one else exists; I am merely energies." Under all circumstances, one should recollect and maintain that frame of mind. . . .
78. The awakened person should worship paired images [of the śaktis], or he should worship them as independent of any ritual.
79. He becomes the single lord of kula. . . .
96. This secret ritual revealed by the Lord is now described. Let it be performed in the company of an outer energy [a woman called dūtī].
97. Brahman is ultimate bliss and resides in the body in three ways: the first two are means, the third is the result, all are identical with bliss.
98. He who observes the last three is it.

99–100. Enslaved beings who are deprived of the three Ms are completely deprived of bliss. Those who perform the sacrifice without the three Ms, which are sources of bliss, also go to a dreadful hell.

100–101. The distinctive feature of feminine energy—śakti—is that she is identical with the owner of the energy. Her selection, therefore, should be made regardless of her appearance, caste, etc.

101–102. Since such identity is beyond all worldly or supraworldly associations, this energy is given three different names in my master's tradition—

caused, subsequently caused, and co-caused. She is like that which is threefold, directly or indirectly. Thus she is threefold in two ways.

103. As succintly summarized by the *Sarvācarahṛdaya*: "It is said that there are six energies already mentioned that bestow enjoyment and liberation."

104. Emanation and reabsorption are engendered by both [partners]. Thus their union is the ultimate reality.

105. When the dūtī is present, both of them engage in mutual worship, finding satisfaction in each other; they worship the main circle by means of an innermost process. The organ of consciousness produces bliss.

106–107. Thus is the main circle; the secondary circles are inferior to it. The term *cakra* [circle] is associated with some verbal roots meaning: to expand; to be satisfied; to sever bonds and to act efficiently. So the circle shines, is satisfied, breaks, and performs action.

That which generates bliss and should be used in worship because it enraptures the heart.

107. And again, externally the sacrifice is a satisfaction hailed as an expansion.

108–109. The energetic zeal of consciousness may be due to external substances, flowers, perfumes and incense, which act upon the breath; also to food, from which pleasure is derived. This zeal is aroused when the possessor of the energy imagines the sexual satisfaction, and so penetrates into the main circle.

110. This is how [the couple] should, with the help of suitable substances, mutually satisfy their secondary circles so that these become united with the main circle.

110–111. This is what is stated in the *Triśirastantra*: "He whose interior faculties are unified in the midst of the six sense activities, becomes absorbed into the Rudra."

111–112. In the intense awareness of one's own nature, which becomes evident with the extension of varied enjoyments, related to their respective secondary wheels, the divine energies find access one by one to the central circle of consciousness.

113. For those attached to their own ego and who, due to their prejudices concerning "I" and "you," are deprived of such a realization. The energies of their secondary circles remain distinct; they are neither vibrating nor endowed with plenitude.

113–114. Turning to each other, the couple formed by the energy and the owner of it, filled with the rays coming from the energies of the secondary circles, reach their full potency.

114–115. When the couple is absorbed into the superior space, there occurs an intense agitation due to this contact. The secondary circles are stirred and identified with this sacred space.

115–116. Thus this union, wherein all differrentiated knowledge gradually fades away for the couple who are in such a state. Consciousness itself, the unitive friction of the flows of emission gradually appears. Such is the highest, permanent and most noble abode. It is the universal bliss composed of both. The supreme kaula is neither quiescent nor emergent, but it is their original cause, which produces the "rested" and the "risen."

117. With this consciousness, he who wants to reach this undivided state must make it his own repeatedly. The nature of divine consciousness is boundless and undivided from the perspective of the goddess.

118–119. The blissful person penetrates into the undivided space, which is the source of the emission, by watching how the quiescent and emergent modalities referred to as "this" and "that" arise and cease.

119–120. The two emerge simultaneously in the source and owner of śakti. If both reach this domain at the same time and by way of reciprocity, this is emergence; but if they reach it only within themselves, this is the quiescent aspect. Nonetheless both actually form a united pair in quiescence as well as in emergence.

121. Although both are equally aware of the quiescent and emergent states, the energy alone, and not the owner, is capable of developing emanation. . . .

122–123. To woman alone, treatises state that her median way fully expands. By means of her alone should the guru impart the entire secret doctrine; and through her superior body, by the practice of union . . . it is imparted to men.

124. According to Maheśī, the mouth of the yoginī is superior because she is endowed with a pure, superior substance.

124–125. Due to this superiority according to Maheśī, the "mouth of the yogini" is affirmed to be the principal form of the circle and from there is knowledge obtained. This knowledge beyond duality cannot be described in writing and it is stated to be transmitted from mouth to mouth.

126. And the mouth is the main wheel. How could we possibly account for our own consciousness in writing? They gain access to the boundless place, those who, during this double emission—the rested and risen places—grasp the reality of the emission preceding them, and become firmly established.

127. Those wishing to acquire supernatural power must nourish oneself on the ejaculated form.

128–129. Then, let them worship it alone because of its pure form; it is close to consciousness; it goes from the mouth [of the yoginī] to [the adept's] own mouth and vice versa. Bestower of immortality and eternal youth, it is named kula, supreme.

129–132. As for those who have not reached full enlightenment, they too will obtain knowledge by taking part in the sacrifice which attains completion by ejaculation, after they have worshiped the divine energies of the main circle evoked during this sacrifice. And there, in the circle of energy they worship these divinities in accordance with the method mentioned, with the help [of the emergent form] full of bliss, starting from the outside: Ganeśa, with his attendants in the four spatial directions, the couple of Kula masters [Śiva and the energy] in the center; the three goddesses at the three beams of light and, externally four goddesses at each point. The sage should also worship a twelve-spoked wheel or the eight, or else the sixty-four. . . .

133. He should repeat the worship of those same divinities, and they should be performed not only in the circle of energy, but also in the sacred domain of one's own body.

133–135. Because the consciousness of the heart is developed by means of any practice that arrives at the quiescent form of Śiva, one then gains access to the rested state, called the calmed sea.

When one becomes settled in that rested state, the whole group of the divinities of the central circle becomes inert, ceasing to fluctuate, suspended in the void, in undivided bliss.

135–136. [The energies] of the secondary circles—sight, hearing—also participate in this energy, for they depend on the energies of the central circle; immersed in non-bliss, they remain immobile, yearning for bliss.

136–137. Having no contact with the supreme reality, all the energies of the sense organs remain immobile. They are deprived of their own natures and crave for them.

137–138. Due to an internal longing, things overflow with their own essence and obtain a sacred state owing to this satisfaction, which are poured out as an [offering] to its self.

139. Through this offering of their respective objects to the self, there is an outpouring of a stream, which causes consciousness to overflow and . . . there is an intense agitation of virile potency. And, as already stated, the Lord of the circle also expands vigorously.

140. Consequently, the flow is threefold: unitive, risen and rested. . . .

142–143. After entering the awakened condition, the veins rest, and absorption on the winds ascending and descending currents in the central channel, the motions of the circles, the junctions and joints, Śiva, who dwells in the body endowed with 72,000 channels, unites each mode of consciousness and liberates its ceaseless movement.

144. A person should become firmly established in this union as Śiva.

145. At the level of Bhairava, he should remain within the union, being separated and free. The state is characterized by the full attainment of a reality devoid of space and time.

146–147. After withdrawing from all beings, one should concentrate on Being, which occurs after restraining the sun and moon from either dissolution or dissemination.

147–148. Thus the sound vibration, which is perfect self-awareness, arises in the sphere of union during absorption in the consciousness of the triple flow. The resonance is the power of the mantra.

148–149. He alone concentrates on the emergence of the mantra who, in this very resonance, with a desire to obtain the result of emergence, remains absorbed in the mantra.

149–150. With full awareness of consciousness, just as the secondary circles rush suddenly into the central circle of consciousness and identify with it, that, with the help of sound, he should simultaneously perform japa.

150–151. According to the *Yogasaṃcāra* cherished by the yoginī, there is a lotus that rests hidden in an ever-unfolding circle resting inside the triangle. Attached to this lotus, there resides a stem whose root is adorned with a sixteen-petal circle.

152–153. The shoot is emitted [on three conditions]: 1. Owing to the successive frictions of the two lotuses strung on the stem standing upright in the center. 2. Owing to the union of ovum and sperm in the three-petaled lotus. 3. Owing to the unitive friction in fire of the energy waves of the fully magnificent rays of the sun and the moon.

153–154. By means of the mudrā, he suddenly becomes rooted in the fourth state wherein moon, sun and fire are united, internally takes hold of the processes of emanation, etc. . . .

154–155. The power of the mantra consists in an awareness by the person who possesses śakti of the potency of the mantra. When they penetrate into this khecarī-mudrā, they embrace, rejoice, laugh, and play the game of love.

156. This awareness manifests the following eight stages: non-manifested, resonance, and roaring sound, heard sound, murmur, resonance, and end of the resonance. As to the unuttered and unbroken sound, this is related to union.

156–157. He gains access to the set of eight circles when he practices spontaneous japa inside the supreme space and achieves the state of the eight bhairavas itself, which is divided into eight phases.

157–158. During union, in the back and forth movement, in the certainty, in dual hearing, dual sight, the initial contact of both organs, in sexual union and at the two extremities of the body: these are the unified pairings.

158–159. There is an undefined sound which comes from the heart and which, moving through the chest, is expressed in the throat, and ends up on the lips. After hearing it at the center of both circles, he enjoys the ultimate appeasement.

159–160. The supreme Bhairava residing there as supreme sound, is divided into eight phases, made of light, and of sound vibrations and of touch. It is called eminent pervasion.

160–161. The eight bhairavas are given eight names. . . . This pervasion extends from the half-moon to the transcendental.

161–163. He who, in his every act and place remains heedful of this pervasion, being undefiled, is one liberated-in-life, and he identifies with the supreme Bhairava. Anybody conceived during such a union is known as a "yoginī's son"; he is Rudra, the worthy recipient of the repository of knowledge. According to the *Vīrāvaliśāstra*, an infant in the womb possesses the form of Śiva himself.

164–166. This sacrifice is termed "original" or primordial because through it the essence is extracted, and because it is the original sacrifice. . . .

166–168. By means of the couple, he is free from resorting to vows, and yoga . . . the guru, by evoking the original sacrifice, becomes engaged and lays on the female body. He meditates on the lotus [woman] in the form of the moon, and then on himself in the form of the sun. Then he intimately merges together these two bases constituted of science and knowledge.

169. Because this doctrine is a profound secret, I am not expressing it lucidly. He who is interested in this teaching can read the scriptures.

171–173. The body itself is the supreme circle, the eminent, auspicious liṅga, the chosen abode of the divine energies and the place of the highest worship. It is indeed the principle maṇḍala composed of the triple trident, consisting of lotus, circle, and space.

There, all energies are endlessly worshiped, both externally and internally. Then, in full awareness of his own mantra, he should perform the process of emanation and reabsorption. He is placed in contact with the blissful and manifold sexual fluid issuing from the circle of consciousness.

174–175. Through this contact, the wheel of consciousness suddenly awakens and he who has mastered it reaches the supreme reality, where all his bodily energies become satiated. . . .

183–185. In a cremation ground representing the void, which is visited by yoginīs and perfected beings (*siddhas*), a place of play that is fearsome, which contains a circle of rays, a location where darkness is overcome, which is devoid of differentiated thinking, a location of bliss and funeral pyres: who cannot be lead to perfection in this dreadful place?

186–187. The master may thus initiate disciples, but only one out of one hundred thousand is worthy of such an initiation.

Source: *Tantraloka* by Abhinavagupta, edited by R. C. Dwivedi and N. Rastogi (Delhi Motilal Banarsidass, 1987) Chapter 29; translated by Carl Olson.

Selections from the *Yoginīhṛdaya* with the Commentary of Amṛtānanda

The Goddess Says:

It is to say that I, Śiva, take responsibility upon myself for [this process] until it is revealed that I am, by my active consciousness, the one that questions. [This question is announced under the form: "The Goddess] says," to the last person of the singular totality. [The use of the] past explains itself by the eternal character of what will be said. It is not of today, since it is not submitted to time. [The verbal form is employed by him to designate what is beyond words] of which no one is a witness because it is inaccessible to the senses. [The use of the expression:] "Bhairava says" explains itself the same way. [It is necessary therefore to understand it as:] Myself, I am supreme Śiva whose nature is light, wanting to spill my grace on the universe and inviting me [for it] in the process [four plans of Speech:] the Supreme, the Seer, the Way, and the Revealed, I being made questioner because of valuable consciousness, then I give an answer by my light, I descend [in this world] Tantra: here is something that signifies [the first words of our text]. It is that which is called the Mahāsvacchanda.

God, the eternal Śiva, being held himself in her [double] condition of master and of disciple, sends down the Tantra by phrases [forming] questions and answers:

God of Gods, great God, expansion of perfect plenitude, this Vāmakeśvaratantra contains numerous things unknown (1): Condescend to say to them entirely, O Bhairava!

The supreme Śiva is Bhairava, so named because, demonstrating, keeping, and reabsorbing [the universe], he carries it, stops it, and vomits it out. "God of the gods": this God is the illuminator of the gods, it is said then of those whose nature shines, like the sun, etc. This grand God possesses by nature the highest light. Here is what it wants to say: the nature of your being is greatest light, You alone make the universe shine, whereas You, no one can make you shine (or illuminate you). . . .

"Expansion of perfect fullness": expansion is consciousness. The expansion of perfect fullness is then intelligence, which has the universe for its object. Such is the nature [of Śiva], it is this of which he is made. Since You are omniscient, You alone must make Yourself known to everyone. No one can apprehend anything about You. . . .

Bhairava Says:

Listen, Goddess, the great secret, the heart of the Yoginī, supreme. (2) I adore you at the present time, by love for you that which is hidden in all particulars and has been [always] received on earth by a teaching given by mouth to ear. (3)

[This big secret is] "supreme," supereminent, because it transcends all knowledge. One will say indeed farther: "When one reaches knowledge, O Woman of beautiful hips! one immediately reaches the khecara stage" (v. 5). "Listen" to this: it is agreeable to the voice of consciousness.

"By love for You": because I am perfectly merged and united with You, I tell it to you "today," because, a cause of his extreme secret, it had not been said again by anyone. For this same reason, it "must be especially secret." This is to say that [that secret teaching] must be apprehended meditatively by intense meditative contemplation of the nature of "Me" absolute of his own self.

To underline this idea of an extreme secret, [Tantra] says that [teaching must not be given to others]. . . .

[This big secret] must not be given to those who are not worthy:

It is not necessary to entrust it to the disciples of others, not to unbelievers, O Goddess! Not to those who have little ardor for hearing it, neither to those who do not give of their wealth (4)

One cannot confer it to [a candidate] who was examined and put to the test during a half year. When one possesses knowledge of it, O Woman of beautiful hips! One reaches immediately the khecara stage. (5)

It means to say that [in reaching the khecara stage] one immediately reaches Reality: one becomes free in life. . . .

O supreme Goddess! The relative agreement with the Goddess Tripurā is threefold: The relative agreement of the cakra and those concerning the mantra and the cult. (6)

Supreme goddess, she is triple, her nature being light, conscious awareness and perfect fusion [of these two aspects]. . . .

To the extent that one won't have the knowledge of this triple agreement, one won't possess the supreme inherent authority of the cakra of Tripurā. (7)

To the extent that one won't have consciousness of the triple agreement that is to be described [now], one won't possess the supreme authority inherent to the cakra of the very awareness of the supreme Tripurā, formed of the collection of the categories of the manifestation, relevant to the expert of the knowledge and the knowable. Authority is the capacity to grant favor and restraint: so he is the king in the life of this world. It is in this sense that one is so-called supreme. It is about the authority of the supreme Lord himself, to whom, in all the worlds, nothing can become an obstacle. The one, then, who possesses this supreme authority will be the supreme Lord himself. Who knows it will arrive immediately at the state of khecara and who ignores it won't arrive there. The thing is established then in a positive and negative way that also indicates he could pursue [by our text] and, implicitly, the one who is qualified [to receive the teaching], as well as the object [of the work] and the relation [between these elements]. This qualified adept is the one who wants liberation. The object is the divinity who is conscious of herself and she could pursue liberation. As for the connection [between these elements], it is the being [who joins] what one desires to obtain to what one is permitted to obtain. Now begins *exposure to the relative convention of the cakra:*

This cakra allows, in the sense of the emanation, five energies and, within those of the dissolution, four fires. He is born therefore of the conjunction of five energies and four fires. (8)

When this supreme energy, taking by her own will this aspect of the universe, she sees herself as luminous, then appears the cakra. (9)

Of the empty letter A [and] of what is finally by emission: from the bindu, vibrant consciousness, (10)

"The letter A is empty: it is all together empty and the letter A is empty because the entire cosmic expansion is excluded some. It is then the supreme Śiva. . . . The letter A, first of all phonemes, light, is the supreme Śiva." To that same topic, the revelation [says]: "The brahman is A" (Ait. Up. 3.6). "Of what is finally by emission," it is to say finally that He produces emission. [Indeed, it is] "of the bindu, vibrant consciousness," that is born of the sun, a synthesis of fire and the moon, called Kāma and of which nature is the perfect fusion of Śiva and Śakti. . . . the realization of the bindu named kāma, fuses perfectly of Śiva and Śakti, who are vibration consisting of two bindus, white and red, which are fire and moon. It is said that the most dynamic form of consciousness is born of the conjunction of the white bindu and red: from the vibration of the bindu which is a perfect fusion of A and HA.

Whose supreme nature is light and that is united to the lighting wave [of energy], flows the baindavacakra, place [of birth] of the cosmic wave, made of the triple mātṛ[kā]. (11)

["Whose supreme nature is light and that is united with the lightning wave:] of the contact of fire and consciousness are born with the light, as butter becomes clarified [due to the contact with fire]. The stream of the energy of awareness. In effect the nature of light is supreme. "And that is united with the lighning wave": it is the wave of energy of lightning awareness that springs in the middle of the two bindus under the shape of the demi-Kalā of HA: from the union [of kāma] with this one. From this akṣara kamakalā "is born" the baindavacakra made from the triple mātṛ[kā], place [of birth] of the wave of the universe. By "place [of birth] of the cosmic wave" it is necessary to understand that this wave, these streams, these are the 36 tattvas and that she is their ground in the sense that she is the cause of their appearance. "The triple mātṛ[kā]," these are the [seeds of speech]: mark, way, settled. Of her, it is with the appearance of a fourth bindu, named Sadāśiva, resulting from the coalescence of these [other elements] that unfold the central triangle, the baindavacakra.". . .

This one has three different shapes then.

There are then three different shapes of this cakra, whose nature is that of one triangle. The word "then" aims here [at the appearance of] new features in the [cakra] that are described: the one is himself here first the nature of a triangle, then, because of the emission, he reaches the condition of energy and, with reabsorption, the one of fire. It is in this sense that he becomes triple. This that makes him understand.

[There appear] dharma and adharma, those [four kinds of] ātman, as well as the knowing subject, the knowable and the knowledge. (12) Its nature is then of one increasing womb. It is immense, a mass of consciousness and happiness. To this nondual cakra [corresponds] one division in nine mantras. (13)

This [navayoni] is present in the [in accordance with cakra], eight points, under the form of Ambikā. Surrounded by vowels, it is the dynamism of consciousness, the fire of the reabsorption. And is placed on the throne that forms the bindu. (14)

This nondual cakra, whose nature is that of nondual womb, is a mass of consciousness and happiness; consciousness being the aspect of dynamic consciousness and happiness, the one evolution of the cosmos. These two [elements] form a mass in this sense that they form something interior and exterior that is perfectly compact and finished. It is "immense," this is to say that being made of consciousness is not limited by extension, time, nor formal configuration. . . .

The [first of the two cakras] possesses ten points is a single luminous form born of the effulgence of the nine triangles. It makes the ten phonemes sparkle, of that one that precedes Śakti to the first of nine [following]. (15) It is the support for the light of the ten coarse and subtle elements.

By "nine triangles," [it is necessary to understand] the [original] triangle and the navayonicakra. The word triangle designates [indeed here] the baindava-[cakra] situated in the middle of the [central] triangle. The widespread effulgence around them by the baindava and those "nine triangles" (= navayoni), the brightness that is inherent to them, takes thus, while changing, the, shape of the ten points [of the following cakra]. Śakti is the letter RA. It is what the Uddhārordhvatantra, indicates about the subject of the extraction of the bīja of the Rāmaśakti: "Candra, Śakti, Mahāśakti, Brahmnī, Kāmikā, etc." What comes before Śakti, the letter RA, is YA. While starting then with the letter YA, preceding Sakti, and some going until the last of these nine phonemes, one arrives at KṢA. Thus is shown the shape of the ten [phonemes in question]. Their sparkling is connected to awareness. It is necessary to understand that [it owes itself to produce at this level] an awareness of the ten phonemes of YA to KṢA.

The five coarse elements are the earth, fire, air, and ether; the five subtle elements: odor, flavor, shape, touch, and sound. The ten elements have a single tenfold light because this one serves to support them. As the objects, earth, etc., have the nature of Śiva and the nature of the YA phonemes, etc., it is energy, this cakra is to be formed by ten triangles and to have for its nature time, light, and consciousness. While saying that [this cakra is the support of the tattvas] of the earth, etc., and of the phonemes [of YA] until KṢA, one makes appear that the nature of the three cakras—the first has ten points and the [two] others—are those of the preservation of the cosmos.

The second cakra of ten points is described :

The lightning shape of the second to the ten points [is associated with the] krodhīśa phonemes, etc. (16)

What is the sense of this passage? It is that when the cakra of the bindu, of the central triangle and the one with eight points are illuminated by the double clarity of light and the hold of consciousness shining at the center, born are the two cakras at ten angles, thus the letters KA, etc., [the elements] its, etc., and the letters YA, etc., and [the elements] earth, etc., produce themselves to reflect this tenfold effulgence. . . .

The cakra with fourteen points is said [to sustain]:

By continuation of the transformation of the luminescence of the four [first] cakras conjoins [with the one with ten points, appears] under a form of fourteen points and while having for nature the perception and the organs of the senses, [the cakra follows] makes for the expansion, to the highest sense, of the phonemes of khecarī in jayā [and that], thus, it is made of the luminescence of raudrī flashing under forms of fire and energy. (17–18)

The fourth [first] cakra consists of the bindu. The [central] triangle, the cakra has eight points and the first has ten points. It shines with quadruple luminescence. As [these cakras] are distant [from the one with fourteen points], one doesn't distinguish them [on this last level] with the luminescence [and not the composing parts]. As in the case of one forest, made of many trees, one doesn't distinguish [from afar the trees] that compose it. Whereas because of its proximity to the second cakra with ten points and of its conjunction with the quadruple luminescence, one will be able to distinguish the composing elements and the quadruple luminescence [of the other cakras with the one with fourteen points, this one] resulting from the transformation of it [cakra] with ten points. "Under a form with fourteen points and while having for its nature the perception and the organs of the senses": perception is knowledge. But this word also connotes action. The organs [mentioned here] are then the ten senses [of apperception and action]. . . . That it is the central cakra and not another that, becoming the triangle, then the cakra has eight points, then the two have ten points, it is transformed into a cakra with fourteen points, which are light and awareness and provides the fourteen phonemes of TA to BHA and of the fourteen organs of perception, it is to say senses of apperception, hearing, etc., of those of action, speech, etc., plus the internal sense, intellect, principle of individuation and psychism. . . .

[Finally there appear] the squares, forms of Jyeṣṭhā and the triple tower, forms of Vāmā.

That which possesses three times four angles, or points, the quadrilaterals, shapes the Jyeṣṭhā, it is the [external] squares. The triple tower, or triple circumference, is a form of Vāmā. The expression "triple tower" designates also the two lotuses situated at the interior of the three circles. . . .

Another way to represent this same cakra is to say then:

The [first] triangle arises from consciousness; the eight triangles, of the Śāntyatīta [kalā]; (19) the two [cakras] ten points as well as the one in the fourteen, of Śānti[kalā]. That which forms a circle of eight petals is the brilliance of the vidyākalā. The lotus of sixteen petals, manifests effulgence, [is] in the body of the Prathiṣṭha[kalā. Finally] when the squares shine then appears the aspect of the nivṛttikalā. (21)

In the ninth cakra, however, from the trailokyamohana to the first, O Sureśvarī! One meets nāda, kalā, Jyesthā, Raudrī and Vāmā, (22) as well as Visaghnī, Dūtarī, and Sarvānandā, in this order. Nāda and bindu are undivided, Kalā is the will for proper nature, (23) Jyeṣṭhā is knowledge and all of the rest is activity. Thus the cakra is triple, it is a form of Kāmakalā, its essential nature being expansion. (24)

[First, one is] the energy Śāntā, who is indivisible. This indivisibility contains what is restful, its nature being that of consciousness. It is why, also, Nāda and Bindu, which make the energy śāntā, are without divisions. The second cakra: squares and lotuses have sixteen petals, are forms of Nāda and Bindu, they, are then also made of the energy śāntā. Kalā, then, possesses by its own nature will. This own nature is [indeed] dynamic. It is to say that the lotus with eight petals is made of will energy. Jyeṣṭhā, she, is knowledge; her own nature is not anything else then knowledge. The cakra with fourteen points is then made from energy of knowledge. "The whole remains activity": it has for form the five energies named Raudrī, Vāmā, Viṣaghnī, Dūtarī, and Sarvānandā.

They correspond to the five cakras that are two to ten angles, the one has eight angles, the central triangle and the bindu, all aspects of energy.

In Akula, in what one names Viṣu, in what raises energy and in fire, since in the navel, the anāhata, the [vi]śudha, [the cakra of] the uvula and between the eyebrows, (25) in the moon, in its half, then in nirodhinī, nāda, nādānta and śakti, then in vyāpikā and in the domain of samanā and unmanā, (26) finally in the mahābindhu, he mediates then on the triple cakra.

Until the ājñā [the meditation cakra] is said with kalā; [of her] until unmanī she is sakala-niṣkala. To the supreme state, she is without kalā. She finds herself this way being triple. On the forehead, she has the form of a circle similar to one lamp. . . . (27–28)

Pure and empty consciousness: this meditation is "without kalā." The meditator finds himself within triple being. . . . The sudden burst of the [first stage, the one of bindu] is comparable to that of a lamp. . . .

[Nāda presents itself as] a stick between two bindus, of the form of a penis, iridescent as a jewel, [with one duration] of a sixteenth [of more. Duration] two times [least for] nādantā, flaming as lightning, (30) in the form of a plow, a bindu being attached to him on the right. However, what shines afterwards is śakti, which is the aspect of one [feature] that raises above on the left of the two bindus. (31)

Nāda has the form of a right line between two bindus—that of a penis. One names the penis tubular body situated between the two testicles: here to what it resembles. It "shimmers like a jewel": its color is that of the ruby. . . .

"Blazing like lightning": its burst being similar to the one of lightning to "the shape of a plow": of a stick in shape of a plowshare. "A bindu being attached to him on the right," it is to say that being placed between two bindus, it is against the one situated to its right. The number to multiply by two is sixteen. . . .

Vyāpikā is born afterwards when bindu, by its game, takes a triangular aspect. Samanā, then, is made of a single line placed right between two bindus. Then, unmanā, when the game of the bindus produce a right line. The body of śakti, etc., shines from a burst similar to the twelve suns, the fractions of more [of the statement] of these [kalā] to leave from śakti are: of the more. Then two times [less that] this total amount, then two times [less] again for manomanī. After what [comes] unmanī. (32–34)

Vyāpikā is the triangular figure formed by the three Vāmā energies, etc., that are the bindu in its game. . . .

It is also from this same bindu and by its game [that appears] unmanā, that is a right line. . . .

Higher than it [again], it is there the supremely great, that is not limited in time, space, that is beautiful by nature and that stirs supreme happiness. (35)

"That stirs the supreme happiness": the happiness is also contained in the experience of a particular thing, a sound for example, etc. [But] this [happiness] is without length. It is why one says here "stired by the supreme happiness" [what is all something else]. That one wants to say, in effect?—that which is prior has all things existing in triple time and triple forms, that doesn't limit (or doesn't divide) neither time nor space, what is supremely big, that whose beauty is spontaneous, staying in the fullness of happiness of a common enjoyment and merging with the supreme Śiva, supreme light, the energy of consciousness, it is Mahātripurasundarī. . . .

When this supreme kalā knows the lightning of itself, then, taking the aspect of Ambikā, she expresses herself as supreme speech. (36)

This supreme kalā is the energy of consciousness: this one fragment of the collection of the phonemes. . . .

Source: *Le coeur de la yoginī: Yoginīhṛdaya avec le commentaire Dīpikā d'Amṛtānanda*, translated by André Padoux (Paris: Collège de France, 1994); translated from the French by Carl Olson.

NOTES

CHAPTER 6 KRISHNA DEVOTIONALISM

1. John Brockington, *The Sanskrit Epics* (Leiden: E.J. Brill, 1998), 26.
2. James L. Fitzgerald, "India's Fifth Veda: The Mahābhārata's Presentation of Itself," *Journal of South Asian Literature* 20/1 (1985): 126–28.
3. Brockington, *Sanskrit Epics*, 34.
4. Jan Gonda, *Die Religionen Indiens I: Veda und älterer Hinduismus* (Stuttgart: W. Kohlhammer Verlag, 1960), 42, 220.
5. Alf Hiltebeitel, *Rethinking the Mahābhārata: A Reader's Guide to the Education of the Dharma King* (Chicago: University of Chicago Press, 2001), 18–19.
6. James L. Fitzgerald, "The Many Voices of the Mahābhārata," *Journal of the American Oriental Society* 123/4 (2003): 811.
7. Yaroslav Vassilkov, "The Mahābhārata's Typological Definition Reconsidered," *Indo-Iranian Journal* 38/3 (1995): 255.
8. David Dean Shulman, "Devana and Daiva," in *Ritual, State, and History in South Asia: Essays in Honour of J.C. Heesterman*, edited by D.H.A. Kloff and M.S. Oort (Leiden: E. J. Brill, 1992), 359.
9. Alf Hiltebeitel, "Śiva, the Goddess, and the Disguises of the Pāṇḍavas and Draupadī," *History of Religions* 12/1–2 (1980): 147–74.
10. Alf Hiltebeitel, *The Ritual of Battle: Krishna in the Mahābhārata* (Ithaca: Cornell University Press, 1976), 318.
11. Madeleine Biardeau, *Études de mythologie hindoue (I–V),*" Bulletin de l'École Française de l'Extrême-Orient 54 (1968): 19–45; 55 (1969): 5–105 (1971): 17–89; 63 (1976): 111–263; 65 (1978): 87–238.
12. John Stratton Hawley, *Three Bhakti Voices: Mirabai, Surdas, and Kabir in Their Times and Ours* (New Delhi: Oxford Univeristy Press, 2005), 252, 255–256.
13. Ibid., 246.

CHAPTER 7 RAMA DEVOTIONALISM

1. J. L. Brockington, *Righteous Rāma: The Evolution of an Epic* (Delhi: Oxford University Press, 1985), 94–95.
2. Robert P. Goldman and Sally J. Sutherland Goldman, "Rāmāyaṇa," in *The Hindu World*, edited by Sushil Mittal and Gene Thursby (New York: Routledge, 2004), 76.
3. Brockington, *Righteous Rāma*, 10.

4. Julia Leslie, *Authority and Meaning in Indian Religions: Hinduism and the Case of Vāmīki* (Aldeershot: Ashgate, 2003), 80–94.
5. Frank Whaling, *The Rise of the Religious Significance of Rāma* (Delhi: Motilal Banarsidass, 1980), 31, note 2.

CHAPTER 9 GODDESS DEVOTION AND TANTRA

1. Malcolm McLean, *Devoted to the Goddess: The Life and Work of Ramprasad* (Albany: State University of New York Press, 1998), 35.
2. Ibid., 31.
3. Rachel Fell McDermott, *Mother of My Heart, Daughter of My Dreams: Kālī and Umā in the Devotional Poetry of Bengal* (New York: Oxford Univeristy Press, 2001), 3.

INDEX

Abhinavagupta of Kashmir Śaivism, 409, 478–485, 507, 555–562
Aditi, 18, 21, 24, 354
Advaita Vedānta school, 76–77, 232
Agamas, 408
Agni (god of fire), 15, 24–25, 152, 346
Aitareya Āraṇyaka, 4
Aitareya Upaniṣad, 28
Aksapāda Gotama, 74
Ālvārs of Tamilnadu, 152
Āṇṭāl, 152–154, 172–191
Appar, 408
Āraṇyakas (forest teachings), 7, 28
Arjuna, 226–230, 357–358, 362, 364, 366, 368, 519
artha, 240
Aryaman, 16
asceticism, 407
ashes, 429–430, 447, 493
Āśrama Upaniṣad, 30, 46–48
Aśvins (twin deities), 13–14, 226
Atharva Veda Saṃhitā, 7, 10
ātman (self), 29, 31–37, 77, 145–147, 202–212, 478, 480–484
avidyā (ignorance), 119, 127, 129, 136–137
Ayodhyā, 342–343, 346
Āyus (long life), 22

Bādarāyaṇa, 76
bandhu (inherent connections), 11
Basava (or Basavaṇṇa), 409
Basava Purāṇa, 409–410, 499–502
Benares, 377, 381–382
Bhagavad Gītā, 77, 228, 348
Bhāgavata Purāṇa, 23, 234–253, 324
Bhairava, 508, 538
bhakti (devotion to god), 152, 211–212, 232, 372, 379; two kinds, 233
Bharata, 342–343, 347, 351, 354–355
bhāṣya, 73
bhava (emotions), 318–320, 322, 324, 329
Bhoja, King, 76
body, 142–143
Brahmā, 355–356, 400, 489
Brahman, 2, 26, 29, 32, 36–38, 131–147, 202–212, 236–237, 362, 380, 481, 485, 530–531, 533
Brāhmaṇas (sacred ritual texts), 7, 11–12, 28
Bṛhadāraṇyaka Upaniṣad, 28
Bṛhaspati, 20
buddhi (intellect), 106–109, 135, 141

Caitanya, 232–233, 306–318, 504, 519–520
Caitanya Caritāmṛta (of Kṛṣṇadāsa Kavirāja), 306–318
cakra (mystical diagrams), 438, 508, 522, 546–547, 551, 565–567
Campantar, 408
Caṇḍīdāsa, 231
Candikā, 503–504
caste (*jāti*), 71
causation, 102
Cekkilār, 410
celibacy, 430–431
chandas, 12
Chāndogya Upaniṣad, 28
Chinnamastā, 544
cow, 13–14, 16, 31, 304
Cuntarar, 408

Dādū, 348, 386–392
Dakṣa, 21–22, 415–419
Dānu, 17
darśana (visual contemplation), 312
Darśanas (Hindu philosophical systems), 73
Daśaratha, King, 350–351
death, 68–70, 545
Devakī, 235–237
Devī Māhātmya, 503, 508–514
dharma, 49–72, 89–91, 93–95, 226, 228, 240, 315, 344, 346–347
Dharmaāstras, 50
Dharmasūtras, 1, 49
dhi (insight), 1
dhyāna (meditation), 353
Dignāga, 74
Draupadī, 226–227
Durgā, 503, 505
dūtī, 557
Dvaita Vedānta school, 77
Dvāpara Yuga, 395, 486

Earth, 13

fire-sacrifices (*homā*), 25–27
food, 64–65

gaṇas (deformed figures), 418
Gaṇeśa, 393, 419–425, 559
Ganges, 347, 351, 366, 381, 504, 520
Garuḍa, 244, 346, 366, 418, 423
Gauḍapāda, 76
Gauḍīya Vaiṣṇava tradition, 232, 504
Gāyatrī-mantra, 433, 440
Gītā Govinda (of Jayadeva), 231, 253–267
gopīs, 232, 241, 243, 246–253, 293–306, 319–320
gopuram (temple pyramids), 4
Gorakhnāth, 407
Gorakṣa Śataka, 407, 436–443
Gosvāmī, Jīva, 233
Gosvāmī, Rūpa, 233
Govardhana, Mount, 247–249, 273–274
grace, 449–451, 469–471, 473–474, 477, 481, 491, 498, 536–537, 541–542
Gṛhyasutras, 49
Guha, 347
guṇas (strands), 103–104, 112, 116, 119, 121, 127–128, 236, 245, 328
Gupta, M., 505
Gupta dynasty, 225
guru, 368–371, 536, 538–539, 542, 558, 562

hagiography, 234
Hanumān, 345–347, 352–353, 393, 398–402
Harivaṃś, Śrī Hit, 237, 283–293
Harivaṃśa, 225
Haṭha yoga, 436
Homer, 225, 341
horse, 22–23, 27
horse sacrifice, 354
hotṛ priest, 15, 48

iḍa, 439–441
Indra, 16–18, 22, 24, 35–36, 152, 226, 347, 511
inference, 83–86, 429
initiation (*dikṣā*), 54–55, 541–542
interpretation, 91–93, 96–100
Īśa Upaniṣad, 28
Īśvara, 117–118
Īśvarakrishna, 76, 100–114
Itihāsas, 224

Jagannatha temple in Puri, 311, 526
Jaimini, 75
Jaṭāyus, 349, 352
jīva (self, soul), 33, 134–135, 313, 396, 439
jñāna, 110
Jñāneśvara or Jñānadeva, 348–357, 368
Jyotisa (astronomy), 12

Kabīr, 348–349, 368–377
Kaikeyī, 343, 347, 351, 354–355
Kālī, 426, 503–518, 544–545, 549–551, 554
Kāliya, 242–245
kali yuga, 393, 395, 416, 419, 486, 532
kalpa, 436
Kalpasūtras, 12, 49
kāma (desire), 240, 320

Kāma or Kāmadeva, 250, 296, 493
Kaṃsa, 236–240
Kaṇāda, 74
Kānphaṭas, 407
Kapila, 76
kārikās (verses), 73
karma, 477
Kashmir Śaivism, 409
Kaṭha Upaniṣad, 28, 38–45
Kaula tradition, 409, 506–507
Kauravas, 225–230
Kauṣātaki Brāhmaṇa Upaniṣad, 28
Kena Upaniṣad, 28
kevala (solitary, isolation), 113
kīrtana (chanting), 315, 320, 520
Krishna, 224–331, 363–364, 504, 519–520
kṛta yuga, 486
Kubera, 350
Kula (clan), 506, 508
Kulārṇava Tantra, 506–507, 534–543
Kumāra, 159–160
Kumārila, 75
kuṇḍālinī, 440, 522, 547–548
Kurukṣetra, 229

Lakṣmaṇa, 342, 346, 351, 355, 401
Lakṣmī, 155, 195–196, 352, 367
Lakṣmī Tantra, 154, 191–202
līlā. *See* play
liṅga (male organ, sign, mark), 407, 430, 439, 483–497
Liṅgāyatas (Vīraśaivas), 409
love, 458–460

madness, 317–318
Mādhva, 77, 155–156, 216–223
Mahābhārata, 1, 224–231, 341
Mahādēviyakka, 409, 493–499
Mahānārāyaṇa Upaniṣad, 28
Mahānubhāva tradition, 232–233
Mahāvidyās, 507
Mahiṣa, 503
Maitrāyaṇi Upaniṣad, 28
Maitrī Upaniṣad, 29
manas (mind), 107–108
Mānava Dharmaśāstra. *See Manusmṛti* (Laws of Manu)
maṇḍala (mystical diagrams), 8, 562
Māṇḍūkya Upaniṣad, 28
Māṇikkavācakar, 408, 455–460
mantra, 7–10, 26, 536–537, 539, 541–542, 547, 549, 554–555, 560
Manu, 17
Manusmṛti (Laws of Manu), 50–52
Mārīca, 342, 344, 352, 365
Mārkaṇḍeya Purāṇa, 503, 508–514
Maruts, 16–17, 22
Matsya (fish *avatāra*), 156–159
māyā (unreal, illusion, cognitive error), 371, 393, 410–411, 426, 430, 476, 478, 481, 496, 527

McLean, Malcolm, 506
Mīmāṃsā school of philosophy, 73, 75–76, 89–100
Mīrābāī, 231, 276–283, 504
Miśra, Vācaspati, 100–114
Mitra, 16, 22
mokṣa (liberation), 29, 77, 134, 228, 318, 550
mudras (hand gestures), 307, 547–548, 554, 561
mukti (liberation), 546
Muṇḍaka Upaniṣad, 28
muni (ascetic), 342

Naciketas, 38–45
nāḍīs (channels), 438, 443
Nālāyira Divyaprabandham (Four Thousand Divine Compositions), 154
Nammālvār, 152–153, 165–172
Nanda, 236, 239–240, 243–244, 246, 304
Nandi, 412, 419
Nārada, 349–350
Narasiṃha (half-man, half-lion *avatāra*), 161–163
Nārāyaṇa, 210, 244, 393
Naṭarāja: Śiva as, 408, 445–446
Nāthamuni, 154
Nātha tradition, 407
Nāyanārs, 407–408
Nikhilananda, Swami, 505–506
nyāsa, 553, 555
Nyāya school of Hindu philosophy, 73–74, 78–89

Pāñcarātra, 154, 427
Pāṇḍavas in *Mahābhārata*, 225–230
Pāṇini, *Aṣṭādhyāyi*, 11
Paṇis, 18
Paramahaṃsa Upaniṣad, 45–46
Paramārthasāra, 478–485
Pārvatī, 393, 418–424, 426, 503, 541
pāśa(fetter), 408, 476
Pāśupatas, 407, 427–436
Paśupata Sūtra, 407, 427–436
paśus (creatures), 408, 427
Patañjali, 76
Patañjali *(Mahābhāṣya*, Great Commentary), 11
pativrata (ideal wife), 343
perception, 78–83, 108, 429
Periya Purāṇa (by Cēkkilār), 410
piṅgalā, 439–441
play (*līlā*), 233–234, 252, 287, 306–318
power, 120–121
Prabhākara, 75
Prajāpati, 22, 26, 35–36, 417
prakṛti (primal matter), 76, 101–102, 110–113, 193–194, 478, 481, 519
pralaya (cosmic dissolution), 230, 312
prāṇa (breath), 122–123, 439, 442–443
prasāda (blessed food, grace), 326
Praśastapāda, 74
Praśna Upaniṣad, 28
Pratyabhijñā (recognition school), 409
prema (love, devotion), 307–308, 312, 314, 318–320, 322–324, 532
priest (Brahmin), 51
Pṛthivī (earth goddess), 478, 481
pūjā, 152, 508
Purāṇas, 1, 151–152
purification, 66–71
puruṣa (self, spirit), 24–25, 76, 105–110, 112–113, 115, 519
Pūṣan, 22
Puṣṭimārga (path of grace), 232
Pūtanā, 240–242, 325

Rādhā, 231, 233, 253–267, 271–272, 308, 325, 331, 519
Rādhāvallabha, 232
rāgānugā bhakti, 320
Raidās, 348, 377–386
Rākṣasas (demons), 26
Raktabīja, 504, 510–512
Rāma, 341–406, 519, 524, 527, 531
Rāmacaritmānas (The Sacred Lake of Rāma's Deeds of Tulsīdās), 349, 393–406
Ramakrishna, 505–506, 518–534
Rāmānuja, 77, 153, 155, 202–212
Rāmāyaṇa (of Vālmīki), 224, 341–347, 349–356
Ramprasād Sen, 504–505, 514–518
rasa (aesthetic emotion), 233, 251–253, 324, 328–330
rati (pleasure), 322–323, 326–327, 329
Rāüḷ Guṇḍam, 233–234
Rāvaṇa, 342–345, 352–353, 365, 400–401, 527
rebirth (*saṁsāra*), 77
Rig Veda, 7–24, 28, 49
ṛṣi (wise man), 2, 7
ṛta (principle of cosmic order and dharma), 2
Rudra, 16. *See also* Siva
Rukmiṇī, 233
Rūpa Gosvāmī, 318–331

Śabara, 75
sacrifice, 415–419
Sadyojoti, 408
Śaiva Siddhānta, 408
Śaivism, 348, 407–503
Śaivite Nāyanārs. *See* Nāyanārs
Śakti (power), 154, 194–196, 408, 422, 440, 442, 476, 478–481, 508, 530, 538, 542, 556, 565
Śāktism, 503–518
samādhi (trance, absorption), 114, 386, 428, 477, 522–524, 532–533
sāmans (chants), 9, 31
Sāma Veda Samhitā, 7, 9
Śaṃhita, 7
Sāṃkhya, 76
Sāṃkhyakārikā (of Īśvarakrishna), 100–114
saṃnyāsin (renouncer), 30
Śaṅkara, 76–77, 128–147, 232
sankīrtan (devotional singing), 307, 313, 316
Sanskrit, 1–2, 75, 151, 357

Sant tradition, 348, 385
Saṣṭitantra (Science of Sixty Topics), 76
Śatapatha Brāhmaṇa, 11, 25–27
Śatrughna, 355
satya (truth), 2
scripture, 4
self-surrender, 199–201
Śeṣa (Remainder), 237
śikṣa (pronunciation and phonetics), 12
Sītā in *Rāmāyaṇa*, 342–347, 351, 353, 401–402, 519, 524
Śiva, 29, 393, 407–502, 519, 535–536, 539–542, 544, 554, 559–563, 565, 570
sky, 13
Śloka meter, 50
smṛti (remembered texts), 1, 50, 99, 377, 409
Soma (god of the sacrificial drink), 9, 15–20
Somanātha, P., 409, 499–502
śrāddha (faith), 323
Śrautasūtras, 12, 49
Śrīcakra, 507
Śrīvidyā tradition, 508
śruti (revelation), 1, 7, 50, 99, 151, 377, 409
staff (*tridaṇda*), 75
Subāhu, 342
sublation (*bādha*), 139–140
Sugrīva, 344–345, 352–353, 398
Śūnyasampādane, 485–499
superimposition, 129–130, 144
Sūrdās, 231, 268–276
Sūrsāgar (of Sūrdās), 231
Sūtas (bards), 225
sūtra (shortened formulae), 1, 49, 73
Śvetaketu, 33–35
Śvetāsvatara Upaniṣad, 28–29

tāṇḍava dance, 425–426
Tantra, 503–570
Tantraloka, 507, 555–562
tapas (literally, heat and asceticism), 2, 410
Tāra, 155, 505, 550–551
Tāṭakā, 342
tejas (light, splendor), 480
Teṅkalai (southern) school of Tamil, 155
Tēvāram, 407–408, 444–455
tikā (gloss), 73
time (*kāla*), 545
Tiruvāśagam (of Māṇikkavācakar), 455–460
Tiruvāymoli (of Nammālvār), 152–157
Toḍala Tantra, 507, 543–555
Tretā Yuga, 341, 403, 486
Trika tradition, 409
Tripurā, 410–415, 508, 564
Tripurasundarī, 508, 544
Tulasīdās, 341, 349, 393–406
Tvaṣṭṛ, 16–17, 22–23

Udayama, 73
udgātṛ priest, 31
Udyotakara, 74
Uma, 504–505
Umāpati, 408, 471–477
Upaniṣads, 7, 28–48
Uṣas (goddess dawn), 13–14

vacanas (what is said), 409
Vācaspati Miśra, 74
Vaiśeṣika school, 73–75, 78–89
Vaiṣṇava Ālvārs. *See* Ālvārs of Tamilnadu
Vaiṣṇavism, 151–223, 348
Vālin, 345
Vallabha, 232, 293–306
Vālmiki, 341–392, 349–350
Vāmana (dwarf *avatāra*), 163–165, 237
Varāha (boar *avatāra*), 160–161
vārtittika (subcommentary), 73
Varuṇa, 15–16, 22
Vātsyāyana, 74
Vāyu (wind god), 226
Vedāṅga (subsidiary limbs of the Vedas), 12, 49
Vedānta, 29, 75–77, 202, 530
Vedānta Deśika, 155, 213–216
Vedāntasūtra (of Badarayana), 128–147
Vedas, 1–4, 7–27, 60–61, 93–96, 364
verbal testimony, 87–98
Vibhīśśana, 347
vidyā (knowledge), 77, 129, 431, 508, 543
Vijñānabhikṣu, 76
Vipra, 2
Viraśaivas, 409
Virocana, 35
Viṣṇu, 16, 29, 155–165, 236, 342, 346, 350, 354–355, 365, 381, 400, 418–419, 422, 486, 511, 535
Viśvāmitra, 342, 355–356
Viṭhobā (Viṣṇu) in Pandharpur, 232–233
Vṛndāvana, 314–315
Vṛtra, 17–18, 241, 347
vyākaraṇa (grammar), 12
Vyāsa, 76, 224, 341–342, 363
vyūha (divine emanations), 154, 191–194

waters, 25
writing, 4

Yajur Veda Saṃhitā, 7, 9, 11
Yamunā River, 242–244, 250, 303
yantra (mystical diagrams), 507, 539
yoga (discipline), 114–115, 428, 433–434, 536, 540–541, 546
Yoga system of Patañjali, 76, 114–128
Yoginīs, 507–508
Yognīhṛdaya (The Heart of the Yoginī), 507–508, 562–570
yoni (female sexual organ), 407, 438, 520
Yudhiṣthra in *Mahābhārata*, 226–230
Yuktidīpikā (Light of Argumentation), 76

ABOUT THE AUTHOR

PROFESSOR CARL OLSON has taught at Allegheny College since 1981. The college has appointed him to the National Endowment for the Humanities Chair (1991–1994), Teacher-Scholar Professorship of the Humanities (2000–2003), and chairperson. During 2002, he was appointed to a Visiting Fellowship at Clare Hall, University of Cambridge, and was elected a Permanent Fellow of Clare Hall by its board of trustees.

Professor Olson has published over two hundred articles and reviews for various journals. He has served as review editor for the *International Journal of Hindu Studies* since 1996. He has also published the following books: *The Book of the Goddess Past and Present: An Introduction of Her Religion* (1983); *The Mysterious Play of Kali: An Interpretive Study of Ramakrishna* (1990); *The Theology and Philosophy of Eliade: A Search for the Centre* (1992); *The Indian Renouncer and Postmodern Poison: A Cross-Cultural Encounter* (1997); *Zen and the Art of Postmodern Philosophy: Two Paths of Liberation from the Representational Mode of Thinking* (2000); and *Indian Philosophers and Postmodern Thinkers: Dialogues on the Margins of Culture* (2002); *The Different Paths of Buddhism: A Narrative – Historical Introduction* (2005); *Original Buddhist Sources: A Reader* (2005).